# NOVELL'S

## Certified Web Designer
## Study Guide

JIM BOWMAN

Novell.
**PRESS**

Novell Press, San Jose

**Novell's Certified Web Designer Study Guide**

Published by
**Novell Press**
**2180 Fortune Drive**
**San Jose, CA 95131**

Library of Congress Catalog Card No.: 98-70589

ISBN: 0-7645-4548-5

Printed in the United States of America

10 9 8 7 6 5 4 3 2 1

1P/RX/QW/ZY/FC

Distributed in the United States by IDG Books Worldwide, Inc.

Distributed by Macmillan Canada for Canada; by Transworld Publishers Limited in the United Kingdom; by IDG Norge Books for Norway; by IDG Sweden Books for Sweden; by Woodslane Pty. Ltd. for Australia; by Woodslane New Zealand Ltd. for New Zealand; by Addison Wesley Longman Singapore Pte Ltd. for Singapore, Malaysia, Thailand, and Indonesia; by Distribuidora Norma S.A.-Colombia for Colombia; by Intersoft for South Africa; by International Thomson Publishing for Germany, Austria, and Switzerland; by Toppan Company Ltd. for Japan; by Distribuidora Cuspide for Argentina; by Livraria Cultura for Brazil; by Ediciencia S.A. for Ecuador; by Addison-Wesley Publishing Company for Korea; by Ediciones ZETA S.C.R. Ltda. for Peru; by WS Computer Publishing Corporation, Inc., for the Philippines; by Unalis Corporation for Taiwan; by Contemporanea de Ediciones for Venezuela; by Computer Book & Magazine Store for Puerto Rico; by Express Computer Distributors for the Caribbean and West Indies. Authorized Sales Agent: Anthony Rudkin Associates for the Middle East and North Africa.

For general information on IDG Books Worldwide's books in the U.S., please call our Consumer Customer Service department at 800-762-2974. For reseller information, including discounts and premium sales, please call our Reseller Customer Service department at 800-434-3422.

For information on where to purchase IDG Books Worldwide's books outside the U.S., please contact our International Sales department at 650-655-3200 or fax 650-655-3295.

For information on foreign language translations, please contact our Foreign & Subsidiary Rights department at 650-655-3021 or fax 650-655-3281.

For sales inquiries and special prices for bulk quantities, please contact our Sales department at 650-655-3200 or write to the address above.

For information on using IDG Books Worldwide's books in the classroom or for ordering examination copies, please contact our Educational Sales department at 800-434-2086.

For press review copies, author interviews, or other publicity information, please contact our Public Relations department at 650-655-3000 or fax 650-655-3299.

For authorization to photocopy items for corporate, personal, or educational use, please contact Copyright Clearance Center, 222 Rosewood Drive, Danvers, MA 01923, or fax 978-750-4470.

For general information on Novell Press books in the U.S., including information on discounts and premiums, contact IDG Books at 800-434-3422 or 650-655-3200. For information on where to purchase Novell Press books outside the U.S., contact IDG Books International at 650-655-3021 or fax 650-655-3295.

John Kilcullen, *CEO, IDG Books Worldwide, Inc.*
Steven Berkowitz, *President, IDG Books Worldwide, Inc.*
Brenda McLaughlin, *Senior Vice President & Group Publisher, IDG Books Worldwide, Inc.*

The IDG Books Worldwide logo is a trademark under exclusive license to IDG Books Worldwide, Inc., from International Data Group, Inc.

KC Sue, *Publisher, Novell Press, Novell, Inc.*

Novell Press and the Novell Press logo are trademarks of Novell, Inc.

# NOVELL'S

## Certified Web Designer
## Study Guide

# Welcome to Novell Press

Novell Press, the world's leading provider of networking books, is the premier source for the most timely and useful information in the networking industry. Novell Press books cover fundamental networking issues as they emerge — from today's Novell and third-party products to the concepts and strategies that will guide the industry's future. The result is a broad spectrum of titles for the benefit of those involved in networking at any level: end user, department administrator, developer, systems manager, or network architect.

Novell Press books are written by experts with the full participation of Novell's technical, managerial, and marketing staff. The books are exhaustively reviewed by Novell's own technicians and are published only on the basis of final released software, never on prereleased versions.

Novell Press at IDG Books Worldwide is an exciting partnership between two companies at the forefront of the knowledge and communications revolution. The Press is implementing an ambitious publishing program to develop new networking titles centered on the current versions of intraNetWare, GroupWise, BorderManager, ManageWise, and networking integration products.

Novell Press books are translated into 14 languages and are available at bookstores around the world.

*KC Sue, Publisher*
*Novell Press, Novell, Inc.*

## Novell Press

**Publisher**
*KC Sue*

**Marketing Manager**
*Marcy Shanti*

## IDG Books Worldwide

**Acquisitions Editor**
*Jim Sumser*

**Development Editor**
*Stefan Grünwedel*

**Technical Editor**
*Brett Spackman*

**Copy Editor**
*Nicole Fountain*

**Project Coordinator**
*Ritchie Durdin*

**Quality Control Specialists**
*Mick Arellano*
*Mark Schumann*

**Graphics and Production Specialists**
*Mario F. Amador*
*Vincent F. Burns*
*Linda J. Marousek*
*Hector Mendoza*
*Dina F Quan*
*Elsie Yim*

**Illustrator**
*David Puckett*

**Proofreader**
*Christine Sabooni*

**Indexer**
*C² Editorial Services*

**Cover Photography**
*© 1998 Steve Edson / Photonica*

## About the Author

Jim Bowman, Master CNE, Certified Internet Business Strategist, Certified Web Designer, and Certified Intranet Manager, is a former product marketing engineer for Novell. He has won regional and international awards for technical-writing projects produced for Novell and Apple Computer. Jim Bowman also speaks at NetWare Users International conferences. He is a prolific author of Internet and networking titles, including *Novell's Guide to Web Site Management* and *Novell's Certified Internet Business Strategist Study Guide.* His publishing accomplishments also include feature articles and photographs in recreation magazines, including *Bay and Delta Yachtsman, Dirt Rider, Dirt Bike,* and *Cycle News.*

*To Martha and Porter*

# Preface

**T**his book serves two purposes. Primarily, it is a study guide for those who want to earn Novell's Certified Web Designer certificate. However, it is also a guide to designing and creating Web sites. If you are just getting started, you will probably be surprised at how easy it is to create your first Web page. All you need is a computer, a text-editor program, such as Windows Notepad, and a browser (Netscape Communicator is included on this book's CD-ROM). In my seminars, attendees learn to create a basic Web page in less than 15 minutes. Everything they learn after that helps them to create better Web pages.

In this book, I cover far more than I do in my seminars. This book presents the information taught in the following Novell Education courses:

- ▸ Course 654, Web Authoring and Publishing

- ▸ Course 655, Advanced Web Authoring

- ▸ Course 660, Designing Effective Web Sites

To earn Novell's Certified Web Designer certificate, you need to pass certification tests for each of these classes, plus the test for the Certified Internet Business Strategist certificate. The Certified Internet Business Strategist is the entry-level certification track in Novell's Certified Internet Professional program and is a prerequisite to the Certified Web Designer program. The Certified Internet Business Strategist track teaches how to plan and manage the development of a Web site and how to use Netscape Communicator to access a variety of Internet services.

To help you prepare for the Certified Internet Business Strategist exam, I wrote *Novell's Certified Internet Business Strategist Study Guide*, available from Novell Press. This book picks up where that book leaves off.

Although the Internet Business Strategist certificate is listed as a prerequisite for the Certified Web Designer program, you do not have to earn your certificate before using this book. The only skills you really need before you use this book are the ability to use your Windows-based computer and the ability to use Netscape Navigator or a comparable browser. You need these skills to test the Web pages you'll learn to create.

If you would like to earn the Certified Web Designer certificate, hands-on exercises and study questions throughout this book will help you test your progress and your understanding of Web design concepts. When you think you are ready to take the exam, you can call 1-800-RED-EXAM for test registration information. These tests are offered throughout the world at the same test centers that administer tests for Novell's famous Certified Novell Engineer certification.

I hope you'll find Web site development to be fun. I know I have. I've created Web sites for employers, for myself, and for clubs that I belong to. I've even created a Web site for you. This book's CD-ROM contains a sample Web site that illustrates most of the concepts presented in this book. You can view this Web site without a Web server (you'll learn how in Chapter 2), and you can copy these Web pages and edit them to create your own. Let's get started!

## How This Book Is Organized

This book is divided into 3 parts and 15 chapters.

### Part I: Web Page Authoring

Part I presents the information that corresponds to Novell Education Course 654, Web Authoring and Publishing. In this part, you learn how to prepare for Web site construction, how to build Web pages and sites with HTML commands called tags, and how to build Web sites with NetObjects Fusion. This part concentrates on the basics for creating Web pages and Web sites.

Chapter 1 begins with guidelines and instructions for setting up a computer on which you can build your Web sites. Contrary to what you might have heard, you don't need a Web server to start creating Web pages. All you need is a Web browser such as Netscape Communicator, which is provided on this book's CD-ROM.

In Chapter 2, you learn how to create your first Web page and format it with HTML tags. You also learn how to view the finished page in your browser without the help of a Web server. This chapter describes how to use many of the basic tags for text formatting and alignment.

Chapter 3 describes how to format Web page text into lists and tables and how to add images to your Web pages.

Once you've learned to create Web pages in Chapters 2 and 3, Chapter 4 shows you how to link them together to create a Web site. Links are the glue that holds a Web site together. In this chapter, you learn how to link to other locations in the same Web page, to other Web pages in the same Web site, and to pages in other Web sites.

Chapter 5 shows you how to use frames, forms, and other advanced features in your Web site. This chapter describes ways to publicize your finished Web site and introduces software tools that you can use to build your Web site faster, test it, and maintain it with ease.

The final chapter in Part I shows you how to build Web sites with NetObjects Fusion. In this chapter, you will see how NetObjects Fusion helps you complete the tasks described in Chapters 2 through 5 in less time and often with more precision and consistency. A trial version of NetObjects Fusion is included on this book's CD for your evaluation.

### Part II: Designing Effective Web Sites

Part II covers the material that corresponds to Novell Education Course 660, Designing Effective Web Sites. After you've mastered the basic Web page skills covered in Part I, Part II explains how to design, create, and publish a complete Web site. The emphasis in this part is on creating a logical structure for your Web site and creating a consistent look or theme.

Chapter 7 introduces the roles a Web designer plays and describes the Web design process recommended by Novell. This chapter also discusses Web site architecture and storyboarding, which is a method of visualizing your Web site before you begin building it.

A very important component in Web design is the use of Web page images, which is the subject of Chapter 8. This chapter describes many ways to use, misuse, and avoid misuse of images. A very important part of this chapter focuses on keeping image file sizes small so that they add more to your Web page than their download time detracts.

Multimedia is another design element that can positively or negatively impact your Web pages, and Chapter 9 addresses this issue. In this chapter, you learn how to add sounds, animations, and movies to Web pages.

Chapter 10 builds upon the information in Chapters 7 through 9 and discusses how to apply and publish your Web site design. In this chapter, you learn additional tips and tricks for laying out Web pages and using type, and you learn how to test and publish your Web site when it is done.

### Part III: Using Web Page Programs and Scripts

Part III covers the material that corresponds to Novell Education Course 655, Advanced Web Page Authoring. This part explains how to use a variety of Web page programming tools to make your Web pages both dynamic and interactive.

Chapter 11 describes how to use special Web server commands called Server Side Include (SSI) commands to add variable data to Web pages. This chapter also explains how to use extended SSI commands supported by the Novell Web Server, and how to manage SSI command processing on the Novell Web Server.

Common Gateway Interface (CGI) programs are introduced in Chapter 12. Your Web pages can use CGI programs to interact with databases, electronic commerce servers, and other Web features that are not supported by HTML alone. This chapter explains how to call CGI programs from Web pages.

In Chapter 13, you learn to write simple Perl scripts and how to modify Perl scripts that others have written. Perl scripts are a form of CGI programming and are much easier to write than many other types of programs. By the end of this chapter, you will know how to write a basic Perl script that can display data in a Web page.

JavaScript is another type program that is relatively easy to write, and Chapter 14 explains how to write simple JavaScripts and modify JavaScripts others have written. Unlike CGI scripts, JavaScripts operate in browsers and give you much more control over the browser window and its contents.

The final chapter in this book shows you how to add Java applets to your Web pages. Java applets require programming expertise to create, but they are relatively easy to add to a Web page once they are complete. This book's CD includes several free applets you can use on your Web pages, and this chapter explains how to use them.

At the back of this book, you'll find three appendixes. Appendix A lists the answers to the exercises in this book, and Appendix B provides additional information about publishing Web sites on Web servers from Novell. Appendix C lists the software components on this book's CD-ROM and where you can find installation instructions for each component.

If you practice what you read about in this book, you'll be ready to work as a Web Designer when you finish, and you'll be ready to take the Certified Web Designer exams. You can take the corresponding exam after you finish each part of the book, or you can wait and take them all when you are done.

### Getting More Information

As this book goes to press, Novell is working on new products and programs that will improve upon those discussed in this guide. To keep informed on issues that affect this book and the products described in it, visit the following Web sites:

`www.adventurec.com`

This is my Web site, and it contains updates to this book and information on other books and speaking engagements. My e-mail address is `jbowman@adventurec.com`.

`www.novell.com`

Go to the Novell Web site to find product announcements and software updates.

`www.novell.com/programs/press`

The Novell Press Web site lists all of the Novell Press books and upcoming titles.

`www.novell.com/netboss`

This is the Novell Education Web site for Internet training programs. If you'd like to earn a Novell Certified Internet Professional certificate, check out this Web site.

`www.idgbooks.com`

The IDG Books Worldwide Web site lists books from all of the publisher's product lines, including the Novell Press division.

## Other Books by the Author

*Novell's Certified Web Designer Study Guide* is my third Novell Press book. The following are descriptions of my other two books.

*Novell's Guide to Web Site Management* is a complete guide to creating and managing Web sites using the Novell Web Server, a copy of which is included on the book's CD-ROM. This book covers the installation, configuration, and maintenance of the Novell Web Server, as well as instructions for using Novell software for TCP/IP connectivity and routing, the Novell Domain Name System (DNS) server, the Novell Dynamic Host Configuration Protocol (DHCP) server, and the Novell IPX/IP Gateway server. Additional sections cover TCP/IP basics, Web client setup, and Web page construction.

*Novell's Certified Internet Business Strategist Study Guide* covers the information in Novell Education Course 600, Internet Business Strategies; and Course 650, Mastering the 'Net with Netscape Communicator. This book helps Web development team members plan and manage the development of a Web site. It also explains how to use Netscape Navigator and other Netscape Communicator components that enable you to use Internet services beyond those offered by the World Wide Web.

# Acknowledgments

I'd like to thank all the people who have contributed to the Certified Web Designer program in general and to this book in particular. Paula Moreira and Brad Wayment are the Novell Education program managers who created the current version of Novell Education's Certified Internet Professional program, and Paula and her staff were very helpful in giving me the support I needed to earn my Certified Web Designer certificate and develop this book. If you want classroom instruction, the Novell Certified Internet Professional program is excellent.

Thanks to Brett Spackman for his fine technical review of this book and to Karl Childs and Mary Ireland for sharing the Course 660 materials and inviting me to the first Course 660 class. Brett Spackman is an Internal Webmaster for Novell and works on Novell's internal Web site, called Innerweb. Karl is one of the course developers for Course 660 and works for Mary. Thanks also to Marci Orler and Steve Schwartz of the Novell sales staff.

As usual, the Novell Press staff of KC Sue, Marcy Shanti, and Robin Wheatley excelled at keeping me in touch with the appropriate groups within Novell and getting me the information I needed. I want to extend special congratulations and best wishes to Robin in her new marriage and new life outside of Novell.

Without the efforts of Jim Sumser, this book would have never been started, and without the editing efforts of Stefan Grünwedel and Nicole Fountain, and the production efforts coordinated by Ritchie Durdin, it never would have been finished. I thank these IDG Books Worldwide employees and all the others that worked on this book behind the scenes.

Most importantly, I'd like to thank my wife, Carol, and my children, Matthew and Rebecca, for their support and understanding while I worked on this book. Carol and her mother, Martha, helped work on the puzzles in this book and took up many of my household responsibilities while I worked long hours in the office. I'm very fortunate to be able to do the kind of work I like, and to have a wonderful family that supports me.

# Contents at a Glance

Preface . . . . . . . . . . . . . . . . . . . . . . . . . . . . . . . . . . . . . . . . . . . . .ix
Acknowledgments . . . . . . . . . . . . . . . . . . . . . . . . . . . . . . . . . . . .xv

## Part I    Web Page Authoring    1

Chapter  1    Preparing for Learning . . . . . . . . . . . . . . . . . . . . . . . . .3
Chapter  2    Creating Web Pages . . . . . . . . . . . . . . . . . . . . . . . . . . .17
Chapter  3    Using Lists, Tables, and Images . . . . . . . . . . . . . . . . . . .49
Chapter  4    Linking Web Pages . . . . . . . . . . . . . . . . . . . . . . . . . . . .81
Chapter  5    Using Advanced Web Page Features . . . . . . . . . . . . . . .123
Chapter  6    Creating Web Sites with NetObjects Fusion . . . . . . . . .169

## Part II    Designing Effective Web Sites    203

Chapter  7    Web Design Basics . . . . . . . . . . . . . . . . . . . . . . . . . . .205
Chapter  8    Creating and Adapting Web Graphics . . . . . . . . . . . . . .231
Chapter  9    Adding Multimedia to Web Pages . . . . . . . . . . . . . . . . .303
Chapter 10    Applying and Publishing Your Design . . . . . . . . . . . . . .343

## Part III    Using Web Page Programs and Scripts    393

Chapter 11    Using SSI Commands . . . . . . . . . . . . . . . . . . . . . . . . . .395
Chapter 12    Using CGI Programs and Scripts . . . . . . . . . . . . . . . . . .453
Chapter 13    Using Perl Scripts . . . . . . . . . . . . . . . . . . . . . . . . . . . .483
Chapter 14    Using JavaScripts . . . . . . . . . . . . . . . . . . . . . . . . . . . . .527
Chapter 15    Using Java Applets . . . . . . . . . . . . . . . . . . . . . . . . . . . .589

Appendix A    Answers to Exercises . . . . . . . . . . . . . . . . . . . . . . . . .623
Appendix B    Publishing Web Pages on Web Servers
              from Novell . . . . . . . . . . . . . . . . . . . . . . . . . . . . . . .661
Appendix C    What's on the CD-ROM? . . . . . . . . . . . . . . . . . . . . . . .669

Index . . . . . . . . . . . . . . . . . . . . . . . . . . . . . . . . . . . . . . . . . . . . . .681

# Contents

Preface . . . . . . . . . . . . . . . . . . . . . . . . . . . . . . . . . . . . . . . . . . . . . .ix

Acknowledgments . . . . . . . . . . . . . . . . . . . . . . . . . . . . . . . . . . . . .xv

## Part I    Web Page Authoring

**Chapter 1**        Preparing for Learning . . . . . . . . . . . . . . . . . . . . . . . . . . . .3

Setting up Standalone Web Clients . . . . . . . . . . . . . . . . . . . . . . . . . . . . . .6

Setting up Dial-up Internet Web Clients . . . . . . . . . . . . . . . . . . . . . . . . .6

   Preparing the Computer . . . . . . . . . . . . . . . . . . . . . . . . . . . . . . . . .7

   Installing Netscape Communicator . . . . . . . . . . . . . . . . . . . . . . . . . .9

   Getting an Internet Access Account . . . . . . . . . . . . . . . . . . . . . . . .11

   Solving Internet Access Problems . . . . . . . . . . . . . . . . . . . . . . . . . .14

Setting up a LAN Web Client . . . . . . . . . . . . . . . . . . . . . . . . . . . . . . .15

Setting up a Web Server for Testing . . . . . . . . . . . . . . . . . . . . . . . . . . .16

Summary . . . . . . . . . . . . . . . . . . . . . . . . . . . . . . . . . . . . . . . . . . . . . .16

**Chapter 2**        Creating Web Pages . . . . . . . . . . . . . . . . . . . . . . . . . . . .17

Web Page Basics . . . . . . . . . . . . . . . . . . . . . . . . . . . . . . . . . . . . . . . . .18

Web Page Anatomy . . . . . . . . . . . . . . . . . . . . . . . . . . . . . . . . . . . . . .19

Changing Text Appearance . . . . . . . . . . . . . . . . . . . . . . . . . . . . . . . . .23

   Using Physical Style Tags . . . . . . . . . . . . . . . . . . . . . . . . . . . . . . . .26

   Using Logical Style Tags . . . . . . . . . . . . . . . . . . . . . . . . . . . . . . . .29

Adjusting Line Spacing and Margins . . . . . . . . . . . . . . . . . . . . . . . . . . .33

Adding Special Characters to HTML Files . . . . . . . . . . . . . . . . . . . . . .36

Summary . . . . . . . . . . . . . . . . . . . . . . . . . . . . . . . . . . . . . . . . . . . . . .37

**Chapter 3**        Using Lists, Tables, and Images . . . . . . . . . . . . . . . . . . . .49

Creating Lists . . . . . . . . . . . . . . . . . . . . . . . . . . . . . . . . . . . . . . . . . . .50

   Unordered Lists . . . . . . . . . . . . . . . . . . . . . . . . . . . . . . . . . . . . . .51

   Ordered Lists . . . . . . . . . . . . . . . . . . . . . . . . . . . . . . . . . . . . . . . .52

   Definition Lists . . . . . . . . . . . . . . . . . . . . . . . . . . . . . . . . . . . . . . .53

   Nested Lists . . . . . . . . . . . . . . . . . . . . . . . . . . . . . . . . . . . . . . . . .54

Building Tables . . . . . . . . . . . . . . . . . . . . . . . . . . . . . . . . . . . . . . . . . . . . . . . .56
Displaying Images . . . . . . . . . . . . . . . . . . . . . . . . . . . . . . . . . . . . . . . . . . . . . .62
    Creating Images . . . . . . . . . . . . . . . . . . . . . . . . . . . . . . . . . . . . . . . . .64
    Adding Background Images to Web Pages . . . . . . . . . . . . . . . . . . . . . . . .65
    Adding Foreground Images to Web Pages . . . . . . . . . . . . . . . . . . . . . . . .65
    Storing Image Files . . . . . . . . . . . . . . . . . . . . . . . . . . . . . . . . . . . . . . . .68
Summary . . . . . . . . . . . . . . . . . . . . . . . . . . . . . . . . . . . . . . . . . . . . . . . . . . . . .71

**Chapter 4**    Linking Web Pages . . . . . . . . . . . . . . . . . . . . . . . . . . . . . .81
Intradocument Links . . . . . . . . . . . . . . . . . . . . . . . . . . . . . . . . . . . . . . . . . . . .82
Interdocument Links . . . . . . . . . . . . . . . . . . . . . . . . . . . . . . . . . . . . . . . . . . . .87
    Components of URLs . . . . . . . . . . . . . . . . . . . . . . . . . . . . . . . . . . . . . . .87
    Examples of Interdocument Links . . . . . . . . . . . . . . . . . . . . . . . . . . . . . .95
Links to Headings in Other Documents . . . . . . . . . . . . . . . . . . . . . . . . . . . . . .96
Image Map Links . . . . . . . . . . . . . . . . . . . . . . . . . . . . . . . . . . . . . . . . . . . . . .97
    How an Image Map Works . . . . . . . . . . . . . . . . . . . . . . . . . . . . . . . . . . .98
    Using Server-side Image Maps . . . . . . . . . . . . . . . . . . . . . . . . . . . . . . . .98
    Using Client-side Image Maps . . . . . . . . . . . . . . . . . . . . . . . . . . . . . . . .102
Creating a Portable Web Site . . . . . . . . . . . . . . . . . . . . . . . . . . . . . . . . . . . .104
Summary . . . . . . . . . . . . . . . . . . . . . . . . . . . . . . . . . . . . . . . . . . . . . . . . . . . .108

**Chapter 5**    Using Advanced Web Page Features . . . . . . . . . . . . . . . . .123
Using Frames . . . . . . . . . . . . . . . . . . . . . . . . . . . . . . . . . . . . . . . . . . . . . . . . .124
    Creating Frameset Documents . . . . . . . . . . . . . . . . . . . . . . . . . . . . . . . .126
    Creating Nested Framesets . . . . . . . . . . . . . . . . . . . . . . . . . . . . . . . . . .130
    Supporting "No Frame" Browsers . . . . . . . . . . . . . . . . . . . . . . . . . . . . .131
    Creating Links to Frames and Windows . . . . . . . . . . . . . . . . . . . . . . . . .132
Creating Forms . . . . . . . . . . . . . . . . . . . . . . . . . . . . . . . . . . . . . . . . . . . . . . .134
    Creating a Basic Form . . . . . . . . . . . . . . . . . . . . . . . . . . . . . . . . . . . . .135
    Creating Form Elements . . . . . . . . . . . . . . . . . . . . . . . . . . . . . . . . . . . .138
Publicizing Your Web Site . . . . . . . . . . . . . . . . . . . . . . . . . . . . . . . . . . . . . . .145
    Preparing Pages for Search Engine Registration . . . . . . . . . . . . . . . . . . .146
    Registering Your Site with Search Engines . . . . . . . . . . . . . . . . . . . . . . .149
Defining the HTML Version for Web Pages . . . . . . . . . . . . . . . . . . . . . . . . . .150

Using Web Site Management Tools . . . . . . . . . . . . . . . . . . . . . . . . . . . . . .151
    Web Page Development Tools (HTML Editors) . . . . . . . . . . . . . . . . . . . . . .151
    Web Site Development Tools . . . . . . . . . . . . . . . . . . . . . . . . . . . . . . . . .153
    Validation Tools . . . . . . . . . . . . . . . . . . . . . . . . . . . . . . . . . . . . . . . . .153
    Conversion Utilities . . . . . . . . . . . . . . . . . . . . . . . . . . . . . . . . . . . . . .153
    Graphics Programs and Utilities . . . . . . . . . . . . . . . . . . . . . . . . . . . . . .154
    Web Page Accessory Tools . . . . . . . . . . . . . . . . . . . . . . . . . . . . . . . . .154
Why Learn HTML Tags Anyway? . . . . . . . . . . . . . . . . . . . . . . . . . . . . . . .155
Summary . . . . . . . . . . . . . . . . . . . . . . . . . . . . . . . . . . . . . . . . . . . . . . .156

**Chapter 6**      Creating Web Sites with NetObjects Fusion . . . . . . . . . . .**169**
Building a Web Site . . . . . . . . . . . . . . . . . . . . . . . . . . . . . . . . . . . . . . . .170
    Starting a New Web Site . . . . . . . . . . . . . . . . . . . . . . . . . . . . . . . . . . .171
    Changing the Display in Site View . . . . . . . . . . . . . . . . . . . . . . . . . . . . .173
    Renaming Web Pages . . . . . . . . . . . . . . . . . . . . . . . . . . . . . . . . . . . . .174
    Adding Pages . . . . . . . . . . . . . . . . . . . . . . . . . . . . . . . . . . . . . . . . . .175
    Deleting Pages . . . . . . . . . . . . . . . . . . . . . . . . . . . . . . . . . . . . . . . . .176
    Moving Pages . . . . . . . . . . . . . . . . . . . . . . . . . . . . . . . . . . . . . . . . . .176
Building Web Pages . . . . . . . . . . . . . . . . . . . . . . . . . . . . . . . . . . . . . . .176
    Web Page Architecture . . . . . . . . . . . . . . . . . . . . . . . . . . . . . . . . . . . .177
    Selecting a Site Style . . . . . . . . . . . . . . . . . . . . . . . . . . . . . . . . . . . . .178
    Selecting Pages to Edit . . . . . . . . . . . . . . . . . . . . . . . . . . . . . . . . . . . .179
    Adding Text . . . . . . . . . . . . . . . . . . . . . . . . . . . . . . . . . . . . . . . . . .180
    Adding Graphics . . . . . . . . . . . . . . . . . . . . . . . . . . . . . . . . . . . . . . . .181
Previewing the Web Site . . . . . . . . . . . . . . . . . . . . . . . . . . . . . . . . . . . .182
Creating Text Links . . . . . . . . . . . . . . . . . . . . . . . . . . . . . . . . . . . . . . .183
Making Image Maps . . . . . . . . . . . . . . . . . . . . . . . . . . . . . . . . . . . . . . .184
Importing Web Pages . . . . . . . . . . . . . . . . . . . . . . . . . . . . . . . . . . . . . .185
Creating Forms . . . . . . . . . . . . . . . . . . . . . . . . . . . . . . . . . . . . . . . . . .185
Adding a Site Map . . . . . . . . . . . . . . . . . . . . . . . . . . . . . . . . . . . . . . . .187
Adding Multimedia to Web Pages . . . . . . . . . . . . . . . . . . . . . . . . . . . . . .188
Publishing the Web Site . . . . . . . . . . . . . . . . . . . . . . . . . . . . . . . . . . . . .189
    Configuring Staging and Publishing Locations . . . . . . . . . . . . . . . . . . . . .189
    Staging and Publishing the Web Site . . . . . . . . . . . . . . . . . . . . . . . . . . .191
Summary . . . . . . . . . . . . . . . . . . . . . . . . . . . . . . . . . . . . . . . . . . . . . . .192

# Part II    Designing Effective Web Sites

**Chapter 7**    Web Design Basics . . . . . . . . . . . . . . . . . . . . . . . . . . . . . .**205**

What Does a Web Designer Do? . . . . . . . . . . . . . . . . . . . . . . . . . . . . . .206

   Publication Design . . . . . . . . . . . . . . . . . . . . . . . . . . .207

   Graphic Design . . . . . . . . . . . . . . . . . . . . . . . . . . . . . .208

   Marketing . . . . . . . . . . . . . . . . . . . . . . . . . . . . . . . . . .208

   Web Design . . . . . . . . . . . . . . . . . . . . . . . . . . . . . . . .208

How to Design a Web Site . . . . . . . . . . . . . . . . . . . . . . . . .210

Defining Site Goals . . . . . . . . . . . . . . . . . . . . . . . . . . . . . .211

Web Site Design Guidelines . . . . . . . . . . . . . . . . . . . . . . . .213

   Web Site Architecture . . . . . . . . . . . . . . . . . . . . . . . .213

   Page Design Guidelines . . . . . . . . . . . . . . . . . . . . . . . .219

Storyboarding . . . . . . . . . . . . . . . . . . . . . . . . . . . . . . . . . .224

Summary . . . . . . . . . . . . . . . . . . . . . . . . . . . . . . . . . . . . .226

**Chapter 8**    Creating and Adapting Web Graphics . . . . . . . . . . . . . .**231**

Understanding Web Image Design Issues . . . . . . . . . . . . . . . . . . . . . . .233

   How Bitmaps Work . . . . . . . . . . . . . . . . . . . . . . . . . . .233

   Common Web Image Maladies . . . . . . . . . . . . . . . . . . .239

Choosing a Web Image Format . . . . . . . . . . . . . . . . . . . . . . . . . . . . . .250

   Graphic Interchange Format . . . . . . . . . . . . . . . . . . . .250

   Joint Photographic Experts Group Format . . . . . . . . . . .252

   Portable Network Graphics Format . . . . . . . . . . . . . . .253

Introduction to Adobe Photoshop . . . . . . . . . . . . . . . . . . . . . . . . . . . .255

   Starting Photoshop . . . . . . . . . . . . . . . . . . . . . . . . . . .256

   Opening Image Files in Photoshop . . . . . . . . . . . . . . . .257

   Choosing a Photoshop Color Mode . . . . . . . . . . . . . . .257

   Switching to Indexed Color Mode . . . . . . . . . . . . . . . .259

   Choosing a Photoshop File Format . . . . . . . . . . . . . . . .263

   Creating Image Objects in Photoshop . . . . . . . . . . . . . .264

   Disabling Anti-aliasing . . . . . . . . . . . . . . . . . . . . . . . . .265

   Loading and Choosing Web Color Swatches . . . . . . . . . .265

Optimizing Images (All Formats) . . . . . . . . . . . . . . . . . . . . . . . . . . . . .268

   Cropping Images . . . . . . . . . . . . . . . . . . . . . . . . . . . .268

   Displaying Alternate Images . . . . . . . . . . . . . . . . . . . .269

Specifying Image Dimensions . . . . . . . . . . . . . . . . . . . . . . . . .269
Creating and Optimizing GIF Images . . . . . . . . . . . . . . . . . . . . . . .270
Creating GIF Images . . . . . . . . . . . . . . . . . . . . . . . . . . . . . .270
Reducing Image File Size . . . . . . . . . . . . . . . . . . . . . . . . . .271
Creating Interlaced GIFs . . . . . . . . . . . . . . . . . . . . . . . . . . .274
Choosing Transparent Colors . . . . . . . . . . . . . . . . . . . . . . . .274
Converting Other Image Formats to GIF . . . . . . . . . . . . . . . . . . .275
Creating and Optimizing JPEG Images . . . . . . . . . . . . . . . . . . . . .278
Converting Other Images to JPEG . . . . . . . . . . . . . . . . . . . . . . .280
Guidelines for Creating Rules, Bullets, and Buttons . . . . . . . . . . . . . . .280
Creating and Optimizing Background Graphics . . . . . . . . . . . . . . . . .281
Testing Your Web Images . . . . . . . . . . . . . . . . . . . . . . . . . . . . .284
Summary . . . . . . . . . . . . . . . . . . . . . . . . . . . . . . . . . . . . . .285

**Chapter 9**    Adding Multimedia to Web Pages . . . . . . . . . . . . . . . . .**303**
Why Use Multimedia? . . . . . . . . . . . . . . . . . . . . . . . . . . . . . . .304
How Multimedia Operates on the Web . . . . . . . . . . . . . . . . . . . . . .305
Plug-ins and Helper Applications . . . . . . . . . . . . . . . . . . . . . . .306
MIME Types . . . . . . . . . . . . . . . . . . . . . . . . . . . . . . . . . .307
Playing Multimedia Files . . . . . . . . . . . . . . . . . . . . . . . . . . . . . .310
Obtaining Multimedia Files . . . . . . . . . . . . . . . . . . . . . . . . . .310
Calling Multimedia Files from Web Pages . . . . . . . . . . . . . . . . . . .311
Providing Instructions for Plug-ins and Helper Applications . . . . . . . . . . .314
Multimedia Guidelines . . . . . . . . . . . . . . . . . . . . . . . . . . . . . . .316
General Guidelines . . . . . . . . . . . . . . . . . . . . . . . . . . . . . . .316
Animation Guidelines . . . . . . . . . . . . . . . . . . . . . . . . . . . . . .320
Guidelines for Sounds . . . . . . . . . . . . . . . . . . . . . . . . . . . . .328
Video Guidelines . . . . . . . . . . . . . . . . . . . . . . . . . . . . . . . .331
Summary . . . . . . . . . . . . . . . . . . . . . . . . . . . . . . . . . . . . . .333

**Chapter 10**    Applying and Publishing Your Design . . . . . . . . . . . . . . .**343**
Supporting Multiple Browsers . . . . . . . . . . . . . . . . . . . . . . . . . . .344
Positioning Text and Graphics . . . . . . . . . . . . . . . . . . . . . . . . . . .346
Selecting a Page Size . . . . . . . . . . . . . . . . . . . . . . . . . . . . . .347
Aligning with HTML Tags . . . . . . . . . . . . . . . . . . . . . . . . . . . .349
Aligning with Art . . . . . . . . . . . . . . . . . . . . . . . . . . . . . . . .350

Aligning with Tables . . . . . . . . . . . . . . . . . . . . . . . . . . . . . . . . . . . . .350
Aligning with Frames . . . . . . . . . . . . . . . . . . . . . . . . . . . . . . . . . . . . .352
Balancing Left-justified Pages . . . . . . . . . . . . . . . . . . . . . . . . . . . . . .354
Adding Navigation Aids to Web Sites . . . . . . . . . . . . . . . . . . . . . . . . . . . .354
Navigation Tools . . . . . . . . . . . . . . . . . . . . . . . . . . . . . . . . . . . . . . .354
Guidelines . . . . . . . . . . . . . . . . . . . . . . . . . . . . . . . . . . . . . . . . . . .361
Using Graphical and HTML Type . . . . . . . . . . . . . . . . . . . . . . . . . . . . . .362
Typography 101 . . . . . . . . . . . . . . . . . . . . . . . . . . . . . . . . . . . . . . . .363
Typography Guidelines for the Web . . . . . . . . . . . . . . . . . . . . . . . . .367
Creating Graphical Type in Photoshop . . . . . . . . . . . . . . . . . . . . . . .368
Selecting Browser-safe Colors for HTML Text . . . . . . . . . . . . . . . . . .371
Creating Type Effects with HTML . . . . . . . . . . . . . . . . . . . . . . . . . .372
Supporting Visually Impaired Visitors . . . . . . . . . . . . . . . . . . . . . . . . . . .374
Testing Your Web Site . . . . . . . . . . . . . . . . . . . . . . . . . . . . . . . . . . . . .374
Prototyping Guidelines . . . . . . . . . . . . . . . . . . . . . . . . . . . . . . . . . .375
Functionality Testing Guidelines . . . . . . . . . . . . . . . . . . . . . . . . . . . .376
User Testing Guidelines . . . . . . . . . . . . . . . . . . . . . . . . . . . . . . . . .377
Publishing Your Web Site . . . . . . . . . . . . . . . . . . . . . . . . . . . . . . . . . . .379
Setting up the Web Server or Server Account . . . . . . . . . . . . . . . . . .379
Copying Web Site Files to a Web Server . . . . . . . . . . . . . . . . . . . . . .380
Copying Special Web Site Files to Special Directories . . . . . . . . . . . . . .380
Establishing a Feedback Channel . . . . . . . . . . . . . . . . . . . . . . . . . . .381
Publicizing Your Web Site . . . . . . . . . . . . . . . . . . . . . . . . . . . . . . . . . . .381
Summary . . . . . . . . . . . . . . . . . . . . . . . . . . . . . . . . . . . . . . . . . . . . . .382

# Part III   Using Web Page Programs and Scripts

**Chapter 11**   Using SSI Commands . . . . . . . . . . . . . . . . . . . . . . . . . . . . .**395**
How SSI Commands Work . . . . . . . . . . . . . . . . . . . . . . . . . . . . . . . . . . .398
Enabling SSI-Command Processing . . . . . . . . . . . . . . . . . . . . . . . . . . . . .399
Specifying a File Extension for Parsed-HTML Files . . . . . . . . . . . . . . . .399
Enabling SSI Processing for a Specific Directory . . . . . . . . . . . . . . . . . .401
Using SSI Commands on Web Pages . . . . . . . . . . . . . . . . . . . . . . . . . . . .407
Entering the SSI Commands . . . . . . . . . . . . . . . . . . . . . . . . . . . . . . .407
Distinguishing SSI Commands from HTML Comments . . . . . . . . . . . . . .408
Specifying Filenames and Paths in SSI Commands . . . . . . . . . . . . . . . . .409

NCSA Server SSI Commands . . . . . . . . . . . . . . . . . . . . . . . . . . . . . .413

    The config Command . . . . . . . . . . . . . . . . . . . . . . . . . . . . .414

    The echo Command . . . . . . . . . . . . . . . . . . . . . . . . . . . . .418

    The flastmod Command . . . . . . . . . . . . . . . . . . . . . . . . . . .422

    The fsize Command . . . . . . . . . . . . . . . . . . . . . . . . . . . . .423

    The include Command . . . . . . . . . . . . . . . . . . . . . . . . . . .423

Novell Web Server SSI Commands . . . . . . . . . . . . . . . . . . . . . . . . .424

    The append Command . . . . . . . . . . . . . . . . . . . . . . . . . . .425

    The break Command . . . . . . . . . . . . . . . . . . . . . . . . . . . .426

    The calc Command . . . . . . . . . . . . . . . . . . . . . . . . . . . . .427

    The count Command . . . . . . . . . . . . . . . . . . . . . . . . . . . .428

    The exec Command . . . . . . . . . . . . . . . . . . . . . . . . . . . . .429

    The if Command . . . . . . . . . . . . . . . . . . . . . . . . . . . . . .429

    The goto Command . . . . . . . . . . . . . . . . . . . . . . . . . . . . .431

    The label Command . . . . . . . . . . . . . . . . . . . . . . . . . . . .432

Processing Forms with SSI Commands . . . . . . . . . . . . . . . . . . . . . .432

Troubleshooting Tips . . . . . . . . . . . . . . . . . . . . . . . . . . . . . . . . . .435

When to Use SSI Commands . . . . . . . . . . . . . . . . . . . . . . . . . . . .436

Summary . . . . . . . . . . . . . . . . . . . . . . . . . . . . . . . . . . . . . . . . . .438

**Chapter 12**   Using CGI Programs and Scripts . . . . . . . . . . . . . . . . . . .**453**

Why Use CGI? . . . . . . . . . . . . . . . . . . . . . . . . . . . . . . . . . . . . . .454

How CGI Works . . . . . . . . . . . . . . . . . . . . . . . . . . . . . . . . . . . . .456

CGI on the Novell Web Server . . . . . . . . . . . . . . . . . . . . . . . . . . .458

CGI Program Types . . . . . . . . . . . . . . . . . . . . . . . . . . . . . . . . . . .463

    NETBASIC . . . . . . . . . . . . . . . . . . . . . . . . . . . . . . . . . . .464

    PERL . . . . . . . . . . . . . . . . . . . . . . . . . . . . . . . . . . . . . .464

    REMOTE CGI (RCGI) . . . . . . . . . . . . . . . . . . . . . . . . . . .465

    LOCAL CGI (LCGI) . . . . . . . . . . . . . . . . . . . . . . . . . . . . .467

Putting CGI to Work . . . . . . . . . . . . . . . . . . . . . . . . . . . . . . . . . .467

    Obtaining or Creating CGI Programs . . . . . . . . . . . . . . . . . . .468

    Specifying CGI Program and Script Directories . . . . . . . . . . . . .469

    Placing CGI Scripts and Programs in Directories . . . . . . . . . . . .474

    Loading the CGI Program or Interpreter . . . . . . . . . . . . . . . . .474

    Calling CGI Programs from Your Web Pages . . . . . . . . . . . . . . .475

Safeguarding Your Server . . . . . . . . . . . . . . . . . . . . . . . . . . . . . . .476

Troubleshooting Tips . . . . . . . . . . . . . . . . . . . . . . . . . . . . . . . . . . . . . . . .477

Summary . . . . . . . . . . . . . . . . . . . . . . . . . . . . . . . . . . . . . . . . . . . . . . . . .478

**Chapter 13**     Using Perl Scripts . . . . . . . . . . . . . . . . . . . . . . . . . . . . . . **483**

Using Perl on the Novell Web Server . . . . . . . . . . . . . . . . . . . . . . . . . . . . .485

Writing Your First Perl Script . . . . . . . . . . . . . . . . . . . . . . . . . . . . . . . . . .486

Punctuating Perl Scripts . . . . . . . . . . . . . . . . . . . . . . . . . . . . . . . . . . . . . .488

    Semicolons . . . . . . . . . . . . . . . . . . . . . . . . . . . . . . . . . . . . . . . . . . .489

    Quotation Marks . . . . . . . . . . . . . . . . . . . . . . . . . . . . . . . . . . . . . . .489

    Backslash . . . . . . . . . . . . . . . . . . . . . . . . . . . . . . . . . . . . . . . . . . . .489

    Pound Sign . . . . . . . . . . . . . . . . . . . . . . . . . . . . . . . . . . . . . . . . . . .490

Converting a Web Page to a Perl Script . . . . . . . . . . . . . . . . . . . . . . . . . .490

Processing Forms . . . . . . . . . . . . . . . . . . . . . . . . . . . . . . . . . . . . . . . . . .491

    Recording Form Data . . . . . . . . . . . . . . . . . . . . . . . . . . . . . . . . . . .492

    Processing Form Data . . . . . . . . . . . . . . . . . . . . . . . . . . . . . . . . . . .500

    If and Else Branching Statements . . . . . . . . . . . . . . . . . . . . . . . . . . .502

Modifying Perl Scripts for the Novell Web Server . . . . . . . . . . . . . . . . . . .507

    The First Line . . . . . . . . . . . . . . . . . . . . . . . . . . . . . . . . . . . . . . . . .508

    HTML Output . . . . . . . . . . . . . . . . . . . . . . . . . . . . . . . . . . . . . . . .508

    HTML Headers . . . . . . . . . . . . . . . . . . . . . . . . . . . . . . . . . . . . . . .509

    Testing, Testing, 1, 2, 3, and 4 . . . . . . . . . . . . . . . . . . . . . . . . . . . . .509

Troubleshooting . . . . . . . . . . . . . . . . . . . . . . . . . . . . . . . . . . . . . . . . . . .510

    Using the Novell Web Server Perl Consoles . . . . . . . . . . . . . . . . . . .510

    Common Perl Script Problems . . . . . . . . . . . . . . . . . . . . . . . . . . . . .513

Summary . . . . . . . . . . . . . . . . . . . . . . . . . . . . . . . . . . . . . . . . . . . . . . . . .515

**Chapter 14**     Using JavaScripts . . . . . . . . . . . . . . . . . . . . . . . . . . . . . . . **527**

What Is JavaScript? . . . . . . . . . . . . . . . . . . . . . . . . . . . . . . . . . . . . . . . . .528

Why Use JavaScript? . . . . . . . . . . . . . . . . . . . . . . . . . . . . . . . . . . . . . . . .529

    Improved User Interface Controls . . . . . . . . . . . . . . . . . . . . . . . . . .530

    Form Preprocessing . . . . . . . . . . . . . . . . . . . . . . . . . . . . . . . . . . . .530

    Form Processing . . . . . . . . . . . . . . . . . . . . . . . . . . . . . . . . . . . . . . .530

Enabling and Disabling JavaScript in the Browser . . . . . . . . . . . . . . . . . . .531

Writing Your First JavaScript . . . . . . . . . . . . . . . . . . . . . . . . . . . . . . . . . .532

Punctuating JavaScripts . . . . . . . . . . . . . . . . . . . . . . . . . . . . . . . . . . . . . .534

Hiding JavaScripts from Unenlightened Browsers . . . . . . . . . . . . . . . . . . .536

Using Literal and Variable Data ................................. 538
  Data Types ................................................ 539
  Literals .................................................. 540
  Variables ................................................. 540
Using Form Data and Other Object Data ......................... 542
  Object Hierarchy .......................................... 543
  Object Descriptions ....................................... 545
  Property Descriptions ..................................... 547
  Object and Property Naming Conventions .................... 548
  Accessing Object Property Values .......................... 552
Processing Data ............................................... 552
  Expressions ............................................... 553
  Operators ................................................. 554
  Using Flow-control Statements ............................. 556
  Using Functions ........................................... 558
  Using Events and Event Handlers ........................... 563
  Using Methods ............................................. 566
Using the JavaScript Interactive Window ....................... 569
Linking to JavaScript Functions and Methods ................... 570
Two Kinds of JavaScripts ...................................... 571
Modifying JavaScripts ......................................... 572
Security Issues ............................................... 573
JavaScript Versus Java ........................................ 574
Getting More Information on JavaScript ........................ 575
Troubleshooting ............................................... 576
Summary ....................................................... 578

**Chapter 15**    Using Java Applets ............................ **589**
What Is Java? ................................................. 590
Why Use Java? ................................................. 591
Preparing the Browser ......................................... 593
  Choosing a Browser ........................................ 593
  Enabling and Disabling Java in the Browser ................ 594
Preparing the Novell Web Server ............................... 595
  Verifying Long Name Space Support ......................... 595
  Calculating Memory Requirements for Long Filenames ........ 595

Enabling Long Filename Support . . . . . . . . . . . . . . . . . . . . . . . . . . . . . .596
Locating Java Applets . . . . . . . . . . . . . . . . . . . . . . . . . . . . . . . . . . . . . .597
Calling Java Applets from Web Pages . . . . . . . . . . . . . . . . . . . . . . . . . .598
  Placing the Applets . . . . . . . . . . . . . . . . . . . . . . . . . . . . . . . . . . . . .599
  Using the Applet Tags . . . . . . . . . . . . . . . . . . . . . . . . . . . . . . . . . . . .600
  Testing Applets . . . . . . . . . . . . . . . . . . . . . . . . . . . . . . . . . . . . . . . .605
Java Versus JavaScript . . . . . . . . . . . . . . . . . . . . . . . . . . . . . . . . . . . . .606
Security Issues . . . . . . . . . . . . . . . . . . . . . . . . . . . . . . . . . . . . . . . . . . .607
  Java Security . . . . . . . . . . . . . . . . . . . . . . . . . . . . . . . . . . . . . . . . . .607
  Known Java Security Holes . . . . . . . . . . . . . . . . . . . . . . . . . . . . . . . .609
Java on NetWare . . . . . . . . . . . . . . . . . . . . . . . . . . . . . . . . . . . . . . . . .609
Troubleshooting . . . . . . . . . . . . . . . . . . . . . . . . . . . . . . . . . . . . . . . . .611
Summary . . . . . . . . . . . . . . . . . . . . . . . . . . . . . . . . . . . . . . . . . . . . . . .613

**Appendix A**   Answers to Exercises . . . . . . . . . . . . . . . . . . . . . . . . . . . .**623**

**Appendix B**   Publishing Web Pages on Web Servers from Novell . . . . . .**661**
Common Web Publishing Issues . . . . . . . . . . . . . . . . . . . . . . . . . . . . . .662
Publishing on a Novell Web Server . . . . . . . . . . . . . . . . . . . . . . . . . . . .664
  Copying Files to the Server . . . . . . . . . . . . . . . . . . . . . . . . . . . . . . .664
  Adding an Additional Index Filename . . . . . . . . . . . . . . . . . . . . . . . .665
  Configuring SSI Processing . . . . . . . . . . . . . . . . . . . . . . . . . . . . . . . .666
Publishing on Netscape Web Servers for NetWare . . . . . . . . . . . . . . . . .666
  Copying Files to the Server . . . . . . . . . . . . . . . . . . . . . . . . . . . . . . .666
  Configuring SSI Processing . . . . . . . . . . . . . . . . . . . . . . . . . . . . . . . .667

**Appendix C**   What's on the CD-ROM? . . . . . . . . . . . . . . . . . . . . . . . . .**669**
CD-ROM Contents . . . . . . . . . . . . . . . . . . . . . . . . . . . . . . . . . . . . . . . .670
Installing the Demonstration
Web Site on a Web Server . . . . . . . . . . . . . . . . . . . . . . . . . . . . . . . . . . .673
  Installing on a Novell Web Server . . . . . . . . . . . . . . . . . . . . . . . . . . .673
  Installing on Netscape Web Servers for NetWare . . . . . . . . . . . . . . . .676

**Index** . . . . . . . . . . . . . . . . . . . . . . . . . . . . . . . . . . . . . . . . . . . . . . . . .**681**

# PART I

# Web Page Authoring

**CHAPTER 1**

# Preparing for Learning

To practice the skills taught in this book, you need to create Web pages. If you want to earn the Certified Web Designer certificate, practice is the best way to learn and retain what you have learned. If you want to get a job as a Web Designer, the best proof of your skills is a working Web site. Imagine walking into a job interview, sitting down at the interviewer's computer, and bringing up your own Web site! It can be done, and you'll learn how to do this in this book.

**IMPORTANT**

**The information in this chapter is designed to help you set up a workstation on which you can practice creating and viewing Web sites. The Certified Web Designer exam does not cover the information provided in this chapter, so you do not have to study this chapter to prepare for the exam.**

I realize that everyone has access to different types of computer services, so this chapter provides instructions and guidelines for setting up three different types of practice environments. These are:

- A standalone Web client with no Web server connection

- A dial-up Internet Web client with an Internet connection and Web storage space

- A local area network (LAN) Web client with a connection to an intranet Web server or an Internet Web server

With a standalone Web client, you can practice most of the skills in this book. If you want to show off your Web site in an interview, you can copy it to a laptop and bring the laptop to the interview. I sometimes use this approach to demonstrate Web sites in my seminars.

Figure 1.1 shows the two most common ways to connect your computer to the Internet. The dial-up connection is typically used for personal and small business accounts. The LAN connection is usually used by larger businesses that have full-time connections to the Internet.

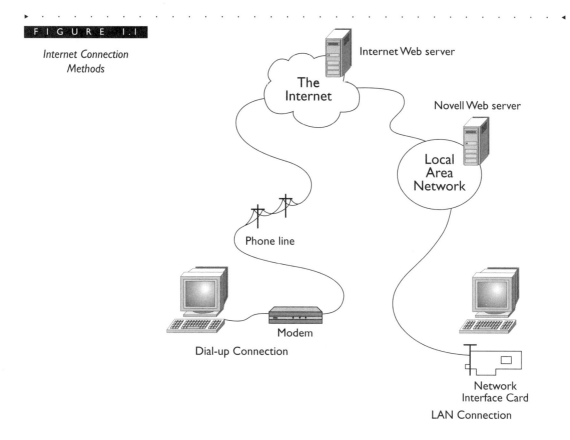

**FIGURE 1.1**

*Internet Connection Methods*

With a dial-up Web client, an Internet account, and Web storage space, you can create Web sites on your local computer, copy them to the Web storage space, and they will be published on the Internet for you. After your Web site is published, anyone who knows your Web site address can view it from any Internet-connected computer.

If you set up a LAN Web client with a connection to a Novell Web Server, you can practice every skill described in this book. However, if the LAN is not connected to the Internet, Web sites that you store on the server will only be available to local network users. There aren't that many skills in this book that require a Novell Web Server, so if you have access to a different type of Web server, go ahead and use it.

The following sections describe how to set up standalone, dial-up, and LAN Web clients, and where you can find information on setting up a Novell Web Server.

## Setting up Standalone Web Clients

A standalone Web client is a dial-up or LAN Web client without a connection to a Web server. Basically, a standalone Web client is any computer with a browser. To set up a standalone Web client, just install the browser as described in the sections for setting up dial-up and LAN clients. You can skip any instructions related to setting up dial-up or LAN connections. You can always add these connections later.

When you start the browser without a network connection, the browser might display a message stating that the network is unavailable. To begin using the browser, acknowledge the message. You won't be able to access Web servers without a dial-up or LAN connection, but you will be able to browse the demonstration Web site on this book's CD-ROM, and you will be able to browse the Web pages and Web sites you'll learn to create in later chapters.

## Setting up Dial-up Internet Web Clients

A dial-up Web client is a computer that has an installed browser and is configured to establish a temporary Internet connection. Typically, the temporary Internet connection is made through a modem over a phone line, but there are other options available.

To set up a standalone or Internet Web client, you need to do the following:

1 • Prepare the computer for the browser software and a dial-up connection.

2 • Install and configure the browser software (Netscape Communicator is included on this book's CD-ROM).

3 • Establish an Internet access account.

If you already have a computer with an installed browser or an Internet connection, you can skip some or all of these steps. Figure 1.2 is a flowchart diagram you can use to locate and complete only those tasks that haven't already been done. The following sections describe the procedures for completing the tasks in Figure 1.2.

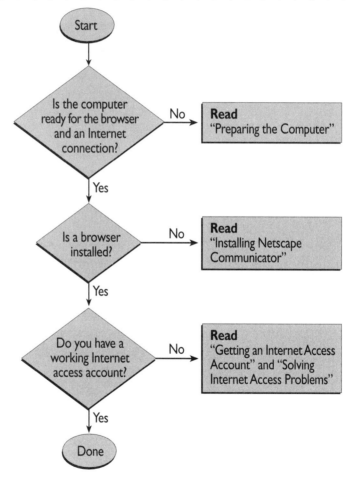

**FIGURE 1.2**

*Web Client Setup Flowchart*

## PREPARING THE COMPUTER

Before you can use a browser, you must prepare your computer for the browser and an Internet connection. This means you need the proper hardware and software, and you need the physical Internet connection.

Table 1.1 lists the hardware and software that must be installed to support the Netscape Communicator browser.

### TABLE 1.1

*Hardware and Software*
*Requirements*

| COMPONENT | NETWARE CLIENT REQUIREMENTS |
|---|---|
| Computer | A computer that uses an Intel 80486 (SX or DX), Pentium, or later processor |
| Memory | Windows 3.x, 95, NT 3.51, and NT 4.0: 16MB RAM. 24MB required when using the Netcaster component. |
| Disk Space | Netscape Communicator: 25 to 35MB, depending on the components installed |
| 256-color display | This is a requirement for Netscape Communicator. |
| Modem and telephone line | For dial-up connections, you need a modem and a telephone line that you can use to call the remote location. The minimum modem speed is 14.4Kb. |
| Windows 3.x, Windows 95, or Windows NT | Netscape Communicator runs on these Windows operating systems, as well as others. |
| Dial-up Network Software | Dial-up network software is provided with Windows 95 and Windows NT; if you are using Windows 3.x, you can use the dial-up software provided with the 16-bit version of Netscape Communicator. |

To prepare a computer for Communicator, you first need to install any required hardware, such as additional memory or a modem. The modem must be connected to a telephone line. For instructions on installing this hardware, see the product manuals.

**NOTE**

**For dial-up connections, a modem and phone line combination is the most popular. However, in many areas there are other alternatives you might want to consider. Wireless modems give you the traveling convenience of cellular phones, while Integrated Services Digital Network (ISDN) modems provide faster speeds than phone line modems, and cable modems offer connection speeds that are unreachable by phone and ISDN technologies. All these technologies can be substituted for the modem and phone line, but you will need the special equipment they require.**

Next, if Microsoft Windows is not already installed, you should install it as described in the product manual.

## INSTALLING NETSCAPE COMMUNICATOR

This section describes how to install Netscape Communicator on computers that use Windows 3.1, Windows 95, and Windows NT.

**NOTE**

**If you are creating a dial-up Web client on a Windows NT workstation, you must install the Windows dial-up networking software before you install Netscape communicator. For instructions on installing the dial-up networking software, see your Windows documentation or Novell's Guide to Web Site Management.**

**If you are creating a dial-up Web client on a Windows 95 workstation, the Netscape Communicator setup program will set up dial-up networking for you, but you might need your Windows 95 distribution software (diskettes, CD, or Cab files) to complete the installation.**

To install dial-up Netscape Communicator from the CD-ROM that comes with this book, do the following:

**1** • Place this book's CD-ROM in the CD-ROM drive.

**2** • At the workstation, start Windows, select File → Run, and enter one of the following commands:

Windows 3.1: *d*:\BROWSER\DIALUP\16BIT\SETUP

Windows 95 or NT: *d*:\BROWSER\DIALUP\32BIT\SETUP

**3** • When the welcome dialog box appears, click Next.

**4** • When the license dialog box appears, click Yes.

**5** • When the setup dialog box appears, click Next to accept the default path shown, or click Browse to select a new destination.

If you are upgrading an earlier version of Netscape Communicator or Netscape Navigator, use the default path (unless you used a custom path for the previous installation). Specifying the path to the previous installation allows the Setup program to adopt your existing configuration settings and bookmarks.

**TIP**

**To display a dialog that allows you to limit the number of Netscape Communicator components installed, click Custom. A dialog will appear later in this procedure that allows you to select which components Setup installs.**

**6** • If the options dialog appears, use the checkboxes to select which Netscape Communicator components you want to install.

**7** • If the Setup Associations dialog appears, select the file types that you want associated with Netscape Communicator and click Next. If you are going to be creating graphics with an image editing program, I recommend that you clear the checkboxes for JPEG and GIF image files.

**8** • If an information dialog box appears about multimedia, click OK.

**9** • When the Select Folder dialog box appears, name the program group in which the Netscape Communicator program icon will be installed, and then click Next.

**10** • When the Start Copying Files dialog box appears, click Install.

After you click Install, the setup program begins copying files to the computer.

**11** • If you are installing on Windows 3.1 and are prompted to set up your modem, click Yes if you have one or click No if you are setting up a standalone Web client. To set up your modem, follow the onscreen instructions.

**12** • When the Read Me dialog box appears, click Yes or No.

**13** • To close the README file display, press Alt+F4.

**14** • When the setup complete dialog box appears, click OK.

**15** • When you are prompted to restart the computer, select one of the options and click OK.

You must restart the computer before using Netscape Communicator. This completes the Netscape Communicator installation.

To start Netscape Communicator, double-click the Netscape Communicator icon. If Netscape Communicator prompts you to set up an Internet account, you can start the account setup by using the procedure in the next section. If you don't want to set up an account, use the dialog controls to exit the dialog.

If you have upgraded a dial-up version of Netscape Communicator, your dial-up account should be ready for use. If you have not set up a dial-up connection, the browser is now ready for use as a standalone client.

## GETTING AN INTERNET ACCESS ACCOUNT

After you install your browser, you must sign up for an Internet access account to gain access to the Internet and the World Wide Web. Browsers, such as Netscape Communicator, cannot surf the Net until they have a physical connection to it. A modem and a telephone line work together to establish a connection from your computer to an Internet Service Provider (ISP). The ISP completes the connection to the Internet. An Internet access account is a service account that you establish with an ISP so that your computer has an onramp to the Internet information superhighway.

### Setting up an Account Using Netscape Communicator

The Netscape Communicator software on this book's CD includes an Account Setup wizard that you can use to configure Netscape Communicator for an existing account or to establish a new account. If your modem is properly connected and you have a credit card, you can establish a new Internet account from the United States or Canada using the Account Setup wizard.

To set up an account using the Account Setup wizard, close Netscape Communicator and open the Netscape Account Setup program by double-clicking its icon or choosing it from the Start menu. To complete the account setup, follow the instructions in the wizard dialogs. You can get additional information by clicking the Help button.

 **If you have already started Netscape Communicator and the program is prompting you to set up an account, you don't need to quit. You can begin setting up the account now.**

**NOTE**

If you have trouble using the Account Setup wizard, you can get more information from the Netscape product documentation by doing the following:

**1** • If the browser is not open, start Netscape Navigator.

**2** • If the Account Setup wizard is open on a Windows 3.1 workstation, use the dialog controls to exit the wizard. With Windows 95 and NT workstations, you can leave the wizard open, switch to the Navigator window, and select File → New → Navigator Window. This opens a new window that you can use to display the product documentation.

**3** • In the browser window, select File → Open Page.

**4** • Use the Open Page dialog to select the following page:

`d:\BROWSER\DIALUP\DOCS\INDEX.HTM`.

**5** • Click Open to open the home page for the dial-up browser documentation.

**6** • To display the instructions for setting up an Internet account, click the link for the chapter titled *Using Account Setup*.

After you open the product documentation, you can read it online or print it using your the File menu Print command. If Windows is configured for printing, the Print command will work.

### Setting up an Account for a Different Browser

If you have purchased your computer or modem recently, chances are good that you already have Internet access software you can use to establish an Internet access account. To establish an Internet access account with software that came with your computer or modem, review your hardware documentation for instructions on establishing Internet access accounts.

If you don't want to establish an account with one of the ISPs supported by the Netscape Communicator install or by software provided with your computer, you can call a local service provider or one of the ISPs listed in Table 1.2.

**NOTE**

**Some online service providers require you to use their custom software to publish Web pages on the Internet. When you are choosing an ISP, be sure to choose one that permits you to publish standard Web pages. Standard Web pages are text files that contain hyperText Markup Language (HTML) tags. You'll learn more about these files in the next chapter. You need these types of browsers so you can view the Web pages you'll learn to create using this guide.**

### TABLE 1.2

*Partial List of Internet
Service Providers*

| ISP | URL | PHONE NUMBER |
| --- | --- | --- |
| Ameritech.net | www.ameritech.net | 800-327-9346 |
| Bell Atlantic Internet Solutions | www.bellatlantic.net | 800-638-2026 |
| BellSouth.net Internet Services | www.bellsouth.net | 800-436-8638 |
| Concentric Network | www.cris.com | 800-939-4262 |
| EarthLink Network | www.earthlink.com | 800-395-8425 |
| Netcom | www.netcom.com | 800-638-2661 |
| Pacific Bell Internet | public.pacbell.net | 800-708-4638 |
| Southwestern Bell Internet Services | www.swbell.net | 800-638-4357 |
| Sprint | www.sprint.com | 800-545-5040 |
| SPRYNET | www.sprynet.com | 800-447-2956 |

If you have access to an Internet account, you can get a more complete list of ISPs by browsing to:

`http://thelist.internet.com`

As you set up your Internet access account, be sure to write down, print, or save the following:

▸ Any account information you receive

▸ At least two local phone numbers from any telephone access number lists you see

▸ Any setup instructions

▸ Technical support phone numbers

The process of setting up an Internet access account is usually completed by placing a phone call from your computer using Internet access software. If the phone call gets interrupted, or you later need to reconfigure your computer, the information in the previous list can help you recover quickly.

## SOLVING INTERNET ACCESS PROBLEMS

When you are having trouble accessing the Internet, contact your ISP. If you can reach the ISP Web site, you might be able to solve your problem by reading documents posted on their support Web pages. If you can't reach the ISP Web site, you'll need to use the telephone.

Before you contact the ISP, get prepared to answer some, or all, of the following questions:

▸ When was the last time you successfully connected to the Internet?

▸ Did you make any changes to your computer between then and now?

▸ What computer hardware, operating system, and browser software are you using?

▸ Do you hear a dial tone when the computer places the call?

▸ Does the login or authentication process complete?

▸ Does an error message appear and what does it say? (Write down the message and any error numbers that appear.)

▸ Which Internet services can you use?

▸ Which Internet services don't work?

If you don't know how to answer these questions, your ISP can help you. However, if you can answer these questions, you might be able to solve the problem yourself or help the ISP solve the problem faster.

**TIP**

**A complete troubleshooting discussion about Internet access problems is beyond the scope of this book. For more troubleshooting information, see the support Web page for your ISP or *Novell's Guide to Web Site Management*, published by Novell Press. This book provides detailed instructions on setting up Web clients and testing connections to Web servers.**

## Setting up a LAN Web Client

The procedure for setting up a LAN Web client is similar to the procedure for setting up dial-up Web clients. The difference is that LAN Web clients use a network interface card to connect to a local network. Instead of installing and configuring a modem and dial-up software, you must configure a local area network (LAN) connection. After the LAN connection is configured, the browser automatically uses the network connection each time it starts.

Setting up a LAN connection requires you to use network addresses that conform to those used by the other computers on your network. If the addresses are not set up correctly, your LAN connection might not work and it might interfere with other network communications. For instructions on setting up LAN Web clients, see your LAN administrator.

**TIP**

**If you are a LAN administrator, Windows 95, Windows NT 4.0, and both NetWare and intraNetWare include software that you can use to connect LAN clients to the Internet. For more information, see the product documentation or *Novell's Guide to Web Site Management*, published by Novell Press. LAN versions of Netscape Communicator are located on this book's CD-ROM in the following directory: *d:\BROWSER\STANDARD\*.**

## Setting up a Web Server for Testing

To practice all the skills in this book, you need to set up a Novell Web Server and establish a connection to it. The Novell Education courses currently cover some tasks that are unique to the Novell Web Server. As these courses are updated, I expect that they will cover similar procedures on the following new Web servers from Novell:

- Netscape Enterprise Server for NetWare

- Netscape FastTrack Server for NetWare

If you prefer to use a Web server other than the Novell Web Server, go ahead. There aren't many procedures that are unique to the Novell Web Server, so you should be able to pass the certification tests by just memorizing the information in this guide. If you want to install and use the Novell Web Server, *Novell's Guide to Web Site Management* provides complete installation instructions and includes a CD-ROM with the Novell Web Server 3.1 software.

## Summary

This chapter provides guidelines for preparing your computer for Internet connections with Netscape Communicator. Because the Certified Web Designer exam does not cover the information in this chapter, there are no study exercises.

# CHAPTER 2

# Creating Web Pages

**W**eb pages are the building blocks of Web sites. A Web site is a collection of Web pages that serves a common goal and is managed as a group. This chapter describes how to create individual Web pages. In Chapter 4, you'll learn how to connect Web pages together to create Web sites.

As you will see, creating a basic Web page is easy, and you can use a Web browser to view your results quickly — with or without an Internet connection. In this chapter, you'll learn the four pairs of commands you must use for every Web page. You will also learn how to dress up your Web pages with bold text, headings, and other features.

## Web Page Basics

Web pages are text files that you can create or edit with text editor programs and most word processors. A *text file* is a file that contains only standard alphanumeric symbols — in other words, letters, numbers, and some other symbols. By itself, a text file does not display special type formatting like bold text, italics, or superscript. The text file format is the simplest file format and can be created and viewed with almost any computer, so you can create Web pages on almost any computer.

If Web pages are text files, and if text files do not display type formatting, how can you create cool Web pages that have special text formatting features? The answer is simple: Web page format commands are created using text file characters. To separate these formatting commands from the text you want to appear on the page, you put the formatting commands between less than (<) and greater than (>) symbols; for example, *<command>*. Any text appearing between these symbols is treated as a command and does not appear on the Web page.

Web page formatting commands are called tags, and these tags are defined by the *HyperText Markup Language* (HTML) standard. HTML uses a set of tags that are a subset of those used by the *Standard Generalized Markup Language* (SGML) standard, which is a standard used in the publishing industry.

**IMPORTANT**

**Novell's Course 654, Web Authoring and Publishing, describes the tags defined in HTML version 3.2, which was defined by the World Wide Web Consortium. You can review the standard by browsing:**

```
www.w3.org/pub/WWW/TR/REC-html32.html
```

HTML tags usually appear in pairs, marking the beginning and end of special formatting. To create a sentence with one word in bold text, for example, you could enter the following:

```
This sentence has one <B>bold</B> word.
```

In this example, the <B> tag marks the beginning of the bold text and the </B> signals the end of the bold text. The difference between a start tag and the end tag is the forward slash character (/). The forward slash character always signals the end of formatting.

Web-page formatting, or HTML formatting, is that simple. To create simple Web pages, you only need to learn the basic HTML tag set.

## Web Page Anatomy

Figure 2.1 shows the minimum set of tags that define a Web page and its structure. These tags create a Web page titled "Put title here." The only content on the page is the text: "Put Web page content here."

**FIGURE 2.1**

*Minimum Set of Web Page Tags*

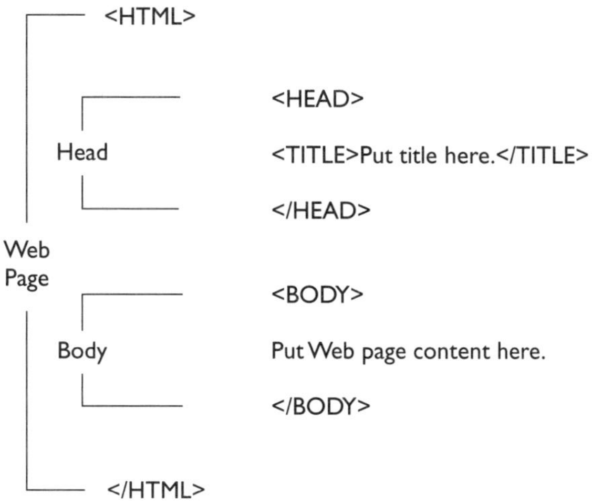

```
            ┌─── <HTML>
            │
            │          ┌─── <HEAD>
            │          │
       Head │          │    <TITLE>Put title here.</TITLE>
            │          │
  Web       │          └─── </HEAD>
  Page      │
            │          ┌─── <BODY>
            │          │
       Body │          │    Put Web page content here.
            │          │
            │          └─── </BODY>
            │
            └─── </HTML>
```

**NOTE** The tags in the Figure 2.1 use uppercase letters, but **HTML** tags are not case-sensitive. In other words, you can use uppercase and/or lowercase letters in your tags. The indentation in this figure is also optional. When browsers display Web page files, they ignore extra spaces, tabs, and extra lines unless the **<PRE>** tags are used. (The **<PRE>** tags are described later in this chapter.)

The <HTML> and </HTML> tags define the beginning and end of your HTML document (the Web page). The opening and closing <HTML> tags may eventually become obsolete because browsers use the file name extension to determine the file type. Many browsers no longer require the <HTML> tags.

The <BODY> and </BODY> tags mark the beginning and end of everything that actually appears on the Web page. This is the body section of the HTML file. To enter text on the Web page, simply add text between the body tags. To add graphics, tables, and other Web page features, you add additional tags. Everything that you want to appear on the Web page must be defined in the body section of the file.

The <HEAD> tags define the document head, which lists text and commands that do not appear in the Web page body. Initially, the <TITLE> tags are the only tags you'll use in the head. In Chapter 5, you'll learn how to put META tags in the head, and in Part III, you'll learn how to place JavaScript functions here as well.

The <TITLE> tags define the title of your Web page. Your Web page title is important because viewers of your Web page see this in several places. First, the title appears in a user's browser when the user opens your Web page. Second, the title appears in the viewer's bookmark list whenever a bookmark is created for your page. Finally, the title appears in a list whenever a user searches the Web for something and your Web page meets the search criteria. Because users use the title to access your Web page, a title should be short (to fit in bookmark lists) and descriptive.

Figure 2.2 shows how a browser displays a Web page that has no title. Because no title is present, Netscape Navigator 4 displays only the Netscape title at the top of the page. Other browsers, such as Netscape Navigator 3, display a URL at the top of the page when there is no page title.

*Web Page Without a Title*

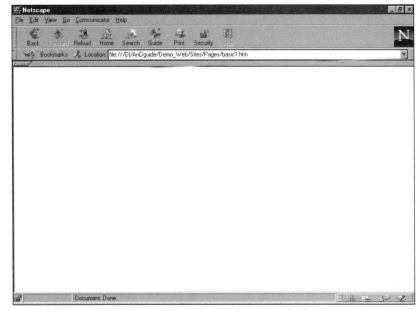

This book's CD-ROM includes a demonstration Web site that you can use to view the sample files in this book. You can view this file on the demonstration Web site by inserting the CD-ROM into your computer's CD-ROM drive and using your browser to open the following Web page:

```
d:/DemoWeb2/Sites/Pages/basic1.htm
```

**TIP**

**The home page for the demonstration Web site is at: d:/DemoWeb2/index.htm.**

**To open a Web page from the CD-ROM in Netscape Navigator, start Navigator, select File → Open Page, click Choose File, locate the file with the Open file dialog, click Open, and then click Open again. After you open the Web page file, it appears in the browser window. All the Web tags introduced in this chapter are processed by the browser and do not require a Web server for processing or display.**

The following example provides a title and some text for the Web page:

```
<HTML>

<HEAD><TITLE>Basic Web Page</TITLE></HEAD>

<BODY>

Basic Web text.

</BODY>

</HTML>
```

Notice that the Web page head and body are not indented in this example, and the <HEAD> and <TITLE> tags appear on the same line. The sequence of the tags is important; the indentation and line breaks are unimportant. You can combine tags on a single line or put them on separate lines to make the file easier to read. Make your files as easy to read as possible.

Figure 2.3 shows how this page displays in a browser. The Web page title appears on the title bar and the text appears on the page. This is a simple Web page, but it is a Web page — and it works! You could publish this page on your Web server by simply copying this file to a published directory on a Web server (See Appendix B). To view the second example on the CD-ROM, open the following Web page:

```
d:/DemoWeb2/Sites/Pages/basic2.htm
```

 **Exercise 2.1: If you're preparing to take the certification exam, or if you want to practice what you learned in this section, turn to the end of this chapter and complete Exercise 2.1. When you are done, continue reading here to prepare for the next exercise.**

*A Basic Web Page*

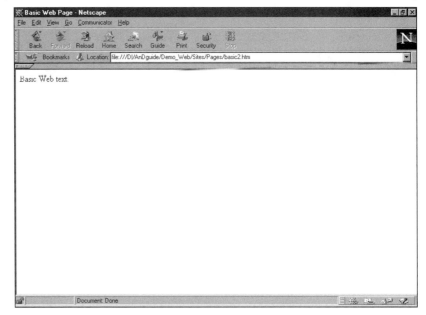

## Changing Text Appearance

If you successfully created a Web page in Exercise 2.1, you are now a Web page author! Okay, that Web page was pretty plain, but it was a Web page. Everything else you'll learn about creating Web pages will be an extension of what you have already learned. The rest of this chapter describes how to format the text that you add to Web pages.

Earlier in this chapter, an example showed how to use the bold tags, <B> and </B>, to create bold text on a Web page. The HTML standard defines many tags you can use to format the text on your Web pages. Figure 2.4 shows some of the ways you can change the appearance of text on your Web page.

▶ . . . . . . . . . . . . . . . . . . . . . . . ◀

| FIGURE 2.4 | |
|---|---|
| *Examples of Text Formatting* | |

Underlined type, **Boldface type**, *Italic type*, ***Boldface, italic type***

Sentence with subscript text. Sentence with superscript text.

Teletype text looks like it was typed on a typewriter.

SMALL TEXT APPEARS SMALLER THAN NORMAL TEXT.

**BIG** TEXT APPEARS BIGGER THAN NORMAL TEXT.

Blink tags cause your text to blink in the browser.

Font size 1, Font size 2, Font size 3, Font size 4, Font size 5, Font size 6,

# Font size 7

Font size +1, Font size +2, Font size +3, Font size +4

The following HTML code shows the text and tags used to create the Web page shown in Figure 2.4:

```
<HTML>

<HEAD>

    <TITLE>Simple Formatting Tags</TITLE>

</HEAD>

<BODY TEXT="#0000FF" BGCOLOR="#FFFFFF">

<P><U>Underlined type,</U><B>Boldface type,</B> <I>Italic
type,</I> <B><I>Boldface, italic type</I></B></P>

<P>Sentence with <SUB><FONT
COLOR="#FF0000">Subscript</FONT></SUB> text. Sentence with
<SUP><FONT COLOR="#FF0000">Superscript</FONT></SUP> text.

</P>

<P><TT><FONT COLOR="#FF0000">Teletype</FONT></TT> text looks
like it was typed on a typewriter. </P>

<P><SMALL>SMALL</SMALL> TEXT APPEARS SMALLER THAN NORMAL
TEXT. </P>
```

```
<P><BIG>BIG</BIG> TEXT APPEARS BIGGER THAN NORMAL TEXT. </P>

<P><BLINK><FONT COLOR="#FF0000">Blink</FONT></BLINK> tags
cause your text to blink in the browser. </P>

<P><FONT SIZE=+1>Font size +1,</FONT> <FONT COLOR="#FF0000"
SIZE=+2>Font

size +2,</FONT> <FONT SIZE=+3>Font size +3,</FONT> <FONT
COLOR="#00FF00" SIZE=+4>Font

size +4</FONT> </P>

<P><FONT COLOR="#000000"><FONT SIZE=-1>Font size -1,</FONT>
<FONT SIZE=-2>Font size -2,</FONT> <FONT SIZE=-3>Font size -
3,</FONT> <FONT SIZE=-4>Font size=-4</FONT></FONT> </P>

</BODY>

</HTML>
```

You can view this file on the demonstration Web site by opening the following page:

```
d:/DemoWeb2/Sites/Pages/basic3.htm
```

**NOTE**

**All the tags used to create the Web page shown in Figure 2.4 are described in Table 2.1.**

Notice that certain tags, such as the <FONT SIZE =+1> tag, can have different settings, or *attributes*. In this example, FONT is the tag name, SIZE is the attribute, and +1 is the value assigned to the attribute. A tag can have multiple attributes, and each attribute must be separated from the tag name and the other attributes by one or more character spaces. For example: <FONT SIZE=+1 COLOR=#000000>.

In the code example, notice you can surround text with more than one type of tag to create *combined effects*, such as the bold italic text that appears on the first line of the Web page in Figure 2.4.

Novell Education Course 654 divides text formatting tags into two groups: physical style tags and logical style tags. The following sections describe the differences between these tags and list tags that you can use to format text on your Web pages.

## USING PHYSICAL STYLE TAGS

Physical style tags are named for the typestyle they create. For example, the italic tags identify text to appear in an italic typeface. Logical style tags, however, are named for the type of content they represent. For example, acronym tags identify text that represents acronyms. The acronym tag name doesn't define the physical type appearance, it defines a type of content.

Table 2.1 lists some physical HTML tags that can be used to change the appearance of text in a Web page.

TABLE 2.1

*Physical Style Tags*

| STYLE | TAG (HTML VERSION) | ATTRIBUTES (VALUES) | DESCRIPTION |
|---|---|---|---|
| Base font size | `<BASEFONT >` (HTML 3.2) | | This tag defines the default font size for Web page text. |
| | | `SIZE=n` | The `SIZE` attribute defines a relative size between 1 and 7. Size 1 is the smallest, size 2 is the default value if no size value is specified, and size 3 corresponds to the default font size used in the absence of the `<BASEFONT>` tag. |
| Big | `<BIG> </BIG>` (HTML 3.2) | | The `<BIG>` tags cause the browser to display the marked text in a larger-than-normal font. |
| Blink | `<BLINK> </BLINK>` (Netscape browser only) | | The `<BLINK>` tags mark text the browser will alternately hide and display. |
| Body | `<BODY> </BODY>` (HTML 2.0) | | The `<BODY>` tag has several possible attributes (you learned about this tag earlier in the chapter). |
| | | `BACKGROUND= (/path/ file.ext)` | The `BACKGROUND` attribute specifies a graphic file that appears as a background for all the text on the Web page. This file is usually a small image the browser *tiles* to cover the entire background. This feature is similar to the wallpaper feature in Windows 95. |
| | | `TEXT= rrggbb` | The `TEXT` attribute determines the color of all nonlink text on a page. |

**T A B L E  2.1**

*Physical Style Tags*

| STYLE | TAG (HTML VERSION) | ATTRIBUTES (VALUES) | DESCRIPTION |
|---|---|---|---|
| | | ALINK= *rrggbb* <br><br> LINK= *rrggbb* <br><br> VLINK= *rrggbb* | The ALINK, LINK, and VLINK attributes define the color of active, unvisited, and visited links on the page. |
| | | BGCOLOR= *rrggbb* | The BGCOLOR attribute defines the background color to use when a background image is not defined. |
| | | **Color examples:** White: ffffff Red: ff0000 Green: 00ff00 Blue: 0000ff Black: 000000 | The value *rrggbb* is a hexadecimal number that defines how much red (*rr*), green (*gg*), and blue (*bb*) appear in the attribute's color. A 00 value indicates the minimum value (or no color). An ff value indicates the maximum value or color intensity. |
| Bold | <B> </B> (HTML 2.0) | | <BOLD> tags mark text to appear in **boldface** type. |
| Font | <FONT> </FONT> (HTML 3.2) | | <FONT> tags mark text to appear in a different size or color. |
| | | SIZE=(1 to 7, +1 to +4, and -1 to -4) | The SIZE attribute defines the relative size of the typeface. Size 1 is the smallest size, size 7 is largest. When a plus or minus symbol appears before the size value, it determines how much larger or smaller the text appears. |
| | | COLOR= *rrggbb* | The COLOR attribute uses the same color values used with the <BODY> tag. |
| | (HTML 4.0) | FACE="*typeface1, typeface2*" | The FACE attribute specifies one or more preferred typefaces or fonts for the text. The first font listed is the preferred font and the remaining fonts are alternates in order of preference. If none of the listed fonts are installed on the browser user's computer, one of the available fonts is used. |

*(continued)*

**T A B L E  2.1**

*Physical Style Tags*
*(continued)*

| STYLE | TAG<br>(HTML VERSION) | ATTRIBUTES<br>(VALUES) | DESCRIPTION |
|---|---|---|---|
| Italic | `<I> </I>`<br>(HTML 2.0) | | `<ITALIC>` tags mark text to appear in *italic* typeface. |
| Small | `<SMALL> </SMALL>`<br>(HTML 3.2) | | The `<SMALL>` tags mark text that the browser displays in a smaller-than-normal font. |
| Subscript | `<SUB> </SUB>`<br>(HTML 3.2) | | Subscript tags mark text to appear in <sub>subscript</sub> form |
| Superscript | `<SUP> </SUP>`<br>(HTML 3.2) | | Superscript tags mark text to appear in <sup>superscript</sup> form. |
| Strike-through | `<S> </S>`<br>`<STRIKE> </STRIKE>`<br>(HTML 2.0) | | Both of these pairs of tags are used to indicate text that has been deleted from a document. |
| Teletype | `<TT> </TT>`<br>(HTML 2.0) | | Teletype tags mark text to appear as if it were typed on a typewriter or teletype that uses a `fixed width for each character.` |
| Underline | `<U> </U>`<br>(HTML 2.0) | | These tags underline text in your Web page. |

**Table 2.1 lists the RBG color codes for five basic colors. For a more complete listing of colors, view the RGB Hex Triplet Color Chart at the following URL:**

`www.phoenix.net/~jacobson/rgb.html`

In the sample file for Figure 2.4, one HTML tag — the `<P>` tag — has not yet been explained. The `<P>` tag is one of several tags that control line spacing on a Web page, and is described later in this chapter.

The HTML versions listed in Table 2.1 show which versions of HTML support the listed tags. HTML 2.0 is the first widely adopted standard for HTML tags. HTML 3.0 was a working standard to which browser manufacturers developed software, but it was later replaced by HTML 3.2. The tags defined in HTML 2.0

are supported in later versions, but same tags support additional attributes in never versions. The latest official release is HTML 4.0.

**For information on a specfic version of HTML, browse to:**

**HTML version 2.0:** `www.w3.org/MarkUp/html-spec/`

**HTML version 3.2:** `www.w3.org/TR/REC-html32.html`

**HTML version 4:** `www.w3.org/TR/REC-html40/`

**To view online HTML handbooks, visit the following locations:**

**The Web Developer's Virtual Library:** `www.stars.com/`

**Netscape's Online Handbook:**
`www.netscape.com/eng/mozilla/3.0/handbook/`

**Microsoft Internet Explorer 3.0 Author's Guide and HTML Reference:**
`www.microsoft.com/workshop/author/newhtml/htmlr000.htm`

**The URLs for files or Web pages on some operating systems are case sensitive. If you enter a URL that doesn't work, check to be sure that you used the correct case. For example, on UNIX systems** `www.test.com/Index.htm` **and** `www.test.com/index.htm` **are two different file names.**

**TIP**

## USING LOGICAL STYLE TAGS

Logical style tags identify specific types of content, such as headings or addresses, rather than physical type characteristics, such as bold or italic. Because logical style tag names don't specify a physical appearance, browser developers have more freedom to choose how to display text marked with these tags. Most browsers support some of these logical style tags by changing the appearance of the marked text and ignore the other logical style tags.

Figure 2.5 shows a Web page featuring some logical style tags.

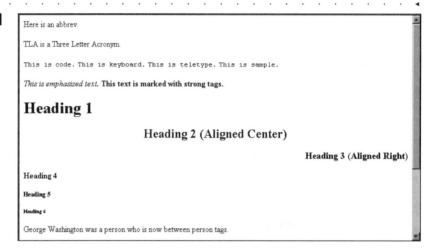

F I G U R E  2.5

*Logical Style Tags*

> Here is an abbrev.
>
> TLA is a Three Letter Acronym.
>
> This is code. This is keyboard. This is teletype. This is sample.
>
> *This is emphasized text.* **This text is marked with strong tags.**
>
> # Heading 1
>
> ## Heading 2 (Aligned Center)
>
> ### Heading 3 (Aligned Right)
>
> **Heading 4**
>
> **Heading 5**
>
> **Heading 6**
>
> George Washington was a person who is now between person tags.

Some lines don't show any special formatting because browsers ignore tags they do not support.

**NOTE**

**Some utility programs use HTML logical tags, even though your browser doesn't support them. For example, you might use the `<ACRONYM>` tags to mark acronyms in your Web page, and then run a utility to compile and sort the list of acronyms.**

To see how the Figure 2.5 logical style tags appear in your browser, view the following demonstration Web page:

`d:/DemoWeb2/Sites/Pages/logical.htm`

To view the tags used in the sample file with Netscape Navigator 4, select View → Page Source.

Notice the third line in Figure 2.5. This line uses a different tag for each sentence, yet all four sentences appear in the same monospace font. In this case, the browser supports all four of the tags in the same way. Each browser can support logical style tags differently. For example, one browser might use bold for text between `<STRONG>` and `</STRONG>` tags, while another might use a larger type size.

Table 2.2 describes some of the most common logical style tags.

TABLE 2.2

*Logical Style Tags*

| STYLE | TAG (HTML VERSION) | DESCRIPTION |
|---|---|---|
| Abbreviation | `<ABBREV> </ABBREV>` (HTML 3.0) | This tag marks text that represents an abbreviation. You might use this tag to highlight abbreviations defined elsewhere in the document. |
| Acronym | `<ACRONYM> </ACRONYM>` (HTML 3.0) | Acronym tags mark text that represents an acronym. You might use this tag to highlight acronyms defined elsewhere in the document. |
| Address | `<ADDRESS> </ADDRESS>` (HTML 2.0) | This tag marks special text, such as an e-mail address. You might use this tag to highlight a Web page author's name, e-mail address, or postal address. |
| Citation | `<CITE> </CITE>` (HTML 2.0) | The `<CITE>` tags can be used to mark text that is a citation from a book or other published work. |
| Code | `<CODE> </CODE>` (HTML 2.0) | Code tags mark text representing computer code. The `<CODE>` tags typically display text in a monospace font—similar to the fonts you get when you use the teletype (`<TT>`), keyboard (`<KBD>`), and sample (`<SAMP>`) tags. |
| Deleted | `<DEL> </DEL>` | These tags mark text deleted from an earlier version of a document. These tags are often used in legal documents. For example, a browser might display deleted text by using strikethrough formatting. |
| Definition | `<DFN> </DFN>` (HTML 3.2) | The `<DFN>` tags can be used to mark new terms that you are defining on your Web page. |
| Emphasize | `<EM> </EM>` (HTML 2.0) | These tags mark text you want to emphasize. You can use other tags, such as bold and italic, to emphasize text, or you can use the `<EM>` and `<STRONG>` tags to let the browser determine how to emphasize your text. Typically, the emphasize tags produce italic text. |
| Heading | `<H1> </H1>` `<H2> </H2>` `<H3> </H3>` `<H4> </H4>` | This formats the surrounded text as a heading. Headings are used in documents, as in this book, to create titles for different sections. Headings help to organize a document and break up what might otherwise appear as a solid wall of text. Typically, the `<H1>` tags display bold text in a large font size, and the `<H6>` tags display text in a smaller font size. |

*(continued)*

**T A B L E 2 . 2**

*Logical Style Tags*
*(continued)*

| STYLE | TAG (HTML VERSION) | DESCRIPTION |
|---|---|---|
| | `<H5> </H5>`<br>`<H6> </H6>`<br>(HTML 2.0) | The default position for headings is on the left, but you can use the ALIGN attribute to position the heading LEFT, CENTER, or RIGHT. For example:<br>`<H1 ALIGN=CENTER>Centered Head</H1>` |
| Inserted | `<INS> </INS>` | These tags mark text that has been inserted into a document (just as the `<DEL>` tags highlight deleted text). The `<INS>` and `<DEL>` tags enable you to mark changes made to documents. |
| Keyboard | `<KBD> </KBD>`<br>(HTML 2.0) | These tags mark text that represents keyboard-entered text. Typically, browsers display keyboard text in monospace fonts — similar to the fonts used for teletype (`<TT>`) and code (`<CODE>`), and sample (`<SAMP>`) tags. |
| Person | `<PERSON> </PERSON>`<br>(HTML 3.0) | Person tags mark text identifying a person. For example, you might want to use this tag to identify the actors in a play script. |
| Sample | `<SAMP> </SAMP>`<br>(HTML 3.2) | The `<SAMP>` tag can be used to identify sample commands and computer output in your Web pages. Typically, browsers display this text in monospace fonts — similar to the fonts used for keyboard (`<KBD>`), teletype (`<TT>`), and code (`<CODE>`) tags. |
| Strong | `<STRONG> </STRONG>`<br>(HTML 2.0) | The `<STRONG>` tag is used for text that should be emphasized. You can use other tags, such as the bold and italic tags to emphasize text, or you can use the `<STRONG>` tags and let the browser determine how to emphasize your text. Typically, the `<STRONG>` tags produce bold text. |
| Variable | `<VAR> </VAR>`<br>(HTML 2.0) | These tags are used to mark variable names or other text that serves as a placeholder for other information. |

**NOTE**

**Some utility programs might use tags not specified in the HTML specifications. For example, the `<DEL>` and `<INS>` tags are described in Course 654, but they are not in the HTML specifications.**

**TIP**

**Whenever you start using a new logical style tag, it is wise to test that tag in the browsers you want to support. You don't want to create 200 Web pages with a tag that your browser ignores or displays in a way that you don't appreciate.**

**Exercise 2.2: If you're preparing to take the certification exam, or if you want to practice what you learned in this section, turn to the end of this chapter and complete Exercise 2.2. When you are done, continue reading here to prepare for the next exercise.**

## Adjusting Line Spacing and Margins

So far, you've seen how to set up a basic Web page and change the appearance of the type on the page. As a Web author, you have some control over the width and length of the Web page, but the user has ultimate control. For example, users define the Web page width when they open the browser and adjust the window size. If the window width becomes narrower, the length of the document becomes longer as the browser automatically adjusts the text to fit in the smaller window. If the user makes the window wider, the document length becomes shorter.

As a Web author, you control the vertical spacing (line breaks) in your document and the indentation from the margin. Table 2.3 lists HTML tags that control the *position* of the text on the page.

TABLE 2.3

*Line Spacing and Margin Tags*

| STYLE | TAG (HTML VERSION) | ATTRIBUTES (VALUES) | DESCRIPTION SAMPLE FILE |
|---|---|---|---|
| Block quote | `<BLOCKQUOTE> </BLOCKQUOTE>` (HTML 2.0) | | Indents the paragraph between The `<BLOCKQUOTE>` tags from both the right and left margins. Sample file: *d*:/DemoWeb2/Sites/Pages/blkquote.htm |
| Center line | `<CENTER> </CENTER>` (HTML 3.2) | | Centers the line of text in the browser window. Sample file: *d*:/DemoWeb2/Sites/Pages/linebrk.htm |
| Comments | `<!--comments>` (HTML 2.0) | | Enables you to include comments that are hidden from Web-page visitors. Sample files: all of the files in this list |

*(continued)*

T A B L E  2.3

*Line Spacing and Margin*
*Tags (continued)*

| STYLE | TAG (HTML VERSION) | ATTRIBUTES (VALUES) | DESCRIPTION SAMPLE FILE |
|---|---|---|---|
| Document division | `<DIV> </DIV>` (HTML 3.2) | | The division tags mark a section of text that is to be aligned with the ALIGN attribute. |
| | | `ALIGN=(LEFT, RIGHT, or CENTER)` | The `ALIGN` attribute determines the alignment of the text in the document division. The default alignment is LEFT. |
| Horizontal rule | `<HR>` (HTML 2.0) | | Creates a horizontal rule (or line) across the Web page. |
| | | `SIZE= (1-99)` | The `SIZE` attribute determines the thickness of the rule. |
| | | `WIDTH= (1-100)%` or *n* | The `WIDTH` attribute determines the width of the rule. When the % symbol is specified, this attribute sets the percentage of the page the rule covers. When a number is entered without the % symbol, the width is defined in pixels. |
| | | `ALIGN=(LEFT, RIGHT, or CENTER)` | The `ALIGN` parameter determines the alignment of the rule. The default alignment is LEFT. |
| | | `NOSHADE` | The `NOSHADE` attribute creates a solid rule with no shading. Sample file: *d*:/DemoWeb2/Sites/Pages/horzrul.htm |
| New line (break) | `<BR>` (HTML 2.0) | | Starts a new line; does not create an extra blank line. |
| | | `CLEAR= (LEFT or RIGHT)` | The `CLEAR` attribute starts the next text line on the next available line if the specified margin (left or right) is clear. This option can be used to prevent text from wrapping around an image. Sample file: *d*:/DemoWeb2/Sites/Pages/linebrk.htm |
| No line break | `<NOBR> </NOBR>` (HTML 3.0) | | Prevents a line of text from being split into two or more lines. Sample file: *d*:/DemoWeb2/Sites/Pages/linebrk.htm |

**T A B L E   2.3**

*Line Spacing and Margin
Tags*

| STYLE | TAG (HTML VERSION) | ATTRIBUTES (VALUES) | DESCRIPTION SAMPLE FILE |
|-------|--------------------|--------------------|--------------------------|
| Paragraph | `<P> </P>` (HTML 2.0) | | Marks the beginning and end of a paragraph. Creates one blank line after the paragraph. Sample file: *d*:/DemoWeb2/Sites/Pages/linebrk.htm |
| Preformatted text | `<PRE> </PRE>` (HTML 2.0) | | Causes the browser to display the space characters and line breaks in the surrounded text exactly as it appears in the HTML file. Sample file: *d*:/DemoWeb2/Sites/Pages/pre_fmt.htm |

**NOTE**

**The sample files mentioned in Table 2.3 demonstrate how the various tags can be used. You can use your browser to view both the finished page and the source HTML text and tags. To view the source HTML in Netscape Navigator 4, select View → Page Source.**

The break and new paragraph tags listed in Table 2.3 are necessary, as browsers ignore any formatting that is not created with HTML tags. For example, if you write a paragraph in the body of your HTML file and then hit enter twice to create a blank line between paragraphs, browsers ignore those blank lines. Browsers also ignore multiple space characters and tab characters.

To force browsers to use the formatting of your HTML file, you can use the `<PRE>` tags. When you use the `<PRE>` tags, all line endings and spaces between the tags are preserved.

**TIP**

**Browsers also ignore multiple `<P>` tags when there is no text between them. For example, if you entered three new paragraph tags, `<P><P><P>`, the browser would skip just one line before starting the next paragraph. To trick the browser into supporting multiple new paragraph tags, enter each tag as follows: `<P> `**

**The ` ` value inserts an invisible nonbreaking space character into the paragraph so the paragraph is not empty. This special character is introduced in the next section.**

**Exercise 2.3: If you're preparing to take the certification exam, or if you want to practice what you learned in this section, turn to the end of this chapter and complete Exercise 2.3. When you are done, continue reading here to prepare for the next exercise.**

## Adding Special Characters to HTML Files

At some point, you may want to include a less-than (<) or greater-than (>) symbol on your Web page. If you simply type the symbol, your browser will interpret it as part of an HTML tag. At best, the symbol will not appear on your Web page. The worst case is the browser will interpret the symbol as a valid HTML tag and display your page in some bizarre manner you didn't intend.

To ensure that symbols actually appear as the intended symbols, you must occasionally enter some special text that browsers will recognize as symbols. Table 2.4 shows how to display a variety of special characters on your Web pages.

| TABLE 2.4 | SYMBOL | CHARACTER | HTML CODE |
| --- | --- | --- | --- |
| *Special Character Codes* | Ampersand | & | `&amp;` |
| | Copyright | © | `&#169;` |
| | Greater-than | > | `&gt;` |
| | Less-than | < | `&lt;` |
| | Nonbreaking Space | Produces a single blank character or space. | ` ` |
| | Quotation Marks | " | `&quote;` |
| | Registered Trademark | ™ | `&reg;` |

To view a sample file with special characters, open the following demonstration Web page:

```
d:/DemoWeb2/Sites/Pages/symbol.htm
```

Some symbols, such as parentheses and the dollar symbol ($), can be entered directly in an HTML file, and others such as the ampersand symbol require special codes. If you are unsure if a symbol requires a code, just enter the symbol in the Web page. If the symbol does not appear properly, you need to use a special HTML code.

**You can see a list of additional special characters on the following Web page:**

```
www.uni-passau.de/~ramsch/iso8859-1.html
```

**Exercises 2.4 and 2.5: If you're preparing to take the certification exam, or if you want to practice what you learned in this section, turn to the end of this chapter and complete Exercises 2.4 and 2.5.**

## Summary

In this chapter, you learned that Web pages are text files with Hypertext Markup Language (HTML) tags. HTML tags define the beginning and end of the Web page, and they divide the Web page into two components: the head and the body.

HTML tags also let you control how text appears on the Web page. Physical style tags are HTML tags that define the appearance of text, and logical style tags are HTML tags that define the content between the tags.

Because browsers ignore the line endings in HTML files, you must use HTML tags to start new lines and paragraphs on Web pages. Additional HTML tags enable you to create rules, and to position paragraphs on the left, right, or center of the browser window.

When you want to enter special characters, such as < and > on Web pages, you need to enter special character sequences like &lt; and &gt;. Otherwise, these characters are interpreted as HTML commands.

This chapter showed you how to create a basic Web page and format text on that page. In the next chapter, you'll learn how to dress up pages with lists, tables, and images.

## PUZZLE 2.1: CREATING WEB PAGES

The following word puzzle contains many of the terms discussed in this chapter. See if you can find all the words. As you search for the words, ask yourself why the word is in the list, and how it was used in this chapter. If you don't know the answers to these questions, you might want to review the chapter.

```
A   M   P   E   R   S   A   N   D   G   B   R   U   X   T
L   U   C   M   Y   N   O   R   C   A   I   G   R   W   E
P   F   E   T   O   U   Q   K   C   O   L   B   L   G   Z
H   O   N   S   B   H   N   K   R   L   V   B   A   I   I
A   F   T   B   G   J   G   N   H   A   F   P   C   S   S
N   Y   E   N   C   R   I   I   T   C   M   K   I   S   K
U   W   R   L   O   A   L   L   D   I   A   K   G   T   R
M   M   I   U   L   F   A   B   I   S   T   V   O   R   Y
E   M   N   I   O   A   E   P   W   Y   E   L   L   O   H
R   D   N   C   R   N   M   S   P   H   M   I   E   N   B
I   K   D   H   L   M   G   S   A   P   F   N   H   G   O
C   E   A   R   E   S   W   O   R   B   O   K   S   F   D
O   T   E   T   I   P   U   S   V   L   N   Q   K   A   Y
D   D   H   T   M   L   R   B   Y   I   T   W   J   D   B
E   T   E   X   T   D   P   E   L   V   D   V   Y   B   K
```

| | | | |
|---|---|---|---|
| ALINK | blink | link | site |
| acronym | body | logical | size |
| align | bookmark | meta | small |
| alphanumeric | browser | PRE | strong |
| ampersand | center | page | text |
| BGCOLOR | code | physical | title |
| BLOCKQUOT | DIV | RGB | URL |
| background | font | SGML | VLINK |
| basefont | HTML | SUB | Web |
| big | head | SUP | width |

**EXERCISE 2.1: CREATING A WEB PAGE**

Now that you know what needs to be in an HTML file, why not create a Web page? It's easy, and doing it will give your confidence a big boost.

To create a Web page, do the following:

**1** • Open the text editor or word processor program that you want to use to create the HTML file. Windows Notepad will work.

**NOTE**

**If you use a word processor, be sure that the program permits you to save the file in text format. To improve your understanding of HTML, I recommend that you do not use Web page and Web site development tools until after they are introduced later in Chapters 5 and 6.**

**2** • Create a new file with the required HTML tags and the following text:

Title: **My First Web Page**

Body content: **This is my first Web page.**

**3** • Save the file in text file format as MYPAGE1.HTM.

**NOTE**

**Most Web servers and browsers expect HTML files to use the HTM or HTML file extension. Some text editors and word processors, however, save text files with the default TXT extension if you do not specify an extension. If you plan to publish your Web pages on one of the Web servers from Novell, I recommend that you use the HTML extension. If you plan to publish your Web pages on a different type of Web server, ask your Web server administrator to tell you which extension to use.**

**4** • View the file with your browser and verify that the title appears at the top of the browser window and the body content appears in the Web page display area. If you have trouble with this exercise and want to see the correct results, view the Web page and its source HTML tags on this book's CD-ROM at:

*d:*/DemoWeb2/Answers/mypage1.htm

**TIP**

**The URL for a file on your computer is:**

file:///d:/path/filename.htm

where *d* is the drive letter, *path* specifies the file's directory, and *filename* is the name you give to the file.

**TIP**

**When viewing a Web page in your browser, you can quickly view the HTML tags for that page by using a menu command. To view the tags in Netscape Navigator 4, select View → Page Source.**

**EXERCISE 2.2: FORMATTING TEXT**

In this exercise, you'll add some text formatting to liven up that Web page you created in Exercise 2.1.

To complete this exercise, do the following:

**1** • Use a text editor or word processor program to open the file you created in Exercise 2.1. This file is also on this book's CD-ROM at:

*d:*/DemoWeb2/Answers/mypage1.htm

**2** • Add a heading to the body titled **My First Web Page**. This should be a level-1 heading, and it should be positioned in the center of the page.

**3** • Format the word *My* in the heading so that it blinks.

**4** • Format the sentence below the heading so the entire sentence appears in blue and the word *my* appears in italics.

**5** • Save the file and display it in your browser. Your Web page should appear as shown in Figure 2.6. The source file for this exercise is on this book's CD-ROM at:

*d:*/DemoWeb2/Answers/mypage2.htm

**FIGURE 2.6**

*Exercise 2.2 Result*

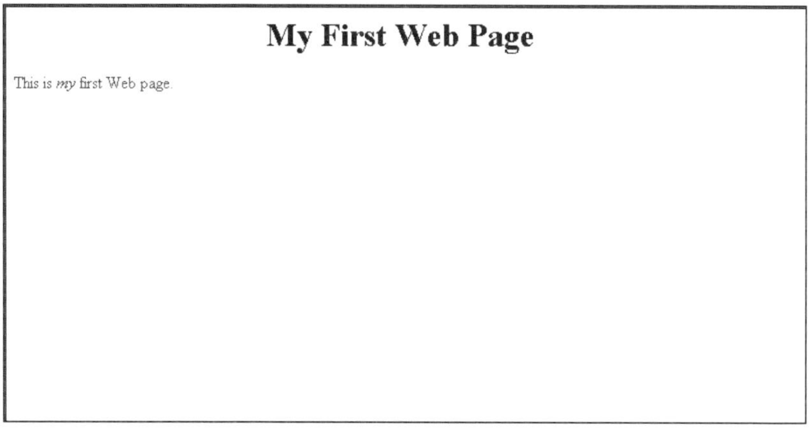

# My First Web Page

This is *my* first Web page.

### EXERCISE 2.3: POSITIONING TEXT

In this exercise, you'll improve the Web page you created in Exercise 2.2 by adding some alignment tags and a horizontal rule.

To complete this exercise, do the following:

1 • Use a text editor or word processor program to open the file you created in Exercise 2.2. This file is also on this book's CD-ROM at:

   *d:*/DemoWeb2/Answers/mypage2.htm

2 • Use <CENTER> tags to center the last sentence on the page.

3 • Add a horizontal rule below the last sentence and set it to 50 percent of the page width.

4 • Add the following sentences below the horizontal rule:

**This paragraph is aligned left.**

**This paragraph is centered.**

**This paragraph is aligned right.**

5 • Format each sentence in Step 4 as a separate paragraph that is aligned as defined in the sentence. There should be one blank line space between paragraphs.

6 • Add a second horizontal rule below the last sentence and set it to use the default settings.-

7 • Enter the numbers 1, 2, and 3, and format them so they appear on different lines with no blank lines between them. Use <CENTER> tags to center these lines.

**8** • Save the file and display it in your browser. Your Web page should appear like the one shown in Figure 2.7. The source file for this exercise is on this book's CD-ROM at:

*d:/DemoWeb2/Answers/mypage3.htm*

FIGURE 2.7

*Exercise 2.3 Result*

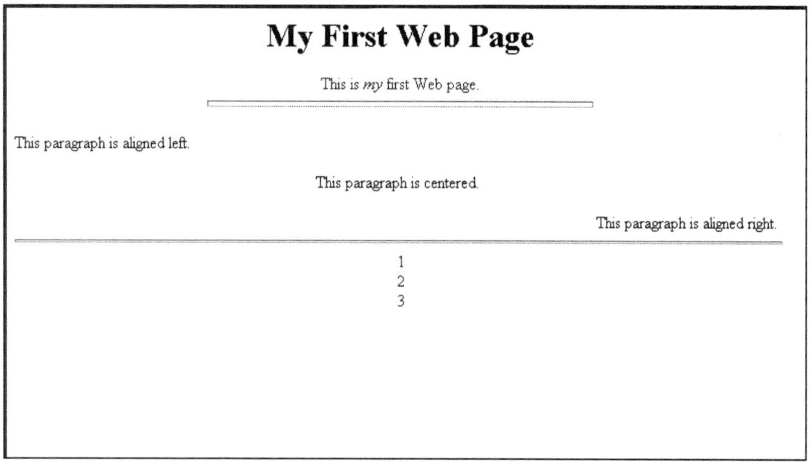

**My First Web Page**

This is *my* first Web page.

This paragraph is aligned left.

This paragraph is centered.

This paragraph is aligned right.

1
2
3

## EXERCISE 2.4: ADDING SPECIAL CHARACTERS

In this exercise, you'll add special characters to the Web page you created in Exercise 2.3.

To complete this exercise, do the following:

**1** • Use a text editor or word processor program to open the file you created in Exercise 2.3. This file is also on this book's CD-ROM at:

*d:*/DemoWeb2/Answers/mypage3.htm

**2** • In the first of the three numbered paragraphs, place a less-than symbol (<) in front of the number and a greater-than symbol (>) after the number.

**3** • In the second of the three numbered paragraphs, place quotation marks on either side of the number.

**4** • After the last sentence in the file, create a new paragraph with the word Novell, and place the registered trademark symbol after Novell. Center this line in the browser.

**5** • Save the file and display it in your browser. Your Web page should appear like that shown in Figure 2.8. The source file for this exercise is on this book's CD-ROM at:

*d:*/DemoWeb2/Answers/mypage4.htm

FIGURE 2.8

*Exercise 2.4 Result*

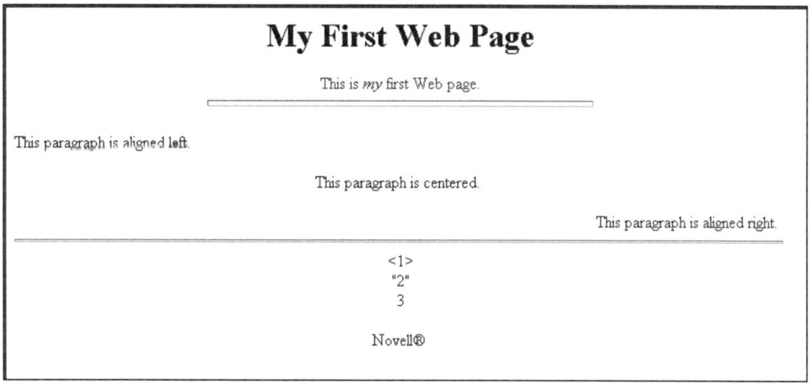

# My First Web Page

This is *my* first Web page.

This paragraph is aligned left.

This paragraph is centered.

This paragraph is aligned right.

<1>
"2"
3

Novell®

### EXERCISE 2.5

The best way to prepare for the Course 654 exam is to practice using all of the tags and attributes described in this chapter. You might be asked to name or enter any of these tags, and you'll need to understand the differences between tags that produce similar results. The following questions help you prepare for this test:

1 • HTML is a subset of which standard?

   Answer: . . . . . . . . . . . . . . . . . . . . . . . . . . . . . . . . . . . . . .

2 • Name the two parts of an HTML document.

   a. . . . . . . . . . . . . . . . . . . . . . . . . . . . . . . . . . . . . . . . . .

   b. . . . . . . . . . . . . . . . . . . . . . . . . . . . . . . . . . . . . . . . . .

3 • What file format do you use when saving a Web page file?

   Answer: . . . . . . . . . . . . . . . . . . . . . . . . . . . . . . . . . . . . . .

4 • Which tag pair causes a browser to display the non-HTML line breaks and spaces entered in a Web page file?

   Answer: . . . . . . . . . . . . . . . . . . . . . . . . . . . . . . . . . . . . . .

5 • Name three places where a Web page title can appear.

   a. . . . . . . . . . . . . . . . . . . . . . . . . . . . . . . . . . . . . . . . . .

   b. . . . . . . . . . . . . . . . . . . . . . . . . . . . . . . . . . . . . . . . . .

   c. . . . . . . . . . . . . . . . . . . . . . . . . . . . . . . . . . . . . . . . . .

6 • List the two tag pairs that produce subscript and superscript type.

   a. Subscript: . . . . . . . . . . . . . . . . . . . . . . . . . . . . . . . . . . .

   b. Superscript: . . . . . . . . . . . . . . . . . . . . . . . . . . . . . . . . . .

**7** • Which heading tag attribute allows you to position the heading in the left margin, the center, or the right margin?

Answer: . . . . . . . . . . . . . . . . . . . . . . . . . . . . . . . . . . . . . . . . . .

**8** • Write down the complete opening blockquote tag.

Answer: . . . . . . . . . . . . . . . . . . . . . . . . . . . . . . . . . . . . . . . . . .

**9** • Write down the HTML character sequence that produces a nonbreaking space character.

Answer: . . . . . . . . . . . . . . . . . . . . . . . . . . . . . . . . . . . . . . . . . .

**10** • Write down the HTML character sequence that produces an ampersand character (&).

Answer: . . . . . . . . . . . . . . . . . . . . . . . . . . . . . . . . . . . . . . . . . .

# CHAPTER 3

# Using Lists, Tables, and Images

The previous chapter described how to create a basic Web page and format text on that page. This chapter describes how to enhance your Web pages with lists, tables, and images.

## Creating Lists

Lists are a great way to organize information on your Web pages. You can use HTML tags to create the following kinds of lists:

- Unordered lists

- Ordered (numbered or lettered) lists

- Definition lists

- Nested lists

Figure 3.1 shows how the three types of lists appear on a Web page.

| FIGURE 3.1 | |
|---|---|
| *Examples of Lists* | In the following example lists, notice that the sample unordered list does not display a list title, but the sample ordered list does. If you enter text after the start list tag and before the first \<li\> tag, that text becomes a list title, which appears on its own line above the list. Also, note the indentation of List titles. |

The following is an unordered list:

- Item 1
- Item 2
- Item 3

The following is an ordered (numbered) list:

Ordered List
1. Item 1
2. Item 2
3. Item 3

The following is a definition list:

Topic #1
    Description of Topic #1.
Topic #2
    Description of Topic #2.
Topic #3
    Description of Topic #3.

Figure 3.1 shows a portion of the demonstration Web page that contains different kinds of lists. To view the complete page in your browser, open this page:

```
d:/DemoWeb2/Sites/Pages/lists.htm
```

Lists convey information on your Web pages clearly and concisely.

## UNORDERED LISTS

*Unordered lists* organize nonsequential items. In plain unordered lists, each list item begins on a new line without any preceding symbols. In bulleted lists, each item is preceded by a bullet, which highlights the beginning of a list item with a circle or square symbol. The following is an example of an unordered HTML list:

```
<UL>List Heading

<LI>Item 1

<LI>Item 2

<LI>Item 3

</UL>
```

Notice the list structure: as with most of the HTML tags you've used so far, there is an opening tag and a closing tag. There is also a list item tag, <LI>, for each item within the list. Remember that, unless the <PRE> tags are used, the browser ignores line endings. The <LI> tag is required to identify the start of a new list item. For example, the following list tags produce the same result as the previous set:

```
<UL>List Heading

<LI>Item 1<LI>Item 2<LI>Item 3

</UL>
```

**NOTE**

**Closing </LI> tags are not required.**

Use the HTML tags shown in Table 3.1 to create unordered lists.

T A B L E  3.1

*Unordered List Tags*

| STYLE | TAG (HTML VERSION) | ATTRIBUTES (VALUES) | DESCRIPTION |
|-------|-------------------|--------------------|-------------|
| List start | `<UL>` (HTML 2.0) | | Marks the beginning of an unordered list. Any text placed after this tag and before the first list item (`<LI>`) tag appears as a heading for the list. |
| | | PLAIN | The PLAIN attribute causes the list to appear without bullets. Note: This attribute does not require a value. Use it as you use the others (for example, `<UL PLAIN>`). |
| List item | `<LI>` (HTML 2.0) | | Starts a new list item on its own line. |
| | | TYPE=(DISC, CIRCLE, or SQUARE) | The TYPE attribute determines the type of bullet that appears for this item and all the following items until another type is specified. DISC specifies a solid circle, CIRCLE specifies a hollow circle, and square displays a square. |
| | | | Note that some browsers ignore the TYPE attribute, or display circles as squares. |
| List end | `</UL>` (HTML 2.0) | | Marks the end of the unordered list. |

## ORDERED LISTS

*Ordered lists* are numbered lists best used to organize sequential items, such as procedures or outlines. Ordered lists use the same structure as unordered lists. Table 3.2 lists the HTML tags you can use to create ordered lists.

TABLE 3.2

*Ordered List Tags*

| STYLE | TAG (HTML VERSION) | ATTRIBUTES (VALUES) | DESCRIPTION |
|---|---|---|---|
| List start | `<OL>` (HTML 2.0) | | Marks the beginning of an ordered list. Any text placed after this tag and before the first `<LI>` tag appears as a heading for the list. |
| | | `START=` (*number* or *letter*) | The `START` attribute specifies the first list item number or letter. The default start number is 1. |
| List item | `<LI>` (HTML 2.0) | | Starts a new list item on its own line. |
| | | `TYPE=` (1, I, i, A, a) | The `TYPE` attribute determines the type of number or letter that appears for this item and all the following items until another type is specified. The default value is Arabic numerals (1, 2, 3...). Types I and i specify uppercase and lowercase roman numerals. Types A and a specify uppercase and lowercase letters. |
| List end | `</OL>` (HTML 2.0) | | Marks the end of the ordered list. |

## DEFINITION LISTS

*Definition lists* are a good way to present groups of definitions, such as in a glossary. The following tags illustrate the structure of definition lists:

```
<P><B>Definition List</P></B>

<DL>

<DT>Topic #1

<DD>Description of Topic #1.

<DT>Topic #2

<DD>Description of Topic #2.

<DT> Topic #3
```

```
<DD>Description of Topic #3.

</DL>
```

As with the other list types, definition lists begin and end with tags that define the list type. The difference is that definition lists have two item types — topics and descriptions. If this list was for a glossary, each topic would correspond to a term and each description would correspond to the definition. Use the HTML tags shown in Table 3.3 to create definition lists.

TABLE 3.3

*Definition List Tags*

| STYLE | TAG (HTML VERSION) | DESCRIPTION |
|---|---|---|
| Definition list start | `<DL>` (HTML 2.0) | Marks the beginning of a definition list. Any text placed after this tag and before the first definition topic (`<DT>`) tag appears as a heading for the list. |
| Definition topic | `<DT>` (HTML 2.0) | Marks the beginning of a topic name. Each topic name appears flush left on a separate line. |
|  |  | If you use the `<DT>` tag without the definition list start (`<DL>`) tag or the definition description (`<DD>`) tags, your definition will follow on the same line, immediately after the topic name. |
| Definition description | `<DD>` (HTML 2.0) | Marks the start of a topic description; the description is indented automatically. |
| Definition list end | `</DL>` (HTML 2.0) | Marks the end of the definition list. |

**TIP**

**If the definition tags don't create line breaks where you want them, remember, you can use a `<BR>` tag to create a line break (in other words, to create a new line).**

## NESTED LISTS

Nested lists are lists within lists. Figure 3.2 shows a nested list.

FIGURE 3.2

*Nested List*

The following is a nested list:

1. First primary list item
2. Secondary List #1
   - Item 1
   - Item 2
   - Item 3
3. Secondary List #2
   1. Item 1
   2. Item 2
   3. Item 3
4. Secondary List #3
   - Item 1
   - Item 2
   - Item 3

To create a nested list, you simply create lists within lists. The browser recognizes subordinate lists and indents them automatically. The following HTML tags created the nested list in Figure 3.2:

```
<OL>

<LI>First primary list item

<LI>Secondary List #1

<UL TYPE=SQUARE>

<LI>Item 1

<LI>Item 2

<LI>Item 3<!--End of secondary list #1-->

</UL>

<LI>Secondary List #2

<OL>

<LI>Item 1

<LI>Item 2

<LI>Item 3<!--End of secondary list #2-->

</OL>

<LI>Secondary List #3
```

```
<UL TYPE=CIRCLE>

<LI>Item 1

<LI>Item 2

<LI>Item 3<!--End of secondary list #3--><!--End of primary
list-->

</UL>

</OL>
```

**NOTE**

**Novell Education Course 654 recommends that you limit nesting to three levels. Beyond three levels, nested lists are hard to read.**

**Exercise 3.1: If you're preparing to take the certification exam, or if you want to practice what you learned in this section, turn to the end of this chapter and complete Exercise 3.1. When you are done, continue reading here to prepare for the next exercise.**

## Building Tables

As with lists, tables can help to organize information on a Web page. Figure 3.3 shows a sample table.

*Sample Table*

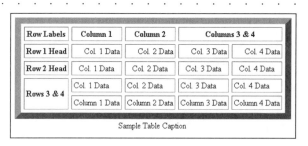

The HTML structure for tables is similar to that for lists. Each table begins and ends with HTML tags that mark the start and finish of the table. The difference is that the items between the start and end tags define table rows instead of list items. The following HTML tags demonstrate how to define rows in an HTML table:

```
<TABLE>

<TR></TR>

<TR></TR>

</TABLE>
```

These tags create a table with two rows and no columns. Because there are no columns, this table won't display. To add columns, you have to define the column cells in each row with table head tags (<TH>) and table data tags (<TD>). Table head tags typically display bold text and are used for row and column headings. Table data tags are used to display table cell data. The following HTML tags create a table with two rows and three columns:

```
<TABLE>

<TR><TH>Rows<TH>Column 1<TH>Column 2</TR>

<TR><TH>1<TD>Data<TD>Data</TR>

<TR><TH>2<TD>Data<TD>Data</TR>

</TABLE>
```

Because the first row lists all of the column headings, each column cell is defined with a <TH> tag. Rows 2 and 3 start with a <TH> tag to define the row heading, and the remaining cells are defined with <TD> tags.

The important thing to remember when creating tables is that you must account for every column in every row, otherwise some rows will be shorter than others. For example, suppose I had no data for row 2, column 2 in the previous example. If I omitted the column cell definition for this cell, the data for column 3 would appear in column 2, and there would be no table cell for column 3. The table would be wrong, and if I were using borders for the table, it would also be ugly. To avoid this, I need to define the column cell without contents as follows:

```
<TABLE>

<TR><TH>Rows<TH>Column 1<TH>Column 2</TR>

<TR><TH>1<TD><TD>Data</TR>
```

```
<TR><TH>2<TD>Data<TD>Data</TR>

</TABLE>
```

The two adjacent <TD> tags indicate that the first represents an empty cell. Table 3.4 lists the most common table tags.

T A B L E  3.4

*Table Tags*

| STYLE | TAG (HTML VERSION) | ATTRIBUTES (VALUES) | DESCRIPTION SAMPLE FILE |
|---|---|---|---|
| Table start | <TABLE> (HTML 3.2) | | Marks the beginning of a table. |
| | | CELLPADDING= (*number*) | The CELLPADDING attribute defines the number of pixels between the cell border and the cell contents. |
| | | CELLSPACING= (*number*) | The CELLSPACING attribute defines the number of pixels between the cell borders. |
| | | BORDER= (*number*) | The BORDER attribute creates a border around the table and defines the border thickness in pixels. |
| | | ALIGN= (LEFT or RIGHT) | The ALIGN attribute defines whether the table is aligned with the left or right margins of the page. The default alignment is left. |
| | | BACKGROUND= filename.ext | BACKGROUND identifies a background image for the table, which tiles to fill the table. Images are described later in this chapter. |
| | | BGCOLOR= *#rrggbb* | BGCOLOR specifies a background color for the table using the same hexadecimal values that are used for text colors. |
| | | WIDTH= *x or x%* | The WIDTH attribute specifies the table width in pixels, or in a percentage of the window size. |

T A B L E  3.4

*Table Tags*

| STYLE | TAG (HTML VERSION) | ATTRIBUTES (VALUES) | DESCRIPTION SAMPLE FILE |
|---|---|---|---|
| Table caption **(Netscape)** | `<CAPTION>` `</CAPTION>` `<TC> </TC>` (HTML 3.2) | | Both of these tag pairs mark text that appears as a label or caption for the table. |
| | | `ALIGN=` (`TOP` or `BOTTOM`) | When entered in the caption start tag, the `ALIGN` attribute defines whether the caption appears at the top or the bottom of the table. The default alignment is top. |
| Table caption **(Internet Explorer)** | `<CAPTION>` `</CAPTION>` `<TC> </TC>` (HTML 3.2) | | Both of these tag pairs mark text that appears as a label or caption for the table. |
| | | `VALIGN=` (`TOP` or `BOTTOM`) | When entered in the caption start tag, the `VALIGN` attribute defines whether the caption appears at the top or the bottom of the table. The default alignment is top. |
| | | `ALIGN=` (`LEFT`, `RIGHT`, or `CENTER`) | In Internet Explorer, the `ALIGN` attribute controls the horizontal placement of the caption. |
| Table row | `<TR> </TR>` (HTML 3.2) | | Defines the beginning and end of a row of cells. The table head and all rows below it must use these tags. |
| | | `ALIGN=` (`LEFT`, `CENTER`, or `RIGHT`) | The `ALIGN` attribute defines the horizontal placement of cell data for the entire row. |
| | | `VALIGN=` (`TOP`, `MIDDLE`, or `BOTTOM`) | The `VALIGN` attribute defines the vertical placement of cell data for the entire row. |
| Table heading | `<TH> </TH>` (HTML 3.2) | | Defines table cells that are either row, or column, heads. |
| | | `ALIGN=` (`LEFT`, `CENTER`, or `RIGHT`) | The `ALIGN` attribute defines the horizontal placement of the cell data. |

*(continued)*

· · · · ·

**T A B L E  3.4**

*Table Tags (continued)*

| STYLE | TAG (HTML VERSION) | ATTRIBUTES (VALUES) | DESCRIPTION SAMPLE FILE |
|-------|--------------------|---------------------|-------------------------|
| | | VALIGN= (top, middle, or bottom) | The VALIGN attribute defines the vertical alignment of cell data. |
| | | ROWSPAN= (*number*) | The ROWSPAN attribute joins the specified cell with the specified number of cells below it. |
| | | COLSPAN= (*number*) | The COLSPAN attribute joins the specified cell with the specified number of cells to the right of it. |
| | | NOWRAP | The NOWRAP attribute forces the browser to make the cell wide enough to display the table head on one line. |
| Table cell data | `<TD> </TD>` (HTML 3.2) | Uses the same attributes as `<TH>` tags. | Marks the beginning and end of all table cells that are not row, or column, heads. |
| Table end | `</TABLE>` (HTML 3.2) | | Marks the end of a table. |

The following HTML tags produced the table in Figure 3.3. Table 3.4 defines these tags.

```
<TABLE BORDER=12 CELLSPACING=6 CELLPADDING=3 >

<TR>

<TH>Row Labels

<TH>Column 1

<TH>Column 2

<TH colspan=2>Columns 3 &amp; 4

</TR>

<TR align=right>

<TH>Row 1 Head

<TD >Col. 1 Data
```

```
<TD>Col. 2 Data

<TD>Col. 3 Data

<TD>Col. 4 Data

</TR>

<TR align=center>

<TH>Row 2 Head

<TD >Col. 1 Data

<TD>Col. 2 Data

<TD>Col. 3 Data

<TD>Col. 4 Data

</TR>

<TR align=left>

<TH rowspan=2>Rows 3 &amp; 4

<TD>Col. 1 Data

<TD>Col. 2 Data

<TD>Col. 3 Data

<TD>Col. 4 Data

</TR>

<TR>

<TD>Column 1 Data

<TD>Column 2 Data

<TD>Column 3 Data

<TD>Column 4 Data

</TR>

<CAPTION align=bottom>
```

```
<P>Sample Table</P>

</CAPTION>

</TABLE>
```

Notice the ROWSPAN and COLSPAN attributes listed in table head tags in the previous example. These attributes enable you to merge cells together to create a single cell that spans two or more rows or columns (see Figure 3.3). When you use these attributes, you must omit the cell definitions for any cells that become part of the larger cell.

The default alignment for tables is with the left margin. To change the alignment, surround the complete table with <DIV> tags and use the ALIGN attribute to set the alignment to RIGHT, LEFT, or CENTER. You can also center tables by surrounding the table tags with <CENTER> tags. These alignment tags are introduced in Chapter 2.

**TIP**

**When you create tables with borders, an empty table cell (no data) will not have a border. To ensure that a border appears around the empty table cell, insert a character that won't be visible in the table. I use the nonbreaking space character ( ).**

**Exercise 3.2: If you're preparing to take the certification exam, or if you want to practice what you learned in this section, turn to the end of this chapter and complete Exercise 3.2. When you are done, continue reading here to prepare for the next exercise.**

## Displaying Images

A graphic image is a good way to breathe life into an otherwise dull text page. Graphic images can be used to

- Clarify concepts

- Help organize a page

 ▶ Establish a theme for a group of Web pages

 ▶ Grab a viewer's attention instantly

 ▶ Entertain the viewer

When you add images to a Web page, you add them to the background or the foreground. Both background and foreground pictures are added to the body of the Web page, but each type of image behaves differently.

Background images are like the Wallpaper feature in Microsoft Windows. You can specify backgrounds for Web pages and tables. If the image is larger than the Web page or table, Web page viewers see one copy. If the image is smaller, the image is tiled to fill the entire background. When your Web page uses both foreground and background images, the foreground images appear on top of the background image.

Foreground images are usually just called images or inline images. These images can be placed inline with text anywhere in the body, and they are often placed in table cells. Tables are often used to precisely control the placement of images, but you can also use alignment attributes within the image tag, `<IMG>`, to control the placement of images.

A special type of foreground image is the thumbnail image, which is a reduced version of a larger image. Large images can take much longer to download than small images, and this can frustrate Web site visitors — especially when they don't want to see the image. Thumbnail images help prevent this by quickly displaying smaller images that represent the larger pictures. To give your Web site visitors access to the larger pictures, you can turn the thumbnails into links to the larger pictures. You'll learn how to do this in the next chapter.

To add a background or foreground image to a Web page, you need to do the following:

**1** • Create a graphic and save it in a format that browsers can view.

**2** • Store the graphic image file in a directory your browser users can access.

**3** • For background images, use the `BACKGROUND` attribute in `<BODY>` or `<TABLE>` tags to specify the background image.

**4** • For foreground images, add an image tag, <IMG>, for each image.

**5** • View your Web page to verify that the image appears as you intended.

The following sections explain the different image file formats, and how to add graphic images to your Web pages.

## CREATING IMAGES

To create images for Web pages you need to use a computer graphics program, a scanner, or an electronic camera. Graphics programs, such as Adobe Photoshop, enable you to create graphics and save them in formats that browsers can display. If you don't want to create your own graphics, you can buy clipart or use a scanner or electronic camera to copy images or photos into the computer.

To create thumbnail images for Web pages, you need to use graphics or utility programs to save a reduced copy of the image. If you want your Web site visitors to view both the thumbnail and the original size version, you need two image files: the original and the thumbnail.

 **Chapter 8 provides more information on creating and modifying Web images.**

**NOTE**

When you create or convert images, you must be sure to use the correct format. Browsers can support several image formats, but the two most common are

▸ Joint Photographic Experts Group (JPEG)

▸ Graphic Interchange Format (GIF)

JPEG images support millions of colors, and are best used for large photos or illustrations requiring more than 256 colors. JPEG images should be stored with a JPG extension.

GIF images support up to 256 colors and load quickly. GIF is a good format for small photographs, buttons, icons, and other simple illustrations (especially those with solid colors). GIF files should be stored with a GIF extension.

Two popular GIF formats are noninterlaced and interlaced. The noninterlaced version is the standard version and is usually just called a GIF image. When a browser displays a GIF image using a slower communication line, such as a 28.8 modem connection, the image gradually appears from the top down.

Interlaced images build the image in stages. As with standard GIF images, interlaced images display from the top down, but each stage gradually shows more image detail. The result is that the entire image appears more quickly and gradually comes into focus. The speed at which the image comes into focus is determined by the file size and the network communications speed. For small files or fast, unburdened networks, the interlaced GIF can be displayed so quickly that the transition is unnoticeable.

To create interlaced GIF images, you need a program or utility that permits you to save to this type of file. You don't have to do anything special to the image — the graphics program or utility automatically translates the source image into an interlaced GIF when you select that file type. The interlaced GIF format is newer than the noninterlaced format and is sometimes referenced using its standard number: GIF 89a. (The older format is GIF 87.) Adobe Photoshop, LViewPro, WinGIF, and PaintShopPro can save interlaced GIF images.

## ADDING BACKGROUND IMAGES TO WEB PAGES

After you create a background image, you can add it to a Web page or table using the BACKGROUND attribute of the <BODY> or <TABLE> tag. For example:

```
<BODY BACKGROUND="path/fi/lename.ext">
```

```
<TABLE BACKGROUND="path/fi/lename.ext">
```

The filename and path variables indicate the image filename and where it is stored, and they must use forward slashes. Because Web sites are often developed on workstations and later transferred to Web servers, it is important to choose the location where you store the image file, and the path you use to specify the file, carefully. For information on storing image files and specifying paths to them, see "Storing Image Files," which appears later in this chapter.

## ADDING FOREGROUND IMAGES TO WEB PAGES

To display a foreground image on your Web page, you must add an image tag, <IMG>, to your HTML file. The image tag specifies the name and location of your image file, and the placement of the image on the page. Table 3.5 shows the format of the image tag. Figure 3.4 shows a sample Web page with images and captions in a variety of positions.

T A B L E   3 . 5

*Image Tag Attributes*

| | ATTRIBUTES (VALUES) | DESCRIPTION |
|---|---|---|
| Image | `<IMG>` (HTML 2.0) | Indicates the browser is to place a graphics file on the Web page. |
| | `SRC=` (*path/filename*) | The `SRC` (source) attribute is required; it identifies the path and filename of the graphics file to be displayed. The following are sample paths: `SRC=filename.ext` `SRC=subdirectory/filename.ext` |
| | `ALIGN=` (`LEFT`, `RIGHT`, `TOP`, `MIDDLE`, or `BOTTOM`) | The `ALIGN` attribute places the image on the left, or on the right, side of the window. If you specify top, middle, or bottom, the image is placed in the left margin and the next line of text is positioned to the right of the image (even with the top, middle, or bottom of the image). |
| | `ALT=("text")` | The `ALT` attribute specifies a name that appears in place of an image when a browser cannot display images, or when the user is viewing the page in text-only mode. If one or more space characters appear in the text string, the quotation marks are required to prevent the additional words from being interpreted as attributes. Use straight quotes ("), not "curly" quotes. |
| | `WIDTH=` *n* or *n*% | The `WIDTH` and `HEIGHT` attributes define a rectangular area in which the image appears. |
| | `HEIGHT=` *n* or *n*% | If the rectangular area doesn't match the image size, it is scaled to fit the area. If these dimensions are specified with a % sign, the dimensions represent a percentage of the browser window's width or height. If the dimensions are specified without a % sign, the dimensions represent the pixel measurements of the image area. |
| | `BORDER=`*n* | The `BORDER` attribute defines an image border width in pixels. The border appears only when the image serves as an image link. If this attribute is set to 0, no border appears. Image links are described in Chapter 4. |

*Image Captions*

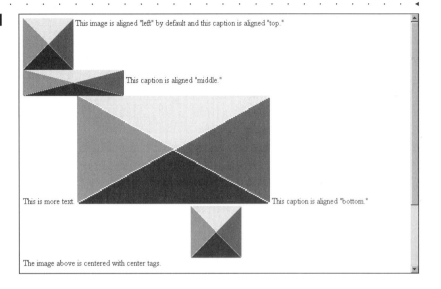

You can view the complete demonstration Web page and its source HTML text by opening the following page:

`d:/DemoWeb2/Sites/Pages/images.htm`

When entering an image tag, remember the following:

- ▸ Some browsers cannot display images, and some Web page visitors may disable image loading to speed the display of Web pages. The `ALT` attribute enables you to specify text that will appear in place of the image. This alternate text is often displayed between brackets (for example, [Alternate Text]) to indicate an image link, but the brackets are not required.

- ▸ The `ALIGN` attribute can place images adjacent to the left or right margins. To center an image, place the image tag between `<CENTER>` and `</CENTER>` tags.

- ▸ If text preceding a left-aligned image tag is not separated from the image by a line break (`<BR>` or `<P>`), the image appears *in line* with the text, which is to the right of the preceding text and on the same line. Additional text can follow the inline image on the same line.

▸ The top, middle, and bottom values of the ALIGN attribute define the placement (top, middle, or bottom) of image captions. The caption begins with the text that immediately follows the image tag and ends when the first line break appears.

▸ When you specify a width and height for an image, the text portion of the page displays faster because the browser reserves space for the image file and continues to download text. Without the graphic dimensions, the browser must download the complete image file before it can continue displaying text on the page.

▸ The path to the image file must use forward slashes and can use relative path references.

This last point deserves more discussion. The filename and path variables indicate the image filename and where it is stored. Because Web sites are often developed on workstations and later transferred to Web servers, it is important to choose the location where you store the image file, and the path you use to specify the file, carefully. For information on storing image files and specifying paths to them, read the next section.

**To prevent an image from overlapping text or another image, use either the `<BR CLEAR=LEFT>` or the `<BR CLEAR=RIGHT>` tags before the image tag. These tags are described in Chapter 2.**

TIP

## STORING IMAGE FILES

After you create an image file, you need to save or copy it to a location that browser users can access. When a browser loads a Web page, it locates all the references to image files — and other types of files, as well — and downloads those files to the browser. If the browser cannot access the image file, the image file won't appear on the Web page.

The simple solution to storing image files is to place them in the same directory as the Web page that uses them. When the Web page and image files are both in the same directory, a path is not required. You just enter the filename as shown in the following example:

```
<BODY BACKGROUND="filename.ext">

<IMG SRC="filename.ext">
```

The same directory solution doesn't work for all situations. For example, what if you want to use the same graphic for two different Web pages that are stored in two different directories? You could copy the image file to each directory, but that wastes disk space and makes file maintenance more difficult. After all, how do you remember where all the copies are when it is time to update images?

As you build a Web site from Web page and image files, you'll probably want to organize these files in your own way. You might want to create a single directory for all shared image files and place nonshared image files in the same directory as the Web pages in which they appear. If there are too many Web page and image files in the same directory, you might want to move the image files to a subdirectory.

When you specify an image within a Web page that requires a path to another directory, you can use two types of paths: absolute and relative. Absolute paths explicitly define a Web server and a path from a specific Web server directory. Absolute paths are equivalent to a URL and are required when you access files on a different Web server. The disadvantage of absolute paths is that different paths are required for files on your local computer and on a Web server. If you use absolute paths in your Web pages, you can specify paths for files on the local computer (file:///...) or on a Web server (http://...), but the same path will not work on both.

Relative paths define a path to an image file — or any other file — that is relative to the location of the Web page file. Relative paths work on a local computer or on a Web server. Whenever you reference a file that is stored on the same computer as the Web page, you should use relative references. In Chapter 4, Linking Web Pages, you'll learn more about using absolute references. For now, you can store image files in the same directory as the Web page that uses them, or you can reference image files using relative references, which are listed in Table 3.6.

**T A B L E   3 . 6**

*Relative File References*

| RELATIVE | EXAMPLE | REFERENCE TYPE |
|---|---|---|
| File Relative Reference | file.ext | Refers to a file in the same directory as the source Web page. |
| Subdirectory Relative Reference | Directory/file.ext | Refers to a file in the specified subdirectory of the directory where the Web page is stored. |
| Parent Directory Relative Reference | ../file.ext | Refers to a file in the parent directory of the directory in which the Web page is stored. |
| Parent Directory Relative Reference | ../directory/file.ext | Specifies a file path that begins with the parent directory of the directory in which the Web page is stored. To specify a directory higher in the file structure, add additional relative references (../) to the beginning of the reference. |

Notice that none of the relative references in Table 3.6 begin with a forward slash. A preceding forward slash refers to a specific directory on the Web server. Relative paths always start with a file name, directory name, or period.

Figure 3.5 shows a sample directory tree that we can use to see how relative references can be used in the HOME.HTM file. Table 3.7 lists the explicit and relative paths that you can use in HOME.HTM to reference the graphics in this tree.

The document root directory shown in Figure 3.5 is a special directory that has been configured as the default root of all browser access to the Web server. Although this directory can be positioned anywhere on any Web server hard disk, from the browser user's point of view, this serves as the root of all file access to the server. To specify an explicit path from the document root directory to an image file, begin the path with a forward slash as shown in Table 3.7. (You will learn more about the document root directory in Chapter 4.)

 **Exercises 3.3 and 3.4: If you're preparing to take the certification exam, or if you want to practice what you learned in this section, turn to the end of this chapter and complete Exercises 3.3 and 3.4.**

**FIGURE 3.5**

*Sample Web Server Directory*

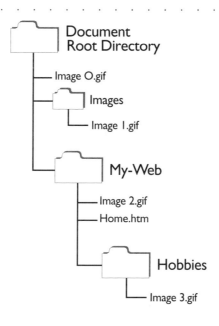

Document Root Directory

— Image O.gif

Images

— Image 1.gif

My-Web

— Image 2.gif
— Home.htm

Hobbies

— Image 3.gif

**TABLE 3.7**

*Sample Explicit and Relative References*

| IMAGE FILE | EXPLICIT REFERENCE | RELATIVE REFERENCE |
|------------|--------------------|--------------------|
| Image0.gif | /Image0.gif | ../Image0.gif |
| Image1.gif | /Images/Image1.gif | ../Images/Image1.gif |
| Image2.gif | /My_Web/Image2.gif | Image2.gif |
| Image3.gif | /My_Web/Hobbies/Image3.gif | Hobbies/Image3.gif |

## Summary

This chapter described how to create lists and tables, and how to place images on your Web pages.

You can use HTML tags to create unordered lists, ordered lists, and definition lists. All lists begin and end with tags that define the list type. Each item within the list must also be identified with a tag. List tag attributes enable you to define different bullet types and numbering methods for lists.

As with lists, tables begin and end with a tag that identifies the table as a table. The table rows and columns are defined one row at a time. Within each row, table head tags and table data tags classify and define each of the column cells for the table.

When placing images on Web pages, you can place them in the background of Web pages or tables, or you can place them in the foreground. Foreground images appear over the background. To align images on a Web page, you can use the ALIGN attribute in the <IMG> tag, and you can use the CLEAR attribute in the <BR> tag.

With the knowledge you've gained in Chapters 2 and 3, you should be able to create some good looking Web pages. In the next chapter, you'll learn how to connect Web pages together to build Web sites.

## PUZZLE 3.1: USING LISTS, TABLES, AND IMAGES

The following word puzzle contains many of the terms discussed in this chapter. See if you can find all the words. As you search for the words, ask yourself why the word is in the list and how it was used in this chapter. If you don't know the answers to these questions, you might want to review the chapter.

```
C  E  L  L  S  P  A  C  I  N  G  E  P  J  G
W  E  P  D  G  B  O  R  D  E  R  F  I  G  K
I  P  L  Y  N  H  I  S  H  D  R  B  N  M  R
D  N  A  L  T  U  K  A  E  R  B  A  M  E  G
T  B  O  L  P  F  O  R  E  G  R  O  U  N  D
H  G  N  I  K  A  E  R  B  N  O  N  L  Q  E
D  C  A  S  T  D  D  N  G  R  W  P  O  L  S
J  O  P  T  R  I  I  D  L  K  I  I  C  I  L
O  L  S  O  S  A  N  R  I  X  C  R  M  C  C
V  O  L  C  L  G  T  I  E  N  I  A  A  L  B
I  R  O  P  I  U  R  L  F  C  G  P  B  E  P
P  G  C  L  E  C  A  L  R  E  T  N  I  A  N
O  T  A  B  L  E  T  Q  O  I  D  O  T  R  R
S  V  T  N  A  P  S  W  O  R  I  H  R  X  C
S  R  I  H  R  K  U  N  O  W  R  A  P  Y  J
```

| | | | |
|---|---|---|---|
| ALT | circle | image | ROWSPAN |
| align | clear | interlace | row |
| BGCOLOR | column | JPEG | SRC |
| background | definition | list | square |
| border | directory | NOWRAP | start |
| break | disc | nonbreaking | table |
| CELLPADDING | foreground | ordered | type |
| CELLSPACING | GIF | path | URL |
| COLSPAN | HTTP | pixel | VALIGN |
| caption | IMG | plain | width |

## EXERCISE 3.1: CREATING LISTS

In this exercise, you'll use lists to improve the appearance of a Web page. To complete this exercise, do the following:

**1** • Use a text editor or word processor program to open the following file on this book's CD-ROM:

   *d*:/DemoWeb2/Answers/lists.htm

   I've already typed the text for you. You just need to add the HTML tags to format it.

**2** • Add the HTML tags that will create the unordered list shown in Figure 3.6.

**3** • Add the tags that will create the ordered list shown in Figure 3.6.

**4** • Add the tags that will create the definition list shown in Figure 3.6.

**5** • Save the file and display it in your browser. Your Web page should appear as shown in Figure 3.6. The correct HTML code for this exercise is on this book's CD-ROM at:

   *d*:/DemoWeb2/Answers/lists2.htm

---

### FIGURE 3.6

*Exercise 3.1 Result*

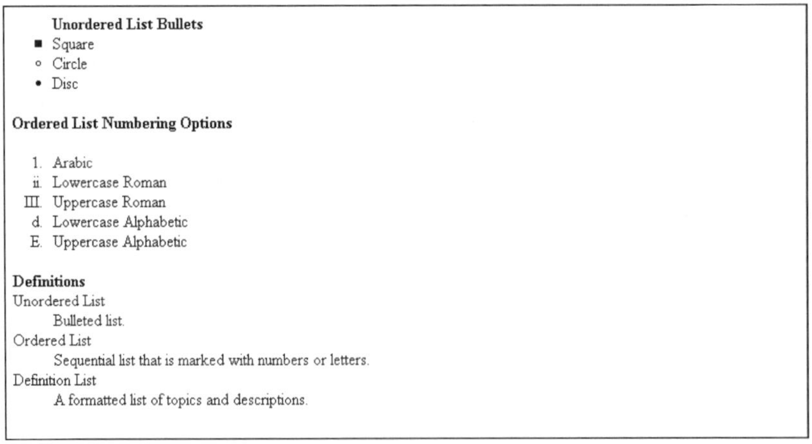

**Unordered List Bullets**
- ▪ Square
- ○ Circle
- • Disc

**Ordered List Numbering Options**

1.  Arabic
ii.  Lowercase Roman
III.  Uppercase Roman
d.  Lowercase Alphabetic
E.  Uppercase Alphabetic

**Definitions**
Unordered List
   Bulleted list.
Ordered List
   Sequential list that is marked with numbers or letters.
Definition List
   A formatted list of topics and descriptions.

## EXERCISE 3.2: BUILDING TABLES

In this exercise, you create a table for a Web page. To complete this exercise, do the following:

**1 •** Use a text editor or word processor program to open the following file on this book's CD-ROM:

*d:/DemoWeb2/Answers/basic.htm*

This file contains the basic set of HTML commands required for any Web page.

**2 •** Title the Web page "My Table."

**3 •** Add the tags that will create the table shown in Figure 3.7. You'll need to know the following:

a. The border is 3 pixels wide.

b. Without an extra tag, the contents of the Row 1, Column 1 cell will appear on one line. The tag you need is defined in Chapter 2.

c. The text that appears above the table is a caption.

**TIP**

**To save yourself some work, create the first table row, and then use Copy and Paste commands to create the additional rows.**

**4 •** Save the file and display it in your browser. Your Web page should appear as shown in Figure 3.7. The correct HTML code for this exercise is on this book's CD-ROM at:

*d:/DemoWeb2/Answers/table.htm*

**FIGURE 3.7**

*Exercise 3.2 Result*

| My First Table | | |
|---|---|---|
| Row 1, Column 1 | Column 2 | Column 3 |
| Row 2 | | y |
| Row 3 | x | z |

For extra practice, change the table you created so that the column heads for Columns 2 and 3 become one column head that reads "Other Columns." Also change the heads for Rows 2 and 3 to become one row head that reads "Other Rows." The correct HTML code for this updated table is on the CD at:

▶ *d:/DemoWeb2/Answers/table2.htm*

## EXERCISE 3.3: DISPLAYING IMAGES

In this exercise, you add images to the background and foreground of a Web page. To complete this exercise, do the following:

**1** • Use a text editor or word processor program to open the following file on this book's CD-ROM:

*d*:/DemoWeb2/Answers/basic.htm

This file contains the basic set of HTML commands required for any Web page.

**2** • Title the Web page "Images."

**3** • Add the tags that will create the Web page shown in Figure 3.8. You'll need to know the following:

a. The background image can be found on the CD at:
*d*:/DemoWeb2/Answers/Image3.gif

b. The foreground image can be found on the CD at:
*d*:/DemoWeb2/Answers/square.gif

c. Specify the following alternate text for each foreground image: [Square].

d. Aligning the images in the first line is easier than you might expect. Remember, the browser won't start new lines until you add a tag to tell it to do so.

e. To avoid overlapping images below the first row, you'll need to use the <BR> tag with the CLEAR attribute as described in Chapter 2.

**TIP**

**To save yourself some work, create the image tag and then use Copy and Paste commands to create the additional tags.**

**4** • Save the file and display it in your browser.

Your Web page should appear as shown in Figure 3.8. The correct HTML code for this exercise is on this book's CD-ROM at: *d:/DemoWeb2/Answers/image.htm*

**F I G U R E  3.8**

*Exercise 3.3 Result*

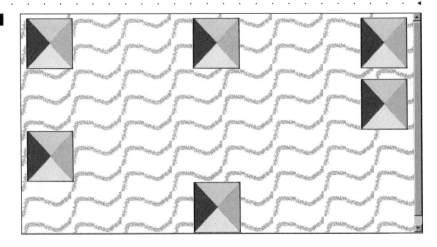

If you have trouble, consider the following:

▶ If an image doesn't appear on the page, the image tag is written incorrectly or the browser can't find the image file. If you haven't done so already, copy the image file to the directory where your Web page file resides.

▶ If an image appears in the wrong location on the page, the only problem is the alignment. The image path must be correct, or the image wouldn't appear.

▶ If image alignment is difficult, start with one foreground image and view the file in your browser. Add foreground images one at a time and view the file after each addition.

When you have finished the Web page, reduce the browser window size until the images at the top of the page overlap. Notice that the other images don't overlap. This demonstrates the importance of the <BR> tag and its CLEAR attribute.

**EXERCISE 3.4: UNDERSTANDING LISTS, TABLES, AND IMAGES**

The following exercise tests your understanding of lists, tables, and images. To complete this exercise, do the following:

**1** • List the three bullet type attributes you can use for unordered lists.

a. . . . . . . . . . . . . . . . . . . . . . . . . . . . . . . . . . . . . . .

b. . . . . . . . . . . . . . . . . . . . . . . . . . . . . . . . . . . . . . .

c. . . . . . . . . . . . . . . . . . . . . . . . . . . . . . . . . . . . . . .

**2** • List the five type attributes you can use for ordered lists.

a. . . . . . . . . . . . . . . . . . . . . . . . . . . . . . . . . . . . . . .

b. . . . . . . . . . . . . . . . . . . . . . . . . . . . . . . . . . . . . . .

c. . . . . . . . . . . . . . . . . . . . . . . . . . . . . . . . . . . . . . .

d. . . . . . . . . . . . . . . . . . . . . . . . . . . . . . . . . . . . . . .

e. . . . . . . . . . . . . . . . . . . . . . . . . . . . . . . . . . . . . . .

**3** • What is a nested list? . . . . . . . . . . . . . . . . . . . . . . . . . . . . . . . . .

**4** • When text appears between the list start tag and the first list item tag in ordered and unordered lists, how is this text formatted?

Answer: . . . . . . . . . . . . . . . . . . . . . . . . . . . . . . . . . . . . . .

**5** • Tables are defined one _____ at a time.

**6** • What is the difference between <TH> and <TD> tags?

Answer: . . . . . . . . . . . . . . . . . . . . . . . . . . . . . . . . . . . . . .

**7** • Name the two attributes that enable you to merge two or more table cells together.

a. . . . . . . . . . . . . . . . . . . . .     b. . . . . . . . . . . . . . . . . . . . .

**8** • Which attribute defines the number of pixels between a cell border and a cell's contents?

Answer: . . . . . . . . . . . . . . . . . . . . . . . . . . . . . . . . . . . . . .

**9** • Write the complete tag that will place a table adjacent to the right margin with a border that is 5 pixels thick.

Answer: . . . . . . . . . . . . . . . . . . . . . . . . . . . . . . . . . . . . . .

**10** • Name the two most popular graphic formats for Web pages.

a. . . . . . . . . . . . . . . . . . . . . . . . .　　b. . . . . . . . . . . . . . . . . . . . .

**11** • You want to put pictures of your company's products on the home page, but you also want the home page to load quickly. What type of image should you consider?

Answer: . . . . . . . . . . . . . . . . . . . . . . . . . . . . . . . . . . . . . .

**12** • Which type of image appears in stages, gradually coming into focus?

Answer: . . . . . . . . . . . . . . . . . . . . . . . . . . . . . . . . . . . . . .

**13** • Write the complete tag that assigns the BACKGROUND.GIF file to a Web page. This file is in the same directory as the Web page.

Answer: . . . . . . . . . . . . . . . . . . . . . . . . . . . . . . . . . . . . . .

**14** • Write the complete set of tags that place the WOW.GIF file in the center of a Web page. This file is in the COOL directory, which is a subdirectory of the directory that stores the Web page.

Answer: . . . . . . . . . . . . . . . . . . . . . . . . . . . . . . . . . . . . . .

**15** • Write the complete tag that you can use to separate two images so they don't overlap each other on the right side of the Web page.

Answer: . . . . . . . . . . . . . . . . . . . . . . . . . . . . . . . . . . . . . .

# Linking Web Pages

In Chapters 2 and 3, you learned how to create Web pages. In this chapter, you'll learn how to create the hypertext and image links that tie the various pages of a Web site together (and to other sites). You can create several different kinds of text and graphic links. In this chapter, you'll learn how to create:

- ▸ Intradocument text and image links

- ▸ Interdocument text and image links

- ▸ Links to headings in other documents

- ▸ Server-side and client-side image maps

The final section in this chapter discusses how to use your Web page links so your Web site is easily transferred from computer to computer.

## Intradocument Links

Let's suppose your Web page is now quite long, but you aren't yet ready to split it into multiple Web pages. What you should do is create some intradocument links. *Intradocument links* enable people viewing the page to:

- ▸ Move to the top of the page

- ▸ Skip to the bottom of the page

- ▸ Jump to text that further explains a concept

- ▸ Jump to a particular heading on the page by selecting a link from a table of contents at the top of the page

Figure 4.1 shows an example of a page with a table of contents at the top. To skip to any heading, someone viewing the page could click the appropriate underlined title in the table of contents.

FIGURE 4.1

*Intradocument Links*

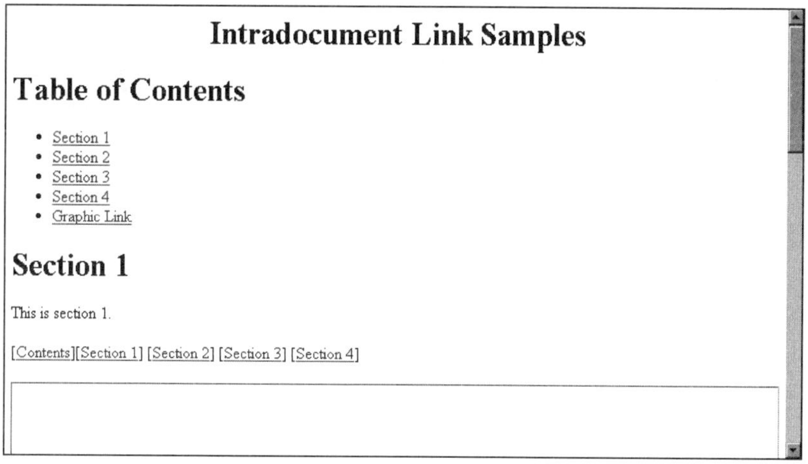

### Intradocument Link Samples

## Table of Contents

- Section 1
- Section 2
- Section 3
- Section 4
- Graphic Link

## Section 1

This is section 1.

[Contents][Section 1] [Section 2] [Section 3] [Section 4]

To create an intradocument link, you must insert two types of *anchor* tags in the HTML file for the page: link anchors and named anchors. *Link anchor* tags surround the text that becomes hypertext; they define the destination of the link. The following is an example of a link anchor:

```
<A HREF="#sect1">Section 1</A>
```

The text "Section 1" between the opening and closing anchor tags (`<A>` and `</A>`) becomes a hypertext link on the Web page. The HREF (hypertext reference) attribute identifies the named anchor, which is the destination of the link. In this example, when a user clicks on the text "Section 1," the browser displays the portion of the Web page containing the *sect1* named anchor.

*Named anchor tags* serve as a signpost or destination for the link anchor tags. Some HTML editing tools refer to named anchor tags as *link targets*. The following is the named anchor that corresponds to the previous example:

```
<H1><A NAME="sect1"></A>Section 1</H1>
```

The link anchor tags use the HREF attribute, and the named anchor tags use the NAME attribute. Notice the named anchor tags do not surround any text. The sole purpose of the named anchor tags is to mark the destination of a link. In this example, the destination is the heading labeled Section 1. Table 4.1 shows the format of the anchor commands for intradocument links.

<table>
<tr><td colspan="4">T A B L E   4.1</td></tr>
<tr><td colspan="4">*Intradocument Link Tags*</td></tr>
</table>

| NAME | TAG (HTML VERSION) | ATTRIBUTES (VALUES) | DESCRIPTION |
|---|---|---|---|
| Anchor start | `<A>` (HTML 2.0) | | The anchor start tag marks the beginning of link and named anchors. |
| | | `HREF=` `"#name"` | If the `HREF` attribute is used with the # symbol; the anchor marks the beginning of an intradocument link. Any text between the opening and closing anchor tags becomes a hypertext link to the named anchor that bears the same name. |
| | | `NAME=` `"name"` | If the `NAME` attribute is used, the named anchor marks the location to which an intradocument link will jump.<br><br>The quotation marks shown are required only if the name contains any space characters. |
| Anchor end | `</A>` (HTML 2.0) | | The anchor end tag marks the end of a link anchor or a named anchor. |

The following HTML code shows the tags that produced the intradocument links in Figure 4.1:

```
<H1><A NAME="contents"></A>Table of Contents</H1>


<UL>

<LI><A HREF="#sect1">Section 1</A>

<LI><A HREF="#sect2">Section 2</A>

<LI><A HREF="#sect3">Section 3</A>

<LI><A HREF="#sect4">Section 4</A>

<LI><A HREF="#graphic">Graphic Link</A>

</UL>


<H1><A NAME="sect1"></A>Section 1</H1>
```

```
<P>This is section 1.</P>
<P>[<A HREF="#contents">Contents</A>]
[<A HREF="#sect1">Section 1</A>] [<A HREF="#sect2">Section
2</A>] [<A HREF="#sect3">Section 3</A>]
[<A HREF="#sect4">Section 4</A>]</P>

<P><HR size=100></P>


<H1><A NAME="sect2"></A>Section 2</H1>
<P>This is section 2.</P>

<P>[<A HREF="#contents">Contents</A>]
[<A HREF="#sect1">Section 1</A>]
[<A HREF="#sect2">Section2</A>]
[<A HREF="#sect3">Section 3</A>]
[<A HREF="#sect4">Section 4</A>]</P>

<P><HR size=100></P>


<H1><A NAME="sect3"></A>Section 3</H1>
<P>This is section 3.</P>
<P>[<A HREF="#contents">Contents</A>]
[<A HREF="#sect1">Section 1</A>]
[<A HREF="#sect2">Section 2</A>]
[<A HREF="#sect3">Section 3</A>]
[<A HREF="#sect4">Section 4</A>]</P>

<P><HR size=100></P>


<H1><A NAME="sect4"></A>Section 4</H1>
<P>This is section 4.</P>
<P>[<A HREF="#contents">Contents</A>]
[<A HREF="#sect1">Section 1</A>]
[<A HREF="#sect2">Section 2</A>]
```

```
[<A HREF="#sect3">Section 3</A>]
[<A HREF="#sect4">Section
4</A>]</P>
<P><HR size=100></P>


<P>This is section 4.</P>
<P><A NAME="graphic"></A><A HREF="#contents"><IMG
SRC="../../images/square.jpg"</A></P>
```

Look at the code for the table of contents at the start of the file. The list item (<LI>) tags format the table of contents as a bulleted list. Each line in the list is a hypertext link to a named anchor in another part of the document. The destination for each item in the table of contents is a named anchor, which is placed in the corresponding heading.

If you look at the last line in the example, you'll see an image link. The difference between a hypertext link and an image link is what appears between the start and end link anchor tags. If text appears between the anchor tags, it is a hypertext link. If an image tag appears between the anchor tags, it is an image link.

**TIP**

**By default, image links display a colored border. The border color is defined by the <BODY> tag link color attributes as described in Chapter 2, and the border width is defined by the <IMG> tag BORDER attribute as described in Chapter 3. To hide the border, specify BORDER=0 in the <IMG> tag.**

You can view this sample file on the demonstration Web site by opening the following page:

*d:/DemoWeb2/Sites/Links/intralnk.htm*

If you look at this Web page in your browser, you'll notice a border around the image, which is the same color as a hypertext link. This border indicates the image is also a link. Later in this chapter, you'll see how to divide a graphic into separate regions that link to different locations.

**Exercise 4.1: If you're preparing to take the certification exam, or if you want to practice what you learned in this section, turn to the end of this chapter and complete Exercise 4.1. When you are done, continue reading here to prepare for the next exercise.**

## Interdocument Links

When one Web page just isn't enough, or when you want to provide a link to someone else's Web page, you need to create an *interdocument link*. You've already learned most of what you need to know to create an interdocument link. The following is an example of an interdocument link:

```
<A HREF="url">Text or image tag.</A>
```

The difference between this link anchor example and the link anchors you learned about earlier in this chapter is the Uniform Resource Locator (URL). The URL serves as an address for the link destination and is explained in the next section.

### COMPONENTS OF URLS

To link to another Web page, you must specify the page's URL. A URL is a combination of the Internet address of the destination Web server and the path to the destination file on that server.

The format for a URL is as follows:

```
protocol://host_name:port/path/filename.ext
```

The format for an interdocument link with a complete URL is as follows:

```
<A HREF="protocol://host_name:port/path/filename.ext">Text
or image tag.</A>
```

Each of the variables in the URL has a default value and can be omitted. The following sections look more closely at these variables.

### Protocol

The *protocol* portion of a URL specifies which Internet protocol to use to access the destination file. Each Internet service conforms to a protocol or specification, which defines how the service operates and how clients and servers communicate with each other. The protocol for communications between a Web browser and a Web server is the HyperText Transfer Protocol (HTTP); this is the default protocol for link anchors. Table 4.2 lists some common Internet protocols that can be supported by Web browsers.

| TABLE 4.2 | PROTOCOL | DESCRIPTION |
|---|---|---|
| *Protocols for Interdocument Links* | File | Access a file on a local hard disk |
| | FTP | Access a file on an FTP (File Transfer Protocol) server |
| | Gopher | Access files through a Gopher menu system on a Gopher server |
| | HTTP | Access a file on a Web server |
| | MailTo | Send e-mail to a specified address |
| | News | Access news documents on a news server |
| | Telnet | Start a terminal emulation session on a Telnet server |

So far, the URLs in this book have used the HTTP protocol to access Web pages on Web servers, and the File protocol to access Web pages on your local computer.

In general, when you specify a URL in a Web page or a Web browser, you can omit the HTTP:// portion of the URL if the destination file is a Web page. This is because HTTP is the default protocol for Web browsing and Web page links. Remember, when you specify HTTP, or accept HTTP by default, the expectation is that the requested file is stored on a Web server. Table 4.3 lists sample URL formats with, and without, the protocol specification.

**TIP**

**Use the File protocol in your browser to display Web pages on your computer — but don't use the File protocol in a link anchor. As you'll learn later in this chapter, whenever possible, you should use relative references in your links. Explicit references, such as those created with the File protocol, do not work when a file is moved from your computer to a Web server.**

| TABLE 4.3 | SAMPLE | RESULT |
|---|---|---|
| Sample URL Formats with Different Protocol Specifications | http://host_name/path/filename.ext | Searches for the HTML file *filename.ext* in directory *path* on host *host_name*. |
| | *host_name/path/filename.ext* | When entered in HTML browsers or HTML files, this URL takes you to the HTML file *filename.ext* in directory *path* on host *host_name*. |
| | file:///d:/path/filename.ext | When entered in an HTML browser, this URL takes you to the file *filename.ext* in directory *path* on drive d:. |

### Host Name

The *host name* portion of a URL specifies the Internet server that stores the destination file and provides the service requested by the specified (or default) protocol. For Web servers, the destination host is a Web server. For FTP servers, the destination server is an FTP server. The host name can be either of the following:

- An Internet Protocol (IP) address, which is the network address of the host computer

- A host name defined by a name service, such as the Domain Name System (DNS)

A host name is an alias to the IP address of the destination server. Names are much easier to remember than IP addresses, which are numbers, such as 130.57.163.43. When a user specifies a host name in a URL or clicks a link that refers to a host name, the browser computer looks up the name in a name service and gets the IP address. The browser uses the IP address — not the host name — to complete the link.

When you specify a URL in a link (or when you're browsing the Web), you have several options. You can:

- Specify a host name.

- Specify the IP address.

> ▸ Omit the host name (this refers to the default host, which is the Web server on which the source file containing the link is stored).

You cannot omit the host name if the destination file is on a *remote server,* which is any server other than the Web server where your Web page is stored.

Table 4.4 lists URL sample formats for different host name specifications.

| TABLE 4.4 | SAMPLE | RESULT |
|---|---|---|
| *Sample URL Formats with Different Host Name Specifications* | http://host_name/path/filename.ext | Searches for the file *filename.ext* in directory *path* on host *host_name*. |
| | *Host_name/path/filename.ext* | When entered in HTML browsers or HTML files, this URL searches for the file *filename.ext* in directory *path* on host *host_name*. |
| | http:/path/filename.ext | When entered as part of a link, this URL searches for the file *filename.ext* in directory *path* on the same server on which the source HTML file resides. |
| | */path/filename.ext* | When entered as part of a link, this URL searches for the file *filename.ext* in the directory *path* on the same server on which the source HTML file resides. |

### Port

The *port* component of a URL specifies the TCP/IP port number of the destination service. Because the default value for the TCP/IP port number is usually correct, you probably won't ever need to enter this in a URL. Most standard TCP/IP services, such as Web servers, use *a well-known port number,* which is a specific number reserved for that service. If the port number is omitted from a URL, the well-known port number is used as the default.

**The well-known port number for Web servers is 80.**

NOTE

## Path

The path portion of a URL defines the path from the starting directory to the destination file. When you specify the path, you can choose from the following types of starting directories:

- ▸ The directory in which the source HTML file is stored

- ▸ The document root directory on a Web server

- ▸ A virtual directory on a Web server

**Source Web Page Directory**     In Chapter 3, you learned how to use relative paths to specify an image file path based on the location of the Web page file. You can use these same relative paths to specify a link destination. For example, you can use the following anchor tags to specify link destinations with relative references:

```
<A HREF="filename.htm">
```

```
<A HREF="dir1/filename.htm">
```

```
<A HREF="../dir1/filename.htm">
```

Because you are referring to another Web page on the same Web server, you can omit the protocol, hostname, and port from your URL. In the example above, the URLs are relative references from the current Web page file (which is the source file) to another Web page file (which is the destination file). The first anchor tag refers to a Web page in the same directory as the source file, while the second refers to a destination file in a subdirectory below the source file, and the third refers to a subdirectory of the source file's parent directory.

**Document Root Directory**     The document root is the root directory for general public access to a Web server. You are probably familiar with the root directories for your computer. A root directory is the highest-level directory on each volume (disk): the directory that contains all the named directories. From a Web site visitor's perspective, the document root directory functions like a volume root directory. The difference between the two is that the document root directory can be set to any directory on the Web server. It does not have to be set to the volume root directory.

Web site visitors can only view Web pages that are stored in the document root directory or in other directories called virtual directories (more on these later). This allows Web server managers to have private storage areas for server configuration files and public areas for browser access.

When you publish a Web site (as described in Appendix B), you copy your Web pages to the document root directory, a virtual directory, or a subdirectory of one of these directories. If you are creating internal links, which are links to other files within your Web site, you should use relative file references. If you plan your file structure properly, as described later in this chapter, the file path is usually shorter, and the links work equally well on your local computer or the Web server.

When you are creating external links (links that refer to a file on another Web server), you must include the host name and specify the path from either the document root directory or a virtual directory. The URL format is:

```
http://host_name/dir1/filename.htm
```

Because the document root directory is the default directory for Web server URLs, you do not include it when you refer to files in this directory. For example, the previous example refers to FILENAME.HTM in the DIR1 subdirectory of the document root. The following URL refers to the file INDEX.HTM in the document root directory:

```
http://host_name/index.htm
```

**TIP**

**If you've browsed the Web, you already know you can display Web pages just by entering a host name, such as** `www.novell.com`. **When you enter a URL without a filename, the Web server looks for a default filename in the Web server's document root directory. You'll learn more about filenames later in this chapter.**

Although it is not recommended, you can create an internal link using a reference from the document root directory or a virtual directory. To specify the path from the document root directory or a virtual directory, place a forward slash at the start of the path, as follows:

```
/dir1/filename.htm
```

A reference from a document root directory or a virtual directory is called an *absolute* or *explicit* reference. When you include the host name in a URL, you are creating an absolute reference. The path must be specified from the document root directory or a virtual directory. When you omit the hostname, the only difference between an absolute reference and a relative reference is the starting forward slash. Use it for absolute references and omit it for relative references.

**Virtual Directories**    Virtual directories are special Web server directories that the Web server manager defines as public directories. These directories can be within, or outside of, the document root directory. The Web server manager gives each virtual directory a special name, or alias, that can be used to access the file in URLs.

To create an external link with an absolute reference to a file in a virtual directory, enter a URL with the following format:

```
http://host_name/virtual_directory_name/path/filename.htm
```

The difference between references to the document root directory and those to a virtual directory is that you must specify the virtual directory name in the path.

To create an internal link with an absolute reference to a virtual directory file, use the following URL format:

```
/virtual_directory_name/path/filename.htm
```

As with internal references to the document root directory, a virtual directory absolute path must begin with a forward slash.

Table 4.5 lists additional examples of URL formats that use the different path specifications.

| TABLE 4.5 | SAMPLE | RESULT |
|---|---|---|
| *Sample URL Formats with Different Path Specifications* | http://host_name/path/filename.ext | Searches for the file *filename.ext* in directory *path* on host *host_name*. This directory path starts at the document root directory. |
| | *host_name/path/filename.ext* | When entered in HTML browsers or HTML files, this URL searches for the file *filename.ext* in directory *path* on host *host_name*. This directory path starts at the document root directory. |
| | /path/filename.ext | When entered as part of a link, this URL searches for the file *filename.ext* in directory *path* on the local server. This directory path starts at the document root directory. |

*(continued)*

| TABLE 4.5 | SAMPLE | RESULT |
| --- | --- | --- |
| *Sample URL Formats with Different Path Specifications (continued)* | */filename.ext* | When entered as part of a link, this URL searches for the file *filename.ext* in the document root directory on the local server. |
| | *dir1/filename.ext* | When entered as part of a link, this URL searches for the file *filename.ext* in directory *dir1*, which is a subdirectory of the directory in which the source HTML file resides. |
| | *filename.ext* | When entered as part of a link, this URL searches for the file *filename.ext* in the directory in which the source HTML file resides. |
| | *../dir1/filename.ext* | When entered as part of a link, this URL searches for the file *filename.ext* in directory *dir1*. This directory path starts in the directory above the directory in which the source HTML file resides. |
| | *../filename.ext* | When entered as part of a link, this URL searches for the file *filename.ext* in the directory above the directory in which the source HTML file resides. |
| | *../../filename.ext* | When entered as part of a link, this URL searches for the file *filename.ext* in the directory, which is two levels above the directory in which the source HTML file resides. |

**NOTE**

**The absolute and relative paths described in this chapter can be used to refer to any file from a Web page. For example, you can use any of these paths to specify the location of an image file.**

### Filename

The *filename* portion of the URL specifies the file you want to access. As with other components of a URL, the filename portion is optional. If this link is to a Web server and the filename is omitted, the destination Web server searches for a file that uses the *index* file name. By default, the index file name is index.html on the Netscape Web servers for NetWare and on UNIX Web servers, and it is index.htm on Novell Web Servers..

**NOTE**

**The Web server administrator can change the default name of the index file. Other common index filenames are home.html and homepage.html. The Netscape Web servers for NetWare also support home.html by default.**

If the filename is omitted and the index file is not found at the URL-specified location, the Web server might generate an index Web page for the directory defined in the URL (whether explicitly defined or implied by default). All Novell Web servers offer an automatic index feature, which permits the Web server to generate a list of all the files in the specified directory automatically. Each entry in the list includes the name of a file and serves as a hypertext link to the file. For this feature to work, the Web server administrator must enable automatic indexing for the specified directory.

## EXAMPLES OF INTERDOCUMENT LINKS

For a little extra practice, Table 4.6 lists sample links with a variety of URL formats. Notice that the paths for image graphics files use the same path structure as the links.

**TABLE 4.6**

*Examples of Links
Containing URLs*

| SAMPLE | RESULT |
|---|---|
| <A HREF="http://*host_name/path/ filename.ext*">Sample Link.</A> | Sample Link becomes a hypertext link to the file *filename.ext* in directory *path*, which is in the document root directory on host *host_name*. |
| <A HREF="*host_name/path/filename.ext*"> <img src="*/images/graphic.jpg*"></A> | The graphic *graphic.jpg* is an image link to the file *filename.ext* in directory *path*, which is in the document root directory on host *host_name*.<br><br>The *graphic.jpg* file is in the images subdirectory of the document root directory on the local server. |
| <A HREF=" */path/filename.ext*"> Master Link.</A> | Master Link becomes a hypertext link to the file *filename.ext* in directory *path*, which is a subdirectory of the document root directory on the local server. |
| <A HREF="*/dir1/filename.ext*"> <img src="*graphic.gif*"></A> | The graphic *graphic.gif* is an image link to the file *filename.ext* in directory *dir1*, which is in the document root directory of the local server.<br><br>The *graphic.gif* file is in the same directory as the source HTML file. |

*(continued)*

**TABLE 4.6**

*Examples of Links*
*Containing URLs*
*(continued)*

| SAMPLE | RESULT |
|---|---|
| <A HREF="/filename.ext"> Twisted Link.</A> | Twisted Link becomes a hypertext link to the file *filename.ext* in the document root directory on the local server. |
| <A HREF="dir1/filename.ext"> <img src="../image.gif"></A> | The graphic *image.gif* is an image link to the file *filename.ext* in directory *dir1*, which is in the same directory as the source HTML file. The *image.gif* file is in the parent directory containing the directory that contains the source HTML file. |
| <A HREF="filename.ext"> Sample Link.</A> | Sample Link is a hypertext link to the file *filename.ext*, which is in the same directory as the source HTML file. |
| <A HREF="../dir1/filename.ext"> <img src="image.gif"></A> | The graphic *image.gif* is an image link to the file *filename.ext* in directory *dir1*, which is in the parent directory of the directory that contains the source HTML file. The *image.gif* file is in the directory that contains the source HTML file. |

# Links to Headings in Other Documents

In this section, you'll put together what you've learned about intradocument and interdocument links to create links that take browsers to a specific section of another HTML file. The format for this type of link combines the two other link types with which you're already familiar. The format is:

```
<A HREF="protocol://host_name:port/path/filename#name">Text
or image tag. </A>
```

As with intradocument links, you must create a named anchor in the destination document. The format for the named anchor is the same, as follows:

```
<A NAME="name">Link Destination. </A>
```

**Exercise 4.2:** If you're preparing to take the certification exam, or if you want to practice what you learned in this section, turn to the end of this chapter and complete Exercise 4.2. When you are done, continue reading here to prepare for the next exercise.

## Image Map Links

So far, you've seen graphic images that activate only a single link. Click anywhere on the graphic and that link is activated.

*Image map links* (usually referred to as *image maps*) allow a single graphic to activate multiple links. Image maps enable you to divide an image into separate areas or *hot spots* and assign a different link to each area. After you create an image map, the location of a user's mouse click determines which link is activated. Figure 4.2 shows a sample Web page that displays an image map.

FIGURE 4.2

*Web Page with an Image Map*

### Client-Side Image Map Example

**Select your travel destination:**

Hawaii   Alaska   Baltic Sea   Hong Kong

You can view the Web page shown in Figure 4.2 on the demonstration Web site by opening the following page:

```
d:/DemoWeb2/Sites/Links/clntmap.htm
```

The image shown on the sample Web page is a single image that appears as four separate buttons.

NOTE

**If you click any of the buttons, the browser will *attempt* to display one of four links, which are all valid Web destinations. If you do not have an Internet connection, the links will be unsuccessful. To stop a Netscape Navigator 4 browser from an attempt to display the link destination, select View → Stop Page Loading, or click the Stop button.**

Two types of image maps exist: server-side image maps and client-side image maps. Both image map types produce the same results, but *server-side image maps* depend on a Web server for processing. *Client-side image maps* depend on the browser software for processing. To understand the required processing, you must know how image maps work.

### HOW AN IMAGE MAP WORKS

When a user clicks a portion of an image map, two types of processing are required. First, the browser must determine the coordinates of the mouse click within the image. Second, the browser, or server, must use those coordinates to select a destination URL from a table of coordinates and links. For server-side image maps, the table of coordinates and links is stored in a separate file and is similar to the following:

```
rect http://www.visit.hawaii.org/ 0,0 95,29

rect http://www.juneau.com 97,0 191,29

rect http://www.btc.se/ 194,1 288,29

rect http://www.hkta.org/ 290,0 385,29
```

Each line in this example defines a rectangle within the source image. The URL is the link destination, and the coordinates are the pixel coordinates defining the link area. Unless you enjoy counting pixels, you'll want to use an image map utility program to create your image maps. These utility programs enable you to use your mouse to select the regions for each link.

### USING SERVER-SIDE IMAGE MAPS

The primary advantage to server-side image maps is that more browsers support them. Client-side image maps are relatively new, and older browsers don't support them. (The section on client-side image maps explains which browsers can use client-side image maps.) If you know some of your Web site visitors are using older browsers, you might want to use server-side image maps.

To use server-side image maps, you must do the following:

- ▶ Verify that your Web server supports image maps

▸ Create the image

▸ Create the map file and place it on the server

▸ Add image map link tags to your Web page

The following sections explain how to complete these tasks.

### Verifying Server-Side Image Map Support

Server-side image map support is a server feature that is provided by Web servers, such as the Web servers from Novell. To verify that you can use server-side image maps, contact your Web server manager or refer to your Web server documentation. You need to answer the following:

▸ Can you use server-side image maps?

▸ Where do you place your image map files?

▸ Which type of Web server are you using, NCSA or CERN?

Some image map utilities, such as the Mapedit utility on this book's CD, need to know which type of Web server you are using. The Web servers from Novell are based on the National Center for Super Computing Applications (NCSA) Web server.

### Creating the Image

Create an image for an image map in the same way you create any other image for a Web page. As explained in Chapter 3, the file should be stored in GIF or JPEG format and stored with your Web site files.

The image for an image map is divided into regions, so you should create the image with this in mind. Visual borders, buttons, and logos help to indicate where the user can click within the graphic. Also, plan your images so the "hot spots" for your links are large enough for users to click easily.

### Creating the Map File and Placing it on the Server

After you create your image, you are ready to create the image map file, which contains the image coordinates and URLs for your image map links. The best way to create an image map file is to use an image map editor such as Mapedit. The

CD-ROM provided with this book includes a 30-day trial version of the Mapedit utility.

**The instructions for installing Mapedit are in Appendix C. To get the latest version of Mapedit, browse the following location:**

`www.boutell.com/mapedit`

For instructions on creating the image map file, refer to the documentation for your image map editor. In the next exercise, you'll learn to install and create an image map with Mapedit.

After you create the image map file, place it in the image map directory on your Web server, or in one of your own directories if it is enabled to support server-side image maps. The Netscape Web servers for NetWare support image maps in any directory. On the Novell Web Server, the default image map directory is SYS:\WEB\MAPS. If you don't have rights to the image map directory, you will need your administrator's help to place this file on the Web server.

**NOTE**

**When you create an image map file for the Novell Web Server, which uses a separate MAPS directory, you must use explicit references or relative references from the document root directory or a virtual directory. For example, you cannot use a relative path such as filename.htm#END unless that file is in the new current directory, MAPS. To refer to a label in the source file, you should use a path such as /Sales/report.htm#END. You can use the shorter relative reference (filename.htm#END) on the Netscape Web Servers for NetWare when the source and map files are in the same directory.**

### Entering the Server-Side Link Tags

After you create the image and image map files, and place them in the appropriate places on the Web server, all the pieces are in place for your image map link. The format for the image map link is as follows:

```
<A HREF="/maps/filename.map"><IMG SRC="/path/filename.ext"
ISMAP></A>
```

This is the same as the other link tags, except for the following differences:

- ▶ The filename in the link start tag is required and must identify an image map file on the Web server.

- ▶ The image file tag contains the ISMAP attribute, which identifies the image as a server-side image map.

Notice that the URL in the example image link begins with a forward slash, which indicates the reference is from the document root directory or a virtual directory. In this example from a Novell Web Server installation, the reference is actually to the MAPS virtual directory (SYS:WEB\MAPS).

The server-side image map link example on the demonstration Web site is as follows:

```
<A HREF="/maps/travel.map"><IMG SRC="../images/travel.gif"
ISMAP> </a>
```

You can test this link on the demonstration Web site by selecting the appropriate link on the following page:

```
d:/DemoWeb2/Sites/Links/index.htm
```

If you test the image map on this page, you'll find the browser displays an error message for any button you click. The reason is you are using the image map without the help of a Web server. If you watch the status bar at the bottom of a Netscape Navigator browser, you'll see the browser is looking for a map file and calculating the coordinates of the mouse pointer.

To see this work on your own Web server, you can install the demonstration Web site on your Web server as described in Appendix C.

**NOTE**

**The image map example presented at the beginning of this section works because it is a client-side image map. A server-side image map will not work when you access the files on the CD-ROM.**

**Exercise 4.3: If you're preparing to take the certification exam, or if you want to practice what you learned in this section, turn to the end of this chapter and complete Exercise 4.3. When you are done, continue reading here to prepare for the next exercise.**

## USING CLIENT-SIDE IMAGE MAPS

When you know your Web site visitors have browsers that support client-side image maps, you should use these over server-side image maps. Client-side image maps have the following advantages:

▶ Browsers process client-side image maps, so you can test them on your local computer.

▶ Client-side image maps display the link destination in the status area, so visitors know where a link will take them.

▶ Client-side image maps do not require server processing, so your server has more resources to support other Web server tasks.

▶ Client-side image maps store link information in the same file as the HTML tags, so it is easier to locate and update link information.

To use client-side image maps, you must do the following:

▶ Verify that the browsers your customers are using support client-side image maps

▶ Create the image

▶ Place an image tag in the source HTML file

▶ Use an image map utility to create the image map table in the HTML file

The following sections explain how to complete these tasks.

### Verifying Browser Support for Client-Side Image Maps

Client-side image maps are supported by the following browsers:

▶ Netscape 2.0 beta 4 or better

▶ Microsoft Internet Explorer

▶ Spyglass Mosaic 2.1 and derivatives thereof

If your Web site visitors are using older versions of these browsers, the users can click the image map, but the links won't work. One way to support older browsers is to have a hypertext link somewhere on the page that leads to an alternative page with hypertext and image links.

### Creating the Image

Create an image for a client-side image map in the same way you would create an image for a server-side image map.

### Adding the Image Tag

Before you create the image map table, enter an image tag for the image in the source HTML file. Enter the image tag using the format described in Chapter 3. The image map utility will look for this tag when you start the utility.

### Creating the Image Map Table with a Utility

After you create your image and enter your image tag, you are ready to create the image map table, which contains the image coordinates and URLs for your image map links. The best way to create an image map table is to use an image map editor.

A trial copy of the MAPEDIT utility is free on this book's CD-ROM; an unlimited-use copy is currently $25 — well worth the money. The CD-ROM also includes a trial copy of NetObjects Fusion, which provides tools for creating client-side image maps on your Web pages.

For instructions on creating the image map file, refer to the documentation for your image map editor. Appendix C and Exercise 4.3 describe how to install Mapedit. The next exercise describes how to create client-side image maps with Mapedit.

The following sample code shows the image map table and tags used in the client-side image map example on the demonstration Web site:

```
<P><IMG SRC="../../images/travel.gif" usemap="#travel"> </P>


<map name="travel">

<area shape="rect" coords="1,1,95,29"
href="http://www.visit.hawaii.org">

<area shape="rect" coords="97,1,191,29"
```

```
href="http://www.juneau.com">

<area shape="rect" coords="192,0,289,29"
href="http://www.btc.se">

<area shape="rect" coords="290,1,385,28"
href="http://www.hkta.org">

<area shape="default" nohref>

</map>
```

The image tag in the first line includes the USEMAP attribute and a label (#travel) that looks like a reference to named anchor. The USEMAP attribute identifies the image as a client-side image map and the label directs the browser to the <MAP> tag that defines the start of the image map table. The image map table is similar to the image map table used for server-side image maps.

As with server-side image maps, the best way to create an image map table is to use an image map editor. The image map editor enables you to create the image map table by dragging your mouse over the picture. Without the image map utility, you might have to guess at the pixel coordinates for each region and experiment repeatedly until you get it right.

 **Exercise 4.4: If you're preparing to take the certification exam, or if you want to practice what you learned in this section, turn to the end of this chapter and complete Exercise 4.4. When you are done, continue reading here to prepare for the next exercise.**

## Creating a Portable Web Site

Novell Education Course 654 defines the following steps for creating a Web site:

1 • Plan the Web site.

2 • Create the Web pages.

3 • Test the Web pages.

**4** • Publish the Web site.

**5** • Maintain the Web site.

You've already learned to create Web pages in the previous chapters, and if you've been completing the exercises, you've probably learned something about testing them as well. In Part II, you will learn about planning and publishing Web sites. However, one important part of planning is directly related to the topic of this chapter. To create portable Web sites, you must plan your Web site file structure correctly and use relative paths in your links.

A portable Web site is one that is easily transferred from one location to another. If the Web site is truly portable, it will run in all locations. Typically, Web sites are developed on a client computer and later transferred to a Web server. You'll want to do this for the following reasons:

▸ Your Web server is not ready, but you want to start creating and testing Web pages

▸ You want to test your Web pages privately, before you publish them on a Web server for others to view

As you browse your way through this guide, you will likely be surprised at how many Web features are actually implemented or executed by the browser, not the Web server. When you develop and test your Web site on a local computer, you can practice and test about 90 percent of the skills described in Parts I and II and about 50 percent of the skills described in Part III.

Some Web page features, including some of those described in Part III, can be tested only with a Web server. However, you want to avoid editing Web page files on an active Web server because people might be using the Web server and may see Web pages that you aren't ready to share. Some word processors lock files that you are editing, which can prevent Web site visitors from seeing a Web page (they get an error instead). It's best to build the Web site, or portions of the Web site, on your local computer and then transfer the files to the Web server (see Appendix B).

If you are using features that can't be tested on your local computer, you should test all other features before transferring your Web site files to the Web server, and then test your Web pages when you expect the least amount of Web site traffic.

Another alternative is to set up a test Web server. The test Web server is sometimes called a staging Web server and can be used for testing and for content review before publishing the site to a public Web server.

To create a portable Web site, you need to create a directory structure that will work on every development workstation, staging Web server, and production Web server. For example, if you know that you will put your Web site files in the document root directory on your Web server, create a directory on your development client that serves the same function. Figure 4.3 shows an example of a directory structure that can be copied from a development client to a Web server.

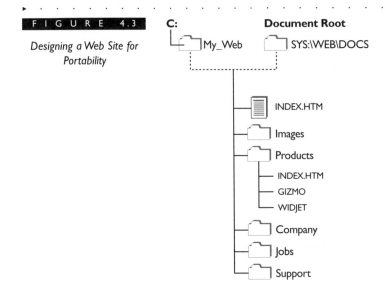

**FIGURE 4.3**

*Designing a Web Site for Portability*

The file structure shown in Figure 4.3 is designed to run on a local computer or a Web server, but it is the relative links within the Web pages that make this possible. For example, suppose I started creating this Web site on a local computer and put a link on every Web page that points back to the home page, INDEX.HTM. If I use the absolute path C:\My_Web\INDEX.HTM to refer to this file, I'd have to change every link before I could use these links on a Web server. If I use relative paths, such as ..\INDEX.HTM, the links work on both platforms. Let's take a closer look.

Consider the INDEX.HTM file in the Products directory. I can create a link back to the home page using any of the following paths:

```
C:\My_Web\INDEX.HTM
```

```
\INDEX.HTM
```

```
..\INDEX.HTM
```

The first path tells the browser to look on the C drive, which is usually not appropriate for a Web server. The second path points to the document root directory, which does not exist on the local computer. The third path tells the browser to look in the parent directory for the INDEX.HTM file. This works on the local computer and on the Web server. On the local computer, the file is found in the MY_WEB directory; on the example Web server, the file is found in the SYS:\WEB\DOCS directory.

To view the Web site on the local computer, just open the home page file as you would any other HTML file on the local computer. Once the home page is open, you can use the links you have created to move from Web page to Web page. As long as you have used relative references, the links will work. Navigating the Web site on the local computer is virtually identical to navigating a Web site on a Web server!

When you are ready to copy your local Web site to a Web server, just copy all of the files and folders from your local Web site directory to the Web server document root directory, or to one of the other Web server published directories. In the example shown in Figure 4.3, I would copy the contents of MY_WEB (excluding the MY_WEB directory) to the SYS:\WEB\DOCS directory.

**You can develop your Web site on a NetWare or intraNetWare file server, too. Simply map a drive to the NetWare server and develop your Web site as if you were developing on a local drive. The advantage to this approach is that you can share your Web site with other NetWare clients.**

TIP

**Exercise 4.5: If you're preparing to take the certification exam, or if you want to practice what you learned in this section, turn to the end of this chapter and complete Exercise 4.5.**

## Summary

In this chapter, you learned to create hypertext and image links that link your Web page to internal and external Web pages. Internal Web pages are the other Web pages on your Web server; external Web pages are stored on other Web servers. You also learned to link to named anchors within the source file or to named anchors in a different file. These links between Web pages are the glue that holds your Web site together.

URL components are important for the following reasons:

- ▸ URLs must be specified when you add graphics to a Web page, create links, or specify the location of a server-side image map file.

- ▸ URLs have default values for each component. What you leave out of a URL can be just as important as what you put in it.

Server-side and client-side image maps allow you to attach multiple links to a single graphic. Finally, you learned that relative references in your links make your Web site portable and enable you to use the Web site on your local computer or on a Web server.

## PUZZLE 4.1: LINKING WEB PAGES

The following word puzzle contains many of the terms discussed in this chapter. See if you can find all of the words. As you search for the words, ask yourself why the word is in the list and how it was used in this chapter. If you don't know the answers to these questions, you might want to review the chapter.

```
T  E  N  L  E  T  H  A  B  S  O  L  U  T  E
N  N  I  N  D  E  X  G  R  M  A  I  L  T  O
E  B  E  N  I  L  R  E  D  N  U  A  T  P  S
M  O  E  M  U  A  V  L  R  U  U  K  X  W  F
U  R  L  Q  U  R  M  E  T  T  Q  F  E  R  H
C  D  I  R  E  C  T  O  R  Y  O  N  T  T  O
O  E  F  S  V  N  O  I  D  O  Z  M  R  P  S
D  R  C  D  I  R  V  D  E  L  P  G  E  A  T
R  O  Y  T  I  L  I  B  A  T  R  O  P  M  T
E  H  C  C  L  I  E  N  T  R  O  A  Y  R  U
T  C  I  U  Z  I  R  H  N  H  T  M  H  S  K
N  N  M  E  M  E  S  C  E  H  O  N  E  N  W
I  A  A  I  T  E  S  M  M  P  M  M  I  R  N
B  H  G  X  W  A  N  R  A  Z  A  L  E  A  W
M  R  E  H  P  O  G  T  N  P  D  O  Z  V  K
```

| | | | |
|---|---|---|---|
| absolute | GOPHER | internal | remote |
| anchor | HREF | intradocument | root |
| border | HTTP | link | server |
| client | home | MAILTO | TELNET |
| directory | host | map | URL |
| document | hypertext | NCSA | USEMAP |
| domain | ISMAP | news | underline |
| external | image | path | virtual |
| FTP | index | port | |
| file | interdocument | portability | |

## EXERCISE 4.1: CREATING INTRADOCUMENT LINKS

In this exercise, you will update a Web page to include intradocument links. To complete this exercise, do the following:

**1** • Use a text editor or word processor program to open the following file on this book's CD-ROM:

*d:*/DemoWeb2/Answers/intralnk.htm

I've already typed the text for you. You just need to add the HTML tags to create links.

**2** • Add link anchor labels to the following headings:

➤ The book title, "My Great Novel"

➤ The Contents heading in the table of contents

➤ The heading for each of the five chapters

Label the book title "home," the contents heading "contents," and the other headings "chapx," where x is the chapter number.

**3** • Adjacent to the image tag at the end of the file, add a link label tag named "the end."

**4** • For each of the chapters in the table of contents, create an intradocument link to the label for that chapter.

**5** • In the table of contents, locate the The End entry and add an intradocument link to the link label you created in Step 3.

**6** • Copy the following file to the directory where you are modifying this Web page:

*d:*/DemoWeb2/Answers/home.gif

**7** • Add the tags that will make the HOME.GIF image an intradocument link back to the home label in the book title.

**8** • **Extra Credit**\*\* For a little extra fun, locate the chapter headings listed at the end of each chapter and turn these into links to the appropriate chapter headings. Adding these extra links is a great service to your Web page visitors. It makes it very easy for them to navigate your Web pages.

**After you add the links at the end of the first chapter, use the Copy and Paste commands to duplicate them at the other locations.**

TIP

**9** • Save the file and display it in your browser. Your Web page should appear as shown in Figure 4.4.

**10** • Test all of your links to be sure they work properly. The correct HTML code for this exercise is on this book's CD-ROM at:

*d:/DemoWeb2/Answers/intra2.htm*

▶ . . . . . . . . . . . . . . . . . . . . . . . . . . . ◀

FIGURE 4.4

*Exercise 4.1 Result*

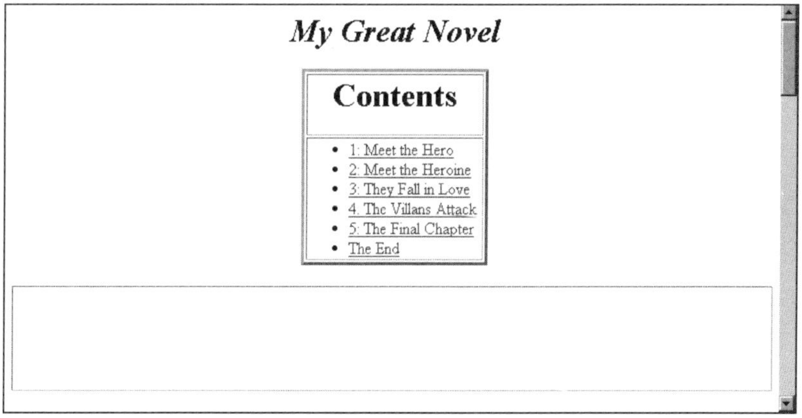

*My Great Novel*

**Contents**

- 1: Meet the Hero
- 2: Meet the Heroine
- 3: They Fall in Love
- 4. The Villans Attack
- 5: The Final Chapter
- The End

## EXERCISE 4.2: CREATING INTERDOCUMENT LINKS

In this exercise, you will update a Web page to include interdocument links to internal and external Web pages. To complete this exercise, do the following:

**1** • Use a text editor or word processor program to open the following file on this book's CD-ROM:

   d:/DemoWeb2/Answers/link.htm

   I've already typed the text for you. You just need to add the HTML tags to create links.

**2** • Locate the Intralink Practice Page list item and turn it into a link to the Web page you created in Exercise 4.1.

**3** • Make the other list items into links to the following Web sites:

   ▸ Novell: www.novell.com

   ▸ Novell Press: www.novell.com/programs/press

   ▸ IDG Books Worldwide: www.idgbooks.com

   ▸ Adventure Communications: www.adventurec.com

**4** • **Extra Credit**\*\* At the end of the table, add a link to Chapter 4 on the Web page you created in Exercise 4.1.

**5** • Save the file and display it in your browser. Your Web page should appear as shown in Figure 4.5.

**6** • Test all of your links to be sure they work properly. If you don't have an Internet connection, the external links won't work. To test these links without an Internet connection, move the mouse cursor over each link and watch the status message area in the browser. When the mouse is over a link, the link destination appears in the status message area. The correct HTML code for this exercise is on this book's CD-ROM at:

*d:/DemoWeb2/Answers/link2.htm*

FIGURE 4.5

*Exercise 4.2 Result*

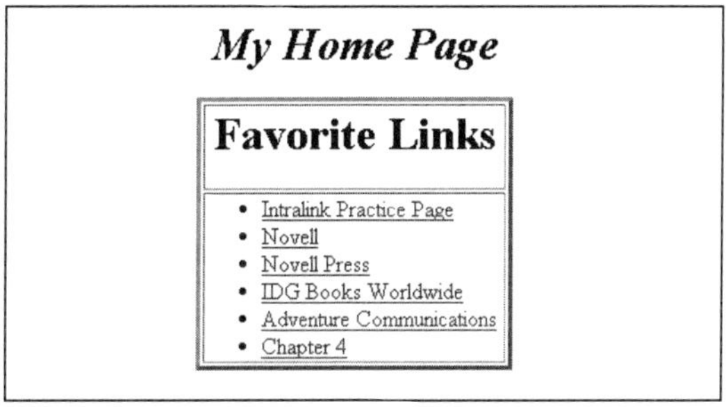

*My Home Page*

**Favorite Links**

- Intralink Practice Page
- Novell
- Novell Press
- IDG Books Worldwide
- Adventure Communications
- Chapter 4

## EXERCISE 4.3: CREATING A SERVER-SIDE IMAGE MAP

In this exercise, you will use Mapedit to create a server-side image map. I've already created an image for you to use. To complete this exercise, do the following:

**1** • Copy the buttons.gif file from this book's CD-ROM to the directory where you are creating your Web pages. The path to the file is:

*d:/DemoWeb2/Answers/buttons.gif*

**2** • Install Mapedit as follows:

a. Start Windows and open one of the following installation utilities on this book's CD:

Windows 3.1: `d:\DemoWeb2\Mapedit\mapdst.exe`

Windows 95 and NT: `d:\DemoWeb2\Mapedit\map32dst.exe`

b. Follow the instructions to complete the installation and start Mapedit.

**3** • If Mapedit isn't started, start it now by double-clicking the icon that was created during installation.

**4** • In Mapedit, select File → Open/Create.

**5** • In the dialog box that appears, do the following:

a. In the Map or HTML File text box, enter the path and the name of the server-side map file to create. Use the path to the directory where your files are stored, and name the map file "chapters.map." When you specify a map file extension, Mapedit knows you want to create a server-side image map.

b. In the Image Filename text box, enter the path and filename of the BUTTONS.GIF image you copied from the CD.

c. If you know your Web server uses the CERN method, select CERN. Otherwise, leave the NCSA button selected.

d. Click OK.

**6** • When you are prompted to create the map file, click Yes.

**7** • To create the first "hot spot" region and assign a URL to it, do the following:

    a. Click in one corner of the Chapter 1 area. The rectangle selection tool is selected by default.

    b. Move the mouse to the opposite corner of the area and click again.

    c. When the dialog box appears, enter the URL for the link destination. In this exercise, you are creating an imagemap that will take visitors to other areas of the same page, so the URL is "#chap1."

You have just created the first hot spot.

**8** • Using the procedure in Step 7 as a guide, create hot spots for the other five chapters.

**9** • To save the map file, select File → Save.

**10** • To quit Mapedit, select File → Exit.

**11** • Use a text editor or word processor to open the map file you just created. The map file should look similar to the following:

```
rect #chap1 1,0 100,48

rect #chap2 101,2 199,48

rect #chap3 201,1 299,48

rect #chap4 300,2 399,47

rect #chap5 399,2 498,48
```

Depending on your accuracy, the pixel numbers may be different. If you want to be more exact, you can adjust the numbers in the text editor. In relatively large areas, accuracy isn't as important because visitors usually click somewhere in the middle of the area.

**12** • Now prepare a Web page to use the image map file. Use a text editor or word processor to open the Web page you created in Exercise 4.1. If you didn't do this exercise, you can open the following file on this book's CD-ROM:

*d:/DemoWeb2/Answers/intra2.htm*

**13** • Locate the group of chapter references at the end of Chapter 1, and insert an image tag for the BUTTONS.GIF image before these references.

**14** • Make the BUTTONS.GIF image tag an image link to the map file you created earlier in this exercise.

**15** • Save the file and display it in your browser.

**16** • Select the link to Chapter 1. Your Web page should appear as shown in Figure 4.6.

**17** • Move the mouse over the image map and watch the status message area. As you move the mouse, the status message area should show the name of the image map file and the coordinates of the cursor within the image. The browser cannot show you a link destination because the server determines this after the mouse click. The correct HTML code for this exercise is on this book's CD-ROM at:

*d:/DemoWeb2/Answers/ssmap.htm*

| FIGURE 4.6 | |
| --- | --- |
| *Exercise 4.3 Result* | |

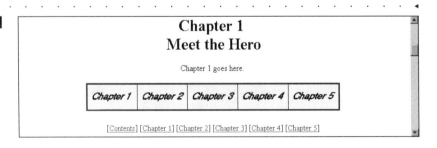

**Chapter 1**
**Meet the Hero**

Chapter 1 goes here.

| Chapter 1 | Chapter 2 | Chapter 3 | Chapter 4 | Chapter 5 |
| --- | --- | --- | --- | --- |

[Contents] [Chapter 1] [Chapter 2] [Chapter 3] [Chapter 4] [Chapter 5]

**EXERCISE 4.4: CREATING A CLIENT-SIDE IMAGE MAP**

In this exercise, you will use Mapedit to create a client-side image map. I've already created an image for you to use. To complete this exercise, do the following:

**1** • If you didn't complete Exercise 4.3, do the following:

a. Copy the BUTTONS.GIF file from this book's CD-ROM to the directory where you are creating your Web pages.

b. Install Mapedit as follows:

   i) Start Windows and open one of the following installation utilities on this book's CD:

   Windows 3.1: `d:\DemoWeb2\Mapedit\mapdst.exe`

   Windows 95 and NT: `d:\DemoWeb2\Mapedit\map32dst.exe`

   ii) Follow the instructions to complete the installation and start Mapedit.

**2** • Use a text editor or word processor program to open the following file on this book's CD-ROM:

*d:/DemoWeb2/Answers/intra2.htm*

**3** • Locate the group of chapter references at the end of Chapter 1, and insert an image tag for the BUTTONS.GIF image before these references.

**4** • Save the file to your computer as CSMAP.HTM.

**5** • If Mapedit isn't started, start it now by double-clicking the icon that was created during installation.

**6** • In Mapedit, select File → Open/Create.

**7** • In the dialog box that appears, do the following:

a. In the Map or HTML File text box, enter the path and the name of the CSMAP.HTM file you saved earlier. When you specify an HTML file extension, Mapedit knows you want to create a client-side image map.

b. In the Image Filename text box, enter the path and filename of the BUTTONS.GIF image you copied from the CD. If you use the Browse button to select the HTML file, Mapedit prompts you to select one of the graphics in this file.

c. Click OK.

**8** • To create the first "hot spot" region and assign a URL to it, do the following:

a. Click in one corner of the Chapter 1 area. The rectangle selection tool is selected by default.

b. Move the mouse to the opposite corner of the area and click again.

c. When the dialog box appears, enter the URL for the link destination. In this exercise you are creating an imagemap that will take visitors to other areas of the same page, so the URL is "#chap1."

You have just created the first hot spot.

**9** • Using the procedure in Step 7 as a guide, create hot spots for the other four chapters.

**10** • To save the map file, select File → Save.

**11** • To quit Mapedit, select File → Exit.

**12** • Use a text editor or word processor to open the CSMAP.HTM file you just created, and do the following:

a. Look at the image tag to see the attribute that Mapedit added.

b. Look at the map tags Mapedit added to the end of the file.

**13** • In your browser, open the CSMAP.HTM page and select the link to Chapter 1. Your Web page should appear as shown in Figure 4.6. The appearance will be the same as that for a server-side image map.

**14** • Click each of the hot spots in the image map to verify that all links are working. As you move the mouse over the image map, the status message area should show the link destination for each hot spot. The correct HTML code for this exercise is on this book's CD-ROM at:

*d:/DemoWeb2/Answers/csmap.htm*

**EXERCISE 4.5: UNDERSTANDING LINKS AND IMAGE MAPS**

The following exercise tests your understanding of links and image maps. To complete this exercise, do the following:

1 • Write the complete tag that marks a link destination in a Web page and names it "Doc Brown."

   Answer: . . . . . . . . . . . . . . . . . . . . . . . . . . . . . . . . . . . . . .

2 • Write the complete set of tags that mark the text "Doctor Brown" as a link to the label "Doc Brown" on the same Web page.

   Answer: . . . . . . . . . . . . . . . . . . . . . . . . . . . . . . . . . . . . . .

3 • Write the complete set of tags that mark the text "Novell" as a link to the document root directory of www.novell.com.

   Answer: . . . . . . . . . . . . . . . . . . . . . . . . . . . . . . . . . . . . . .

4 • Write the shortest possible set of tags that link the image file BANNER.GIF to a file named HOMEPAGE.HTM, which is stored in the same directory as the source Web page.

   Answer: . . . . . . . . . . . . . . . . . . . . . . . . . . . . . . . . . . . . . .

5 • Write the set of tags that use an absolute reference to mark the text "ACME Corporation" as a link to the "ACMEHOME.HTM" file in the document root directory of www.acme.com.

   Answer: . . . . . . . . . . . . . . . . . . . . . . . . . . . . . . . . . . . . . .

6 • A _____ link displays a Web page on a different Web server.

   Answer: . . . . . . . . . . . . . . . . . . . . . . . . . . . . . . . . . . . . . .

**7** • When you create a server-side image map, which attribute must be added to the <IMG> tag?

Answer: . . . . . . . . . . . . . . . . . . . . . . . . . . . . . . . . . . . . . .

**8** • When you create a link for a server-side image map, what is the extension of the destination file?

Answer: . . . . . . . . . . . . . . . . . . . . . . . . . . . . . . . . . . . . . .

**9** • When you create a client-side image map, which attribute must be added to the <IMG> tag?

Answer: . . . . . . . . . . . . . . . . . . . . . . . . . . . . . . . . . . . . . .

**10** • When you create a client-side image map, does the image map require link anchor tags?

Answer: . . . . . . . . . . . . . . . . . . . . . . . . . . . . . . . . . . . . . .

**11** • What is a hot spot?

Answer: . . . . . . . . . . . . . . . . . . . . . . . . . . . . . . . . . . . . . .

**12** • In a link anchor tag, which character precedes a reference to a named anchor label?

Answer: . . . . . . . . . . . . . . . . . . . . . . . . . . . . . . . . . . . . . .

**13** • List the five steps Novell recommends in Course 654 for creating Web sites.

Answer: . . . . . . . . . . . . . . . . . . . . . . . . . . . . . . . . . . . . . .

# CHAPTER 5

# Using Advanced
# Web Page Features

**C**hapters 2 through 4 described how to create Web pages and link them together to create Web sites. This chapter describes how to add the following advanced features to your Web site:

▸ Frames that enable you to display multiple Web pages simultaneously

▸ Forms that you can use to collect data from Web site visitors

▸ Information that Internet search engines can use to publicize your Web site

While none of these features is required to build a Web site, they are commonly used by many first-class Web sites. The final sections of this chapter describe some useful Web site development tools and discuss why it is important to use Web site tools and to understand HTML tags.

## Using Frames

Frames are an HTML 3.2 feature that you can use to divide a browser window into separate areas, each of which can display independent Web pages. A collection of frames is called a *frameset*. Figure 5.1 shows a frameset of two horizontal frames. In this example, the upper frame is a fixed frame that only displays the Web site banner. The lower frame is a scrollable frame that can be used to browse the Web site. This type of frameset is useful when you want to be sure that information such as a logo or copyright statement remains on the screen while visitors browse part of your Web site.

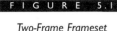

*Two-Frame Frameset*

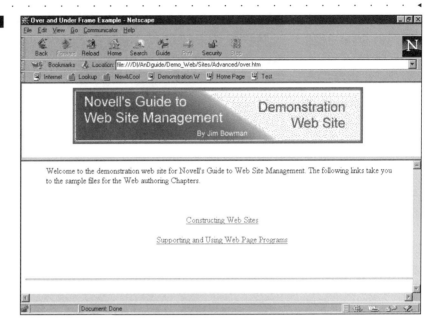

Another common use of frames is for displaying a table of contents for part, or all, of your Web site. In the frameset shown in Figure 5.2, the table of contents always displays in the left frame and the contents that the user selects appear in the right frame. Framesets can be configured to display frames horizontally, vertically, or in combinations. For more examples of frame sets, browse the demonstration Web site at:

```
d:/DemoWeb2/Sites/Advanced/frames.htm
```

This section describes how to create frameset documents and how to create links to other frames and browser windows.

FIGURE 5.2

*Table of Contents Frameset*

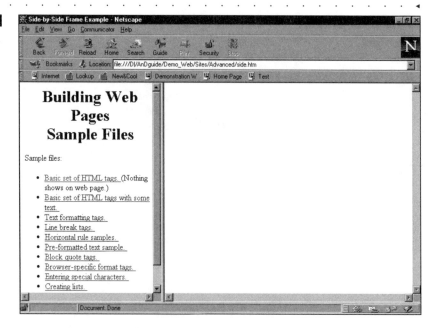

## CREATING FRAMESET DOCUMENTS

To create framesets, you need to create a special variation of a Web page called a frameset document. You create these frameset documents using the same tools you use to create Web pages. The following is the frameset document that creates the frameset shown in Figure 5.1:

```
<HTML>

<HEAD>

    <TITLE>Over and Under Frame Example</TITLE>

</HEAD>

<!--filename over.htm-->


<FRAMESET ROWS="35%, *">

    <FRAME SRC=logo.htm NORESIZE>
```

```
<FRAME SRC=home.htm SCROLLING=yes>
```

```
</FRAMESET>
```

```
</HTML>
```

The differences between the Web page documents, described in the previous chapters, and a frameset document are as follows:

▸ The frameset document uses <FRAMESET> tags instead of <BODY> tags.

▸ The tags between the <FRAMESET> tags are limited to special tags for framesets.

Think of a frameset as a home for your Web pages and the frames as the rooms. A frameset document creates the room structure in which you display your Web pages. To create this structure, you use <FRAMESET> tags.

Each pair of <FRAMESET> tags defines a set of frames that are arranged in either rows or columns. To define the number of rows or columns for the frameset, use either the ROWS or COLS (columns) attribute in the opening <FRAMESET> tag as follows:

```
<FRAMESET ROWS="value list">
```

```
<FRAMESET COLS="value list">
```

The value list is a series of values that define both the number of frames and the size of the frames. The total number of values defines the total number of frames in the frame set. Each value is separated from the others by commas and defines the size of the frame using one of the following value types:

▸ Percentage—For example, a "50%, 20%, 30%" value list creates three frames that divide the available space in the respective portions.

▸ Relative scale—A "2*, *" value list assigns two-thirds of the available space to the first frame and the remaining space to the second frame.

▸ Pixel count—A "500, *" value list creates a row frame that is 500 pixels tall or a column frame that is 500 pixels wide. The remaining space is assigned to the second frame.

An asterisk in the value list (*) tells the browser to divide the available space between the columns and rows that are defined with asterisks. If a factor is listed with the asterisk, the row or column gets a proportional amount of space based on the other columns marked with asterisks. For example, "3*, *" creates two rows or columns, the first of which uses three-fourths of the available space. The "2*, 3*" defines two rows or columns, the first of which uses two-fifths of the available space. Table 5.1 lists the <FRAMESET> tag attributes.

**For some framesets, relative frame sizes (such as 35 percent or *) are better than pixel counts. Remember browser users define the size of their windows. Frames that are defined with pixel counts do not change dimensions when the user resizes a window.**

TIP

| TABLE 5.1 | ATTRIBUTE | DESCRIPTION |
|---|---|---|
| <FRAMESET> Tag Attributes | (Values) BORDER="n" (Netscape) | This optional attribute specifies the pixel width of the divider between frames. It only works with Netscape browsers. |
| | COLS="*,*,*" | This attribute is described in the text preceding this table. |
| | FRAMEBORDER= "yes or no" (Netscape) | The optional FRAMEBORDER attribute specifies whether or not a border will appear between frames. |
| | FRAMEBORDER= "0" (Microsoft) | The optional FRAMEBORDER attribute specifies whether or not a border will appear between frames. For Internet Explorer browsers, the 0 value hides the border. |
| | ROWS= "*,*,*" | This attribute is described in the text preceding this table. |

After you define a frameset, you must define what each frame contains. A frame can display a Web page or, as you'll see in the next section, a frame can contain another frameset. To define frames that display Web pages, use `<FRAME>` tags as follows:

```
<FRAMESET ROWS="50%, *">

    <FRAME SRC=one.htm>

    <FRAME SRC=two.htm>

</FRAMESET>
```

Notice that a closing frame tag is not required. As with link anchor tags and image tags, the SRC attribute defines a file to display. When the frame SRC attribute defines an HTML file, a Web page appears in the frame. The Web page is a separate file that you have created as described in previous chapters. Additional attributes define how the frame appears and how it behaves. Table 5.2 lists the `<FRAME>` tag attributes.

| TABLE 5.2 | ATTRIBUTE (Values) | DESCRIPTION |
| --- | --- | --- |
| `<FRAME>` *Tag Attributes* | SRC="url" | The optional source (SRC) attribute defines the URL of the Web page for the frame. If this attribute is omitted, the frame remains blank. |
| | NAME="*name*" | The optional NAME attribute specifies a name for the frame. Frame names are case sensitive and must begin with an alphanumeric character. |
| | | The name is required only when you want to have a link in a different frame change the content of this frame. For example, if you have a table of contents in the left frame and you want links in the left frame to display contents in the right frame, you need to assign a name to the right frame. |
| | SCROLLING= (yes, no, auto) | The SCROLLING attribute defines when scroll bars appear in the frame. A yes value displays scroll bars all the time, whether they are needed or not, and a no value never displays scroll bars. The default value is auto, which displays scroll bars only when they are needed. |

*(continued)*

| ATTRIBUTE | DESCRIPTION |
|---|---|
| NORESIZE | The NORESIZE attribute locks the frame size so users cannot change the size of the frame. When the NORESIZE option is absent, users can click and drag the dividers between frames to resize them. |
| MARGINHEIGHT | The MARGINHEIGHT attribute defines, in pixels, the margin height that appears above and below the Web page content in the frame. |
| MARGINWIDTH | The MARGINWIDTH attribute defines, in pixels, the margin width that appears to the sides of the Web page content in the frame. |

**T A B L E   5.2**

⟨FRAME⟩ *Tag Attributes*
*(continued)*

**NOTE**

**When you create frameset documents, remember the title defined in the head of your frameset document is the title browser users see. Although the individual frames display Web pages, the Web page titles for these Web pages do not replace the frameset title in the browser window.**

## CREATING NESTED FRAMESETS

A single frameset enables you to create rows or columns, but not both. However, once you've used a frameset to define two or more frames, you can replace any of those frames with another frameset, which is called a nested frameset. A nested frameset further divides a frame into either rows or columns. For example, you can create a frameset that divides the browser window into two rows, and then you can divide one of the rows into columns with a second pair of ⟨FRAMESET⟩ tags. The following example illustrates how to do this.

```
<FRAMESET ROWS="50%, *">

    <FRAMESET COLS="50%, *">

        <FRAME SRC=one.htm>

        <FRAME SRC=two.htm>

    </FRAMESET>
```

```
<FRAME SRC=three.htm>
```

```
</FRAMESET>
```

In this example, the first frameset creates two row frames that each occupy 50 percent of the browser window. The second frameset replaces the frame tag for the first row, so it divides the first row frame into two column frames that each use 50 percent of the row frame.

Often, nested framesets are used to divide a window into both rows and columns. The trickiest part of using nested framesets is to decide which way to divide the browser window first. The best way to decide is to draw your frames on a piece of paper. If any row stretches across the entire browser window, you need to define rows first. The same is true for columns.

## SUPPORTING "NO FRAME" BROWSERS

Frames are still a relatively new browser feature; they are supported by Netscape Navigator 2.0 and later and by Microsoft Internet Explorer 3.0 and later. If you expect Web site visitors who use other browsers, you can use the `<NOFRAME>` and `</NOFRAME>` tags within the `<FRAMESET>` tags to provide HTML content for these browsers. Here is an example:

```
<FRAMESET ROWS="50%, *">

  <FRAME SRC=one.htm>

  <FRAME SRC=two.htm>

  <NOFRAME>

        <CENTER>

        Your Browser does not support frames.

        <P>Click <A HREF="filename.htm">here</A> to see a
non-frame version of this page.

        </CENTER>

  </NOFRAME>

</FRAMESET>
```

In this example, the text between the `<NOFRAME>` tags explains why the Web page is otherwise empty and provides a link to an alternative Web page. Without the link, the only way a Web site visitor could move on would be to use the Back button or enter a new URL.

## CREATING LINKS TO FRAMES AND WINDOWS

The `<FRAME>` tags in the frameset document define the initial pages that appear in the frameset. If you use standard links in the Web pages for these frames, those links will cause the browser to display each new Web page in the frame from which the link is selected. To display a new Web page in a different frame or window, you need to add the TARGET attribute to the link's tag. You can use the TARGET attribute in the following link tags:

- ► `<A HREF="url" TARGET="name">`

- ► `<AREA SHAPE="shape" COORDS="values" HREF="url" TARGET="name">`

- ► `<FORM ACTION="url" TARGET="name">`

The first two examples above use the anchor tag (`<A>`) and `<AREA>` tag, both of which are described in Chapter 4. The `<AREA>` tag is usually created by an image map utility when you are creating client-side image maps. The last tag is the `<FORM>` tag, which is introduced later in this chapter.

The name value for the TARGET attribute specifies the name of the window or frame that will display the new Web page. If this name matches a frame name defined in the current frameset, the named frame displays the Web page. If the name doesn't match a frame name, the destination Web page is displayed in a new browser window that is named with the name in the TARGET attribute.

The TARGET attribute supports four special targets that Netscape calls magic targets. These targets give you additional control over where the Web page appears. Table 5.3 describes these targets. For a live example of how they work, browse the demonstration Web site at:

`d:/DemoWeb2/Sites/Advanced/parent.htm`

| TABLE 5.3 | MAGIC TARGET | DESCRIPTION |
|---|---|---|
| *Magic Targets* | TARGET="_blank" | The _blank target opens the Web page in a new browser window—be careful with this. If you use many of these targets, an inexperienced browser user can unwittingly use up all his computer resources with multiple open browsers. |
| | | Also, note that when a browser user selects a link with this target, the browser back button can't take the user back to the Web page in the other browser window. You might want to add a link back to the previous page if you want to use this type of target. |
| | TARGET="_self" | The _self target opens the Web page in the same frame as the source link. This target enables you to use the current frame when you've defined a different default frame with the <BASE> tag, which is described after this table. |
| | TARGET="_parent" | The _parent target opens the Web page in the parent frameset frame. If the current frameset is built in a single frameset document, the parent frame is the entire browser window, and this target displays the Web page in the browser window without frames. |
| | | If the current frameset is defined in a nested frameset, the parent frameset frame is the frame in which the child frameset document is displayed. Use the demonstration Web site to see how this works. |
| | | Note that this magic target is disabled in the topmost window because that window is its own parent. |
| | TARGET="_top" | The _top target displays the Web page in the topmost window, which is the browser window without any frames. |

When the Web page for one of your frames contains many links that target another frame (for instance, when you are creating a table of contents), it is easier to define a new default target frame than it is to specify the same target in every link. To specify a default target for all of the links in a document, use the <BASE> tag as follows:

```
<BASE TARGET="name">
```

In the `<BASE>` tag, the target name can use a frame name, a name for a new window, or any of the magic target names.

**Exercise 5.1: If you're preparing to take the certification exam, or if you want to practice what you learned in this section, turn to the end of this chapter and complete Exercise 5.1. When you are done, continue reading here to prepare for the next exercise.**

## Creating Forms

HTML forms are the most popular tool for collecting data from Web site visitors. In Part III, Using Web Page Programs and Scripts, you'll learn some ways to process form data with SSI commands and CGI scripts. In this chapter, you'll learn how to build the forms and add `ACTION` attributes that determine where the form data is sent. Figure 5.3 shows a sample form from the demonstration Web site.

FIGURE 5.3

*Sample Form*

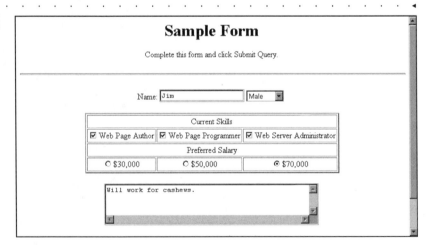

Each form element, such as a text box or a button, is defined by HTML tags. Like lists and tables, the elements of a form are grouped together between opening and closing HTML tags: `<FORM>` and `</FORM>`.

You can include a number of different elements in your Web page forms. Some common form elements are:

- ▸ Text input boxes

- ▸ Large text input areas

- ▸ Menu option lists

- ▸ Checkboxes

- ▸ Radio buttons

- ▸ Submit and Reset buttons

You can use forms to conduct surveys, register product users, or collect orders for your products. When the Web page visitors see a form, they can ignore it or fill in the information. Nothing happens until they click the button to send the input information. (By default, this button is called the Submit Query button, but you can choose a different name.) When a user clicks the Submit Query button, the data is sent to a location defined in the opening form tag.

The following sections describe how to create a basic form and how to add form elements to the form.

## CREATING A BASIC FORM

The following code shows the basic set of tags that create a form:

```
<FORM METHOD=method ACTION=action>


<!-- insert one or more form elements here -->


<INPUT TYPE=submit>
</FORM>
```

As mentioned earlier, the opening and closing <FORM> tags group the individual form elements into a form. The <INPUT> tag with the attribute TYPE=submit creates a Submit Query button. You'll learn more about the <INPUT> tag and the Submit Query button later in this chapter. For now, just remember that when the user clicks the Submit Query button, all of the data in the form elements between the <FORM> tags is sent to the destination defined by the ACTION attribute in the opening <FORM> tag.

**IMPORTANT**

**When you are creating forms, do not create forms within a form. This is called nesting, and while it is permitted with some HTML features, it is not permitted when creating forms.**

The opening <FORM> tag attributes are METHOD and ACTION. The METHOD attribute defines how data is sent to the destination; the ACTION attribute defines where the data is sent. The following subsections describe how to use each of these attributes.

### Using the METHOD Attribute

The two values for the METHOD attribute are GET and POST. The default value is GET. If the method attribute is omitted, or if the POST value is not entered in uppercase letters, the form data is sent to the Web server using the GET method.

**GET** The GET method appends all form data to the end of the URL in the HTTP header. The HTTP header is the first message sent to a server when a browser makes a request. If the user clicks the Submit Query button in the sample form shown in Figure 5.3, the following URL is sent to the Web server:

```
http://www.adventurec.com/DemoWeb2/Sites/Advanced/results.htm
?your_name=Jim&menu=Male&c1=on&c2=on&c3=on&one=3&comments=
Will+work+for+cashews.
```

In this sample URL, the question mark and the text that follows it is called the *query string* portion of the URL. The query string contains a variable name for each form component and the data values entered for that component. For example, *your_name* is a variable assigned to the first text box form element, and Jim is the value entered in that form element. The equals signs indicate which variables correspond to which values, the ampersand symbols separate the variable and value pairs, and the plus symbols replace any spaces in the values.

You can experiment with the sample form by accessing it on the demonstration Web site at:

`d:/DemoWeb2/Sites/Advanced/forms.htm`

The GET method works fine for small forms, but it does have some disadvantages. For example, the length of the URL is limited. If a form contains too much data, the limit will be exceeded and part of the data will be lost. The other disadvantage to the GET method is related to security. HTTP headers are recorded in Web server access logs and can be recorded in error logs as well. If you don't want Web server administrators to see the form data, don't use the GET method.

**POST**  The POST method sends the HTTP header first without the data, and then it sends the form data in a separate message. The message containing the form data includes information that identifies how much data is enclosed in the message.

The POST method is generally the preferred choice for data transfer. You don't have to worry about truncated data or Web server logs; however, don't develop a false sense of security. The POST method doesn't encrypt the transferred data, so it is still visible to network spies; they just have to work a little harder to see it.

### Using the ACTION Attribute

As mentioned earlier, the ACTION attribute defines the destination of the form data; and as you might guess, this destination is defined by a URL. In the sample form for this chapter, I specified a Web page as the destination: ACTION= "results.htm", however, the destination is usually one of the following:

- ▸ A Server Side Include (SSI) Web page that uses SSI commands to save the data to a Web server text file

- ▸ A Common Gateway Interface (CGI) program or script

- ▸ A server-side JavaScript such as those supported by the Netscape Enterprise Server for NetWare

In Chapter 11, you'll see an example that shows how form data can be sent to a file using SSI commands. The most common destinations for form data, however, are CGI programs and scripts, which are described in Chapter 12. Server-side JavaScripts are introduced in Chapter 14.

## CREATING FORM ELEMENTS

In this section, you'll learn how to create the following types of form elements:

- ▸ Text input boxes

- ▸ Large text input areas

- ▸ Menu option lists

- ▸ Checkboxes

- ▸ Radio buttons

- ▸ Submit and Reset buttons

The only required form element is a submit button, which initiates the data transfer to the Web server. A single button form can launch a CGI script or a JavaScript or display another Web page, but you must use additional form elements if you want to send data to the destination.

### Text Input Boxes

Text input boxes provide room for users to enter a single line of text. Figure 5.4 shows a sample text input box. The format for creating a text input box is:

```
<INPUT TYPE=type NAME=name VALUE=text SIZE=nn MAXLENGTH=nn
MIN=nn MAX=nn>
```

The TYPE and NAME attributes are required; the others are optional. Table 5.4 lists the values you can use with the TYPE attribute.

▸ . . . . . . . . . . . . . . . . . . . . . . . . . . . . . . ◂

**FIGURE 5.4**

*Text Input Box*

| TABLE 5.4 | VALUE | DESCRIPTION |
|---|---|---|
| *Type Attribute Values* | text | Use the text value to display a standard input box for text. The input box displays all characters entered. |
| | password | Use the password value when you want the browser to display an asterisk for each character the user enters. This value is used to prevent others from reading what the user types. |
| | hidden | Use the hidden value when you don't want the browser to display any text in the text box. As a Web page author, you might use the hidden value to hide data in a form. For example, you might create a hidden text box that identifies an account name or user name for users who fill out a form. |
| | range | Use the range value to restrict text box entries to integer numbers (no decimals or fractions) between the values set by the min and max attributes.<br><br>This is an HTML 3.0 feature this was not adopted in HTML 3.2. This might not work in your browser. |

The NAME attribute specifies the name of the variable representing the data entered in this box. Variable names cannot include spaces, but may include the underscore character (_), and variable names must be unique. For example, you can't use the same variable name for more than one form element. You must also use names that are different from JavaScript and environmental variables, which you'll learn more about in Part III.

The VALUE attribute defines the default entry for the text box. For example, you can use the VALUE attribute to display "Enter your name here." in the text box.

The rest of the attributes define the size and acceptable contents for the text box. The SIZE attribute specifies the size of the text box in characters, while the MAXLENGTH attribute defines how many characters can be entered in the box. When the SIZE attribute is smaller than the MAXLENGTH attribute, the text box will scroll when users enter more than the number of characters defined by the SIZE attribute.

When the TYPE attribute is set to range, the MIN and MAX attributes define the minimum and maximum values that can be entered in the text box. These attributes require integer number values.

### Large Text Input Areas

This type of text box provides room for users to enter multiple lines of text, as shown in Figure 5.5. The format for creating a large text input area is:

```
<TEXTAREA NAME=name COLS=nn ROWS=nn WRAP=option>Default
text.</TEXTAREA>
```

The NAME attribute is required and specifies the name of the variable representing the data entered in this box. The COLS and ROWS attributes define the number of columns and rows the text box displays. As with text input boxes, the user can enter more text than will fit in the display area. The text within the text box will scroll when necessary to display the additional characters.

▶ . . . . . . . . . . . . . . . . . . . . . . . . . . . . . . . . . ◀

**FIGURE 5.5**

*Large Text Input Area*

The WRAP attribute defines what happens when text typed on a single line extends beyond the borders of the text area. If the WRAP attribute is set to OFF, a new line does not begin until the browser user presses Enter. The text area will scroll, enabling the user to create very long lines.

When the WRAP attribute is set to SOFT or HARD, long text lines automatically wrap to create new lines when the line exceeds the visible length of the text area. The difference between the SOFT and HARD options is that the HARD option sends line-ending characters when the form is submitted and the SOFT option does not.

The text between the opening and closing <TEXTAREA> tags defines the default entry for the text box. For example, you can enter text here to display "Enter your comments here." in the text box.

### Menu Option Lists

Menu option lists enable Web page visitors to select one or more options from a list that you define. Depending on the options you choose, the option list can appear as a drop-down list or as a scrollable list, both shown in Figure 5.6. To create a menu option list, use the <SELECT> and <OPTION> tags as follows:

```
<SELECT NAME=name SIZE=nn MULTI>
```

```
<OPTION VALUE=value>Option 1 description.
```

. . . . . .

```
<OPTION VALUE=value>Option 2 description.

<OPTION VALUE=value selected>Option 3 description.

</SELECT>
```

The `<SELECT NAME=name>` and `</SELECT>` tags mark the beginning and the end of the menu option list. Table 5.5 describes the `<SELECT>` tag attributes.

► . . . . . . . . . . . . . . . . . . . . . . . . . . . . . . . . ◄

**FIGURE 5.6**

*Drop-Down (left) and Scrollable (right) List*

**TABLE 5.5**

`<SELECT>` *Tag Attributes*

| ATTRIBUTE | DESCRIPTION |
|-----------|-------------|
| NAME | The NAME attribute is required; it specifies the name of the variable representing the data option selected in this box. |
| SIZE=nn | The SIZE attribute specifies how many options are simultaneously visible on the Web page. The default value is 1. When the SIZE attribute specifies two or more options and is set to fewer than the total number of options, the menu option list displays a scroll box. |
| MULTI | The MULTI attribute is optional. When this attribute is included, users can select multiple options by holding down the Ctrl key as they click options. |

To add an option to a menu option list, you enter an `<OPTION>` tag and a description of the option. The option description appears as a menu option on the Web page. Unless you use the `VALUE` attribute with the `<OPTION>` tag, the option description is sent back to the Web server when a Web page visitor selects the option.

The `VALUE` attribute for the `<OPTION>` tag can be used to send a value to the Web server in place of the option description. This attribute can help you minimize the amount of data sent to the Web server. For example, the following tag would send the value 007 to the Web server instead of the longer description:

```
<OPTION VALUE=007>A famous secret agent from England.
```

You can use the `SELECTED` attribute to designate a default option for the menu option list. Table 5.6 shows the attributes that correspond to the `<OPTION>` tag.

| TABLE 5.6 | ATTRIBUTE | DESCRIPTION |
|---|---|---|
| `<OPTION>` Tag Attributes | VALUE | The VALUE attribute defines a value sent to the Web server in place of the option description, which is the text following the `<OPTION>` tag. |
| | SELECTED | The SELECTED attribute defines the default option in the menu option list. If a default option is not designated, the first option becomes the default option. |

### Checkboxes

Checkboxes let visitors select (or deselect) one or more options. Figure 5.7 shows some sample checkboxes. The format for creating a checkbox is as follows:

```
<INPUT TYPE=checkbox NAME=name VALUE=value CHECKED>Checkbox
description.
```

The text following the closing bracket of the INPUT tag is the option description, which appears on the actual Web page with the checkbox. Table 5.7 describes the checkbox option attributes.

| FIGURE 5.7 | ☐ Web Page Author  ☐ Web Page Programmer  ☐ Web Server Administrator |
|---|---|
| Checkbox Options | |

| TABLE 5.7 | ATTRIBUTE | DESCRIPTION |
|---|---|---|
| Checkbox Option Attributes | TYPE=checkbox | When the TYPE attribute is set to checkbox, the `<INPUT>` tag creates a checkbox option. |
| | NAME | The NAME attribute provides a variable name associated with the status of the checkbox. |
| | VALUE | The VALUE attribute defines a value sent to the Web server when the checkbox is checked. For example, you might use the value y to indicate yes, the checkbox is checked. |
| | CHECKED | The CHECKED attribute is similar to the selected attribute for menu option lists. Use the checked attribute to check a checkbox when the Web page appears. You can use the checked attribute on as many checkboxes as you want. |

When form data is sent to the Web server, the default value for checked options is on. If you use the VALUE attribute to specify a different value, this value is sent to the Web server instead of the on value. No data is sent to the Web server if the checkbox is unchecked. When you use multiple checkboxes, use a unique name in the NAME attribute for each checkbox. If you do not use unique names and your checkboxes use the same values, you won't know which checkboxes have been checked.

**Radio Buttons**

Radio buttons operate like the station-selection buttons on a car radio. When you select one button, you automatically deselect the previous choice. Use radio buttons when you want visitors to select only one item from a group of choices. (Use checkboxes to allow users to enable or disable several options independently of one another.) Figure 5.8 shows a sample group of radio buttons. The format to create a radio button is as follows:

```
<INPUT TYPE=radio NAME=name VALUE=value CHECKED>Radio button
description.
```

The text following the closing bracket of the <INPUT> tag is the option description, which appears on the actual Web page. Table 5.8 describes the radio button option attributes.

**FIGURE 5.8**

| ○ $30,000 | ○ $50,000 | ○ $70,000 |

*Radio Buttons*

**TABLE 5.8**

*Radio Button Option Attributes*

| ATTRIBUTE | DESCRIPTION |
| --- | --- |
| TYPE=radio | When the TYPE attribute is set to radio, the <INPUT> tag creates a radio button option. |
| NAME | The NAME attribute provides a variable name for a group of radio buttons. |
| VALUE | The VALUE attribute defines a value sent to the Web server when the radio button is selected. For example, you might use the values 1, 2, and 3 for each of three radio buttons. The value sent with the form data then indicates which radio button is selected. |

*(continued)*

| TABLE 5.8 | ATTRIBUTE | DESCRIPTION |
|---|---|---|
| Radio Button Option Attributes (continued) | CHECKED | Use the CHECKED attribute to select a default radio button when the Web page appears. You can use the CHECKED attribute on only one radio button. |

Use the NAME attribute to create a group of radio button options. Browser users can only select one radio button in each radio button group. If you use different NAME attribute values for each radio button, you've created multiple groups. The browser enables users to select one item within each of the groups.

**Most other HTML groups are created by using starting and ending tags. Radio button groups are an exception to the general rule.**

NOTE

When form data is sent to the Web server, the default value for the selected radio button option is on. This causes a problem when more than one radio button appears on a Web page. If any button is selected, the Web server receives the value on. How do you know which button the user selected? For this reason, you should always use the VALUE attribute to assign a unique value to each radio button within a group. This unique value identifies the selected radio button. If a visitor does not select any radio button, no data is sent to the Web server.

### Submit Button

The Submit button makes things happen; it sends the form data to the Web server for processing. The Submit button doesn't have to be named "Submit," but it must be included within the opening and closing <FORM> tags to enable form processing. The format for creating a submit button is as follows:

```
<INPUT TYPE=submit VALUE="button name">
```

The submit value of the TYPE attribute causes a Submit button to appear on the Web page. The VALUE attribute specifies the text that appears on the button. If the VALUE attribute is omitted, the name of the submit button is "Submit Query."

**As with all HTML tag attributes, quotation marks are required when the attribute value contains one or more character spaces.**

IMPORTANT

### Reset Button

The Reset button enables Web page visitors to erase all input and display the default form values. You don't have to name the Reset button "Reset." The format for creating a Reset button is as follows:

```
<INPUT TYPE=reset VALUE="button name">
```

When you make reset the value of the TYPE attribute, a reset button appears on your Web page. The VALUE attribute defines the name of the reset button. If the VALUE attribute is omitted, the name of the reset button will be "Reset."

 **Exercise 5.2: If you're preparing to take the certification exam, or if you want to practice what you learned in this section, turn to the end of this chapter and complete Exercise 5.2. When you are done, continue reading here to prepare for the next exercise.**

## Publicizing Your Web Site

After you've worked hard to create your Web site, how do you get the word out? The process is somewhat different for intranet and Internet Web sites. If you are managing an intranet Web site, you have a relatively small audience that you can reach by e-mail, voicemail, newsletter, or bulletin board. Just give your audience your Web site's URL.

If you have set up an Internet Web site, the world is your audience; but how do you reach everyone? You can advertise with TV, radio, and magazines. You can place your URL on your business cards. You can also send e-mail to newsgroups, and ask other Web sites to create links to your site.

There are many ways to advertise your Internet Web site. One way is to register with Internet search engines. Many people use search engines to locate information. If your Web site is registered with a search engine and someone searches for a keyword that is on your site, the search engine displays a link to the corresponding Web page on your Web site. This section describes how to prepare your Web pages for registration and how to register them with search engines.

### PREPARING PAGES FOR SEARCH ENGINE REGISTRATION

When a user locates your Web page with a search engine, the user sees a link to your Web site and some introductory information about your Web site (see Figure 5.9). Of course, the user usually sees links to many other Web sites as well. To entice the user to your Web site, you need to make sure your site information accurately lists the purpose and scope of your Web site.

▶ · · · · · · · · · · · · · · · · · · · · · · · · · · · · · · · · · · · · ◀

F I G U R E   5 . 9

*Yahoo Search Results*

The site information displayed by search engines sometimes comes from registration forms that you complete as described in the next section. Other times, the site information is taken from your Web pages. To prepare your Web pages for search engine registration, you can do the following:

▶ Make sure your Web page titles accurately describe the Web pages they label.

▶ Add <META> tags to the Web page document head to register information about your Web site.

▶ Place site information at the beginning of your home page.

▶ Use the ALT attribute in image tags to define your Web page images.

Search engines use software tools called robots or spiders to roam the Web and index Web sites. The information displayed by search engines can come from your Web page titles, Web page content, and tags within your Web pages. Often, the site information is taken from <META> tags in the document head. The <META> tags enable you to define Web site and Web page information that is invisible to Web page visitors, but visible to search engines and other Web tools. The following HTML code lists common <META> tags that you can use in the document head:

```
<HEAD>

<TITLE>Adventure Communications Home Page</TITLE>

<META NAME="Author" CONTENT="Jim Bowman">

<META NAME="Generator" CONTENT="NetObjects Fusion 2.0.1 for
Windows">

<META NAME="Classification" CONTENT="Computers, Internet,
WWW">

<META NAME="Description" CONTENT="Home page for Novell Press
author Jim Bowman, who writes and speaks about the Internet,
the World Wide Web, and related topics.">

<META NAME="KeyWords" CONTENT=" Jim Bowman, Adventure
Communications, Novell, WWW, World Wide Web, Web, book,
books, speaker, speakers, speaking, author, Novell Web
Server, Novell DNS Server, Novell DHCP, Novell IPX/IP
Gateway, Novell Client 32, Internet, TCP/IP, seminar, HTML,
DNS, DHCP, SSI, CGI, Perl, JavaScript, Java">

</HEAD>
```

The format for two types of <META> tags is:

```
<META NAME="value" CONTENT="content">

<META HTTP-EQUIV="value" CONTENT="content">
```

Table 5.9 defines some of the content types you can define with the NAME attribute, and Table 5.10 defines some of the content types you can define with the HTTP-EQUIV attribute.

| NAME **ATTRIBUTE** VALUE | CONTENT **ATTRIBUTE** VALUE | DESCRIPTION VALUE |
| --- | --- | --- |
| Author | Author name, e-mail address, or other identification | Identifies the Web page author or Web site administrator. |
| Classification | Identifies how the page should be classified by the search engine | You should browse search engine Web sites to see how they classify Web sites that are similar to yours. The search engine Web site might have instructions on what they want you to enter for the classification. |
| Description | A description of your Web site | This description often appears on the search engine Web page under the title of your Web page. If you don't enter a description, the search engine may use the first few lines of your Web page content. |
| Generator | HTML editor identification | Typically, HTML editors (such as those offered by NetObjects, Netscape, and Adobe) enter this automatically. It is not required for Internet search engines. |
| KeyWords | Keywords that describe your Web site content | Some Internet catalogs use these keywords to index your Web site. Search engines typically index all of the words in your Web site, so you only need to enter keywords that are not listed in your site but are reasonable alternatives for your content. |

| TABLE 5.10 | HTTP-EQUIV ATTRIBUTE VALUE | CONTENT ATTRIBUTE VALUE | DESCRIPTION |
|---|---|---|---|
| <META> *Tag* HTTP-EQUIV *and* CONTENT *Attribute Values* | Expires | Date and time in the following format: "Mon, 1 Dec 1997 05:49:32 PST" | Identifies an expiration date and time for the Web page. Cache servers can use this date to determine when to load a new copy of the Web page. |
| | Pragma | "no cache" | When this <META> tag is included, cache servers that support it will not cache the Web page. |

## REGISTERING YOUR SITE WITH SEARCH ENGINES

After you prepare your Web pages for search engine registration, you can wait for the search engines to find you, or you can tell them where to look. Telling a search engine about your Web site is the quickest way to get registered.

To register with search engines, you can register through a third party that registers your Web site with multiple search engines, or you can directly register with each search engine. Typically, you browse the registration Web site and look for a link named Add URL, Add Web Site, or Register Web Site.

**To register your Web site with some of the popular search engines, use the Add URL links on the following search engine Web sites:**

**Yahoo!:** www.yahoo.com

**AltaVista:** altavista.digital.com

**Excite:** www.excite.com

**HOTBOT:** www.hotbot.com

**Infoseek:** www.infoseek.com

**Lycos:** www.lycos.com

**WebCrawler:** www.webcrawler.com

For more information on registering with search engines, read the registration instructions on these Web sites. To locate more search engines, use the search forms on these Web sites.

Submit It! is an Internet business that registers your Web site with many search engines at once. Submit It! offers free registration for about 20 search engines and fee-based registration for larger groups of search engines. Its URL is: www.submit-it.com.

## Defining the HTML Version for Web Pages

HTML is an evolving specification for which there have been three official releases: HTML 2.0, HTML 3.2, and HTML 4. However, software developers, in their race to help bring new features to market and define the specifications, have also created software that conforms to an unofficial HTML 3.0 specification. As you have probably noticed in some of the tables in this guide, software developers, such as Netscape and Microsoft, can and have implemented additional features that might be unavailable or different in a competitor's product.

When you are creating your Web pages, which version should you follow? Should you implement features that are specific to one browser developer? There are many ways to tackle these issues, one of which is to create duplicate Web sites that specifically address specific browser vendors or HTML versions. The most conservative route is to pick an HTML standard and develop for that. Most of the tags described in this guide are for HTML 3.2, although many were available in HTML 2.0. Chapter 2 provides the URLs for these standards.

If you choose to develop your Web site for a specific version of HTML, you can define that version in your Web pages with what is called the document type declaration. When you include a document type declaration, Web tools that read this information know which version of HTML you want to use. This is useful when you are using Web validation tools, which are introduced later in this chapter. These tools can be used to analyze your Web pages and, if you have declared a document type, they can provide reports that show where your Web pages might not conform to the HTML specifications.

To include a documentation type declaration in your Web page, place one of the following on the first line of your Web page, above the document head:

▸  `<!DOCTYPE HTML PUBLIC "-//W3C//DTD HTML 4.0//EN">`

▸  HTML 3.2: `<DOCTYPE HTML PUBLIC "-//W3C//DTD HTML 3.2//EN">`

▸  HTML 2.0: `<DOCTYPE HTML PUBLIC "-//IETF/./DTD HTML 2.0//EN">`

## Using Web Site Management Tools

Web site management tools help you create your Web site faster and make it easier to maintain and update your Web site. These tools can be divided into the following groups:

▸  Web page development tools

▸  Web site development tools

▸  Validation tools

▸  Conversion utilities

▸  Graphics programs and utilities

▸  Web page accessory tools

The following subsections describe the functions of these types of Web site management tools and list products that perform those functions.

### WEB PAGE DEVELOPMENT TOOLS (HTML EDITORS)

Web page development tools hide much of the HTML complexity from you and help you to create Web pages and Web sites quickly. These software tools, which are often called HTML editors, help you create individual Web pages and can contain tools that help you link these individual pages to others.

HTML editors usually operate like word processors or graphics software that you might already be familiar with. For example, to create a bold word with an HTML editor, you double-click the word and select the Bold command from a menu or toolbar. The HTML editor automatically inserts the bold tags into your HTML file and displays the word in boldface type. You don't have to remember the tag names, and you don't have to view them on the page as you create your Web page.

You will appreciate HTML editors when it's time to enter special tags, symbols, and colors that are hard to remember. For example, some HTML editors provide tables of symbols and colors that you can enter by clicking a table cell—instead of entering a hard-to-remember character code or color code. Many HTML editors can also be configured to publish your Web pages for you at the click of a mouse. When you select the publish command, the HTML editor copies your Web pages to a directory on your Web server.

Before you purchase an HTML editor, review the software you already have. WordPerfect and Microsoft Word both allow you to save files in HTML format, and Netscape Communicator and Netscape Navigator Gold both include an HTML editor that you can start from your browser window. Although the NetObjects Fusion product is considered a Web site development tool, you can use it to create Web pages, and an evaluation copy is provided free on this book's CD-ROM. If you need to purchase a Web page development tool, Table 5.11 lists some of the HTML editing tools available.

(Netscape Communicator is provided on this book's CD-ROM.)

| TABLE 5.11 | PRODUCT | URL |
|---|---|---|
| *Web Page Development Tools* | Adobe PageMill | www.adobe.com |
| | Corel WordPerfect | www.corel.com |
| | HomeSite | www.allaire.com |
| | HotDog | www.sausage.com |
| | HoTMetaL Pro | www.sq.com |
| | Microsoft Word | www.microsoft.com |
| | Netscape Communicator and Netscape Navigator Gold | www.netscape.com |

## WEB SITE DEVELOPMENT TOOLS

Web site development tools help you create an entire Web site of linked Web pages. These tools are sometimes called Web site managers because they manage the links between the Web pages. Without links, Web pages are individual Web pages. The links provide the glue that holds a Web site together.

Web site development tools often contain additional tools that provide functionality beyond link management. For example, NetObjects Fusion enables you to create Web pages and Web sites simultaneously, and it provides database connectivity and publishing options. Table 5.12 lists some Web site development tools.

| TABLE 5.12 | PRODUCT | URL |
|---|---|---|
| *Web Site Development Tools* | Adobe SiteMill | `www.adobe.com` (currently only for Macintosh) |
| | NetObjects Fusion | `www.netobjects.com` (NetObjects Fusion is provided on this book's CD-ROM.) |
| | Macromedia Backstage | `www.macromedia.com` |

## VALIDATION TOOLS

Validation tools are software programs that can read your Web page files and generate error and statistics reports. Using the information in these reports, you can correct Web page errors and then retest the files to be sure the errors have indeed been corrected. Table 5.13 lists several validation tools.

| TABLE 5.13 | PRODUCT | URL |
|---|---|---|
| *Validation Tools* | CSE 3310 HTML Validator | `www.htmlvalidator.com` |
| | Doctor HTML | `www3.imagiware.com/RxHTML` |
| | Weblint | `www.unipress.com/cgi-bin/WWWeblint` |

## CONVERSION UTILITIES

Conversion utilities are programs that convert existing document files into Web page files. As mentioned earlier, both Microsoft Word and WordPerfect allow you to convert files to HTML files. Table 5.14 lists some additional programs that let you convert document files to Web page files.

| TABLE 5.14 | PRODUCT | URL |
|---|---|---|
| *Conversion Utility Tools* | HTML Transit | www.infoaccess.com |
| | PostScript-to-HTML | www.unive.it/guida/HTMLdocs/PCTOOLS/ pc_doc_man.html |

## GRAPHICS PROGRAMS AND UTILITIES

As mentioned in Chapter 4, graphics programs and utilities either allow you to create Web page images, or they allow you to convert other image files into Web page image files. Table 5.15 lists some of these programs and utilities.

| TABLE 5.15 | PRODUCT | URL |
|---|---|---|
| *Web Site Development Tools* | Adobe Photoshop | www.adobe.com (A trial version of Adobe Photoshop is included on the CD that comes with this book.) |
| | GIF Movie Gear | www.gamani.com (A trial version of GIF Movie Gear is included on the CD that comes with this book.) |
| | LView Pro | www.lview.com |
| | Paint Shop Pro | www.jasc.com |
| | ThumbsPlus | www.cerious.com |
| | WinGIF | www.best.com/~adamb/GIF-doswin.html (shareware) |

## WEB PAGE ACCESSORY TOOLS

Web page accessory tools, which are also called HTML accessories, are those Web page tools that don't fit into the other groups. Some software tools create guest books, some register your Web site with Internet search engines, and others help you create image maps. Table 5.16 lists some HTML accessory programs.

| TABLE 5.16 | PRODUCT | URL |
|---|---|---|
| Web Page Accessory Tools | Forms Plus | www.lantel.com/spiral/fplus |
| | Guestbook*Star | www.Webgenie.com/Software/Guestar |
| | Mapedit | www.boutell.com/mapedit<br>(A trial version of Mapedit is included on the CD that comes with this book.) |
| | Web Promotion Spider | www.beherenow.com/spider |

**TIP**

**There are many HTML accessories available. To locate additional programs, use Internet search engines to search for "Web authoring tools."**

## Why Learn HTML Tags Anyway?

Web page and Web site development tools do a fine job inserting HTML tags for you, so why should you bother to learn HTML in the first place? Here are some very good reasons to learn HTML:

▸ Web page and Web site development tools cost money. You can start creating Web pages with text editors you already have and upgrade later when you can justify the expense.

▸ An understanding of HTML can help you troubleshoot Web page problems.

▸ If you know HTML, you can look at the document source in other people's Web pages and learn how they created them.

▸ Each HTML editor is designed to support a specific version of HTML and possibly some specific vendor extensions. You might need to know HTML to add features not supported by an HTML editor or to change HTML tags that you don't want in your Web page.

- ▸ If you plan to take the certification test for Novell Course 654, you'll need to know how to use the HTML tags described in Part I of this book.

When you are creating your first Web sites, you might want to start with a text editor or word processor and just enter the HTML tags. This will save you money, and help you learn HTML. If you will be working with tens or hundreds of Web pages, or if you don't have the patience to learn HTML, you'll want to consider Web page or Web site development software.

 **Exercise 5.3: If you're preparing to take the certification exam, or if you want to practice what you learned in this section, turn to the end of this chapter and complete Exercise 5.3.**

## Summary

In this chapter, you learned how to create Web page frames and forms and how you can publicize your Web site.

Frameset documents use `<FRAMESET>` and `<FRAME>` tags to define the frame structure that appears in the browser. `<FRAME>` tags define the initial Web page that appears in each frame, and the frame options. To define links that display Web pages in other frames, you need to use the `<TARGET>` tag.

Forms and form elements enable you to collect data from Web page visitors. When you create forms, keep the following in mind:

- ▸ Start every form with the `<FORM METHOD=`*method*` ACTION=`*action*`>` tag.

- ▸ Use the `METHOD` attribute to specify the method as either POST or GET. If you omit this attribute, the form uses the GET method.

- ▸ Use the `ACTION` attribute to identify the destination of form data.

- ▸ Create a Submit Query button, which can initiate form processing.

▸ Close the form with the </FORM> tag.

▸ Don't nest forms; that is, don't place a form within a form.

To prepare for search engine registration of your Web site, add information using the <TITLE> and <META> tags in the document head of your Web pages. You can either wait for search engines to discover your Web site, or you can register with the search engines through a service provider or by completing a form on the search engine Web site.

## PUZZLE 5.1: ADVANCED WEB PAGE FEATURES

The following word puzzle contains many of the terms discussed in this chapter. See if you can find all of the words. As you search for the words, ask yourself why the word is in the list and how it was used in this chapter. If you don't know the answers to these questions, you might want to review the chapter.

```
M  A  R  G  I  N  H  E  I  G  H  T  J  X  H
E  C  H  E  C  K  B  O  X  R  A  N  G  E  A
T  O  N  L  D  E  M  A  R  F  O  N  A  C  I
H  E  T  M  A  R  G  I  N  W  I  D  T  H  T
O  P  A  S  S  W  O  R  D  L  E  I  F  T  L
D  Y  R  R  E  H  E  B  L  R  O  R  R  G  U
M  T  G  E  T  N  A  O  E  N  A  R  A  N  M
E  C  E  D  G  S  R  Z  S  M  V  E  M  E  R
N  O  T  I  E  C  I  R  E  A  A  D  E  L  O
U  D  N  P  S  S  K  S  L  T  E  R  T  X  F
D  E  A  S  E  Q  U  E  K  X  O  F  A  D
F  R  C  R  Q  T  E  M  C  I  W  B  D  M  P
W  R  O  B  O  T  S  E  T  I  M  B  U  S  O
S  N  E  D  D  I  H  S  E  A  R  C  H  D  S
N  A  M  E  T  C  O  I  D  A  R  E  S  E  T
```

| | | | |
|---|---|---|---|
| action | frame | method | SRC |
| base | get | NOFRAME | scrolling |
| border | header | NORESIZE | search |
| checkbox | hidden | name | selected |
| checked | MARGINHEIGHT | password | size |
| DOCTYPE | MARGINWIDTH | post | spiders |
| engine | MAXLENGTH | radio | submit |
| FRAMEBORDER | META | range | target |
| FRAMESET | MULTI | reset | value |
| form | menu | robots | wrap |

## EXERCISE 5.1: USING FRAMES

In this exercise, you will create a frameset that uses a table of contents in one frame to determine the contents of the other. To complete this exercise, do the following:

1 • Use a text editor or word processor to open the following file on this book's CD-ROM:

   *d:/DemoWeb2/Answers/basic.htm*

   You can use this file as a starting point for your frameset document.

2 • Using the BASIC.HTM file, or a new file, create a frameset document that does the following:

   ▶ Creates two columns, the first of which uses 30 percent of the browser window

   ▶ Displays the FRAME1.HTM file in the first column. Name this frame frame1.

   ▶ Displays the FRAME2.HTM file in the second column. Name this frame frame2.

3 • For browsers that don't support frames, add the following text using the correct tags:

   **To view this Web page, you must use a frame-enabled browser, such as Netscape Navigator 2.0 and later and Microsoft Internet Explorer 3.0 and later.**

4 • Save the frameset file as FRAMESET.HTM.

5 • Copy the following files from the CD to the directory where you saved your frameset document:

   *d:/DemoWeb2/Answers/frame1.htm*
   *d:/DemoWeb2/Answers/frame2.htm*
   *d:/DemoWeb2/Answers/chap1.htm*
   *d:/DemoWeb2/Answers/chap2.htm*

*d:*/DemoWeb2/Answers/chap3.htm
*d:*/DemoWeb2/Answers/chap4.htm
*d:*/DemoWeb2/Answers/chap5.htm

**6** • Open the FRAMESET.HTM file in your browser. Your Web page should appear as shown in Figure 5.10.

**7** • Test the links in the table of contents. After a link takes you away from the table of contents, you can use the Back command to redisplay the table of contents.

**8** • Use the ⟨BASE⟩ tag to set Frame 2 as the new default target for the table of contents in FRAME1.HTM.

**9** • Open or reload the FRAMESET.HTM file in your browser.

**10** • Test the links in the table of contents. This time, the chapters you select should appear in Frame 2. The correct HTML code for this exercise is on this book's CD-ROM at:

*d:*/DemoWeb2/Answers/frameset.htm
*d:*/DemoWeb2/Answers/frame1.htm

FIGURE 5.10

*Exercise 5.1 Result*

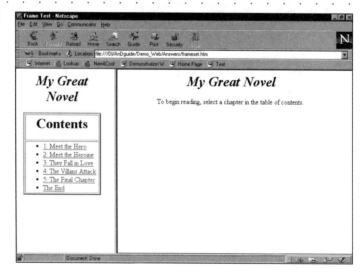

**EXERCISE 5.2: CREATING FORMS**

In this exercise, you will create a form that includes each of the form elements introduced in this chapter. To complete this exercise, do the following:

**1** • Use a text editor or word processor to open the following file on this book's CD-ROM:

*d:/DemoWeb2/Answers/form.htm*

This file contains a table that will organize the form elements you enter. Tables generally give you more control over the placement of form elements than other HTML tags.

**2** • Enter form tags before and after the table. Set the ACTION attribute in the opening form tag to FORM.HTM. Omit the METHOD attribute to select the default method, GET.

**3** • Locate the Customer Name table cell and enter a text input box so it appears on the line below the customer name heading. Set the NAME attribute to **name**.

**4** • Locate the Topping Types table cell and, below that heading, create checkboxes for the following:

▸ Cheese

▸ Meat

▸ Vegetables

See Figure 5.11 for the correct positioning of the checkboxes. Use the names listed above as the checkbox names.

**5** • Locate the Size table cell and, below that heading, create radio buttons for the following:

▸ Small

> ▸ Medium

> ▸ Large

See Figure 5.11 for the correct positioning of the radio buttons. Name this group **size** and set the value of each button to the names listed above.

**6** • Locate the Dining Area table cell, and below that heading create a drop-down menu option list with the following entries:

> ▸ Take out

> ▸ Deliver

> ▸ Inside dining

> ▸ Patio dining

Make **Inside dining** the preselected option, and set the NAME attribute to **dining**.

**7** • Locate the Toppings table cell and, below that heading, create a large text input area with the following default text:

**Enter a list of toppings here.**

Make the text input area 40 columns wide and 5 rows tall, and set the NAME attribute to **toppings**.

**8** • Locate the Order Pizza table cell, and change this text into a form Submit button named **Order Pizza**.

**9** • Locate the Clear Form table cell and change this text into a form Reset button named **Clear Form**.

**10** • Save the form file as FORM.HTM.

**11** • Open the FORM.HTM file in your browser. Your Web page should appear as shown in Figure 5.11.

**12** • Fill out the form and click "Order Pizza." Because the ACTION attribute is set to display the FORM.HTM page, the page reappears with an empty form. Notice the URL. You should see your menu selections appended to the end of the URL. This is how the GET method sends data to Web servers. If any of your form entries are missing in the URL, it could be that you didn't name that form element.

FIGURE 5.11

*Exercise 5.2 Result*

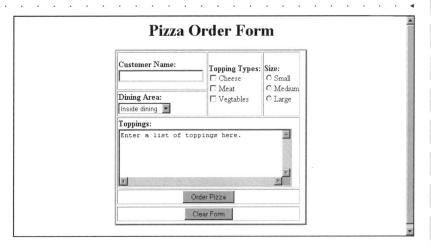

## EXERCISE 5.3: UNDERSTANDING ADVANCED WEB PAGE FEATURES

This exercise tests your understanding of the advanced Web page features described in this chapter. To complete this exercise, answer the following questions:

**1** • Do you use the `<BODY>` tag in a frameset document?

Answer: . . . . . . . . . . . . . . . . . . . . . . . . . . .

**2** • Write the opening tag that divides a browser window into two columns, the first of which uses 25 percent of the page.

Answer: . . . . . . . . . . . . . . . . . . . . . . . . . . .

**3** • How tall is the second row in the following tag: `<FRAMESET ROWS="200, 250, *">`?

Answer: . . . . . . . . . . . . . . . . . . . . . . . . . . .

**4** • When you create a nested frameset that defines both rows and columns, how do you determine what to define first?

Answer: . . . . . . . . . . . . . . . . . . . . . . . . . . .

**5** • Which opening tag marks the beginning of text that is visible only to browsers that don't support frames?

Answer: . . . . . . . . . . . . . . . . . . . . . . . . . . .

**6** • Which link anchor tag attribute can you use to display a link destination in a different frame?

Answer: . . . . . . . . . . . . . . . . . . . . . . . . . . .

**7** • Write the complete tag that begins a form and causes form data to be sent separately from the URL to a Web page named FORM.HTM.

Answer: . . . . . . . . . . . . . . . . . . . . . . . . . . .

**8** • List the attribute that causes each of the following form elements to become the default value:

a. Checkbox: . . . . . . . . . . . . . . . . . . . . . . . . . . . . . . . . . . . . . . . . . . . . .

b. Radio button: . . . . . . . . . . . . . . . . . . . . . . . . . . . . . . . . . . . . . . . . . .

c. Menu option: . . . . . . . . . . . . . . . . . . . . . . . . . . . . . . . . . . . . . . . . . . .

**9** • Which form element is required in every form?

Answer: . . . . . . . . . . . . . . . . . . . . . . . . . . . . . . . . . . . . . . . . . . . . . . . . .

**10** • Which attribute is required in every form element?

Answer: . . . . . . . . . . . . . . . . . . . . . . . . . . . . . . . . . . . . . . . . . . . . . . . . .

**11** • Write the complete set of tags that creates a text area named **comments** that is 60 columns wide, 10 rows tall, and contains the default text **Enter comments here**.

Answer: . . . . . . . . . . . . . . . . . . . . . . . . . . . . . . . . . . . . . . . . . . . . . . . . .

**12** • Which attribute value must be identical for all of the radio buttons in the same group?

Answer: . . . . . . . . . . . . . . . . . . . . . . . . . . . . . . . . . . . . . . . . . . . . . . . . .

**13** • List the purpose of each of the following values for the <META> tag NAME attribute:

a. Author: . . . . . . . . . . . . . . . . . . . . . . . . . . . . . . . . . . . . . . . . . . . . . . .

b. Classification: . . . . . . . . . . . . . . . . . . . . . . . . . . . . . . . . . . . . . . . . . .

c. Description: . . . . . . . . . . . . . . . . . . . . . . . . . . . . . . . . . . . . . . . . . . . .

d. Generator: . . . . . . . . . . . . . . . . . . . . . . . . . . . . . . . . . . . . . . . . . . . . .

e. Keywords: . . . . . . . . . . . . . . . . . . . . . . . . . . . . . . . . . . . . . . . . . . . . .

**14** • Where do you place <META> tags?

Answer: . . . . . . . . . . . . . . . . . . . . . . . . . . . . . . . . . . . . . . . . . . . . . . . . .

**15** • List the purpose of each of the following values for the <META> tag HTTP-EQUIV attribute:

a. Expires: . . . . . . . . . . . . . . . . . . . . . . . . . . . . . . . . . .

b. Pragma: . . . . . . . . . . . . . . . . . . . . . . . . . . . . . . . . . . .

**16** • <META> tags include either the NAME or the HTTP=EQUIV attribute and what other attribute?

Answer: . . . . . . . . . . . . . . . . . . . . . . . . . . . . . . . . . . . .

**17** • Write the complete document type declarations for HTML 2.0 and HTML 3.2 documents:

a. . . . . . . . . . . . . . . . . . . . . . . . . . . . . . . . . . . . . . . .

b. . . . . . . . . . . . . . . . . . . . . . . . . . . . . . . . . . . . . . . .

**18** • Match the following types of Web site management tools with their appropriate descriptions.

*Web Site Management Tool Types*

A. Web page development tools. . .

B. Web site development tools. . .

C. Validation tools. . .

D. Conversion utilities. . .

E. Graphics programs and utilities. . .

F. Web page accessory tools. . .

*Descriptions*

a. . . . .translate a word processing file into a Web page file.

b. . . . .check a Web page file for errors.

c. . . . .use a word-processor interface and insert HTML tags for you.

d. . . . .perform a variety of functions that don't fit into the other categories.

e. . . . .manage the links between Web pages for you.

f.  . . . .help you create Web images.

# CHAPTER 6

# Creating Web Sites with NetObjects Fusion

**C**hapter 5 introduced Web site development tools, one of which is NetObjects Fusion. NetObjects is an award-winning Web site development tool that can greatly increase the productivity of your Web site construction projects.

Although there are other Web site development tools available, there just isn't enough room in one course to give them all equal coverage. To give you some experience with a Web site tool that you can use to create Web sites or Web pages, Novell chose NetObjects Fusion. This chapter provides an introduction to creating Web sites with NetObjects Fusion.

**IMPORTANT**

**Although NetObjects is presented as an example of a Web site management tool, Novell Education does require that you learn some of the product's features to pass the Course 654 exam. This chapter describes the features that are covered in Course 654.**

**This book's CD includes NetObjects Fusion, and Appendix C provides instructions for installing the product. The product documentation is provided in the \NetObjects\Documentation directory in PDF format. To view this documentation, you need the Adobe Acrobat application or browser plug-in. For more information on Adobe Acrobat, browse www.adobe.com.**

## Building a Web Site

Chapters 2, 3, and 5 explained how to build Web pages one page at a time, and Chapter 4 described how to link the pages together to create a Web site. However, before you start creating a Web site, you should first plan your Web site's structure and style. You'll learn more about Web site design in Part II, but you'll get an introduction in this chapter. Unlike most Web page development tools, NetObjects Fusion incorporates the design process into the development of a Web site.

With NetObjects Fusion, you create the Web site first, and then you add content to your Web pages. Figure 6.1 shows the NetObjects Fusion site view, which displays the architecture of a Web site.

Each of the objects in Figure 6.1 represents a Web page, and the lines between the pages show the structure of the site. The topmost page is the home page, and all of the Web pages that directly connect to the home page are called *children* of the home page. The home page is a *parent* to these children. Child Web pages that share the same parent are *peers*. These terms are used to describe the relationship between the Web pages in the site.

F I G U R E 6.1

*NetObjects Fusion Site View*

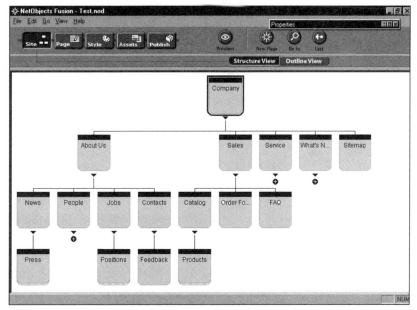

The lines between the parent and child pages also represent links, which NetObjects Fusion adds automatically when you create a Web page. The automatic links are a powerful feature. Not only does NetObjects Fusion add the links for you, it automatically revises them if you delete or move Web pages. Think of all the link anchor tags you don't have to create or edit!

This section describes how to start a new Web site, and how to add, delete, and move Web pages. In the following section, you'll learn how to add to, or change, the content of Web pages.

## STARTING A NEW WEB SITE

NetObjects Fusion gives you several ways to start a Web site. You can import an existing Web site into a NetObjects Fusion Web site, or you can use one of the Web site templates provided with the product. The Web site templates, which are called

AutoSite templates, are basically premade Web sites that you can customize for your own needs. If you create a Web site that you want to use as a template for another Web site, NetObjects Fusion lets you use your site to create a new custom template.

Of course, if you don't have an existing Web site and none of the AutoSite templates will meet your needs, you can always create a Web site from scratch.

To start a new Web site with or without a template, do the following:

**I** • Start NetObjects Fusion by selecting Start → Programs → NetObjects Fusion → NetObjects Fusion 2.02. If this is the first time you have started NetObjects Fusion, the New Site dialog box appears (Figure 6.2).

**2** • If the New Site dialog box does not appear, select File → New Site.

**3** • Name the new Web site in the New Site dialog box.

**4** • In the source area of the New Site dialog box, select what you want to use to create the new site. The Blank option creates a new blank site with a single home page. To select an AutoSite template, click AutoSite template and select a template from the drop-down list. For information on using custom templates, or importing local and remote Web sites, see the NetObjects Fusion documentation.

**5** • If you want to change the storage location of the Web site files, click Change and select a new location.

**6** • Click OK to create the Web site.

**FIGURE 6.2**

*New Site Dialog Box*

After you click OK, NetObjects Fusion stores the site in a directory that is named for the Web site name you chose. For example, if you named the site "Test," the Web site directory name is Test. Unless you specify an alternate location, this directory is stored in the NetObjects Fusion 2.02\User Sites\directory.

The initial contents of the new Web site directory are a Web site file and a directory named "Assets." The site filename is the site name with a NOD extension. For example, the filename for a site named "Test" is TEST.NOD. The site file is a special NetObjects Fusion file, not an HTML file. Later in this chapter, you'll learn how to publish NetObjects Fusion sites to the HTML file format described earlier in this book.

The Assets directory is the directory that contains all of the support files for your Web site. The support files are independent files, such as image files, that are used by your Web site.

After you open a new or existing Web site, NetObjects Fusion displays the site in site view, and it displays the floating Tools and Properties palettes. You can use these palettes to change the Site view display and rename Web pages.

## CHANGING THE DISPLAY IN SITE VIEW

The floating Tools and Properties palettes shown in Figure 6.3 enable you to customize the Site view appearance. These palettes appear in both Site view and Page view, but their contents change depending on the view you have selected. (You'll learn more about Page view later in this chapter.) To minimize or expand the size of one of these palettes, double-click the title bar. To move a palette, drag the title bar.

The Tool palette provides three tools for Site view. The selection tool (arrow) enables you to select Web pages for editing. When a Web page is selected, a blue border appears around the page in Site view. After you select a page, you can move or delete it, add child pages, or change some of the page properties. You'll learn how to do some of these things later in this chapter.

To reduce or enlarge the display in the site view window, select one of the magnifying glass tools in the tool palette and click the site view display.

FIGURE 6.3

Site View Properties and
Tools Palettes

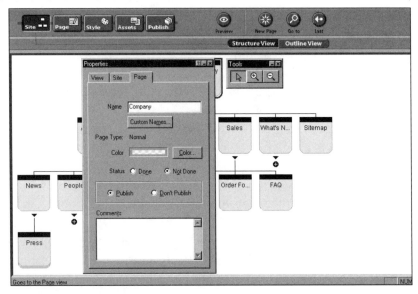

The Properties palette contains three tabs that present configuration options you can change. To change the orientation or background color for site view, use the options on the View tab. To specify a site author, use the Site tab, and to change a Web page color, use the Page tab. In the next section, you'll learn how to use the Page tab to change the page names.

## RENAMING WEB PAGES

You can rename a Web site page at any time. It is a good idea to choose a short name, as the Web page name is the default name for the page title, the page banner, and any link buttons that refer to this page. The page title corresponds to the Web page title defined in the document head, the banner is a title that appears on the Web page, and the link buttons actually appear on other Web pages and link to the page you are naming. If you prefer to use different names for the title, banner, and buttons, you can do that too.

There are two ways to change the Web page name that appears in Site view. The first is to click the page name and type a new name. The second way is to use the

Properties palette as follows:

**1** • If you are not already in Site view, select Site view by clicking the Site button near the top of the NetObjects Fusion window. You can also select Go → Site.

**2** • Open the Properties palette and select the Page tab.

**3** • Enter the new page name in the Name text box.

To specify custom names for Web page features, such as the title, banner, or link buttons, do the following:

**1** • Select Site view and display the Properties palette Page tab as described in the previous procedure.

**2** • Click Custom Names.

**3** • Use this dialog box to specify new names, or to select a file extension for the Web page.

**4** • Click OK.

When you change the Site view page name, you'll see the new name immediately in Site view. If you define custom names for the banner or buttons, you'll have to change to Page view to see your changes. If you define a custom name for a page title, you'll have to preview the site to see the title. You'll learn more about Page view and Preview later when you learn how to build Web pages. First, you need to learn how to add, delete, and move the Web pages you will be building.

## ADDING PAGES

After you start building your new site, one of the first things you'll want to do is start adding pages, especially if you started a blank site. To add a page, simply click the parent page to select it, then click the New Page button at the top of the NetObjects Fusion window. You can also select Edit → New Page.

After you create a new page, an untitled page appears below the selected parent. To name the page, click the name and type the new name. For more information on where this name is used and how to use custom names, see the preceding section.

### DELETING PAGES

To delete a page in Site view, click the page to select it, press Delete, and click Yes to confirm the deletion. You can also select the page, and then select Edit → Delete Page.

### MOVING PAGES

Moving pages with NetObjects Fusion is easier than moving them with some other Web page tools. All you have to do is select the page to be moved and drag it over another page. When you move a Web page over another, an arrow appears on the border to show where the Web page will be moved to. If the arrow appears to either side of the Web page, the Web page is moved to that side and becomes a peer. If the arrow appears below the Web page, the moved Web page becomes a child page. You control where the arrow appears by placing the Web page closest to the border where you want the arrow to appear.

As you'll see in the following exercise, when you move a Web page, NetObjects fusion automatically updates all links on the affected pages.

 **Exercise 6.1: If you're preparing to take the certification exam, or if you want to practice what you learned in this section, turn to the end of this chapter and complete Exercise 6.1. When you are done, continue reading here to prepare for the next exercise.**

## Building Web Pages

After you set up your Web site architecture in Site view, it's time to add some content to those Web pages. Before you begin, however, you need to learn how NetObjects Fusion builds Web pages. This section describes the Web page architecture used by NetObjects Fusion, and how to select Styles and add text and images to the Web pages.

## WEB PAGE ARCHITECTURE

To ensure that Web pages use a consistent style, NetObjects Fusion provides two features that enable you to control the design of many Web pages at once. These features are MasterBorders and Styles.

Figure 6.4 shows a NetObjects Fusion Web page in Page view. Notice that it is divided into two areas, the MasterBorder area and the Layout area.

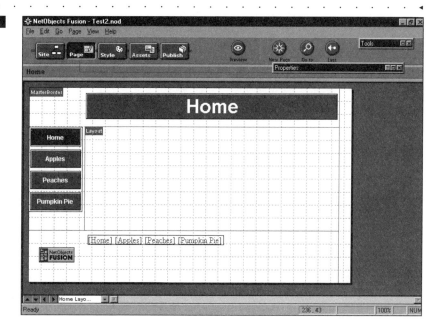

In its default configuration, the MasterBorder area surrounds the Layout area. The MasterBorder stores objects that appear on many Web pages; the Layout area contains the content that is unique to the Web page. The MasterBorder is a good place to add a company logo or an administrator's e-mail address. You add these items once, and they appear on every page that uses the MasterBorder.

In the MasterBorder, the banner, graphic buttons, and text links are all special components that NetObjects Fusion automatically creates for the default MasterBorder. There are other special components, as well. If you want to change the default MasterBorder, you can use the Properties and Tools palettes to add or delete components and to change their position. When your MasterBorder is complete, you can save your changes in a new MasterBorder, which you can apply to any Web page in the site. Each Web page can have its own MasterBorder, or you can use the same MasterBorder for groups of pages. For more information on working with MasterBorders, see the product documentation.

If you don't like the default style of the banner and buttons that appear in the default MasterBorder, there are about 50 other styles to choose from. Styles can define many features including the following:

▸ Background graphics

▸ Banner images and text styles

▸ Primary and secondary navigation button images

▸ Link colors

If you can't find a style you like, you can always create your own. When you create and select your own style, NetObjects Fusion uses your style components to build the MasterBorder.

The difference between MasterBorders and Styles is that MasterBorders define which components appear in the MasterBorder and which positions they occupy. Styles define the colors and images of the special objects that the MasterBorder displays. For example, if you choose to display the NetObjects Fusion navigation button bar, which it will create for you, the MasterBorder defines where the button bar appears and the Style defines which graphics are used to display the buttons.

While you can create a different MasterBorder for every page, you select a Style for the entire Web site. Some Style components can be overridden on a page-by-page basis, but the chosen Style provides the base design for the entire Web site.

## SELECTING A SITE STYLE

To select a site Style, do the following:

I • Open the site in NetObjects Fusion. NetObjects always loads that last site worked on when you start the program. To select another site, select File → Open Site and use the dialog box to locate the *filename*.nod file for your Web site. The default location for Web sites is *d*:NetObjects Fusion 2.02\User Sites\.

**2** • Select Style view by clicking the Style button or selecting Go → Style. The Style view window appears as shown in Figure 6.5.

**3** • Select a style from the list in the left frame.

**4** • Click the Set Style button above the style list.

The new style takes effect immediately. To see the changes, click the Page button to return to Page view.

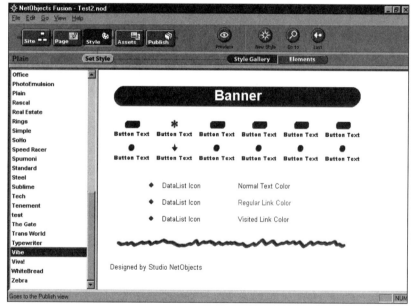

FIGURE 6.5

*Style View*

## SELECTING PAGES TO EDIT

So far, this chapter has described how to select pages in Site view and how to switch to Page view to see the page. You don't have to go through Site view to select pages. You can use the Go menu or the triangle buttons in the lower-left corner of the window (see Figure 6.4).

When you select the Up arrow in Page view, the program displays the parent Web page. When you select the Down arrow, NetObjects Fusion displays the first child page below the current Web page. The left and right arrows select peer Web pages that appear in Site view to the left or right of the current page.

## ADDING TEXT

When you begin work on your Web pages, you can add text to MasterBorders or to the Layout area. Adding text is a three-step process. First you define a text box on the page, next you add the text, and finally you format the text.

To add text to a Web page, do the following:

**1** • Open the Web site and view the page you want to change in Page view.

**2** • In the Tools palette, select the text tool. The text tool is the button with the letter A (see Figure 6.6).

**3** • On the Web page, click and drag to create a text box. Handles will appear on the text box you create. To resize the box, simply drag one of the handles. To move the text box, click the border away from a handle and drag the text box.

**4** • To add text to a text box, click in the text box and start typing.

**5** • To format text in a text box, select the text as you would in a word processor and select the desired formatting from the Text page in the Properties palette.

**NOTE**

**The Text tab only appears in the Properties palette when you select text.**

The Properties palette Text tab enables you to enter most of the text formatting options that you learned about in the previous chapters. To stop editing a text box, just click anywhere outside of the text box.

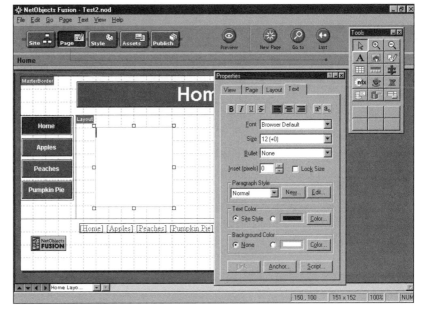

## ADDING GRAPHICS

Before you can add a graphic to a Web page, you must create the graphic as described in Chapter 3. When the image is ready, you can add it to a Web page in much the same manner that you add text.

To add an image to a Web page, do the following:

**1** • Open the Web site and view the page you want to change in Page view.

**2** • In the Tools palette, select the image tool. The image tool is the button to the right of the text tool (see Figure 6.6).

**3** • On the Web page, click and drag to create an image box. When you release the mouse button, a dialog box will prompt you for the location of the image file you want to use.

**4** • Use the file dialog box to select the image file. The image appears in an image box with handles. To resize the image box, drag one of the handles. To move the text box, click the border away from a handle and drag the image box.

**5** • To change the image alignment or specify alternate text for the image, use the Picture tab in the Properties palette.

**NOTE**

**The Picture tab only appears in the Properties palette when you select an image.**

The Properties palette Picture tab enables you to enter most of the image formatting options that you learned about in Chapter 3. To stop editing an image, just click anywhere outside of the image box.

## Previewing the Web Site

As mentioned earlier, NetObjects Fusion stores all Web site data in a file named *filename*.nod and stores supporting files in a directory named Assets. Web browsers cannot view the NOD files, so before you can view your Web pages, you must tell NetObjects Fusion to create them. NetObjects provides three options for creating Web pages: Preview, Staging, and Publishing.

Preview quickly creates Web pages that you can view in your browser on your local PC. Staging and Publishing, which are described later in this chapter, create full working Web sites that you can transfer to a Web server. The difference between Preview and Staging or Publishing is that Preview creates Web pages that use explicit file references, not relative references. This enables Preview to generate a preview Web site quickly, but the Preview Web site won't work on a Web server.

To prepare NetObjects Fusion for Preview, select Edit → Preferences, select the Preview options, and click OK. If you have more than one browser installed on your computer, you can choose a preview browser. You can also choose to preview the entire site or the current page automatically.

To preview your Web site at any time, click the Preview button in the NetObjects Fusion Window.

After you click Preview, NetObjects Fusion creates the HTML files for your Web site, launches your browser, and displays the Web site home page in the browser. All of the local links on your Web pages will work. The only features you cannot use are links to external sites and features that require a Web server for processing.

**To preview a single Web page, press and hold the Control key when you click Preview.**

TIP

**Exercise 6.2: If you're preparing to take the certification exam, or if you want to practice what you learned in this section, turn to the end of this chapter and complete Exercise 6.2. When you are done, continue reading here to prepare for the next exercise.**

## Creating Text Links

After you add text to a Web page, you can turn any text into an internal or external link.

To create a text link, do the following:

**I** • In Page view, highlight the text that will become a link.

**2** • In the Properties palette Text tab, click Link.

**3** • To create an internal link, choose the Internal Link tab and choose a page from the list on this tab.

**4** • To create an external link, choose the External Link tab and enter a destination URL.

**5** • Click Link.

After you create a text link, the linked text displays in the link color defined in the Style.

## Making Image Maps

NetObjects Fusion enables you to create client-side image maps for your Web pages quickly and easily.

To create a client-side image map, do the following:

1 • Create an image for the image map using the guidelines in Chapters 3 and 4.

2 • Place the image map on a Web page as described earlier in this chapter.

3 • Display the image in Page view, and select the image tool in the Tools palette. Notice the secondary tools at the bottom of the Tools palette. The three secondary tools with red dots are the tools you use to define hot spots in the image. The tools enable you to define rectangle-, ellipse-, and polygon-shaped hot spots.

4 • Select a hot spot tool.

5 • To define a rectangle or ellipse area, click and drag the cursor. When you release the mouse button, the link dialog box appears.

6 • To define a polygon area, click a corner of the area you want to mark and then click on additional area borders to define the shape. When the shape is defined, double-click to stop editing the polygon.

The easiest way to learn to use this tool is to experiment with it. To delete a hot spot, select its border and click delete.

When you double-click the mouse button, the link dialog box appears.

7 • Use the link dialog box to define internal or external links just as you would for text links. After you define the link destination, the hot spot is marked on the image. This hot spot does not show on published Web pages.

## Importing Web Pages

If you want to start managing an existing Web site with NetObjects Fusion, you should import the entire Web site as introduced in "Starting a New Web Site," which appears earlier in this chapter. There might be times, however, when you want to import a single page from an existing Web site. When you import a single page, the entire contents of the page appear in the layout area of a NetObjects Fusion Web page.

To import a single Web page, do the following:

1 • Create the NetObjects Fusion page that will contain the imported Web page.

2 • Display the page in Page view. If there are objects in the layout area, such as text and graphics, consider copying them to different pages. The Web page you import will overlay existing Web page objects.

3 • Select File → Import Page.

4 • Use the Open dialog box to select and open the Web page you want to import.

After you import the Web page, the Web page contents appear as objects in the NetObjects Fusion Web page. You can resize and move these objects just as you would any other NetObjects Fusion object.

## Creating Forms

Chapter 5 explains how to create forms using HTML tags. To create forms with NetObjects Fusion, you use Form tools. You can create one form per Web page.

To create a form with NetObjects Fusion, do the following:

1 • Select the Web page to contain the form and choose Page view.

**2** • In the Tools palette, select the Form tool. The Form tool is the lower-right tool in the primary Tools palette (see Figure 6.7). After you select the Form tool, form element tools appear in the secondary tool palette.

**3** • To add a submit button, do the following:

**a.** Click the Button tool and drag the mouse in the layout area where you want the button to appear. The button appears with the word Text on it.

**b.** In the Properties palette, select the Button tab.

**c.** In the Text area of the Button tab, click Text, enter a name for the submit button in the text box, and click Submit.

You can use this same procedure to create a reset button; just click Reset instead of Submit on the Properties palette.

**4** • To define the action for a form, do the following:

**a.** Select any form element and display the Properties palette tab for that element.

**b.** Click Settings.

**c.** In the Form Settings dialog box that appears, click Browse to select a script file that is stored on your local computer. When you publish the Web site, this file will be copied to the Web server.

**d.** In the Action text box, enter the URL of the CGI script that will process the form data.

Select either the Post or the Get method.

**5** • To add other form elements, do the following:

**a.** Click a form element tool in the Tools palette and drag the mouse in the layout area where you want the form element to appear. A blank element appears.

**b.** In the Properties palette, select the tab for the form element.

Use the properties on the form element tab to define the form element.

For more information on creating specific form elements, see the NetObjects Fusion documentation.

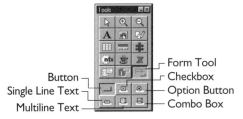

Button —
Single Line Text —
Multiline Text —

— Form Tool
— Checkbox
— Option Button
— Combo Box

## Adding a Site Map

A site map is a pictorial view of your Web site, similar to the view you see in Site view. NetObjects Fusion includes a Java-based utility that can present a site map to your Web site visitors. The site map enables visitors to see where they are within your Web site and lets them jump to another Web page immediately.

To add the NetObjects Fusion site map to your Web site, do the following:

1 • Display your Web site's home page in Site view.

2 • In the primary Tools palette, select the NetObjects Components tool. It's the tool with the letters *nfx* on it.

3 • In the secondary Tools palette, select the Site Mapper tool. The Site Mapper tool looks like a three-page Web site in Site view.

4 • Click and drag the mouse to mark the area where you want the Site Mapper activation button to appear. The Site Map button appears. You can add this button to the MasterBorder or the layout area. You can also replace the button image with your own.

**5** • To change the Site Mapper button image, select the Site Map button, and select a new image using the Component tab on the Properties palette. You can create a new site map button image using the guidelines provided in Chapter 3. To select the new image from the Component tab, click the image item in the component list, click the browse button (...), and select the new image file.

After you add a site map to your home page, users can access the site map by clicking the site map button. When the site map appears, it displays in a separate browser window. The pages the visitors select appear in the original browser window.

## Adding Multimedia to Web Pages

NetObjects Fusion supports several types of multimedia, which include the following:

▸ Sound files

▸ Movie or video files

▸ Java applets

▸ Shockwave files

▸ ActiveX controls

Sound, movie, and video files produce just what their names imply. Java applets are mini applications that often provide special sound, video, or animation effects, and Shockwave files can contain both animation and sounds. ActiveX controls operate like mini programs that add animation, sound, movies, or custom features to the Web page.

The latest versions of most browsers support Java applets, and Microsoft Internet Explorer version 3.0 and later supports ActiveX controls. To listen or view the other multimedia files, browser users typically need to download and install a plug-in, which is an accessory program that can present the file for the browser. For more information on using these types of multimedia with NetObjects Fusion, see the product documentation.

## Publishing the Web Site

When you think your Web site is complete, it's time to test it, and if it tests out okay, it's time to publish it. While Preview mode is good for testing the visual appearance of your Web pages, Preview mode does not create a complete, independent version of the Web site. To test your Web site fully, you need to *stage* the Web site. After the staged Web site passes your tests, you can *publish* your Web site with confidence.

When you stage the Web site, NetObjects Fusion translates the NOD file into the HTML files for your Web site. The program stores these files in a location you define with additional directories that contain support files (such as image files). The staged Web site contains copies of all the files required by your Web site and uses relative link paths. You can stage to your local computer, or you can stage directly to a Web server for testing.

When you publish your Web site, NetObjects Fusion creates the same set of files that it creates for staging. Technically, there is no difference between staging and publishing. However, because most Web masters set up a Web site testing area and a separate Web site publishing area, NetObjects Fusion enables you to configure two ways to publish your Web site. After you configure staging and publishing, you can stage or publish your Web site with just two mouse clicks.

### CONFIGURING STAGING AND PUBLISHING LOCATIONS

When you configure NetObjects Fusion for staging and publishing, you configure two locations for publishing your Web site. The staging location is typically your local computer, a network file server, or a private location on a Web server. The publishing location is a public location on the Web server that will serve your Web site files to the Internet or intranet. Having two locations configured makes it easy to switch between staging and publishing quickly, as your needs dictate.

To configure staging and publishing locations, do the following:

1 • Click the Publish button near the top of the NetObjects Fusion window. This selects the Publish view.

2 • Click the Settings button. The program displays the Configure Publish dialog box shown in Figure 6.8. The Stage and Publish tabs are identical and enable you to define staging and publishing locations. The Modify tab enables you to create alternate versions of the Web site. For more information on the Modify tab options, see the NetObjects Fusion documentation.

3 • Select the tab for the location you want to define, which is either Stage or Publish.

4 • In the location area of the tab, select Local or Remote.

Select Local if you will be publishing to the local computer or a network file server. You can use this option to publish to any file server or Web server that you can select using file selection dialog boxes on your computer.

Select Remote if you will be publishing to Web server through a File Transfer Protocol (FTP) server. Typically, Internet Web servers also operate as FTP servers, and both servers share a common file space. Clients use FTP to store Web site files on the Web server because most Web servers can only serve files — they do not receive files.

If you are uncertain about whether to use the Local or Remote option, contact your Web server administrator. You will also need to know which Web server directories to use for staging and publishing.

5 • If you are publishing to a local directory, use the Browse button to select the destination directory.

**6** • If you are publishing to a remote FTP directory, click Configure. The program displays the Remote dialog box, which you can use to specify an FTP server, the destination directories for Web site files, and your FTP account information. For more information on configuring these options, see the NetObjects Fusion product documentation.

**7** • In the Files area, define a filename and extension for the home page.

**8** • When the configuration is complete, click OK.

*Configure Publish
Dialog Box*

## STAGING AND PUBLISHING THE WEB SITE

After you configure the staging location, it is easy to stage or publish your Web site quickly. To stage or publish the Web site, do the following:

**1** • Select Publish view.

**2** • Click Stage or Publish.

After you click Stage or Publish, the program creates the Web site files in the location you configured (see the previous section). To access your Web site in a local directory, open the home page in your browser. To access your Web site on a Web server, specify your Web site URL. If you don't know the URL, see your Web server administrator.

**Exercises 6.3 and 6.4: If you're preparing to take the certification exam, or if you want to practice what you learned in this section, turn to the end of this chapter and complete Exercises 6.3 and 6.4.**

## Summary

In this chapter, you learned to use NetObjects Fusion to create Web sites. With NetObjects Fusion, you can use Site view to add Web pages to your site and define the site's structure. To apply a style to all of the pages in your site, you can use the controls in Style view.

When you are ready to work on individual pages, you need to switch to Page view. You can use MasterBorders to display banners, titles, logos, and navigation buttons in the Web page margins. The layout area is where all the unique page content appears.

To add content to MasterBorders or the layout area, you need to use the appropriate tool in the Tools palette. To further define the appearance or operation of any Web page element, use the appropriate tab on the Properties palette.

When you are done creating the Web site, use the Publish view to configure staging and publishing locations for the Web site. Once staging and publishing are configured, staging or publishing is as easy as clicking either the Stage or the Publish button in Publish view.

## PUZZLE 6.1: CREATING WEB SITES WITH NETOBJECTS FUSION

The following word puzzle contains many of the terms discussed in this chapter. See if you can find all the words. As you search for the words, ask yourself why the word is in the list and how it was used in this chapter. If you don't know the answers to these questions, you might want to review the chapter.

```
R  S  E  I  T  R  E  P  O  R  P  A  M  N  Q
D  E  L  E  T  E  G  A  M  I  R  U  O  G  W
T  C  D  G  Q  X  Y  C  H  I  L  D  R  E  N
N  N  E  R  M  U  L  T  I  M  E  D  I  A  O
E  E  L  N  O  I  T  A  C  O  L  V  V  S  I
R  R  T  P  U  B  L  I  S  H  E  I  W  S  S
A  E  I  O  Z  R  R  D  P  R  G  S  E  E  U
P  F  T  P  B  E  L  E  P  A  I  R  B  T  F
A  E  O  I  N  J  T  C  T  T  L  E  U  S  S
G  R  H  N  S  A  E  I  E  S  N  E  T  P  T
E  P  A  S  L  O  O  C  M  F  A  P  T  O  A
Q  B  K  P  T  N  T  R  T  P  H  M  O  T  G
F  T  M  L  A  Y  O  U  T  S  O  G  N  V  E
P  E  W  Y  K  F  L  N  A  M  E  R  O  X  Z
T  O  O  L  S  G  D  E  K  B  A  X  T  O  Y
```

| | | | |
|---|---|---|---|
| assets | hot | navigation | site |
| autosite | image | NetObjects | spot |
| banner | import | page | stage |
| button | layout | palette | style |
| children | location | parent | template |
| delete | MASTERBORDER | peers | title |
| FTP | map | preferences | tools |
| form | multimedia | preview | URL |
| fusion | NOD | properties | view |
| go | name | publish | Web |

## EXERCISE 6.1: CREATING A WEB SITE

In this exercise, you'll create a Web site and practice adding, deleting, and moving Web pages in it. You'll also get a look at the default navigation links that NetObjects Fusion adds to Web pages.

To complete this exercise, do the following:

1 • If NetObjects Fusion is not installed, install it as described in Appendix C.

2 • Start NetObjects Fusion and create a new Web site using the Company Internet AutoSite template. Name the site "Company."

3 • View the home page by double-clicking the Company page, or by selecting it and clicking the Page button above the Site view window.

4 • At the top of the page, note the link button for Service. Scroll down to the bottom of the page and locate the text link for Service. The Service button is an image link. It is common to provide both image and text links so browser users who cannot or do not want to display graphics can still navigate the site.

5 • Click the Site view button above the Page view window. You can also switch to Site view by selecting Go → Site.

6 • Delete the Service Web page and its children. This deletes pages from your new site, not the template. You can use the template at any time to create a new site that contains the Service pages.

7 • Select the Company page and switch back to Page view. Notice that the links for the Service page are gone.

8 • Switch back to Site view, add a child page to the home page, and name it "Partners."

9 • Select the Company page, switch back to Page view, and look for the links to the new page.

**10** • In Site view, move the Partners Web page to the left of the Sales page.

**11** • View the Company Web page in Page view and note the change in position of the links to the Partners page.

This completes Exercise 6.1. You can quit NetObjects Fusion by choosing File → Exit.

**TIP**

**Before you quit NetObjects Fusion, you might want to look at some of the other Web pages in the Company Internet template. You might also want to create additional Web sites using other templates so you can view them. While the templates do not provide a unique design (all other NetObjects Fusion users have them), they do provide a quick and easy way to show management what can be done. With a few quick changes to a template, you might be able to help management visualize a new Web site and get its approval to get started.**

## EXERCISE 6.2: BUILDING WEB PAGES

In this exercise, you create a new Web site, change the Web site style, and add text and graphics to your home page.

To complete this exercise, do the following:

1 • Start NetObjects Fusion and create a new Web site using the Blank template. Name the site "MyCompany."

2 • Add three pages to your Web site, and name them "Sales," "Marketing," and "Operations." This step creates some additional navigation buttons that will make the home page look more complete.

3 • Display the Home page in Page view and look at the default style, which is named *Plain*.

4 • Switch to Style view and apply the Rascal Style to the Web site.

5 • Switch back to Page view and view all four of your Web site pages. Notice that all Web pages use the same style.

6 • Switch to Style view and apply the Vibe Style to the Web site.

7 • Display the Home page in Page view and add a text box to the Layout area that contains the following: "Welcome to the MyCompany Home Page!" Use Figure 6.9 to determine the approximate position of the text box. It is not important to be precise. The goal of this step is to give you some experience placing text on a page.

8 • Use the Properties palette Text tab to format the text to use centered, boldface, size 18 (+2) type.

9 • Place the following graphic from this book's CD on the page as shown in Figure 6.9:
   *d*:\DEMO_WEB\ANSWERS\SQUARE.GIF

**10** • Add the second text box in Figure 6.9 and format the text as shown. The *New!* headline is formatted as a level-one head. To define headings and other paragraph formats, use the Paragraph Style combo box on the Properties palette Text tab. To create the bulleted list, use the Bullet option on the Text Tab. You will use these bullets in the next exercise to create links to other Web pages.

**11** • Preview the Web site and test all the links.

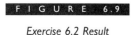

FIGURE 6.9

*Exercise 6.2 Result*

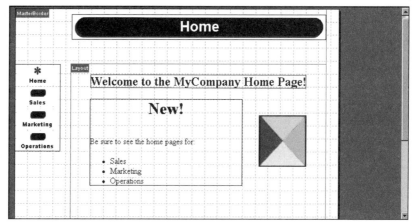

## EXERCISE 6.3: ENHANCING AND PUBLISHING WEB PAGES

In this exercise, you'll add a text link, an image map, and a site map to a Web site. You'll also import a Web page, modify a form, and publish the Web site on your local computer.

To complete this exercise, do the following:

**1** • Start NetObjects Fusion and create a new Web site using the Company Internet AutoSite template. Name the site "Internet."

**2** • Display the home page (Company) in Page view.

**3** • To get some practice creating a text link, do the following:

a. Replace the first paragraph on the page with the following paragraph:

"Check out our new products!"

b. In the paragraph you just entered, make the words "new products!" a text link to the Products page.

**4** • To practice creating an image map, do this:

a. Select the Sitemap page and display it in Page view.

b. Create hotspots on the image map image for the following Web pages, which correspond to the pages in Site view:

▸ Company

▸ About Us

▸ Sales

▸ Service

▸ What's New

Don't confuse this image with the Site Mapper feature. This is a graphic image to which you'll add hot spots. You'll use the Site Mapper feature later in this exercise.

Although you can create all these hots pots with the rectangle tool, try creating some with the ellipse and polygon tools, just for practice. To delete any hot spot, just select it and press Delete.

**5** • Import a page by doing the following:

a. Create a new page below the Company page and title it "Test Page."

b. Import the following HTML file from this book's CD:

*d*:\DEMO_WEB\ANSWERS\MYPAGE4.HTM

Notice the alignment of the imported objects. For some additional practice, try repositioning the objects and choosing a MasterBorder for the page.

**6** • To experiment with a form, follow these steps:

a. Display the Register page in Page view.

b. Locate the Submit button and rename it "Send Form."

c. Reposition the Clear button and rename it "Reset Form." For extra experience, replace the Age Group checkboxes with a radio button group or a combo box.

**7** • Use the SiteMapper tool to create a site map for the Web site. Place the site map button in the MasterBorder on the home page.

**8** • To practice staging the Web site on your local computer, do the following:

a. Display the configuration settings for the staging location and write down the directory location and home page filename for the staged Web site. You can accept the defaults or change them, but you'll need to know the path and filename to test the staged Web site.

b. Stage the Web site.

**9** • Open the staged home page in your browser, test your links, and view your work. If you want to make changes to the Web site, switch back to NetObjects Fusion, make the changes, stage the site, and then view it again in your browser. You might have to reload some Web pages to see your changes.

## EXERCISE 6.4: USING NETOBJECTS FUSION

Novell Course 654 introduces NetObjects Fusion as an example of a site management program and provides overviews of the procedures described in this chapter. To prepare for the Course 654 exam, be sure you know the purposes of all the major controls in the NetObjects Fusion window, the tools in the Tools palette, and the differences between preview, staging, and publishing.

This exercise reviews your knowledge of the NetObject Fusion controls and features. To complete this exercise, answer the following questions:

**1** • List two ways to add a page to a Web site.

a. . . . . . . . . . . . . . . . . . . . . . . . . . . . . . . . . . . . .

b. . . . . . . . . . . . . . . . . . . . . . . . . . . . . . . . . . . . .

**2** • If you drag a Web page in Site view over another Web page, how can you make sure that the dragged Web page becomes a child of the page it is dragged to?

Answer: . . . . . . . . . . . . . . . . . . . . . . . . . . . . . . . . .

**3** • Which feature defines which Web page objects appear in the margins and where they are placed?

Answer: . . . . . . . . . . . . . . . . . . . . . . . . . . . . . . . . .

**4** • Which feature defines the appearance of common elements, such as background graphics and link colors, that appear throughout the Web site?

Answer: . . . . . . . . . . . . . . . . . . . . . . . . . . . . . . . . .

**5** • How can you change pages in Page view without switching to Site view?

Answer: . . . . . . . . . . . . . . . . . . . . . . . . . . . . . . . . .

**6** • Which control do you use to create an image map?

Answer: . . . . . . . . . . . . . . . . . . . . . . . . . . . . . . . . . . . . .

**7** • Which control creates a site map?

Answer: . . . . . . . . . . . . . . . . . . . . . . . . . . . . . . . . . . . . .

**8** • Which control provides the fastest way to see what your Web site will look like?

Answer: . . . . . . . . . . . . . . . . . . . . . . . . . . . . . . . . . . . . .

**9** • Which feature provides the best way to test your Web site before release?

Answer: . . . . . . . . . . . . . . . . . . . . . . . . . . . . . . . . . . . . .

**10** • Which control enables you to select a Web page to import?

Answer: . . . . . . . . . . . . . . . . . . . . . . . . . . . . . . . . . . . . .

**11** • Where do you find the controls for creating forms?

Answer: . . . . . . . . . . . . . . . . . . . . . . . . . . . . . . . . . . . . .

**12** • List five types of multimedia that NetObjects Fusion supports.

a. . . . . . . . . . . . . . . . . . . . . . . . . . . . . . . . . . . . .

b. . . . . . . . . . . . . . . . . . . . . . . . . . . . . . . . . . . . .

c. . . . . . . . . . . . . . . . . . . . . . . . . . . . . . . . . . . . .

d. . . . . . . . . . . . . . . . . . . . . . . . . . . . . . . . . . . . .

e. . . . . . . . . . . . . . . . . . . . . . . . . . . . . . . . . . . . .

# PART II

# Designing Effective
# Web Sites

# CHAPTER 7

# Web Design Basics

**P**erhaps you've volunteered to create a Web site for your department, your company, or your club—or maybe you were volunteered. What do you do next? You could start creating and publishing Web pages, but without a Web site design, the Web site is likely to be disorganized and less effective. Books, buildings, and businesses require designs and plans to achieve their goals, and Web sites are no different. Consider the following:

> ▸ Like a book, a Web site is a publication that is available for others to view.

> ▸ Like a building, a Web site has a structure and must conform to certain common guidelines.

> ▸ Like a business, a Web site has an image that can attract customers or drive them away.

This chapter introduces the role of the Web site designer, the skills a Web site designer needs, and a procedure for designing and producing a Web site. This chapter also describes how to set goals for your Web site and introduces guidelines you can use to design the complete site and the pages within the site. Finally, this chapter introduces storyboarding, which is a technique for planning and visualizing a production, such as a Web site, before you start construction.

## What Does a Web Designer Do?

A Web designer can be responsible for part or all of the development of a Web site. At a minimum, the Web designer is responsible for the appearance of one or more areas of the Web site. However, if the designer works for a small company, she might be responsible for the site architecture, the site appearance, and the site content as well.

To properly design an entire Web site, the design team needs skills in the following areas:

> ▸ Publication design

▸ Graphic design

▸ Marketing

▸ Web design

**IMPORTANT** **If you are planning to take the exam for Novell Education Course 660, Designing Effective Web Sites, you might be asked about these four skill areas on the exam. In Course 660,** the *publication design* **skill area is called** *design principles,* **and the Web design skill set is referred to as** *Internet experience.*

If you are a one-person design team, you'll probably have strengths in one or more of these areas and need to develop skills in the other areas. If you are leading a design team, or if you are a design team member, you might want to pick one of these areas as your specialty and have other team members do the same. The following sections describe each of these skill areas and how they contribute to the Web site design.

## PUBLICATION DESIGN

Although the Web offers capabilities not available in standard print publications, many of the publication design principles apply to the Web. For example, the composition of each Web page should appear balanced, and images, text, and multimedia components should look like they belong together. Common design elements on each page should establish a theme that makes it clear the pages are part of the same Web site. A common theme or *look* is especially important for Web sites because it is so easy for a user to link out of your Web site or link in from another Web site. The Web site design helps visitors know when they are in your Web site and when they have left it.

Other important publication design principles that apply to the Web are technical accuracy and good writing skills. The best-looking publications, whether they are in print or on the Web, will quickly lose credibility and respect if they are inaccurate or difficult to read. Most professional, printed publications are assembled by a team that includes writers, editors, and graphic designers. If you can provide all of these services, great! If not, you might want to look for team members that can contribute in the areas where you might need help.

## GRAPHIC DESIGN

One specialty of publications design is graphic design. Graphic designers create illustrations, select and crop photos, and add rules and bullets to pages to make them more interesting and appealing. Artistic talent and an understanding of design principles, such as color, contrast, and balance all contribute to the designer's ability to create images and pages that catch the eye and invite the Web page visitor to take a closer look.

## MARKETING

Just about every Web site serves as a marketing tool of some kind. Your Web site might be marketing products or services for your company, it might be designed to improve the image of your company, or it might represent an organization with a message to deliver. Regardless of the marketing goals, at the very least, you want to market your Web site. All your hard work on the Web site will be useless if you cannot bring people to your Web site to view what you have created.

As with any publication, marketing skills are an important part of the formula for success. The success of your Web site can be judged by a variety of measures that include product sales, site visits (which are also called hits), ads sold, and customer responses. One way to encourage customer responses is to offer a free gift or a discount for those who respond.

As a Web designer, it is in your best interest to develop marketing skills or find a team member who can help. One of the easiest ways to develop marketing skills and ideas is to surf the Web and see what other organizations are doing. This is also a good way to learn what works and what doesn't in publication and graphic design.

## WEB DESIGN

Although the Web design team needs publication design, graphic design, and marketing skills, the most important skill required is that of adapting these skills to the Web. People with skills in traditional publication design, graphic design, and marketing need help adapting to the Web environment. Although many of the design principles are the same, the Web introduces new challenges and opportunities, such as the following:

- ▸ Support for sounds, animation, and video

- ▸ Support for user input and responses

- ▸ Special graphic format requirements

- ▸ Differences in Internet access speeds

- ▸ Differences in Web page appearance caused by different browsers and different computer capabilities

Traditional designers are likely to recognize good page designs and layouts when they see them, but designing an interactive Web site requires user interface design, which has no equivalent in the paper publishing world. Web navigation principles are also different. Most books are designed to be read from front to back. Books don't have Forward, Back, and Home buttons, and touching words and pictures rarely takes you to another book or another country.

Because the Web is different from other traditional forms of publishing and marketing, it is important for the Web designer to become familiar with the available Web technologies. For example, traditional marketers and designers might conduct a survey using the postal service as the delivery tool, but as a Web designer, you might create a survey Web page instead. This Web page might store survey data in a database or send it in an e-mail message to the survey administrator. The Web offers many opportunities to improve upon the approaches used for traditional design and marketing, and when you know what these opportunities are, you can develop your Web site to its fullest potential.

As you work on your Web site, and when it is finished and available to your audience, it is important to keep abreast of the latest tools and utilities for creating and maintaining Web sites. The Web technologies are constantly evolving, and the Web designer that follows these changes is best prepared to take advantage of new tools that can make Web site development and maintenance easier and more enjoyable.

## How to Design a Web Site

Novell's Course 660, Designing Effective Web Sites, identifies the following steps for designing and publishing a Web site:

1 • Define the Web site goals.

2 • Create a storyboard.

3 • Produce the Web site content.

4 • Develop a Web site prototype.

5 • Test the prototype.

6 • Revise the prototype and publish the finished Web site.

**TIP**

**If you are planning to take the certification exam for Course 660, Designing Effective Web Sites, you should know these steps and their order.**

This chapter describes how to set goals for your Web site and provides guidelines for designing Web sites and Web pages. Your Web site design will start to take shape in the storyboard phase, which is described later in this chapter, and will continue to be defined and refined as you develop your Web site content.

Most of this book is about creating Web site content. Part I describes how to create HTML text, tables, and forms. Chapter 8 explains how to create and optimize Web images, and Chapter 9 shows you how to add multimedia to your Web pages. In the last part of this book, you'll learn how to use Web page programs to add yet more features to your Web site.

When your Web site content is complete, it's time to assemble a prototype and see if your Web site is ready for publishing. Chapter 10 provides guidelines for testing and publishing your Web site.

Although Web site testing is listed as Step 5 in the previous list, it is important to get feedback on your project at each of the steps listed. For example, after you determine your Web site goals, ask for comments from management, other team members, and other departments. Do the same after you've developed a storyboard, and as you develop individual content pieces, such as articles, images, and animation. Getting feedback from your management and peers encourages their support and can help you avoid making mistakes that are difficult to correct later when the Web site is almost complete.

## Defining Site Goals

The first step in the Web site design process is to determine the goal, or goals, for your Web site. Sometimes the goal seems obvious. For example, your company wants to sell more products, or it wants to cut customer support calls by posting customer service information on the Web. These are worthy goals if you are selling products on your Web site, and if your customers are Internet visitors, but these are poor goals if your company can't sell products on the Web or if your customers don't have computers.

Good Web site goals consider the needs of your business and your customers. The following are some common business goals for Web sites:

- Generate more sales leads for existing channels

- Sell products over a new channel: the Internet

- Increase business or product visibility

- Improve the company image

- Demonstrate your company's commitment to new technologies

- Attract new customers

- Keep pace with your competition or move ahead by offering new and innovative services

- Improve customer satisfaction by offering alternative and possibly more convenient ways to access your business

Many businesses will want to achieve more than one of these goals and, when this is the case, you will want to establish priorities for your goals. Few businesses have unrestricted resources. In most cases, you'll have a specified time and budget to get a Web site up and running. Setting priorities enables you to focus on the most important goals first.

While you are selecting and prioritizing your goals, it's wise to conduct an audience analysis to see if you can achieve your goals with your expected audience. To get to know your audience, ask questions such as the following:

- Do our current customers use the Internet?

- Can we expect to gain new customers from the Internet?

- What will entice customers to come to our Web site?

- Will our Web site visitors have e-mail addresses?

- How often do they use the Internet?

- How experienced are they at using the Internet?

- Do they access the Internet from slow home connections or from faster connections at work?

- Do they purchase products on the Internet?

- Do they expect Internet services from you that are similar to those offered by your competitors?

When you have a clear understanding of your company goals and the needs of your Web site audience, you are ready to start designing your Web site. As you develop the design and Web site content, keep your goals and audience in mind. Many of the tougher design decisions are easier when you ask pointed questions. Consider which approach is more in line with the project goals and which approach best serves the Web site audience.

*Novell's Certified Internet Business Strategist Study Guide,* available from **Novell Press,** provides additional information on setting business goals for **Web** sites and analyzing your audience.

**TIP**

## Web Site Design Guidelines

When you translate your Web site goals into a design, you'll need to develop a Web site architecture and Web page design guidelines. The Web site architecture defines the organization of your Web pages and how visitors navigate your Web site. The page design guidelines define the appearance of your Web pages, the functionality they contain, and other guidelines that determine how the pages are developed. The following sections provide more information on designing a Web site architecture and creating page design guidelines.

### WEB SITE ARCHITECTURE

A Web site's *architecture* is the organization of the pages (content) that make up the site (Figure 7.1). If all of your Web site information fits on one Web page, you don't need to define an architecture. However, when your Web site contains 1,000 pages, how will your visitors find what they are looking for? After they find what they need, how can they find the next item they need?

*Web Site Architecture*

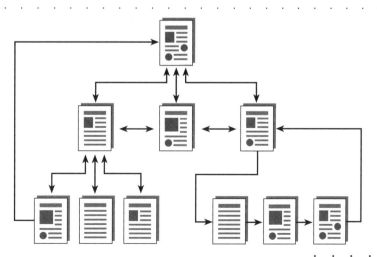

The Web site architecture defines the links between all the Web pages in your site. It is the navigation structure that guides visitors through your site. To a large extent, each visitor's opinion of your site is based on his or her ability to find something useful or entertaining at your site. One of your challenges as a Web designer is to design a Web site architecture that makes it easy for your visitors to find all the great content you are publishing.

Each Web site usually has a single home page that serves as the primary point of entry to the site. This page typically identifies the site and its purpose and contains links to other pages in the site. In a large site, however, there just isn't enough room on the home page to link to every other page. To solve this problem, the home page links to a secondary set of pages that form the second level of the Web site, and these pages contain links to pages in the third level. If there are still too many other pages, additional levels are created.

This process of adding levels to the Web site architecture is much like organizing computer files in directories or folders. The goal is the same: you want to save some information and store it where it can be found easily. You also want to travel through the minimum number of folders to get to the files when you need them.

As the Web site designer, you choose how to structure the Web site content. It is common for a business site home page to link to second-level pages that serve as area home pages, which correspond to organizational departments, geographic locations, or products. These area home pages contain links to third-level Web pages that provide the content for these areas.

Although Web technology allows you to create a Web site in which every page links to every other page, this "mesh" approach doesn't create a structure, and in large Web sites it produces more confusion than convenience. As mentioned earlier, you might not have room on your Web pages to link to every other Web page.

To begin your architectural design, create a sketch similar to that in Figure 7.1. Start with a home page. Next, start dividing the proposed content into areas and add these area home pages to the second level in your sketch. As you add pages, consider how you want users to be able to navigate between Web pages. As you add additional levels of Web pages, you'll find that each area develops one of the following structures:

- ▶ Linear layout

- ▶ Hierarchical layout

▶ Combined linear and hierarchical layout

Each of these structures has certain advantages and disadvantages. When evaluated as a whole, most Web sites use the combined layout; however, it is very common for individual Web site areas to use any of the three. The following sections describe each of these layouts and provide examples of when to use them. After these structures are described, an additional section provides guidelines for designing your Web site architecture.

### Linear Layout

When you use a *linear layout,* you organize the Web site or area in a unidirectional path from start to finish—similar to the pages in a book. Web site visitors view the home page, and then the next page, and so on. Figure 7.2 illustrates a linear layout.

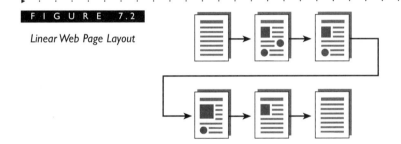

**FIGURE 7.2**

*Linear Web Page Layout*

A linear layout provides a rigid structure that is particularly well suited for procedure instructions. This type of layout gives the site developer a great deal of control over the visitors' path through the material presented. Some people like this kind of Web site structure, but others do not. As a Web designer, your job is to know your audience and to provide the structure most comfortable to them.

If you are using the demonstration Web site on the CD-ROM, you can view a sample linear layout at the following URL:

```
file:///d:/DemoWeb2/Design/Basics/index.htm
```

### Hierarchical Layout

A *hierarchical layout* has a tree-like structure. The Web site's home page is the root, which links to multiple Web pages that branch off to provide additional information. Figure 7.3 illustrates a hierarchical Web page layout.

**FIGURE 7.3**

*Hierarchical Web Page
Layout*

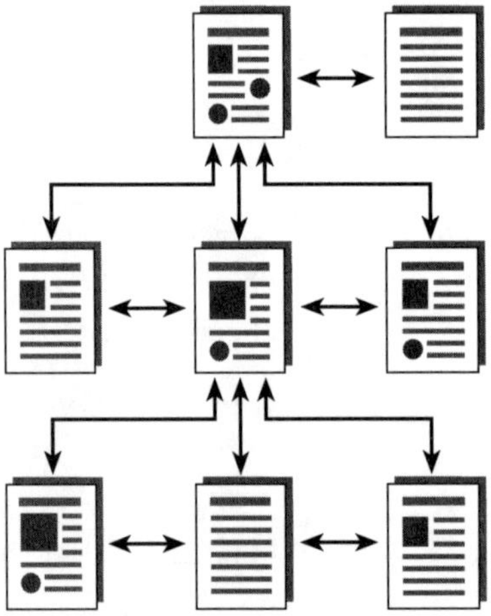

A hierarchical layout provides a flexible structure that gives site visitors more control over the information they view. For example, at any Web page, the visitor can usually link to the parent-level Web page, the child-level Web page, or peer Web pages at the same level. Although it isn't shown in Figure 7.3, the Web pages at the lowest level often link back to the home page or a second-level Web page so visitors can easily navigate to another branch of the Web site.

If you are using the demonstration Web site on the CD-ROM, you can view a sample hierarchical layout at the following URL:

```
file:///d:/DemoWeb2/Design/Basics/index.htm
```

### Combined Layout

As you might expect, a *combined layout* is a combination of the linear and hierarchical layouts. Figure 7.1, which appears earlier in this chapter, illustrates a combined Web page layout.

You can give visitors to your Web site the best of both worlds by combining linear and hierarchical layouts within your site. Use linear page layout for information that would be confusing if presented out of sequence. Use hierarchical layout for information that can be compartmentalized and understood by itself, without reference to other Web pages.

### Additional Navigation Support Structures

In addition to the layout structures introduced earlier, many Web sites use the following special navigation structures:

- Front door or entry Web pages

- Utility navigation features, such as indexes and site maps

Some sites use a *front door* or *entry* Web page as the entry point to the Web site. The difference between an entry Web page and a home page is that the entry page usually contains information that you want visitors to see before they enter the site. For example, a front door Web page might prompt a visitor to enter a user name and password before he enters your site. An entry Web page might display special news bulletins or promotions, or it might let visitors know that they need to download and install additional software (plug-ins) to view Web site features. After users complete whatever actions are required, they can click a link on the entry page to link to the site's home page.

*Utility navigation* structures, which are also known as metacontent structures, are Web pages or areas devoted to making your Web site more usable. Utility structures are different from other Web pages because they assist with site navigation without providing content. For example, you might create Web pages that present a site index, a table of contents, or a site map (site maps are introduced in Chapter 6). Site visitors use these utility navigation structures to locate the content pages they want to browse. Chapter 10 provides more information on utility navigation structures.

### Architectural Guidelines

Web site architecture is an important part of the design process. You can use it to give users as much browsing guidance or freedom as you choose. Chapter 10 provides more information on navigation controls, but you might want to consider the following guidelines while you are designing the Web site architecture:

- Place the most popular information close to the home page.

- Reposition Web pages that have too many links.

- Minimize topical links.

- Provide links for visitors that "pop in" to the middle of your Web site using search engines or links from other Web sites.

- Control visitor access to links that take them away from your site.

- Avoid orphan pages that have no links to their parent pages or the site home page. These are dead ends.

As you develop your Web site architecture, try to anticipate what Web content visitors will want most and minimize the number of links it takes to get there. Although a software update link might logically belong on a Web page 6 levels below the home page, you might want to create a direct link to one of the top levels if 90 percent of your visitors are visiting your site to get this page.

Also, review your architectural sketch for Web pages that have too many links to other Web pages. If a Web page at a lower level has many links to other pages, you might want to move it up to a higher level so visitors will find it quicker.

*Topical navigation* links connect a topic in the Web page content area to additional information in another Web page. You might use topical links to connect Web page text or thumbnail images to full size images. Another common use for topical links is as a cross-reference to a definition or a white paper. As you design your Web site architecture, try to minimize the need for topical links to other branches of the tree. While there are controls that enable a user to link back to the page that presented the topic, it can be easy for the visitor to chase other links in the other branch and later have trouble returning to the page where she started.

Chapter 4 introduces intradocument links, which are a form of internal navigation that enables you to refer to specific areas of a Web page. From a site design point of view, intradocument links are largely a content issue. However, when you are designing the Web site, it is important to remember that search engines and other Web sites can create links that bring your site visitors into almost any location within your Web site. For this reason, it is very important to carefully consider the navigation controls you place on each Web page. With careful planning, you might be able to redirect one of these "pop in" visitors to areas that will convert them to regular site visitors and customers.

You should also give special consideration to your external Web site links, which take users to other Web sites. Place these links on the home page or on a page that is just a link away from the home page, and design them so it is clear that the user will exit your site if they select the link. If you have a home page link on all your Web pages and a special Web page with external links close by, a user is never more than a couple of clicks from the external Web sites. However, if your internal and external links look the same and are scattered throughout your Web site, visitors are likely to be startled when they click a link and suddenly find themselves somewhere else.

## PAGE DESIGN GUIDELINES

A well-designed Web site is both informative and visually attractive. The easiest way to get acquainted with Web-site design is to browse the Web. As you look at each Web page, ask yourself these questions:

- ▸ Does the look of the page entice you to read the text?

- ▸ Does the page quickly tell you what information it contains?

- ▸ Does the page include graphics that inspire emotion, such as happiness, sadness, fear, or anticipation?

- ▸ Are the links easy to locate and read or are they buried in paragraphs?

- ▸ Do the graphics take so long to download you lose interest in the Web page?

The balance between text, colors, and graphics is a key design decision. *Text* is a common form of information delivery, but it often takes more time to interpret text than it does to interpret graphics. The effective use of color and graphics can quickly entice Web surfers to read further or to bookmark your Web page. However, graphics files are larger than text files, so they take more time to travel across the Web. A Web page heavy on graphics, which takes a long time to load, can be less effective than a Web page light on graphics that loads quickly.

As you design your Web site, consider developing your own guidelines for your Web pages. It is a good idea to develop guidelines for the common design elements that appear on every page and additional guidelines that apply to the content on each page. These guidelines are especially important when you are creating a large Web site, where different designers are often responsible for different areas. Developing Web site guidelines helps ensure consistency among the pages in your site.

The following sections provide guidelines for defining Web page layout and content.

### Page Layout Guidelines

A well-designed Web site has a look and feel that is unique and consistent throughout. To develop a consistent look, designers create coordinated sets of page elements that they repeat on every page. These page elements can include:

- Company logos

- Page banners

- Text headings

- Body text

- Bullets

- Rules

- Background colors or images

- Navigation buttons

Designers coordinate these page elements by using a consistent color scheme and a consistent layout for each page. While some sites might use different layouts for different areas of the Web site, the best designs usually have a layout that is consistent throughout. To create unique layouts for individual Web site areas, the designers add special graphic elements or banners that distinguish the Web site area, but still conform to the site guidelines. The goal is to develop a design that all designers can support and that Web site visitors will find pleasing and consistent.

Designers often create Web sites that portray a theme. Like theme parks, Web sites can use colors, fonts, sounds, and images to portray an environment that is business like, happy, gloomy, mysterious, or futuristic. The theme can be anything you want as long as it is appropriate for your business and your audience.

Another technique often used by designers is the metaphor. For example, a business Web site for a department store could be designed to appear as a department store catalog or an actual building. The front door page into the site might feature an image of a front door, and the home page might resemble a hallway leading to the many different departments. As visitors click different departments, new pages appear, featuring the products in those departments. Metaphors are especially useful when they add entertainment value or make the Web site architecture easier to understand.

Establishing a Web site theme or metaphor requires graphic design skills that are beyond the scope of this book. However, as you or your graphic designers create your Web site theme, consider the following guidelines for using color:

- Use contrasting colors to distinguish foreground text colors from background colors or images. For example, use dark or saturated colors on a light background or vice versa. Black, red, green, and blue can be used on white or yellow, but you should avoid low contrast color combinations such as yellow on white.

- Select background images that won't interfere with the readability of foreground text.

- Use colors to highlight links, headlines, pull quotes, and other Web page features you want visitors to notice.

- Pick colors that are browser-safe. You'll learn more about browser-safe colors in Chapter 8.

- Define the theme colors for your Web site page elements and publish these for the team members. All team members should use these colors to keep the Web site appearance consistent.

While the Web site theme establishes the look of your Web site, much of the feel of the Web site is defined by the page layout you choose and the controls you provide. One of the first decisions you must make during the design process is the size of the Web page you will design.

In some ways, designing for a particular Web page size can be futile because the user can change the browser window size at any time. However, the smallest computer displays usually display 640×480 pixels, so this is a reasonable lowest common denominator if you want your Web page to appear the same on all computers. Of course, the actual Web page area is less because the browser uses part of this area to display browser controls. Whatever page size you choose, you should use that size throughout your site so visitors only need to adjust their browser once. (For more information on selecting a page size, see Chapter 10.)

If you decide to design for a larger size Web page, it is a good idea to lay out your Web page so the title, controls, and the most important information is still visible to those with small display areas. This approach permits these visitors to navigate your Web site without scrolling, and if your content is compelling enough, the information they can see might tempt them to scroll to learn more.

As you plan your page layout, remember to include an area for navigation controls. Controls that often appear on Web pages are buttons or links for Home, Forward, Back, and some of the top-level Web pages. These are the controls that you want to be visible to all visitors. Controls labeled "Forward," or "Next" are particularly useful for guiding visitors through your site. You might also want to include a link for submitting comments or suggestions for your Web site. (Navigation controls are discussed in more detail in Chapter 10.)

In addition to your color theme and navigation controls, you might want to add a company logo or banner to each Web page and perhaps other elements, such as the Webmaster's e-mail address. As you complete your layout, remember that the page elements you add to your basic layout will be repeated on every Web page. You want to be sure to leave enough room for the actual Web page content and enough free space, which is called white space in printing circles, so that the pages do not look too cluttered.

The other reason to limit your total number of Web page elements is that each element increases the combined file size of the Web page, which increases the time it takes for visitors to download it. Those with 28.8K modem connections can download about 1Kbps. If you need to support modem users, you might want to establish a guideline for a maximum combined Web page size that designers can create (for example 50K). Another approach is to create an alternate Web site for those who use modem connections and optimize each site for the connections your visitors will use.

**NOTE** **Chapters 8 and 9 provide guidelines for optimizing Web page images and multimedia components. You can use these guidelines to minimize the size of the page layout elements and page content.**

### Content Guidelines

Your Web page layout serves as the backdrop or scene for your Web page star, which is your Web site content. Although your Web site theme is important, be careful not to put so much effort into it that there aren't enough resources to develop quality content. Your visitors will sing your praises if your Web site is attractive *and* useful, but they aren't likely to stay or return if the site is not useful.

As you define each Web page during your design, define a goal for that page and a title. As described in Chapter 2, Web page titles are very important because they describe your pages in the browser window, in bookmarks, and in search engine reports. The title should be descriptive and short so that the entire title appears in these locations.

The purpose of some pages is to deliver information, but other pages collect data from visitors or act as signposts to other Web pages. While you are defining Web pages, be sure to include some pages that reward your visitors for dropping by. For example, some sites offer free screen savers or wallpaper images if the visitor signs a guest log. Others might offer discount coupons for company products. The visitor departs with a neat graphic, and your business has a new sales lead.

While you are planning your Web site, you should also be thinking about how you can keep the Web site interesting and useful for repeat visitors. If you want visitors to come back, you need to have content on the Web site that looks like it will be updated, and you need to be sure to update it. The most obvious ways to encourage return visitors are to offer new promotions and add new useful information. Another way is to add new technologies, such as animations and interactive training programs, that make the existing information more interesting or more useful.

When it is time to write the Web page content, use experienced writers and editors if possible, and strive for clear and concise writing. Long Web pages can be difficult to read, so consider breaking long documents into several shorter pages. Also, use graphics and multimedia when they can help make your point better than mere text. Just be careful not to add so much flash that your message gets lost in the fireworks.

To draw visitors into your Web pages, consider adding pull quotes, which are those quotations that magazines often enlarge in the middle of the page to pull you into an article. You might also highlight keywords or add special icons, images, or animation to draw the visitor's attention to the Web page content. Remember that your work is wasted if no one reads it. Creating a Web site is only part of the challenge. The only way to reach your Web site goals is to get people to read the pages and take the action you want them to take.

## Storyboarding

Implementing a Web site architecture and design can involve a substantial amount of work. *Storyboarding* is a technique for planning and visualizing presentations before you commit to building them. Storyboarding is often used to plan movies, multimedia titles, and other complex productions. The purpose of a storyboard is to give the Web site developer—or prospective client—an overall view of the Web site as it's being developed. Storyboarding can help you recognize inconsistencies or an unbalanced structure.

At the start of a project, you use a storyboard to make notes and sketches that simulate the finished product. No single way exists to create a storyboard. You can create notes and sketches on pieces of paper or cardboard, and you can lay out the storyboard as sheets on a wall or floor in the shape of your Web site architecture. You can also develop a storyboard on a computer using a flowcharting tool, a word processing program, or a graphics program. NetObjects Fusion, which is included on this book's CD, is an excellent tool for creating a storyboard because you can quickly apply a style to many pages and view the structure in Site view. (NetObjects Fusion was introduced in Chapter 6.) Figure 7.4 shows how you might lay out a series of notes and sketches to create a storyboard for a Web site.

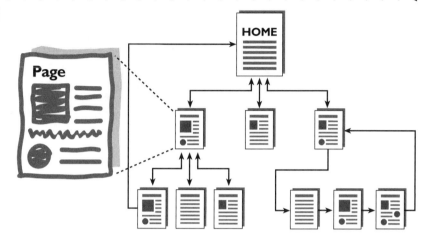

FIGURE 7.4

*An Example of
Storyboarding*

As you refine your storyboard, you may want to include the following information for each Web page:

▸ Web page title and file name

▸ Main heading

▸ Subheadings

▸ Purpose of page

▸ Content description

▸ Rough sketches of graphics or a list of graphics

▸ List of links

Your storyboard should present as much visual information as possible at each stage of development. Initially, you might only have titles for each Web page. As you define the common elements for each page, sketch those on your storyboard pages. Beauty isn't important at this stage, but function is critical. The storyboard serves as the first prototype of your Web site. You'll get the best feedback and team support when it is easy for team members to visualize what you're creating.

▶ . . . . . . . . . . . . . . . . . . . . . . . . . ◀

## Summary

This chapter introduces the role of the Web Designer and explains that, as a Web designer, you need to develop skills in publication design, graphic design, marketing, and Web design. This chapter also defines the following steps for designing and producing Web sites:

1 • Define the Web site goals.

2 • Create a storyboard.

3 • Produce the Web site content.

4 • Develop a Web site prototype.

5 • Test the prototype.

6 • Revise the prototype and publish the finished Web site.

Before or during the storyboard creation process, you need to create a Web site architecture, which determines how Web site visitors navigate your Web site. You also need to define the common page elements that appear on all Web pages and create the theme for your Web site.

Storyboarding is a procedure for developing a visual prototype of your Web site. You can use a storyboard to help team members and management visualize the Web site architecture and theme you are creating.

 **Another way to apply a consistent style on multiple Web pages is to use Cascading Style Sheets (CSS). CSS is a new HTML standard that is part of the Dynamic HTML standard. You can learn more about CSS and Dynamic HTML by browsing the following locations:**

**World Wide Web Consortium:** www.w3.org/

**The Web Developers Virtual Library:** www.stars.com/

The following word puzzle contains many of the terms discussed in this chapter. See if you can find all the words. As you search for the words, ask yourself why the word is in the list and how it was used in this chapter. If you don't know the answers to these questions, you might want to review the chapter.

```
A  T  P  R  O  M  O  T  I  O  N  S  U  G  D
J  R  K  C  O  N  T  E  N  T  O  B  C  N  E
L  A  C  I  H  C  R  A  R  E  I  H  O  I  V
H  U  A  H  C  O  N  S  I  S  T  E  N  T  E
S  D  B  P  I  S  N  L  S  S  A  S  T  E  L
I  I  D  A  U  T  A  O  E  P  G  I  R  K  O
L  E  E  R  U  O  E  T  I  P  I  V  A  R  P
B  N  E  G  G  R  C  C  R  T  V  E  S  A  T
U  C  F  S  S  Y  O  O  T  T  A  R  T  M  O
P  E  N  T  R  B  T  H  M  U  N  M  Q  U  P
U  M  O  U  E  O  I  I  P  B  R  O  I  H  I
B  E  W  O  T  A  T  R  L  A  I  E  R  N  C
L  H  G  Y  I  R  L  I  O  I  T  N  M  F  A
I  T  P  A  R  D  E  M  D  O  T  E  E  O  L
C  E  Z  L  W  N  G  I  S  E  D  U  M  D  H
```

| | | |
|---|---|---|
| animation | front | publish |
| architecture | goal | revise |
| audience | graphic | storyboard |
| combined | hierarchical | test |
| consistent | home | theme |
| content | layout | title |
| contrast | marketing | topical |
| design | metaphor | utility |
| develop | navigation | web |
| door | promotions | writers |
| editors | prototype | |
| feedback | public | |

**EXERCISE 7.1: UNDERSTANDING WEB DESIGN BASICS**

Review your knowledge of the Web design basics presented in this chapter by answering the following questions:

1 • List the four skills required by a Web designer or a Web team.

a. . . . . . . . . . . . . . . . . . . . . . . . . . . . . . . . . . . . . . . . . . . . . . . . . . . .

b. . . . . . . . . . . . . . . . . . . . . . . . . . . . . . . . . . . . . . . . . . . . . . . . . . . .

c. . . . . . . . . . . . . . . . . . . . . . . . . . . . . . . . . . . . . . . . . . . . . . . . . . . .

d. . . . . . . . . . . . . . . . . . . . . . . . . . . . . . . . . . . . . . . . . . . . . . . . . . . .

2 • List the six steps for designing and publishing a Web site.

a. . . . . . . . . . . . . . . . . . . . . . . . . . . . . . . . . . . . . . . . . . . . . . . . . . . .

b. . . . . . . . . . . . . . . . . . . . . . . . . . . . . . . . . . . . . . . . . . . . . . . . . . . .

c. . . . . . . . . . . . . . . . . . . . . . . . . . . . . . . . . . . . . . . . . . . . . . . . . . . .

d. . . . . . . . . . . . . . . . . . . . . . . . . . . . . . . . . . . . . . . . . . . . . . . . . . . .

e. . . . . . . . . . . . . . . . . . . . . . . . . . . . . . . . . . . . . . . . . . . . . . . . . . . .

f. . . . . . . . . . . . . . . . . . . . . . . . . . . . . . . . . . . . . . . . . . . . . . . . . . . .

3 • After each stage of Web site design and development, what should you request from peers and management?

Answer: . . . . . . . . . . . . . . . . . . . . . . . . . . . . . . . . . . . . . . . . . . . . . .

4 • Who should you consider when you are defining your Web site goals?

Answer: . . . . . . . . . . . . . . . . . . . . . . . . . . . . . . . . . . . . . . . . . . . . . .

5 • What does the Web site architecture determine for your visitors?

Answer: . . . . . . . . . . . . . . . . . . . . . . . . . . . . . . . . . . . . . . . . . . . . . .

**6** • What is the name of the top-level Web page for most Web sites?

Answer: . . . . . . . . . . . . . . . . . . . . . . . . . . . . . . . . . . . . . . . . . . .

**7** • What type of layout guides Web site visitors on a predetermined path through your Web site?

Answer: . . . . . . . . . . . . . . . . . . . . . . . . . . . . . . . . . . . . . . . . . . .

**8** • Which Web site layout uses a tree-like structure?

Answer: . . . . . . . . . . . . . . . . . . . . . . . . . . . . . . . . . . . . . . . . . . .

**9** • What is the name for the type of layout that uses the layouts described in Questions 7 and 8?

Answer: . . . . . . . . . . . . . . . . . . . . . . . . . . . . . . . . . . . . . . . . . . .

**10** • What purpose does a front door or entry Web page serve?

Answer: . . . . . . . . . . . . . . . . . . . . . . . . . . . . . . . . . . . . . . . . . . .

**11** • What is the general name for Web pages that contain a site index, site map, or table of contents?

Answer: . . . . . . . . . . . . . . . . . . . . . . . . . . . . . . . . . . . . . . . . . . .

**12** • Where should you place your Web site's most popular information?

Answer: . . . . . . . . . . . . . . . . . . . . . . . . . . . . . . . . . . . . . . . . . . .

**13** • Why are orphan Web pages a problem?

Answer: . . . . . . . . . . . . . . . . . . . . . . . . . . . . . . . . . . . . . . . . . . .

**14** • What is the smallest common computer display size?

Answer: . . . . . . . . . . . . . . . . . . . . . . . . . . . . . . . . . . . . . . . . . . .

**15** • What types of controls should appear on every Web page?

Answer: . . . . . . . . . . . . . . . . . . . . . . . . . . . . . . . . . . . . . . . .

**16** • What is the purpose of a storyboard?

Answer: . . . . . . . . . . . . . . . . . . . . . . . . . . . . . . . . . . . . . . . .

# CHAPTER 8

# Creating and Adapting
# Web Graphics

**C**hapter 3 introduces the two primary Web image formats (GIF and JPEG) and describes how to use image files on your Web pages. Before you can use image files, however, you need to create them. Web designers often create Web graphics by doing the following:

- ▸ Creating new images in image-editing programs

- ▸ Modifying commercial clip art images using image-editing programs

- ▸ Scanning art and photographs from existing materials and modifying them with image-editing programs

Creating and adapting images for the Web is a different process than those methods used for paper publishing. In paper publishing, image quality is usually more important than file size. In Web publishing, however, large file sizes require long download times. Also, Web pages must appear on many different platforms, each of which might or might not display the same screen area or the same number of colors. Good image design practices can improve the download speed of your Web pages and ensure a consistent quality across multiple platforms. Poor image designs can make your images unintelligible.

This chapter begins by describing how Web graphics operate and providing some examples of what can go wrong with Web images. The following section presents the three principle Web image formats and describes how to choose the right one to use. The rest of the chapter describes how to create, convert, and optimize images for the Web, and how to use these images for special Web page elements, such as bullets and backgrounds. The final section explains how to test your Web images in your browser quickly.

**NOTE**

**As with Novell Education Course 660, this chapter refers to Adobe Photoshop as an example of a Web image editor. In this chapter, you'll learn to create and edit Web images with Photoshop. Although many of the procedures in this chapter will be different for other image editors, the basic principles will be the same.**

# Understanding Web Image Design Issues

Chapter 3 recommends that you use the Graphic Interchange Format (GIF) for simple illustrations and the Joint Photographic Experts Group (JPEG) format for scanned photographs. In the following sections, you'll learn how bitmap images operate, and you'll see some of the problems created when you choose the wrong format, or when your Web page viewers use computers that are set up differently than yours. After you finish this section, you'll understand why GIF and JPEG images are used for different purposes.

## HOW BITMAPS WORK

When you create or edit images for the Web, you cannot avoid learning about image size, resolution, bit depth, and palettes. These settings define your image workspace and the colors you can use in the image. If you don't pick values for these settings, the image editor will pick values for you.

Learning how bitmaps work is cheap insurance. Although most image editors permit you to change settings after you have created an image, these setting changes can introduce image problems that take hours to correct. Sometimes, it is easier to redo an image than to convert it.

The following sections introduce the primary settings that control how bitmaps operate. These sections define terms that are used throughout the rest of the chapter.

### Image Size and Resolution

Bitmap images display as a grid of colored squares, which are often called bits. A bitmap is simply a map of all the bits that form an image. Figure 8.1 shows how these bits appear when a graphic image is enlarged.

**FIGURE 8.1**

*Bitmap Graphics*

The image in Figure 8.1 shows that shapes and text are both composed of bits. In this example, all of the bits are either black or white, but you can use image-editing programs to color the bits individually or as part of text, or object, areas. The image in Figure 8.1 was enlarged to make the bits more obvious. The rough edges are much less obvious at the actual size.

In graphics programs, the bitmap bits are usually called *pixels*. Pixels are the individual dots that display color on computer displays. When you are creating bitmaps for Web pages, each bit that you include in your image will display as one pixel in a browser window. This isn't an accident, this is the way bitmaps work. Because of this, you have to design your Web images for browsers using principles that are different from paper image designs.

When you create a bitmap, the first thing you need to do is define the size of the grid (the image size) and the image resolution, which defines the size of the bits. Image resolution is usually measured in dots-per-inch (dpi), and 72 dpi is generally accepted as standard for computer displays. At 72 dpi, each square inch of an image is 72 pixels wide, 72 pixels tall, and contains a total of 5,184 pixels.

Programs such as Adobe Photoshop enable you to define the image height and width in pixels or in other units such as inches, centimeters, or picas (a typesetting measurement unit). Photoshop also requires that you specify a resolution for each image or accept the default resolution.

If you aren't used to working with pixels, you might choose to define your image size in inches and then select 72 dpi as the resolution. This is a good approach; however, it is important to know that your Web image dimensions are still defined in pixels—not inches. The image editor simply translates your inch measurements into pixel measurements (1 inch equals 72 bits).

In the "Common Web Image Maladies" section, later in this chapter, you'll see that image size and resolution together have a direct effect on the size of the image file, which affects the download time. You'll also see that mismatches between the resolutions on different computer displays can cause an image to appear larger or smaller than intended. Before we get to the maladies section, however, it's important to learn about bit depth, which creates a few maladies of its own.

### Bit Depth

Bit depth is an overly technical term that specifies how many colors can be displayed in an image. In a bitmap image, color information is provided for each bit in the image. The bit depth term is derived from the number of data bits in the binary numbers that define each color in the image. Table 8.1 lists the most common bit depths and the number of colors they support.

| TABLE 8.1 | BIT DEPTH | TOTAL COLORS |
|---|---|---|
| *Common Bit Depths* | 1 | 2 |
| | 2 | 4 |
| | 4 | 16 |
| | 6 | 64 |
| | 8 | 256 |
| | 16 | 65,536 |
| | 24 | 16.7+ million |
| | 32 | 16.7+ million with 256 grayscale alpha channel |

Bit depth is often used to describe an image file. For example, a bitmap image that uses a bit depth of 24 is called a *24-bit image*. This terminology also applies to computer displays and display adapters. Most displays support 24-bit color, but your adapter could be an 8-bit adapter (which would limit the colors on your display to only 256). Later in this chapter, you'll see that mismatches between the bit depths of image files, displays, and adapters is the cause of many Web image maladies, but there are ways to minimize these problems.

For the GIF format, which supports bit depths between 1 and 8, bit depth directly affects the size of an image file. To understand this better, let's consider the 8-bit bit depth, which uses 8 data bits to define each color. This means that each bit's color in an image file is specified with a binary number between 0000 0000 and 1111 1111. When you multiply these 8 bits times the number of pixels, you can see that you get a much larger file than one that uses only 2 bits to define pixel colors. Larger bit-depths provide more colors to choose from, but they create larger files, which take longer to download.

**TIP**

**The mathematical relationship between bit depths, the binary numbers they use, and the total number of colors makes it easy to calculate the total number of colors based on the bit depth. To calculate the total number of colors calculate $2^x$, where the exponent x is equal to the bit depth. For example, $2^8 = 256$, so 8-bit images support up to 256 colors.**

If you haven't created Web images yet, don't worry about specifying Web colors as binary numbers. Most image editors enable you to choose colors from charts or tables, or you can specify colors using hexadecimal or decimal values. In Chapter 2, you learned how to specify font colors using the hexadecimal values 00-FF for red, green, and blue. Decimal values enable you to select the same colors using numbers between 0 and 255.

GIF files support a maximum bit depth of 8, which is much smaller than the 24-bit bit depth used for JPEG files. The smaller bit-depth of GIF images, and the smaller files they create, is one of the reasons GIF images are generally preferred over JPEG images. However, the increased number of colors in 24-bit JPEG images enables image detail not possible with 8-bit GIFs, which is why JPEG images are usually used for scanned photographs and other art with large amounts of color and detail.

### Palettes

A palette is a collection of predefined colors that can be used to create and display images. Palettes are used by image editors to create images that use 8-bit color or less, and they are used by operating systems to define colors for 8-bit adapters. The 8-bit adjective is important here. When you use a 24-bit image format, such as JPEG, you don't use a color palette. The 24-bit binary number for each image bit can define any one of about 16.7 million colors, so color selection is not a problem.

For 8-bit images (such as GIFs) and for 8-bit display adapters, however, color selection is limited to just 256 colors. Figure 8.2 shows a simplified view of how 8-bit image files use palettes to select image colors.

**FIGURE 8.2**

*8-bit Image File Components*

**Image Area**

| | | |
|---|---|---|
| 0000 0001 | 0101 0001 | 1111 1111 |
| 1111 0001 | 0101 0101 | 1100 1100 |
| 1101 1101 | 0110 1111 | |

**Color Lookup Table**

| 8-bit Number | 24-bit Color Value (Hex) |
|---|---|
| 0000 0001 | FF 00 FF |
| 0000 0010 | FF 00 00 |
| 0000 0011 | 00 FF FF |

In Figure 8.2, the image area of the file is simply a grid that contains the 8-bit binary color definitions for each image pixel. The color lookup table within the file maps each one of the 8-bit color definitions to a 24-bit color definition. The color lookup table enables you to pick your 256 colors from any of the 16.7 million colors provided by 24-bit numbers. (I listed the hexadecimal values of 24-bit numbers in Figure 8.2 to keep the figure smaller.)

The terms *color lookup table* and *palette* are often interchanged. In general, color lookup tables are the color definitions and palettes are the pictorial representations of those tables. For example, most image editors enable you to choose colors by clicking the colored squares in palettes. Image editors also enable you to store your color selections in one or more color lookup tables. Each time you start a new image, you can accept a default color lookup table or choose a different table so you can use custom colors.

The palette approach to color selection is great because it defines all colors in standard 24-bit values that can be interpreted equally by both 8-bit and 24-bit display adapters. This means you can create images that appear equally on both types of adapters. Without the palette approach, there would have been separate color-numbering systems for 8-bit and 24-bit colors, and you would have to design all of your images for one or the other.

Of course, I wouldn't be explaining all of this if there weren't design issues associated with the differences between 8-bit and 24-bit color systems. The problem is that many Windows and Macintosh systems use 8-bit display adapters, and these systems use fixed 256-color palettes that are different from each other. Because these systems can only display the colors in their palettes, browsers must convert the colors in your image to the colors supported by the operating system where the images are displayed (as shown in Figure 8.3).

F I G U R E   8.3

*Color Conversion for
8-bit Images*

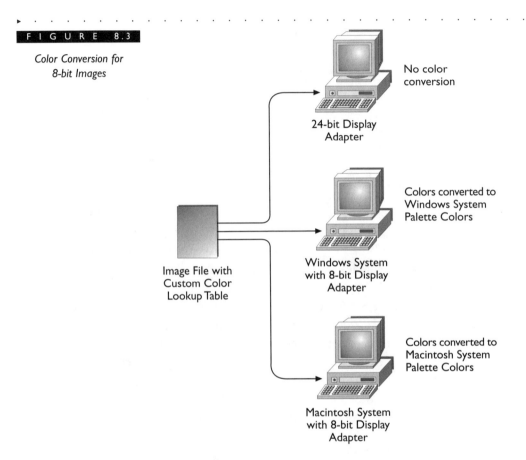

The biggest danger in color conversion occurs when the foreground and background colors in an image are similar. When this happens, both foreground and background colors can be converted to the same color, which can cause text, image detail, or other image information to disappear. Fortunately, this problem can be solved by designing images with enough contrast that foreground and background images will not be translated to the same color. We can also minimize some of the color conversion by using color lookup tables that specify the 216 colors that are common to both Windows and Macintosh systems. You'll learn more about this later in this chapter.

**Exercise 8.1: If you're preparing to take the certification exam, or if you want to practice what you learned in this section, turn to the end of this chapter and complete Exercise 8.1. When you are done, continue reading here to prepare for the next exercise.**

## COMMON WEB IMAGE MALADIES

Now that you know how bitmap images work, let's take a look at some common problems that occur when images are added to Web pages. This section addresses the following problems:

▸ Images take too long to download

▸ Images appear too large or too small in browser

▸ Colored dots appear in an image

▸ Significant image detail is lost

▸ The wrong colors appear in the browser

There are design solutions for all of these problems. In many cases, however, you need to apply the solution before you create the image file. The following sections describe these problems and their solutions. Later in this chapter, you'll learn to create images using procedures that account for these problems.

### Images Take Too Long to Download

The source of this problem is file size. The only way to shorten the download time for images is to reduce their file size. However, when you just can't reduce the file size any more, there are tricks you can use to make the Web page and image appear faster. The following sections describe how to reduce image file size, display the Web page faster, and make an image appear sooner.

**Reducing File Size**   The primary way to reduce an image file size is to reduce the image size. When you have less information in the file, the file size is smaller. Because most browser users use displays that measure 640×480 or 800×600 pixels, your images should not exceed these dimensions. If you want Web page visitors to see other images or text with an image, your image dimensions need to be smaller. It's a good practice to make the image as small as possible.

For GIF images, you can further reduce the image file size by deleting colors from the color table. For example, if you convert an 8-bit image to a 2-bit image that uses only four colors, you can reduce the file size by deleting the color table entries for those other 252 24-bit color values. When you reduce the colors, the color data for each image bit is also smaller because there are fewer colors to choose from. You'll learn how to do this later in this chapter.

JPEG images always use 24-bit color, so you can't reduce their color depth, but you can reduce their file size when you save the file. Like GIF images, JPEG images use file compression techniques to reduce the file size. However, the JPEG format enables you to select several image-quality levels when the file is saved, and each level uses a different compression format. Often, you can use the lowest-quality level to create an acceptable Web page image that is considerably smaller than the original and downloads much faster.

**Reducing Web Page Delays Caused by Embedded Images** Remember the HTML image tag (<IMG>) WIDTH and HEIGHT attributes described in Chapter 3? These attributes play a very important part in displaying your Web page when it contains images. When these attributes are used to define the pixel dimensions of an image, the browser quickly displays the entire Web page with reserved areas for the images it will download later. This results in quick display of the Web page so Web page visitors can read the Web page text while the images continue to download. You can accomplish this with an image tag similar to the following:

```
<IMG SRC="image.gif" HEIGHT=25 WIDTH=25>
```

When you omit the height and width parameters from the image tag, the browser must download the entire image and calculate its dimensions before it can display the rest of the Web page. This can waste the Web page visitor's time and give him incentive to visit someone else's site.

There are two ways to get the image pixel measurements in your Web pages. The first way is to look them up in the image editor, and you'll learn how to do this with Photoshop later in this chapter. The other way is to use HTML editors, such as Netscape Composer or NetObjects Fusion, to insert your images. These programs automatically calculate the pixel dimensions and create the image tags for you.

**Displaying Images Faster Using Interlacing** Chapter 3 introduced interlaced GIF images, which display an image in stages as shown in Figure 8.4. You can also create interlaced JPEG images, although some browsers need a plug-in to display them.

Interlaced GIFs require slightly larger files than noninterlaced GIFs, but they start displaying quicker (see Table 8.3, later in this chapter). Interlaced GIFs can make your Web pages more interesting and entice visitors to wait until the image download is complete. Interlaced GIFs can also provide the visitor with enough information to help her determine if the image is worth waiting for.

Interlaced image files use an internal property, called *row order,* to control when rows appear during interlacing. When the row order is set to regular, the image appears without the interlacing effect.

Interlaced GIFs create a tradeoff situation where you, as the designer, need to pick which is more important—total download time, or quicker (but initially poorer) image resolution. The good news is that you have the choice.

As you'll see later in this chapter, creating interlaced images is as easy as checking a checkbox when you export a file to GIF format. Interlaced images do not require special file preparation.

### Images Appear Too Large or Too Small in a Browser

If you are used to creating images for printers that use 300 or 600 dpi, you know that these resolutions provide sharper images and more detail than those that use the 72 dpi setting recommended in this chapter. And if you are like me, your first inclination will be to use the higher resolution settings for your Web images. After all, more is better, right? Wrong.

As mentioned earlier, Macintosh displays typically use 72 dpi and, depending on display and display adapter specifications, Windows displays usually use between 75 to 100 dpi. These are physical limits built into the display. To get a higher resolution, you have to buy a different display and display adapter; and even if you do invest in the more expensive higher resolution equipment, your Web page visitors probably won't. The bottom line is—you need to design your Web page images to use between 72 and 100 dpi.

When an image appears larger than you expected, it is probably because the resolution on the destination display is lower than your image was designed for. Figure 8.5 shows an example of two images. The first image uses 72 dpi and is displayed on a computer monitor that supports 72 dpi. The second image is a 300-dpi image displayed on the same monitor. The monitor can only display 72 dots per inch, so the image designed for 300 dpi becomes very large.

You can see these images and all the examples for this chapter on the demonstration Web site at *d*:/DemoWeb2/Design/Graphics/index.htm.

When an image appears smaller than you expected, the destination display is probably using a higher resolution than your image is designed for. For example, if your image uses 72 dpi, and is displayed on a Windows system that uses 80 dpi, each image dot will be smaller and the entire image will be smaller.

It's a good practice to design your images for 72 dpi. The worst that can happen is that your images will appear slightly smaller on some systems, which is much better than having them so large that Web page visitors are forced to scroll to see the rest of the image.

**NOTE**

**When images appear too large in the browser, you can use the <IMG> tag WIDTH and HEIGHT attributes to resize the image. This changes the display size, but it does not change the file size. Web site visitors will still have to wait longer for the Web page to download.**

### Colored Dots Appear in an Image

Colored dots can appear in both GIF and JPEG images, but they appear for different reasons. When the dots appear in a pattern, the effect is called *dithering*. When the dots appear in an apparently random fashion, this is called *noise*. The following sections explain why the dots appear and how to design images so they won't appear—or so they'll appear according to a plan.

FIGURE 8.5

*Different Resolutions on the Same Display*

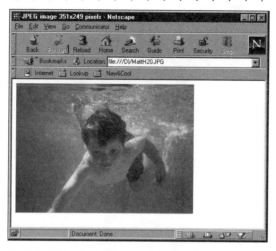

**Dithering**   When colored dots appear in a consistent pattern, it's called dithering. Figure 8.6 shows an example of a JPEG image with dithering. In this example, the letters are dithered and the area surrounding the letters contains noise. You'll learn more about noise in the next section.

Browsers and 8-bit display adapters use dithering to simulate image colors that the display adapter doesn't support. Remember that 8-bit display adapters can only display the colors in the System palette. To create the illusion of additional colors, dithering uses a mixture of colored pixels from the system palette. When viewed as a group, the pixels appear as the missing color.

Dithering can be intentional or accidental. To demonstrate dithering in Figure 8.6, I created a JPEG image with lettering that uses a color not found in the system palette on my computer, and then I set my computer to display only 256 colors. When I opened the image in my browser, the browser dithered the lettering.

When I tried this procedure with a GIF image, the results were very different. Instead of dithering to support the missing color, the browser simply converted the color to the most similar color in my system palette. To force a GIF image to dither, you need to specify dithering when you save the file. Otherwise, all colors that don't match those in the system palette will be converted for you.

In the previous examples, the dithering was intentional. To prevent dithering on 8-bit display systems, you must limit your image colors to the 216 colors shared by both the Windows and Macintosh system palettes. These colors are called the *browser-safe colors*. When you use these colors, both operating systems can display the colors, and dithering is not required. The sidebar "Which Colors are Browser Safe?" provides more information on these colors and their values.

**Noise**   Noise is a problem that plagues only JPEG images. When random colored dots appear in JPEG images, it is not dithering. Noise is created by the way JPEG images are compressed and stored. This noise usually appears in large areas of solid color. This noise doesn't appear in images with subtle shading and color differences because it blends in. Figure 8.7 shows an image with some random noise pixels.

## WHICH COLORS ARE BROWSER SAFE?

Both the Windows and Macintosh operating systems reserve 40 colors in their 256-color system palette for the operating system. These colors are unique to each operating system and should not be used for Web images unless you know all your viewers are using the same operating system.

The remaining 216 colors were chosen from the 16.7 million colors by dividing the red, green, and blue color values into equal segments. The result is that all colors in the browser-safe color palette use the hexadecimal or decimal values listed in Table 8.2.

To calculate the total number of colors supported by these 6 browser-safe color values, just multiply 6 (values of red) ×6 (values of green) ×6 (values of blue). The result is 216. If you always use these color values for your images, or if you select palette colors that use these values, your images will not dither and image colors will not be converted to other colors.

| TABLE 8.2 | HEXADECIMAL VALUE | DECIMAL VALUE |
|---|---|---|
| *Browser-Safe Color Values* | 00 | 00 |
| | 33 | 51 |
| | 66 | 102 |
| | 99 | 153 |
| | CC | 204 |
| | FF | 255 |

FIGURE 8.7

*Random "Noise" Pixels*

The noise in Figure 8.7 was actually intensified when I captured the image from a browser window. The screen capture program added noise to the noise, so your images will probably look better than this.

To capture the noise shown in Figure 8.7, I created a JPEG image that uses large areas of solid color and only browser-safe colors. The large areas of solid color promoted noise, and the browser-safe colors eliminated dithering.

Notice how the noise intensifies around the color changes. This effect softens the edges in images and creates more subtle changes between colors. This is good for photographs and other *continuous tone* images. This is not good when you want to present art with a high contrast and sharp edges.

The solution to the noise problem with JPEG images is to use GIF images instead. In simple illustrations with a limited number of colors, there is no reason to use the JPEG format. Use the JPEG format only for images, such as scanned photos or captured video, where continuous tones and large numbers of colors are required to display the detail in the image.

### Significant Image Detail Loss

Simple images use few colors; detailed images use many colors to represent highlights, textures, and shading. When you have a problem with detail loss, it is usually due to a mismatch between the colors in the original image and the colors that the destination computer can display. Figure 8.8 shows a loss of detail between two images.

FIGURE 8.8

*Detail Loss*

When you are using JPEG images, there is not much that you can do about the detail loss. If the remote computer can't display 16.7 million colors, you have to decide if the translated image quality in 8-bit browsers is acceptable, or if you need to select a new image.

When you are using GIF images, there should not be any detail loss between systems. If there is, it could be that you are not using browser-safe colors. For example, you might have chosen foreground and background colors that are too close in value and are translated to the same color in the system palette.

The best way to preview your images is to view them in a browser at different color depths. Later in this chapter, you'll learn how to change the bit depth in Windows so you can preview what your audience will see on your Web pages.

### The Wrong Colors Appear in the Browser

If you've read the preceding sections of this chapter, you probably know why the wrong colors appear in a browser. This problem is caused by mismatches between the colors in your image and the colors in the system palette on the destination computer. As described earlier, the solution to this problem is to use browser-safe colors in your images so that no color translation is required. Another solution is to save your GIF images with dithering so the image editor can simulate the desired colors with browser-safe colors.

### "Halos" Appear Around Foreground Images

Halos are colored lines or images, which are often white, that appear between a foreground image and the Web page background (see Figure 8.9). There are several ways to prevent halos from appearing. To understand which method is best for your images, you need to understand how halos are created.

FIGURE 8.9

*Halos*

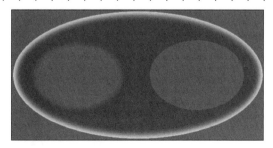

Halos are the result of the solution to another Web image problem: How do you create images in shapes other than rectangles and squares? All image files are rectangular or square. You can't change this, but fortunately there are ways to make images appear in different shapes.

One solution to the shape problem is to create your image with the same background color that your Web page uses. For example, you could create a star-shaped image with a blue background and use the same shade of blue for your Web page background. The star would appear in the shape of a star, even though the image is actually square.

The "matching background" approach works fine when the background doesn't have a pattern. When the background image does have a pattern, aligning it with a matching background inside the foreground image can be very difficult. To solve this problem, image formats, such as GIF, support the definition of *transparent* colors.

Transparent colors are colors that you define when you save an image. The transparent color definitions are stored in the image file, and when the browser displays the image, it ignores all transparent colors and lets the background color or pattern show through.

Transparent colors are a great solution to the problem of boring rectangular and square images. However, when the transparent colors disappear, there are often additional colors around the image that are introduced by an imaging technique called *anti-aliasing*. These additional colors create the halo around the foreground image.

Anti-aliasing is a technique for smoothing out the jagged edges that appear when you add shapes and text to bitmap programs (see Figure 8.10).

FIGURE 8.10

*Aliased and Anti-Aliased Objects*

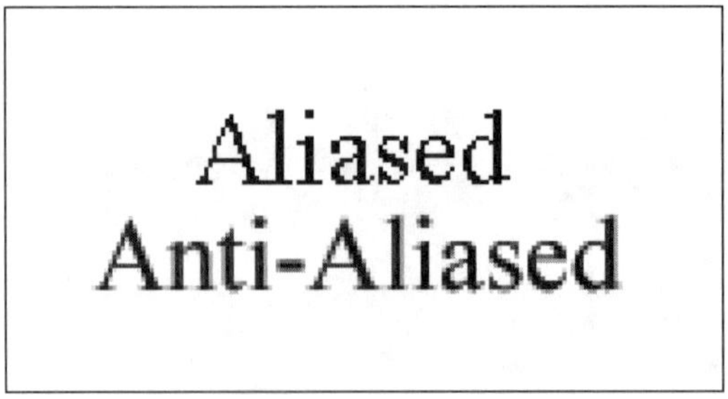

Aliased
Anti-Aliased

Objects and text that display rough edges are called *aliased objects* and *aliased text*. Anti-aliasing adds intermediate colors or shades of gray between an object or text and the background color, which visually softens the jagged edges of aliased objects.

Anti-aliasing is another one of those neat features that solves one problem and creates another. When you specify the background color of your image as transparent, the intermediate colors between the transparent background and your foreground image remain, and these create the halo. For example, if you specified white as the transparent background color, any anti-aliased objects and text would have borders that included off-white pixels, and these produce a white halo.

One solution to the halo problem is to turn off anti-aliasing when you create the objects and text in your images. The aliased edges that remain are usually far less objectionable than halos. You'll learn how to turn off anti-aliasing later in this chapter.

Another solution to halos is to specify multiple transparent colors, one for each of the colors that are used by the anti-aliasing. Because this produces the same visual result as aliased images, the first solution is easier. Specifying multiple transparent colors to hide anti-aliasing should only be used when it's too late to correct the problem another way. You'll learn how to specify transparent colors later in this chapter.

The final solution for hiding halos is to create the image using the same background color as the Web page, or the predominate background color in a background pattern. When you use this approach, anti-aliasing creates intermediate colors between objects and the background color, and these intermediate colors are hardly noticeable. The small oval on the left side of Figure 8.9 anti-aliases into the color behind it without displaying a distracting halo.

### Images Appear Brighter on Some Systems

Typically, Macintosh and SGI displays are brighter than those used by computers that run Windows. This causes Web images to appear brighter on Macintosh and SGI displays and darker on PC displays. One of the new features introduced by the Portable Network Graphics (PNG) format, which is introduced in the next section, is an image setting that enables you to compensate for these differences.

If you are concerned about differences in the brightness display, you can do one of the following:

  ▸ Create PNG Web images (PNG is not widely supported)

> ▸ Test your images on multiple systems and adjust them for an intermediate brightness level

> ▸ Design images on the platform you prefer and accept the differences

One way to simulate the appearance of images on different computers is to adjust the brightness of your display. For example, if you are working on a PC, you can place a Macintosh next to it, preview an image on both computers, and mark the brightness setting on the PC that most closely matches the image appearance on a Macintosh.

**Exercise 8.2: If you're preparing to take the certification exam, or if you want to practice what you learned in this section, turn to the end of this chapter and complete Exercise 8.2. When you are done, continue reading here to prepare for the next exercise.**

## Choosing a Web Image Format

Choosing a Web image format is the first step toward creating a new image or converting an existing image. In Chapter 3 and in the earlier sections of this chapter, you learned some of the guidelines for selecting an image format. However, these guidelines were based solely on image content. What if you want to create images for animation or coordinate an image and the Web page background so they blend together well?

The following sections summarize the guidelines for using the GIF and JPEG formats, and they provide additional information particular to these formats. The third section introduces the PNG format, which is a relatively new format that may eventually become the preferred one for Web images.

### GRAPHIC INTERCHANGE FORMAT

GIF files support an additional feature that has not yet been introduced — animation. Although the GIF format is generally used for all images except photographs, there may be times when you'll want to convert photographs to GIF images to take advantage of animation or transparency. You'll want to do this when the benefits of the GIF features outweigh the loss in image quality.

The following sections introduce animation and summarize the features of GIF images.

### Animation

Animation is the newest feature of the GIF format. When you create an animated GIF file, you store a series of GIF images in the same file. When the GIF is displayed, it displays the series of images to produce the animation.

Because animated GIFs store more images, the file sizes are larger. However, as with interlacing, animated GIFs can start displaying before the entire file is downloaded. The feature that enables this is called *streaming*. Streamed files can be displayed while they download.

The GIF features described in this book are provided by two different versions of the GIF specification. GIF89a is the latest specification and supports all of the GIF features presented here. The GIF87a specification supports all of the GIF89a features, except animation. You'll learn more about animation in Chapter 9.

### GIF Feature Summary

The following list summarizes the features supported by GIF files:

- ▸ User-selectable support for between 2 and 256 colors (1-bit to 8-bit color depths)

- ▸ Animation (GIF89a)

- ▸ Multiple transparent colors

- ▸ Interlacing

- ▸ Relatively small file size

- ▸ Supported by most graphical browsers

The primary disadvantage to using GIFs is the limited number of colors they support. Although GIFs support up to 256 colors, only 216 of those are browser-safe. Using the other 40 colors forces the browser to substitute different colors on different operating systems. Of course, when you need more colors than GIF files support, you can use the JPEG format.

## JOINT PHOTOGRAPHIC EXPERTS GROUP FORMAT

As described earlier, the JPEG format is used primarily for photographs; however, there are special graphical effects that JPEG images display better than GIF images. For example, many image editors enable special effects, such as gradients, textures, and blurs. To display these effects, the image editor adds colors to the image, and these added colors usually aren't browser safe. When you want to create images with these effects, you might want to use the JPEG format.

**TIP** **Most image editors do not permit you to add special effects requiring additional colors to GIF images. If you want to use these special effects, you need to start with another file format, such as JPEG, and later convert to GIF. You'll lose some quality when you convert, but if you use dithering and a little experimentation, you might be able to achieve the effect you are looking for.**

One feature of JPEG images that has not been introduced is adjustable file compression. When you save JPEG images, most image editors enable you to select from multiple levels of compression. Of course, there are tradeoffs. Although more compression does reduce the file size, it also reduces the image quality and increases the time required to display the image. Usually, the best way to determine the optimum compression is to save several copies of the image with different compression levels and then preview each image in a browser.

**TIP** **You do not have to add an image to a Web page to preview it in a browser. Browsers, such as Netscape Communicator, enable you to open GIF and JPEG images just as you would a Web page. When you open an image file instead of a Web page, the image appears in the upper-left corner of the browser window.**

The following summarizes the features supported by JPEG files:

▶ Support for 16.7 million colors (24-bit color depth)

▶ Support for multiple levels of compression

▶ Supported by most graphical browsers

▶ Interlacing (Progressive format)

**NOTE**

**GIF images that are interlaced are called *interlaced GIFs*; JPEG images produce an effect similiar to interlacing when stored with the Progressive file format. While some browsers directly support interlaced JPEG images, others require plug-in software.**

The following list summarizes the disadvantages of using JPEG files:

▸ Relatively large file size

▸ Noise is added to large areas of solid colors

Before you create JPEG images, consider the disadvantages carefully. Often, you can replace a photograph with line art that uses a smaller file size and loads faster. While special effects can look great, you should consider whether or not Web site visitors will wait for larger images to download.

When a JPEG image is the right solution, consider using compression and other optimization techniques to reduce the file size and display images faster. You'll learn more techniques for optimizing images later in this chapter.

**TIP**

**If your Web site plans call for you to scan existing art from brochures or magazines, scan these images early in the construction phase to see how well they convert to Web images. You might have problems with issues, such as glares, that will require revising or recreating art.**

## PORTABLE NETWORK GRAPHICS FORMAT

Portable Network Graphics (PNG) format is a relatively new image format that is designed specifically for the Internet. Because PNG images are not supported in older browsers, this chapter focuses on the GIF and JPEG formats. However, PNG has been endorsed by the World Wide Web Consortium and is supported in the latest versions of Netscape Navigator and Microsoft Internet Explorer. The following sections introduce the PNG format features and provide some guidelines for using PNG files.

### PNG Features

PNG files support the following features:

▸ Image quality that is comparable to JPEG

> ‣ Support for 8-bit, 24-bit, and 32-bit color depths

> ‣ Multiple transparent colors

> ‣ Interlacing

> ‣ Multiple file compression options

> ‣ Cross-platform support

PNG features include features from both the GIF and JPEG feature sets, and some features that are unique to PNG. For example, only PNG can support the 8-, 24-, and 32-bit color depths. Also, PNG files store data about the platform on which they are developed. The Gamma setting, which is a measure of display brightness, is different for Windows and Macintosh computers. The Gamma data stored in PNG files enables browsers to compensate for these differences so images appear more consistently between different platforms.

One downside to PNG images is that they can be slightly larger than similar JPEG files. Depending on your design requirements, however, the additional benefits of PNG can be worth the cost in file size.

### Usage Guidelines

At the time of this writing, using the PNG format is a little risky because only the following browsers support PNG images:

> ‣ Netscape Navigator (4.1 and later)

> ‣ SPRYNET Mosaic

> ‣ WinCIM CompuServe (2.01 and later)

> ‣ Microsoft Internet Explorer (4.0b1 and later)

If your Web page visitor is using a browser that doesn't recognize PNG images, the user must install a plug-in that supports PNG images or all your hard work is unavailable. The solutions to this problem are to:

▸ Avoid using PNG images until enough of your Web audience upgrades to browsers that support PNG.

▸ Create alternate sites for Web visitors that use PNG-aware browsers.

▸ Cater to the Netscape browsers, which support an additional ⟨IMG⟩ tag attribute that enables you to specify an alternate image file.

The second option is not very practical because it requires so much additional effort. If you know that most of your Web page visitors use Netscape Navigator 1.1 or later, the third option is worth considering.

The ⟨IMG⟩ tag attribute that enables you to specify an alternate file is LOWSRC, and it is a Netscape extension that is not part of the HTML specifications. The original intent of this attribute was to specify a low-quality image that would quickly appear and display in the browser until a higher-quality image replaces it.

To support multiple files with the LOWSRC attribute, enter an image tag similar to the following:

```
<IMG LOWSRC="image.jpg"SRC="image.png"HEIGHT=500 WIDTH=500
ALT="picture">
```

When a Navigator browser attempts to display this image, it first loads the image specified by the LOWSRC attribute. Next, it attempts to display the image specified by the SRC attribute. If the browser supports PNG files, the PNG file appears in place of the LOWSRC file. If the browser doesn't support PNG files, the LOWSRC file remains on display in the browser.

 **Exercise 8.3: If you're preparing to take the certification exam, or if you want to practice what you learned in this section, turn to the end of this chapter and complete Exercise 8.3. When you are done, continue reading here to prepare for the next exercise.**

## Introduction to Adobe Photoshop

During the rest of this chapter, you'll learn to create GIF and JPEG images using Adobe Photoshop, which is an excellent image-editing program that supports many bitmap image formats (including the GIF, JPEG, and PNG formats). One of the prerequisites for Novell Education Course 660 is a familiarity with Adobe Photoshop. If you aren't already familiar with Photoshop, this section will help you get acquainted.

The CD-ROM included with this book provides a trial version of Adobe Photoshop. For instructions on installing Photoshop, refer to Appendix C.

## STARTING PHOTOSHOP

After Photoshop is installed, start the program as you would any other Windows program. In Windows 3.1, open the program group for Adobe Photoshop and double-click the program icon. In Windows 95 and Windows NT, select Start→ Programs→Adobe→Photoshop→Adobe Photoshop. After Photoshop starts, it displays a window and tool palettes similar to those shown in Figure 8.11.

FIGURE 8.11

*Adobe Photoshop Window and Tool Palettes*

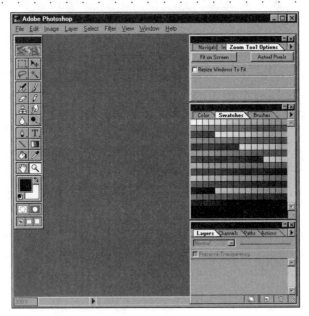

## OPENING IMAGE FILES IN PHOTOSHOP

After you start Photoshop, you can open existing images or create new images. To open an existing image, select File→Open, and use the Open dialog box to choose a file.

To begin a new image in Photoshop, do the following:

**1** • Start Photoshop and select File→New. The New dialog box appears.

**2** • Define your new image as follows:

▸ Specify a filename in the Name text box.

▸ In the Image Size area, specify a width, height, and resolution for the image.

▸ In the Mode drop-down list, select RGB Color. (You'll learn more about this in the next section.)

▸ In the Contents area, select a white image background, the background color currently selected in the tool palette, or a transparent background.

**3** • Click OK.

After you click OK, Photoshop displays an image-editing window that uses the dimensions you specified.

To edit an image, use the tools in the tool palette. Some of these tools are similar to tools you have probably used in other image-editing programs, such as the Paint program provided with Windows. For more information on using the Photoshop tools, see the product documentation.

## CHOOSING A PHOTOSHOP COLOR MODE

Photoshop supports many different color modes, each of which is designed to produce colored images for specific types of media format. For example, there is a *grayscale* mode for creating images without colors, the *RGB color* mode is for creating 32-bit color images, and the *indexed color* mode is for creating 8-bit (or less) color images that use palettes. If you've read the preceding pages in this chapter, you should be able to guess which modes are used for JPEG, PNG, and GIF images. The following sections provide additional information on the RGB and indexed color modes, and describe when to use them.

### RGB Color Mode

Typically, you begin new Web images in Photoshop using RGB color mode, which enables you to create 24- and 32-bit color images. As with the HTML color tags you learned about in Chapter 2, the RGB color mode defines colors by specifying the amounts of red, green, and blue to display. The maximum values for red, green, and blue create white, while the minimum values create black. The RGB approach to defining colors is the same approach used for displaying color on computer monitors and televisions.

Unlike HTML, Photoshop uses a decimal-numbering system to select the values of the red, green, and blue color components. Earlier in this chapter, Table 8.2 showed the browser-safe color values in both hexadecimal and decimal formats. Both formats specify binary color values, they just specify the values using different numbering systems. Fortunately, you'll usually select Photoshop colors from a palette or color-picker dialog box. However, you'll want to know the browser-safe color values in Table 8.2 because these values are displayed in Photoshop and give you an instant indication of whether or not the color you have selected is browser-safe.

To create JPEG and PNG images, you should use the RGB color mode. Although you can convert GIF images to the JPEG and PNG formats, this creates larger image files. This is not worthwhile, however, unless you plan to enhance the images with 24-bit or 32-bit color.

### Indexed Color Mode

The indexed color mode can be used to create 1- to 8-bit color images. In this mode, your color choice is limited to the colors in the image color palette you select. You can choose from standard palettes, you can customize a standard palette, or you can create new palettes.

Because indexed color mode supports fewer colors, many of the Photoshop special effects, such as gradients, are disabled. This is because these special features use many of those 16.7 million colors to create different types of transitions between image colors. Because indexed color mode doesn't support 16.7 million colors, these special effects are disabled. For these reasons, Photoshop does not permit you to create a new document in indexed color mode. You must start with another mode (such as RGB), and then switch to indexed color mode.

Photoshop enables you to export RGB color mode images to GIF images and to save indexed color mode images as GIF images. Because RGB color mode creates images with more color data than GIF files support, you cannot directly save RGB color mode images to GIF files. You must either export the image, or convert to indexed color mode and save the file.

When you want to create a GIF image, the choice of color modes is yours. If you want to use only browser safe colors, you can switch to indexed color mode and select the Web palette provided with Photoshop. The Web palette contains only browser-safe colors and any color you choose is automatically converted to a browser-safe color. The next section describes how to switch to indexed color mode and select the Web palette.

If you want to give yourself the maximum number of features when creating images, you can choose the RGB color mode and plan to later export or convert the image. It is still easy to select browser-safe colors because Photoshop provides a feature called *swatches*, which enable you to pick colors from colored squares in a color table. Although the swatches might appear in a palette, RGB color mode images are not restricted to the colors in the swatches palette.

**TIP**

**Although RGB color mode gives you more options, it also gives you more responsibility. If you decide to use special effects that require more than 256 colors, test these effects before you spend days creating the perfect work of art. You might find that the effect does not convert well to GIF, or the lower-image quality after conversion is acceptable, or that you can reduce the image degradation by using dithering when you save the GIF file.**

## SWITCHING TO INDEXED COLOR MODE

When you are working with Web images, there are two reasons for switching color modes to indexed color mode. The first reason is to create a new GIF image; and the second is to convert an existing image so that it can be saved as a GIF image. The procedures for switching and converting are virtually identical. The difference is the color palette you select.

When you switch to indexed color mode before you add any content to the image, I recommend that you select the Web palette provided with Photoshop 4.0. This palette supports only the 216 browser-safe colors, so your image colors will be consistent in Windows and Macintosh browsers. If you are designing an image for just one of these platforms, you can select System (Windows) palette or System (Macintosh) palette to support all 256 colors supported by that platform.

**If you are using an earlier version of Photoshop that does not include a Web palette, or if you are using a different image editor and need a Web palette, browse the following Web pages:**

`www.lynda.com/files`

`www.oit.itd.umich.edu/projects/DMS/answers/colorguide`

**Once you've located a Web palette file, which may be called an Internet color palette, you can install it by copying the file to the Color Palettes folder in the Photoshop folder on your computer.**

When you are converting an existing image to indexed color mode from any other color mode (such as RGB), the image contains existing colors that might or might not match the Web and System palettes. Photoshop provides two special palette selections for converting images and adapting to color mismatches. One of these palettes is the Exact palette, which you can only select when the image to be converted contains less than 256 colors. This palette setting automatically creates a custom palette for the image that includes all of the colors in the original image, whether they are browser safe or not.

The Adaptive palette setting is the palette setting to use when the original image contains more than 256 colors. This setting creates a custom-image palette using the original colors and a mathematical formula that calculates the best colors to use to minimize image quality degradation. As with the Exact palette setting, colors are chosen to optimize image quality and are not limited to browser-safe colors.

In most cases, you should use the Adaptive or Exact palettes when converting files to indexed color mode. These palettes don't change the browser display on 8-bit color computers because all colors are converted to the System palette colors anyway. However, when these GIF images are displayed on 24-bit color computers, the image quality is greatly enhanced because it uses the optimized colors in the color palette instead of the System palette colors.

To switch or convert an image to indexed color mode, do the following:

**1** • Start Photoshop and open the file you want to change. If you are converting an image with more than 256 colors, or more colors than are supported by the bit depth you plan to select, Photoshop will delete colors from the image, and this can cause important image details to disappear. The next step enables you to select colors you want to keep during the conversion.

**2** • To specify areas that contain colors you want to keep, use the Marquee tool to select the areas (see Figure 8.12). To select more than one area, press the shift key while you select additional areas.

*Multiple Selected Areas*

**3** • Select Image → Mode → indexed color. Photoshop displays the indexed color dialog box shown in Figure 8.13.

**NOTE**

**If Photoshop prompts you to "Flatten Layers," you will have to flatten the layers before switching modes. Layers store different parts of your image so you can edit and move these parts independently of the others. When you flatten layers, you combine the information in all layers into a single layer. If you want to preserve multiple layers, save the file in Photoshop format before you switch modes. When you are ready to switch modes, click OK.**

FIGURE   8.13

*Indexed Color Dialog Box*

**4** • In the Palette drop-down list, choose the palette for the converted image. For best results, choose Web for new images and Adaptive for converted images.

**5** • In the Color Depth drop-down list, select a color depth.

If you previously chose the Web palette, the color depth is set to Other, and the number of colors is set to 216. You should use this setting. Later in this chapter, you'll learn how to reduce the number of colors (and the file size) after you have finished creating your image.

If you previously chose Adaptive, you can select any bit depth. To maximize the image quality (and the file size), choose 8 bits/pixel. To reduce the file size (and possibly the image quality), choose a lower bit depth.

**6** • Read the value in the Colors text box to verify that Photoshop is converting the image the way you want. The value in this text box is determined by the palette and bit depth you select. If this value is wrong, check your other settings. You should not need to change this value.

**7** • In the Dither drop-down list, select the Dither option you want to use. To prevent dithering, select None. Pattern-based dithering creates an obvious pattern of dithered pixels. Diffusion dithering dithers the image in such a way that it prevents noticeable patterns.

**8** • Click OK.

After you click OK, Photoshop converts the image to indexed color mode and displays the image as it would appear on computers that use the same number of colors as yours.

**WARNING**

**If you have just converted an image, you have two very important options that you will lose if you are not careful. Remember that, in most cases, image information (and quality) is lost when you convert an image to indexed color mode. To undo your conversion and keep the original file unmodified, you can select Edit→Undo Mode Change. To keep the original file intact for future editing or conversions, save a copy of the converted file by choosing File→Save As.**

The next section describes the file formats that Photoshop supports.

## CHOOSING A PHOTOSHOP FILE FORMAT

When you create a new document in Photoshop, as described earlier in this chapter, the default file format is the Photoshop document format, which creates files with the PSD extension. To convert a file to a Web image format, or any other format, choose File→Save As. You can also save copies of a PSD document using the File→Save a Copy and File→Export commands. You can use Photoshop to save image files using the following formats:

- CompuServe GIF (GIF)

- JPEG (JPE or JPEG)

- PCX (PCX)

- Photoshop Encapsulated Postscript (EPS)

- PICT (PCT or PIC)

- PNG (PNG)

- Raw (RAW)

- Targa (TGA, VDA, ICB, or VST)

> ▸ Tagged Image File Format (TIF)

> ▸ Windows Bitmap (BMP or RLE)

You can export Photoshop images to the following formats:

> ▸ GIF89a (GIF)

> ▸ Adobe Illustrator EPS (AI, AI3, AI4, AI5, or AI6)

Remember that you cannot save images in RGB color mode directly to GIF, though you can export images to GIF. You must first convert them to indexed color mode.

Conversely, you cannot save images from indexed color mode directly to JPEG. Instead, you must first convert the image to RGB color mode as described later in this chapter.

When you create images in RGB color mode, you should consider keeping copies of both the original RGB color image in PSD format and the saved Web image document. Often, the color and compression options you choose for a Web image file result in lost image quality, which you cannot replace. If you create and edit your images in the PSD format, you can save several Web images with different settings, and you can save the image to other file formats. This can be useful when you want to use one of your favorite Web images as a Windows wallpaper or screen saver image.

## CREATING IMAGE OBJECTS IN PHOTOSHOP

If you are accustomed to creating images with rectangle and oval tools in other image-editing programs, you might be a little dismayed to find these tools missing from the Photoshop tools menu. However, there are ways to create these shapes with other tools.

For example, you can use the Marquee tool to select rectangular and oval areas, and then you can use the Paint Bucket tool to fill these selected areas with color. You can also use the Lasso and Polygon Lasso tools to select irregular shaped areas, and then you can fill these areas with the Paint Bucket tool.

A complete discussion of this topic is beyond the scope of this book. However, you can get more information on these tools and their use from the Photoshop documentation.

### DISABLING ANTI-ALIASING

Anti-aliasing, which was introduced earlier in the section about halos, adds additional colors to an image to visually soften the jagged edges of bitmap image objects. Anti-aliased edges provide a nice aesthetic touch to many images, but there are times when you'll want to disable anti-aliasing for the following reasons:

▸ Anti-aliasing adds additional colors to the image, which creates larger files if the image is converted from RGB color mode to indexed color mode. (Anti-aliasing is disabled in indexed color mode.)

▸ Anti-aliasing can cause halos to appear between foreground and background images when transparent colors are used.

Some Photoshop tools, such as the Lasso, Text, and some Marquee tools, let you enable or disable anti-aliasing when you use them. A complete discussion of how to use these tools is beyond the scope of this chapter, but Figure 8.14 shows the checkbox that lets you enable or disable anti-aliasing for the Lasso tool. Check the checkbox to enable anti-aliasing, clear the checkbox to disable it. You'll learn more about anti-aliasing with the Text tool in Chapter 10. For more information on using the Lasso and Marquee tools, refer to the Photoshop product documentation.

FIGURE 8.14

*Lasso Tool Options*

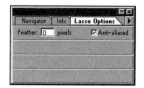

### LOADING AND CHOOSING WEB COLOR SWATCHES

Adobe Photoshop provides two palettes for selecting colors for your images: the Color Picker and Swatches (Figure 8.15). The Color Picker enables you to select any color by clicking in the Foreground Color area, or by entering numerical color values in the window. The advantage of the Color Picker is that you can choose any color, the disadvantage is that you can easily select a color that isn't browser safe.

Color swatches are colored squares that appear in the Swatches palette. You can think of this palette as a storage area for the colors you prefer to use. If you create or load a swatches palette that contains only browser-safe colors, you will have a safe place from which to choose colors for your Web graphics.

The following sections describe how to load a browser-safe swatches palette and how to select colors from the palette after it is loaded.

**FIGURE 8.15**

*Photoshop Color Picker and Swatches Palette*

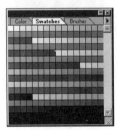

### Loading a Browser-Safe Swatch Palette

The default Swatches palette in Photoshop contains 122 colors and is not browser safe. Before you begin creating Web images, you should locate and load a browser-safe swatches palette as follows:

I • Download a browser-safe swatches palette from the Web. To find browser-safe swatches palettes, use an Internet search engine, or use the Web site in the following paragraph.

**You can get a browser-safe swatches palette by downloading the BCLUT2.ACO file from** www.lynda.com. **This palette contains the 216 browser-safe colors.**

**2** • Store the browser-safe swatches palette in the Palettes folder for Adobe Photoshop (default: *d*:\Adobe\Photoshop\Palettes).

**3** • Start Photoshop, and if the Swatches palette is not visible, select Windows → Show Swatches.

**4** • Click the arrow to the right of the tabs in the Swatches palette, and then select Replace Swatches from the menu that appears.

**5** • When the Load dialog box appears, use this dialog box to locate and select the swatches palette file you downloaded from the Internet.

After you load the Swatches palette, Photoshop uses those swatches until you change them. For information on editing the Swatches palette or appending additional palettes to it, see the Photoshop documentation.

### Selecting Browser-Safe Colors

After you load a browser-safe swatches palette, selecting browser-safe foreground color is as easy as clicking a color in the Swatches palette. If the Swatches palette is not visible, select Windows → Show Swatches, and then select your color.

**To verify that the colors in the Swatches palette are truly browser safe, you can use the Color Picker. To open the Color Picker, click the foreground color square in the tools palette. To see if a color is browser safe, click the color in the Swatches palette and read the R, G, and B settings in the Color Picker. The color is browser safe if all three of these settings use one of the following values: 0, 51, 102, 153, 204, 255 (these are multiples of 51).**

**Exercise 8.4: If you're preparing to take the certification exam, or if you want to practice what you learned in this section, turn to the end of this chapter and complete Exercise 8.4. When you are done, continue reading here to prepare for the next exercise.**

## Optimizing Images (All Formats)

There are some optimizing techniques that apply to all images, regardless of the image format you use. The following sections describe how to reduce or crop an image size with Photoshop, how to speed up image display by specifying image dimensions, and how to use a small image file as a temporary placeholder for a larger, higher-quality image.

### CROPPING IMAGES

When you crop an image, you select a portion of an image to keep, and you discard the rest. Cropping reduces the size of any image, and therefore reduces the time it takes to download. When an image file is too large, consider cropping the image to remove any unnecessary information.

To crop an image in Photoshop, do the following:

1 • In the Tools palette, click and hold the Marquee tool until the additional tools appear, and then select the Crop tool (see Figure 8.16).

Crop tool

FIGURE 8.16

*Photoshop Cropping Tool*

2 • Click and drag the Crop tool over the image to select the image area to keep.

**3** • Press Enter to crop the image.

After you crop the image, the image area is reduced to the size you selected. To undo a crop, select Edit→Undo Crop.

## DISPLAYING ALTERNATE IMAGES

When a Web page contains images that are large or use many colors, the Web page can take a long time to download. One way to improve the download speed for a Web page is to display a temporary image that downloads quickly, and then replace the temporary image later with a higher-quality image. This feature is supported only in Netscape browsers, but it can produce an animated effect as the first image is replaced by the second. To load two images in this manner, add the LOWSRC attribute to the <IMG> tag as follows:

```
<IMG LOWSRC="image.gif" SRC="image.jpg" HEIGHT=500 WIDTH=500
ALT="picture">
```

When a Navigator browser attempts to display this image, it first loads the image specified by the LOWSRC attribute. Next, it attempts to display the image specified by the SRC attribute. If the Web page viewer is using a browser other than Navigator, the LOWSRC attribute is ignored and the browser displays only the image specified by the SRC attribute.

## SPECIFYING IMAGE DIMENSIONS

Earlier in this chapter, I explained that Web pages appear faster when you include the HEIGHT and WIDTH attributes in your image tags. For example:

```
<IMG SRC="image.gif" HEIGHT=25 WIDTH=25>
```

Many HTML editors automatically create these tags and attributes when you use them to place an image on a Web page. If you are manually entering your image tags, you can look up the image dimensions in Photoshop by opening the image file and selecting Image→Image Size. After you select this command, Photoshop displays a dialog box that includes the pixel dimensions of your image.

## Creating and Optimizing GIF Images

Earlier in this chapter, I introduced the following ways to improve the display performance of GIF images:

- Reduce the image file size

- Speed up the image display using interlacing

I also introduced transparent colors, which you can use to create irregular-shaped foreground images. Now that you know more about using Photoshop, the following sections will show you how to use Photoshop to create GIF images, how to optimize GIF images for Web pages, and how to select transparent colors.

### CREATING GIF IMAGES

There are so many ways to create GIF images using Photoshop that getting started can be confusing. The following procedure summarizes the tasks you need to complete and references the other sections of this chapter that describe how to complete each of these tasks.

To create a GIF image with Photoshop, do the following:

1 • Start Photoshop and open a new image file in RGB color mode as described earlier in this chapter.

2 • If you want to use special effects, such as gradients, blurs, and anti-aliasing, do the following:

a. Create your image in RGB color mode using the browser-safe color swatches wherever possible. The procedure for selecting browser-safe color swatches was described earlier in the chapter.

b. If you need to specify transparent colors for the image, switch to indexed color mode as described earlier in this chapter.

c. Export the image to a GIF file as described later in this chapter. If you do not need to specify transparent colors, you can export the image from RGB color mode as described in the "Exporting GIF Images from RGB Color Mode" section. Otherwise, export the image from Indexed color mode as described in "Choosing Transparent Colors" section.

**3** • If you want to minimize your opportunities to use colors that are not browser safe, do the following:

a. Switch to indexed color mode, as described earlier in this chapter.

b. Create your image in indexed color mode using the browser-safe color swatches. The procedure for selecting browser-safe color swatches was described previously in this chapter.

c. Export the image to a GIF file as described in the "Choosing Transparent Colors" section of this chapter.

After you export the GIF image, the file is ready to use on your Web pages.

## REDUCING IMAGE FILE SIZE

After you create a GIF image, the only ways to further reduce the size of the image file are to crop the image (as described previously) and to reduce the number of colors in the color palette. The following are three ways to reduce colors with Photoshop:

▸ Specify a bit depth less than 8-bit when you convert an image to indexed color mode. (See "Switching to Indexed Color Mode", earlier in this chapter.)

▸ Convert an indexed color mode image to RGB color mode, and then convert back to Indexed Color mode with a lower bit depth setting.

▸ Specify fewer colors when you export an image from RGB color mode to GIF format.

To give you an idea of how reducing the number of colors reduces the file size, Table 8.3 lists the file sizes for a sample photograph that I exported to a variety of bit depths. The image size was about 3.5 × 5 inches at 72 dpi.

TABLE 8.3

*Sample File Sizes for*
*a GIF Image*

| BIT DEPTH | COLORS | NONINTERLACED FILE SIZE | INTERLACED FILE SIZE |
|-----------|--------|-------------------------|----------------------|
| 3-bit | 8 | 19K | 19K |
| 4-bit | 16 | 23K | 25K |
| 5-bit | 32 | 29K | 31K |
| 6-bit | 64 | 37K | 40K |
| 7-bit | 128 | 46K | 50K |
| 8-bit | 256 | 59K | 63K |

The following sections explain how to reduce color depth using the RGB color mode conversion and export methods.

### Converting to RGB Color Mode and Back

Converting to RGB color mode from indexed color mode is easy because RGB color mode supports all of the indexed color mode features and more. To convert to RGB color mode, simply select Image → Mode → RGB Color. The conversion is almost instantaneous.

To complete the color reduction, convert back to indexed color mode as described earlier in "Switching to Indexed Color Mode." Because the image has already been reduced to 256 colors or less, the default palette will be the Exact palette. To reduce the color depth, select the Adaptive palette, and then select a new color depth.

### Exporting GIF Images from RGB Color Mode

Photoshop enables you to export GIF images from both RGB color mode images and indexed color mode images; however, you can only reduce the color depth when you export from RGB color mode. When you export a GIF image from RGB color mode, Photoshop lets you define a bit depth for the exported image and enable or disable interlacing.

To reduce image colors while exporting a GIF image, do the following:

**1** • If the image is not in RGB Color mode, switch to RGB color mode as described in the previous section.

**2** • Select File → Export → GIF89a Export. When you export from RGB color mode, Photoshop displays the dialog box shown in Figure 8.17.

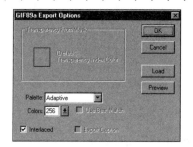

F I G U R E   8.17

*Export Dialog in RGB Color Mode*

**3** • In the Palette drop-down list, choose the Adaptive palette. If the Exact palette is selected, the image already contains fewer than 256 colors; however, you can reduce the number of colors further if you select the Adaptive palette.

**4** • In the Colors drop-down list, select the number of colors for the exported image.

**5** • To preview how your image will appear with the reduced number of colors, click Preview, and then click OK when you are done.

**6** • To enable or disable interlacing in the exported GIF, check or clear the Interlaced checkbox.

**7** • Click OK. Photoshop displays a dialog box for saving files.

**8** • Select a folder and a name for the exported file, and then click Save.

After you export the GIF image, you can use it in your Web pages or open it with Photoshop to make additional changes. If you need to specify transparent colors for the image, you can do so by opening the image file and exporting the image from indexed color mode as described later in this chapter.

### CREATING INTERLACED GIFS

Interlaced GIFs, which are introduced in Chapter 3 and illustrated in Figure 8.4, are created when you export a GIF image. To enable or disable interlacing, check or clear the Interlaced checkbox. For instructions on exporting GIFs, see "Exporting GIF Images from RGB Color Mode," which appears earlier in this chapter, or refer to the next section, which describes how to export GIF images from indexed color mode.

### CHOOSING TRANSPARENT COLORS

As with Interlacing, you enable the transparent color feature for GIFs when you export them. Photoshop enables you to select multiple transparent colors; however, you must export GIF images from indexed color mode to display the dialog box that lets you select transparent colors.

To choose transparent colors for an image, do the following:

1 • If you have not yet switched to indexed color mode, switch to indexed color mode now. The procedure for this is described earlier in this chapter.

2 • Select File → Export → GIF89a Export. Photoshop displays the dialog box shown in Figure 8.18. If you export from RGB color mode, Photoshop displays a similar dialog box without the color palette.

3 • Use the eyedropper to click the colors you want to make transparent.

You can click colors in the image or in the color palette below the image. After you select a color as transparent, a black border appears around the color in the palette and all image-preview areas that use that color change to gray. If you make a mistake, click Cancel to return to the original image.

FIGURE 8.18

*Export Dialog Box in Indexed Color Mode*

4 • To enable or disable interlacing in the exported GIF, check or clear the Interlace checkbox.

5 • Click OK. Photoshop displays a dialog box for saving files.

6 • Select a folder and a name for the exported file, and then click Save.

After you export the GIF image, you can use it in your Web pages or open it with Photoshop to make additional changes.

## Converting Other Image Formats to GIF

If you have a favorite image in another file format, chances are good that you can convert that image to a GIF image. Even when the image is already in JPEG or PNG format, you might want to convert it to GIF to take advantage of GIF features, such as small file size, transparency, and animation.

Photoshop recognizes many popular image formats including the vector-based format used by Adobe Illustrator. Photoshop can also directly import images from TWAIN-compliant scanners. If you can open the image with Photoshop, you can export it to GIF.

**NOTE**

**For more information on vector-based art, see the sidebar titled "Computer Graphic Types." For more information on Photoshop's capability to work with scanners, see the Photoshop documentation.**

To convert an image file to GIF with Photoshop, do the following:

**1** • Select File → Open, and use the Open dialog box to locate and open the image file. Be sure All Formats is selected in the Files of Type drop-down list.

**2** • If you need to specify transparent colors for the image, switch to indexed color mode as described previously in this chapter.

**3** • Export the image to a GIF file as described earlier in this chapter. If you do not need to specify transparent colors, you can export the image from RGB Color mode as described in "Exporting GIF Images from RGB Color Mode." Otherwise, export the image from indexed color mode as described in "Choosing Transparent Colors."

**Exercise 8.5: If you're preparing to take the certification exam, or if you want to practice what you learned in this section, turn to the end of this chapter and complete Exercise 8.5. When you are done, continue reading here to prepare for the next exercise.**

## COMPUTER GRAPHIC TYPES

When you start creating images for Web pages, you can choose between two types of graphics programs: bitmap programs and vector-graphics graphics programs. Although all Web images must eventually be saved as bitmap graphics, it is common to create images using some other program type, and then convert the image to a bitmap later. The following sections introduce bitmap, and vector, graphics.

### Bitmap Graphics

When you create a bitmap image, you can add text, shapes, and colors; however, as soon as you add something to the image, it becomes part of the entire image. For example, if I add the word *Hello* to a scanned photograph, the word becomes part of the image, just as if I had painted it on the photograph. Now, because the word is part of the image, the only way to remove the word is to paint something over it, or erase it and fill the void with something else.

The *paint* approach to building images is the important difference between bitmap graphics and vector graphics. Some programs, such as Adobe Photoshop, enable you to paint your image in layers, which makes it easy to remove something by removing its layer. However, layered images are still created by painting images on the layers. The next section describes how vector graphics are different.

### Vector Graphics

Vector-graphics programs store image data as a collection of objects. As with bitmapped graphics, you can add text and shapes. The difference is that after a text or shape is added to the image, it remains an independent object. Each object can be selected independently of the others and modified using any of the tools provided by the vector-graphics program. For example, you could draw a circle with a vector-graphics program and later resize, recolor, or delete the circle without affecting the appearance of any other objects.

The advantage of using vector-graphics images is that they can be easier to create and update. For some people, it is much easier to build art with the shapes tools and more comforting to know that the shapes can be modified later. Of course, there are disadvantages to vector-graphics programs. For example, bitmap graphics programs enable you to erase part of a circle. With vector-graphic programs, you can't erase part of a circle. Instead, you have to use another shape to hide what you don't want visible.

Another advantage of vector graphics is that they are *resolution independent*. Although vector-graphics images are stored as objects instead of dots, they are always converted to bitmaps when displayed or printed. The object nature of the file data, however, enables the same file to be used to display an image at 72 dpi on a monitor or 600 dpi on a laser printer. With bitmaps, you need to create two separate images to get optimal display on both a monitor and a printer.

In the end, any Web graphics that you create must be converted to bitmaps. If you prefer to use vector-graphics programs, however, you can use a program, such as Adobe Illustrator, to create your vector graphics. You can then use a bitmap image editor, such as Adobe Photoshop, to convert your image.

When you convert a vector-graphics program with Photoshop, the process is called *rasterizing*. Rasterizing paints a bitmap image into computer memory using the object commands stored in the original vector-graphics file. When the bitmap is complete, it is saved to a file that can be edited by bitmap editors, such as Photoshop. Photoshop enables you to save bitmaps to all three Web image formats.

## Creating and Optimizing JPEG Images

Creating a JPEG image with Photoshop is easier than creating a GIF because you don't have to convert to indexed color mode or export the image. You can create JPEG images in RGB color mode and save them with varying levels of image quality and compression. You can also save JPEG images in the progressive format, which produces an interlaced image. The following procedure summarizes the tasks for creating JPEG images and references other sections of this chapter that describe how to complete each of these tasks.

To create a JPEG image with Photoshop, do the following:

**1** • Start Photoshop and open a new image file in RGB color mode as described earlier in this chapter.

**2** • Create your image in RGB color mode using the browser-safe color swatches wherever possible. The procedure for selecting browser-safe color swatches was described previously in this chapter.

**3** • To preserve the Photoshop layers in your original image and create a JPEG version of the file, do the following:

    a. Save the original image as a Photoshop document file with the PSD extension. Layers store different parts of your image so you can edit and move these parts independently of the others. The JPEG format does not support layers. If you save the original layers, you can edit them later and create a new JPEG image from that file.

    b. Select File → Save A Copy. Photoshop displays the Save a Copy dialog box, which permits you to enter a file name for the new file and select a folder in which to store it.

    c. Skip Step 4 and continue with Step 5.

**4** • To convert your original image to a JPEG image, do the following:

    a. Select Layer → Flatten Image. Layers store different parts of your image so you can edit and move these parts independently of the others. The JPEG format does not support layers. This step removes the layers so you can save the image in other formats.

b. Select File→Save As. Photoshop displays the Save As dialog box, which enables you to enter a file name for the new file and select a folder in which to store it.

**5** • Complete the Save dialog box as follows:

a. In the Save As drop-down list, select the JPEG format.

b. Enter a filename with the JPG extension, select a folder for the file, and click Save. Photoshop displays the JPEG Options dialog box shown in Figure 8.19.

**6** • To choose the levels of image quality and compression you want to use, click and drag the triangle in the Image Options area.

**7** • To create an interlaced JPEG, click the Progressive Format radio button and select the number of scans used to display the image.

**8** • Click OK.

After you click OK, the file is ready to use on your Web pages.

▶ . . . . . . . . . . . . . . . . . . . . . . . . . . . . . . . . . . . . ◀

**F I G U R E   8.19**

*JPEG Options Dialog Box*

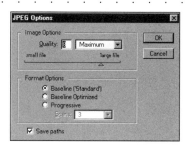

## Converting Other Images to JPEG

If you have a favorite image in another file format, chances are good that you can convert that image to a JPEG image. Photoshop recognizes many popular image formats, including the vector-based format used by Adobe Illustrator. Photoshop can also directly import images from TWAIN-compliant scanners. If you can open the image with Photoshop, you can convert it to JPEG format.

**NOTE** Remember that the JPEG format is best used for scanned photographs and other images that use millions of colors. When you are converting image files, be sure to convert them to the correct format. Converting line art images with less than 256 colors (such as GIF images) can create oversized files that display poorly.

**NOTE** For more information on vector-based art, see the sidebar titled "Computer Graphic Types." For more information on Photoshop's capability to work with scanners, see the Photoshop documentation.

To convert an image file to JPEG format with Photoshop, do the following:

**1** • Select File → Open, and use the Open dialog box to locate and open the image file. Be sure All Formats is selected in the Files of Type drop-down list.

**2** • If the image is a GIF image, switch to RGB color mode as described earlier in this chapter.

**3** • Save the file in JPEG format as described in the previous section.

## Guidelines for Creating Rules, Bullets, and Buttons

Now that you know how to create Web images, you can design your own rules, bullets, and buttons for your Web pages. After you create these images, just use the HTML <IMG> tag to insert them where you want them in Web pages. Figure 8.20 shows some sample rules, bullets, and buttons.

*Rules, Bullets, and Buttons*

The following are some tips for using images as rules, bullets, and buttons:

- ▸ Rules made up of vertical and horizontal lines do not require anti-aliasing.

- ▸ The edges of square and rectangular buttons and bullets do not require anti-aliasing.

- ▸ Keep the size of bullets small (preferably less than 25×25 pixels).

- ▸ Although buttons are typically larger than bullets, keeping the file size small will improve Web page performance.

- ▸ Use the background space around an image to establish Web page positioning. For example, you can use this technique to ensure consistent spacing between a bullet image and the text that follows it.

- ▸ You can use transparent colors to hide the background colors and halo pixels of irregularly shaped rules, bullets, and buttons.

- ▸ You can also match the image background to the Web page background color to create the appearance of irregularly shaped objects.

## Creating and Optimizing Background Graphics

Chapter 3 describes how to add background graphics to Web pages using the following HTML tags:

```
<BODY BACKGROUND="path/filename.ext">

<TABLE BACKGROUND="path/filename.ext">
```

To create background images, you can create GIF, JPEG, or PNG images using the guidelines provided earlier in this chapter. Before you create a background image, however, you should decide whether you want to create a full screen image or a tiling image. This section provides some background image examples and guidelines for designing background images.

A full screen background image is an image that is designed to appear only once on the Web page. Because the image does not repeat, a full-screen background image is sometimes called a *nontiling image*. Figure 8.21 shows an example of a full-screen background image.

**F I G U R E   8.21**

*Full-Screen
Background Image*

**Sample Page with Full-Size Background Image**

This page uses nested unordered lists to position text to the right of the vertical bar.
The background image uses less than 3 KB.

The advantage of the full-screen background image is that you have more design flexibility because you have more area to work with. As you might guess, the disadvantage is that the larger work area creates a larger file size, which slows the Web page's download time.

A tiling background image is one that is smaller than the Web page display area. Because the image is smaller, the browser automatically repeats or tiles the image across and down the Web page. Figure 8.22 shows an example of a tiling background image.

FIGURE 8.22

*Tiling Background Image*

**Sample Page with Tiling Background**

The 25x25 pixel background image uses less than 1 KB

Of course, the advantage of a tiling background is that it is smaller and downloads faster. Although the image is repeated, it only has to download once. Once the browser receives the downloaded file, the browser repeats the image in the background. Figure 8.23 shows a special application of a tiling image that creates a sidebar.

FIGURE 8.23

*Vertically Tiling Background Image*

**Sample Page with Vertical Tiling Background**

This page uses a table to position text to the right of the blue border.
The backgroud image uses less than 1 KB.

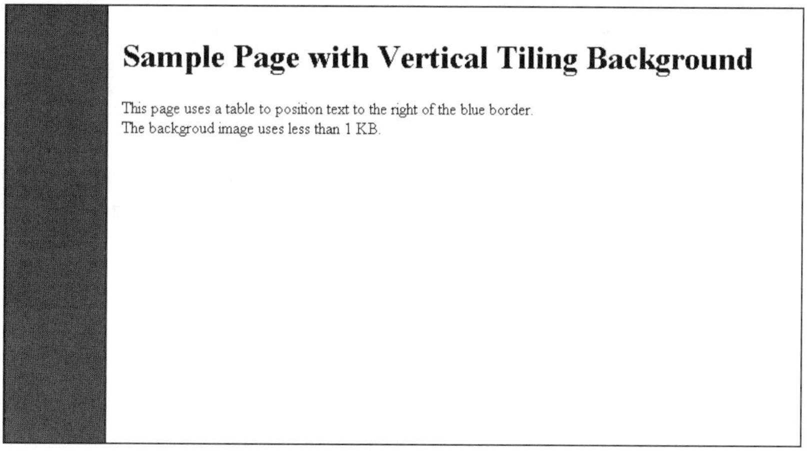

The background image in Figure 8.23 is so wide that it only tiles vertically. This enables the Web designer to divide the Web page into vertical areas and create some interesting visual effects.

When you are creating background images, consider the following guidelines:

▸ To present a smaller image as a full-screen image that won't tile, create a colored or transparent border that makes the full size of the image wider and taller than the Web page appears on most monitors. Because many pages use white backgrounds, a white border often appears transparent to the viewer.

▸ To prevent images from tiling horizontally, make the image width 1,000 pixels, which is wider than most monitors will display.

▸ To prevent images from tiling vertically, make the image height 1,200 pixels. Of course, if the total Web page length is longer, the image will tile.

▸ Tiling can produce a noticeable pattern that can be distracting. To minimize this, use light colors and avoid details and patterns near the image border that will be difficult to match to the other copies of the tiled image.

▸ Because 24-bit and 8-bit color images support a different number of colors, it can be difficult to coordinate foreground and background image colors if they use different color depths. Consider using the same file format and color depth for foreground and background images.

 **Exercise 8.6: If you're preparing to take the certification exam, or if you want to practice what you learned in this section, turn to the end of this chapter and complete Exercise 8.6.**

## Testing Your Web Images

After you create Web images that you hope will look great on displays that support 8-bit, 24-bit, or 32-bit color, how do you test them? You can view any Web image in the Netscape Navigator browser by selecting File → Open Page and selecting the image file just as you would a Web page file.

If you are creating your images on a computer that supports 24-bit or 32-bit color, the browser will display your images using these settings, and the images will look just the same as they did in Photoshop. To see how the images look in systems that support fewer colors, you need to view the images on a different system, or change the color depth system settings for your computer.

The following procedure describes how to change the color depth setting on Windows 95 and Windows NT 4.0 systems:

**1** • Select Start → Settings → Control Panel.

**2** • When the Control Panel window opens, double-click the Display control panel.

**3** • Click the Settings tab.

**4** • In the Color Palette drop-down list, select a new color depth.

**5** • Click OK.

**6** • If you are prompted to restart Windows, you must restart Windows to begin using the new color depth setting.

After you change the color depth setting for Windows, you can change it back at any time using the preceding procedure.

## Summary

This chapter describes the many issues that affect Web page images, and how to create images for the Web. Bitmap images are grids of pixels; a color value is assigned to each pixel. The size of a bitmap image file is determined by the number of pixels it contains and the number of colors that each pixel can have. Image file size is important because it determines how long it takes to download and display the image.

GIF images use a color palette to specify a set of colors to use. A browser-safe color palette is one that includes only the 216 colors that are provided by both the

Windows and Macintosh operating systems. When you create an image with a browser-safe palette, computers that support only 256 colors will display all of the colors in your image.

Good image design and construction skills can help you do the following:

- Keep file sizes small and download times quicker

- Correctly size images

- Use dithering to simulate colors or eliminate dithering when it is not wanted

- Avoid unwanted "noise" pixels in images

- Minimize image quality loss

- Ensure that colors appear consistently on different types of computers

- Use transparency or coordinated background colors to create the appearance of irregularly shaped objects and avoid "halos"

- Use anti-aliasing to smooth image object edges, or use aliasing to reduce the number of image colors and avoid halos

- Preview images at different brightness settings to see how images appear on Windows and Macintosh computers

The three Web image formats described in this chapter are GIF, JPEG, and PNG. Most browsers support GIF and JPEG images without plug-ins. The PNG image format was designed to overcome the shortcomings of the GIF and JPEG formats, but it is not widely supported at this time.

GIF images support animation, transparent colors, and interlacing, and are best used for line art and images with less than 256 colors.

JPEG images support 16.7 million colors, multiple levels of compression, and interlacing, though some browsers require plug-ins to display interlaced JPEGs. JPEG images are typically used to display photographs.

PNG images support up to 32-bit color depths, transparent colors, multiple levels of compression, and interlacing. To present PNG images with alternate images for Netscape Browsers, you can use the LOWSRC attribute in the <IMG> tag.

This chapter described how to create GIF and JPEG images with Adobe Photoshop. The Photoshop RGB color mode enables you to create images with millions of colors; but, you can limit your color selection to browser-safe colors by loading browser-safe color swatches and using these to color your images. You can create GIF or JPEG images in RGB color mode. The indexed color mode supports up to 256 colors and can be used to prepare GIF images.

All image formats download and display faster when you crop the image. To display a Web page faster, specify the image dimensions in your <IMG> tags with the HEIGHT and WIDTH attributes. To temporarily display lower-quality images before a higher-quality image loads, use the LOWSRC attribute in your <IMG> tags. The LOWSRC attribute only works with Netscape browsers.

You can create Web images that serve as rules, bullets, buttons, and background images. The basic rules for creating and optimizing these types of images are all the same, but this chapter does provide additional guidelines for creating these types of objects.

When you are done creating Web images, you can test them in your browser. If some of your Web audience will be using computers that support 256 colors or less, you might want to change your computer display settings to see how your images will appear on those systems.

## PUZZLE 8.1: CREATING AND ADAPTING WEB GRAPHICS

The following word puzzle contains many of the terms discussed in this chapter. See if you can find all the words. As you search for the words, ask yourself if you know why the word is in the list and how it was used in this chapter. If you don't know the answers to these questions, you might want to review the chapter.

```
L  G  I  F  B  Q  U  A  L  I  T  Y  P  E  S
A  G  T  H  P  A  R  G  O  T  O  H  P  S  E
M  I  M  A  G  E  C  A  L  R  E  T  N  I  H
I  N  D  E  X  E  D  K  P  N  G  D  D  O  C
C  O  L  O  R  J  P  E  G  C  T  I  E  N  T
E  V  I  S  S  E  R  G  O  R  P  W  S  O  A
D  A  O  L  N  W  O  D  A  O  O  P  I  D  W
A  L  I  A  S  E  D  N  K  P  J  U  G  E  S
X  P  H  O  T  O  S  H  O  P  C  K  N  D  P
E  L  C  O  M  P  R  E  S  S  I  O  N  D  A
H  T  M  L  A  N  I  M  A  T  I  O  N  E  L
N  B  G  R  E  H  T  I  D  N  Q  L  H  B  E
S  S  E  N  T  H  G  I  R  B  T  T  A  M  T
V  N  O  I  T  U  L  O  S  E  R  I  L  E  T
T  H  G  I  E  H  P  I  X  E  L  B  O  W  E
```

| | | | |
|---|---|---|---|
| aliased | design | indexed | progressive |
| animation | dither | interlace | quality |
| anti | download | JPEG | RGB |
| background | embedded | lookup | resolution |
| bit | GIF | noise | swatches |
| brightness | HTML | PNG | transparent |
| color | halo | palette | type |
| compression | height | photograph | width |
| crop | hexadecimal | photoshop | |
| decimal | image | pixel | |

## EXERCISE 8.1: UNDERSTANDING BITMAP IMAGES

The following questions test your understanding of bitmap images. To complete this exercise, answer the questions.

**1 •** List two names for the dots that make up a bitmap image.

a. . . . . . . . . . . . . . . . . . . . . . . . . . . . . . . . . . . . . . . . . . . . . .

b. . . . . . . . . . . . . . . . . . . . . . . . . . . . . . . . . . . . . . . . . . . . . .

**2 •** What is the generally accepted resolution for creating Web images?

Answer: . . . . . . . . . . . . . . . . . . . . . . . . . . . . . . . . . . . . . . . .

**3 •** What is the technical term that defines the number of colors supported by an image or computer display?

Answer: . . . . . . . . . . . . . . . . . . . . . . . . . . . . . . . . . . . . . . . .

**4 •** When an image uses 8 bits to define colors, how many colors can it display?

Answer: . . . . . . . . . . . . . . . . . . . . . . . . . . . . . . . . . . . . . . . .

**5 •** When an image uses 24 bits to define colors, how many colors can it display?

Answer: . . . . . . . . . . . . . . . . . . . . . . . . . . . . . . . . . . . . . . . .

**6 •** What is the maximum number of colors that a GIF image can display?

Answer: . . . . . . . . . . . . . . . . . . . . . . . . . . . . . . . . . . . . . . . .

**7 •** How many colors can a JPEG image display?

Answer: . . . . . . . . . . . . . . . . . . . . . . . . . . . . . . . . . . . . . . . .

**8** • What is a palette?

Answer: . . . . . . . . . . . . . . . . . . . . . . . . . . . . . . . . . . . . . . . . . . .

**9** • Do JPEG images use palettes?

Answer: . . . . . . . . . . . . . . . . . . . . . . . . . . . . . . . . . . . . . . . . . . .

**10** • How many colors are shared by both the Windows and Macintosh system palettes?

Answer: . . . . . . . . . . . . . . . . . . . . . . . . . . . . . . . . . . . . . . . . . . .

## EXERCISE 8.2: UNDERSTANDING WEB IMAGE PROBLEMS

This exercise tests your understanding of common Web image problems. To complete this exercise, answer the following questions.

**1** • List three ways to reduce the file size and download time for an image.

a. . . . . . . . . . . . . . . . . . . . . . . . . . . . . . . . . . . . . . . . . . . . . . .

b. . . . . . . . . . . . . . . . . . . . . . . . . . . . . . . . . . . . . . . . . . . . . . .

c. . . . . . . . . . . . . . . . . . . . . . . . . . . . . . . . . . . . . . . . . . . . . . .

**2** • How can you speed up the display of Web pages that include images?

Answer: . . . . . . . . . . . . . . . . . . . . . . . . . . . . . . . . . . . . . . . . . .

**3** • How does interlacing affect the display of an image?

Answer: . . . . . . . . . . . . . . . . . . . . . . . . . . . . . . . . . . . . . . . . . .

**4** • If an image appears much larger in the browser than you intended, what might be wrong?

Answer: . . . . . . . . . . . . . . . . . . . . . . . . . . . . . . . . . . . . . . . . . .

**5** • What is dithering?

Answer: . . . . . . . . . . . . . . . . . . . . . . . . . . . . . . . . . . . . . . . . . .

**6** • Which image format is affected by noise?

Answer: . . . . . . . . . . . . . . . . . . . . . . . . . . . . . . . . . . . . . . . . . .

**7** • What is one negative side effect of reducing colors?

Answer: . . . . . . . . . . . . . . . . . . . . . . . . . . . . . . . . . . . . . . . . . .

**8** • What causes halos?

Answer: . . . . . . . . . . . . . . . . . . . . . . . . . . . . . . . . . . . . . .

**9** • Aliased images display _____ edges and anti-aliased images display _____ edges.

**10** • What is the shape of all Web images?

Answer: . . . . . . . . . . . . . . . . . . . . . . . . . . . . . . . . . . . . . .

**11** • How can you create the illusion of an irregular shape without using transparent colors?

Answer: . . . . . . . . . . . . . . . . . . . . . . . . . . . . . . . . . . . . . .

**12** • Web images appear brighter on which types of computer displays?

Answer: . . . . . . . . . . . . . . . . . . . . . . . . . . . . . . . . . . . . . .

**EXERCISE 8.3: CHOOSING A WEB IMAGE FORMAT**

This exercise tests your understanding of the Web image formats introduced in this chapter. To complete this exercise, answer the following questions.

**1** • Which image format supports animation?

Answer: . . . . . . . . . . . . . . . . . . . . . . . . . . . . . . . . .

**2** • Which image formats support transparent colors?

Answer: . . . . . . . . . . . . . . . . . . . . . . . . . . . . . . . . .

**3** • What does streaming do?

Answer: . . . . . . . . . . . . . . . . . . . . . . . . . . . . . . . . .

**4** • Which image formats are supported by most browsers?

Answer: . . . . . . . . . . . . . . . . . . . . . . . . . . . . . . . . .

**5** • Why is JPEG a better format for displaying photographs?

Answer: . . . . . . . . . . . . . . . . . . . . . . . . . . . . . . . . .

**6** • When you increase the compression used for a JPEG image, what happens to the image quality?

Answer: . . . . . . . . . . . . . . . . . . . . . . . . . . . . . . . . .

**7** • What JPEG image format creates an interlaced image?

Answer: . . . . . . . . . . . . . . . . . . . . . . . . . . . . . . . . .

**8** • Which image format is designed to address the differences in display brightness on different computer systems?

Answer: . . . . . . . . . . . . . . . . . . . . . . . . . . . . . . . . .

**9** • Which image format requires a plug-in on most older browsers?

Answer: . . . . . . . . . . . . . . . . . . . . . . . . . . . . . . . . . . . . . .

**10** • Which browser supports the LOWSRC attribute, and why would you use this attribute with a PNG image?

Answer: . . . . . . . . . . . . . . . . . . . . . . . . . . . . . . . . . . . . . .

**EXERCISE 8.4: USING ADOBE PHOTOSHOP**

The following exercise gives you a chance to practice what you've learned about Adobe Photoshop. In this exercise, you'll use Photoshop to create a GIF image that includes aliased and anti-aliased objects. You'll create this image using a browser-safe color palette, and you'll view the results in a browser window. To complete this exercise, do the following:

1 • If you have not yet installed Adobe Photoshop, install it now as described in Appendix D.

2 • Connect your browser to the Internet and download the browser-safe color swatches, BCLUT2.ACO, from www.lynda.com.

3 • Start Photoshop and create a new image in RGB color mode that is 500 pixels wide, 250 pixels tall, and uses the correct resolution for Web page images.

4 • Replace the Photoshop default swatches with the browser-safe color swatches.

5 • Display the Color Picker and Swatches palette.

6 • Click a color in the Swatches palette and read the R, G, and B values in the Color Picker window.

7 • Write down the six decimal values that are used to create all of the colors in the browser-safe palette. You will have to click several different color swatches to find them all.

a. . . . . . . . . . . . . . . . . . . . . . . . . . . . . . . . . . . . . .

b. . . . . . . . . . . . . . . . . . . . . . . . . . . . . . . . . . . . . .

c. . . . . . . . . . . . . . . . . . . . . . . . . . . . . . . . . . . . . .

d. . . . . . . . . . . . . . . . . . . . . . . . . . . . . . . . . . . . . .

e. . . . . . . . . . . . . . . . . . . . . . . . . . . . . . . . . . . . .

f. . . . . . . . . . . . . . . . . . . . . . . . . . . . . . . . . . . . .

**8** • Close the Color Picker Window.

**9** • Create an anti-aliased oval as follows:

a. Select a dark blue color from the Swatches palette.

b. Select the Marquee tool in the Tool palette.

c. If the Options palette is not visible and is not displaying the Marquee options page, select Window → Show Options, and then select the Options tab.

d. In the Shape drop-down list, select Elliptical.

e. Check the Anti-aliased checkbox in the Options palette.

f. In the Feather text box, enter **6**. This creates a wide feather that will emphasize the anti-aliasing.

g. In the image area, click and drag to create a large oval that covers most of the image area.

**TIP** **If you need to redraw the oval, choose Select → None and then redraw the oval.**

h. To color the selected area, click the Paint Bucket tool in the Tool palette, and then click inside the oval. Notice the blurry edge of the oval; this is exaggerated anti-aliasing. To view this up close, click the Zoom (magnifying glass) tool and then click on the image. To zoom in further, click again. To zoom out, press the Alt key while clicking with the Zoom tool.

**10** • To view the halo that would appear on a dark-colored background, do the following:

a. Choose Select → None.

b. Click on a dark red color in the Swatches palette.

c. Click the Paint Bucket tool, and then click in the area outside of the oval. Notice the white halo that surrounds the oval.

11 • Now create a smaller oval inside the large oval as follows:

a. Click the Marquee tool, and then click and drag to create an oval within the oval that occupies the left half of the oval. When you create the new oval, keep its edge inside the anti-aliasing of the larger oval.

b. Click the Paint Bucket tool, and then click inside the new oval. Notice that the red foreground color now anti-aliases to the blue background, so there is no white halo.

12 • Now create another small oval without anti-aliasing as follows:

a. Click the Marquee tool to select it.

b. In the Options palette, clear the Anti-aliased checkbox.

c. In the Feather text box, enter **0**.

d. Click and drag to create an oval within the large oval that occupies the right half of the oval. As before, when you create the new oval, keep its edge inside the anti-aliasing of the larger oval.

e. Click the Paint Bucket tool, and then click inside the new oval.

f. Use the Zoom tool to examine the edge of the aliased oval. Notice there is no anti-aliasing. Aliased images use fewer colors and do not create halos.

13 • Save the image using the Photoshop document (PSD) format.

**The trial version of Adobe Photoshop does not allow you to save, export, or print images.**

IMPORTANT

14 • Switch to indexed color mode using the Adaptive palette and Diffusion dithering.

15 • Save the image using the GIF format as follows:

    a. Select File → Save A Copy. Photoshop displays the Save A Copy dialog box.

    b. In the Save As drop-down list, select CompuServe GIF.

    c. Use the other dialog box controls to select a destination folder and name the file with a GIF extension, and then click Save.

    d. When the GIF89a Options dialog box appears, click Interlaced, and then click OK.

    e. When Photoshop displays the dialog box that says that some settings can't be saved, read the message and click OK.

16 • Open the image in your browser as follows:

    a. Open Netscape Navigator.

    b. Select File → Open Page.

    c. Click Choose File, and then use the dialog box that appears to select your GIF image file. (In the Files of Type drop-down list, you'll need to select All Files.)

    d. Click Open.

    Compare your image with the image on the demonstration Web site at: `d:/DemoWeb2/Design/Images/halo.gif`

## EXERCISE 8.5: CREATING GIF IMAGES

In this exercise, you'll reduce the colors in a GIF image, select some transparent colors, and then create a two-frame animation by displaying two images in succession on a Web page. To complete this exercise, do the following:

**1** • Using Windows Explorer or File Manager, look up and write down the size of the following file:

`d:/DemoWeb2/Design/Images/halo.gif`

Size: . . . . . . . . . . . . . . . . . . . . . . . . . . .

This image is 8-bit.

**2** • Using Photoshop, open the file listed in Step 1.

**3** • Reduce the image file size as follows:

a. Convert the image to RGB color mode.

b. Convert the image back to indexed color mode using the Adaptive palette, 4-bit color depth, and Diffusion dithering. Notice the reduction in image quality.

**4** • Export the image to GIF format with a single transparent color as follows:

a. Select the command that exports images to GIF format.

b. When the export dialog box appears, use the Eyedropper tool to select the red color as transparent. Be sure to click in the middle of one of the red areas.

c. Click OK, and then name the file HALO2.GIF.

**IMPORTANT**

**The trial version of Adobe Photoshop does not permit you to save, export, or print images.**

**5** • Open the HALO2.GIF file to see the changes. Notice the red and white halos around the large oval and the small oval on the left. The gray area represents the transparent color.

**6** • Export the image again, make all colors except the four darkest shades of blue transparent, and save the image as HALO3.GIF.

**7** • Look up and write down the file sizes for the HALO2.GIF and HALO3.GIF files.

   HALO2.GIF: . . . . . . . . . . . . . . . . . . . . . . . . . . . .

   HALO3.GIF: . . . . . . . . . . . . . . . . . . . . . . . . . . . .

**8** • Using a text editor or word processor, open the following Web page for editing:

   `d:DemoWeb2/Answers/halo.htm`

**9** • Modify the `<IMG>` tag so that the Web page will display the HALO3.GIF file before it displays the HALO.GIF file.

**10** • Save the Web page as HALO2.HTM in the same directory where you stored the HALO.GIF and HALO3.GIF files. (You can copy these image files from the CD at d:DemoWeb2/Design/Images/.)

**11** • Open the modified Web page in Netscape Navigator.

If you've completed this exercise correctly, the HALO2.HTM will display the smaller HALO3.GIF image and then the HALO.GIF image in its place, creating a simple two-frame animation. You can compare your exercise results to the files I created by browsing the following page:

`d:/DemoWeb2/Answers/halo2.htm`

**EXERCISE 8.6: GUIDELINES FOR CREATING SPECIAL WEB PAGE ELEMENTS**

This exercise tests your understanding of the guidelines introduced for creating rules, bullets, buttons, and background images. To complete this exercise, answer the following questions:

1 • Which object edges do not need anti-aliasing?

   Answer: . . . . . . . . . . . . . . . . . . . . . . . . . . . . . . . . . . . . . . . . .

2 • How can you control the space between a bullet image and the text that follows it?

   Answer: . . . . . . . . . . . . . . . . . . . . . . . . . . . . . . . . . . . . . . . . .

3 • What is the term that describes a background image that is repeated on the Web page?

   Answer: . . . . . . . . . . . . . . . . . . . . . . . . . . . . . . . . . . . . . . . . .

4 • A _____ background appears just once on a Web page.

5 • Which background image type offers the most design flexibility?

   Answer: . . . . . . . . . . . . . . . . . . . . . . . . . . . . . . . . . . . . . . . . .

6 • How can you prevent an image from tiling horizontally?

   Answer: . . . . . . . . . . . . . . . . . . . . . . . . . . . . . . . . . . . . . . . . .

# CHAPTER 9

# Adding Multimedia
# to Web Pages

**W**hat is multimedia? Outside of the world of computers, there are many types of media. For example, there is television, books, and radios. When we are surfing the Web, however, the computer is our media. Can you have multimedia on a single media?

When we use computers, every type of information delivery method is considered a different form of media. Display text, sound, and animation are all different forms of media. If you view text on the screen and, at the same time, receive information from a different media, you are experiencing multimedia.

I find this interesting because, by the computer definition, television is multimedia. Many people consider scanned photographs to be a separate form of computer media, making the combination of display text and a photograph a form of multimedia. I guess that means this book is a multimedia presentation?

The previous chapter explained that the JPEG image format is good for photographs, and it showed how to create a simple animation effect by sequentially displaying two different images. If your multimedia needs require photograph or line art images, Chapter 8 provides guidelines for creating and managing Web images.

This chapter explains how to create multimedia Web pages by adding animation, sounds, and video. Although animation, sounds, and video play differently, the process for adding each type of media to a Web page is almost identical. The rest of this chapter explains how multimedia operates with Web pages and how to play multimedia files. The final section of this chapter provides general guidelines for using multimedia and provides additional guidelines for each media type.

## Why Use Multimedia?

Multimedia can be exciting. Imagine the browser user cruising to your Web page. At first, the screen paints some text and a few images. Ho, hum. Suddenly, music starts playing and your visitor is tapping her foot. A moment later, a video starts playing. Now there is sound and motion, and what was otherwise a static Web page has come to life.

One of the primary reasons to use multimedia on your Web site is to excite and entertain your Web audience. However, there are times when multimedia can be a better tool than the text and images normally placed on Web pages. For example, why describe a sound when you can play it? Often, a simple animation can communicate how something works more efficiently than words. In addition, a few minutes of video can often communicate more emotion than many pages of text.

Of course, text and images are often a better solution than multimedia. In general, text and images take less time to create, and download faster. Your multimedia message is worthless if you can't afford to develop it or if Web page visitors won't wait to see it.

The secret to effective use of multimedia on the Web is choice. Good Web sites offer multimedia in ways that enable the user to choose whether or not she wants to view or hear multimedia information. Good multimedia design lets Web page visitors get information the old-fashioned way through text and images, or through the more exciting offerings of animation, sounds, and video. Offering users a choice avoids alienating them and tempts them to see what they might be missing.

## How Multimedia Operates on the Web

As with the images described in Chapter 8, animations, sounds, and video are stored in files. This shouldn't surprise you. Everything on computers is stored in files; and as with images, using multimedia on the Web is a three-step process. The first step is to create the multimedia file, the second step is to copy the file to the Web server that will publish the file, and the final step is to call the file from your Web page with an HTML tag.

As with images, creating an animation, sound, or video is the hard part. For the most part, adding multimedia to your Web page is simply a matter of using the right HTML tag and attributes. The difference, however, is that most animations, sounds, and videos require a plug-in or helper application. Plug-ins and helper applications are software programs that display or play files that the browser does not support on its own. Only when your Web page visitors have the correct plug-ins or helper applications, can they play your multimedia files.

Figure 9.1 shows what happens when a user directly requests a multimedia file, or selects a Web page that automatically loads a multimedia file.

▶ · · · · · · · · · · · · · · · · · · · · · · · · · · · · · · · · · · · · ◀

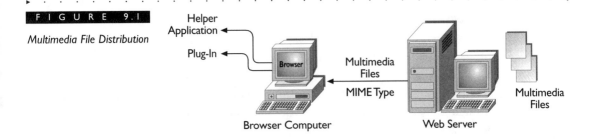

FIGURE 9.1

*Multimedia File Distribution*

Helper Application

Plug-In

Browser

Multimedia Files

MIME Type

Browser Computer

Web Server

Multimedia Files

As with HTML files and image files, the Web server sends a multimedia file to the browser when it is requested. However, most browsers are designed to display HTML, text, and image files. Some browsers support additional types of media files, but no browser supports all types. If the browser receives a file type it supports, it displays or plays the file contents. If it receives another type of file, it does one of the following:

▶ Launches a plug-in application that can play or display the file in a browser window

▶ Launches a helper application to display or play the file

▶ Prompts the user to search for, and download, a plug-in or helper application or to save the file locally

The following sections provide more information on plug-ins and helper applications and describe how browsers use MIME types to determine which plug-in or helper application to launch.

## PLUG-INS AND HELPER APPLICATIONS

Plug-ins and helper applications are programs that browsers use to display or play files the browser can't open. Plug-ins extend the functionality of the browser so the browser can play a file in the current window or in an additional browser window. Helper applications are standard applications that the browser can call to display or play a file.

A browser, for example, can be configured to display a word-processing document, such as one in Adobe System's Portable Document Format (PDF), in one of two ways. The PDF file can be displayed in a browser window using the Adobe Acrobat Reader plug-in, or the browser can be configured to launch the Adobe Acrobat Reader program (the helper application), which runs as a separate program from the browser. (For more information on PDF files, see the sidebar titled "More About PDF Files.")

Often, a plug-in is the most convenient solution for displaying a media file. Plug-ins are usually free and are optimized for viewing or listening to a file. While some applications are designed only for viewing or playing, others are designed for creating media. Most applications that create media are not free, so it is less likely that your Web audience will have these applications or buy them.

As a multimedia Web author, you need to understand plug-ins and helper applications because your audience may not. What good is your multimedia message if your audience can't play it? If a Web page visitor can't play or hear something on your Web page, the Web page visitor blames you. A good multimedia designer plans for this situation and provides Web page visitors with the information they need to get, and install, plug-ins and helper applications. Fortunately, most of these applications are available on the Web so, in most cases, all you need to do is explain what the browser user needs and point him to the right Web site to get it.

## MIME TYPES

The Multipurpose Internet Mail Extension (MIME) standard defines one way that Internet computers can exchange files between different platforms. The MIME type identifies the type of file that is being sent to an Internet computer. A MIME type definition at the browser determines how each browser responds to the files associated with your Web page. Figure 9.2 shows how MIME types are passed from the Web server to the Web browser.

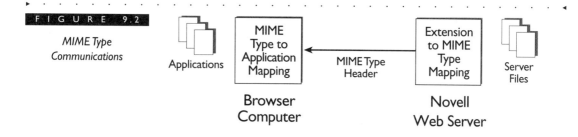

**FIGURE 9.2**

*MIME Type Communications*

Applications — MIME Type to Application Mapping — Browser Computer ← MIME Type Header — Extension to MIME Type Mapping — Server Files — Novell Web Server

## More About PDF Files

Portable Document Format (PDF) documents are popular on the Web for the following reasons:

- ▸ Unlike HTML documents, PDF files can contain both text and graphics in one file.

- ▸ Printing a PDF file prints all text and graphics in the file.

- ▸ Copying information from a PDF file to another computer format is more difficult than copying HTML text and Web images.

If you download software or product literature from the Web, chances are good that you'll download a PDF document someday. Many manufacturers use this format to distribute product manuals and related information on the Web. To view this documentation, you can use the Adobe Acrobat Reader plug-in or standalone viewer application.

If you want to distribute documents in PDF files, you'll need to use the Adobe Distiller or PDFWriter applications to create the PDF files. For more information on these products and the Acrobat Reader applications, browse to www.adobe.com.

Each MIME type definition includes a type, a subtype, and a list of file extensions. For example, the Web server MIME type definitions for some of the file types you already know how to use are:

```
image/gif      gif

image/jpeg     jpeg jpg jpe

text/html      html htm

text/plain     txt
```

In the sample above, the text before the forward slash specifies the type. The text after the slash defines a subtype, while the extensions that follow define which files are assigned to the MIME types and subtypes.

At the server, the MIME type configuration determines what MIME type is sent with each file the Web server distributes. Each time a file is requested, the Web server looks at the file extension and uses that to set the MIME type. Most Web servers come with a default list of MIME types. If a new MIME type is created, the Web server administrator must add the MIME type to the server. Otherwise, the Web server automatically includes the default MIME type with the files it distributes.

**NOTE**

**The default MIME type is text/html, so the browser will always try to display any file that doesn't include a MIME type, regardless of the file content. If Web site visitors are seeing an unintelligible series of characters on your Web pages, it could be that the Web server is not configured to support the file type you are using. Contact your Web server administrator and ask him to add the correct MIME type for the file format you are using.**

**To view a list of current MIME types, browse to** `ftp.isi.edu/in-notes/iana/assignments/media-types/media-types`.

At the browser, a separate MIME type configuration tells the browser how to respond to each MIME type. Depending on the browser configuration, it might respond to a MIME type by launching a plug-in or helper application, or by prompting the user to save the file.

At this point, you might be wondering why browsers don't use the file extension mapping in the operating system to determine how to handle a file. After all, IBM-compatible PCs use the file extension to determine which application to launch.

The MIME type is required because the local operating system might not be configured to support files with a particular extension. Also, it is the browser that determines whether to launch a plug-in or helper application, or save the file. MIME types enable you to configure your browser to respond to downloaded files independently of the operating system configuration.

As a Web page designer, you won't have to worry too much about MIME types. Most plug-in installations automatically set the MIME types in the browser for the particular kind of file the plug-in supports. However, there are certain situations where a previously working Web page stops working or works differently. When this happens, it is usually caused by a change in the MIME type definitions at the browser. The browser user may have installed a new plug-in that also supports that MIME type, or the browser user may have selected a helper application that supports the MIME type. These actions can result in multiple entries for a MIME type, and when this happens, the wrong plug-in or helper application might be called to process your Web page files.

Although you can't prevent users from changing their MIME types, you might want to provide a troubleshooting tips Web page to let users know which plug-ins and helper applications you recommend. You might also provide instructions for removing conflicting plug-ins and editing the browser MIME type definitions.

## Playing Multimedia Files

Playing multimedia files is a three-step process. First you need to obtain the multimedia file and store it where it is available to the Web page. Second, you need to add a tag to your Web page to call the multimedia file; and third, you should provide some kind of instructions that help users locate and install any plug-ins or helper applications your multimedia file requires. The following sections describe how to complete these tasks.

### OBTAINING MULTIMEDIA FILES

Before you can publish multimedia files on your computer, you must create them, buy them, or obtain freeware versions. After you get the files, you need to store them on your Web server with your Web pages.

To create animation, sound, and video files, you need to use special applications, which are different from the applications that you use to create Web pages and images. Although this chapter does introduce how to create animated GIFs, a complete discussion of how to create multimedia files is beyond the scope of this chapter.

To locate multimedia files that are free or available for purchase, search the Web. You can also search your local computer store. Some companies sell clip art collections that include sounds and animation. If you buy software that permits you to create multimedia files, it may come with samples that you may use on your Web site for free. (Just be sure to check for copyright restrictions.)

When you get your multimedia files, store them in the same directory as the Web page that will call them, or store them in a shared directory. When the multimedia file is available for publishing, you are ready to add the tags to call the file.

## CALLING MULTIMEDIA FILES FROM WEB PAGES

There are two ways to add multimedia to your Web page. The first way is to call multimedia files directly from the Web page as it loads. This is called *inline media* because it is treated as an additional Web page element that appears inline with the others.

The other way to call multimedia files is with a link from the Web page. Multimedia files that are downloaded this way are called *Referenced media* because the user must reference or click the link before the multimedia file plays.

From the visitor's perspective, the primary difference between inline and referenced media is choice. Inline media is downloaded and started whether the user wants it or not. Although the user can interrupt the media playback by stopping the page loading, the media playback does start without the user's prior approval. If the user doesn't have the correct plug-in to play the file, a message may appear in the browser.

Referenced media, on the other hand, does not play until the Web page visitor clicks the link. If the user doesn't reference the multimedia file, she will never have to worry about what plug-in or helper application it needed.

The following sections describe how to call multimedia files as inline or referenced media.

### Calling Inline Media

The exact method for starting an inline media file is determined by the type of file you are playing and the plug-in or application that plays it. However, you can start many multimedia files with the <EMBED> tag, which uses the following format:

```
<EMBED SRC="filename" HEIGHT="pixels" WIDTH="pixels">
```

As with the <IMG> tag, the SRC attribute specifies the name of the file to be opened, which could be an animation file, a sound file, a video file, or some other type of file that is brand new. The <EMBED> tag is the tag for opening any kind of file that is not covered by another HTML tag.

The HEIGHT and WIDTH attributes define a portion of the Web page that is dedicated to the media file. For sounds, these attributes define the dimensions of a control console that the Web page user can use to control the sound (Figure 9.3). For animations and videos, the media file area might display only the animation or video, or it might include a control panel also. (For information on displaying a control panel for QuickTime videos, see the sidebar titled "Adding a Control Panel to QuickTime Videos.")

*Audio Control Console*

Depending on the type of media and the features supported by the browser, plug-in, or application that displays it, there may be additional attributes that you can use to control the media playback. Table 9.1 lists some of the attributes supported by different media types. Both of the supporting applications listed in Table 9.1 support additional attributes. For more information on which attributes you can use, you need to refer to the documentation for the plug-in and helper applications you think your Web page visitors will use.

**Adding a Control Panel to QuickTime Videos**

To display a control panel that Web page visitors can use to control a QuickTime video, you must increase the height of the video display area by 24 pixels. To determine the height of a video, do the following:

1 • Open the MoviePlayer application that comes with the QuickTime program, and then open the video file you want to publish.

2 • Select Movie → Get Info.

3 • From the right-hand pop-up menu, select Size.

4 • Note the size and close the MoviePlayer application.

Once you have the correct movie height, you can add 24 pixels to this height and specify the new value in the HTML tag that calls your video file.

TABLE 9.1

*Sample EMBED Tag*
*Attributes*

| ATTRIBUTE | SUPPORTING APPLICATIONS | DESCRIPTION |
|---|---|---|
| SRC | LiveAudio, QuickTime | Specifies the media file to play. |
| HEIGHT | LiveAudio, QuickTime | Defines the height (in pixels) of the media display area or the media control panel. |
| WIDTH | LiveAudio, QuickTime | Configures the width (in pixels) of the media display area or the media control panel. |
| HIDDEN | LiveAudio, QuickTime | When set to TRUE, this attribute hides the playback control panel and automatically starts playback when the Web page is loaded. |
| AUTOSTART | LiveAudio, QuickTime | When set to TRUE, this attribute starts the media play when the Web page is downloaded. When set to False, the browser user must use the control panel to start the media play. |
| LOOP | LiveAudio, QuickTime | Specifies how many times the media plays. When set to FALSE, the media plays once. |
| ALIGN | LiveAudio | Aligns the media display area on the Web page. Valid values are TOP, BOTTOM, CENTER, BASELINE, LEFT, RIGHT, TEXTTOP, MIDDLE, ABSMIDDLE, ABSBOTTOM. |
| PLUGINSPAGE | QuickTime | Defines a URL for a Web page that enables the user to download the plug-in that plays the media file. |

One example of another tag that plays multimedia files is the <BGSOUND> tag, which plays sounds and is supported only by Internet Explorer. This tag uses the following format:

```
<BGSOUND SRC="filename" LOOP="number">
```

As with the other HTML tags, the SRC attribute defines the file to be played, and the LOOP attribute specifies how many times the file is to be played.

### Calling Referenced Media

There are two ways to reference multimedia from a Web page. The first way is to create a link that specifies the file to be played, and the second is to create a link to a Web page that automatically plays the media file. When you link directly to the media file, the browser plays only the single media file. When you link to a Web page that automatically plays the file, the Web page can play more than one media file.

The difference between calling an inline media file and a referenced media file is very subtle when you are calling a Web page that displays the media file automatically. In this case, you are referencing a Web page that includes an inline media file reference. With respect to the first Web page, the media file is a referenced media file only if you make it clear to the user in the first Web page that the link starts a multimedia file.

To call a referenced multimedia file, enter a link similar to the following:

```
<A HREF="file_or_page" HEIGHT="pixels" WIDTH="pixels">Play
the music!</A> (WAV file, 30K)
```

The *Play the music!* link text makes it clear that the link will play some sort of sound. Whether the link calls a sound file or a Web page that automatically plays a sound file is unimportant. What is important is that the Web page visitor can choose to play or ignore the sound. The information after the link tells the visitor what kind of file the link starts and the file size. The user can choose to wait for the file or pass it by.

## PROVIDING INSTRUCTIONS FOR PLUG-INS AND HELPER APPLICATIONS

There are two general approaches to alerting your audience about plug-ins and helper applications. The first approach uses a *front door* Web page to let people know what they need before they enter the Web area that uses multimedia. Typically, the front door is a Web page that describes what plug-in is needed and how to get and install it. Usually, the front door page includes a link to a Web site where the user can download the plug-in. If this Web site provides good instructions for installing and using the plug-in, your front door can refer the visitor to that site for instructions.

The second approach lets users discover the plug-in requirement the hard way. For example, if Netscape Navigator does not know how to support a file, it displays the dialog box shown in Figure 9.4.

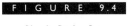

*Plug-In Dialog Box*

When the browser user sees a dialog box like this, he can do the following:

- ▸ Click More Info to learn how to download a plug-in that can process the file

- ▸ Click Pick App to choose a local program that can read the file

- ▸ Click Save File to download the file to your computer

- ▸ Click Cancel

If the user clicks More Info, a Web page appears that explains how to download and install the requested plug-in. After the plug-in is installed, the user can navigate back to the Web page where he found the link, click the link, and Navigator will start the plug-in and process the file. Depending on the type of file it is, Navigator will display a document, play sounds, or do whatever the program is designed to do.

I think the front door approach is a good one. The user finds out, up front, that the Web site or area uses files that require plug-ins. Then, she can decide if she wants to install the plug-in or avoid links that are likely to prompt her to download and install a plug-in. As a designer, the choice is yours. If your users are frequent Web surfers and very knowledgeable, they might not need the extra guidance the front door approach provides.

 **Exercise 9.1: If you're preparing to take the certification exam, or if you want to practice what you learned in this section, turn to the end of this chapter and complete Exercise 9.1. When you are done, continue reading here to prepare for the next exercise.**

## Multimedia Guidelines

In the perfect Web world, your entire Web site could be a multimedia presentation. There would be no limits on file size, all your Web site visitors would have top-speed connections to your Web site, and they would all use sound and graphics hardware that can support anything your Web site could dish out. Unfortunately, the Web isn't there yet. Consider the following:

- Usually, it takes considerably more time to create a multimedia file than it takes to create an HTML file.

- Although the software that creates sound files might be provided with your computer, you will probably have to purchase additional hardware to record sounds and video, and you'll need additional software tools to create animation and video files

- The creation of multimedia requires new skills. You'll need to learn these skills or hire someone to create your files for you.

- Multimedia files require considerably larger file sizes than HTML or image files, and this can place a burden on those who visit your site using modem connections.

Although multimedia can be expensive to develop and deliver, its contribution to a Web site is often worth more than the cost. The following sections provide general guidelines for developing multimedia and specific guidelines for animation, sounds, and videos.

### GENERAL GUIDELINES

As a Web designer, it is your responsibility to choose when to use multimedia on your Web sites. The goal is to get as much benefit as possible from your Web development budget and minimize the download times for your Web site visitors. The following sections provide general guidelines for using multimedia and discuss copyright issues that affect you whenever you use material that is developed by someone else.

### When to Use Multimedia

As a Web page designer, you will probably have more multimedia ideas than you have the time, budget, and bandwidth to develop and distribute. Don't let this frustrate you. The challenge is to identify the areas where you can get the most benefit from multimedia and then get started. When you finish adding multimedia to the most important areas, you can start in other areas. By rolling out your multimedia in stages, you create a Web site that is constantly changing, and this tempts visitors to come back again to see what's new.

When you are choosing which multimedia ideas to develop first, consider the following:

▸ All multimedia files should support or contribute to the goals you have for your Web site.

▸ Multimedia can communicate sound and visual information that is difficult to describe with words and static images.

▸ Multimedia can represent dynamic processes.

▸ Used in moderation, multimedia can be stimulating and entertaining. Too much multimedia, however, can be distracting or annoying.

▸ The entertainment value of any multimedia must adequately reward the visitor for waiting during the file download period.

When you are developing a Web site with constrained resources, the first point above is the most important. Unless the sole purpose of your Web site is entertainment, most visitors will arrive looking for something other than a multimedia presentation. As a Web designer, your goal should be to give visitors what they are looking for, and to enhance that information with multimedia when it contributes to your Web site's goals.

### Designing for Minimum Download Times

As with Web page images, your multimedia files should be designed and optimized for minimum download times. If your Web page visitors use 28.8 modems, they will receive your Web site files at approximately 1K per second. At this rate, a 50K file takes 50 seconds to download. Fortunately, there are ways to improve download times.

**Download times are much less critical when your audience connects to the Web server from a Local Area Network (LAN). For relatively current information on Internet audiences, browse the surveys conducted by Georgia Tech's Graphics, Visualization, and Usability Center at** `www.cc.gatech.edu/gvu/user_surveys`.

In the last chapter, you learned that you could minimize the size of images by reducing their size and quality. This also holds true for multimedia. For example, animation and videos are composed of a series of image frames that are played back at a specified speed. Higher-quality animation and video use more image frames and play them faster, and this creates more information that must be stored in the multimedia file. Larger images also require more file space. Sometimes, a reduction in the size or number of frames in an animation or video provides a substantially lower file size with a minimal reduction in quality.

Although sound files play differently from images, animation, and video, they store information in a similar manner and can be optimized too. Remember the bit depths that were used to specify the number of image colors in Chapter 8? These bit depths are also used to define the different sound levels that can be stored in a file. Just as a 16-bit color depth provides more image detail than 8-bit color depth, a 16-bit sound file produces more audio depth and quality than an 8-bit sound file. The sampling rate of a sound file, which is functionally similar to the frame rate of animation or video, also affects the sound quality and file size. Larger sampling rates produce larger files and better-quality sound.

Other image optimization techniques work for multimedia too. For example, if the multimedia format and plug-ins you select support streaming, a multimedia file can begin playing before its download is complete. One trick that you can use with sound files is to call the sound file from a tag near the end of your Web page. This approach lets the entire Web page load before the sound starts downloading. Later, while the visitor is viewing the rest of the page, the sound starts playing.

As with creating images, you can achieve the largest reductions in multimedia file size when you are creating or editing the multimedia file. There just isn't enough room to describe how to do this in all types of files, so Table 9.2 summarizes file optimization guidelines you can use for multimedia files. For specific instructions on performing these tasks, see the product documentation for your multimedia tools.

| TABLE 9.2 | MULTIMEDIA TYPE | OPTIMIZATION TECHNIQUES |
|---|---|---|
| *Multimedia File Optimization Techniques* | Animation | * Reduce the image size<br>* Reduce the color bit depth<br>* Reduce the number of colors used<br>* Reduce the number of frames<br>* Use streaming animation formats and plug-ins<br>* Use formats that offer file compression |
| | Sound | * Reduce the sound bit depth<br>* Reduce the sampling rate<br>* Use monaural sound instead of stereo<br>* Start the sound near the end of the Web page<br>* Use streaming sound formats and plug-ins<br>* Use formats that offer file compression<br>* Use short repeating sound clips for background music |
| | Video | * Reduce the image size<br>* Reduce the number of frames<br>* Use streaming animation formats and plug-ins<br>* Use formats that offer file compression |

### Copyright Issues

Most of us learn to create multimedia by copying and modifying other people's work. For example, my first animations were based on clip art I had purchased, and the first sounds I used were clip sounds. Clip art and clip sounds are great tools for getting started because their license usually permits you to use them on the Web.

When creating Web images and multimedia files, it is very important to avoid copyright violation. With microphones, scanners, and video cameras, it is easy for us to create personal multimedia files that later end up on the Web. Capturing sounds and images for our own personal use might or might not violate copyright laws, but publishing other people's work on the Web does violate them. The only time you can publish someone else's work is when you have permission from that person.

There are many free images, sounds, animations, and videos on the Internet. You can also purchase multimedia files as part of collections that are intended for your personal publishing. Before you publish someone else's work, take the time to review any copyright statements and guidelines provided with the work. You might be required to give the artist credit, or your rights might be restricted to certain types of publishing. A little research up front can avoid costly litigation later.

## ANIMATION GUIDELINES

Chapter 8 describes how to create a simple, two-frame animation by sequentially displaying two images. The first is displayed with the LOWSRC attribute, and the second is displayed by the SRC attribute. Animations are simply collections of images that, when played in sequence, create the illusion of movement or change. The following are some examples of how you might use animation on a Web page:

▸ Animate an advertisement, link, or headline to attract viewers to it

▸ Change the appearance of a button or menu when a user activates a Web page control to show a Web page response

▸ Illustrate a dynamic process that is difficult to describe with words and static images

While you can also use video to illustrate dynamic processes, animation files are typically smaller than video files and can cost less to develop. Sometimes an animation is superior to a video because the animation can illustrate a single process, such as the operation of a single gear in a watch. In this example, a video would require extensive editing to hide all of the other gears that draw attention away from the one the animation illustrates.

When you are planning animation for your Web pages, consider the following:

▸ Unless your Web page is about animation, have only one or two animations running when the page loads. Animation draws the readers' attention faster than static images or text, but too many animations are distracting.

▸ Avoid animating text that you want visitors to read. It is difficult to read moving text.

The procedure for starting animations was described earlier in this chapter. Also, be sure to review the "General Guidelines" section earlier in this chapter before you start creating and using animation files. This section introduces the animation formats you can use, and the plug-ins and helper applications that support them (see Table 9.3). Unless you plan to use animation files that someone else has already created, you'll need to choose an animation format to get started. Table 9.4 provides additional information on the plug-ins and helper applications listed in Table 9.3.

| TABLE 9.3 Animation File Formats | ANIMATION FORMAT (EXTENSIONS) | COMPATIBLE PLUG-INS AND HELPER APPLICATIONS |
|---|---|---|
| | Animated GIFs (.gif) | None required |
| | Authorware | Shockwave Authorware Shockwave The Works |
| | Director (.dir, .dxr, .dcr) | Shockwave Shockwave The Works |
| | Flash (.spl, .swf) | Shockwave Shockwave Flash Shockwave The Works |
| | Java (.class) | None required |
| | JavaScript | None required |
| | Virtual Reality Modeling Language (.wrl, .wrz) | Live3D |

TABLE 9.4

Sound File Plug-Ins

| PLUG-IN | PROVIDER | URL | STREAMING? |
|---|---|---|---|
| Live3D | Netscape | home.netscape.com | |
| Shockwave Shockwave Flash Shockwave The Works Shockwave Authorware | Macromedia | www.macromedia.com | Yes |

**For more information on plug-ins for Netscape Navigator and Microsoft Explorer, browse the following pages, respectively:**

`home.netscape.com/comprod/products/navigator/`
`version_2.0/plugins/index.html`

`www.microsoft.com/ie/download`

**To view the plug-ins available for Internet Explorer, you must use Internet Explorer when you access the Microsoft Web site.**

The following sections provide additional information on animation file formats, plug-ins, and helper applications.

### Animated GIF

Chapter 8 introduced animated GIFs as an extension of the GIF89a image format. Animated GIFs create animations by repeating a series of GIF images at a predetermined speed. Although animated GIFs don't support sound, they are extremely popular because recent versions of Netscape Navigator and Microsoft Explorer support them without plug-ins. When your Web page displays animated GIFs, you can assume that most of the Internet users in the world can see them. Many of the animated banners, buttons, and images on the Web are animated GIFs.

**To view some examples of animated GIFs, or to locate free animated GIFs that you can use on your Web pages, browse the following sites:**

**Electric GIFs:** `www.electricgifs.com`

**2Cool Animations:** `www.gifanimations.com`

**Yahoo!:** `www.yahoo.com/Arts/Visual_Arts/Animation/`
`Computer_Animation/Animated_GIFs/Collections`

**Before using an animated GIF from one of these sites, be sure to read and abide by any copyright information and restrictions posted there. Also, be careful to avoid using animated GIFs that use trademarked or copyrighted material that the GIF creator doesn't have permission to use.**

When compared with other animation formats, animated GIFs are relatively easy to create, and their file sizes are relatively small (although the small size is due in part to the lack of support for sound, three-dimensional imaging, and other features offered by other formats). Because GIF images store multiple, complete images instead of just the image information that changes between frames, GIF compression is less than ideal. However, no other animation format is as widely supported as GIF89a.

To create an animated GIF, you need to use both a GIF editing tool and a GIF animation tool. Typically, these are two separate tools, though they could be integrated. First, you create a series of GIF images that become your animation frames, and then you import them into the GIF animation tool to create the animation file and set the animation playback controls. Table 9.5 lists some of the GIF Animation products you can purchase on the Web. Most of these products offer trial versions that are free for a specified period. For unlimited use of a product, however, you need to purchase the product.

**T A B L E   9.5**

*GIF Animation Products*

| PRODUCT | WEB SITE |
|---------|----------|
| Animagic GIF Animator | `rtlsoft.com/animagic` |
| GIF Construction Set | `www.mindworkshop.com/alchemy/gifcon.html` |
| GIF Movie Gear (formerly Cel Assembler) This book's CD includes a trial version of GIF Movie Gear. | `www.gamani.com` |
| Ulead GIF Animator | `www.ulead.com` |
| WWW GIF Animator | `stud1.tuwien.ac.at/~e8925005` |

 **To locate additional tools for working with animated GIFs, browse to** `www.tucows.com`.

If you decide to create an animated GIF, consider the following guidelines, many of which apply to other types of animation as well.

▸ To keep the animation file size small, use a minimum number of colors and the smallest image area size possible.

▶ When preparing images to place in an animation, use the same size and positioning for all images so it is easier to align the frames in the animation file.

▶ When defining an animated GIF, you can set the file to display the first image until the file download is complete and the animation starts. When you choose this option, select an appropriate first image that users can view while they wait.

▶ If the animated GIF plays just once, the final animation frame will be displayed until the visitor leaves your Web page. Be sure to choose a final frame that is appropriate.

▶ For repeating animations, select the frames so that there is a natural transition between the last frame and the first frame. Otherwise, each repetition will display an unnatural jump.

▶ The frames between the start and end frames are the transition frames. You can blur portions of the image in these frames to smooth transitions, and because visitors don't see these frames as long, you can spend less time on these images than on the start and end frames.

▶ Because animated GIFs are called with the `<IMG>` tag instead of the `<EMBED>` tag, you can use the `LOWSRC` attribute to display the animation first and the `SRC` attribute to display a replacement static image. You can also reverse this process.

▶ To add animation to a large image, consider dividing the image into parts and aligning the parts with a table. After you do this, you can animate one or more parts using smaller image files. For example, you could divide a portrait image so that one eye blinks.

For an example of how to create an animated GIF, see the sidebar titled "Creating Animated GIFs with GIF Movie Gear."

## Creating Animated GIFs with GIF Movie Gear

GIF Movie Gear is an animated GIF creation tool that you can download from the Internet. The trial version of GIF Movie Gear is free for 30 days and is included on this book's CD. To create an animated GIF with this program, do the following:

1 • Create GIF images for each animation frame in an image editor, such as Adobe Photoshop.

2 • Start GIF Movie Gear and select File → Insert Frame to open a frame for the animation. Continue to insert additional frames until all of your image frames are loaded.

3 • Click and drag frames to rearrange them as necessary.

4 • To set the animation controls for each frame, click the frame, select Edit → Frame Properties, and when the Frame Properties dialog box appears, edit the settings. (To select properties for all frames, select Edit → Global Frame Properties.)

5 • To set special transition effects for each frame, select a transition effect from the Animation drop-down list in the Frame Properties dialog box.

The No Disposal Method and Leave Alone settings draw the new frame over the old one. The Background Color setting replaces each frame with the background color before it draws the next frame, and the Restore Previous setting redisplays the previous frame before displaying the next frame.

6 • To preview the animation, select View → Animation Preview.

7 • To optimize the animation, select Tools → Optimize Animation, and use the dialog box that appears to reduce your animation file size as much as possible.

8 • To save the animation, select File → Save and use the save dialog box to save the file.

*(continued)*

---

### Creating Animated GIFs with GIF Movie Gear *(continued)*

**9** • To preview the animation in your browser, open the saved file just as you would a Web page. The animation will play in the browser.

**10** • To add the animation to a Web page, use the <IMG> tag as described in Chapter 3.

If you want GIF Movie Gear to create the tag for you, select Tools → HTML. When the HTML Code dialog box appears, click Copy Code to copy the HTML tag shown in the dialog box. You can now open your HTML file and paste this tag into your Web page.

---

### Director, Authorware, and Flash

Director, Authorware, and Flash are all multimedia products from Macromedia. Director is Macromedia's flagship multimedia tool, which supports animation, interactivity, and sound. Authorware is an online training development package that shares many of the features found in Director and Flash.

While Director and Authorware use bitmap images to create animations, Flash uses vector-graphics images, which are introduced in a sidebar in Chapter 8. Flash animations use less file space and can be enlarged with no loss of image quality.

To view Authorware, Director, and Flash files, Web page visitors must install the Shockwave plug-in, which is available free from the Macromedia Web site. As shown in Table 9.3, different versions of the Shockwave plug-in are offered and each supports different combinations of the Macromedia animation formats.

 **Web sites that use Macromedia media files are often called *shocked* Web sites. To view examples of these types of animations, browse the Shockzone Gallery Guide at** www.macromedia.com/shockzone/guide.

### Java and JavaScript

As you'll learn in Chapters 14 and 15, Java and JavaScript are two different programming tools that you can use with your Web pages. Typically, programmers create animations with these tools by using programming commands to move an image across the page, or by changing images so that a single image appears to be moving or changing.

Because Java and JavaScript are programming tools, they are not as well suited for animation as some of the other tools described in this chapter. For example, Java and JavaScript do not include commands that permit you to integrate sound with your moving and changing images. Another limitation of Java is that you have to learn to program before you can use it. JavaScript, however, is relatively easy to learn, but takes more effort than some of the other animation tools.

One advantage of Java and JavaScript is that these programs are supported in Netscape Navigator 3.0, Internet Explorer 3.0, and later versions of these products. As with animated GIFs, no plug-ins are required to view animations created with Java and JavaScript.

For an example of an animated JavaScript, browse this book's CD at:

```
d:/DemoWeb2/Programs/JavaScpt/ticker.htm
```

### Virtual Reality Modeling Language

Virtual Reality Modeling Language (VRML) is an industry-standard description language for creating virtual, three-dimensional worlds. For example, you can use VRML to create a Web site that is modeled after a house. This "house world" would appear to be three-dimensional and enable users to move from room to room. Animation provides the visual effects that make the visitor feel that he is actually moving through the house.

Although VRML is designed to create virtual worlds, you can use it to create three-dimensional images and animations that appear without the backdrop of a virtual world. VRML files are ASCII text files that contain modeling instructions instead of a series of bitmapped images. The VRML plug-in uses these instructions to create virtual worlds or objects. Because the modeling instructions often require less file space than bitmap animation, VRML files can be relatively small and can download faster than bitmap animations.

VRML animations and worlds are still relatively uncommon and can be used to surprise and amaze your Web page visitors. Virtual worlds also offer interesting possibilities for training and entertainment. Before you start virtual construction, however, be aware that three-dimensional projects can be costly to develop. Three dimensional designers are harder to find and, hey, it takes time to build a world. Also, because this technology is relatively new, 3-D developers and viewers can expect more software crashes and fewer development tools until this market matures.

**Exercise 9.2: If you're preparing to take the certification exam, or if you want to practice what you learned in this section, turn to the end of this chapter and complete Exercise 9.2. When you are done, continue reading here to prepare for the next exercise.**

## GUIDELINES FOR SOUNDS

Although sound files can be very large, you can often download them in the background while the user is viewing the rest of the Web page. You can also set up sounds so they continue to play as users browse from page to page in your Web site. Just be sure to provide the controls on each page that enable the user to stop the sound.

Sound enriches the visitor's experience with your Web page and can be used to communicate emotion, deliver information, and play music or other audio broadcast programs. The following are some examples of how sounds might be used on a Web page:

▸ Background music to soothe frustrated customers visiting a customer support Web site

▸ Faulty motor sounds to help auto mechanics troubleshoot problems

▸ Samples of music for sale

▸ Inspiring speeches from celebrities or corporate executive officers

**For an example of a Web site that relies heavily on sound files, visit the National Public Radio Web site at** www.npr.org.

The procedure for starting sounds is described earlier in this chapter. Also, be sure to review the "General Guidelines" section before you start creating and using sound files. This section introduces the sound formats that you can use, and the plug-ins and helper applications that support them (Table 9.6). Unless you plan to use sound files that someone else has already created, you'll need to choose a sound format to get started. Table 9.7 provides additional information on the plug-ins and helper applications listed in Table 9.6.

**TABLE 9.6**

*Sound File Formats*

| SOUND FORMAT (EXTENSIONS) | SOUND DEPTH | SAMPLING | COMPATIBLE PLUG-INS AND HELPER APPLICATIONS |
|---|---|---|---|
| Audio Interchange File Format (.aiff, .aif, .aiffc) | 8-bit, 16-bit | Up to 48kHz | Beatnik, Live Audio, QuickTime application, QuickTime plug-in |
| Musical Instrument Digital Interface (.midi) | N/A | N/A | Beatnik, Live Audio, QuickTime application, QuickTime plug-in |
| u-Law (.au) | 8-bit | Up to 44kHz | Live Audio, Netscape Audio Player |
| Real Audio (.ra, .ram) | 16-bit | 8kHz | Real Player |
| Waveform Audio (.wav) | 8-bit, 16-bit | Up to 44kHz | Beatnik, Live Audio, Microsoft Media Player |

**TABLE 9.7**

*Sound File Plug-Ins*

| PLUG-IN | PROVIDER | URL | STREAMING? |
|---|---|---|---|
| Beatnik | Headspace | www.headspace.com | Yes |
| Live Audio | Netscape (provided with Netscape Navigator) | www.netscape.com | |
| Microsoft Media Player | Microsoft | www.microsoft.com | |
| Netscape Audio Player | Netscape (provided with Netscape Navigator) | www.netscape.com | |
| QuickTime | Apple Computer | www.apple.com/quicktime/ | Yes |
| Real Player Real Video | Progressive Networks | www.realaudio.com | Yes |

The following sections provide additional information on sound file formats, plug-ins, and helper applications.

### Audio Interchange File Format

The Audio Interchange File Format was originally developed by Apple for the Macintosh and is now supported by most plug-ins on most platforms. The QuickTime plug-in and application both support this format so sound can be included in QuickTime movies.

### Beatnik

Beatnik is a plug-in by Headspace, Inc. that is designed to play sounds on Windows 95, Windows NT, and Macintosh Power PC computers without special sound card requirements. As of this writing, Headspace recommends using Beatnik on Netscape Navigator 3.01 and later and provides only limited support for Microsoft Explorer. While Beatnik supports other file formats as listed in Table 9.6, it also supports its own Rich Music Format (RMF).

### Musical Instrument Digital Interface

Unlike other sound file formats, Musical Instrument Digital Interface (MIDI) files do not store samples of sound. Instead, MIDI files store instructions that create sounds on MIDI sound cards and MIDI musical instruments. Instead of storing a recording of sound, MIDI files store the musical notes and rhythm information required to create the music. The result is a much smaller file that produces quality that is limited only by the sound card or musical instrument on which it is played.

### LiveAudio

LiveAudio is a plug-in that is provided with Netscape Navigator. You can expect Navigator users to be able to play sound files that use the following formats: Audio Interchange File Format, u-Law, MIDI, and Waveform Audio.

### RealAudio

RealAudio is a sound format that is best known for its streaming capabilities and good compression rates. RealAudio files can easily support 30 minutes of audio, making them ideal for speeches, radio programs, and other forms of broadcast information.

RealAudio files can be played by the RealPlayer plug-in, which is available free from Progressive Networks. To use RealAudio files on your Web page, you need to use Progressive Networks software on your server, and your Web page visitors must have sound cards installed in their computers. Unlike the other sound file formats that can be called with the <EMBED> tag, RealAudio files are started by creating a link to a metafile. The metafile is an ASCII text file that contains the URL of the sound file to play and uses the RAM (RealAudio metafile) extension.

**u-Law**

The u-Law format, pronounced mu-law, is often used to store and play sounds on UNIX machines; however, it is supported by plug-ins on most platforms. The Netscape Audio Player plug-in plays this type of file. Before Netscape Navigator 3.0, this plug-in was known as NAPLAYER.

**Waveform Audio**

The waveform audio format is the default multimedia sound format for Windows 3.1, 95, and NT workstations, and is supported by plug-ins for both Microsoft Explorer and Netscape Navigator. Even if the browser user removes the plug-in that supports waveform audio files, the user can still download and play mono and stereo sound files using the Media Player software distributed with Windows.

 **Exercise 9.3: If you're preparing to take the certification exam, or if you want to practice what you learned in this section, turn to the end of this chapter and complete Exercise 9.3. When you are done, continue reading here to prepare for the next exercise.**

## VIDEO GUIDELINES

Sometimes there is no better way to describe something than to show a video of it. The following are some examples of how you might use videos on a Web page:

- Playback a speech or broadcast where the speaker's image and personality enhance the message.

- Illustrate a dynamic process that is difficult to describe with words and static images.

- Preview a movie or video you want to promote.

The procedure for starting videos was described earlier in this chapter. Also, be sure to review the "General Guidelines" section before you start creating and using video files. This section introduces the video formats that you can use and the plug-ins and helper applications that support them (Table 9.8). Unless you plan to use video files that someone else has already created, you'll need to choose a video format to get started. Table 9.9 provides additional information on the plug-ins and helper applications listed in Table 9.8.

| T A B L E  9.8 Video File Formats | VIDEO FORMAT (EXTENSIONS) | COMPATIBLE PLUG-INS AND HELPER APPLICATIONS |
| --- | --- | --- |
| | Motion Picture Experts Group (.mpeg) | NET TOOB |
| | QuickTime (.mov, .qt) | NET TOOB, QuickTime application, QuickTime plug-in |
| | RealVideo (.rv, .rm) | Real Player |
| | Video for Windows (.avi) | NET TOOB, QuickTime 2.0 plug-in Video for Windows plug-in |

T A B L E  9.9

Video File Plug-Ins

| PLUG-IN | PROVIDER | URL | STREAMING? |
| --- | --- | --- | --- |
| NET TOOB | Digital Bitcasting Corp. | www.duplexx.com | Yes |
| QuickTime | Apple Computer | www.apple.com/quicktime | Yes |
| Real Player | Progressive Networks | www.realaudio.com | Yes |
| Video for Windows plug-in | Netscape. Provided with Netscape Navigator. | www.netscape.com | |

The following sections provide additional information on video file formats, plug-ins, and helper applications.

### Motion Picture Experts Group

The Motion Picture Experts Group (MPEG) file format was developed as a standard by the International Standards Organization (ISO). MPEG files are relatively small, but they offer modest quality. The MPEG video format is the only video format introduced in this chapter that is not closely tied to a particular manufacturer. MPEG plug-ins are available on all platforms.

### QuickTime

The QuickTime video format was developed by Apple computer, and Apple's QuickTime plug-in and QuickTime player are often used to view QuickTime files.

QuickTime movies can include both video and sounds. When adding sounds to QuickTime movies, you can use the following sound formats: Audio Interchange File Format, MIDI, MPEG Layer 2, u-Law, and waveform audio.

The QuickTime 2.0 plug-in plays both QuickTime and Video for Windows formats and provides limited support for MPEG files.

**NOTE** **When QuickTime movies are developed on a Macintosh, Internet Explorer users might have trouble viewing movies that are saved with the .mov extension.**

### RealVideo

RealVideo is a video format from Progressive Networks, by the same people who developed the RealAudio format. As with RealAudio, RealVideo offers good compression and quality. You can play both RealAudio and RealVideo files with the RealPlayer 4.0 plug-in from Progressive Networks.

### Video for Windows

The Audio/Visual Interleaved (.avi) format is the default multimedia video format for Windows 3.1, 95, and NT workstations and is supported by plug-ins for both Microsoft Explorer and Netscape Navigator. Even if the browser user removes the plug-in that supports waveform audio files, the user can still download and play video files using the Media Player software distributed with Windows.

**Exercises 9.4 and 9.5: If you're preparing to take the certification exam, or if you want to practice what you learned in this section, turn to the end of this chapter and complete Exercises 9.4 and 9.5.**

## Summary

This chapter introduced multimedia and described how multimedia works, how to play multimedia, and guidelines for using multimedia. The multimedia described in this chapter include animations, sounds, and videos. These types of multimedia are stored in files.

To play a multimedia file, you use an HTML tag to reference the file in a manner that is similar to referencing an image file. One of the differences is that many multimedia files require plug-in or helper applications, which play the multimedia file. To determine whether the browser, a plug-in, or a helper application plays a file, the browser reads the MIME type, which the Web server sends to the browser with the multimedia file.

While you can find many multimedia files on the Web, to create a multimedia file, you usually need to use special software and hardware. To create animation, you need animation software, and both sound and video require hardware and software for recording.

To play multimedia in Web pages, you can use HTML tags to refer to inline media or referenced media. Inline media is a multimedia file that is called directly from your Web page as it loads. Referenced media is a multimedia file that is not loaded until the Web page visitor clicks a link that refers to the file. Inline media is typically called with the <EMBED> tag, and referenced media is usually called with an anchor tag, <A>.

When you use multimedia on your Web pages, it is courteous to let your Web page visitors know in advance which plug-ins they need to view your multimedia files. You can do this with a front door page to the Web site or area that uses multimedia, or you can add information on your Web pages near the links that call the multimedia files.

As with image files, you can reduce the size and download time for most multimedia files by reducing the amount of detail in the file and the size of the file. For sound files, detail is measured in bit depth, and size is measured in terms of sampling frequency and length. For animations and video, sounds, colors, frames, and image size all contribute to the finished size of the file.

The following word puzzle contains many of the terms discussed in this chapter. See if you can find all the words. As you search for the words, ask yourself why the word is in the list and how it was used in this chapter. If you don't know the answers to these questions, you might want to review the chapter.

```
P  L  A  Y  B  A  C  K  C  M  E  D  O  M  H
L  T  S  A  M  P  L  I  N  G  E  Z  U  D  T
U  N  A  C  H  M  H  V  I  C  L  L  T  F  P
G  D  U  O  R  E  M  O  N  C  T  A  P  T  E
I  A  D  N  H  H  L  E  T  I  S  V  I  H  D
N  O  I  S  S  E  R  P  M  O  C  A  R  G  N
S  L  O  O  G  E  N  E  E  I  G  J  C  I  E
P  N  A  L  F  N  D  I  F  R  M  R  S  R  D
A  W  C  E  O  I  I  Q  L  M  R  V  A  Y  D
G  O  R  E  A  C  I  M  A  N  Y  D  V  P  I
E  D  O  D  N  O  I  T  A  M  I  N  A  O  H
D  N  B  E  L  I  F  A  T  E  M  J  J  C  R
O  U  A  B  D  D  L  O  W  S  R  C  J  F  L
O  O  T  M  P  I  H  E  I  G  H  T  D  I  W
R  S  G  E  P  M  V  K  D  N  U  O  S  G  B
```

| | | | |
|---|---|---|---|
| ASCII | download | JavaScript | photograph |
| acrobat | dynamic | LOWSRC | playback |
| animation | embed | MIDI | plugin |
| audio | GIF | MIME | referenced |
| BGSOUND | HREF | MPEG | sampling |
| compression | height | metafile | sound |
| console | helper | modem | streaming |
| copyright | hidden | multimedia | VRML |
| depth | inline | PDF | video |
| door | Java | PLUGINSPAGE | width |

## EXERCISE 9.1: UNDERSTANDING MULTIMEDIA

This exercise tests your understanding of multimedia, how it operates with the Web, and how to play multimedia files on your Web pages. To complete this exercise, answer the following questions:

**1** • List two uses for multimedia.

    a. . . . . . . . . . . . . . . . . . . . . . . . . . . . . . . . . . . . . .

    b. . . . . . . . . . . . . . . . . . . . . . . . . . . . . . . . . . . . . .

**2** • List two advantages that text and image Web pages have over multimedia Web pages.

    a. . . . . . . . . . . . . . . . . . . . . . . . . . . . . . . . . . . . . .

    b. . . . . . . . . . . . . . . . . . . . . . . . . . . . . . . . . . . . . .

**3** • Which type of program extends the functionality of a browser?

    Answer: . . . . . . . . . . . . . . . . . . . . . . . . . . . . . . . . .

**4** • Which type of program displays or plays a file when the browser and its extensions cannot open the file?

    Answer: . . . . . . . . . . . . . . . . . . . . . . . . . . . . . . . . .

**5** • Which file format is often used to distribute product documentation for software that is distributed online?

    Answer: . . . . . . . . . . . . . . . . . . . . . . . . . . . . . . . . .

**6** • What does a Web server include with a downloaded file to identify the file type?

    Answer: . . . . . . . . . . . . . . . . . . . . . . . . . . . . . . . . .

**7** • A browser is suddenly using a different browser extension to display a media file. What might have happened?

Answer: . . . . . . . . . . . . . . . . . . . . . . . . . . . . . . . . . . . . .

**8** • Which HTML tag is typically used to play inline media files?

Answer: . . . . . . . . . . . . . . . . . . . . . . . . . . . . . . . . . . . . .

**9** • Which HTML tag is typically used to play referenced media files?

Answer: . . . . . . . . . . . . . . . . . . . . . . . . . . . . . . . . . . . . .

**10** • Which type of media file plays when the Web page is downloaded?

Answer: . . . . . . . . . . . . . . . . . . . . . . . . . . . . . . . . . . . . .

**11** • When playing sounds, what is the purpose of the HEIGHT and WIDTH attributes?

Answer: . . . . . . . . . . . . . . . . . . . . . . . . . . . . . . . . . . . . .

**12** • What is the purpose of the HIDDEN attribute?

Answer: . . . . . . . . . . . . . . . . . . . . . . . . . . . . . . . . . . . . .

**13** • What is the purpose of the PLUGINSPAGE attribute?

Answer: . . . . . . . . . . . . . . . . . . . . . . . . . . . . . . . . . . . . .

**14** • What Internet Explorer HTML tag enables you to play background sounds?

Answer: . . . . . . . . . . . . . . . . . . . . . . . . . . . . . . . . . . . . .

## EXERCISE 9.2: UNDERSTANDING ANIMATION GUIDELINES

This exercise tests your understanding of the animation guidelines described in this chapter. To complete this exercise, answer the following questions:

**1** • List three ways to reduce the size of animation files.

a. . . . . . . . . . . . . . . . . . . . . . . . . . . . . . . . . . . . . . . . . . .

b. . . . . . . . . . . . . . . . . . . . . . . . . . . . . . . . . . . . . . . . . . .

c. . . . . . . . . . . . . . . . . . . . . . . . . . . . . . . . . . . . . . . . . . .

**2** • When should you worry about copyright restrictions for animation files?

Answer: . . . . . . . . . . . . . . . . . . . . . . . . . . . . . . . . . . . . . .

**3** • List three purposes for using animation on a Web page.

a. . . . . . . . . . . . . . . . . . . . . . . . . . . . . . . . . . . . . . . . . . .

b. . . . . . . . . . . . . . . . . . . . . . . . . . . . . . . . . . . . . . . . . . .

c. . . . . . . . . . . . . . . . . . . . . . . . . . . . . . . . . . . . . . . . . . .

**4** • List two advantages that animation files have over video files.

a. . . . . . . . . . . . . . . . . . . . . . . . . . . . . . . . . . . . . . . . . . .

b. . . . . . . . . . . . . . . . . . . . . . . . . . . . . . . . . . . . . . . . . . .

**5** • Can you have too many animations on a page? Why?

Answer: . . . . . . . . . . . . . . . . . . . . . . . . . . . . . . . . . . . . . .

**6** • Which animation file format do you play using the <IMG> tag?

Answer: . . . . . . . . . . . . . . . . . . . . . . . . . . . . . . . . . . . . . .

**7** • Which animation file format was developed to create virtual worlds?

Answer: . . . . . . . . . . . . . . . . . . . . . . . . . . . . . . . . . . . . . . . . .

**8** • Which plug-in plays AUTHORWARE, DIRECTOR, and FLASH animation files?

Answer: . . . . . . . . . . . . . . . . . . . . . . . . . . . . . . . . . . . . . . . . .

**9** • Which three animation formats play in most browsers without a plug-in?

a. . . . . . . . . . . . . . . . . . . . . . . . . . . . . . . . . . . . . . . . . . . .

b. . . . . . . . . . . . . . . . . . . . . . . . . . . . . . . . . . . . . . . . . . . .

c. . . . . . . . . . . . . . . . . . . . . . . . . . . . . . . . . . . . . . . . . . . .

**10** • What is unique about the Flash file format?

Answer: . . . . . . . . . . . . . . . . . . . . . . . . . . . . . . . . . . . . . . . . .

**11** • List two disadvantages to using Java and JavaScript to create animations.

a. . . . . . . . . . . . . . . . . . . . . . . . . . . . . . . . . . . . . . . . . . . .

b. . . . . . . . . . . . . . . . . . . . . . . . . . . . . . . . . . . . . . . . . . . .

**12** • What is the file format for VRML files?

Answer: . . . . . . . . . . . . . . . . . . . . . . . . . . . . . . . . . . . . . . . . .

## EXERCISE 9.3: UNDERSTANDING GUIDELINES FOR SOUNDS

This exercise tests your understanding of guidelines presented in this chapter for using sound files. To complete this exercise, answer the following questions:

**1** • List three ways to reduce the size of sound files.

a. . . . . . . . . . . . . . . . . . . . . . . . . . . . . . . . . . . . . .

b. . . . . . . . . . . . . . . . . . . . . . . . . . . . . . . . . . . . . .

c. . . . . . . . . . . . . . . . . . . . . . . . . . . . . . . . . . . . . .

**2** • How can you minimize the download time for HTML pages that use background sounds?

Answer: . . . . . . . . . . . . . . . . . . . . . . . . . . . . . . . . . .

**3** • Which sound file format was developed by Apple Computer?

Answer: . . . . . . . . . . . . . . . . . . . . . . . . . . . . . . . . . .

**4** • Which sound file format does not store sampled sounds?

Answer: . . . . . . . . . . . . . . . . . . . . . . . . . . . . . . . . . .

**5** • Which sound file format is most common on UNIX computers?

Answer: . . . . . . . . . . . . . . . . . . . . . . . . . . . . . . . . . .

**6** • Which sound file format is most common on Windows computers?

Answer: . . . . . . . . . . . . . . . . . . . . . . . . . . . . . . . . . .

**7** • What is different about the procedure for starting RealAudio sounds?

Answer: . . . . . . . . . . . . . . . . . . . . . . . . . . . . . . . . . .

**EXERCISE 9.4: UNDERSTANDING VIDEO GUIDELINES**

This exercise tests your understanding of the video guidelines presented in this chapter. To complete this exercise, answer the following questions:

**1** • Which video file format was developed by the International Standards Organization (ISO)?

Answer: . . . . . . . . . . . . . . . . . . . . . . . . . . . . . . . . . . . . . . .

**2** • Which video file format was developed by Apple Computer?

Answer: . . . . . . . . . . . . . . . . . . . . . . . . . . . . . . . . . . . . . . .

**3** • Progressive Networks developed which video file format?

Answer: . . . . . . . . . . . . . . . . . . . . . . . . . . . . . . . . . . . . . . .

**4** • All Windows computers support which video file format?

Answer: . . . . . . . . . . . . . . . . . . . . . . . . . . . . . . . . . . . . . . .

**5** • List two ways to reduce the size of video files.

a. . . . . . . . . . . . . . . . . . . . . . . . . . . . . . . . . . . . . . . . . . . .

b. . . . . . . . . . . . . . . . . . . . . . . . . . . . . . . . . . . . . . . . . . . .

### EXERCISE 9.5: USING MULTIMEDIA

In this exercise, you add multimedia to a Web page and test your Web page. To complete this exercise, do the following:

**1** • Use a text editor or word-processor program to open the following file on this book's CD-ROM:

*d*:/DemoWeb2/Answers/spin.htm

**2** • Below the line that says "Time flys!," add an HTML tag that calls an animated GIF file named SPIN.GIF. This image is 100 pixels tall and 100 pixels wide.

**3** • Below the line that says "Use the control panel to play the sound." add an HTML tag that calls a sound file named HELLO.WAV and displays a control panel that is 60 pixels tall and 146 pixels wide.

**4** • Save the modified Web page to your computer using the correct extension of HTML files.

**5** • Copy the following files from the CD to the same directory where you stored your modified Web page:

*d*:/DemoWeb2/Answers/spin.gif
*d*:/DemoWeb2/Answers/hello.wav

**6** • Open your modified Web page and view the changes. Your Web page should be similar to the following file on the CD:

*d*:/DemoWeb2/Answers/spin2.htm

**7** • Play the sound.

**8** • Stop the animation.

**9** • Extra credit: Use the trial version of GIF Movie Gear that is provided on the CD to open the SPIN.GIF file and reverse the direction of the spinning arrow.

# CHAPTER 10

# Applying and Publishing Your Design

If you have been creating your Web site while reading this book, you started the design in Chapter 7, learned about images and multimedia in Chapters 8 and 9, and are now returning to design issues in this chapter. This chapter introduces design issues and techniques that are easier to understand once you are familiar with all of the HTML and image issues that apply to Web design.

This chapter starts with an introduction to some of the design issues that affect your Web pages when your visitors use different types of browsers. The following sections present instructions and guidelines for positioning Web page elements and using Web navigation tools. Additional sections provide guidelines for using graphical and HTML text and supporting visually impaired visitors. You'll want to consider these guidelines and issues as you create your Web site.

As you complete each phase of your Web site design and implementation, you should consider testing your Web site as described later in this chapter. When your Web site is complete, the final sections provide guidelines for publishing and publicizing your Web site.

## Supporting Multiple Browsers

One of the challenges that all Web designers have to contend with is the different feature sets supported by Web browsers. Not only are the feature sets different between different manufacturers, but they are different between different versions of the same browser. Feature sets can also differ between the platforms supported by the same version of a browser. For example, table cells that look fine on a Windows computer, may appear narrower on a Macintosh computer, and this can change the line breaks in table cells, making a professionally designed table look garbled.

The differences between browsers are caused by several issues. First, each browser is designed to support a specific HTML specification (for example, HTML version 3.2). This accounts for most of the differences between different versions of the same browser. Second, competition and impatience with the standard-development process have driven browser vendors to develop their own extensions to the HTML specifications. Sometimes these extensions are added to the next version of the HTML specification, and other times they aren't. Popular extensions are usually added and are eventually supported by all browsers.

As a Web designer, you need to consider the differences between browsers as you design and build your Web site. If you are designing for an intranet audience that uses only one type of browser, you can design for a specific version of that browser and use any extensions supported by the browser. If you are designing for an Internet audience, you'll probably want to design for a specific browser and version and avoid using tags that are extensions to the HTML specification to which the browser conforms.

Unfortunately, it is not always easy to recognize HTML extensions as you are creating Web pages. If you are using an HTML editor, such as Netscape Composer, it will insert tags and attributes that Netscape Navigator supports. You might use a tag or attribute that you read about in a magazine article and later find out that some browsers don't support it.

Throughout this book, I've highlighted the areas where I know about the browser differences, and I'll introduce more of these differences later in this chapter. However, the best way to determine the support for a tag or attribute is to use it in a Web page, and then view the page in each of the browsers your audience might use. You'll learn more about testing Web sites and pages later in this chapter.

The following are some examples of HTML tags and attributes that are supported differently in browsers:

- ▸ While the ⟨HR⟩ tag is supported in most browsers, the WIDTH, SIZE, and ALIGN attributes might or might not be supported.

- ▸ The ⟨CENTER⟩ tag is supported by Netscape Navigator and Internet Explorer 3.0 and later. Some other browsers don't support it.

- ▸ The fonts used for the ⟨H1⟩, ⟨P⟩, ⟨LI⟩, ⟨I⟩, and ⟨B⟩ tags are determined by the browser defaults or by the browser user, if the user chooses to override the defaults.

**NOTE** **The user generally selects a variable-width (proportional) font and a fixed-width (monospaced) font. The browser determines which tags use which fonts.**

Fortunately, browsers ignore unrecognized tags and attributes. If you do use a tag or attribute that is not supported by a browser, the browser user will still see your Web page; it will just appear as if the unsupported tag or attribute is missing.

**TIP**

**When creating the content for Web pages that will be viewed by different browsers, avoid references to specific browser commands and controls, such as the File→Save command or the Back button. These controls might have different names in different browsers. For example, some browsers have a Reload button and others have a Refresh button.**

**To make your content correct for multiple browsers, write your instructions using generic phrases instead of commands. For example, ask users to "save the file" or "go back to the previous page." In the case of commands, such as Reload and Refresh, however, you might have to choose the term that applies to the majority of your audience.**

## Positioning Text and Graphics

Chapter 2 shows how to position text on Web pages using basic HTML tags; however, you can use advanced features to position text and graphics with more precision. Many of the techniques described in this section are not obvious because they are workarounds. HTML is not designed for page layout, so clever Web designers around the globe have come up with tricks for using other Web page features to control page layout.

To control the positioning of text, foreground images, and background images, for example, designers often use one or more of the following:

- ▶ HTML tags

- ▶ Spacer art

- ▶ Tables

- ▶ Frames

The following sections describe how to select a page size for your Web pages and how to align Web page elements using the above features.

**TIP**

**Some of the alignment techniques described in the following sections are not supported in all browsers. Before you use these techniques throughout a site—test them. After you know which techniques you prefer, use the same techniques on all of your Web pages to provide a consistent look and to make updates easier.**

## SELECTING A PAGE SIZE

Before you start creating your Web pages, it is wise to select a standard page size for all of the pages in your site. Otherwise, site visitors might have to resize their browser window for different pages or spend time scrolling. Choosing a standard page size presents a consistent view of your Web site, which gives your Web site a more professional appearance.

Unfortunately, there is no perfect page size. The maximum page size for each visitor is determined by his computer display capabilities, the space used by browser controls, and the size of the browser window. To determine the maximum number of pixels available for your Web page, total the pixels supported by the computer display and subtract the pixel dimensions of the browser title bar, menu bar, toolbars, scroll bars, and borders. The remaining area is available for Web pages if the browser user doesn't reduce the size of the window. Table 10.1 lists the dimensions of some of the more popular display areas and the dimensions for the Web page display area.

| T A B L E  10.1 | DISPLAY AREA IN PIXELS | BROWER AREA WIDTH (NO SCROLL-BAR) | BROWSER AREA WIDTH WITH SCROLL-BAR | BROWSER AREA HEIGHT WITH STANDARD TOOLBARS | BROWSER AREA HEIGHT WITH TEXT-ONLY TOOLBARS |
|---|---|---|---|---|---|
| *Netscape Navigator 4 Page Areas* | 640 × 400 | 578 | 565 | 254 | 275 |
| | 640 × 480 | 578 | 565 | 334 | 355 |
| | 800 × 600 | 738 | 725 | 454 | 475 |
| | 1024 × 768 | 962 | 949 | 622 | 643 |

The computer display area is determined by the size of the computer display and the capabilities of the graphics adapter. The most popular display sizes are 14- to 20-inch displays, but the graphics adapters determine the actual number of pixels displayed. For example, a 14-inch computer display can display either 640 × 480 pixels or 800 × 600 pixels if the graphics adapter supports both these settings.

While the 640 × 400 size is used by some laptops, the most common display area supported by computers is 640 × 480. If you want your complete page to be visible on most computers without scrolling, determine the maximum page size your target browser displays on a 640 × 480 display and make that your standard page size.

If the 640 × 480 page size is too small for your needs, you might choose to support 800 × 600 display areas, or you might choose to use the 640 pixel width and create longer Web pages. Horizontal scrolling is very annoying, especially when you have to do it to read the end of each text line. While many designers strive to minimize horizontal and vertical scrolling, vertical scrolling is reasonable if you have provided enough information at the top of the page to convince the visitor that the offscreen contents are worth the effort of scrolling.

To test the page size you select, create a colored foreground image of that size, create a Web page that contains only that image, and view the Web page in your target browser on your target display size. If scroll bars appear, your target page size is too large. If background space appears around the image, you are not using all of the available page area. Later in this chapter, you learn more about testing Web pages, and you will find URLs for some Web sites that enable you to test Web page areas.

When you start creating Web pages, the actual page size displayed in the browser window is determined by the page contents. To create a Web page of a minimum width, you need to create a table or image that is that wide. To create a page of a specified length, add contents to the page until the page reaches that length, or use an image that matches that length. The easiest way to establish the page area is to create a background image that uses the page dimensions.

**NOTE**

**You can't count on the length of text lines to establish the page width. Browsers adjust the page width of text lines based on the width of other elements, such as tables and images. Text appears in the window based on the page width set by other page elements and based on the fonts the browser user selects.**

Once you establish your page size, publish this for everyone on the design team. If anyone creates content that is wider or longer than the preferred page size, scrollbars might appear or content might appear to run off of the background image. Remember, it is the content on each Web page that determines the total page size. There are no page size tags in HTML.

**NOTE**

**If you have experimented with NetObjects Fusion, which is introduced in Chapter 6, you might have discovered page size settings in that program. NetObjects Fusion uses tables to create the masterborder and layout areas, as well as other areas within these areas. You'll see this if you look at the page source HTML for a NetObjects Fusion Web page. NetObjects Fusion defines the page size by creating a table that matches the page size. The information you enter in NetObjects Fusion pages is actually entered in cells of the master table.**

## ALIGNING WITH HTML TAGS

Chapter 2 introduces HTML tags that you can use to position text and images on a Web page. All content that you enter is positioned from the upper-left corner of the Web page. Content on each line is displayed from left to right unless HTML tags specify otherwise. Each new line adds length to the Web page.

When you are positioning images on a page, Internet Explorer browsers support special <IMG> tag attributes that enable you to position a foreground image from the upper-left corner of the page accurately. If the majority of your Web site visitors will be using Internet Explorer, you might want to use these attributes. To position an image for Internet Explorer users, enter a tag similar to the following:

```
<IMG SRC=filename.ext TOPMARGIN=100 LEFTMARGIN=50 ALT="Image">
```

This tag positions the foreground image, *filename.ext*, 100 pixels from the top of the page and 50 pixels from the left margin. Of course, as described in Chapter 8, you should include the image dimensions with the HEIGHT and WIDTH attributes to improve the Web page display speed.

Another handy HTML tag for positioning Web page content is the <UL> tag introduced in Chapter 3 for creating lists. The <UL> tag indents the caption for a list. This indent is similar to the indent produced by the Tab key in word-processor programs. Add additional <UL> tags, and the result is similar to pressing the Tab key additional times. To return to the left margin, however, you need to add the corresponding closing tags, `</UL>`. For example, the following HTML tags indent a line of text the equivalent of two tabs:

```
<UL><UL>This is indented text.</UL></UL>
```

## ALIGNING WITH ART

Chapter 8 describes how to create Web images. Sometimes, you can use Web images to position your Web page objects.

One way to position text or foreground images is to add them to the background image. The advantage to this approach is that you can place elements in the background with pixel accuracy.

Another way to control the positioning of Web page objects with art is to create spacer art. Foreground Web images appear inline with text and other images, so other objects can appear to the left or right of a foreground image, but they can't appear over or under the image. This means that you can use an image to move other objects to the left or the right. For example, I can use an image that is 100 pixels wide to position a line of text 100 pixels from the left margin.

The important thing to remember when creating spacer art is that it must appear invisible, otherwise it is a foreground image. To create invisible spacer art, create the art in the same color as the background, or create the art using a single color, and then specify that color as a transparent color. Chapter 8 explained how to create transparent artwork.

## ALIGNING WITH TABLES

Chapter 3 described how to organize text in HTML tables, but you can also add images to tables. Many Web pages use tables to create multiple columns and margins, and to position images. Most people don't realize they are viewing tables because the table borders are not displayed. Figure 10.1 shows a Web page that uses a table to organize the page elements. I set the border to 1 pixel so you can see the table cells, but the borders are hidden on the finished page. Figure 10.3 shows this page without the borders.

*Table-Aligned Web Page*

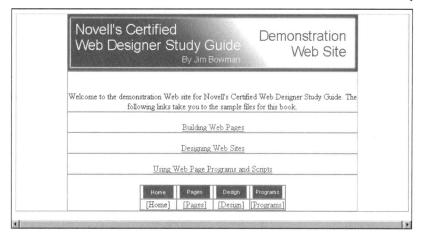

You can view the finished and border versions of this page on the demonstration Web site at the following locations:

*d:/DemoWeb2/Design/Apply/table2.htm* (finished Web page)

*d:/DemoWeb2/Design/Apply/table.htm* (unfinished Web page with borders)

The following are some guidelines to keep in mind when using tables to organize Web pages:

▸ To set the cell width for a column, use the WIDTH attribute in the cell tag (<TD> or <TR>), or place transparent art in an empty cell.

▸ You can define a different background color for each table cell by adding the BGCOLOR attribute to the cell tag.

▸ To position objects within table cells, use the ALIGN (horizontal alignment) and VALIGN (vertical alignment) attributes in the table cell tags.

▸ To display a table with no border, set the BORDER attribute to 0 in the opening <TABLE> tag.

▶ Use tables with fixed widths to center page elements precisely. If you use the <CENTER> or <DIV> tags, the page elements will be centered according to the browser window width, and your page design will be different for every browser window size.

▶ To align images together without any space between them, place them in adjacent table cells and set the BORDER, CELLSPACING, and CELLPADDING attributes to 0. When you place images next to each other without tables, the browser displays some space between each image.

▶ To create margins for your Web page, create a table and leave the left and right columns empty. Use the WIDTH attribute in the cell tags to fix the widths for the margins or specify the relative width percentages.

▶ To set the width for a table, use the WIDTH attribute in the opening <TABLE> tag. If you don't specify a table width, table cells will be stretched and compacted as browser users resize their windows.

For more information on using the table tags and attributes described above, see Chapter 3.

## ALIGNING WITH FRAMES

HTML frames, which were introduced in Chapter 5, enable you to divide the browser window into regions or frames, each of which displays a separate Web page. As shown in Figure 10.2, frames are often used to display information, such as a banner or table of contents, that you want to appear on every Web page. When a user selects a link in the table of contents, the appropriate Web page appears in the target frame. Frames are another tool that you can use to align the objects on your Web pages. As with tables, you can turn off the borders on frames to hide the frame structure.

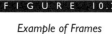
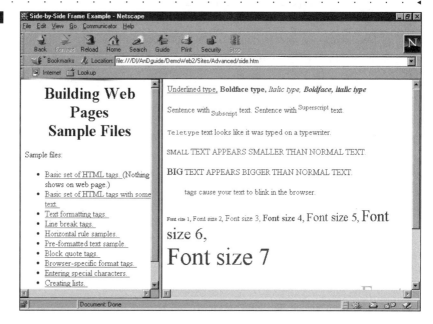

When you are considering which alignment tools to use for your Web page design, remember that frames are a relatively new feature (HTML 3.2) and are not supported by as many browsers as tables. Frames also have some other disadvantages. For example, when a visitor attempts to bookmark a frame, it is the frameset that gets bookmarked; visitors cannot bookmark and return to particular target frames.

Another issue to consider is that some frame links open new browser windows, and when this happens, visitors can't use the Back button to return to a previously viewed page. (They have to switch browser windows.) One way to make this less painful for the visitor is to provide a link in the new browser window that displays the previous page. However, the visitor still has two browser windows open.

If you think frames are the best solution for your Web site, and you want to support nonframe browsers too, consider creating an additional *no-frame* Web site. To give the users a choice between the two Web sites, create a front door Web page with links to the home pages for the frame and no-frame home pages.

## BALANCING LEFT-JUSTIFIED PAGES

One common design problem on the Web is the left-justified Web page that has lots of short lines on the left and lots of white space on the right. Although it is good to design white space into your Web pages, excessive white space is a waste of space, especially when it produces a visual effect that is heavily weighted to one side.

To minimize or eliminate the lopsided effect of left-justified Web pages, consider doing one or more of the following:

- ▸ Combine short lines of text to create a longer line

- ▸ Use wide graphics or right justify graphics to counter balance the left-side content

- ▸ Use weighted images, such as swashes, that appear darker on the right side, to visually increase the content on the right

- ▸ Use tables to organize text in multiple columns

 **Exercise 10.1: If you're preparing to take the certification exam, or if you want to practice what you learned in this section, turn to the end of this chapter and complete Exercise 10.1. When you are done, continue reading here to prepare for the next exercise.**

# Adding Navigation Aids to Web Sites

The navigation aids that you add to your Web site define the Web site structure and determine how visitors access your Web pages. The following sections summarize the navigation tools you can use and provide guidelines for using them as part of your Web site design.

## NAVIGATION TOOLS

The previous chapters introduced the following types of navigation tools:

- ▸ HTML text links

- ▸ Image links

- ▸ Navigation bars

- ▸ Index or table-of-contents frames

- ▸ Site maps

The following sections describe these tools and provide guidelines that apply only to a particular tool. The guidelines section that follows the tool descriptions provides guidelines that apply to all tools.

### HTML Text Links

HTML text links were introduced in Chapter 4, and use the following format:

```
<A HREF=URL>Link text.</A>
```

Although HTML text links can be used anywhere on the page, they are typically used for topical links from within the Web page content or from text versions of navigation bars, index frames, and site maps. When browser users turn off the display of Web images, or when they use browsers that don't support images, text links are the only tools that they can use to navigate your site.

**TIP**

**When you create text links, avoid language, such as "click here." Some text-only browsers don't support mice. Instead, users might use the Tab key to select links, and then press Enter to activate a link.**

### Individual Image Links

Image links were introduced in Chapter 4, and use the following format:

```
<A HREF=URL><IMG SRC=image.ext></A>
```

Image links can be used anywhere on the Web page. The most important thing to consider when creating image links is whether Web site visitors will recognize them as links. Images that appear as buttons are almost always recognized as links, but other images might just appear as images.

To see if your image links are obvious enough, ask coworkers to look at a Web page with images and image links, and ask them to identify the links. If they can identify image links without hesitation, then your Web site visitors probably can too.

If you find that an image is too obscure to be recognized as a link, change the image or add text that clarifies the image's purpose. For example, you can add the word Home to an image link for your home page.

### Navigation Bars

Navigation bars present multiple links in the form of a control panel. Figure 10.3 shows both a text navigation bar and an image-based navigation bar. Because most, but not all, Web site visitors browse with graphical browsers and image viewing enabled, most Web site designs include graphical navigation bars near the top or left margin of the Web page, and place text navigation bars at the bottom of the page. This approach accommodates all users and encourages visitors to view your graphics.

FIGURE   10.3

*Text and Image-Based
Navigation Bars*

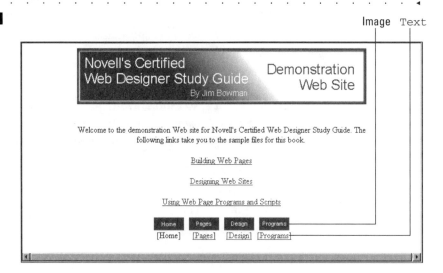

Navigation bars are introduced in multiple chapters because they are formed by combining text links or image links, or by creating image maps (which were introduced in Chapter 4).

**To align text links or image links in a navigation bar, place the links in a table.**

TIP

One of the most popular implementations of navigation bars displays a navigation button or link for every Web page at the current level. For example, this type of navigation bar might display links for the home page and all the pages directly below it. The same navigation bar is then placed on the home page and each of the pages below it.

This type of navigation bar has several benefits. First, it provides a consistent navigation interface on all of the pages it is used on. Second, it reduces the work required to create navigation bars, and third, it can be used to identify which page the user is currently viewing. For example, if the visitor is currently viewing the home page, the link to the home page is highlighted and all others are not.

There are several ways to highlight a link in the navigation bar. In text- or image-based navigation bars, you can do this as follows:

1 • If you are creating a navigation bar composed of image links, create two sets of images: a standard set of images and a set of highlighted images. For example, you might create a group of black buttons to serve as links to each page. You might then create a second set of similar red buttons to serve as highlighted buttons.

2 • Create the navigation bar using the text or image links for all pages. For text navigation bars, just create a single link for each page. For image-based navigation bars, create image links that use the standard images you created in Step 1.

3 • Copy the navigation bar to all pages.

4 • On each page, edit the link for that page so that it appears different than the other links. For text navigation bars, for example, you can remove the link tags so the text appears plain, a visual indication that you can't link to the page because you are already there. For image-based navigation bars, change the <IMAGE> tag filename to reference the highlighted version of the image.

After you customize the link on each Web page, your navigation bar is complete. To provide navigation at lower levels of the site, you can change your primary navigation bar or you can create a secondary navigation tool bar that appears next to the primary bar. Of course, you can use any of the other navigation tools, as well.

### Index Frames

Index frames are frames that contain the equivalent of a table of contents or index for a Web site or Web site area. Figure 10.2, which appears earlier in this chapter, shows an index frame on the left.

Index frames display in the browser window until the visitor leaves the frameset that defines the index frame. When the visitor selects a link, the destination Web page appears in the target frame and the index frame remains unchanged. This form of persistent navigation ensures that the visitor always has access to the navigation controls.

To use an index frame for site navigation, create your frameset as described in Chapter 5, and then add your navigation controls to the frame you want to use as your index frame. Within the index frame, you can use any of the navigation tools. To create the indentation used for a table of contents, you can use the <UL> tags as described earlier in this chapter.

**NOTE**

**When you are considering using index frames, review the frame issues described earlier in the section titled "Aligning with Frames." Frames are not supported by all browsers, and bookmarks and navigation controls sometimes work differently with frames.**

### Site Maps

Chapter 6 introduces site maps as a Java extension for NetObjects Fusion, but you can create site maps using HTML tags, images, and image maps. Figure 10.4 shows a sample site map that is built with HTML tags arranged in a table.

*Table-Based Site Map*

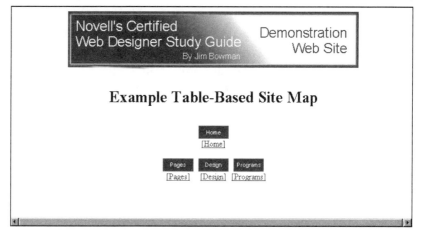

Site maps are a form of utility navigation that provide the following benefits:

▸ Site overview—Visitors see a pictorial representation of the site structure.

▸ Orientation—If you add highlighting that shows the previously visited page, visitors can see where they are in the site.

▸ Free-form navigation—The visitor can select any link in the site map to go directly to the destination page, regardless of the navigation structure.

The most common site map styles are the following:

▸ Table-based site map

▸ Indexed site map

▸ Image map-based site map

▸ Automatically generated site map

Figure 10.4 shows an example of a table-based site map. Each table cell can contain an image link, a text link, or both. To create this type of site map, create a sketch of your Web site architecture, create a table with enough cells to display your Web pages, and then position image and text links in the cells according to their position on the site architecture sketch.

Text-only, table-based site maps download quickly and are supported by all browsers, regardless of whether image viewing is enabled. To speed the download of a table-based site map that uses images, use the same image for all pages, or use a few images to represent the different types of content displayed on Web pages (for example, use a picture icon to represent pages that display pictures only). Reusing images in the site map reduces the download time because an image is only downloaded once, and all copies are created from the downloaded version in the queue.

Indexed site maps use the outline or table of contents format shown earlier in Figure 10.2 for index frames. As with table-based site maps, you can include text links, image links, or both in an indexed site map. The difference between the index frame and the indexed site map is that the indexed site map appears on a separate page from other Web site content. Typically, visitors select the site map link from a navigation bar or another link on the content page, and then they select a link on the site map to select a new destination.

Figure 10.5 shows an image-map site map. To create this type of site map, you need to create an image of your Web site as described in Chapter 8 and assign hot spots to it as described in Chapter 4. The advantage to this type of site map is that you can add lines to your image map to represent links. The disadvantage to this type of site map is that it won't work in text-only browsers.

As described in Chapter 6, NetObjects Fusion can automatically generate a site map. To generate a site map automatically, you need to use a Web utility program that offers this feature. For instructions on creating a site map with NetObjects Fusion, see Chapter 6. For instructions on creating site maps with other utilities, see the appropriate product documentation.

**TIP**

**If your site map is too large for a single Web page, you can create a master-site map and include links to other site maps for specific areas. Also, when you are creating image-map site maps, it is not necessary to show all links in the site map. Instead, just show the principle links that indicate the Web site structure.**

*Image-Map Site Map*

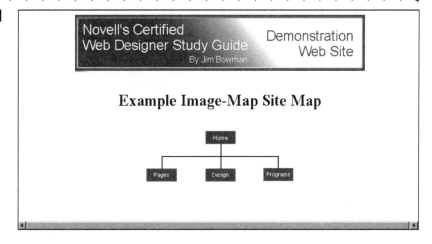

## GUIDELINES

The following are some guidelines to consider when you add navigation controls to your Web site:

- ▸ Design your navigation controls to allow for additions and changes. You might later need to add or delete navigation buttons or pages on your navigation bars and site maps.

- ▸ Use the same link name for all links to a particular page, whether they be in navigation bars, index frames, or elsewhere.

- ▸ When a link is duplicated on many pages, such as a link to a site map, place the link in the same location on all pages.

- ▸ Design navigation controls to coordinate with the colors and fonts in your Web site design.

- ▸ For pages with many images, use an animated image to attract attention to an important link.

▸ Avoid total dependence on navigation features that browsers can disable or might not support. These features include images and frames. Advanced Web page features that users can disable include JavaScript, Java, and ActiveX controls.

▸ At the minimum, always provide at least one link on each page that returns the visitor to the previous page or to the home page. Some browsers do not have equivalents to the Back button, and visitors can get stuck at a Web page if you do not provide the navigation controls to leave.

▸ Optimize link images for minimum file size as described in Chapter 8.

 **Exercise 10.2: If you're preparing to take the certification exam, or if you want to practice what you learned in this section, turn to the end of this chapter and complete Exercise 10.2. When you are done, continue reading here to prepare for the next exercise.**

## Using Graphical and HTML Type

In Chapter 2, you learned to add words and letters to Web pages and format them using HTML tags. This creates HTML type and this type is subject to the limits of HTML and the destination browser settings. For example, if you choose a font that is not available to the destination browser, the browser displays the default font instead.

Graphical type is any words and letters that appear as part of a Web image. The only browser restriction on graphical type is that the browser must be able to display Web images. If the browser doesn't support Web images, or if the user has disabled this feature, the graphical type won't display. Otherwise, graphical type is only limited by the limitations of the Web image format you create it in; and as you'll see in this section, these limits are far less restrictive.

Look around the Web and you'll see many examples of graphical type. Graphical type appears in logos, Web page banners, and on buttons. Graphical type is often used in image maps to present a table of contents or a menu.

Graphical type is not a replacement for HTML type, but it is often used to enhance Web pages for the following reasons:

▶ Graphical type can use any font or font effect your image editor supports.

▶ Graphical type supports more precise positioning of text.

▶ Graphical type can be combined with images to produce effects not possible with HTML text alone.

Although each new generation of HTML provides new features that solve some of the problems of the previous generation, you can't count on browser users to upgrade their systems immediately. The most important benefit of graphical type is that it gives you, the Web page designer, ultimate control over the appearance of your type.

Chapter 2 introduced HTML text formatting, and Chapter 8 described how to create Web images. This Chapter builds upon the information introduced in Chapters 2 and 8 to provide a more complete discussion of using type in Web pages. The following sections introduce some typography fundamentals, provide some guidelines for using type on the Web, and provide additional instructions for using graphical and HTML type.

## TYPOGRAPHY 101

Type design began long before computers during the era of the first printing presses. Although there are more typestyles and principles than I have space to introduce, there are a few basic typestyles and principles that you can use to get started.

### Typestyles

Figure 10.6 shows the three basic typestyles used for publishing with computers: serif, sans serif, and monospaced type. Most of the fonts you will use on your Web pages can be classified as one of these typestyles.

· · · · · · · · · · · · · · · · · · · · · · · · · · · · ·  ◄

**FIGURE  10.6**

*Serif, Sans Serif, and
Monospaced Type*

# Serif Font

# Sans Serif Font

# Monospaced Font

The unique components of serif fonts are the serifs or tails at the bottom of each letter. Serif fonts are generally used for paragraph text, where the serifs help the reader follow the text across the line.

Sans serif fonts are fonts without serifs. These fonts are typically used for headlines, banners, and other text elements where the words are few and you want them to stand out.

Monospaced type is a descendant of the early computer days when most monitors and printers printed all characters into the same size space. In monospaced type an otherwise wide letter M is squeezed into the same size space that the lowercase letter i almost gets lost in. Monospaced type is considered unattractive, but it is still used often to portray computer commands and messages.

You can use either graphical type or HTML type to display these type styles.

### Type-Positioning Controls

Type-positioning controls change the position of letters, words, and lines of text on the page. In Chapter 2, you learned to position text paragraphs in the left and right margins, as well as in the center of the page. You also learned how to start new paragraphs. In typography design circles, however, designers often want more control over their work and use additional features, such as kerning, leading, and baseline shifts to gain this control.

Figure 10.7 shows an example of kerning, which is the process of adding or subtracting small amounts of space between letters to reduce eye fatigue or create special effects. Depending on your image-editing software, kerning can adjust spacing for specific letter combinations or for all the selected characters. You can accomplish a similar effect by adding spaces between letters, but the space character is so wide that it usually makes the text too difficult to read. However, there may be times when you want to add extra spaces between words, and this is called word spacing.

FIGURE 10.7

*Kerning*

# Kerning (Spacing=-1)
# Kerning (Spacing=0)
# Kerning (Spacing=1)
# Kerning (Spacing=2)

Leading (pronounced "ledding") is the term that defines the amount of space between two lines of text. Increased values of leading display more white space, decreased values pack more text on a single page. Figure 10.8 shows examples of different values of leading.

FIGURE 10.8

*Leading*

20
Point
Leading

24
Point
Leading

28
Point
Leading

A baseline shift is illustrated in Figure 10.9. The baseline is the imaginary line on which all characters rest. Typically, text follows the baseline across the page. A baseline shift permits the characters to shift up or down in relation to the primary baseline.

**FIGURE 10.9**

*Baseline Shift and Decorative Typestyles*

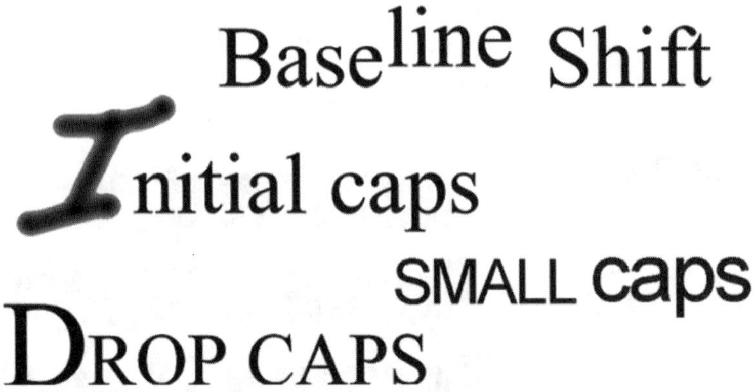

Base<sup>line</sup> Shift

*I*nitial caps

SMALL caps

Dᴿᴼᴾ CAPS

Although HTML text generally uses different leading values for heading text (<H1>, for example) and regular body text, it does not provide specific controls for kerning, leading, and baseline shifts. With graphical type, however, you can position type with pixel accuracy using controls in image editors, such as Photoshop.

### Decorative Type Effects

After you choose a type style, you can use fonts to change the appearance of type. Figure 10.9 introduces some additional type effects you can create independently of fonts.

Small caps are small capital letters that draw attention to a phrase within, or at the beginning of, a paragraph. The smaller font size of the small caps effect balances out the otherwise overbearing effect of all capital letters.

Drop caps and initial caps are typically used at the beginning of a paragraph or chapter. With drop caps, the first letter is significantly larger than the following text; however, it usually appears in a font that is consistent with the text that follows. While initial caps also use a significantly larger first letter, that letter is usually an image or decorative font that stands out from the text that follows.

You can easily create the small caps and drop cap effects in HTML or graphical type. To use the initial caps effect, you'll need to create an image for the initial capital letter.

## TYPOGRAPHY GUIDELINES FOR THE WEB

The following are some guidelines and tips for creating graphical type for Web pages:

▸ Test your fonts before choosing one or more for your Web site. Some fonts display better than others.

▸ Select a readable font size for body text (12 pt for example) and emphasize heading text with a larger font size (16 pt for example), a different color, or a different font.

▸ Avoid using too many fonts. Many Web pages use one sans serif font for headings and one serif font for body text.

▸ Use underlining only with text that serves as a link to another Web page.

▸ Avoid using capital letters to make words stand out. This technique is usually used with typewriters and in other situations where you only have one font to work with. Use bold and italic fonts to highlight words.

▸ When you need a little spelling help, type the text in a word processor first, use the word processor to check the spelling, and then copy the text and paste it in the image. You can paste text directly in the image or into the Photoshop Type Tool dialog box, which is described in the next section.

▸ When placing foreground text over background images, text is easier to read if you select colors that produce a high contrast. For example, black text on white background.

▸ Consider adding figure captions to images. It keeps the caption with the image and aligned the way you choose.

▸ As you develop Web pages, look for opportunities to use both text and graphics. HTML text downloads quickly, but a picture can often be worth a thousand words. Images can also make a page more enjoyable to read.

When you create graphical type, remember that you are creating images, which behave differently from HTML text. You can optimize graphical type images using the same techniques you use to optimize nontext images. For example, you can optimize graphical text images by doing the following:

▸ Use the <IMG> tag WIDTH and HEIGHT attributes so that the Web page displays faster.

▸ Reduce the file size of GIF images by reducing the bit depth or eliminating anti-aliasing.

▸ Use the ALT attribute in the <IMG> tag to specify alternate text that appears when the browser doesn't support images.

**For more information and ideas on using graphical type, browse the following:**
**Cooltype.com:** www.cooltype.com
**NPR Online:** www.npr.org
**PBS Online:** www.pbs.org

## CREATING GRAPHICAL TYPE IN PHOTOSHOP

The Photoshop-type tool enables you to create graphical type quickly, using any of the fonts installed on your computer. You can create colored type, aliased type, and anti-aliased type. Unless you plan to use special graphical effects that require more than 256 colors, create graphical text as GIF images. Because graphical text often contains large areas of solid colors, the JPEG format can introduce noise into your image. As with other line art images, the GIF format enables you to work with fewer colors and reduce the image file size.

**NOTE**

**As with nontext Web images, anti-aliased graphical text images use a larger file size and can display halos. To minimize file size and eliminate halos, use the same techniques described in Chapter 8 for nontext images.**

To create type in Adobe Photoshop, do the following:

**1** • Open or create the image file where you want to add type.

**2** • Select the foreground and background colors for your type. This is especially important when the current foreground color is the same as the background color, or when you plan to use anti-aliasing.

**3** • Select the Type tool and click in the image area. Photoshop displays the Type Tool dialog box shown in Figure 10.10.

**4** • Type text in the text box and use the other controls to format the text.

**5** • To create the type effects described in this chapter, refer to Table 10.2.

**IMPORTANT**

**Some of these effects can be selected in the Type Tool dialog box when the text is created and others must be applied after the text is created. If you create text without an effect that you want to create with the Type Tool dialog box, undo or delete the text and recreate it with the effect.**

**6** • Click OK to place the text in the image area.

After you add text to the image area, you can use any of the Photoshop graphical tools to change the graphical text. You cannot use the text tool to change graphical text, because once the text is added to the image area, Photoshop treats it as an image.

► · · · · · · · · · · · · · · · · · · · · · · · · · · · · · · · · ◄

FIGURE 10.10

Type Tool Dialog Box

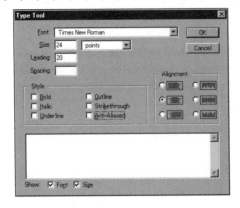

TABLE 10.2

Creating Special Text Effects

| SPECIAL EFFECT | PROCEDURE |
| --- | --- |
| Aliased text | To create text without the extra colors used in anti-aliasing, clear the Anti-Aliased text box in the Text Tool dialog box when you create the text. This creates smaller files with rougher text edges. |
| Anti-aliased text | To create anti-aliased text, check the Anti-Aliased text box in the Text Tool dialog box when you create the text. This creates larger files with smoother text edges. |
| Baseline shift | To create a baseline shift in Photoshop, create your text first, and then use graphics tools, such as the Marquee and Lasso tools, to select and reposition the text. |
| Drop caps | To use the drop caps effect, you need to create two images: the image of the initial letter in the large font size, and the image of the text that follows it. Of course, the text that follows the initial letter should not contain that letter. After you create the two images, use graphics tools, such as the Marquee and Lasso tools, to select and reposition the images. |
| Initial cap | To use the initial cap effect, you need to create two images: the image of the initial letter and the image of the text that follows it. Of course, the text that follows the initial letter should not contain that letter. After you create the two images, use graphics tools, such as the Marquee and Lasso tools, to select and reposition the images. |

**TABLE 10.2**

*Creating Special Text Effects*

| SPECIAL EFFECT | PROCEDURE |
| --- | --- |
| Kerning | In the Text Tool dialog box, enter the number of pixels you want to add or delete between letters in the Spacing text box. |
| | The value you enter is applied to all letters in each word. To reduce spacing, enter a minus symbol before the value you enter. |
| Leading | In the Text Tool dialog box, change the value in the Leading text box. |
| Small caps | To use the small caps effect, you need to create two or more images: the image of the text that precedes the small caps text, the small caps text, and the image of any text that follows the small caps text. After you create the images, use graphics tools, such as the Marquee and Lasso tools, to select and reposition the images. |
| Type styles | To select serif, sans serif, or monospaced type styles, choose a font from the Font drop-down list in the Text tool dialog box. You can preview the font in this dialog box by checking the Show Font checkbox at the bottom of the dialog box. |

## SELECTING BROWSER-SAFE COLORS FOR HTML TEXT

Chapter 8 introduced browser-safe colors, which are colors that appear the same in browsers on different platforms. Chapter 2 described how to specify colors for fonts and backgrounds using tags similar to the following:

```
<BODY BGCOLOR=FFFFFF>

<FONT COLOR=FF0000>This is red text.</FONT>

</BODY>
```

HTML tags use hexadecimal values to represent the same colors that are represented by the decimal numbers introduced in Chapter 8. Although it is annoying that HTML tags use a different numbering system than what is used by many image-editor programs, it is not an insurmountable problem.

Table 10.3 lists the browser-safe hexadecimal color values and the decimal color values that correspond to them. To define text and background colors that will be browser safe, use these values for the red, green, and blue values in your HTML tags.

| TABLE 10.3 | HEXADECIMAL VALUE | DECIMAL VALUE |
|---|---|---|
| Browser-Safe Color Values | 00 | 00 |
| | 33 | 51 |
| | 66 | 102 |
| | 99 | 153 |
| | CC | 204 |
| | FF | 255 |

To use Photoshop to determine the decimal color value for a color in a Web image, do the following:

1 • Open the image in Photoshop.

2 • Select the Eyedropper tool in the Tools palette and click the image color you want to match.

3 • Open the Color Picker by clicking the foreground color square in the Tools palette.

4 • Read the R, G, and B settings in the Color Picker.

If the color you tested is browser safe, you can use Table 10.3 to convert the decimal values to the corresponding hexadecimal values. If the color is not browser safe, you can use a scientific calculator to make the conversion.

## CREATING TYPE EFFECTS WITH HTML

Although HTML type cannot duplicate all of the type effects possible with graphical type, HTML type can display some of them. Table 10.4 shows which effects can be duplicated with HTML type and how to do it.

| | SPECIAL EFFECT | PROCEDURE |
|---|---|---|
| **TABLE 10.4** *Creating Special Text Effects* | Baseline shift | You cannot exactly duplicate a baseline shift with HTML type, but you can use the superscript `<SUP>` and subscript `<SUB>` tags to simulate this. |
| | Drop caps | To create the drop cap effect, use the `<FONT>` tag to create an initial letter that is larger than the following letters. For example: `<FONT=7>H</FONT>ello`. |
| | Initial cap | If you have an image of the initial letter, you can place that image inline with HTML text to produce the initial cap effect. For example: `<IMG SRC=H.gif >ello`. |
| | Kerning | HTML does not provide any controls that support kerning. When kerning is necessary, use graphical type. |
| | Leading | HTML does not provide controls that support leading adjustments, but you can insert varied amounts of white space by using heading tags, such as `<H1>`, which use more leading than standard paragraph text. |
| | Monospaced | HTML supports the following four tags that most browsers display as monospaced type: `<CODE>`, `<KBD>`, `<TT>`, and `<SAMP>`. |
| | Small caps | To create the small caps effect in HTML, use the `<SMALL>` tag as follows: `<SMALL>SMALL TEXT</SMALL>`, *normal text.* |
| | Sans serif | Newer browsers support the `FACE` attribute, which enables you to specify a font, such as a sans serif font, for the Web page. Arial and Helvetica are two sans serif fonts that are available on many computers. |
| | | If the visitor's computer has the specified font, and its browser supports the `FACE` attribute, the selected font is displayed. Otherwise, the attribute is ignored and the default browser font is used. |
| | | Example: `<FONT FACE=HELVETICA>`*sans serif text*`</FONT>` |
| | Serif | As mentioned above for the sans serif style, you can use the `FACE` attribute to select a font. Times and Times New Roman are popular serif fonts. |
| | | Example: `<FONT FACE=Times>`*sans serif text*`</FONT>` |

Exercise 10.3: If you're preparing to take the certification exam, or if you want to practice what you learned in this section, turn to the end of this chapter and complete Exercise 10.3. When you are done, continue reading here to prepare for the next exercise.

## Supporting Visually Impaired Visitors

If you are creating an Internet Web site, you might have visitors that are visually impaired. These visitors depend on speech synthesizers to read the text content of your Web page. To support these visitors, consider doing the following:

▶ Use the ALT attribute in all image tags to specify a meaningful description of the image. Visually impaired visitors won't be able to see the image, but they'll have an idea about what is on the page.

▶ For repetitious graphics, such as bullets, enter the ALT attribute as follows: **ALT=" "**. Otherwise, the speech synthesizer will annoy the visitor by repeating whatever text or symbol (*, for example) you specify.

## Testing Your Web Site

Web site testing is very important. One missing tag can upset the formatting of an entire Web page. A mistake in an anchor tag can produce a page-not-found message, and a misdirected link can create a navigation loop that the visitor cannot exit from without entering a new URL. Testing helps you discover these types of problems before your visitors do.

Consider testing at the following Web site development milestones:

▶ Design complete

▶ Each individual page complete

▸ Prototype complete

▸ Web site published

At each stage of development, your testing should focus on different aspects of the Web site design and function. During the design phase, testing should verify that the site is organized well and meets the needs of the organization and the site visitors. At this stage you might ask users and your site's sponsor to look over your design, storyboard, or initial prototype and make comments. This is user testing, and it is discussed in more detail later in this chapter.

As each Web page is completed, it is important that the page be tested to verify that it appears as it was intended to appear. This is functionality testing, and is described later in this chapter.

Prototypes are unfinished versions of your Web site. You might have many different prototypes, and it is important to perform user and functionality testing for your major releases. For example, if you plan an alpha and beta review of your Web site, you should consider doing a functionality test before each review, and then conduct user and functionality tests during the review. The functionality test before the review checks for major problems that would disrupt the review.

When you think your Web site is ready, it is time to publish it to its audience. Technically, the only difference between a published Web site and a prototype Web site is that one is published, so it is a good idea to think of a published Web site as a published prototype. Because published prototypes can still contain errors, or may still have room for improvement, it is important to continue testing after publishing. If you've done a reasonable amount of testing before publishing, you might choose to let your Web site visitors do your testing. If this is your approach, be sure to give your Web site visitors some way to report errors, issues, and suggestions. The following sections provide guidelines for creating prototypes and conducting functional tests and user tests.

## PROTOTYPING GUIDELINES

Prototyping is one of the steps in the Web design and development process. Your Web site prototype is a preliminary version of your Web site, which can be used for testing and review, but which is not officially published. You can preview this type of site on a local Web server, a local file server, or your local computer.

Your final prototype, however, should be tested using the same type of hardware and Web server software that your finished Web site will use. Otherwise, you might have some surprises when the Web site goes live.

If you publish a prototype site on the Internet for testing, keep the URL a secret. You might also want to create a ROBOTS.TXT file on the Web server that prevents Web search engines from discovering your prototype site and publishing it to the world.

**To learn more about the ROBOTS.TXT file, search for "ROBOTS.TXT" and "standard" on the Internet, see** *Novell's Guide to Web Site Management,* **or browse:** `info.webcrawler.com/mak/projects/robots/robots.html`.

As you are developing your prototype, you can reserve space on pages for different page elements by doing the following:

> ▸ Reserve space for text by creating tables with fixed dimensions. Create one table column for each column of text.

> ▸ Reserve space for images by entering image tags that specify the image dimensions (WIDTH and HEIGHT attributes) and omit the image file name. Use the ALT attribute to indicate what image will appear on the page.

**The <IMG> tag ALT attribute, which this book recommends you use for all images, has another benefit. In newer browsers, the text you specify with the ALT attribute appears when a visitor positions the cursor over an image for a couple of seconds. This makes your ALT text visible to visitors when images are enabled or disabled.**

NOTE

## FUNCTIONALITY TESTING GUIDELINES

Functionality testing verifies that your Web site features work as intended. Functionality testing answers questions, such as the following:

> ▸ Do all the page elements appear where they should?

▶ Do sounds really sound, and do animations really move?

▶ Do links display the correct Web pages?

▶ Is the page appearance acceptable in all supported browsers on all supported platforms?

When you are conducting functionality tests, consider doing the following:

▶ Methodically test all features on every Web page.

▶ View Web pages in several browsers.

▶ Print Web pages from several browsers.

▶ Test Web pages with image display turned off in the browser.

**NOTE**

**Chapter 5 introduced some Web site validation tools that you can use to conduct functionality tests of your Web site.**

**The following Web sites provide useful information for testing the functionality of your Web pages:**
**AgentZ Browser Comparison Page:**
`www.agentz.com/browsers`
**Younis Graphics Web Page Monitor Tester:**
`www.dot.net.au/younis/window.html`

## USER TESTING GUIDELINES

While user testing often includes some functionality testing, the most important component in user testing is the user's impression of your Web site and its ease of use. If your Web site works perfectly but the user gets lost and frustrated, you have a problem. User testing helps discover these types of problems so that you can fix them before publishing your site.

Three popular ways to conduct user testing are the following:

▸ User test sessions

▸ Surveys

▸ Visitor comments

User test sessions usually ask a user to follow a test script, which defines a series of Web pages and interactive tasks you want the user to perform. Your test users can be customers, fellow employees, Web site content editors, your Web master, or anyone else who has an interest in the content and can be objective in their comments. Observers watch the user, and note areas where the user has problems completing the test. The user might also talk aloud to explain her thoughts, so the observers can find out if she is experiencing the site as they intended. The user is also encouraged to write down comments during, or at the end of, the test session.

Surveys are questionnaires that you ask users to complete. There are many ways to conduct surveys. One approach is to create a test script, ask users to follow it, and then ask them to complete a survey. Another approach is to create a survey and publish it in paper or electronic form to solicit comments about your site. You can distribute these surveys using the postal service, e-mail, or online forms. To entice visitors to respond, consider offering freebies, such as an attractive screen shot or a discount coupon for products.

Most people who visit your Web site will probably have e-mail, so one way to continue user testing after you publish your site is to post an e-mail address or a feedback button that visitors can use to provide comments on your Web site. Ask users to send comments and suggestions. This is the least structured approach, but it is the most common method of collecting feedback, and it works.

Whichever form of user testing you use, be sure to schedule some time to review the test results and update your Web site. Chances are good that you'll receive good and bad suggestions. Implement the good suggestions and contemplate the bad ones. Sometimes, a bad suggestion is really a poor explanation, and if you look deeper, you might find the true source of the problem. User testing can help you improve your Web site, but only when you take the time to act on the test results.

## Publishing Your Web Site

Publishing a Web site is a fancy name for copying files to a Web server. Web servers publish files that are stored in special directories that have been configured for Web publishing. You transfer your Web server files to the appropriate directory, and the Web server does the rest.

During the development of your Web site, you might want to publish both prototype Web sites and the final Web site. Before publishing the final product, it is wise to publish a prototype on the same type of equipment that you intend to publish the finished site on. This provides the best simulation of the finished product. Some sites have duplicate Web servers, one for testing and one for publishing. Others have hidden areas on a Web server that are designed for prototype testing and are available only to privileged users, such as the testers.

To publish a prototype or finished Web site, do the following:

1 • Set up a Web server or a server account.

2 • Copy the Web site files to the Web server.

3 • Copy special Web site files to special directories.

4 • Establish a feedback channel.

The following sections provide additional information on these tasks.


### SETTING UP THE WEB SERVER OR SERVER ACCOUNT

You can publish your Web site on your own Web server or on a Web server that your ISP maintains for you. To publish and view your Web site, you'll need to get the following from your Web server administrator or ISP:

▸ Username and password for the Web server

▸ Instructions for copying Web site files to the Web server

▸ The URL for your Web site

You might need a username and password to copy files to the Web server. While some Web servers permit you to copy files to a server using a browser, many Web sites require you to use File Transfer Protocol (FTP) software to transfer files to the Web server. While it takes some additional time to learn to use FTP software, it is usually worth the effort. Browser-based file transfer is often limited to copying one file at a time to directories that already exist. FTP programs enable you to create and delete directories, and to transfer multiple files and directories with a single command.

**For instructions on setting up a Novell Web server, see *Novell's Guide to Web Site Management*.**

NOTE

## COPYING WEB SITE FILES TO A WEB SERVER

To publish your Web site, most of your Web site files need to be copied to a single directory on the Web server. Your home page file goes in this directory, as do all the supporting image and multimedia files. You might use subdirectories to organize your files, but your home page and all subdirectories must be placed in the directory the Web server administrator assigns to your site.

**Appendix B lists the default publishing directories for the Novell Web Server, the Netscape Enterprise Server for NetWare, and the Netscape FastTrack Server for NetWare. If you have set up your own Web server with one of these products, you can use Appendix B to determine which directory to publish your files in.**

NOTE

## COPYING SPECIAL WEB SITE FILES TO SPECIAL DIRECTORIES

While most Web site files are stored in one directory dedicated to your Web site, some files might need to be stored in different directories, or you might need to ask the Web site administrator to configure some of your directories for you. For example, Chapter 4 introduced server-side image maps, which require that a map file be stored on the server. Some Web server administrators might ask you to store your map file in a special directory outside of your directory; others might reconfigure one of your directories to support server-side image maps.

Part III describes Web page programming features that often require special support from the Web server administrator. If you plan to use Server Side Include (SSI) commands, or Common Gateway Interface (CGI) programs, be sure to ask your Web server administrator where you can store these files. To store these files in the proper locations, the Web server might need to extend your rights to use the Web server.

## ESTABLISHING A FEEDBACK CHANNEL

The final step in Web site publishing is user testing, which was described earlier in this chapter. To keep your Web site fit for viewing, provide a way for users to tell you about problems and make suggestions. Then, plan time to respond to user requests.

# Publicizing Your Web Site

Chapter 5 introduces some ways to publicize your Web site. After you have done all the hard work that it takes to design, create, test, and publish a Web site, take some time to publicize the Web site. After all, what good is your Web site if no one visits it?

**NOTE**

**For more information on publicizing Web sites, see *Novell's Certified Internet Business Strategist Study Guide* or *Novell's Guide to Web Site Management* from Novell Press.**

**Exercise 10.4: If you're preparing to take the certification exam, or if you want to practice what you learned in this section, turn to the end of this chapter and complete Exercise 10.4.**

## Summary

This chapter presents guidelines that you can use to implement your Web design. When your Web site will support multiple browsers, the conservative approach to Web site design is to choose a particular version of one browser and develop to the HTML standard supported by that version. If all your Web site visitors will use the same browser, choose a browser and use any of the tags and extensions that browser supports.

To ensure a consistent page appearance on all types of browsers and computer displays, select a target page size and use images and fixed-width tables to establish the page size. To support most computer displays, you can choose a page size based on the 640 × 480 display size. The actual browser display area is the display size minus the areas used for window borders, menu bars, and tool bars.

You can align the elements on your Web pages using HTML tags, art, tables, and frames. The alignment methods you use are partially a matter of preference and partially dependent on what your target browser supports. For example, some browsers do not support frames.

To control navigation for your Web site, you can use text links, image links, navigation bars, index frames, and site maps. Wherever possible, design these controls to coordinate with your Web site design, and use the smallest file size possible. Be particularly careful to provide at least enough navigation options to enable a visitor to return to the previous Web page or the site home page.

As with images, HTML text colors can be translated to other colors if you select colors that are not browser safe. Fortunately, there are just 6 hexadecimal values that are color safe, so it is relatively easy to remember these values and select browser-safe colors for HTML tags. Table 10.3, which appeared earlier in this chapter, shows the hexadecimal and decimal values for browser-safe colors. This table can be used to translate color values between the two numbering systems so you can match colors in HTML tags to colors you use in images.

To enable visually impaired visitors to hear image descriptions, specify the descriptions in <IMG> tags with the ALT attribute. However, specify an empty ALT attribute for repeated images, such as bullets or rules, when the text does not add value and could be annoying to hear repeatedly.

Before you publish your Web site, take some time to test it. Functionality testing verifies that your Web site operates properly, and user testing verifies that users get what they need, or what you want them to have, from your Web site. You can conduct user testing with test sessions and surveys, or you can offer an e-mail address that visitors can use to send comments and suggestions. Whichever approach you use, be sure to take some time to consider the testing results.

To publish a Web site, do the following:

1 • Set up a Web server or a server account.

2 • Copy the Web site files to the Web server.

3 • Copy special Web site files to special directories.

4 • Establish a feedback channel.

To complete Steps 1 through 3, you'll need support from your Web server administrator.

This completes Part II. In Part III, you learn how to add programming to your Web pages.

## PUZZLE 10.1: APPLYING AND PUBLISHING YOUR DESIGN

The following word puzzle contains many of the terms discussed in this chapter. See if you can find all the words. As you search for the words, ask yourself why the word is in the list and how it was used in this chapter. If you don't know the answers to these questions, you might want to review the chapter.

```
U  G  T  F  J  S  T  N  E  T  N  O  C  Q  I
T  N  A  U  V  Y  N  E  P  F  B  R  U  T  M
I  I  B  N  K  E  E  T  U  O  A  E  I  N  P
L  N  L  C  N  V  R  I  B  N  S  C  N  E  A
I  R  E  T  N  R  A  S  L  T  E  A  D  M  I
T  E  P  I  A  U  P  F  I  S  L  P  E  N  R
Y  K  Y  O  V  S  S  O  C  O  I  S  X  G  E
H  C  T  N  I  S  N  O  I  S  N  E  M  I  D
F  A  O  A  G  N  A  K  Z  T  E  S  T  L  B
R  B  T  L  A  O  R  R  E  C  N  A  L  A  B
A  D  O  I  T  Y  T  I  L  I  B  A  E  S  U
M  E  R  T  I  G  R  A  P  H  I  C  A  L  Q
E  E  P  Y  O  G  N  I  D  A  E  L  M  T  H
S  F  M  O  N  O  S  P  A  C  E  D  R  O  P
C  A  P  T  I  A  L  A  I  T  I  N  I  V  E
```

| | | | |
|---|---|---|---|
| alignment | frames | leading | surveys |
| balance | functionality | monospaced | table |
| baseline | graphical | navigation | test |
| contents | HTML | prototype | transparent |
| dimensions | impaired | publicize | type |
| drop | index | questionnaires | usability |
| feedback | initial | site | utility |
| fonts | kerning | spacer | version |

## EXERCISE 10.1: POSITIONING TEXT AND GRAPHICS

Review your knowledge of the browser differences and text- and graphics-positioning techniques presented in this chapter by answering the following questions:

**1** • When a Web page table is displayed in both a Windows browser and a Macintosh browser, which browser might display narrower table cells and cause the table to appear broken?

Answer: . . . . . . . . . . . . . . . . . . . . . . . . . . . . . . . . . . .

**2** • What is the best way to ensure that a browser tag is supported in multiple browsers?

Answer: . . . . . . . . . . . . . . . . . . . . . . . . . . . . . . . . . . .

**3** • What happens when a browser encounters a tag it doesn't support?

Answer: . . . . . . . . . . . . . . . . . . . . . . . . . . . . . . . . . . .

**4** • Why should you avoid referring to the Back button or specific browser menu commands?

Answer: . . . . . . . . . . . . . . . . . . . . . . . . . . . . . . . . . . .

**5** • When selecting a target display size, which size is generally accepted as the least common denominator?

Answer: . . . . . . . . . . . . . . . . . . . . . . . . . . . . . . . . . . .

**6** • What is special about the `<IMG>` tag, `TOPMARGIN`, and `LEFTMARGIN` attributes?

Answer: . . . . . . . . . . . . . . . . . . . . . . . . . . . . . . . . . . .

**7** • What is spacer art?

Answer: . . . . . . . . . . . . . . . . . . . . . . . . . . . . . . . . . . .

**8** • When positioning text and graphics with a table, how do you hide the table?

Answer: . . . . . . . . . . . . . . . . . . . . . . . . . . . . . . . . . . . . . . . . . . .

**9** • How do you create margins with tables?

Answer: . . . . . . . . . . . . . . . . . . . . . . . . . . . . . . . . . . . . . . . . . . .

**10** • Can you bookmark any frame? Why?

Answer: . . . . . . . . . . . . . . . . . . . . . . . . . . . . . . . . . . . . . . . . . . .

**11** • When is the Back button disabled for a frame?

Answer: . . . . . . . . . . . . . . . . . . . . . . . . . . . . . . . . . . . . . . . . . . .

**12** • When creating a Web page, why would you add image swashes that are darker on the right than on the left?

Answer: . . . . . . . . . . . . . . . . . . . . . . . . . . . . . . . . . . . . . . . . . . .

## EXERCISE 10.2: ADDING NAVIGATION AIDS TO WEB SITES

Review your knowledge of the navigation guidelines presented in this chapter by answering the following questions:

**1** • What alignment tool can you use to align individual components in a component bar?

Answer: . . . . . . . . . . . . . . . . . . . . . . . . . . . . . . . . . . . . . .

**2** • In a navigation bar, how can you make one button image appear highlighted to indicate the page the visitor is viewing?

Answer: . . . . . . . . . . . . . . . . . . . . . . . . . . . . . . . . . . . . . .

**3** • What does an index frame display?

Answer: . . . . . . . . . . . . . . . . . . . . . . . . . . . . . . . . . . . . . .

**4** • Why are index frames a form of persistent navigation?

Answer: . . . . . . . . . . . . . . . . . . . . . . . . . . . . . . . . . . . . . .

**5** • List three features that site maps can provide.

a. . . . . . . . . . . . . . . . . . . . . . . . . . . . . . . . . . . . . . .

b. . . . . . . . . . . . . . . . . . . . . . . . . . . . . . . . . . . . . . .

c. . . . . . . . . . . . . . . . . . . . . . . . . . . . . . . . . . . . . . .

**6** • List four site map types.

a. . . . . . . . . . . . . . . . . . . . . . . . . . . . . . . . . . . . . . .

b. . . . . . . . . . . . . . . . . . . . . . . . . . . . . . . . . . . . . . .

c. . . . . . . . . . . . . . . . . . . . . . . . . . . . . . . . . . . . . . .

d. . . . . . . . . . . . . . . . . . . . . . . . . . . . . . . . . . . . . . .

**7** • List two advantages of text-only site maps.

a. . . . . . . . . . . . . . . . . . . . . . . . . . . . . . . . . . . . . . . . . . . . . . . .

b. . . . . . . . . . . . . . . . . . . . . . . . . . . . . . . . . . . . . . . . . . . . . . . .

**8** • How can you add value to a site map with images?

Answer: . . . . . . . . . . . . . . . . . . . . . . . . . . . . . . . . . . . . . . . . . . .

**9** • What is the name for a site map that displays as a table of contents?

Answer: . . . . . . . . . . . . . . . . . . . . . . . . . . . . . . . . . . . . . . . . . . .

**10** • How can you draw a visitor's attention to an important link?

Answer: . . . . . . . . . . . . . . . . . . . . . . . . . . . . . . . . . . . . . . . . . . .

**11** • What can happen when you use only images or frames to display site maps?

Answer: . . . . . . . . . . . . . . . . . . . . . . . . . . . . . . . . . . . . . . . . . . .

## EXERCISE 10.3: USING GRAPHICAL AND HTML TYPE

Review your knowledge of the typography guidelines presented in this chapter by answering the following questions:

**1** • Which form of type appears correctly only when the correct font is installed on, or copied to, the destination browser?

Answer: . . . . . . . . . . . . . . . . . . . . . . . . . . . . . . . . . . . . . . .

**2** • Which form of type appears correctly on destination browsers when the browsers are configured to display images?

Answer: . . . . . . . . . . . . . . . . . . . . . . . . . . . . . . . . . . . . . . .

**3** • List the type styles that are often used to display the following:

Headings: . . . . . . . . . . . . . . . . . . . . . . . . . . . . . . . . . . . . .

Body text: . . . . . . . . . . . . . . . . . . . . . . . . . . . . . . . . . . . . .

Computer text: . . . . . . . . . . . . . . . . . . . . . . . . . . . . . . . . .

**4** • _____ is the adjustment of the spacing between the letters in a word.

**5** • _____ is the adjustment of the spacing between lines of text.

**6** • When should you use underlining with text?

Answer: . . . . . . . . . . . . . . . . . . . . . . . . . . . . . . . . . . . . . . .

**7** • List four type controls that you can select or adjust using the Photoshop Type tool.

a. . . . . . . . . . . . . . . . . . . . . . . . . . . . . . . . . . . . . . .

b. . . . . . . . . . . . . . . . . . . . . . . . . . . . . . . . . . . . . . .

c. . . . . . . . . . . . . . . . . . . . . . . . . . . . . . . . . . . . . . .

d. . . . . . . . . . . . . . . . . . . . . . . . . . . . . . . . . . . . . . .

**8** • Which HTML tag produces the *small caps* effect?

Answer: . . . . . . . . . . . . . . . . . . . . . . . . . . . . . . . . . . .

**9** • Which HTML tag can you use to select a serif font style?

Answer: . . . . . . . . . . . . . . . . . . . . . . . . . . . . . . . . . . .

**10** • Is HTML type subject to the same browser-safe color issues that affect Web images and graphical type?

Answer: . . . . . . . . . . . . . . . . . . . . . . . . . . . . . . . . . . .

## EXERCISE 10.4: TESTING AND PUBLISHING YOUR WEB SITE

Review your knowledge of the testing, prototyping, and publishing guidelines presented in this chapter by answering the following questions:

**1** • What `<IMG>` tag attribute should you use to describe images to visually impaired visitors?

Answer: . . . . . . . . . . . . . . . . . . . . . . . . . . . . . . . . . . . . . . . .

**2** • When should you test your Web site?

Answer: . . . . . . . . . . . . . . . . . . . . . . . . . . . . . . . . . . . . . . . .

**3** • What is the best way to see how your Web pages appear in other types of browsers?

Answer: . . . . . . . . . . . . . . . . . . . . . . . . . . . . . . . . . . . . . . . .

**4** • If you don't have a text-only browser to use for testing, how can you simulate browsing with a text-only browser?

Answer: . . . . . . . . . . . . . . . . . . . . . . . . . . . . . . . . . . . . . . . .

**5** • List three ways to collect feedback from user testing.

a. . . . . . . . . . . . . . . . . . . . . . . . . . . . . . . . . . . . . . . . . .

b. . . . . . . . . . . . . . . . . . . . . . . . . . . . . . . . . . . . . . . . . .

c. . . . . . . . . . . . . . . . . . . . . . . . . . . . . . . . . . . . . . . . . .

**6** • List the four steps for publishing a Web site.

1. . . . . . . . . . . . . . . . . . . . . . . . . . . . . . . . . . . . . . . . . .

2. . . . . . . . . . . . . . . . . . . . . . . . . . . . . . . . . . . . . . . . . .

3. . . . . . . . . . . . . . . . . . . . . . . . . . . . . . . . . . . . . . . . . .

4. . . . . . . . . . . . . . . . . . . . . . . . . . . . . . . . . . . . . . . . . .

# PART III

# Using Web Page Programs and Scripts

# CHAPTER 11

# Using SSI Commands

**S**erver Side Include (SSI) commands are special server commands that perform simple functions to help you dress up your Web page. SSI commands can be used to do the following:

- Display variable information, such as the date, time, and number of times a Web page has been viewed

- Display connection information, such as the Web server name, your workstation IP address, or the URL for the current Web page

- Display file information, such as the name, size, and date the file was last modified

- Add standard "boilerplate" information, such as copyright notices, disclaimers, or blocks of HTML code from a single file and apply it to multiple Web pages

- Process form data and save the results to files or display them on Web pages

Most SSI commands insert dynamic information into Web pages. For example, suppose you want to display the file size of your Web page on the page. You could first view the file size in a directory listing, and then manually enter the file size in your Web page. The file size you enter manually is a static entry, however. The file size listed in the Web page remains the same even if the file size changes. To update the file size information, you must change the HTML file manually.

If you use an SSI command to display the file size, the Web server dynamically includes the *current* file size on the page. If the file size changes, the new file size appears the next time the Web page is loaded.

Table 11.1 lists the SSI commands supported by the Novell Web Server. This chapter describes how SSI commands work, how to support them on the Novell Web Server, and how to use them in Web pages. Each of the commands described in Table 11.1 is explained in more detail later in this chapter.

**NOTE**

As of this writing, Novell Education Course 655, Advanced Web Authoring, covers the use of SSI commands on the Novell Web Server. This chapter contains additional information on using SSI commands on the Netscape Web servers for NetWare, but this information is not on the exam.

| TABLE 11.1 | SSI COMMAND | FUNCTION |
|---|---|---|
| *SSI Commands* | append | Appends data to a file on the Web server |
| | break | Ends the display of the HTML file |
| | calc | Calculates the results of mathematical equations |
| | config | Sets the SSI command display format and error-processing options |
| | count | Records and displays the number of times a Web page has been visited |
| | echo | Displays information on the date, time, file, Web server, connection, or local computer |
| | exec | Launches LCGI programs from within a Web page (LCGI is discussed in Chapter 12) |
| | flastmod | Displays the time and date a file was last modified |
| | fsize | Displays the size of a file |
| | goto | Causes HTML processing to skip to another portion of the file, ignoring the information between the goto command and the destination |
| | if | Permits conditional processing of Web page HTML commands and content |
| | include | Includes all data from another file in your Web page |
| | label | Marks a destination for the goto command |

## How SSI Commands Work

Web servers rely on a special file extension to identify files that contain SSI commands. On the Novell Web Server, the default extension for files with SSI commands is SSI. On the Netscape Web servers for NetWare, it is SHTML.

When a Web server receives a request for an SSI file, it parses the file for SSI commands (see Figure 11.1). *Parsing* is the process by which every line of an HTML file is analyzed to detect SSI commands. When the server detects an SSI command, it processes the command and returns the results to the browser in HTML format.

F I G U R E    II.I

*SSI-Command Processing*

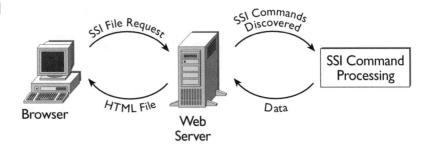

Because SSI files are parsed by the server and contain both HTML and SSI commands, SSI files are often called *parsed-HTML files*. The SSI term comes from the fact that SSI commands are executed on the *server side* of the client-to-server connection and are usually used to *include* data in an HTML file.

The demonstration Web site on the CD-ROM includes examples of SSI commands in action. Those commands won't work when you access the files on the CD-ROM, though. Can you guess why?

The answer is that browsers themselves cannot process SSI commands. SSI commands must be processed on a Web server. Consequently, in order to work, parsed-HTML files must be stored on a Web server. (This also means that, because all SSI processing is performed by the server, SSI commands work with all browsers.)

If you have copied the demonstration Web site to a Web server as described in Appendix C, you can view the SSI command examples at the following URL:

```
http://host_name/DemoWeb2/Programs/SSI/index.htm
```

If your SSI commands don't appear to work on your Web server, don't be alarmed. SSI-command processing must be enabled for specific directories and files before it will work. In the next section, you'll learn how to enable SSI-command processing for a Novell Web Server directory.

## Enabling SSI-Command Processing

Because SSI-command processing requires additional server processing, Web servers (such as the Novell Web Server) let you enable or disable SSI-command processing on a directory-by-directory basis. The default status for most directories is *disabled*. To enable SSI-command processing for a Web page, the Web server administrator needs to:

- ▸ Enable SSI-command processing for the directory in which the SSI files are stored.

- ▸ Publish the parsed-HTML file extension to the Web page authors.

On Novell Web Servers, the default extension for parsed-HTML files is .SSI, but the Web server administrator can change this. The following subsections explain how to set the SSI file extension and enable SSI processing for directories.

### SPECIFYING A FILE EXTENSION FOR PARSED-HTML FILES
You might want to change the parsed-HTML file extension to do the following:

- ▸ If you maintain Novell and UNIX Web servers, or if you plan to upgrade to one of the Netscape Web servers for NetWare, you may want to standardize one parsed-HTML file extension for both platforms. The file extension most often used for parsed-HTML files on UNIX Web servers is .SHTML, and this is the extension used by the Netscape Web servers for NetWare.

- ▸ If you intend to use SSI commands in all of your HTML files, you might want to change the parsed-HTML file extension to .HTM or .HTML.

**NOTE**

**Changing your parsed-HTML file extension to .HTM or .HTML may be useful for testing and experimenting with SSI commands; however, this is not a good practice. The server must parse or process every file that uses a parsed-HTML file extension— regardless of whether it has SSI commands. As a site grows, this can create a processing burden for your Web server. Instead, use different file extensions for HTML and parsed-HTML files; that way you can easily identify which files use SSI commands.**

On the Novell Web Server, the parsed-HTML file extension is set in the MIME. TYP file. The default location for this file is SYS:\WEB\CONFIG\MIME.TYP.

**NOTE**

**The Novell Web Server can simulate the operation of multiple *virtual* Web servers, each of which is called a virtual server. Each virtual server uses a separate MIME.TYP file. For more information on virtual servers, see the Novell Web Server product documentation or *Novell's Guide to Web Site Management*.**

The following MIME.TYP file entry defines the file extension for parsed-HTML files:

```
text/x-server-parsed-html    ssi
```

The entries in the MIME.TYP file are organized in two columns. The entries in the left column identify types of files, and the entries in the right column identify the file extensions that correspond to the file types. In the sample entry, `text/x-server-parsed-html` identifies SSI as the extension for a special kind of text file called `x-server-parsed-html`.

To change the file extension for SSI files, follow these steps:

**1** • Use a text editor to open the MIME.TYP file for a virtual server (Default: SYS:\WEB\CONFIG\MIME.TYP).

**2** • Change the extension in the right-hand column of the following directive:

```
text/x-server-parsed-html    ssi
```

**3** • Save the file and quit the text editor.

**4** • Restart the Web server. The Novell Web Server only reads the MIME.TYP during startup. To restart the Novell Web Server v3.1, enter the following commands at the system console prompt:

**WEBSTOP**
**WEBSTART**

After the Web server restarts, all SSI files on the affected virtual server must use the new file extension.

## ENABLING SSI PROCESSING FOR A SPECIFIC DIRECTORY

SSI processing is usually not enabled for all directories because it requires additional processing power from the server and reduces response times for Web page viewers. This extra processing time is not excessive, but it is best to enable SSI processing only in those directories where it will be used.

On the Novell Web Server, the administrator can control which directories are enabled for SSI-command processing. This enables the administrator to do the following:

▸ Control who creates the parsed-HTML files by enabling SSI-command processing in select directories and using the appropriate NetWare or intraNetWare file system rights to control directory access.

▸ Easily determine the location of parsed-HTML files; parsed-HTML files can only run from the directories that have been enabled.

There are two ways to enable SSI-command processing on the Novell Web Server. The easiest way is to use the Web Manager utility provided with the Novell Web Server. The other way is to edit the Web server ACCESS.CFG configuration file with a text editor. The following sections describe how to enable directories for SSI processing using Web manager or a text editor.

**TIP**

**Discourage Web authors from using SSI commands in CGI scripts. Careless or mischievous Web authors can create scripts that use SSI commands improperly and disable the Web server — either inadvertently or intentionally. To prevent the use of SSI commands in CGI scripts, disable SSI-command processing in the script directories.**

### Using Web Manager

The Web Manager utility (WEBMGR.EXE) is placed in the SYS:\PUBLIC directory when the Novell Web Server is installed. Because this is a Windows-based utility, you may want to create a program icon to launch the utility.

To enable SSI-command processing with Web Manager, do the following:

**1** • To start the Web Manager utility, do the following:

a. From your client computer, map a drive to the SYS volume on your Novell Web Server.

b. Start the WEBMGR.EXE program in SYS:\PUBLIC using the Windows RUN command or a program icon that you have created.

After you start Web Manager, the utility displays the window shown in Figure 11.2.

**F I G U R E    11.2**

*Web Manager Window*

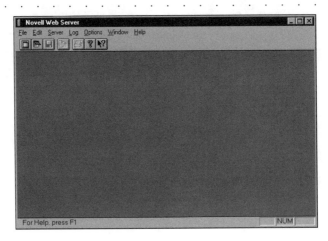

**2** • Choose a virtual server to configure by selecting *File →
virtual_server_name.* After you select the virtual server name, the Web
server configuration dialog box shown in Figure 11.3 appears. Notice
that the virtual server name appears in the dialog box title.

**3** • Choose the Directories page in the dialog box that appears (refer to
Figure 11.4).

FIGURE 11.3

*Web Server Configuration
Dialog Box*

FIGURE 11.4

*Web Manager
Directories Page*

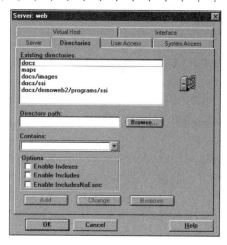

**NOTE**

**If the virtual server name does not appear in the file menu, you might have started Web Manager on a different server than the one you want to configure. For instructions on how to use Web Manager to select virtual servers on other Novell Web Servers, see the product documentation or *Novell's Guide to Web Site Management*.**

**4** • If the directory for which you want to enable SSI commands appears in the Existing directories box, select it.

**5** • If the directory you want does not appear in the Existing directories box, use the Browse button to locate the directory, click Add, and then select your directory in the Existing directories box.

**6** • In the Contains drop-down list, select Documents.

**7** • After you have selected the directory and its contents, check the Enable Includes checkbox, or check the Enable IncludesNoExec checkbox and click Change. The Enable Includes option enables all SSI commands for files in the selected directory. The Enable IncludesNoExec option enables all commands except the exec command. To provide better security for your server, select Enable IncludesNoExec. For more information on the exec command, see the command description that appears later in this chapter.

**NOTE**

**You must click Change. It may be tempting to click OK instead of Change, but this will not change the directory setting.**

**8** • Click OK to save your changes.

**9** • To activate your changes, restart the Novell Web Server as described earlier in this chapter.

After you restart the Novell Web Server, the enabled directories support parsed-HTML files and correctly display SSI command results.

**TIP**

**To learn more about using Web Manager, select Help → Contents within Web Manager, or open the Web Manager Help file on the Web server. The English version of the help file is stored at SYS:\PUBLIC\NLS\ENGLISH\WEBMGR.HLP.**

### Editing the ACCESS.CFG Configuration File

ACCESS.CFG is the virtual server access-control file that determines which directories can use SSI commands. This file also determines who can access the Web server, and contains configuration data for other directory options (such as automatic indexing).

The configuration data for each directory is stored in a group between a pair of <DIRECTORY> tags, which use the same format as HTML tags. The following ACCESS.CFG file entries configure the default SSI-enabled directory on the Novell Web Server:

```
<Directory docs/ssi>

Options Indexes Includes

AllowOverride All

<Limit GET>

order allow,deny

allow from all

</Limit>

</Directory>
```

The opening <DIRECTORY> tag specifies the path to the directory the tags configure. The statements that do not begin with a <DIRECTORY>or <LIMIT> tag are called directives, and these directives configure the Web server. The first word in each directive line is the directive itself, and the remainder of the line represents the value of the directive.

The directive that enables SSI-command processing is the Options directive. When this directive includes the Includes value, all SSI commands are supported in this directory. If this directive contains the value IncludesNOEXEC, all SSI commands except the Exec command are supported.

To enable or disable SSI-command processing with a text editor, do the following:

**1** • Use a text editor to open the virtual server access-control file (default: WEB\CONFIG\ACCESS.CFG).

**2** • Locate the <DIRECTORY> tags for the directory you want to configure. The default installation of the Novell Web Server creates Directory entries for only a few directories. The directory you want to configure might not appear in this file.

**3** • If there are no <DIRECTORY> tags for the directory you want to configure, use the text editor Copy and Paste commands to copy the entry for another directory, and then change the directory name in the starting <DIRECTORY> tag.

**IMPORTANT**

**When you copy the configuration for another directory, you are copying more than the configuration settings for SSI-command processing, so you might create a configuration you don't want.**

**Course 655 describes only the enabling and disabling of SSI processing in the ACCESS.CFG file; it does not describe all the options between the <DIRECTORY> tags. Novell recommends that you configure SSI support using Web Manager.**

**4** • To enable SSI-command processing, locate the Options directive and add either the Includes or the IncludesNOEXEC value.

**5** • To disable SSI-command processing, locate the Options directive and delete the Includes or IncludesNOEXEC value.

**6** • Save the file.

**7** • To activate your changes, restart the Novell Web Server as described earlier in this chapter.

After you restart the Novell Web Server, the enabled directories support parsed-HTML files and correctly display SSI command results.

Exercise 11.1: If you're preparing to take the certification exam, or if you want to practice what you learned in this section, turn to the end of this chapter and complete Exercise 11.1. When you are done, continue reading here to prepare for the next exercise.

## Using SSI Commands on Web Pages

The only differences between a parsed-HTML file and a standard HTML file are the file extension and the SSI commands, themselves. The following subsections describe how to:

▶ Enter SSI commands in HTML files.

▶ Distinguish SSI commands from HTML comments.

▶ Specify filenames and paths within HTML commands.

### ENTERING THE SSI COMMANDS
To use SSI commands on a Web page, do the following:

▶ Add SSI command tags to an existing HTML file or a new file.

▶ Name the file with the parsed-HTML file extension (for example, *filename*.SSI or .SHTML).

▶ Place the file in a directory configured to support SSI-command processing.

The format for an SSI command tag is:

```
<!--#command argument="value" -->
```

The *command* variable in this example represents one of the SSI commands introduced later in this chapter, and *arguments* are used to further define command operation, just as attributes further define HTML tags. To enter a command, enter the command name in the tag and include any arguments the command requires. The command names and arguments are case-sensitive.

**NOTE**

**Although the Novell Web Server ignores the case of command and argument names, the Netscape Web servers for NetWare require that all commands and arguments be entered in lowercase. To make your Web pages portable, enter all command and argument names in lowercase letters.**

**Also, because SSI commands require additional processing by the Web server, a slight delay will occur in the delivery of the Web page to the browser. This delay is usually unnoticeable. If the delay does become noticeable, this may indicate the Web server is overloaded. To reduce the load on the Web server and the delay to browser users, only use the SSI file extension when a file contains SSI commands.**

One of the rules for using SSI commands is that you cannot nest commands. For example, the following command format is not permitted because it contains a command within a command:

```
<!--#command argument="<!--#command argument="value" -->" -->
```

You'll learn more about the SSI commands later in this chapter.

**IMPORTANT**

**Some SSI commands permit you to embed files into an SSI file. Do not use these commands to embed SSI files within SSI files.**

## DISTINGUISHING SSI COMMANDS FROM HTML COMMENTS

Have you noticed the format for SSI commands is similar to the format of HTML comments? The first four and the final three characters are the same for both an SSI command and the HTML <COMMENT> tag. You'll recall the format for an HTML comment is:

```
<!-- Comment -->
```

The similarity is intentional. Browsers cannot interpret SSI commands. All SSI-command processing takes place at the server. Therefore, SSI commands must be disguised as HTML comments so browsers do not attempt to process them. If you view an HTML file with SSI commands on your local computer, you won't see any commands or command results in the browser; the browser ignores comments and a Web server did not process the file.

Because SSI commands are so similar to regular HTML comments, you must be careful not to create an HTML comment accidentally when, in fact, you mean to insert an SSI command.

**NOTE**

**The fifth character in the SSI command is always the # character. To prevent SSI-command errors on your Web pages, avoid using the # character as the first character of your regular HTML comments.**

## SPECIFYING FILENAMES AND PATHS IN SSI COMMANDS

Several SSI commands use arguments that enable you to reference a file. These arguments define a path to a file with which the SSI command works. The `file` argument specifies the path relative to the directory where the source parsed-HTML file is stored. The `virtual` argument specifies the path relative to a *virtual directory* defined on the Web server where the parsed-HTML file is stored. The default virtual directory is the document root directory, but Web server administrators can define other types of virtual directories, as well.

The following subsections provide some examples of how to use the file and virtual arguments.

### The file Argument

With the `file` argument, you must specify a path that begins in the same directory where the source parsed-HTML file resides. Figure 11.5 shows a sample directory tree to illustrate some examples.

*Sample Directory Tree*

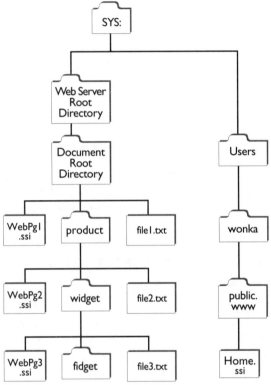

If the destination file is in the same directory as the source parsed-HTML file, you can simply specify the filename for the file. If the file is in a subdirectory below the source file, specify the path and the filename.

Table 11.2 shows the `file` argument statements that each SSI file in Figure 11.5 can include to access the text files.

*Sample* `file` *Argument Paths*

| SOURCE SSI FILE | PATH TO TEXT FILES |
|---|---|
| WebPg1.ssi | file="file1.txt"<br>file="product/file2.txt"<br>file="product/widget/file3.txt" |
| WebPg2.ssi | file="file2.txt"<br>file="widget/file3.txt" |
| WebPg3.ssi | file="file3.txt" |

When you use the file argument, avoid these kinds of paths:

```
file="/path/filename.ext"
```

and

```
file="../path/filename.ext"
```

The leading slash in the first example tells the Web server you are specifying a path from the document root directory. If this is the start of your path, the virtual argument is a better choice. The leading periods and the forward slash in the second example tell the Web server the path is to start in the parent directory of the directory containing the SSI file. The Novell Web Server does not permit you to use relative references to parent directories in SSI commands.

Here are some advantages of using the file argument:

> ▸ When the destination file is in the same directory as the source SSI file or in a subdirectory, the file argument usually requires a shorter path name.

> ▸ When you move a directory on the Web server, all of the file argument references within this directory remain valid because they reference files within this subdirectory.

### The virtual Argument

The path provided with the virtual argument can be used to specify paths that begin in the document root directory, a user Web page directory, or a virtual directory. Here are some advantages of the virtual argument:

> ▸ The virtual argument can be used to specify any destination file on the Web server.

> ▸ When the destination file is in a parent directory of the source SSI file, the virtual argument is the only way to reference the file.

> ▸ The virtual argument can reference files in a user Web page directory. The file argument cannot.

The following subsections describe how to use the virtual argument to access different types of virtual directories.

**Document Root Directory**   If the destination file is in the document root directory, specify the name of the file. If the destination is in a subdirectory of the document root, specify the path to the destination file. The document root directory is the default virtual directory on the Novell Web Server.

All of the SSI files shown in Figure 11.5—except home.ssi—can access the text files using the following virtual argument statements:

```
virtual="file1.txt"
```

or

```
virtual="product/file2.txt"
```

or

```
virtual="product/widget/file3.txt"
```

**User Web Page Directory**   To reference a file in a user Web page directory, enter the virtual argument as follows:

```
virtual="/~username/path/filename.txt"
```

The *tilde* character (~) indicates this is a reference to a user Web page directory. On the Novell Web Server, the username is the NetWare username, which is also the name of the user's home directory. The *path* begins in the directory configured as the public directory for the Web server users (the default is PUBLIC.WWW), and *filename.ext* is the name of the destination file.

To access the home.ssi file in Figure 11.5, you could enter the following virtual argument statement:

```
virtual="/~wonka/home.ssi"
```

**Virtual Directory**   If the destination is a virtual directory, enter the virtual argument as follows:

```
virtual="/virtual_directory_name/path/filename.ext"
```

The virtual directory must be defined in the virtual server SRM.CFG file. For more information on virtual directories, see the Novell Web Server documentation or *Novell's Guide to Web Site Management*.

**Exercise 11.2: If you're preparing to take the certification exam, or if you want to practice what you learned in this section, turn to the end of this chapter and complete Exercise 11.2. When you are done, continue reading here to prepare for the next exercise.**

## NCSA Server SSI Commands

The Novell Web Server supports two types of SSI commands: NCSA SSI commands and Novell Web Server extended commands. The Novell Web Server is modeled after the National Center for Super Computing Applications (NCSA) Web server, which supports a specified set of SSI commands. The Novell Web Server extended commands are additional commands provided by the Novell Web Server and are not part of the NCSA specification. If you practice your Web skills on an NCSA Web server that is not a Novell Web Server, only the NCSA SSI commands operate.

The following commands are supported by Novell Web Server, the Netscape Web servers for NetWare, and NCSA Web servers:

- `config`

- `echo`

- `flastmod`

- `fsize`

- `include`

The following subsections explain how to use each of these SSI commands.

**You can find additional information on NCSA SSI commands at the following URL:**

`hoohoo.ncsa.uiuc.edu/docs/tutorials/includes.html`

## THE config COMMAND

On NCSA Web servers, the `config` command enables you to specify the format of time, date, and file size data sent to a browser by SSI commands. On the Novell Web Server, the `config` command enables you to specify how the Web server handles SSI errors that occur on your Web page.

The `config` command does not display any data; it specifies the format of the data other SSI commands display. This command must be entered before any SSI commands that use its formatting instructions.

The `config` command syntax is as follows:

```
<!--#config timefmt=value sizefmt=value errmsg="text"
onerr="operation"-->
```

Note the single character space after the `config` command. If this space character is omitted, the command is treated as an HTML comment. When the space character is included, the `config` command is recognized as an SSI command.

The following subsections describe how to configure the SSI command display options and the arguments you can use to control SSI error processing.

### Configuring Display Options

The default format for the date and time is:

```
Sunday, 20-Oct-96 09:33:16 PDT
```

The default time format displays the weekday, date, time, and time zone. PDT is an abbreviation for Pacific Daylight Time.

The following example shows the default format for file size data:

```
1K
```

The default file size format displays the file size in kilobytes.

When you only want to set the display options for time and file size, the format for the `config` command is as follows:

```
<!--#config timefmt=value sizefmt=value-->
```

Table 11.3 lists examples of argument values that you can use with the `config` command.

**TABLE 11.3**

*Configuring SSI*
*Display Options*

| ARGUMENT | ARGUMENT VALUE | EXAMPLE | DESCRIPTION |
|---|---|---|---|
| sizefmt | | 9K | If the config command is not used to change the sizefmt value, SSI commands display the file size in kilobytes. |
| sizefmt | abbrev | 9K | File size in kilobytes. |
| sizefmt | bytes | 9,470 | File size in bytes. |
| timefmt | | Sunday, 10-Nov-96 14:28:52 PDT | If the config command is not used to change the timefmt value, SSI commands that display the time or date do so as shown in the sample column. The display includes the day of the week, the date, the time, and the time zone. |
| timefmt | %A | Sunday | Day of the week. |
| timefmt | %a | Sun | Day of the week in abbreviated form. |
| timefmt | %B | September | Month. |
| timefmt | %b | Sep | Month in abbreviated form. |
| timefmt | %c | Wed Sep 03 21:58:06 1997 | Condensed version of the local date and time. |
| timefmt | %D | 11/10/96 | Date in the MM/DD/YY format. |
| timefmt | %d | 03 | Day of the month (0-31). |
| timefmt | %H | 21 | Hour (00-24). |
| timefmt | %I | 09 | Hour (0-12). |
| timefmt | %j | 246 | Day of year (1-365). |
| timefmt | %M | 58 | Minute (0-59). |
| timefmt | %m | 09 | Month (1-12). |

The argument values that begin with the % symbol in Table 11.3 are called date codes. To create custom date codes, you can combine individual date codes as follows:

```
<!--#config timefmt="%a, %D"  -->
```

This `config` command causes the time to be displayed as follows: Sun, 11/10/96. The quotation marks group the argument values. If the quotation marks are omitted, the server tries to interpret any date codes after the first space character as additional arguments. The comma and space character in this example are not required; they are used to make the display easier to read.

**You can see additional date codes on the demonstration Web site at the following locations:**

NOTE

`http://host_name/DemoWeb2/Programs/SSI/datecode.ssi`

`d:/DemoWeb2/Programs/SSI/datecode.ssi`

Table 11.4 provides some additional examples of the `config` command. Table 11.4 shows time and file size formats for every sample `config` command, even though each sample command includes only one argument. Whenever you enter a `config` command, the display options you set are used until you change them. If you don't specify a time or date format, the previously set value is used.

### Configuring SSI-Error Processing

The Novell Web Server extends the function of the NCSA `config` command so you can configure SSI-*error processing*. Without this SSI-error processing, the server displays an error message on the Web page whenever an error occurs. The default server messages are informative, but can be lengthy. Because the server error messages are also displayed on the server, and can be recorded in logs, it is not essential to deliver these messages to the Web page.

You can use the Novell Web Server error-processing features to configure error processing in the following ways:

▸ Suppress server error messages.

▸ Display alternative messages that can be shorter, or more informative, and identify someone to call for technical assistance.

▶ Skip HTML processing for a portion of the file.

▶ Stop Web page processing.

T A B L E   1 1 . 4

*SSI Display Option*
*Examples*

| CONFIG COMMAND | DATE AND TIME DISPLAY | FILE SIZE DISPLAY |
|---|---|---|
| `<!--#config-->(default)` | Sunday, 10-Nov-96 14:28:52 PDT | 9K |
| `<!--#config timefmt="%D"-->` | 11/10/96 | 9K |
| `<!--#config timefmt="%a"-->` | Sun | 9K |
| `<!--#config sizefmt="bytes"-->` | Sun | 9,470 |
| `<!--#config sizefmt="abbrev"-->` | Sun | 9K |

In some cases, the failure of an SSI command can render all, or part, of a Web page useless. If this is the case, skip HTML processing for a section of the page or halt processing altogether.

To configure SSI-error processing, you enter the `config` command with the `onerr` argument and the optional `errmsg` argument as follows:

```
<!--#config onerr="operation" errmsg="text"-->
```

The `errmsg` argument defines the error message that appears when the "on error" argument, `onerr`, is set to `error` or `errorbreak`. Note, the `errmsg` argument defines only a message. The `onerr` argument defines what happens when an error occurs.

Table 11.5 shows a number of ways you can use the `config` command to change SSI-error processing for your Web pages. As with all other HTML tags, quotation marks are required when an argument value contains a space character.

| T A B L E  I I . 5 | |
| --- | --- |
| *Configuring SSI-Error Processing* | |

| #CONFIG COMMAND | DESCRIPTION |
| --- | --- |
| `<!--#config errmsg="text"-->` | Specifies the message *text* that appears when an SSI error occurs and a `config onerr` command specifies the `error` or `errorbreak` values. |
| `<!--#config onerr="goto label"-->` | When an error occurs, execute the `goto` command to jump to the specified label. The `goto` and `label` SSI commands are Novell Web Server extended SSI commands described later in this chapter. |
| `<!--#config onerr="print text"-->` | When an error occurs, print the specified message *text*. |
| `<!--#config onerr=error-->` | When an error occurs, print the message specified by the `config errmsg` command. |
| `<!--#config onerr=break-->` | When an error occurs, execute the Novell Web Server `break` command. |
| `<!--#config onerr=errorbreak-->` | When an error occurs, print the message specified by the `config errmsg` command, and then execute the `break` command. |
| `<!--#config onerr="printbreak text"-->` | When an error occurs, print the specified message *text*, and then execute the `break` command. |

## THE echo COMMAND

The echo SSI command displays the value of a variable within the Web page. When you are using the Novell Web Server, there are three types of variables:

- ▶ Form variables

- ▶ Calculated variables

- ▶ Environment variables

*Form variables* are defined when you assign a name to a form element. *Calculated variables* are created when you use the Novell Web Server calc SSI command. *Environment variables* are predefined by the Web server and describe information about the connection between the remote host (where the browser operates) and the Web server.

The format of the echo command is:

```
<!--#echo var="variable_name" format="fstring"-->
```

The following subsections describe how to use the var and format arguments.

### The var Argument

Variable names are case-sensitive. Environment names must be entered in uppercase letters, while other variables must be entered using the same case used when the variable was defined. Also, the environment variable names are reserved; you can't use environment variable names for form elements or calc command variables.

Table 11.6 lists the environment variables supported by the Novell Web Server. You can view the echo command variables on the Demonstration Web site at the following locations:

```
http://host_name/DemoWeb2/Programs/SSI/ncsa_ssi.ssi#echo

d:/DemoWeb2/Programs/SSI/ncsa_ssi.ssi#echo
```

As you may have guessed, the echo command won't work on your local computer; nevertheless, you can see how the command is used in the sample file.

**T A B L E  I I . 6**

*Environment Variables*

| VARIABLE | DESCRIPTION |
| --- | --- |
| AUTH_TYPE | When users have to authenticate to access a Web page, this variable lists the user authentication method. |
| CONTENT_LENGTH | When the POST method is used with forms (see Chapter 5), this variable contains the length of the data the client sends to the Web server. |
| CONTENT_TYPE | When the POST method is used with forms (see Chapter 5), this variable defines the type of data the client sends to the Web server. |
| DATE_GMT | Greenwich Mean Time (GMT) and date, which is the official time and date in Greenwich, England. |
| DATE_LOCAL | Local data and time at the Web server. |

*(continued)*

**T A B L E  11.6**

*Environment Variables*
*(continued)*

| VARIABLE | DESCRIPTION |
|---|---|
| DOCUMENT_NAME | The name of the file in which the SSI command is placed. |
| DOCUMENT_URI | The Universal Resource Indicator (URI) or URL of the file in which the SSI command is placed. |
| HTTP_ACCEPT | Displays the MIME types supported by the requesting browser. |
| HTTP_REFERER | The URL of the Web page that provided the link to the current page. |
| HTTP_USER_AGENT | Browser software identification. For example: Mozilla/4.03 [en] (Win95; U). |
| LAST_MODIFIED | Date of the last change to the file in which the SSI command is placed. |
| PATH_INFO | When a URL requests a CGI script, HTTP enables additional information, called extra path information, to be included between the script name and the query string. When this information is present, it is stored in this variable. |
| PATH_TRANSLATED | When a URL requests a CGI script, the extra path information can refer to a virtual directory or file. This variable displays the actual path to the specified directory or file. |
| QUERY_STRING | Displays any query string appended to an HTTP request (see Chapter 5). |
| QUERY_STRING_UNESCAPED | Displays a query string with a backslash before any escaped characters. |
| REMOTE_ADDR | IP address of the computer where the Web page is displayed. The remote computer is remote to the Web server. |
| REMOTE_HOST | Name of the computer or host where the Web page is displayed. If this name is not defined in a HOSTS file or in DNS, the IP address appears. |
| REMOTE_IDENT | When the server supports RFC931 identification, this variable contains the name of the remote user. This variable should only be used for log-in. |
| REMOTE_USER | When users have to authenticate to access a Web page, this variable contains the name of the user at the computer where the Web page appears. |
| REQUEST_METHOD | The method used to request a Web page or script. This value is GET, POST, or HEAD. |
| SCRIPT_NAME | When the browser requests a script, this variable contains the script path and name. |
| SERVER_NAME | Name of the Web server processing the SSI file. If DNS does not provide a name, the IP address is displayed. |
| SERVER_PORT | Port number of the Web server processing the SSI file. |
| SERVER_SOFTWARE | Web server software identification. For example: Novell-HTTP-Server/3.1R1. |

**NOTE**

**The environment variables listed in Table 11.6 do not always display values, and may display error messages. For example, the** QUERY_STRING **variable contains no data if the referral link or form does not include data. On the Novell Web Server, the** AUTH_TYPE **and** REMOTE_USER **variables display errors if the Web server is not configured to require authentication for Web page access. Also note that the Novell Web Server does not support all of the variables listed in Table 11.6.**

### The format Argument

On the Novell Web Server, the format argument defines how to display environment variables, form variables, and calculated variables, such as those produced by the calc SSI command. The syntax or structure of an echo command with a format argument is as follows:

```
<!--#echo var="variable_name" format="%[+][width][.prec]type"-->
```

**NOTE**

**The format argument is a Novell Web Server extension; it is not supported on the Netscape Web servers for NetWare.**

The brackets in the format argument indicate that the bracket contents are optional; do not place the brackets in echo commands.

The *type* value is a single character that indicates the type of data to be displayed. When the variable contains text rather than numbers, it is called a string, and the *s* value indicates string data. When the format argument specifies a *width* value for a text variable, the width indicates the number of characters that will be displayed (see Table 11.7).

When the variable contains a number, that number can be formatted as one of several format types. The decimal (d) format presents the number as an integer without a decimal point. The floating point (f) format presents the number with a decimal point and any digits necessary to indicate fractional values. Additional number formats include the scientific notation (g) format and the percent (%) format (see Table 11.7).

**WARNING**

**The Novell Course 655 Student Guide says to use the percent symbol (%) to indicate the percent format, and the Novell Web Server documentation says to use the letter *p*. I couldn't get either format to work with the Novell Web Server.**

When the echo command is used to display a number and the plus sign is included, a plus (+) or minus sign (–) appears before the displayed number. As with string variables, the *width* value specifies the number of characters to be displayed, but as shown in Table 11.7, some variable types ignore the width value.

The precision value, *.prec*, defines how many digits appear in the displayed number. For floating point numbers, the prec value specifies how many digits appear after the decimal point. For decimal variables, the prec value defines the number of digits that appear before the decimal. If the prec value is not specified, the Web server may "fill in" zeros to complete the number of places defined by the width value. Table 11.7 provides examples of how to use the format argument.

### TABLE 11.7

*Format Argument Examples*

| FORMAT ARGUMENT | VARIABLE CONTENTS | FORMATTED RESULT |
|---|---|---|
| format=%5s | Tuesday, 16-Dec-1997 16:21:14 PDT | Tuesd |
| format=%10s | Tuesday, 16-Dec-1997 16:21:14 PDT | Tuesday, 1 |
| format=%5d | 166.667 | 00166 |
| format=%5.3d | 166.667 | 166 |
| format=%5.2f | 166.667 | 166.67 |
| format=%5.2g | 166.667 | 1.7e+002 |

### THE flastmod COMMAND

The flastmod command displays the time and date the specified file was last modified. The two formats for the flastmod command are as follows:

```
<!--#flastmod file="filename.ext"-->
```

and

```
<!--#flastmod virtual="filename.ext"-->
```

The file and virtual arguments are described earlier in this chapter. The `flastmod` command displays the time and date in the following format:

```
Sunday, 20-Oct-96 09:33:16 PDT
```

You can use the `config` command to change the display format for the `flastmod` command.

## THE fsize COMMAND

The `fsize` command displays the size of the specified file. The two formats for the `fsize` command are as follows:

```
<!--#fsize file="filename.ext"-->
```

and

```
<!--#fsize virtual="filename.ext"-->
```

The default configuration displays the file size in kilobytes as follows: 252K. The file and virtual arguments were described earlier in this chapter.

You can use the SSI `config` command to change the display format for the `fsize` command. As with the `flastmod` command, you can enter multiple file and virtual arguments in one `fsize` command to display the sizes of multiple files.

## THE include COMMAND

The `include` command tells the Web server to insert text from the specified file into the Web page. This command makes it easy to insert text from the same file into many Web pages. For example, you could put a copyright statement in one file and have it inserted into all of your Web pages. When the time comes to update the statement, you could update it in one file; and then the change automatically appears on each of the other Web pages the next time they are requested.

The two formats for the `include` command are as follows:

```
<!--#include file="filename.ext"-->
```

and

```
<!--#include virtual="filename.ext"-->
```

The file and virtual arguments were described earlier in this chapter.

**An SSI file cannot include a file with additional SSI commands. An included file should not have an SSI extension.**

NOTE

To see an `include` command example on the demonstration Web site, browse the following locations:

```
http://host_name/DemoWeb2/Programs/SSI/add.ssi
```

```
file:///d:/DemoWeb2/Programs/SSI/add.ssi
```

As mentioned earlier, the `include` command won't work on your local computer, but you can see how the command is used in the sample file.

**While you can include files that contain HTML tags, avoid including complete Web pages with the beginning and ending HTML tags. If you include a complete page within the body of another page, the page display will end when the first closing HTML tag is encountered.**

TIP

**Exercise 11.3: If you're preparing to take the certification exam, or if you want to practice what you learned in this section, turn to the end of this chapter and complete Exercise 11.3. When you are done, continue reading here to prepare for the next exercise.**

## Novell Web Server SSI Commands

For your Web page authoring delight, the Novell Web Server provides additional SSI commands that you can use to spice up those Web pages. The following SSI commands are supported only by the Novell Web Server:

- ► append

- ► break

- ► calc

- count

- exec

- goto

- if

- label

**IMPORTANT** **These commands do not operate on the Netscape Web servers for NetWare. If you customize your Web site for the Novell Web Server and later move the Web site files to a different type of Web server, you'll have to update the files.**

The following subsections describe how to use these commands.

### THE append COMMAND

The append command appends data to the end of a file on the Web server. Do you know why you can't append data to an HTML file? Remember, the last two tags in an HTML file are </BODY> and </HTML>. If you append data after these tags, you change the formatting of the HTML file.

**TIP** **You can append data to a text file, and then use the SSI** include **command to place that text file inside an HTML file. The** include **command is explained earlier in this chapter.**

The format for the append command is as follows:

```
<!--#append file="test.txt" line="&&name1&&, &&name2&&
<tag>"-->
```

The file argument identifies the file to which this data will be appended.

The line argument identifies any variables, text, and HTML tags you want placed in the appended file. To place variables in the appended file, the variables must be preceded and followed by two ampersand characters (&&). Any text, punctuation, space characters, and HTML tags you include in the line argument will be appended with the variable data.

 **NOTE** **Variable names are case-sensitive. Environment variables must be entered in uppercase letters. Other variable names must be entered exactly as they are defined.**

The following append command example appends the visitor's IP address and the local time to a file named append.txt each time the source parsed-HTML file is opened:

```
<!--#append file="append.txt" line="Host=&&REMOTE_HOST&&,
Time=&&DATE_LOCAL&&<br>"-->
```

All of the data specified with the line argument is stored on the same line. To store data on multiple lines, use multiple line arguments within the append command.

You can see an append command example on the demonstration Web site on the following pages:

```
http://host_name/DemoWeb2/Programs/SSI/nw_Web.ssi#append
```

```
d:/DemoWeb2/Programs/SSI/nw_Web.ssi#append
```

### THE break COMMAND

The break command halts all processing of an SSI file. When the server encounters the break command, it stops sending data to the browser. Any SSI command or HTML text that appears after the break command is ignored.

The format of the break command is:

```
<!--#break -->
```

Note the space character after the break command. This space is required. If the space is omitted, the Web server treats the command as a comment.

To view the break command example on the demonstration Web site, browse the following:

```
http://host_name/DemoWeb2/Programs/SSI/nw_Web.ssi#break
```

```
d:/DemoWeb2/Programs/SSI/nw_Web.ssi#break
```

## THE calc COMMAND

The `calc` command enables you to calculate a simple mathematical equation and to assign the result to a variable. The format for the `calc` command is as follows:

```
<!--#calc varname="operation"-->
```

The `calc` command supports the four basic operands: add (+), subtract (-), multiply (*), and divide (/). It also supports variables and the use of parentheses to prioritize operations. To assign a constant value, which is a single number or text string, to a variable, enter the constant value in place of the operation variable.

Unlike most other SSI command arguments, the varname argument name must be replaced with a variable name. The variable name can be an environment variable name, a form element variable name, or a new name that you create. If you are creating a new variable name, be sure to choose a name that is unique on the Web server. If you choose an existing variable name, you'll change the value of that variable instead of creating a new variable. Table 11.8 provides some sample `calc` commands and their result values.

**TABLE 11.8**

*Sample calc Commands*

| CALC COMMAND | VARIABLE VALUE | RESULT |
|---|---|---|
| `<!--#calc c="3"-->` | | c=3 |
| `<!--#calc sum="1+2+3"-->` | | sum=6 |
| `<!--#calc add="a+b"-->` | a=2, b=3 | add=5 |
| `<!--#calc SUM="(2+2)/4 "-->` | | SUM=1 |
| `<!--#calc ADD="2+(2/4)"-->` | | ADD=2 1/2 |
| `<!--#calc serv="SERVER_NAME"-->` | Super_Server | serv=Super_Server |
| `<!--#calc addr="REMOTE_ADDR"-->` | 130.57.163.45 | addr=130.57.163.45 |

**NOTE**

**As with the** append **command, you can enter variables with preceding and trailing double ampersands (&&); however, the double ampersands are not required with the** calc **command. Unless you are copying variable names from another SSI file, omit the double ampersands.**

The result variable from any operation is stored on the Web server and can be used as follows:

▸ Displayed with the echo command

▸ Saved to a file with the append command

▸ Sent to a CGI script with form data

▸ Used as part of another calculation within the file

To assign values to multiple variables, or to calculate multiple values, you can enter multiple calc commands or multiple varname arguments in a single calc command.

## THE count COMMAND

The count command records the number of times a Web page is accessed and displays the number on the Web page. The format of the count command is:

```
<!--#count file="filename.ext"-->
```

The file argument names the text file where the count is stored. If the file does not already exist, the Web server will create the file the first time the count command is executed (which happens when a browser requests the Web page).

Each time the count command runs in your Web page, the Web server increments the count number in the file and sends the incremented number to the browser. You can reset this counter at any time by editing the file with a text editor.

To see the count command example on the demonstration Web site, open one of the following pages:

```
http://host_name/DemoWeb2/Programs/SSI/nw_Web.ssi#count
```

```
d:/DemoWeb2/Programs/SSI/nw_Web.ssi#count
```

## THE exec COMMAND

On the Novell Web Server, the `exec` command enables a Web page author to execute an LCGI program from a Web page. LCGI programs are NLMs that are designed to add functionality to Web pages. (You'll learn about LCGI in Chapter 12, *Using CGI Programs and Scripts.*)

The `exec` command enables authors to execute LCGI programs and NLMs using the rights assigned to the server, itself. This means that Web page authors can write and execute NLMs on their own. Because the server rights level is usually much higher than that of the average user, the `exec` command is often disabled on nonNovell Web Servers. Novell Web Server 3.1 lets you enable or disable the `exec` command when you enable SSI-command processing for a directory.

**NOTE** The `exec` command is not the only way to run an LCGI script from a Web page. In Chapter 12, *Using CGI Programs and Scripts,* you'll learn other ways to run CGI scripts. If you are concerned about rights violations, disable the `exec` command using the Enable IncludesNoExec option as described earlier in this chapter.

**TIP** To disable the exec command on a nonNovell Web server, enter the IncludesNoExec option in the access configuration file for the Web server. For more information, see the documentation for the Web server.

The format for the `exec` command is:

```
<!--#exec cgi="service_type?query_string"-->
```

The *service_type* value identifies the LCGI NLM to run, and the *query_string* value represents data to be passed to the NLM. The service type value must match the LoadableModule directive that is placed in the server's SRM.CFG file. For more information on LCGI, see Chapter 12.

## THE if COMMAND

The `if` command uses a mathematical or logical operator to compare two values. If the result of the comparison is true, the specified operation is performed. If the result is not true, the server continues processing the next line in the file. In computer jargon, this is called conditional branching. The format for the if command is as follows:

```
<!--#if "operand1" operator "operand2" operation-->
```

*Operand1* and *operand2* are the values the if command will compare. The *operator* is the mathematical or logical operator that compares the two values. Table 11.9 lists the operators you can use in an if command.

The following example shows how an if command can be used to control the processing of a Web page:

```
<!--#if "&&NAME&&" contains "Mike" goto "mike"-->

Hi, <!--#echo var="&&NAME&&">. Is this your first visit to
this site?

<!--#goto "continue"-->

<!--#label "mike"-->

Welcome back, Mike!

<!--#label "continue"-->
```

| TABLE 11.9 | OPERATOR | DESCRIPTION |
|---|---|---|
| if *Command Operators* | == | Equal to |
| | != | Not equal to |
| | < | Less than |
| | > | Greater than |
| | >= | Greater than or equal to |
| | <= | Less than or equal to |
| | contains | Operand1 contains the text string in operand2 |

If the NAME variable contains Mike, the goto command sends processing to the line with the mike label command, and the Web page displays: Welcome back, Mike! If the NAME variable does not contain Mike, the goto command is not executed and processing continues on the next line. If the name isn't Mike, the Web page displays a welcome message that includes the name in the NAME variable.

Table 11.10 lists the operations the `if` command can use when the specified condition is true.

## THE goto COMMAND

The `goto` command causes the server to jump to the specified label. The server does not process or display any text, HTML tags, SSI commands, or scripts between the `goto` command and the destination `label` command. The format for the `goto` command is as follows:

```
<!--#goto "label"-->
```

| TABLE 11.10 | OPERATION | DESCRIPTION |
|---|---|---|
| `if` *Command Operations* | goto | Same as for the `goto` command, which is explained in the next section. |
| | print *"text"* | Prints a message you specify. |
| | Error | Prints the current error-message string, defined with the `config` command, as described earlier in this chapter. |
| | Break | Same as for the `break` command described earlier in this chapter. |
| | Errorbreak | Prints the current error message string defined with the `config` command and executes the `break` command. |
| | printbreak *"text"* | Prints a message you specify and executes the `break` command. |

In the following example, the `goto` command causes Grumpy to lose his turn.

```
<!--#label "Happy"-->
Happy's turn.
<!--#goto "Sneezy"-->
<!--#label "Grumpy"-->
Grumpy's turn.
<!--#label Sneezy"-->
Sneezy's turn.
```

## THE label COMMAND

The label command marks a destination to which a goto command can jump. The format of the label command is as follows:

```
<!--#label "name"-->
```

To see how the label command is used, refer to the example for the goto command.

 **Exercise 11.4: If you're preparing to take the certification exam, or if you want to practice what you learned in this section, turn to the end of this chapter and complete Exercise 11.4. When you are done, continue reading here to prepare for the next exercise.**

# Processing Forms with SSI Commands

Now that you've learned about the SSI commands provided with the Novell Web Server, let's see how you can use them to process an HTML form. Figure 11.6 shows a form that appears identical to the form example shown in Chapter 5. This time, however, the form data is processed by SSI commands.

FIGURE 11.6

*Sample HTML Form*

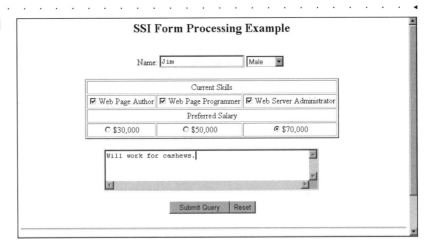

This form collects data from a Web page visitor and stores it on the Novell Web Server in a file named APPEND.TXT. There are two primary differences between the parsed-HTML file for the form in Figure 11.6 and the HTML file used to create the form example in Chapter 5:

▸ The opening `<FORM>` tag for this example calls for a parsed-HTML file instead of an HTML file.

▸ The source parsed-HTML file contains SSI commands that process the form data.

The following is the opening `<FORM>` tag for the sample form:

```
<FORM method=GET action="ssi_form.ssi">
```

When a user clicks the submit button for this form, the GET value for the `METHOD` attribute tells the browser to append the form data to the URL for the file named by the `ACTION` attribute (more on this shortly). The `ACTION` attribute tells the browser to request a parsed-HTML file, which is the same file that contains this form. Figure 11.7 shows what is happening in this example.

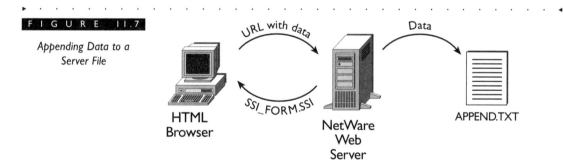

**FIGURE 11.7**

*Appending Data to a Server File*

URL with data

Data

SSI_FORM.SSI

**HTML Browser**

**NetWare Web Server**

**APPEND.TXT**

After a user completes the form and clicks the submit button, the browser creates a request for the SSI_FORM.SSI file and appends the form data to the end of the request. When the server receives the request, it stores the form data in an environmental variable named `QUERY_STRING`; and then the server parses the parsed-HTML file and sends the HTML code and SSI command results back to the browser. The following SSI commands in the parsed-HTML file append the data in the QUERY_STRING variable to a Web server file named APPEND.TXT:

```
<!--#if &&QUERY_STRING&& CONTAINS "your_name" GOTO "END" -->

<!--#if &&QUERY_STRING&& CONTAINS "name" GOTO "APPEND" -->

<!--#goto "END"  -->

<!--#label "APPEND" -->

<!--#append file="append.txt"

   LINE="<P>Name: &&name&&<BR>"

   LINE="Option: &&menu&&<BR>"

   LINE="Checkboxes: 1=&&c1&& 2=&&c2&& 3=&&c3&&<BR>"

   LINE="Radio button: &&one&&<BR>"

   LINE="Comments: &&comments&&</P>"

   LINE="<HR>" -->

<!--#label "END" -->
```

The if commands verify that the QUERY_STRING variable contains new data. (The QUERY_STRING variable is introduced in Chapter 5.) If there is new data, processing skips to the APPEND label, and the following append command appends the data to the APPEND.TXT file.

The variable names listed in the LINE argument values are defined in the source HTML form and are transferred to the Web server when the submit button is clicked. HTML tags are also appended to the text file so the file can be included in a parsed-HTML file for viewing.

If there is no data in the QUERY_STRING variable, SSI processing skips to the END label and no data is saved in the text file.

Before concluding this example, let's see how you can view the data that is stored in the append.txt file. You can:

▸ View the data in a text editor.

▸ Click the "View text file" link at the bottom of the form.

Figure 11.8 shows what happens when you click the link on the form page. The link requests a file named VIEW_APP.SSI, which contains an `include` command that displays the contents of the APPEND.TXT file on its Web page.

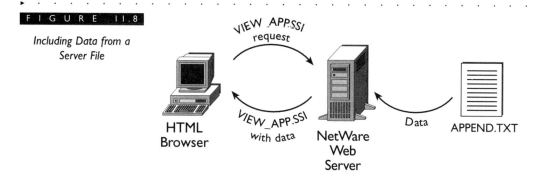

**F I G U R E   11.8**

*Including Data from a Server File*

VIEW_APP.SSI request

VIEW_APP.SSI with data

Data

HTML Browser

NetWare Web Server

APPEND.TXT

To summarize this example, the form stores data in the QUERY_STRING environment variable on the Web server, SSI commands save data in the APPEND.TXT file, and SSI commands display APPEND.TXT file data in a Web page. This is an example of how you can use a Web site to collect data from Web site visitors and store it for future use.

To view the pages used in this example, browse the demonstration Web site at:

```
http://host_name/DemoWeb2/Programs/SSI/ssi_form.ssi
```

```
d:/DemoWeb2/Programs/SSI/ssi_form.ssi
```

## Troubleshooting Tips

The following are some common SSI command problems and their possible causes:

> ▸ Part of the SSI command appears "unprocessed" in the file. **Possible Cause:** The command was entered incorrectly. It was not recognized as an SSI command or as a comment.

▸ Nothing appears where the SSI command result should appear.
**Possible Cause:** The SSI command was treated as a comment or there
was no data to display. Check the command format, check the file
extension, and make sure the file's parent directory has SSI enabled.
Remember, SSI commands must be processed by a Web server. If you
open the SSI file as a file (`file:///d:/path/filename`) and not as a
Web server document (`http://path/filename`), the SSI command
will be treated as an HTML comment.

▸ An error message appears where the SSI command result should
appear. **Possible Cause:** Error messages are produced by the Web
server, so an error message indicates that the command was recognized
as an SSI command. The command arguments might have been entered
incorrectly, or the command might not be supported for the type of
connection in use. Also, a referenced file might be missing.

▸ Some of the argument values for an SSI command argument were
processed, but not all of them. **Possible Cause:** Check for missing
quotation marks. If the value, or values, for an argument include any
space characters, all the values for that argument must be entered
between quotation marks. These should be regular typewriter-style
quotation marks, not the curly quotation marks used by some word
processors.

## When to Use SSI Commands

This chapter describes SSI commands, but the other chapters in this part
describe CGI programs and scripts (which include Perl scripts), JavaScripts, and
Java applets. As you learn to use each of these Web page programming tools, you'll
learn that each has capabilities that might or might not be available in others.
Some tasks cannot be completed with SSI commands. Often, you can accomplish
the same task with more than one tool.

When you can accomplish something with SSI commands or with one of the other tools, consider the following:

- SSI commands are probably the easiest way to complete a task.

- SSI commands usually offer the least amount of custom configuration options.

- SSI commands can impact server performance more than CGI programs and scripts, and will impact performance more than JavaScripts or Java applets.

- If you need to host the same Web site on Novell and nonNovell Web servers, you should use the SHTML file extension and avoid using the Novell-specific SSI commands.

- When you enable SSI processing for a directory, you open the door for people to view the client and server information stored in the environment variables. However, you can control this by limiting who has the rights to create files in the SSI directories and by setting policies on what may be published.

In general, SSI commands offer an easy way to start creating dynamic Web pages. When they won't do what you want them to do, or when they start affecting Web server performance, its time to consider other tools.

 **Exercise 11.5: To test your understanding of the SSI concepts and commands described in this chapter, turn to the end of this chapter and complete Exercise 11.5.**

## Summary

In this chapter you learned how to enter SSI commands in HTML files, how SSI commands are formatted as HTML comments, and how the `file` and `virtual` arguments can be used with SSI commands.

The section called "NCSA Server SSI Commands" introduced you to standard NCSA SSI commands that are supported by the Novell Web Server, and the section titled "Novell Web Server SSI Commands" explained how to use custom SSI commands that are unique to the Novell Web Server.

In the next chapter, you'll learn about the Common Gateway Interface (CGI).

## PUZZLE 11.1: USING SSI COMMANDS

The following word puzzle contains many of the terms discussed in this chapter. See if you can find all the words. As you search for the words, ask yourself why the word is in the list, and how it was used in this chapter. If you don't know the answers to these questions, you might want to review the chapter.

```
C  U  N  E  T  C  O  N  F  I  G  S  I  D  E
L  E  X  X  A  R  J  P  M  E  T  H  O  D  M
A  E  X  T  M  A  C  C  E  S  S  T  H  S  I
C  K  A  E  R  B  T  N  I  R  P  M  C  E  M
V  D  C  N  O  B  T  S  N  M  A  L  E  R  C
K  Y  F  S  F  N  S  I  C  V  A  T  P  V  W
P  Y  J  I  U  I  S  Z  L  I  L  N  O  E  H
A  O  T  O  G  K  T  E  U  R  X  C  Y  R  X
R  P  C  N  A  I  N  F  D  T  F  S  G  D  D
S  W  P  E  M  Y  E  M  E  U  I  A  L  I  U
E  E  R  E  D  O  M  T  S  A  L  F  N  F  Q
D  B  F  C  N  O  M  O  Y  L  E  C  S  A  L
S  M  R  O  F  D  O  N  E  S  T  I  N  G  Z
T  G  N  O  I  T  C  A  W  Z  Z  G  E  I  Q
E  R  R  M  S  G  L  A  B  E  L  I  N  E  O
```

| | | | |
|---|---|---|---|
| access | EXEC | if | PRINTBREAK |
| action | echo | include | parsed |
| append | extension | LCGI | SHTML |
| break | FLASTMOD | label | SIZEFMT |
| CALC | FSIZE | line | SSI |
| CONFIG | file | MIME | server |
| comment | format | method | side |
| count | forms | NCSA | TIMEFMT |
| dynamic | GOTO | nesting | virtual |
| ERRMSG | INCLUDESNOEXEC | operator | WEBMGR |

**EXERCISE II.I: ENABLING SSI COMMAND PROCESSING**

In this exercise, you practice accessing the SSI file extension and enabling SSI-command processing for a directory. Because you might or might not have access to a Novell Web Server, this exercise provides options for both alternatives. If you have access to a Novell Web Server, follow the instructions for Novell Web Server access, or better yet, complete all the steps.

To complete this exercise, do the following:

**1** • If you have access to a Novell Web Server, use a text editor or word-processor program to open the file where the default SSI file extension is defined.

**2** • If you don't have access to a Novell Web Server, use a text editor or word-processor program to open the following file on this book's CD-ROM:

*d*:/DemoWeb2/Answers/MIME.TYP

**3** • Locate and write down the line that defines the default SSI file extension.

. . . . . . . . . . . . . . . . . . . . . . . . . . . . . . . . . . . . . . . .

**4** • Close the file you opened in either Step 1 or Step 2.

**5** • If you have access to a Novell Web Server, do the following to enable SSI-command processing in a directory:

a. If you haven't done so already, copy the demonstration Web site to the Web server as described in Appendix C.

b. Use Web Manager to enable SSI processing for the following directory:

\*path*\DemoWeb2\Programs\SSI

c. To verify that SSI processing is enabled, access the following page:

`http://DemoWeb2/Programs/SSI/ncsa_ssi.ssi`

    d. Scroll down through the Web page and locate the Environment Variables table. If this table contains values in the Values column, SSI is enabled for this directory. If the Values column is empty, SSI-command processing is not enabled for the directory.

**6** • If you don't have access to a Novell Web Server, practice enabling SSI processing for a directory by doing the following:

    a. Use a text editor or word processor program to open the following file on this book's CD-ROM:

    *d:*/DemoWeb2/Answers/access.cfg

    b. Locate and copy the portion of the file that sets the options for the document root directory (docs).

    c. Paste a copy of the document root directory definition at the end of the file.

    d. Change the directory path in the copied text to specify the following directory:

```
\docs\DemoWeb2\Programs\SSI
```

    e. Make the change that enables SSI processing in the directory defined in Step 6d.

    f. Save a copy of the updated file on your local computer.

    g. Verify that you made the correct changes by viewing the following file on this book's CD:

```
d:/DemoWeb2/Answers/access2.cfg
```

### EXERCISE 11.2: UNDERSTANDING SSI COMMAND SYNTAX

This exercise tests your understanding of the SSI-command syntax described in this section. To complete this exercise, answer the following questions.

**1** • Is the following command syntax valid? Why?

```
<!--#command argument="<!--#command argument="value"
-->"-->
```

Answer: . . . . . . . . . . . . . . . . . . . . . . . . . . . . . . . . . . . . . . . . . . .

**2** • Which character distinguishes an SSI command from an HTML comment?

Answer: . . . . . . . . . . . . . . . . . . . . . . . . . . . . . . . . . . . . . . . . . . .

**3** • Do SSI commands work when SSI files are loaded on a client computer? Why?

Answer: . . . . . . . . . . . . . . . . . . . . . . . . . . . . . . . . . . . . . . . . . . .

**4** • The file argument specifies a file relative to _____.

**5** • The virtual argument specifies a file relative _____.

**6** • Is the following argument valid? Why?

```
file="../path/filename.ext"
```

Answer: . . . . . . . . . . . . . . . . . . . . . . . . . . . . . . . . . . . . . . . . . . .

**7** • Is the following argument valid?

```
file="/path/filename.ext"
```

Answer: . . . . . . . . . . . . . . . . . . . . . . . . . . . . . . . . . . . . . . . . . . .

**8** • When a destination file for an SSI command is in a parent directory of the source SSI file, which argument should you use?

Answer: . . . . . . . . . . . . . . . . . . . . . . . . . . . . . . . . . . . . . . . . .

**9** • When a destination file for an SSI command is in a user Web page directory, which argument should you use?

Answer: . . . . . . . . . . . . . . . . . . . . . . . . . . . . . . . . . . . . . . . . .

**10** • When you can use either the file or the virtual argument, which should you choose? Why?

Answer: . . . . . . . . . . . . . . . . . . . . . . . . . . . . . . . . . . . . . . . . .

EXERCISE 11.3: USING NCSA SSI COMMANDS

In this exercise, you create a Web page that uses the NCSA SSI commands. If you have a Web server on which to publish your Web page, you can test it. If not, you can compare the Web page you create to the answer file on this book's CD.

To complete this exercise, do the following:

1 • Use a text editor or word-processor program to open the following file on this book's CD-ROM:

*d*:/DemoWeb2/Answers/ssi.htm

This file gives you a head start on creating the Web page for this exercise. Figure 11.9 shows how this file appears in a browser after you add SSI commands.

FIGURE 11.9

*Result File for Exercise 11.3*

**SSI Practice File**

| Information | Data |
|---|---|
| File | This file was last modified on:<br>Wednesday, December 17 |
| | This file's size is:<br>827 |
| Server | The Web server uses the following software:<br>Novell-HTTP-Server/3.1R1 |
| | The Web server name or IP address is:<br>130.57.128.3 |
| Client | The client IP address is:<br>130.57.128.11 |

*MyCompany*
Street Address
City, State or Province
Postal Code

Country

www.mycompany.com

2 • In the table cell that defines when the file was last modified, add the two SSI commands that produce this information using the following format:

```
Wednesday, December 17
```

In this step and all following steps, add the SSI commands after the ⟨BR⟩ command so the results appear on a separate line. When you are done creating the file, you will save it using the filename SSI_TEST with the appropriate extension.

**3** · In the table cell that defines the file size, add the two SSI commands that display the file size in bytes.

**4** · In the table cell that displays the Web server software information, add the SSI command that displays this information.

**5** · In the table cell that displays the Web server IP address, add the SSI command that displays this information.

**6** · In the table cell that displays the client name or IP address, add the SSI command that displays this information.

**7** · In between the two horizontal rules at the end of the file, enter the SSI command that inserts the following file into the Web page: myco.txt.

**8** · Save this file on your local computer using the filename SSI_TEST and the correct SSI file extension.

**9** · If you have access to a Novell Web Server, do the following:

a. Choose an SSI-enabled directory to which you will copy the files.

The default SSI-enabled directory on the Novell Web Server is:

SYS:\WEB\DOCS\SSI

If you enabled SSI processing for the directory listed in Exercise 11.1, you can use the following directory:

SYS:\WEB\DOCS\DemoWeb2\Programs\SSI

b. Copy the file you have created to the SSI-enabled directory chosen in Step 9a.

    c. Copy the following file from this book's CD to the directory chosen in Step 9a:

    *d:*/DemoWeb2/Answers/myco.txt

    d. Test your SSI-enabled Web page by opening it with one of the following URLs:

    `http://`*hostname*`/ssi/ssi_test.ssi`

    `http://`*hostname*`/DemoWeb2/Programs/SSI/ssi_test.ssi`

**10** • If you do not have access to a Novell Web Server, compare the file you created to the following file on this book's CD:

    `d:/DemoWeb2/Answers/ssi_test.htm`

Your file should closely match the answer file.

**EXERCISE II.4: USING NOVELL WEB SERVER SSI COMMAND**

In this exercise, you use Novell Web Server SSI commands to modify the Web page created in Exercise 11.3. If you have a Web server on which to publish your Web page, you can test it. If not, you can compare the Web page you create to the answer file on this book's CD.

To complete this exercise, do the following:

**I** • Use a text editor or word processor to open the following file on this book's CD-ROM:

```
d:/DemoWeb2/Answers/ssi_test.ssi
```

This file gives you a head start on creating the Web page for this exercise. Figure 11.10 shows how this file appears in a browser after you add SSI commands.

▶ · · · · · · · · · · · · · · · · · · · · · · · · · · · · · · · · · · ◀

**FIGURE II.10**

*Result File for Exercise II.4*

> **SSI Practice File**
>
> Hit count: 7
>
> The sum of 3+4 is 7

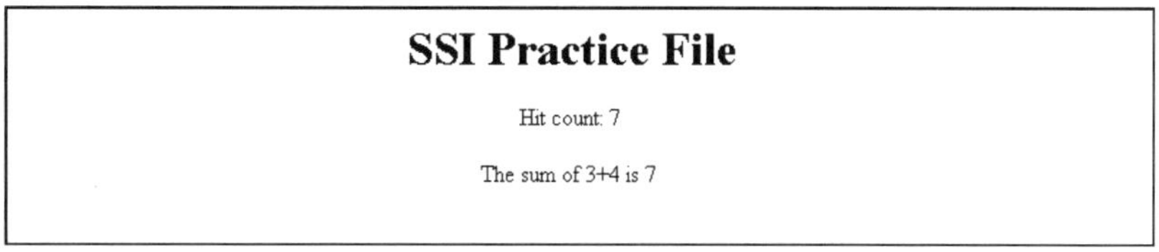

**2** • Between the first <CENTER> tag and the first <TABLE> tag, enter a new line with the text "Hit count:" and the command to display the page count. Name the counter text file "count.txt."

**3** • Immediately after the command you entered in Step 2, add a new line with the command that assigns the sum of 3+4 to a variable named "sum."

**4** • Immediately after the command you entered in Step 3, add a new line that displays **The sum of 3+4 is** and the value of the sum variable. (*Tip:* To display the variable, you use an NCSA SSI command.)

**5** • Immediately after the command you entered in Step 4, add a new line with the command that halts processing of the file.

**6** • Add the HTML formatting tags that will make the text and commands you have entered appear as shown in Figure 11.10.

**7** • Save this file on your local computer using the filename SSITEST2 and the correct SSI file extension.

**8** • If you have access to a Novell Web Server, do the following:

a. Choose an SSI-enabled directory to copy files to.

The default SSI-enabled directory on the Novell Web Server is:

SYS:\WEB\DOCS\SSI

If you enabled SSI processing for the directory listed in Exercise 11.1, you can use the following directory:

SYS:\WEB\DOCS\DemoWeb2\Programs\SSI

b. Copy the file you have created to the SSI-enabled directory chosen in Step 8a.

c. Test your SSI-enabled Web page by opening it with one of the following URLs:

http://*hostname*/ssi/ssitest2.ssi

http://*hostname*/DemoWeb2/Programs/SSI/ssitest2.ssi

**9** • If you do not have access to a Novell Web Server, compare the file you created to the following file on this book's CD:

*d*:/DemoWeb2/Answers/ssitest2.ssi

Your file should closely match the answer file.

## EXERCISE 11.5: USING SSI COMMANDS

This exercise tests your understanding of the SSI concepts and commands described in this chapter. To complete this exercise, answer the following questions:

**1** • Do SSI commands produce static or dynamic information?

Answer: . . . . . . . . . . . . . . . . . . . . . . . . . . . . . . . . .

**2** • Can you test SSI commands without a Web server?

Answer: . . . . . . . . . . . . . . . . . . . . . . . . . . . . . . . . .

**3** • What is the default SSI file extension on the Novell Web Server and where is it defined?

Answer: . . . . . . . . . . . . . . . . . . . . . . . . . . . . . . . . .

**4** • Another name for an SSI file is a _____ HTML file.

**5** • SSI commands should not be used in which type of files?

Answer: . . . . . . . . . . . . . . . . . . . . . . . . . . . . . . . . .

**6** • What is the name of the Web Manager program file provided with the Novell Web Server?

Answer: . . . . . . . . . . . . . . . . . . . . . . . . . . . . . . . . .

**7** • Which two Web Manager options enable SSI processing for a directory on the Novell Web Server?

a. . . . . . . . . . . . . . . . . . . . . . . . . . . . . . . . . .

b. . . . . . . . . . . . . . . . . . . . . . . . . . . . . . . . . .

**8** • Which Novell Web Server file can you edit to enable SSI processing for a directory?

Answer: . . . . . . . . . . . . . . . . . . . . . . . . . . . . . . . . . . . . . . .

**9** • On the Novell Web Server, SSI command names are not case-sensitive, but _____ names are case-sensitive.

**10** • List the five NCSA SSI commands supported on the Novell Web Server.

a. . . . . . . . . . . . . . . . . . . . . . . . . . . . . . . . . . . . . . .

b. . . . . . . . . . . . . . . . . . . . . . . . . . . . . . . . . . . . . . .

c. . . . . . . . . . . . . . . . . . . . . . . . . . . . . . . . . . . . . . .

d. . . . . . . . . . . . . . . . . . . . . . . . . . . . . . . . . . . . . . .

e. . . . . . . . . . . . . . . . . . . . . . . . . . . . . . . . . . . . . . .

**11** • When are quotation marks required around an argument value?

Answer: . . . . . . . . . . . . . . . . . . . . . . . . . . . . . . . . . . . . .

**12** • List the `config` command arguments that set the format for the `flastmod` and `fsize` commands.

a. . . . . . . . . . . . . . . . . . . . . . . . . . . . . . . . . . . . . . .

b. . . . . . . . . . . . . . . . . . . . . . . . . . . . . . . . . . . . . . .

**13** • List three types of variables that the echo command can display on the Novell Web Server.

a. . . . . . . . . . . . . . . . . . . . . . . . . . . . . . . . . . . . . . .

b. . . . . . . . . . . . . . . . . . . . . . . . . . . . . . . . . . . . . . .

c. . . . . . . . . . . . . . . . . . . . . . . . . . . . . . . . . . . . . . .

**14** • What is the `echo` command argument that specifies the variable to be displayed?

Answer: . . . . . . . . . . . . . . . . . . . . . . . . . . . . . . . . . . . .

**15** • Which environment variable displays the client IP address?

Answer: . . . . . . . . . . . . . . . . . . . . . . . . . . . . . . . . . . . .

**16** • What does the `include` SSI command do?

Answer: . . . . . . . . . . . . . . . . . . . . . . . . . . . . . . . . . . . .

**17** • What does the `append` SSI command do?

Answer: . . . . . . . . . . . . . . . . . . . . . . . . . . . . . . . . . . . .

**18** • Write down the complete SSI command that halts processing of a Web page.

Answer: . . . . . . . . . . . . . . . . . . . . . . . . . . . . . . . . . . . .

**19** • Which four mathematical operations does the `calc` command support?

Answer: . . . . . . . . . . . . . . . . . . . . . . . . . . . . . . . . . . . .

**20** • Which SSI command provides for conditional branching?

Answer: . . . . . . . . . . . . . . . . . . . . . . . . . . . . . . . . . . . .

**21** • Which SSI command enables you to store form data on the Novell Web Server?

Answer: . . . . . . . . . . . . . . . . . . . . . . . . . . . . . . . . . . . .

**22** • When you are storing form data on the Novell Web Server, which characters do you place before and after a variable name?

Answer: . . . . . . . . . . . . . . . . . . . . . . . . . . . . . . . . . . . . . . . . . . . .

# CHAPTER 12

# Using CGI Programs and Scripts

**C**ommon Gateway Interface (CGI) is a standard that enables Web pages to interact with external programs called *CGI programs* (or *CGI scripts*). CGI programs and scripts are written to conform with the CGI specifications and can run on the same server as the Web server or on a remote server anywhere on the network. SSI commands and server-side image maps, by contrast, are functions of the Web server software, not separate programs.

Like the SSI commands described in the previous chapter, CGI programs enable you to change the content of Web pages dynamically. CGI programs can do the following:

- ▶ Perform most of the functions provided by SSI commands

- ▶ Collect data from a Web page and save it in a file

- ▶ Collect data from a Web page, perform calculations on the data, and display the results in a new Web page

- ▶ Look up a user name or password and determine if the user should see a Web page

- ▶ Access data in a database and display the results on a Web page

- ▶ Process orders for products, requests for information, and credit card purchases

This chapter describes how CGI works, the CGI program support provided with the Novell Web Server, and how to support and use CGI programs and scripts on the Novell Web Server.

## Why Use CGI?

In Chapter 11, *Using SSI Commands*, you learned how to create dynamic Web pages using SSI commands. CGI programs can do everything that SSI commands can do, and more. For example, suppose you wanted to look up a stock price in a database each time your Web page is loaded. Web servers don't provide SSI commands for this.

CGI programs and scripts, however, enable you to implement custom solutions to your problems. To solve the problem in this example, you can buy or create a program that will do it for you. If this program is CGI compatible, the program can accept data (such as the stock symbol) from the Web server and return a results Web page, which the server sends to a browser. In this example, the results Web page displays the requested stock price.

Here are some services that CGI programs can provide:

- Process Web page form data (for example, data from product order forms or surveys)

- Validate form data and provide response Web pages for incorrect entries

- Display environment and program variables

- Provide information requested from a database

- Score Web-based exams

- Create customized Web pages for particular days of the week, Web page visitors, or Web browsers

- Permit or block access to a Web site based on a user's name and password

Because of the power and flexibility provided by CGI-compatible programming languages, which are described later in this chapter, it is very difficult to list every possible use for CGI programs. While the CGI standard and the particular programming language do place limitations on CGI programs, in most other aspects, CGI program services are only limited by the skill and creativity of the CGI programmer.

When you can choose between a CGI script and an SSI command, consider the following:

▸ CGI scripts can require less server processing time. The Web server delegates processing to a CGI program instead of parsing a complete SSI file.

▸ The programming languages used to create CGI scripts can provide more functions and features than can be provided by SSI command attributes.

▸ You can revise CGI programs that you create. The Web server manufacturer must revise the Web server software to provide new SSI-command functionality.

▸ Many CGI scripts are easily ported to other NCSA Web servers. You can use CGI scripts that other people have created to extend the functionality of your server.

This is not to say there's no advantage to using SSI commands. For one thing, SSI commands are easier to implement — especially for nonprogrammers. However, CGI programs and scripts offer much more versatility.

**NOTE**

**CGI-compatible programs are known by names such as *CGI programs, CGI scripts, extensions,* or *server extensions*. CGI programs are sometimes called *scripts* because they are often developed using scripting languages that produce scripts (similar to DOS batch files). They're sometimes called *extensions* or *server extensions* because they extend the functionality of a Web server to include features that are impossible with HTML alone.**

## How CGI Works

For a better understanding of CGI, look at what happens when a browser requests a Web page. Figure 12.1 is a simplified illustration of the process. When the user requests a Web page directly, with a URL, or indirectly, through a link, the browser requests the file from the Web server. When the server receives the request, it provides the file. That's basically it. The browser asks for the file and the server provides it.

**FIGURE 12.1**

*Simplified HTML File Request*

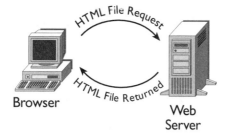

To start a CGI program, you use a URL similar to the following:

`http://host_name/scripts/scriptname`

The scripts variable represents the Web server location of the CGI program or script. The scriptname is the name of the CGI program or script.

Here are several ways to start a CGI program with a URL:

▸ Use the URL in your browser to request the program in the same way you request a Web page.

▸ Use the URL as a link destination within a Web page.

▸ Use the `ACTION` attribute in a `<FORM>` tag to specify the URL of the CGI program (forms are described in Chapter 5).

Forms are a popular way to submit data to a CGI program. Typically, a user completes a form and clicks a button, called the *submit* button. When the user clicks the Submit button, the browser sends the form data in a request for the CGI program. Figure 12.2 shows what happens when a browser requests a CGI program instead of a Web page.

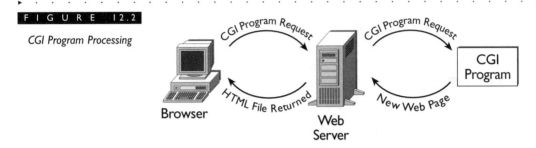

FIGURE 12.2

*CGI Program Processing*

In this example, the user clicks a link or button that causes the browser to call a CGI program, just as the browser might call another Web page. The Web server recognizes the CGI program request and passes any data from the browser to the CGI program, which processes the data and returns a Web page with results to the Web server. The Web server then returns the resulting Web page to the browser.

## CGI on the Novell Web Server

The example in the previous section was simplified to introduce the basic concepts of CGI processing. This section provides more information by showing how CGI works on the Novell Web Server. Figure 12.3 shows the server CGI components that come with the Novell Web Server. Notice that the Perl and NetBasic CGI scripts communicate with the Novell Web Server software through CGI programs called interpreters. CGI scripts are programs that require the help of an interpreter for processing. CGI programs run independently; they do not require interpreters. For more information on interpreters, see the sidebar, "What Is a Command Interpreter?"

The CGI programs that run on the Novell Web Server are written as NetBasic scripts, Perl scripts, or NLMs. To support NetBasic or Perl scripts on a Novell Web Server, you must load the correct CGI interpreter NLM. For each CGI script type (interpreter) and program, you must configure an entry in the Server Resource Management configuration file (SRM.CFG). The entries in the SRM.CFG file define a virtual path to the CGI interpreter or program.

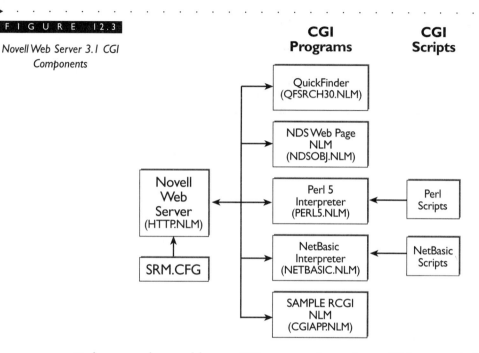

**F I G U R E   12.3**

*Novell Web Server 3.1 CGI Components*

To better understand how a CGI program is used on a Web server, let's look at an example. Figure 12.4 shows the sample HTML form from Chapter 5. The only difference between the form in Figure 12.4 and the form in Chapter 5 is the <FORM> tag ACTION attribute, which calls the echo.pl CGI script when a browser user clicks the submit button. The <FORM> tag from this file is:

```
<FORM METHOD=GET ACTION="/perl/echo.pl">
```

After the browser user enters form data and clicks the submit button, the browser creates a request that includes the CGI program URL (/perl/echo.pl) and the form data. As described in Chapter 5, when the <FORM> tag uses the GET method, the form data is appended to the URL as follows:

```
http://130.57.128.2/perl/echo.pl?your_name=Jim&menu=Male&c1=o
n&c2=on&c3=on&one=3&comments=Will+Work+for+cashews%21
```

## What Is a Command Interpreter?

A command interpreter is a program that can interpret and execute programming language commands. Computers don't understand the English-based programming commands that most programming languages use. To execute a program, the program must be converted to special machine codes that most of us don't want to understand.

When a programmer creates a program, such as a BASIC program, the programmer uses a text editor or word processor to create an ASCII text file. Although the ASCII text file contains programming commands, it is just a text file. To become a program, the text file needs assistance.

One way to execute programs is to use a command interpreter, which is a custom program that can read and execute the commands in text files. To execute a program stored in a text file, you start the interpreter program first, and then you use the interpreter to run the program defined in the text file.

Of course, not all programs are run through interpreters (for example, the interpreter, itself, does not require an interpreter). Another way to execute programs is to use programming tools to convert a text file into an executable program. DOS applications with .EXE extensions are executables that run in DOS without the assistance of an interpreter. NetWare Loadable Modules (NLMs), such as the Novell Web Server QuickFinder and NDS Web page NLMs, are executable programs that do not require interpreters.

For beginners, a command interpreter reduces the programming learning curve. It is relatively easy to start a command interpreter and run your program. It is much more difficult to learn to use additional programming tools to convert a text file into an executable program. Of course, the advantages to creating an executable are that you don't need to have an interpreter to execute the program, and the program usually runs faster as an executable.

**FIGURE 12.4**

*Sample HTML Form*

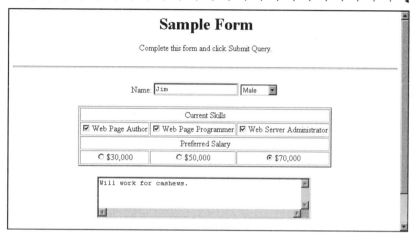

**TIP**

**You can experiment with this on the demonstration Web site at:**

`http://host_name/DemoWeb2/Programs/CGI/cgi_form.htm`

`d:/DemoWeb2/Programs/CGI/cgi_form.htm`

**For instructions on installing the demonstration Web site on your Web server, see Appendix C.**

When the Web server receives the appended data, it stores the information in the QUERY_STRING environment variable. As with SSI commands, CGI programs can access the values in environment variables.

If you try this, you will see the appended data in the location box within your browser. Figure 12.5 shows the Web page that appears in the browser.

F I G U R E   1 2 . 5

*Sample CGI Process Results*

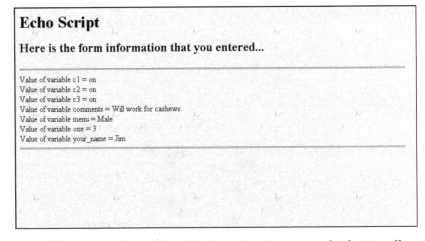

**Echo Script**

**Here is the form information that you entered...**

Value of variable c1 = on
Value of variable c2 = on
Value of variable c3 = on
Value of variable comments = Will work for cashews.
Value of variable menu = Male
Value of variable one = 3
Value of variable your_name = Jim

Figure 12.6 provides an overview of how the form data is processed. The Novell Web Server software (HTTP.NLM) receives the request and uses the information from the SRM.CFG file to determine how to process a request for the /perl/ directory. In this example, the /perl/ directory name is an alias to the directory that contains the Perl interpreter, PERL5.NLM. Whenever the Web server receives a request for this directory, it opens the Perl interpreter and tries to run the Perl script specified after the directory name, which is echo.pl in this example.

F I G U R E   1 2 . 6

*Sample Form Processing
with CGI*

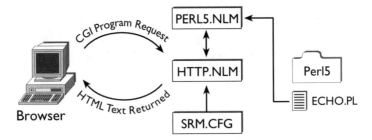

To complete this example, PERL5.NLM loads echo.pl, processes the form data in the QUERY_STRING variable, and returns HTML data to HTTP.NLM, which serves the HTML text to the browser.

HTTP.NLM and PERL5.NLM both conform to the CGI standard and can therefore work together to run Perl programs that output HTML text. In this example, echo.pl is a Perl program that echoes form data back to a browser.

## CGI Program Types

CGI is easier to understand when you know the difference between CGI and CGI programs. CGI is a Web server process that enables the Web server to communicate with other programs. CGI is not a protocol, and on the Novell Web Server, it is not a separate program. CGI is a process and a standard; CGI programs are programs and scripts that communicate with the Web server CGI process.

When you are looking for CGI programs and scripts to use with your Web pages, a familiarity with common CGI programming languages will help you determine if you can easily use the programs you find. Table 12.1 lists the operating systems and programming languages that support CGI programming.

| TABLE 12.1 | OPERATING SYSTEM | LANGUAGES |
|---|---|---|
| CGI Program and Script Languages | NetWare and intraNetWare | C++, Java, NetBasic, Perl |
| | UNIX | C, C++, Java, JavaScript, Perl, shell scripts (Bourne, C, Korn) |
| | Windows | BASIC, Perl, Visual Basic |
| | Macintosh | AppleScript, MacPerl |

C, C++, and Java are programming languages that programmers often use to create executable programs. These programs typically enable complex computing operations and are most efficient, but they require more programming expertise to use.

Script languages such as JavaScript, AppleScript, and the script commands for the Bourne, C, and Korn UNIX shells are typically much easier to use than the full-featured programming languages like C++ and Java. (Shells are programs that provide special commands for communicating with an operating system.) Scripting languages provide a simpler set of programming features, but these features are often enough to get you on your way. If you are new to programming, begin your CGI programming with a scripting language, such as the Perl or NetBasic languages.

On the Novell Web Server, the easiest way to start CGI programming is to write or customize Perl or NetBasic programs. The Perl script described in the previous section runs in the Perl interpreter provided with the Novell Web Server. The Novell Web Server also provides a NetBasic interpreter.

If you are a programmer, you can use ANSI C or Java to create executable CGI programs that run as NLMs on the Novell Web Server. These executable NLMs can be divided into two types of programs, Remote CGI (RCGI) and Local CGI (LCGI) programs.

This section introduces you to the NetBasic and Perl interpreters provided with the Novell Web server and describes the differences between RCGI and LCGI programs.

## NETBASIC

NetBasic is a newer version of the Beginner's All-Purpose Symbolic Instruction Code (BASIC) programming language and is similar to Visual BASIC. To create BASIC programs, you type BASIC commands. To create NetBasic programs, you can use special programs that enable you to drag and drop program components into your new program. This is like using clip art images to create custom illustrations. With NetBasic development tools, you use programming building blocks to build your programs.

Later in this chapter, you'll learn to configure the Novell Web Server to support NetBasic programs. For information on creating NetBasic programs to run on the Novell Web Server, see the *Dynamic Web Page Programmer's Guide*, which is supplied with the Novell Web Server.

## PERL

Perl is short for Practical Extraction and Report Language. When compared with NetBasic, Perl is a relatively new programming language that provides more programming power and flexibility than NetBasic. To create Perl programs for the Novell Web Server, you enter commands in text files, which run in the Perl version 5 interpreter provided with the Novell Web Server.

Later in this chapter, you'll learn to configure the Novell Web Server to support Perl programs. In Chapter 13, you'll learn more about creating and using Perl scripts.

## REMOTE CGI (RCGI)

*Remote CGI (RCGI) programs* are CGI programs that communicate with the Web server software through the Web server TCP/IP stack as shown in Figure 12.7. The alternative to an RCGI program is a Local CGI (LCGI) program, which communicates directly with the Web server software.

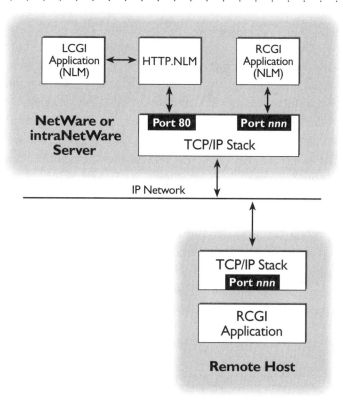

**FIGURE 12.7**

*RCGI Program
Communications*

Note the port numbers in Figure 12.7. In Chapter 4, Linking Web Pages, you learned that the default port number for Web servers is 80, and you learned that port numbers can be specified in URLs. These port numbers serve as addresses for the applications that use the TCP/IP stack. In Figure 12.7, port 80 is the port address for the Novell Web Server software and port *nnn* represents the address of the RCGI application.

RCGI is considered *remote* CGI because the RCGI application can be stored on the local Web server or on remote Web servers. Because the TCP/IP software handles communications between the Web server software and the RCGI application, the RCGI application can be on any Web server that is capable of establishing a TCP/IP connection to the local server. The basic difference between communications with local and remote Web servers is the server host name or IP address.

RCGI is a Novell term that refers specifically to NLMs that run on the Novell Web Server. To create an RCGI program that runs on a Novell Web Server, a programmer must create an RCGI-compatible NLM. Programmers create NLMs with the ANSI C programming language. The Novell Web Server provides source files that provide much of the RCGI functionality. Programmers can use these files to give them a head start on developing RCGI programs.

Remote CGI does not always mean RCGI. For example, in their Web pages, authors can call CGI programs and scripts that are remote to the local Web server. These remote CGI programs and scripts are remote because they operate on a remote server, such as another Novell Web Server or a UnixWare, SunOS, or Solaris host. In this guide, RCGI refers to an NLM on the Novell Web Server, and *remote CGI* refers to programs and scripts that run on remote servers.

When you are trying to decide whether to use CGI scripts with interpreters, custom RCGI NLMs, or remote CGI programs, consider the following:

▸ Interpreted scripts are platform independent. NetBasic and Perl scripts run on any platform that provides the corresponding interpreter program and communicates with the Web server through CGI. RCGI NLMs can only run on NetWare and intraNetWare servers.

▸ Interpreted scripting languages are easier to learn than ANSI C.

▸ Executable RCGI programs (NLMs) operate faster and more efficiently than interpreted languages.

▸ Access to remote CGI programs is dependent on the network connections between the hosts and on the support provided by the remote server administrator.

## LOCAL CGI (LCGI)

As shown previously in Figure 12.7, *local CGI (LCGI)* programs are NLMs that communicate directly with the Web server software. LCGI programs are considered "local" to the Web server software because they must run on the same machine as the Web server software. LCGI programs do not communicate with the Web server software through the TCP/IP stack.

As with RCGI programs, programmers create LCGI NLMs using the ANSI C programming language. The NetBasic and Perl interpreters provided with the Novell Web Server are examples of LCGI programs. They run on the Novell Web Server and communicate directly with the Web server software.

The *local CGI (LCGI)* term is unique to the Novell Web Server. When you browse the World Wide Web, you aren't likely to see the terms LCGI and RCGI. Novell uses these terms to distinguish between the two types of CGI programs that you can use on its server.

Because LCGI NLMs communicate directly with HTTP.NLM, they operate much faster than RCGI NLMs or scripts. LCGI applications do not have to perform the TCP/IP addressing and communications functions required by TCP/IP.

LCGI NLMs are not without drawbacks, however. As with RCGI NLMs, LCGI NLMs run *only* on the NetWare platform. If you want portability, you'll have to create a CGI script first (and run it in an interpreter), and then create a custom LCGI or RCGI NLM later when performance is more important. Use LCGI for optimum performance, use RCGI to make the application available to other Web servers.

## Putting CGI to Work

As with SSI commands, the use of CGI programs and scripts requires support from the Web server administrator and the Web page author. For example, after the Novell Web Server is installed, the CGI programs are ready to run, but you might not have privileges to store CGI programs in the appropriate directories. The Web server administrator can also disable CGI. In this section, you'll learn the steps to properly set up and use CGI. Those steps can be broken down into five main tasks:

1 • Obtain or create CGI programs and scripts

**2** • Specify the CGI program and script directories

**3** • Place CGI programs in the script directories

**4** • Load the CGI NLM or command interpreter

**5** • Call CGI programs from your Web pages

As a Web page author, it is always your responsibility to call the CGI program from your Web pages. However, your ability to manage the other tasks is determined by your access rights to the Web server and your programming experience. Some Web page authors will perform all of these tasks, others will need to delegate some of these responsibilities. Knowing what needs to be done, however, can be very useful when you are trying to understand why your CGI-powered Web pages aren't working. The following subsections describe how to complete these tasks.

## OBTAINING OR CREATING CGI PROGRAMS

At first, the thought of CGI programming may seem a little intimidating, especially if you are not a programmer. Don't let this bother you. If you surf the Web, you'll find lots of CGI scripts available for purchase or as shareware. Some ISPs now offer popular CGI programs as part of their basic Web publishing package.

Some scripts and programs run without modification. If a script needs modification, you can often make the changes yourself using a text editor. Compiled applications, however, require that you obtain the source code and learn enough about programming to create new executable files. The better CGI programs and scripts come with instructions that explain how to set them up on your server.

Figure 12.3 lists the CGI programs that are provided with the Novell Web Server. The Novell Web Server 3.x Examples Toolkit, which is a free download from Novell's Web site, includes some CGI Perl scripts that you can use to dress up your Web site.

**Here are some URLs for CGI program sites:**

**The CGI Collection:** `www.selah.net/cgi.html`

**Dream Catchers CGI Scripts:** `dreamcatchersWeb.com/scripts`

**Kira's Web Toolbox, CGI Library:** `www.lightsphere.com/cgi/`

Many programmers get their start by making minor changes to other people's scripts and programs. After modifying a few scripts, you may want to learn more. Chapter 13 describes how to create simple Perl scripts and how to modify Perl scripts. For more information on customizing scripts and programs, refer to a book on the programming language that interests you.

For specific information on programming CGI programs for the Novell Web Server, refer to the Dynamic Web Page Programmer's Guide, which is provided with the Novell Web Server.

## SPECIFYING CGI PROGRAM AND SCRIPT DIRECTORIES

Before you can use CGI programs and scripts, someone must create the appropriate entries in the appropriate Web server configuration file. On the Novell Web Server, these entries are made in the SRM.CFG file. On UNIX Web servers, the changes are usually made in the SRM.CONF file. Each separate CGI program or interpreter requires its own entry; scripts don't require a separate entry because they use an interpreter.

The default installation of the Novell Web Server configures SRM.CFG to support the CGI programs listed in Table 12.2.

The SRM.CFG entries define a directory and virtual path for each CGI program. For CGI executables, the defined directory specifies where the NLM is stored. For CGI scripts, the defined directory specifies where the interpreter is stored. The CGI program virtual path is used to start CGI programs. It is the first directory name in the URL that refers to a CGI program or script. You'll learn more about this later in this chapter.

TABLE 12.2

*Default CGI Program and*
*Interpreter Locations*

| CGI PROGRAM | DEFAULT DIRECTORY | VIRTUAL PATH |
|---|---|---|
| NetBasic Interpreter | SYS:\INW_WEB\SHARED\LCGI\NETBASIC | /netbasic/ |
| Perl Interpreter | SYS:\INW_WEB\SHARED\LCGI\PERL5 | /perl/ |
| NDS Web Page Program | SYS:\INW_WEB\SHARED\LCGI\NDSOBJ | /nds/ |
| QuickFinder Program | SYS:\INW_WEB\SHARED\LCGI\QFSEARCH | /qfsearch/ |

To use NetBasic or Perl scripts with the default server configuration, place the scripts in the appropriate directories listed in Table 12.3. You do not have to change the Novell Web Server configuration to support these script types.

| TABLE 12.3 | SCRIPT TYPE | DEFAULT LOCATION |
|---|---|---|
| *Default NetBasic and Perl Script Locations* | NetBasic | SYS:\NETBASIC\WEB |
| | Perl | SYS:\INW_WEB\SHARED\DOCS\LCGI\PERL5 |

**NOTE**

**The default location for Perl scripts is very similar to the location for the PERL5 NLM — but it is different. Be sure to place your scripts in the correct directory.**

**Also, if you have used earlier versions of the Novell Web Server, the default script directories are different. You must place your NetBasic and Perl scripts in the directories listed in Table 12.3. The interpreters will no longer find scripts that are stored in the same directory as the NLM.**

The placement of the CGI programs and scripts on the server is very important. The additional power of CGI programs has its benefits and liabilities. Good programmers can do great things with CGI programs. Malicious or inexperienced programmers can disable the Web server. To prevent or minimize server disruption, it is best to place CGI programs and scripts outside of the public directory tree (the document root directory). Notice that all of the directories listed in Tables 12.2 and 12.3 are outside of the default document root directory for the Novell Web Server, SYS:\WEB\DOCS.

Novell recommends that you use the default settings for the CGI programs in Table 12.2; however, you or your administrator can change these settings. To support new RCGI and LCGI programs, you must add new SRM.CFG entries. The following subsections describe how to configure entries for RCGI and LCGI programs, and what access rights should be assigned to these directories.

### Specifying Directories for RCGI and Remote CGI Programs

RCGI programs run on the Novell Web Server, and remote CGI programs run on a remote TCP/IP host. To define a CGI program for the Novell Web Server, you need to add the following directive to the virtual server's SRM.CFG file:

```
RemoteScriptAlias /virtual_path/ hostname:port/path
```

**NOTE** The default path to SRM.CFG is SYS:WEB\CONFIG\SRM.CFG. To add CGI program support to multiple virtual servers, you must separately modify the SRM.CFG file for each virtual server. Each virtual server is configured independently.

RemoteScriptAlias is the directive name that specifies the location of RCGI scripts and programs, and the virtual_path is an alias or alternate name for the actual path that follows. On UNIX servers, the virtual path name is case-sensitive. You can use any name for the virtual path as long as it is unique on the Web server. Two CGI programs cannot use the same virtual path name, and the virtual path name must be different from the names used in the document root directory and for user Web page directories (~jbowman, for example).

Because RCGI programs use TCP/IP to communicate with the Web server, this path must begin with a hostname and port number. The port number is the number of the TCP port that the CGI program uses for TCP/IP communications.

**NOTE** The CGI program port number must be unique on the server. For example, the default port number for the Web server is 80, and the default port number for SSL servers is 443. You cannot use any port number, including ports 80 and 443, if it is already being used by another TCP/IP program.

Novell Web Server 3.1 provides a sample RCGI program that you can use to see how RCGI programs operate on the Novell Web Server. RCGI programmers can also use the included source code for this sample program to start creating a RCGI programs. To support this sample program, you need to enter the following directive in your virtual server's SRM.CFG file:

```
RemoteScriptAlias /cgiproc/
localhost:8003/sys:\inw_web/shared/rcgi/cgiapp/cgiapp.nlm
```

Let's take a closer look at this directive. The hostname and port can reference any network or Internet host. In this example, localhost is an alias name that refers to the host on which the SRM.CFG file is stored. This directive assigns TCP port 8003 to the CGI program CGIAPP.NLM.

To experiment with this sample RCGI program on the Novell Web Server, do the following:

**1** • Add the directive listed above to a virtual server's SRM.CFG file.

**2** • Restart the Novell Web Server.

**3** • At the system console prompt, load the NLM with the following command:

```
LOAD SYS:\INW_WEB\SHARED\RCGI\CGIAPP\CGIAPP.NLM
```

**4** • From a Web client, browse the following location:

```
http://host_name/cgiproc
```

When you browse the sample RCGI program, it displays a Web page that lists some environment variables for your connection to the Novell Web Server.

To use a CGI script or application that runs on a remote server, you must copy a daemon application to the destination host and load it. A daemon is a utility program that starts when the remote host starts and runs in the background. The RCGI daemons provided with the Novell Web Server run on UnixWare, SunOS, and Solaris hosts, and process CGI application requests from the Novell Web Server. These daemons are located on the Novell Web Server in the following default directory:

```
SYS:\WEB\DOCS\TOOLS\RCGID
```

To define an alias and location for an RCGI program on a remote Web server, enter a directive similar to the following:

```
RemoteScriptAlias /rcgid/ remote_host:port#
```

After you modify SRM.CFG, restart the Novell Web Server. After the restart, the server knows how to locate the CGI scripts and programs that Web pages request.

For more information on creating and running RCGI and remote CGI programs, see the Dynamic Web Page Programmer's Guide, which comes with the Novell Web Server.

### Specifying Directories for LCGI Programs

As with RCGI, LCGI program and script locations are defined with directives in the SRM.CFG file. The format for LCGI directive statements is as follows:

```
LoadableModule /virtual_path/ volume:path
```

Because LCGI programs don't communicate with the Web server through TCP/IP, their directives require less information. The LoadableModule directive is required. The virtual_path, volume, and path variables operate the same as they do with the RemoteScriptAlias directive.

Novell Web Server v3.1 includes the following default LCGI entries in SRM.CFG:

```
LoadableModule /nds/
sys:/inw_web/shared/lcgi/ndsobj/ndsobj.nlm

LoadableModule /qfsearch/
sys:/inw_web/shared/lcgi/qfsearch/qfsrch30.nlm

LoadableModule /netbasic/
sys:\inw_web/shared/lcgi/netbasic/cgi2nmx.nlm

LoadableModule /perl/
sys:\inw_web/shared/lcgi/perl5/perl5.nlm
```

If these are the only LCGI programs you need to use, no configuration is necessary. If you want to add LCGI programs to your Web server, you'll need to add directives to the virtual server SRM.CFG file. As with the RemoteScriptAlias directives, any changes that you make to SRM.CFG do not take effect until the next time the Novell Web Server starts up.

### Setting Access Rights for Script Directories

The first rule of CGI program management is to control who has WRITE access to the directories where the CGI programs are stored. To limit access to the CGI program directories, the network administrator should set the NetWare file permissions to READ and FILE SCAN for the [Public] user and limit all other rights to trusted programmers and Web page authors. To prevent accidental server disruption, the network administrator might encourage you to test your programs on a test server before placing them on the production Web server.

## PLACING CGI SCRIPTS AND PROGRAMS IN DIRECTORIES

CGI scripts and programs operate only when they are placed in the directories defined in the SRM.CFG file or in the interpreter application. If your Web page calls a program that is not in the appropriate directory, the browser user will get an error message.

The installation procedure for the Novell Web Server installs the programs and directories listed in Tables 12.2 and 12.3. If you decide to use the default script directories, just copy any new scripts to the appropriate directory.

If you need to add a new CGI program or script interpreter to the Novell Web Server, remember you must do the following:

▸ Add a directive to the SRM.CFG file that refers to the new program.

▸ Restart the Novell Web Server so that it reads the new configuration.

▸ Add the CGI program or interpreter to the new directory.

▸ If you are adding a CGI interpreter, refer to the program documentation to learn which directory you can add scripts to.

▸ Load the CGI program as described in the next section.

## LOADING THE CGI PROGRAM OR INTERPRETER

Some LCGI and RCGI programs automatically load when requested, but others must be loaded before they are requested. If the program is not available to process CGI requests, the browser user will see an error message.

On the Novell Web Server, the NDS Web Page program automatically starts when it is requested, as does the Perl interpreter, PERL5.NLM. The other Novell CGI programs, however, must be started before they are used. The default installation of the Novell Web Server automatically starts these programs using commands in the WEBSTART.NCF and AUTOEXEC.NCF files.

**NCF files are batch files for NetWare servers, which are similar to the BAT files on DOS computers.**

TIP

If you add an LCGI or RCGI program to the Novell Web Server, you need to read the documentation to find out if you need to load an NLM before you use the program. For example, before you can use the sample RCGI program that ships with the Novell Web Server, you or your network administrator must load the NLM at the server with the following command:

```
LOAD CGIAPP
```

**If you want an RCGI NLM to start each time the Novell Web Server starts, you should add a LOAD command for that NLM to the WEBSTART.NCF file, and you should add an UNLOAD command to the WEBSTOP.NCF file. To start editing one of these files at the server console, enter a command similar to the following:** LOAD EDIT WEBSTART.NCF.

TIP

To disable the loading of a CGI program, you or the Web server administrator can remove the appropriate LOAD command from WEBSTART.NCF.

## CALLING CGI PROGRAMS FROM YOUR WEB PAGES

Once your Web server is prepared to run CGI programs, all you have to do is call them from your Web pages. The simplest way to call a CGI program is to add a link to it as follows:

```
<A HREF="/virtual_path/filename.ext">Link text.</A> (Scripts)
```

or

```
<A HREF="/virtual_path/">Link text.</A> (NLMs)
```

Notice the difference between the links for scripts and NLMs. When you call a script, you must specify the virtual path and script filename. When you call an NLM, you specify only the virtual path.

Another way to call a CGI program is to use a `<FORM>` tag as follows:

`<FORM ACTION="/virtual_path/filename.ext">` (Scripts)

`<FORM ACTION="/virtual_path/">` (NLMs)

As with link tags, scripts require a virtual path and script filename, NLMs require only the virtual path.

**NOTE**

**For an example of a form that uses a CGI script, refer back to the section titled "CGI on the Novell Web Server," earlier in this chapter.**

## Safeguarding Your Server

Because CGI programs have server-wide access rights, you should regard them as a security risk. Anyone who has the rights to create and install a CGI program can access any file on the server and can display this information on Web pages. A carelessly or maliciously written program could expose confidential information or bring down the server.

One way to prevent a security breach is to restrict access to CGI program directories. To restrict access to CGI scripts and programs, the default configuration of the Novell Web Server stores all these scripts above the document root directory. WRITE access to the script directories should be limited to only those individuals who install CGI scripts.

**NOTE**

**Although you can enable CGI programs to run in user directories, Novell recommends that you run CGI programs in the default directories.**

Another way to prevent problems is to test scripts before installing them. If your Web server is vital to the operation of your organization, consider using a test Web server to test unproven scripts.

**You can learn more about CGI security by surfing to the following URL:**

**WWW Security FAQ:** `www.w3.org/Security/Faq/www-security-faq.html`

## Troubleshooting Tips

When problems occur with CGI requests, error messages often appear in the browser. Error messages also appear in the server logs. For information on accessing the server logs, see your Web server administrator. Table 12.4 lists some common CGI-related error messages and their possible causes.

TABLE 12.4

*Troubleshooting Tips*

| ERROR MESSAGE | POSSIBLE CAUSE |
|---|---|
| `404 Not Found`<br>`The requested URL /virtual_path/`<br>`was not found on this server.` | This message appears when a Web page calls an LCGI program and the LoadableModule directive for the LCGI program is missing from the SRM.CFG file. |
| `500 Server Error`<br>`Reason: RCGI server refused connection.` | This message appears when a Web page calls an RCGI NLM and the NLM is not loaded at the server. Load the NLM and retry. |
| `500 Server Error`<br>`The server encountered an internal`<br>`error or misconfiguration and was`<br>`unable to complete your request.` | This message appears when a Web page calls a script and the requested script was not found on the server. The script name may be wrong or the script file may be missing. |

**Exercise 12.1: To test your understanding of the CGI concepts and commands described in this chapter, turn to the end of this chapter and complete Exercise 12.1.**

## Summary

In this chapter, you learned about CGI and why you might want to use CGI scripts and programs with your Web pages. The Novell Web server provides interpreters for the NetBasic and Perl programming languages, and it supports both RCGI and LCGI NLMs.

The difference between RCGI and LCGI NLMs is the way they communicate with the Novell Web Server software. The Novell Web Server communicates with RCGI programs through the TCP/IP stack, which lets the RCGI program communicate with other servers as well. The Novell Web Server communicates directly with LCGI NLMs, which increases the efficiency of CGI communications.

To support CGI programs on a Novell Web Server, you need to create or obtain CGI scripts or programs, and modify them for the Web server and for your application. The location of CGI scripts and programs must be defined in the SRM.CFG file and, of course, the scripts or programs must be placed in the defined directories. Some CGI NLMs must be loaded on the server before they can be used, while others are automatically loaded when requested. When in doubt, consult the CGI product documentation.

To call a CGI script or program from a Web page, enter a URL that includes a virtual path or alias. If you are calling a script that requires an interpreter, you must specify the script filename too.

In the final sections of this chapter, you learned about CGI security concerns and the causes of some error messages that might appear when you use CGI scripts and programs.

In the next chapter, you'll learn how to use Perl CGI scripts on your Web pages.

## PUZZLE 12.1: USING CGI PROGRAMS AND SCRIPTS

The following word puzzle contains many of the terms discussed in this chapter. See if you can find all the words. As you search for the words, ask yourself why the word is in the list and how it was used in this chapter. If you don't know the answers to these questions, you might want to review the chapter.

```
E  R  E  T  E  R  P  R  E  T  N  I  R  B  F
L  C  C  P  X  T  N  O  M  M  O  C  E  Z  O
U  G  A  M  T  L  L  E  H  R  E  W  M  L  R
D  I  F  E  E  P  A  F  T  M  L  N  O  Y  M
O  S  R  T  N  R  U  C  O  B  B  C  T  T  X
M  W  E  H  S  O  T  N  I  C  A  M  E  I  I
E  O  T  O  I  G  R  T  A  L  D  S  F  R  N
L  D  N  D  O  R  I  R  H  O  A  R  I  U  U
B  N  I  N  N  A  V  O  R  C  O  M  L  C  N
A  I  G  V  E  M  S  P  Q  A  L  H  E  E  F
D  W  E  B  S  T  A  R  T  L  R  U  N  S  S
A  C  T  I  O  N  W  Y  A  W  E  T  A  G  V
O  I  G  C  L  L  O  A  D  S  U  B  M  I  T
L  P  I  P  C  T  P  I  R  C  S  P  E  R  L
H  T  A  P  A  K  W  O  W  E  B  S  T  O  P
```

| | | | |
|---|---|---|---|
| action | LOCALHOST | NetWare | submit |
| common | load | PERL | TCPIP |
| extension | loadable | path | UNIX |
| filename | local | port | URL |
| form | Macintosh | program | virtual |
| gateway | method | RCGI | WEBSTART |
| interface | module | remote | WEBSTOP |
| interpreter | NCF | SRM | Web |
| LCGI | NLM | script | Windows |
| LOADABLEMODULE | NetBasic | security | |

---

**EXERCISE 12.1: USING CGI PROGRAMS AND SCRIPTS**

This exercise tests your understanding of the CGI concepts and commands described in this chapter. To complete this exercise, answer the following questions.

1 • Which Web server programming feature offers more flexibility and control, SSI commands or CGI programs?

   Answer: . . . . . . . . . . . . . . . . . . . . . . . . . . . . . . . . . . . . . . . . . .

2 • List three ways to start a CGI program.

   a. . . . . . . . . . . . . . . . . . . . . . . . . . . . . . . . . . . . . . . . . . . . .

   b. . . . . . . . . . . . . . . . . . . . . . . . . . . . . . . . . . . . . . . . . . . . .

   c. . . . . . . . . . . . . . . . . . . . . . . . . . . . . . . . . . . . . . . . . . . . .

3 • How does a CGI program access form data that is sent to the Web server with the GET method?

   Answer: . . . . . . . . . . . . . . . . . . . . . . . . . . . . . . . . . . . . . . . . . .

4 • What is the default path and name of the Novell Web Server file that stores the location of CGI programs and scripts? What is this file named on UNIX Web servers?

   Novell servers: . . . . . . . . . . . . . . . . . . . . . . . . . . . . . . . . . . . . .

   UNIX servers: . . . . . . . . . . . . . . . . . . . . . . . . . . . . . . . . . . . . .

5 • Which programming languages can you use to create CGI programs and scripts for NetWare and intraNetWare servers?

   a. . . . . . . . . . . . . . . . . . . . . . . . . . . . . . . . . . . . . . . . . . . . .

   b. . . . . . . . . . . . . . . . . . . . . . . . . . . . . . . . . . . . . . . . . . . . .

   c. . . . . . . . . . . . . . . . . . . . . . . . . . . . . . . . . . . . . . . . . . . . .

   d. . . . . . . . . . . . . . . . . . . . . . . . . . . . . . . . . . . . . . . . . . . . .

**6** • Which programming languages can you use to create CGI programs and scripts for UNIX servers?

a. . . . . . . . . . . . . . . . . . . . . . . . . . . . . . . . . . . . . . . .

b. . . . . . . . . . . . . . . . . . . . . . . . . . . . . . . . . . . . . . . .

c. . . . . . . . . . . . . . . . . . . . . . . . . . . . . . . . . . . . . . . .

d. . . . . . . . . . . . . . . . . . . . . . . . . . . . . . . . . . . . . . . .

e. . . . . . . . . . . . . . . . . . . . . . . . . . . . . . . . . . . . . . . .

**7** • What is the name of the Perl NLM supplied with the Novell Web Server?

Answer: . . . . . . . . . . . . . . . . . . . . . . . . . . . . . . . . . . . .

**8** • On the Novell Web Server, _____ applications communicate with the Web server through TCP/IP and _____ applications communicate directly with the Web server.

**9** • Which configuration file directive identifies the path to an RCGI program?

Answer: . . . . . . . . . . . . . . . . . . . . . . . . . . . . . . . . . . . .

**10** • Which configuration file directive identifies the path to an LCGI program?

Answer: . . . . . . . . . . . . . . . . . . . . . . . . . . . . . . . . . . . .

**11** • The configuration file directive values for LCGI and RCGI programs are almost identical, however, RCGI programs require which two additional values?

a. . . . . . . . . . . . . . . . . . . . . . . . . . . . . . . . . . . . . . . .

b. . . . . . . . . . . . . . . . . . . . . . . . . . . . . . . . . . . . . . . .

**12** • What two things do you need to do before you can run an RCGI program on a remote server?

a. . . . . . . . . . . . . . . . . . . . . . . . . . . . . . . . . . . . . . .

b. . . . . . . . . . . . . . . . . . . . . . . . . . . . . . . . . . . . . . .

**13** • When you call a CGI script from a Web page and that script requires an interpreter, what must the URL include?

Answer: . . . . . . . . . . . . . . . . . . . . . . . . . . . . . . . . . . .

**14** • Do CGI programs create a security risk for the server or the client?

Answer: . . . . . . . . . . . . . . . . . . . . . . . . . . . . . . . . . . .

**15** • What access privileges do CGI programs have to the server?

Answer: . . . . . . . . . . . . . . . . . . . . . . . . . . . . . . . . . . .

# CHAPTER 13

# Using Perl Scripts

In Chapter 12, you learned about how Perl scripts work in the CGI environment on the Novell Web Server. In this chapter, you'll learn to create a simple Perl script and modify existing ones. Don't let the thought of programming intimidate you. The first Perl script in this chapter contains more HTML code than Perl code and is less complicated than HTML tables or forms.

If you are already a programmer and have experience with the C programming language or UNIX shell scripts, you should have no trouble learning Perl. Perl scripts resemble C code and function as a combination of C and UNIX shell scripts. Some of the pattern-matching functions in Perl closely resemble those used in UNIX operations.

If you are not a programmer, get ready to take that first step. By the end of this chapter, you should be able to write simple Perl scripts and modify other people's programs. Teaching Perl script programming is beyond the scope of this book, so learning how to customize Perl scripts for your server is really what this chapter is all about. Perl scripts are available on the following platforms:

- NetWare and intraNetWare

- UNIX

- VMS (DEC)

- Windows 3.x, 95, and NT

- OS/2

- MS-DOS

- Macintosh

- Amiga

Because Perl scripts run on so many different platforms, there is a good chance that there is a Perl script out there on the Web that can help your Web site. If you know what is needed to run the Perl script on your Novell Web Server, you can copy that Perl script, modify it, upgrade your Web site, and show the world that you are a Webmaster!

## Using Perl on the Novell Web Server

Before you start creating your first program, there are a few more things that you should know about using Perl on the Novell Web Server. In Chapter 13, you learned the following:

▸ The Novell Web Server provides a Perl interpreter named Perl5.NLM.

▸ The Novell Web Server supports Perl v5.

▸ The PERL5 NLM automatically starts when a browser requests a Perl script.

▸ Perl scripts are called from Web pages by specifying a virtual path or alias and a program name.

▸ The default location for Perl scripts is SYS:\INW_WEB\SHARED\DOCS\LCGI\PERL5.

To support Perl version 5, the Novell Web Server uses two NLMs: PERL5.NLM and PERLLIB.NLM. PERLLIB is a small file (3K) that is loaded with the Web server NLM (HTTP.NLM) from the WEBSTART.NCF file. PERLLIB stays loaded until the Web server is unloaded. The PERL5 NLM, which is a much larger file (617K), loads when a Perl script is called and automatically unloads after a period of inactivity.

The Perl interpreter is not required for Novell Web Server operation, but Perl scripts cannot run without it. If you want to disable the Perl interpreter, you must comment out or remove the SRM.CFG directive (see Chapter 12) that specifies the path to the PERL5 NLM.

**IMPORTANT**

**You cannot disable the Perl interpreter by commenting out or removing the load command for PERLLIB.NLM in WEBSTART.NCF. PERL5.NLM uses routines in PERLLIB and automatically loads PERLLIB.NLM if it is not already loaded. To disable the loading of PERL5.NLM, you have to disable its access in the SRM.CFG file.**

When the Perl interpreter is first loaded on a Version 3 Novell Web Server, there is no visual indication on the server console. This is a change in operation from Novell Web Server version 2.5, which automatically displayed a Perl console. As you'll learn later in the troubleshooting section, the Perl interpreter provided with Novell Web Server version 3 includes several consoles that you can display or hide.

**TIP**

**The easiest way to find out if the Perl interpreter is loaded is to enter the following command at the server console:** `MODULES PERL5`. **The easiest way to launch the PERL5 NLM is to access a Perl script from a browser. You cannot start the interpreter with the LOAD PERL5 command because the NLM is not stored in the SYSTEM directory. (However, you can start the interpreter with this command:** `LOAD SYS:INW_WEB\SHARED\LCGI\PERL5\PERL5`.**)**

## Writing Your First Perl Script

Okay, your server is ready for Perl scripts. Let's take a look at a simple Perl script:

```
require("cgilib.pl");

print &PrintHeader;


print "<HTML>";

print "<HEAD><TITLE>Hello world!</TITLE></HEAD>";

print "<BODY>";

print "<P>Hello world!</P>";

print "</BODY>";

print "</HTML>";
```

Notice the last six lines of the script. Ignore the print command, the quotation marks, and the trailing semicolon, and what do you have? A simple Web page! Not much magic here. Figure 13.1 shows the results of this program.

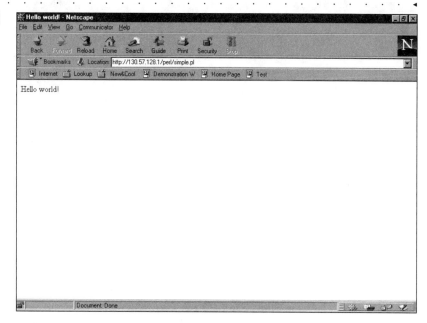

If you have installed the demonstration Web site as described in Appendix C, you can view this example at the following URL:

`http://hostname/Perl/simple.pl`

Let's take a closer look at this simple program. Table 13.1 lists and describes the three Perl commands used in this program.

| PERL COMMAND | DESCRIPTION |
| --- | --- |
| `require("cgilib.pl");` | This command line is required and should be the first line in all of your Perl scripts. This command line allows your Perl script to use commands from a library of CGI-compatible Perl commands. |
| `print &PrintHeader;` | This command line is also required and should be the second line in all of your Perl scripts. This command line prints a Perl subroutine that sends an HTML header to the browser. This header defines the MIME type or contents of the file, which is HTML. |

*(continued)*

| TABLE 13.1 | PERL COMMAND | DESCRIPTION |
|---|---|---|
| *Perl Commands from the Simple Perl Script Program (continued)* | print "*information*"; | This print command sends information to the Web server, which will be forwarded to the browser. This information must be enclosed in quotation marks. In the sample program, this information is HTML tags and text, but as you will see later in this chapter, there are other types of information that can be sent to the browser. |

**IMPORTANT**

**If you have created Perl scripts for earlier versions of the Novell Web Server, the first line of each script must be changed. The CGILIB.PL library name no longer contains a hyphen, so you must delete this hyphen from your Perl scripts.**

This first Perl script doesn't do much, but it does illustrate an important concept. One of the goals of using Perl scripts with Web pages is to create Web pages. When a user activates a Perl script, the user is actually activating a link to a Perl script. This sounds redundant, but the important concept is that the user is activating a link, which takes the user away from the current Web page. Your Perl script might save data to a file, or send e-mail to an Internet user, but it must also display a Web page that serves as the link destination.

Although it is possible to write a Perl script that does not display any HTML data, it is not a good practice. Remember that the browser serves the user. If the user takes an action that executes a Perl script, the user is entitled to a response. If you don't provide some response to the user, and she is using the Netscape Navigator browser, a message appears explaining that the requested document does not contain any data. If she is gracious, she will either think the Web site is malfunctioning or the Web site creator didn't know how to use the Perl script properly.

## Punctuating Perl Scripts

Now that you've looked at a simple Perl script, let's take a look at some useful punctuation for Perl scripts. I'll cover the following:

▶ Semicolon (;)

▶ Quotation marks (")

▶ Backslash (\)

▶ Pound symbol (#)

## SEMICOLONS

Did you notice that every line in the sample program ended with a semicolon (;)? This is a requirement for Perl scripts.

## QUOTATION MARKS

While reviewing the sample program, did you wonder if quotation marks within the HTML text would affect the print statements? They will. Table 13.2 shows a couple of ways to use the Perl print command with HTML text that contains quotation marks.

| TABLE 13.2 | TECHNIQUE | SAMPLE STATEMENT | RESULT |
|---|---|---|---|
| *Perl Punctuation* | Use single quotes in the print statement. | `print 'He said, "Boo."'` | He said, "Boo." |
| | Use a backslash character before any quotation mark symbols. | `print "She said, \"Eek!\""` | She said, "Eek!" |

If you use single quotation marks (') instead of double quotation marks (") with your print statements, you can use all the double quotation marks you want; they are ignored.

## BACKSLASH

Single quotation marks won't work when you want to use both single and double quotation marks in your HTML text. In situations like this, use the backslash character (\) before any character that is not part of the Perl script (see Table 13.2). The backslash is the Perl *literal* character that tells Perl to treat the following character as a displayable character instead of a Perl symbol, such as the literal character or the division operator. If you need to insert a backslash character in your HTML text, use two backslashes.

### POUND SIGN

The last character I'll introduce in this section is the pound symbol (#), which Perl uses to indicate comments. To create a comment in a Perl script, place the pound symbol at the beginning of the comment line as follows:

```
# This is a comment.
```

## Converting a Web Page to a Perl Script

There may be times when you want to convert an existing Web page to a Perl script. For example, if you already have a Web page that is similar to what you want for the output of your Perl script, you may want to edit that page in HTML and then convert the page to a script. If you have a favorite HTML editor, you may prefer to develop your Perl script output in the editor and then convert it to a Perl script.

Now that you are this far into the book, you already have all the skills to convert a Web page to a Perl script and to call that script from a Web page. I'll summarize the procedure in the following steps:

1 • Open the HTML file in your favorite text-editor program.

2 • Save the file with a .pl extension.

3 • Add the two required lines at the beginning of the file:

```
require("cgilib.pl");

print &PrintHeader;
```

4 • Add the following text to the beginning of each HTML line:

```
print '
```

**5** • Add the following characters to the end of each line:

' ;

**6** • Add a backslash before every occurrence of a backslash or single quote within the HTML lines.

**7** • Save your changes.

**8** • Copy the Perl script to the Web server directory that serves Perl scripts.

**9** • Create a Web page that contains a link or a form that calls the Perl script, and copy this page to the Web server.

**10** • Access the Web page on the server and activate the link or form that calls the Perl script.

**11** • Verify that the script runs and displays as you want.

 **Exercise 13.1: If you're preparing to take the certification exam, or if you want to practice what you learned in this section, turn to the end of this chapter and complete Exercise 13.1. When you are done, continue reading here to prepare for the next exercise.**

## Processing Forms

Now we're ready for the neat stuff. You know how to output a Web page in Perl, but what good is that? You already knew how to do that in HTML. What you really want to do is take advantage of Perl's programming capabilities to add something to the Web page that you can't add with HTML. Often, what you'll want to do is take some input from a Web page visitor and return some kind of response. You'll collect the information in a form, your Perl script will take some action on the information, and then the script will display the response in a Web page. This is form processing.

To process form data, a Perl Script has to do the following:

**1** • Record the form data.

**2** • Take some action on the data.

**3** • Print the result of the action to the browser.

## RECORDING FORM DATA

In Chapter 5, you learned how to build forms that can be used to collect data from your Web site visitors. In Chapter 12, you learned that you can send the form data to a Perl script by specifying the script name in the opening <FORM> tag as follows:

```
<FORM METHOD=get ACTION=/perl/name.pl>
```

After a user fills out a form and clicks the Submit button, the form data is sent to the Web server, and the Web server makes it available to the CGI scripts. In Chapter 12, you learned that data sent with the GET method is stored in the QUERY_STRING variable, which can be accessed by CGI programs. Now it's time to learn how CGI programs access the data stored on the Web server.

In most of the Perl scripts you will use, a special Perl function called &ReadParse automatically stores the form data in a special type of variable called an *array*. Commands within the Perl script act on the data in the array and produce results that are sent back to the browser in the form of a Web page. Let's take a closer look at the &ReadParse function, Perl variables and arrays, and the special array that &ReadParse creates.

### The &ReadParse Function

Remember the cgilib.pl Perl library that was introduced earlier in this chapter? It is referenced in the first line of the Perl script and provides a very useful function named &ReadParse, which automatically receives form data and stores it in Perl script variables. The &ReadParse function understands the Get and Post methods, so it is very easy to use. Simply add the following line after the first two lines in the script:

```
&ReadParse;
```

When a Perl script uses the &ReadParse function, the first three lines of the file should be as follows:

```
require("cgilib.pl");

print &PrintHeader;

&ReadParse;
```

When you see the &ReadParse function used in a Perl script, you know that the script will store all your form data in an array variable. But what is an array? How is an array different from a regular variable? Let's take a look at regular Perl variables and then at array variables.

### Perl Scalar Variables

We've used variables in previous chapters. A variable is a special name that we can use to access a special value. For example, when you use the variable name REMOTE_ADDR with the SSI echo command, it returns an IP address (such as 130.57.163.45). The REMOTE_ADDR variable name is recognized by SSI commands and returns a single value.

Perl scripts, like SSI commands, recognize certain variable names. To create a variable name in a Perl script, you enter a name that conforms to the Perl script programming rules for variable names. Standard single-value variables are called *scalar variables* and their names conform to the following rules:

► The first character is $

► The second character is a letter

► The remaining characters are letters, numbers, or underscore ( _ ) characters

The following Perl script lines show sample variable names and how values are assigned to them:

```
#Assign values to variables;

$name="Jim";
```

```
$number="555-1212";

$comment_1="Isn't Perl programming fun!";
```

After a value is assigned to a variable, you can use the variable to refer to that value. The following Perl script lines show how you can print variable values using the variable names:

```
#Print variable values;

print $name, "<BR>";

print $number, "<BR>";

print $comment_1, "<BR>";
```

Notice that the variable names are not encased in quotation marks. The variable names are processed by Perl, which replaces them with the value of the variable. The <BR> tag ensures that the variable values are printed on separate lines in the Web page. The output of these statements is as follows:

```
Jim

555-1212

Isn't Perl programming fun!
```

You can also use a single print statement to print multiple variables. The following statements show different ways to do this:

```
print $name, "<BR>", $number, "<BR>", $comment_1 "<BR>";

print $name, $number, $comment_1;

print $name . $number . $comment_1;
```

The first line above prints the variables on three separate lines as in the previous example. The comma operator enables you to specify multiple variables or text values on the same line. If the commas were omitted, the Perl script would generate an error. You must use an operator between multiple values in a print statement.

The second and third lines print the three variables on the same line because there are no HTML tags that start a new line. The period operator on the third line is used to join the values of multiple string variables. String variables are variables that contain text or symbols that represent something other than a number. While the period operator works in this example, it is best used for other types of program operations. The comma operator works equally well for scalar variables that contain numbers or strings.

When you modify a Perl script, you'll often need to change the values of some of the variables. For example, you might need to change the value of a variable that defines the default directory for source files, or you might need to change the value of a variable that defines the path and filename for your company logo.

### Perl Array Variables

Array variables also store data values, but unlike a single-value variable, a single array can store multiple values. For example, the following Perl script statement stores all three of the variables used in our previous example in one array:

```
@array=("Jim", "555-1212", "Isn't Perl programming fun!");
```

When data is stored in an array, each of the values in the array is assigned its own unique item number, which is called the subscript. The first value in the array is assigned subscript 0, the next value is subscript 1, and the rest of the values are assigned sequence numbers based on their entry order into the array. You can think of an array as a table of subscripts and values that is similar to Table 13.3.

| TABLE 13.3 | SUBSCRIPT | VALUE |
| --- | --- | --- |
| Sample Array in Table Format | 0 | Jim |
| | 1 | 555-1212 |
| | 2 | Isn't Perl programming fun! |

To print these values, we can use the following program statements:

```
#Print variable values;
print $array[0];
print $array[1];
print $array[2];
```

The rules for array variable names are as follows:

▸ When multiple data values are stored in an array at once, the first character in the array name is the @ symbol.

▸ When a single data value is stored or retrieved from an array, the first character in the array is the $ symbol.

▸ The second character in the array name is a letter.

▸ The remaining characters are letters, numbers, or underscore ( _ ) characters

▸ When a single data value is stored or retrieved from an array, the array subscript is enclosed in brackets at the end of the array name. For example, $array[2].

When you modify Perl scripts, you may need to change values in array variables as well as in scalar variables.

### Perl Associative Array Variables

Standard arrays are wonderful because they enable programmers to store lots of data in one place. To access different pieces of data, you use the same variable name and just change the subscript number. But what if you don't know the subscript number for the data you want? Sometimes it would be easier to use a name instead of a subscript number. Associative arrays enable you to do this.

The following Perl script statement is similar to the statement that creates a regular array, but it creates an associative array:

```
%array=("name", "Jim", "number", "555-1212", "comment",
"Isn't Perl programming fun!");
```

The differences in this statement are the % sign in front of the array name and the name and value pairs of data between the parenthesis. The % sign tells Perl that you are creating an associative array. In regular arrays, you specify only the values, and Perl assigns the subscripts for you. In associative arrays, you must specify both subscript names and their corresponding values. You can think of an associative array as a table of subscripts and values that is similar to Table 13.4.

| TABLE 13.4 | SUBSCRIPT | VALUE |
|---|---|---|
| Sample Array in Table Format | "name" | Jim |
| | "number" | 555-1212 |
| | "comment" | Isn't Perl programming fun! |

To print these values, we can use the following program statements:

```
#Print variable values;
print $array{"name"};
print $array{"number"};
print $array{"comment"};
```

As you can see, you refer to associative array variables in much the same way as regular array variables. The difference is that the subscript is enclosed in brace characters and the subscript is a name that appears between double quotation mark characters.

The rules for associative array variable names are as follows:

▸ When multiple data values are stored in an array at once, the first character in the array name is the % symbol.

▸ When a single data value is stored or retrieved from an array, the first character in the array is the $ symbol.

▸ The second character in the array name is a letter.

▸ The remaining characters are letters, numbers, or underscore ( _ ) characters.

▸ When a single data value is stored in or retrieved from an associative array, the array subscript name is enclosed in braces at the end of the array name. For example, $array{"name"}.

Now that you know the structure of scalar variables, array variables, and associate array variable names, you can distinguish these variable names from the other components in Perl scripts.

### The Arrays That &ReadParse Builds

Now, we're ready to see where that form data really goes and what it looks like. As explained earlier, the &ReadParse function stores all form data in an array. The truth is that it stores form data in both a regular array named @in and in an associative array named %in. The term *&ReadParse* is a good one because the function reads the form data and parses, or distributes, it into arrays. Let's look at an example of &ReadParse in action.

Figure 13.2 shows a sample form from the demonstration Web site. This form collects four values and sends them to a Perl script named formdata.pl when the Submit Query button is pressed.

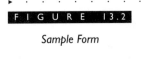

**FIGURE 13.2**

*Sample Form*

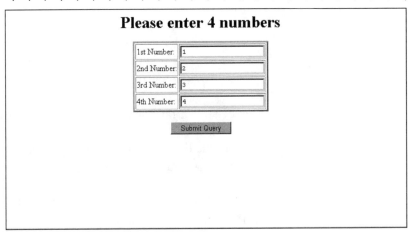

If you have installed the demonstration Web site as described in Appendix C, you can view this example at the following URL:

```
http://hostname/demoweb2/Programs/Perl/number.htm
```

The following are the program statements for the formdata.pl program:

```
require("cgilib.pl");

print &PrintHeader;

&ReadParse;


print "<HTML>";
```

```perl
print "<HEAD><TITLE>Display Form Data</TITLE></HEAD>";
print "<BODY BGCOLOR=\"#FFFFFF\">";


#create table to display array values
print "<CENTER><H1>\"formdata.pl\" Array Values</H1>";
print "<TABLE BORDER=3>";
print "<TR><TH>Array<TH>Subscript<TH>Value";



#print values in regular array @in;
print "<TR><TD>\@in<TD>0<TD>", $in[0];
print "<TR><TD>\@in<TD>1<TD>", $in[1];
print "<TR><TD>\@in<TD>2<TD>", $in[2];
print "<TR><TD>\@in<TD>3<TD>", $in[3];


#print values in associative array %in;
print "<TR><TD>\%in<TD>num1<TD>", $in{num1};
print "<TR><TD>\%in<TD>num2<TD>", $in{num2};
print "<TR><TD>\%in<TD>num3<TD>", $in{num3};
print "<TR><TD>\%in<TD>num4<TD>", $in{num4};


#close table
print "</TABLE></CENTER>";
```

```
print "</BODY>";

print "</HTML>";
```

Figure 13.3 shows the Web page that appears after this program processes the data shown in Figure 13.2.

▶ . . . . . . . . . . . . . . . . . . . . . . . . . . . . . . . . . . . . . . . ◀

FIGURE 13.3

*Array Data from Sample Form*

**"formdata.pl" Array Values**

| Array | Subscript | Value |
|---|---|---|
| @in | 0 | num1=1 |
| @in | 1 | num2=2 |
| @in | 2 | num3=3 |
| @in | 3 | num4=4 |
| %in | num1 | 1 |
| %in | num2 | 2 |
| %in | num3 | 3 |
| %in | num4 | 4 |

Notice that the @in array values produced by &ReadParse use the format *name=value*. The *name* is the variable name defined in the form, and the *value* is the value that is entered into the form. Each value in the @in can be accessed using a number subscript.

The %in array in this example stores the form variable name and variable value as separate entities. The associative array enables programmers to access values using the form variable name as the array subscript.

**TIP**

**If you are just getting started in programming and want to use the &ReadParse program, consider accessing data in the %in array because you can easily perform mathematical operations on that data. Before you can perform mathematical operations on @in array values, you must separate the data values from the form variable names, and this requires additional programming statements.**

## PROCESSING FORM DATA

Now that you know where the &ReadParse function stores your form data and how a program accesses that data, you can write a Perl script that stores form data

This statement defines a new scalar variable, named $total, and assigns the sum of four variable values to $total. If you replace the variable names with numbers, this equation reads as follows: $total = 1 + 2 + 3 + 4. When this statement is processed by Perl with these variable values, the value assigned to $total is 10.

This program prints the following line on a Web page:

```
1 + 2 + 3 + 4 = 10
```

In the sample Perl script, notice the use of commas and quotation marks that produces the printed line. Commas separate the items to be printed. As mentioned earlier, variables are interpreted by Perl and should not be enclosed in quotation marks. To insert the plus signs in the printed statement and the extra space characters, however, these items are enclosed in quotation marks.

This is programming in its simplest form—but it is programming. We collected data from a form, performed a calculation on the data, and returned a response that is based on that data. HTML can't do this. This is an example of a dynamic Web page and the power of CGI programming using Perl scripts.

The goal of this chapter is to show you how to modify existing Perl scripts to run on your Web site. Perl script programming is beyond the scope of this course, so I won't cover much more on the topic. However, because if and else statements are very common in Perl scripts, we will take a quick look at these statements.

## IF AND ELSE BRANCHING STATEMENTS

If and else statements control the *flow* of Perl scripts and enable *branching*, which is the division of program statements into groups that you can selectively execute or ignore. Without flow control statements, the Perl interpreter executes each program statement in sequence from the top to the bottom of the file. This is okay for simple programs, but what if you want to change the flow of execution from one branch to another based on the value of a form variable? The keyword here is *if*.

### If Statements

The simplest form of an if statement is as follows:

```
if (expression) {

  command_statements;

}
```

and prints it out. We're making progress. The next step is to take some action on that data before we print it out.

The following program shows how you can make calculations on form data and display the result in a Web page.

```perl
require("cgilib.pl");

print &PrintHeader;

&ReadParse;


print "<HTML>";

print "<HEAD><TITLE>Display Form Data</TITLE></HEAD>";

print "<BODY BGCOLOR=\"#FFFFFF\">";


#Calculate sum of numbers;

$total = $in{num1} + $in{num2} + $in{num3} + $in{num4};


#Print the numbers and their sum;

print $in{num1}, " \+ ", $in{num2}, " \+ ", $in{num3}, " \+
", $in{num4}, " \= ", $total;


print "</BODY>";

print "</HTML>";
```

If you have installed the demonstration Web site as described in Appendix C, you can view this example at the following URL:

```
http://hostname/demoweb2/Programs/Perl/total.htm
```

The new item in this program is the following equation statement:

```perl
$total = $in{num1} + $in{num2} + $in{num3} + $in{num4};
```

The expression in the if statement is a comparison equation, which compares two values. In most comparison equations, the result of the comparison is either true or false. If the result is true, the command statements between the braces are executed. If the result is false, the command statements are ignored and program processing continues on the next line after the closing brace.

If statements are often called *if/then* statements because *if* the expression is true, *then* the command statements are executed. Table 13.5 lists some comparison operators that can be used in if statements.

| TABLE 13.5 | COMPARISON OPERATOR | FUNCTION | SAMPLE EXPRESSIONS |
|---|---|---|---|
| *Comparison Operators and Sample Expressions* | == | equal | $answer == "Yes" |
| | != | not equal | $b != 20 |
| | < | less than | $c < $temp[3] |
| | > | greater than | 999 > $var{"name"} |
| | <= | less than or equal to | $index <= 33 |
| | >= | greater than or equal to | $a >= (10 + $count) |
| | eq | equal | $name eq "Matt" |
| | ne | not equal | $name ne "Becky" |

The last two operators in Table 13.5 are for comparing text values. The == and != operators compare the mathematical values of variables, the eq and ne operators alphabetically compare text values, which are called string values or strings.

Consider the following example:

```
require("cgilib.pl");

print &PrintHeader;

&ReadParse;


print "<HTML>";

print "<HEAD><TITLE>Display Form Data</TITLE></HEAD>";

print "<BODY BGCOLOR=\"#FFFFFF\">";
```

```
#Check for negative numbers

if ($in{num1} < 0) {

    print "The first number is negative.<BR>";

}


if ($in{num2} < 0) {

    print "The second number is negative.<BR>";

}


if ($in{num3} < 0) {

    print "The third number is negative.<BR>";

}


if ($in{num4} < 0) {

    print "The fourth number is negative.<BR>";

}



print "</BODY>";
print "</HTML>";
```

If you have installed the demonstration Web site as described in Appendix C, you can view this example at the following URL:

```
http://hostname/demoweb2/Programs/Perl/if.htm
```

This program simply checks for negative numbers in the form. If it finds a negative number, it prints out a message on the Web page. If it doesn't find any errors, it doesn't print any messages. The good thing about this program is that it checks the user data to see if it is valid. The bad thing about this program is that it doesn't do anything if the form is completed correctly. We can fix this by using the *if* and *else* statements.

### If and Else Statements

The if statement enables us to execute or omit a single command statement or a group of statements. The if and else statements enable us to choose to execute one group of statements or another group of statements. The format for if and else statement is as follows:

```
if (expression) {

   command_statements;

} else {

   command_statements;

}
```

This form of the if statement translates as follows: if the expression is true, then execute the if command statements, otherwise (or else), execute the else command statements. Let's look at how we can improve our program with the else statement:

```
require("cgilib.pl");

print &PrintHeader;

&ReadParse;


print "<HTML>";

print "<HEAD><TITLE>Display Form Data</TITLE></HEAD>";

print "<BODY BGCOLOR=\"#FFFFFF\">";


#Check for negative numbers and add nonnegative numbers

if ($in{num1} < 0) {

   print "The first number is negative.<BR>";
```

```
} else {

  $sum = $in{num1};

}


if ($in{num2} < 0) {

  print "The second number is negative.<BR>";

} else {

  $sum = $sum + $in{num2};

}


if ($in{num3} < 0) {

  print "The third number is negative.<BR>";

} else {

  $sum = $sum + $in{num3};

}


if ($in{num4} < 0) {

  print "The fourth number is negative.<BR>";

} else {

  $sum = $sum + $in{num4};

}


#print results

print "Sum of nonnegative numbers is: ", $sum;
```

```
print "</BODY>";

print "</HTML>";
```

If you have installed the demonstration Web site as described in Appendix C, you can view this example at the following URL:

```
http://hostname/demoweb2/Programs/Perl/else.htm
```

In each of the if statements in the sample program, the if statement is the same as for the previous example. The difference is that if the *if* expression is false, meaning that the number is 0 or positive, the *else* statement adds the number to the value of nonnegative numbers. The sum of the nonnegative numbers is printed at the end.

**NOTE**

This section introduced *if...then* and *if...then...else* branching. Novell Course 655 also mentions switch branching, which is supported in Java, C, and C++ programming, but not in Perl. If you plan to take the Course 655 exam, you should remember that switch branching is not supported in Perl.

Exercise 13.2: If you're preparing to take the certification exam, or if you want to practice what you learned in this section, turn to the end of this chapter and complete Exercise 13.2. When you are done, continue reading here to prepare for the next exercise.

▶ · · · · · · · · · · · · · · · · · · · · · · · · · · · · · · ◀

## Modifying Perl Scripts for the Novell Web Server

As mentioned earlier, Perl scripts are available on many platforms. Although the basic Perl commands are the same, there are differences that will prevent the programs from working in certain conditions. When you are ready to adapt a Perl script for use on the Novell Web Server, look for the following conditions in the Perl script:

▶ Is the first line correct?

▶ Is the script designed for HTML output?

▶ Does the script provide its own HTML headers?

The following sections provide more information on these issues.

After you modify a Perl script, don't forget to test it before putting it into production.

**The Novell implementation of Perl Version 5 does not support all Perl functions. For more information see the *Dynamic Web Page Programmer's Guide*, provided with the Novell Web Server.**

IMPORTANT

**To locate some free Perl scripts to practice with, browse:**
**Matt's Script Archive:** worldwidemart.com/scripts/
**Prabhjot Gill's Cool Web Sites:** home.echo-on.net/~prabhjot/mycgi.html

## THE FIRST LINE

Remember the first line that is required in Novell Web Server Perl scripts? It is:

```
require("cgilib.pl");
```

This line calls a Perl library that helps your Perl script work with CGI on certain types of Web servers, such as the Novell Web Server. On some UNIX systems the first line in a Perl file is:

```
#!/usr/local/bin/perl
```

This statement identifies the path to the Perl interpreter on a UNIX system and is not required in Novell Web Server Perl scripts. This statement should be replaced by the require statement.

## HTML OUTPUT

Another difference that you should be aware of is that some Perl scripts are designed to print on computer screens and not to browsers through CGI. When you want to use one of these programs, you need to do the following:

▸ Add the HTML print header statement

▸ Add HTML tags to the print statements

The HTML print header statement is the second line that is required in Novell Web Server Perl scripts:

```
print &PrintHeader;
```

If a Perl script is not designed for HTML output, you need to modify the print statements so they include the required HTML tags. In most cases, you will also want to add supplementary formatting tags so the resulting Web page meets your design requirements.

## HTML HEADERS

If you find that your Perl script is designed to output to HTML, you should check for the presence of an HTML header statement, such as the following:

```
print "Content-type: text/html\n\n";
```

This statement accomplishes the same thing as the print &PrintHeader; statement that belongs on line two in a Perl script for a Novell Web Server. When you see this content-type statement in a Perl script, you know the file is designed to print to a Web page. Just make sure the first two lines are correct, and then give your modified Perl script a test.

## TESTING, TESTING, 1, 2, 3, AND 4

When you think your modified Perl script is ready to go, it's good to test it and make sure it works. To test a Perl script:

**1** • Copy the Perl script to the Web server directory that serves Perl scripts.

**2** • Create a Web page that contains a link or a form that calls the Perl script, and copy this page to the Web server.

**3** • Access the Web page on the server and activate the link or form that calls the Perl script.

**4** • Verify that the script runs and displays the response you want.

# Troubleshooting

When you use Perl scripts to process data and generate output Web pages, you have twice as many opportunities to make mistakes. Troubleshooting is easier if you do the following:

- Expect to make mistakes and allot time for testing and troubleshooting

- Make a game of finding your mistakes

Troubleshooting is a lot like playing detective; you need to look for clues and get to know your suspects: Perl, HTML, and yourself. Most people develop good and bad habits. If you find that you habitually leave off semicolons from the end of Perl statements (like me), you should build this into your troubleshooting approach.

The following sections describe how to look for clues on the Novell Web Server Perl consoles, and list common Perl script problems.

## USING THE NOVELL WEB SERVER PERL CONSOLES

The Perl interpreter provided with Novell Web Server 3.*x* provides two consoles that you can use to troubleshoot script problems, the Debug console and the Script Debug console. The following sections describe how to use these consoles.

### The Debug Console

The Debug console displays Perl interpreter activity and can optionally display information on the usage of Perl scripts and procedures. (Perl procedures are not introduced in Course 655.) Figure 13.4 shows an example of the Perl Debug console. The *Return from web-entry* lines mark the ending of a Perl script access. The first three access entries in Figure 13.4 were made with the default console setting. The next two entries, which display file-access information, were made with the file-access option turned on. Notice that the file-access information includes the complete path to the file that is opened.

FIGURE 13.4

*Novell Web Server Perl Debug Console*

```
Return from web-entry
PERL5:freeThreadMemory
PERL5:freeThreadMemory done
Return from web-entry
PERL5:freeThreadMemory
PERL5:freeThreadMemory done
Return from web-entry
PERL5:freeThreadMemory
PERL5:freeThreadMemory done
Return from web-entry
fopen called for sys:/inw_web/shared\DOCS\LCGI\PERL5/simple.pl (013fcc20).
fclose called for sys:/inw_web/shared\DOCS\LCGI\PERL5/simple.pl (013fcc20).
fopen called for SYS:PUBLIC\PERL/cgilib.pl (013fcc20).
fclose called for SYS:PUBLIC\PERL/cgilib.pl (013fcc20).
PERL5:freeThreadMemory
PERL5:freeThreadMemory done
Return from web-entry
fopen called for sys:/inw_web/shared\DOCS\LCGI\PERL5/quotes.pl (013fcc20).
fclose called for sys:/inw_web/shared\DOCS\LCGI\PERL5/quotes.pl (013fcc20).
fopen called for SYS:PUBLIC\PERL/cgilib.pl (013fcc20).
fclose called for SYS:PUBLIC\PERL/cgilib.pl (013fcc20).
PERL5:freeThreadMemory
PERL5:freeThreadMemory done
Return from web-entry
```

To start the Debug console, enter the following command at the server console:

`PERL5 DBGON`

After you load the Debug console, you can control it using the commands listed in Table 13.6. If you forget the Debug console commands, you can display them on the server console by entering the following command: `PERL5`.

**IMPORTANT**

**This command won't work if PERL5.NLM is not loaded. To start PERL5.NLM, initiate a Perl script at a browser or enter the following command:** `LOAD SYS:\INW_WEB\SHARED\LCGI\PERL5\PERL5`.

TABLE 13.6

*Perl Debug Console Commands*

| COMMAND | DESCRIPTION |
| --- | --- |
| PERL5 ACCESS | This command is a toggle command that causes the console to display or hide file path and name information for the accessed Perl scripts. Each time you enter the command, the option changes to the opposite state. |
| PERL5 DBGLOC | This toggle command enables or disables the display of procedure names. |

*(continued)*

| TABLE 13.6 | COMMAND | DESCRIPTION |
|---|---|---|
| *Perl Debug Console Commands (continued)* | PERL5 DBGOFF | The debug off (DGBOFF) command closes the Debug console. |
| | PERL5 DBGON | The debug on (DBGON) command opens the Debug console and must be entered before any of the other commands in this table. |
| | PERL5 FLUSH | The flush command copies the Debug console entries to the following file: SYS:\INW_WEB\ SHARED\LCGI\PERL5\PERL5DBG.LOG. The previous or flushed version of the file is saved as PERL5DBG.BAK. |

### The Script Debug Console

The Script Debug console displays Perl script errors. Figure 13.5 shows an example of the Perl Script Debug console. You can use these error messages to determine what is wrong with your Perl scripts. The first line in a Perl script file is line 1, and the remaining lines are numbered in sequence. When you see an error for a particular line number, be sure to check that line and the line before it. Sometimes an error does not produce a problem until the following line is processed.

FIGURE 13.5

*Novell Web Server Perl Script Debug Console*

In the Figure 13.5 example, the PrintHeader subroutine cannot be found because it is defined in CGILIB.PL and the *require("cgilib.pl");* statement is missing from the script. The second error message appears when a Web page author refers to a script that cannot be found.

To start the Script Debug console, enter the following command at the server console:

```
PERL5 SCRIPT
```

After you load the Script Debug console, you can control it using the commands listed in Table 13.7. If you forget the Script Debug console commands, you can display them on the server console by entering the following command: **PERL5**. This command displays all the commands for both consoles.

**IMPORTANT**

**This command won't work if PERL5.NLM is not loaded. To start PERL5.NLM, initiate a Perl script at a browser or enter the following command:** LOAD SYS:\INW_WEB\SHARED\LCGI\PERL5\PERL5.

| TABLE 13.7 | COMMAND | DESCRIPTION |
|---|---|---|
| *Perl Debug Console Commands* | PERL5 FLUSH | The flush command copies the Debug console entries to the following file: SYS:\INW_WEB\SHARED\LCGI\PERL5\PERL5SCR.LOG. The previous or flushed version of the file is saved as PERL5SCR.BAK. |
| | PERL5 SCRIPT | This toggle command opens or closes the Script Debug console. |

**NOTE**

**The** PERL5 FLUSH **command simultaneously writes the contents of both debug consoles to disk.**

## COMMON PERL SCRIPT PROBLEMS

The first step in troubleshooting a Perl script is to determine if the problem is a Perl script programming error or an HTML formatting error. Look for information in the browser, on the server's Perl console, and in the server log files. Table 13.8 lists some common symptoms and the problems that cause them.

| TABLE 13.8 | SYMPTOM | PROBLEM |
| --- | --- | --- |
| *Common Problems and Their Symptoms* | 404 Not Found message appears in the browser | The requested file was not found on the server. |
| | 500 Server Error message appears in the browser | Perl script processing error. Look on the Web server's Perl console for messages. Often, error messages include a line number. The first line in the file is line 1, and each of the following lines are numbered in sequence. Be sure to check the listed line and the line before it. |
| | | Look for missing semicolons and for colons that appear where semicolons should be. |
| | | Look for symbols in print statements that are for HTML tags or text and not for Perl. Common culprits are quotation marks, and the following symbols: @, %, $, and #. These symbols must be preceded by the backslash character. |
| | 500 Server Error message appears in the browser. Undefined subroutine message appears on the server's Perl console. | The following statement might be missing from the Perl script: require("cgilib.pl"); |
| | 500 Server Error message appears in the browser. Everything looks okay on the server's Perl console. | The following statement might be missing from the Perl script: print &PrintHeader; |
| | The browser displays a message that is similar to the following: Document contains no data | The Perl script is not printing any data to the browser, or the script was not found. |

| TABLE 13.8 | SYMPTOM | PROBLEM |
| --- | --- | --- |
| Common Problems and Their Symptoms | The resulting Web page formatting is incorrect. | This indicates an HTML formatting error. Check the HTML tags in your print statements. |
| | The script runs, but the data is processed incorrectly. | This indicates a Perl processing problem. If the form data appears to be missing, the form may have been empty, or the following statement is missing from the Perl script: &ReadParse; |

**Exercise 13.3: To test your understanding of the Perl programming concepts and commands described in this chapter, turn to the end of this chapter and complete Exercise 13.3.**

## Summary

In this chapter, you reviewed the server requirements for Perl scripts, and you learned how to create your first Perl script. Perl scripts must be punctuated correctly and contain certain statements that prepare the script for the Web server.

You also learned how to convert Web pages to Perl scripts, and how to process forms. Finally, you learned how to convert other people's Perl scripts for the Novell Web Server and how to troubleshoot script processing problems.

In the next chapter, you'll learn another scripting language called JavaScript.

**For more information on Perl, visit:**
**Tom Christiansen's Perl site:** www.perl.com
**The Perl Institute:** www.perl.org
**ActiveState Tool Corp:** www.activestate.com

## PUZZLE 13.1: USING PERL SCRIPTS

The following word puzzle contains many of the terms discussed in this chapter. See if you can find all the words. As you search for the words, ask yourself why the word is in the list and how it was used in this chapter. If you don't know the answers to these questions, you might want to review the chapter.

```
P  R  E  V  R  E  S  F  O  R  M  S  P  T  A
G  R  E  A  D  P  A  R  S  E  S  E  N  N  C
N  O  I  T  A  T  O  U  Q  E  R  E  H  E  T
I  P  T  N  N  O  L  O  C  I  M  E  S  M  I
H  E  T  B  T  W  W  C  U  E  V  X  U  M  O
C  R  P  A  E  H  A  Q  T  I  D  P  L  O  N
N  A  I  C  L  F  E  A  T  B  B  R  F  C  O
A  T  R  K  O  R  T  A  G  P  I  E  W  D  I
R  O  C  S  S  I  L  D  C  L  S  E  B  T
B  R  S  L  N  C  O  D  I  E  L  S  B  G  C
I  A  B  A  O  C  O  M  P  A  R  I  S  O  N
L  R  U  S  C  H  A  E  S  L  E  O  T  N  U
I  R  S  H  T  N  I  R  P  C  P  N  A  I  F
G  A  W  E  Y  O  H  E  L  B  A  I  R  A  V
C  Y  M  D  B  G  O  F  F  N  E  H  T  M  L
```

| | | | |
|---|---|---|---|
| access | DBGLOC | if | script |
| action | DBGOFF | method | semicolon |
| array | DBGON | operator | server |
| associative | dynamic | PERL | statement |
| backslash | else | PERLLIB | subscript |
| branching | expression | print | then |
| cgilib | flush | PrintHeader | variable |
| comment | forms | quotation | WEBSTART |
| comparison | function | ReadParse | |
| console | HTML | require | |

**EXERCISE 13.1: CONVERTING A WEB PAGE**

In this exercise, you will configure a form to call a Perl script, and you will create the Perl script that responds to the form. To simplify the creation of the Perl script, you will convert an existing Web page into a Perl script. To complete this exercise, do the following:

**1 •** To create a Web page to call your Perl script, do the following:

   a. Use a text-editor or word-processor program to open the following file on this book's CD-ROM:

   *d:*/DemoWeb2/Answers/form2.htm

   b. Edit the opening <FORM> tag so that it calls a Perl script named THANKS.PL.

   c. If you have access to a Novell Web Server, save the form file on your Web server as FORM3.HTM.

   d. If you don't have access to a Novell Web Server, save the form file on your local computer as FORM3.HTM and compare this file to the following file on this book's CD-ROM:

   *d:*/DemoWeb2/Answers/form3.htm

**2 •** To convert a Web page to a Perl script, do the following:

   a. Use a text-editor or word-processor program to open the following file on this book's CD-ROM:

   *d:*/DemoWeb2/Answers/thanks.htm

   b. At the beginning of the file, add the two lines required by Perl scripts.

   c. Convert the remaining lines to Perl print statements that will create the response Web page for the form. (Tip: To reduce the total number of print statements, you can combine some of the lines.)

   d. If you have access to a Novell Web Server, save the file as thanks.pl in the appropriate directory.

e. If you don't have access to a Novell Web Server, save the form file on your local computer as THANKS.PL and compare this file to the following file on this book's CD-ROM:

*d:/DemoWeb2/Answers/thanks.pl*

**3** • If you have access to a Novell Web Server, open the FORM3.HTM file on the server, fill out the form, and click Order Pizza.

If you've completed this exercise correctly, the browser should display "Thank you for your order!" If you have problems, compare your files with the answer files on this book's CD-ROM. If the files match and you still have problems, see the troubleshooting section in this chapter.

## EXERCISE 13.2: PROCESSING A FORM

In this exercise, you will update the Perl script from Exercise 13.1 to use form data in its response to a Web page. To complete this exercise, do the following:

1 • To prepare for your Perl script edits, do the following:

a. Use a text-editor or word-processor program to open the following file on this book's CD-ROM:

*d:*/DemoWeb2/Answers/form3.htm

If you completed Exercise 13.1, you can use the file you created in that exercise. They should be the same.

b. Locate the variable names used for each of the form elements and write them down in a form, such as the one shown in Figure 13.6. You need to know these variable names in order to call them in your Perl script. To save time, I've entered the values that each form element can generate. Normally, you would have to determine this.

c. Using what you've learned in this chapter, translate the form variable names into the correct associative array names and write these down in Figure 13.6.

d. Change the opening <FORM> tag to call the Perl script named thanks.pl.

e. Save the file as FORM.HTM

FIGURE 13.6

*Array Variables for FORM3.HTM*

| Form Element | Variable Name | Value | Associative Array Name |
|---|---|---|---|
| Customer Name | | | |
| Take Out Dining Area | | Take out | |
| Delivery Dining Area | | Deliver | |
| Inside Dining Area | | Inside dining | |
| Patio Dining Area | | Patio dining | |

**2** • To practice using form data in your Perl script, do the following:

a. Use a text-editor or word-processor program to open the following file on this book's CD-ROM:

*d:/DemoWeb2/Answers/thanks.pl*

If you completed Exercise 13.1, you can use the file you created in that exercise. They should be the same.

b. Add the line that causes form data to be read into arrays.

c. Edit the heading so that it reads:

```
Thank you, customer name, for your order!
```

(Hint: You are mixing text and a variable on this line, so you'll need to use operators to separate them, and you'll need to be careful how you place quotation marks.)

d. If you have access to a Novell Web Server, save the Perl script on your Web server as thanks.pl, and test it by accessing the FORM4.HTM file. When you first start writing Perl scripts, it's wise to test your scripts often so you don't have too many bugs to correct at once. If your script is working properly, the customer's name should appear in the result Web page.

e. If you don't have access to a Novell Web Server, save the script on your local computer and continue. At the end of this exercise you can compare it to the answer file.

**3** • To practice using branching statements, do the following:

a. Use a text-editor or word-processor program to continue editing the thanks.pl script.

b. After the heading line, enter a print statement that says:

```
"Your pizza will be delivered to   ."
```

Insert the HTML tags that will center this line on the Web page.

c. Edit the print statement created in Step 3b to include a Perl script variable named *deliver* before the period.

d. Above the print statements for the Web page, add four branching statements that assign one of the following values to the *deliver* variable:

the patio

the dining room

the take out counter

your location

(Tip: Remember to use the operator that compares string values. If you have trouble with this step, take a peek at one of the branch statements in the answer file on this book's CD:

*d:/DemoWeb2/Answers/thanks2.pl*

After you get the first branch statement right, try to do the others without peeking.)

e. If you have access to a Novell Web Server, save the file as thanks.pl in the appropriate directory.

f. If you don't have access to a Novell Web Server, save the form file on your local computer as THANKS.PL and compare this file with the following file on this book's CD-ROM:

*d:/DemoWeb2/Answers/thanks2.pl*

**4** · If you have access to a Novell Web Server, open the FORM4.HTM file on the server, fill out the form, and click Order Pizza.

If you've completed this exercise correctly, the browser should display the customer name and the dining location the customer selected as shown in Figure 13.7. If you have problems, compare your files with the answer files on this book's CD-ROM. If the files match and you still have problems, see the troubleshooting section in this chapter.

FIGURE    13.7

*Exercise 13.2 Result*

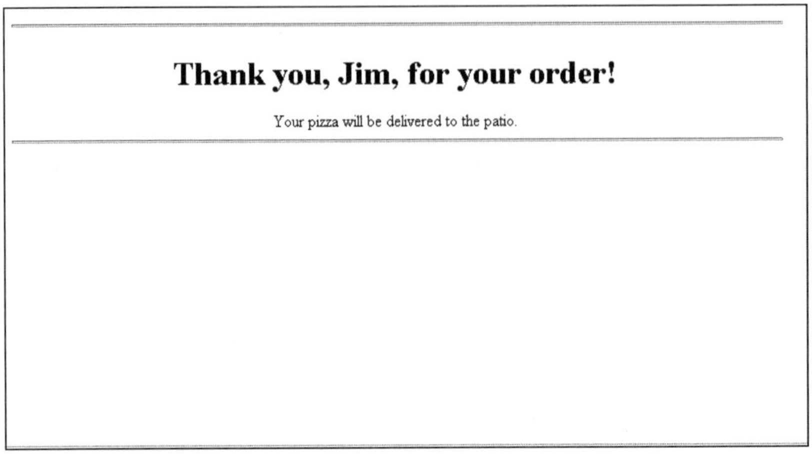

# Thank you, Jim, for your order!

Your pizza will be delivered to the patio.

**EXERCISE 13.3: UNDERSTANDING PERL SCRIPTS**

This exercise tests your understanding of the Perl programming concepts and commands described in this chapter. To complete this exercise, answer the following questions.

**1** • What is the first line that is required in Perl scripts for the Novell Web Server Version 3?

Answer: . . . . . . . . . . . . . . . . . . . . . . . . . . . . . . . . . . . .

**2** • What Perl script statement sends a MIME type header to the browser?

Answer: . . . . . . . . . . . . . . . . . . . . . . . . . . . . . . . . . . . .

**3** • Which characters must precede any HTML code that is sent to the browser?

Answer: . . . . . . . . . . . . . . . . . . . . . . . . . . . . . . . . . . . .

**4** • Which characters must follow any HTML code sent to the browser?

Answer: . . . . . . . . . . . . . . . . . . . . . . . . . . . . . . . . . . . .

**5** • List two ways to include double quotation marks in Perl print statements.

a. . . . . . . . . . . . . . . . . . . . . . . . . . . . . . . . . . . . .

b. . . . . . . . . . . . . . . . . . . . . . . . . . . . . . . . . . . . .

**6** • Which character marks the beginning of a Perl script comment?

Answer: . . . . . . . . . . . . . . . . . . . . . . . . . . . . . . . . . . . .

**7** • The _____ function stores form data in two arrays.

**8** • Label each of the following Perl script variable names as valid or invalid.

a. $test      . . . . . . . . . . . . . . . . . . . . . . . . . .

b. #name      . . . . . . . . . . . . . . . . . . . . . . . . . .

c. $123      . . . . . . . . . . . . . . . . . . . . . . . . . .

d. $a**      . . . . . . . . . . . . . . . . . . . . . . . . . .

e. $one_two   . . . . . . . . . . . . . . . . . . . . . . . .

**9** • What type of variable is $month[3]?

Answer: . . . . . . . . . . . . . . . . . . . . . . . . . . . . . . .

**10** • What type of variable is $data{name}?

Answer: . . . . . . . . . . . . . . . . . . . . . . . . . . . . . . . .

**11** • What is the first word in the branching command described in this chapter?

Answer: . . . . . . . . . . . . . . . . . . . . . . . . . . . . . . . .

**12** • The command statements for a branching command appear between which symbols?

Answer: . . . . . . . . . . . . . . . . . . . . . . . . . . . . . . . .

**13** • The expression in a branching command appears between which symbols?

Answer: . . . . . . . . . . . . . . . . . . . . . . . . . . . . . . . .

**14** • When a branching command contains two sets of command statements, which keyword appears between the sets?

Answer: . . . . . . . . . . . . . . . . . . . . . . . . . . . . . . . .

**15** • List the server console commands that turn on and turn off the Perl
Debug console.

a. . . . . . . . . . . . . . . . . . . . . . . . . . . . . . . . . . . . . . . . . . . .

b. . . . . . . . . . . . . . . . . . . . . . . . . . . . . . . . . . . . . . . . . . .

**16** • List the server console command that turns on and off the Perl Script
Debug console.

Answer: . . . . . . . . . . . . . . . . . . . . . . . . . . . . . . . . . . . . . . .

**17** • List the server console command that copies Perl console data to disk.

Answer: . . . . . . . . . . . . . . . . . . . . . . . . . . . . . . . . . . . . . . .

# CHAPTER 14

# Using JavaScripts

JavaScripts, like the Perl scripts described in Chapter 13, provide another alternative for creating dynamic Web pages. JavaScripts are different from Perl scripts, however, in the following ways:

▸ JavaScripts give the Web page author more control over the user interface within the page.

▸ JavaScripts allow script results to appear on the original Web page; Perl script data is output to a new Web page.

▸ JavaScripts can be embedded in the Web page; Perl scripts are stored as separate files on the Web server.

▸ The browser must support JavaScripts; the browser does not need to be aware of Perl.

▸ JavaScripts can execute on the client, Web server processing is not required.

I'll cover the first three items later in this chapter. The last two deserve more attention now.

Although JavaScript does have many advantages over Perl and other types of CGI programs, CGI programs can be a better choice when you need to support older browsers that are not JavaScript enabled. Because CGI programs execute on the server and output HTML to browsers, implementing CGI requires changes to the server only, not the browsers.

JavaScripts require a compatible browser because the browser acts as an interpreter for the JavaScript commands. The good news here is that you don't need a Web server to test your JavaScripts; all you need is your JavaScript-enabled browser!

## What Is JavaScript?

JavaScript is a scripting language that is less complex than C++ and about as complex as BASIC. The following list shows how Novell Education rates the complexity of JavaScript with other programming languages:

C++
C
Java
Pascal, Perl
JavaScript, BASIC

As this list shows, JavaScript is considered less complex than Perl, which was described in Chapter 13. Don't be concerned about Java being more difficult to learn than Perl. Although we will cover Java in the next chapter, we only cover how to use Java applets (not how to program them), and using Java applets is easier than writing JavaScripts.

And while we're on the topic of programming, the purpose of this chapter is the same as that for the chapter on Perl. The goal here is to learn enough about JavaScript programming that you can use other people's JavaScripts on your Web pages. A complete guide to JavaScript programming is beyond the scope of this chapter, but you will get a good introduction to the basics.

## Why Use JavaScript?

Why would you want to use JavaScript? The answer is the same answer for SSI commands and CGI programs. You use JavaScript to create dynamic Web pages. When you get to the Java chapter, you'll want to use Java applets for the same reason. Standard HTML pages are OK, but dynamic Web pages are cool. JavaScript dynamic Web pages benefit from the following JavaScript features:

▸ Improved user interface controls

▸ Form preprocessing

▸ Form processing

## IMPROVED USER INTERFACE CONTROLS

JavaScript gives you greater control over the user interface than SSI commands or CGI programs. With JavaScript, you can do the following:

▶ Create buttons that activate JavaScripts.

▶ Launch JavaScripts based on user actions, such as mouse movements, mouse clicks, and option selections.

▶ Display JavaScript results on a Web page or in forms.

▶ Display dialog boxes that assist users.

▶ Display messages in the status area at the bottom of the browser window.

▶ Provide controls that enable users to change Web page settings, such as the font size.

## FORM PREPROCESSING

The JavaScript user interface controls enable you to validate user entries in forms locally, before the form is processed by a JavaScript or a CGI program. This is a powerful benefit. After a user completes a text box entry or selects an option, you can immediately respond to invalid entries. This is much better than bouncing messages back and forth between the browser and the server until the form is correct. This saves the user frustration, reduces network traffic, and reduces the load on the Web server.

## FORM PROCESSING

Although JavaScript is a lightweight programming language, it is a programming language nonetheless and can perform many form-processing functions. Because these functions are executed at the browser, JavaScript form processing reduces the load on the Web server. Another advantage of JavaScript form processing is that the scripts are entered directly into the Web page. You don't have to worry about enabling CGI processing or placing the scripts in the correct directory.

The JavaScript user interface controls provide special Web page features, such as the following:

▸   Calculators

▸   Spreadsheets

▸   Worksheets

## Enabling and Disabling JavaScript in the Browser

JavaScripts can only run in browsers that support them. Browsers such as Netscape Navigator 2.0 and later not only support JavaScripts, they give the browser user the ability to enable or disable JavaScript processing. If JavaScript processing is enabled, the browser executes any JavaScripts that are embedded in a Web page. If JavaScript processing is disabled, all JavaScript commands are ignored.

The default configuration for Netscape Navigator enables JavaScript processing. If you have security concerns, you can disable JavaScript.

To enable or disable JavaScript in Netscape Navigator 3, do the following:

**1** •   Open Netscape Navigator 3.

**2** •   In the Options menu, select Network Preferences.

**3** •   Select the Languages tab.

**4** •   To enable JavaScript processing, check the Enable JavaScript checkbox.

**5** •   To disable JavaScript processing, clear the Enable JavaScript checkbox.

**6** •   Click OK.

To enable or disable JavaScript in Netscape Navigator 4.0, do the following:

**1** • Open Netscape Navigator 4.

**2** • Select Edit → Preferences.

**3** • Select the Advanced category.

**4** • To enable JavaScript processing, check the Enable JavaScript checkbox.

**5** • To disable JavaScript processing, clear the Enable JavaScript checkbox.

**6** • Click OK.

## Writing Your First JavaScript

Okay, enough of the introduction. Let's take a look at a simple JavaScript.

```
<SCRIPT LANGUAGE="JavaScript" SRC="filename">

document.write("Hello world!")

</SCRIPT>
```

Pretty intimidating, huh? The first and last lines are basically HTML start and stop tags, `<SCRIPT>` and `</SCRIPT>`. The middle line simply prints "Hello world!" in the browser window.

The simplest way to implement this script in a Web page is to place it in the HTML file between the start and stop `<BODY>` tags as follows:

```
<HTML>

<HEAD>

<TITLE>Hello world. Try JavaScript!</TITLE>

</HEAD>
```

```
<BODY>

<SCRIPT LANGUAGE="JavaScript">
document.write("Hello world!")
</SCRIPT>

</BODY>
</HTML>
```

Figure 14.1 shows the output of this HTML code and JavaScript.

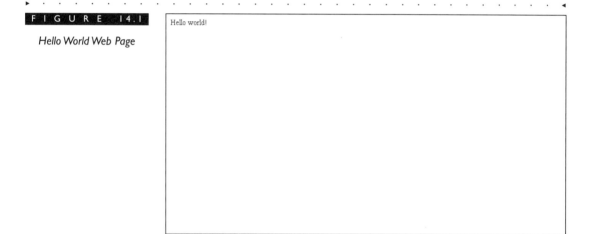

**FIGURE 14.1**

*Hello World Web Page*

Hello world!

Now that we know what the script does, let's take a closer look at its elements. The opening tag is `<SCRIPT LANGUAGE="JavaScript">`, which marks the start of a JavaScript and defines the script language, JavaScript. The `LANGUAGE` attribute is provided to allow for other types of scripting languages in the future. The language attribute is optional because JavaScript is currently the only script language for Web pages.

**NOTE**

**Although the LANGUAGE attribute is optional now, I highly recommend that you always use it in your JavaScript opening tags. Otherwise, a future browser release could instantly render all your Web pages useless if the browser defaulted to some other scripting language or required this attribute.**

The middle line of the script, `document.write("Hello world!")`, prints the "Hello world!" message on the Web page. The `document.write` phrase is called a method, and you'll learn more about methods later in this chapter. Basically, this phrase tells the JavaScript interpreter within the browser to write the text in the document window.

The last line of the script, `</SCRIPT>`, should require no introduction. As with all the other HTML tag pairs described in this book, you must provide a closing tag with that all-important forward slash at the end of a JavaScript.

By the way, did you notice the `SRC="filename"` attribute listed at the beginning of this section? It wasn't used in the sample script. This `<SCRIPT>` tag attribute defines an external file that contains script statements. This attribute enables you to create a script file that can be called from many documents on the same Web server.

## Punctuating JavaScripts

All programming languages have their punctuation requirements, and JavaScript is no different. The following is a brief list of requirements:

▸ JavaScript statements and variable names are case-sensitive. For example, you must enter **document.write** not **Document.Write**.

▸ The semicolon (;) links multiple statements on one line. For example, document.write("Hello world!"); document.write("How are you?"); document.write("I'm fine.").

▸ Quotation marks must appear in pairs.

- A double forward slash marks the start of a single-line comment. For example: //This is a comment.

- A forward slash and an asterisk (/*) mark the beginning of a multiple-line comment. An asterisk and a forward slash mark the end of a multiple-line comment. For example: /* This is a multiple-line comment example for you. */

- Single and multiple line comments can begin after a JavaScript statement on the same line.

For your learning enjoyment, the following sample script provides additional examples of JavaScript punctuation:

```
<SCRIPT LANGUAGE="JavaScript">


// The following line contains two JavaScript statements.
document.write("Hello world!"); document.write("Where am
I?")


document.write("I want to go home.") //Another comment.


/* This is a multiple-line comment.
The following line is ignored because it falls within the
multiple line comment:
document.write("Print me, please.")*/


</SCRIPT>
```

## Hiding JavaScripts from Unenlightened Browsers

As mentioned earlier, JavaScripts must run in a JavaScript-enabled browser. Because not all browsers are enlightened to the JavaScript way, and because some JavaScript-enabled browsers might have JavaScript disabled, it is best to consider these browsers in your Web page design plans.

So, what happens when an unenlightened browser loads a Web page that contains a JavaScript? Figure 14.2 shows what happens when JavaScript is disabled on a Netscape Navigator 4 browser and a Web page contains JavaScript. (Figure 14.3 shows how the Web page appears when JavaScript is enabled.)

**This box displays a scrolling message!**

The JavaScript in this example is supposed to be a scrolling message in the text box. Because JavaScript was disabled in this browser, everything between the `<SCRIPT>` tags is ignored, so the message doesn't appear. If this were an unenlightened browser, the script statements between the `<SCRIPT>` tags might have been displayed in the browser window. Not a pretty picture.

To prevent JavaScript commands from appearing in Web pages on unenlightened browsers, make the entire script an HTML comment as shown in the following example.

```
<HTML>

<HEAD>

<TITLE>Hello world. Try JavaScript!</TITLE>

</HEAD>

<BODY>


<SCRIPT LANGUAGE="JavaScript">

<!-- Hide the script from unenlightened browsers

document.write("Hello world!")

// end the script hiding -->

</SCRIPT>


</BODY>

</HTML>
```

Remember the format of the HTML comment: *<!-- html comment -->*? The following line in the sample script begins the HTML comment:

```
<!-- Hide the script from unenlightened browsers
```

The following line ends the HTML comment:

```
// end the script hiding -->
```

Notice that the line that ends the HTML comment is also a JavaScript comment. This prevents the JavaScript interpreter from trying to interpret the HTML comment close characters (-->).

Also notice that the HTML comment begins and ends between the opening and closing `<SCRIPT>` tags. Nonenlightened browsers ignore HTML tags they don't understand, so the `<SCRIPT>` tags are not a problem.

What happens if you begin or end the HTML comment outside of the <SCRIPT> tags? Consider the following example:

```
<!-- DON'T DO THIS. THIS IS A BAD EXAMPLE!

<SCRIPT LANGUAGE="JavaScript">

// end the script hiding -->

document.write("Hello world!")

</SCRIPT>
```

In this example, nothing appears in a JavaScript-enabled browser because the opening <SCRIPT> tag was ignored as part of an HTML comment. To make the HTML comment work correctly in all browsers, the HTML comment must begin and end within the opening and closing <SCRIPT> tags.

 **Exercise 14.1: If you're preparing to take the certification exam, or if you want to practice what you learned in this section, turn to the end of this chapter and complete exercise 14.1. When you are done, continue reading here to prepare for the next exercise.**

## Using Literal and Variable Data

JavaScripts, like other programming languages, manipulate data. Everything in a JavaScript is either a programming element for manipulating data, or it is the data. After all, if the data is okay as it is, what do we need a program for?

When you modify a JavaScript, you'll need to recognize the data in the JavaScript. In some cases, you'll want to change this data; in other cases, your ability to recognize the data will help you understand how the JavaScript operates and how you can change that operation. The following sections describe JavaScript data types and how they are represented in JavaScripts as literals and variables.

## DATA TYPES

JavaScript supports the following data types:

- ▸ Numbers

- ▸ Strings

- ▸ Boolean

- ▸ Null

The following sections describe these data types.

### Numbers

You are already familiar with numbers. This isn't a trick. JavaScript numbers can be integer numbers (no decimal point) or floating-point numbers, which include a decimal point and can include an exponent. Number data is simply data on which you can perform mathematical calculations and produce a numeric result. The important thing about number data types is that they are different from the string and boolean data types.

### Strings

String data is data that contains letters. The first sample program in this chapter contained the string data: "Hello world!" The key concept to remember here is that string data is evaluated as string data or text—not as numbers. Consider the following example:

```
total = "Hello world!" + 4
```

In this example, the value of the total variable is "Hello world!4." JavaScript recognizes that one of the data values is a string and evaluates the entire equation as if all the values are strings. As you can see, string arithmetic is different from number arithmetic.

### Boolean

The boolean data type has two possible values, true and false, and is often the result of comparing two values. Consider the following expression:

```
4<3
```

There is no equal sign, so we can't refer to this example as an equation. JavaScript refers to this as an expression (we'll spend more time on expressions later in this chapter). Can JavaScript evaluate this expression? We know the expression is false; and surprise, JavaScript also knows this. Boolean data types are very useful for comparing data values.

### Null

The null data type is the loneliest of the data types, for it never contains a value. Because the null data type contains no value, it is not a number, string, or boolean data type. It is a null data type.

## LITERALS

All data within a JavaScript is either literal or variable. In the Hello world! program example, the "Hello world!" data is literal. "Hello world!" is the data.

Literal data is raw data as opposed to data represented by variable names. Literal data is stored in the script and does not change during script execution.

## VARIABLES

Unless you've skipped the preceding chapters, variables are not new to you. Variables are names or placeholders that represent data containers in which you can store data. Unlike literals, you can change variable data values during script execution. When you change variable values, the variable data type automatically changes to correspond to the new data.

If you already have some programming experience, you may have used programming languages that require you to define a particular data type for each variable. JavaScript variables, however, are loosely typed, which means that the interpreter determines the data type by reading the variable contents and analyzing how the data is used in the script. You can use the same variable name for any data type, and you can change data types during the program.

As with other programming languages, JavaScript variable names must conform to certain rules. The JavaScript variable name rules are the same as for C and are as follows:

▸ Variable names can contain letters, numbers, and underscore characters.

▸ The first character in a variable name must be an underscore or a letter.

▸ Variable names cannot contain space characters.

▸ Variable names must be unique.

▸ Keywords are reserved and cannot be used as variable names.

Keywords are special words that are recognized by JavaScript. Remember the `if` statement for Perl? JavaScript has a similar statement and reserves the keyword `if` for this purpose. You cannot use `if` as a variable name for JavaScripts. Table 14.1 lists JavaScript keywords.

| TABLE 14.1 | JAVASCRIPT KEYWORDS | | | |
|---|---|---|---|---|
| *JavaScript Keywords* | abstract | extends | interface | synchronized |
| | boolean | false | long | this |
| | break | final | native | throw |
| | byte | finally | new | throws |
| | case | float | null | transient |
| | catch | for | package | true |
| | char | function | private | try |
| | class | goto | protected | var |
| | const | if | public | void |
| | continue | implements | return | while |
| | default | import | short | with |
| | do | in | static | |
| | double | instance of | super | |
| | else | int | switch | |

**For updates to the JavaScript keywords, review the Reserved Words list in "Appendix A" section of the following Web page:** `developer.netscape.com/library/documentation/ communicator/jsguide4/index.htm`.

## Using Form Data and Other Object Data

Chapter 13 explained that Perl scripts receive form data only after the user clicks the Submit button. Unlike Perl, JavaScript can access the form data at any time. JavaScript can even add data to a form.

JavaScript uses an object model approach to accessing browser and form elements. An object model uses objects to represent the script elements that the script developer wants to control. Figure 14.3 shows some browser and Web page objects.

Form Object
(single element)

Navigator Object     Window Object

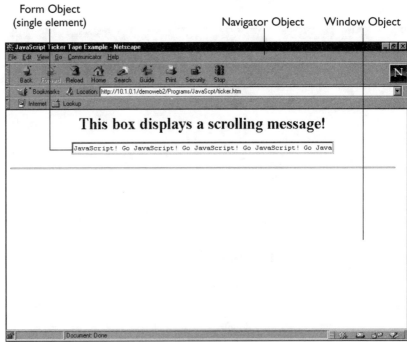

Most of the objects in Figure 14.3 are already familiar to you. The Navigator object represents Netscape Navigator, and the Window object represents the window where you view an HTML document, which is represented by the Document object. When a window contains frames, each frame window is a subordinate window of the topmost window. The form object is made up of one or more elements, each represented by objects.

While you can use JavaScript to create objects, most objects are created by HTML tags. For example, a form object is created with the <FORM> tag. The attributes of the <FORM> tag become *properties* of the form object. Properties are object variables that describe the object or control how it appears. Table 14.2 shows some of the text object properties that control text input boxes in forms.

| TABLE 14.2 | TEXT OBJECT PROPERTY | DESCRIPTION |
|---|---|---|
| *Sample Text Object Properties* | defaultValue | Represents the value assigned with the VALUE attribute when the text input box was created with an HTML tag. |
| | name | Represents the value assigned with the NAME attribute when the text input box was created with an HTML tag. |
| | value | Represents the current value within the text input box. |

Objects and their properties are very useful to JavaScript script developers because JavaScript enables you to read their values and change them. For example, you can display the value from a form text box anywhere on the page, or you can use it in calculations. You can also use a text box to display the results of a script, and we've just begun to explore the possibilities.

To access object data, you need to understand the following:

▸ Object hierarchy

▸ Objects

▸ Properties

▸ Object and property naming conventions

## OBJECT HIERARCHY

If you are already familiar with Novell Directory Services (NDS), you'll notice some similarities between the NDS hierarchy and the JavaScript object hierarchy shown in Figure 14.4.

FIGURE 14.4

*JavaScript Object Hierarchy*

```
navigator          window

plugin             frame

history          document          location

anchor           form             link

button           select           reset

checkbox         submit           text

password         radio            text area
```

The object hierarchy defines the relationship between the browser and Web page objects. The properties of each object include properties unique to that object (such as color) and all child objects. For example, a radio button is not only an object, it is a property of the form that contains it. As you will see later in this chapter, this relationship is used to build the names that you use to access object property data. These names are similar to the distinguished or complete names used by NDS.

**NOTE**

**In some programming languages, the relationship between objects determines how properties are inherited from one object to another. JavaScript objects do not inherit properties from other objects.**

If all Web pages contained no more than one object of each object type, the hierarchy would be unimportant. After all, if you only have one object of a particular type, any reference to that object type is going to identify the correct object.

Web pages, however, can contain many objects of the same type. For example, a Web page can be divided into frames, each of which is a separate window object. Each of the windows can have multiple form objects, and each of the form objects can contain multiple button objects. JavaScript identifies all objects, including a particular form button, by the path in the object hierarchy.

## OBJECT DESCRIPTIONS

Table 14.3 describes some of the objects that are available to JavaScripts.

T A B L E  14.3

*Object Descriptions*

| PARENT OBJECT | OBJECT | DESCRIPTION |
|---|---|---|
| none | navigator | The navigator object stores information about the browser software. |
| none | window | The topmost window is created when the browser window opens. You can create *child* windows using the `<FRAMESET>` tags. You can also use JavaScript commands to create windows. |
| window | frames | Frames are created by the `<FRAME>` tags that appear in `<FRAMESET>` tag pairs. Each frame is a separate window. The window that contains the `<FRAMESET>` tags is the parent window to the frame windows it defines. |
| window or frame | document | Document objects are created by the HTML tags and text that appear between the `<HEAD>` and `<BODY>` tag pairs. |
| window or frame | history | The history object maintains a list of the URLs that the user visits. These are the URLs that appear in the Netscape Navigator Go menu. |
| window or frame | location | The location object stores information on the current URL for a window. |
| document | area | The area object defines an area of an image as an image map or link. Areas are created by HTML tags similar to the following:<br><br>`<MAP NAME="name">`<br><br>`<AREA COORDS="coordinates" HREF="URL">`<br><br>`</MAP>` |
| document | anchor | The anchor object represents the anchors array, which maintains a list of all the named anchors in a document. Named anchors are created by the HTML tags similar to the following:<br><br>`<A NAME=name>text</A>`. |
| document | link | The link object represents the links array, which maintains a list of all the links in a document. Links are created by HTML tags similar to the following: `<A HREF="url">Link text.</A>`. |
| document | form | Form objects are created by the `<FORM>` tag pairs. |

*(continued)*

| TABLE 14.3 |
| :-- |

*Object Descriptions*
*(continued)*

| PARENT OBJECT | OBJECT | DESCRIPTION |
| :-- | :-- | :-- |
| form | button | Button objects are created by HTML tags similar to the following: `<INPUT TYPE="button" NAME=name VALUE="value">`. |
| form | checkbox | Checkbox objects are created by HTML tags similar to the following: `<INPUT TYPE="checkbox" NAME=name VALUE="value">`. |
| form | password | Password objects are created by HTML tags that are similar to the following: `<INPUT TYPE="password" NAME="name" VALUE="value" SIZE=number>`. |
| form | radio | Radio objects are radio buttons that are created by HTML tags that are similar to the following: `<INPUT TYPE="radio" NAME="name" VALUE="value">`. |
| form | reset | Reset objects are reset buttons, which are created by HTML tags that are similar to the following: `<INPUT TYPE="reset" NAME="name" VALUE="value">`. |
| form | select | Select objects are selection or option lists that are created by HTML tags that are similar to the following: `<SELECT NAME="name">` `<OPTION VALUE="value">Option text.` `<OPTION VALUE="value">Option text.` `</SELECT>` |
| form | submit | Submit objects are submit buttons that are created by HTML tags that are similar to the following: `<INPUT TYPE="submit" NAME="name" VALUE="value">`. |
| form | text | Text objects are text input boxes that are created by HTML tags that are similar to the following: `<INPUT TYPE="text" NAME="name" VALUE="value">`. |
| form | textarea | Textarea objects are textarea input boxes, which are created by HTML tags that are similar to the following: `<TEXTAREA NAME="name" ROWS="number" COLS="number">default text</TEXTAREA>` |

Notice that most of the objects listed in Table 14.3 are created by HTML tags, which means that as a Web page author, you have the power to create the objects you want to use in your JavaScripts. Some objects, such as the navigator and history objects, are automatically created when a browser is opened and Web pages are accessed.

**Table 14.3 does not list all of the objects that JavaScript can access. For more information on JavaScript objects, browse to** developer.netscape.com/library/documentation/ communicator/jsguide4/index.htm.

## PROPERTY DESCRIPTIONS

Tables 14.4 through 14.7 describe some of the object properties that you can access from JavaScript.

| TABLE 14.4 | PROPERTY | DESCRIPTION |
| --- | --- | --- |
| *Navigator Object Property Descriptions* | appVersion | Stores the Netscape Navigator version number. For example: 3.0Gold (Win95; U) |
| | appName | Stores the browser application name. For example: Netscape |
| | appCodeName | Stores the browser code name. For example: Mozilla |
| | userAgent | Stores the browser code name and version number. For example: Mozilla/3.0Gold (Win95; U) |

| TABLE 14.5 | PROPERTY | DESCRIPTION |
| --- | --- | --- |
| *Window Object Property Descriptions* | default status | Specifies the default message that appears in the status bar at the bottom of the browser window. |
| | frames[*frame*] | When frames are used, this property can be used to identify one of the frames by name or by its number in the frames array. |
| | length | When frames are used, this property represents the number of frames that are defined in the window object. |
| | parent | When frames are used, *parent* refers to the window or frame that contains a window. |

*(continued)*

| TABLE 14.5 | PROPERTY | DESCRIPTION |
|---|---|---|
| *Window Object Property Descriptions (continued)* | self | Refers to the current window. |
| | status | Specifies the message that appears in the status bar at the bottom of the browser window. |
| | top | Refers to the top window, which is the current window when frames are not used. |
| | window | Refers to the current window. |

| TABLE 14.6 | PROPERTY | DESCRIPTION |
|---|---|---|
| *Document Object Property Descriptions* | alinkColor | The active link color setting specified by the ALINK attribute in the document <BODY> tag. |
| | bgColor | The background color setting specified by the BGCOLOR attribute in the document <BODY> tag. |
| | fgColor | The foreground color setting specified by the TEXT attribute in the document <BODY> tag. |
| | lastModified | The date the document was last modified. |
| | linkColor | The link color setting specified by the LINK attribute in the document <BODY> tag. |
| | referrer | The URL of the document that called the specified document. |
| | title | The title that appears between the <TITLE> tags in the document. |
| | URL | The document URL. |
| | vlinkColor | The visited link color setting specified by the VLINK attribute in the document <BODY> tag. |

## OBJECT AND PROPERTY NAMING CONVENTIONS

To access the object property data using JavaScript, you must specify the correct property name using the following format:

```
window_reference.frame_reference.object_references.property_
name
```

Table 14.8 describes the components of the complete property name.

Let's consider a practical example. Figure 14.5 shows an object hierarchy for a Web page with two frames, both of which contain a form.

Table 14.9 lists some sample names that you can use to access the properties in these objects. We'll discuss the properties in more detail later in this chapter.

**TABLE 14.7**

*Property Descriptions for Objects That Appear in Forms*

| PROPERTY | PARENT FORM OBJECTS | DESCRIPTION |
|---|---|---|
| checked | checkbox, radio | Stores the checked status of the object. |
| defaultChecked | checkbox, radio | Stores the checked status defined by the CHECKED attribute when the object was created. |
| defaultValue | password, text, textarea | For the password and text objects, defaultValue stores the value defined by the VALUE attribute when the object is created.<br>For the textarea object, this property stores the value defined between the <TEXTAREA> and </TEXTAREA> tags. |
| length | radio, select | For a radio object, length stores the number of radio buttons in a radio button group. (All the radio buttons in a group share the same NAME attribute.)<br>For a select object, length stores the number of options in the option list. |
| name | button, checkbox, hidden, password, radio, reset, select, submit, text, textarea | Name stores the value defined by the NAME attribute when the object is created. This is also the object name. |
| value | button, checkbox, hidden, password, radio, reset, submit, text, textarea | Value stores the value defined by the VALUE attribute when the object is created. If the user or your JavaScript changes the object setting, value stores the new setting. |

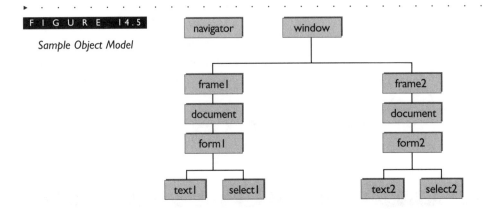

**F I G U R E   14.5**

*Sample Object Model*

| **PROPERTY NAME COMPONENT** | **DESCRIPTION** |
|---|---|
| *window_reference* | The window reference portion of the name can be omitted whenever the property you are accessing is a descendant of the current window. To specify the topmost window in the model, enter "top" as the window reference. |
| *frame_reference* | The frame reference portion of the name refers to any descendant windows of the topmost window. |
| *object_references* | The object references include all objects in the path between the current window and the object property you want to access. |
| *property_name* | The property name is the name of the property you want to access. |

**T A B L E   14.8**

*Property Name Components*

Notice that the location of your JavaScript affects the name you use to access an object property. If you are accessing an object property that is in the same branch of the hierarchy as your JavaScript, you can use the complete name or one of a couple of different abbreviated names (more on the abbreviated names in a moment). If your JavaScript is accessing a property in a different branch of the hierarchy, you must specify the complete name for the property.

**TABLE 14.9**

*Sample Property Names for
Objects in Figure 14.5*

| SCRIPT LOCATION | OBJECT PROPERTY | SAMPLE PROPERTY NAMES |
|---|---|---|
| Frame1 document | Window title | top.document.title <br> parent.document.title |
| Frame1 document | Frame1 name | name <br> self.name <br> top.frame1.name |
| Frame1 document | Frame1 document title | document.title <br> self.document.title <br> top.frame1.document.title |
| Frame1 document | Frame1 document URL | document.url <br> self.document.url <br> top.frame1.document.url |
| Frame1 document | Form1 action | document.form1.action <br> self.document.form1.action <br> top.frame1.document.form1.action |
| Frame1 document | Text1 value | document.form1.text1.value <br> self.document.form1.text1.value <br> top.frame1.document.form1.text1.value |
| Frame2 document | Window title | top.document.title <br> parent.document.title |
| Frame2 document | Frame1 name | top.frame1.name |
| Frame2 document | Frame1 document title | top.frame1.document.title |
| Frame2 document | Frame1 document URL | top.frame1.document.url |
| Frame2 document | Form1 action | top.frame1.document.form1.action |
| Frame2 document | Text1 value | top.frame1.document.form1.text1.value |

JavaScript provides several ways to abbreviate property names when the property and source script are in the same branch of the hierarchy. JavaScript recognizes top, parent, and self as relative references to other windows that are in the same branch of the model as the source script. Top refers to the topmost window, parent refers to the parent of the current window, and self refers to the current window. If no explicit or relative reference is included, JavaScript assumes that the property is a descendant of the current window.

When writing JavaScripts for Web pages with frames, place your
JavaScripts in the highest level frameset document. This simplifies
JavaScript references.

**TIP**

## ACCESSING OBJECT PROPERTY VALUES

Once you know how object and property names are constructed, you can use
these names to access the object properties in your script.

When you want to retrieve a value, use the object property name just as you
would use a variable name. The following script statement prints a property value
in the browser window:

```
document.write(document.url)
```

When you want to change a property value, use the object property name just
as you would use a variable name. The following script statement changes the
value that is displayed in a text box:

```
document.form1.text1.value="This is a test."
```

Some properties are read-only. You cannot change them using this
approach.

**NOTE**

The statement in the example above is an expression, which we'll discuss in the
next section.

Exercise 14.2: If you're preparing to take the certification exam, or if
you want to practice what you learned in this section, turn to the
end of this chapter and complete Exercise 14.2. When you are done,
continue reading here to prepare for the next exercise.

## Processing Data

When you modify a JavaScript, you need to have some notion of how it works
so you can make it work the way you want.

As with Perl, JavaScript is an interpreted language. The JavaScript-enabled browser is the interpreter and it processes a single script statement at a time. Like Perl, JavaScript supports flow-control statements like if that change the script processing order. If no flow-control statements are used, the JavaScript statements are processed in order from first to last.

One of the major differences between Perl and JavaScript is that JavaScript is designed for the browser environment. JavaScript recognizes the objects created by HTML tags and, most importantly, works with them on the same page. One particularly useful JavaScript feature is the event handler that can launch a script when a Web page visitor performs an action, such as click a button or position the cursor over an object.

In this section, I'll introduce the following JavaScript features that are very similar to those described in Chapter 13 for Perl:

- Expressions

- Operators

- Flow control

- Functions

Next, I'll introduce the following new concepts:

- Methods

- Event handlers

## EXPRESSIONS

Expressions are those equations you perform with data. The following are sample expressions:

```
1+2+3+4

X<10*y

count=index+1
```

```
sentence=word1+" "+word2+" "+word3+"."

answer=document.form1.text1.value
```

Notice the use of the data types described earlier in this chapter. You should be able to pick out the literals, the variable names, and the property name.

The first expression above is an arithmetic expression, which evaluates to a number, and the second is a logical expression, which evaluates to be either True or False. You'll learn more about logical expressions in the next section. The last three expressions above are assignment expressions that assign a value to a variable.

Notice the fourth expression, which includes quotation marks. Literal strings, which are those that you don't want interpreted as variables, must be enclosed in quotation marks. In this example, word1, word2, and word3 are variables, and the quotation marks surround space characters that are added to the words.

**You can test your expressions using the JavaScript Interactive Window, which is described later in this chapter.**

NOTE

## OPERATORS

Expressions are built from literals, variables, property names (which are a form of variable), and operators. *Operators* are the symbols that tell JavaScript how to process the literals and variables in the expression. You are probably familiar with many of the JavaScript operators from courses in mathematics. A discussion of them is beyond the scope of this book, but for your convenience, Table 14.10 lists some of the JavaScript operators.

You are probably most familiar with arithmetic and assignment operators. *Arithmetic operators* define an equation that results in a number, and *assignment operators* assign that number to a variable.

*Comparison operators*, however, evaluate to a true or false value. For example, 5<3 evaluates to False, and 7==7 evaluates to true. Notice the double equal sign used in the last example. The single equal sign assigns a value to a variable. The double equal sign compares two values and evaluates to a True or False value.

T A B L E  1 4 . 1 0

*JavaScript Operators*

| OPERATOR TYPE | OPERATOR | DESCRIPTION |
| --- | --- | --- |
| Arithmetic | + | Addition |
| | − | Subtraction |
| | * | Multiplication |
| | / | Division |
| | % | Remainder |
| Assignment | = | Assign value to variable |
| Comparison | < | Less than |
| | > | Greater than |
| | <= | Lesser than or equal to |
| | >= | Greater than or equal to |
| | == | Equal to |
| | != | Not equal to |
| Logical | && | And |
| | \|\| | Or |
| | ! | Not |

The last type of operator introduced here is the *logical operator*, which can return a numeric value or a logical value. For example, the expression EXPR1||EXPR2 is false if the value of either EXPR1 or EXPR2 is false, otherwise, it returns the value of EXPR1. If the value of LIE is true, the value of !LIE is false.

**TIP**

**If you are new to programming, logical operators are a little harder to understand than the others. If you are preparing for the exam, you need to know the logical operators and their descriptions; you don't need to know how to use them.**

JavaScript also supports bitwise, string, and special operators.

## USING FLOW-CONTROL STATEMENTS

As with Perl, JavaScript supports if and else flow-control statements. Although I haven't introduced them yet, Perl and JavaScript also support loop flow-control structures. Flow-control statements enable you to change the flow of statement processing.

### IF Statements

The simplest form of a JavaScript if statement is as follows:

```
if (expression) {

  command_statements

}
```

Note that the only difference between the Perl and JavaScript if statements is that the Perl command statements require a semicolon at the end of each line.

The expression in the if statement is a comparison equation, which compares two values. The result of the comparison is either true or false. If the result is true, the command statements between the braces are executed. If the result is false, the command statements are ignored and program processing continues on the next line after the closing brace.

if statements are often called if, then statements because *if* the expression is true, *then* the command statements are executed. Let's look at an example:

```
<SCRIPT LANGUAGE="JavaScript">

if (document.form1.text1.value < 0) {

  document.write("The first number is negative.<br>")

}


if (document.form1.text2.value < 0) {

  document.write("The second number is negative.<br>")

}

</SCRIPT>
```

This script analyzes two form elements and prints the appropriate statements if one or both elements contain negative numbers.

### ELSE Statements

The `if` statement enables us to execute or omit a single command statement or a group of statements. The `if` and `else` statements enables us to choose to execute one group of statements or another group of statements. The format for `if` and `else` statements is as follows:

```
if (expression) {

  command_statements

} else {

  command_statements

}
```

This form of the if statement translates as follows: if the expression is true, execute the if command statements, otherwise (or else), execute the else command statements. Let's look at another example:

```
<SCRIPT LANGUAGE="JavaScript">

if (document.form1.text1.value < 0) {

  document.write("The number is negative.<br>")

}


else {

  document.write("The number is nonnegative.<br>")

}

</SCRIPT>
```

This script displays "The number is negative" if the value in the text box is negative. It displays "The number is nonnegative" if the text box contains anything other than a negative number.

### Loop-Control Statements

Loop-control statements enable you to execute one or more statements many times. Basically, the program repeats, or loops, through the statements until a specified condition becomes true. The statements might loop until (count==10) or (money<=0).

The following JavaScript statements are used to create loops:

> ▸ for

> ▸ while

> ▸ break

> ▸ continue

One of the easiest scripting mistakes to make is to create a loop that never ends. For example, if a loop was constructed to repeat until the count variable equals 10, but nothing in the script ever changed the count variable to 10, the loop would run forever; or at least until you shut down the browser. If you are modifying a script with loop statements, you might want to avoid making changes in that area of the script, or you might want to learn more about looping.

## USING FUNCTIONS

JavaScript enables you to use functions, which are special scripts that you use throughout a document. Function scripts are loaded into memory when a document loads, but they are not executed until they are called.

Functions provide the following benefits:

> ▸ A function makes one group of statements available to all the scripts in a document.

> ▸ Functions can be called from event handlers, which I cover later in this chapter. Basically, an event handler enables you to launch a function in response to a browser user's action, such as a mouse click or menu selection.

There are two types of functions, user-defined functions and built-in functions. The following two sections describe how to create a function and how to call a function, and a third section introduces some of the built-in JavaScript functions.

### Creating Functions

To create a function, create a JavaScript that includes the following statements:

```
function name(var)

{

script_statements

}
```

The keyword function identifies the function named *name*, which is made up of all the script statements between the opening and closing braces. If one or more values is passed to the function when the function is called, the values are called arguments, and the arguments are assigned to the variables defined in the parentheses following the function name. If the function does not use arguments, the parentheses following the name are empty.

**NOTE**

**Function names cannot use the reserved words listed in Table 14.1.**

Consider the following example:

```
<SCRIPT LANGUAGE="JavaScript">


function label1()

{

document.write(document.form1.text1.value)

}


function sum1(n)

{

total=n+10
```

```
document.write(total)

}


</SCRIPT>
```

In this example, the label1 function prints the text1 value property whenever it is called. The sum1 function does the following:

- ▸ Accepts an argument when it is called

- ▸ Assigns the argument received to variable n

- ▸ Assigns the sum of n + 10 to the variable total

- ▸ Writes the value of total in the document window

Note that you can create multiple functions within the same JavaScript. You can also create multiple scripts within the same document. The only requirement is that you must create a function before you call it. Because scripts are executed in the order in which they appear within the document, many script developers place their functions at the head of the document between the <HEAD> tags. For example:

```
<HTML>

<HEAD><TITLE>Sample Functions</TITLE>


<SCRIPT LANGUAGE="JavaScript">


function label1()

{

document.form1.text1.value=("Update!")

}
```

```
function sum1(n)

{

total=n+10

document.form1.text2.value=total

}


</SCRIPT>

</HEAD>

<BODY>


<FORM NAME=form1>

<INPUT TYPE=text NAME="text1">

<INPUT TYPE=text NAME="text2">

</FORM>


</BODY>

</HTML>
```

Notice that this document creates two empty text boxes. These text boxes are placeholders in which the functions can display results. Also notice that the functions are not called from anywhere within the script. You'll learn how to call functions in the next two sections.

### Calling Functions from Scripts

The following document defines a function and calls the function:

```
<HTML>

<HEAD><TITLE>Sample Function</TITLE>
```

```
<SCRIPT LANGUAGE="JavaScript">


function label1()

{

document.form1.text1.value=("Update!")

}


</SCRIPT>

</HEAD>

<BODY>

<FORM NAME=form1>

<INPUT TYPE=text NAME="text1">

</FORM>

<SCRIPT>

label1()

</SCRIPT>

</BODY>

</HTML>
```

The label1() statement within the <BODY> tags calls the label1 function, which changes the value displayed in the text1 text box to "Update!"

### Built-in Functions

JavaScript includes built-in functions that you can call using the function statement introduced in the previous section. Table 14.11 lists three built-in functions.

TABLE 14.11

*Built-In JavaScript Functions*

| FUNCTION | DESCRIPTION |
|----------|-------------|
| eval | The eval function evaluates a string variable as if it were a mathematical expression or program statement. Consider the following example: `eval ("2+2")`. In this example, the argument includes the quotes and the expression. The quotes around the expression indicate string data, but the eval function evaluates the argument as an expression. |
| parseInt | The parseInt function converts a string variable to an integer value. For example, `parseInt ("2.66")` converts the string "2.66" to the number 2. |
| parseFloat | The parseFloat function converts a string variable to a floating-point value. For example, `parseFloat ("2.66")` converts the string "2.66" to the number 2.66. |

## USING EVENTS AND EVENT HANDLERS

Event handlers give JavaScript developers a great deal of control over Web pages. Event handlers enable JavaScript developers to execute JavaScripts when users access form elements, such as buttons and text boxes, and when users load or unload a document. Use the mouse—go to JavaScript. Load a document—go to JavaScript.

Event handlers are particularly useful for validating form data before the form is processed. You can use event handlers to launch scripts that check to see if a user entered the right number of digits for a telephone number or selected a valid combination of options from several option lists. When forms are processed on a Web server, preprocessing the forms with JavaScript can reduce the load on the Web server and reduce network traffic.

Event handlers are attributes that are entered into the HTML tags for the objects they monitor. The format for event handlers is as follows:

```
<tag attributes event="JavaScript_code">
```

*Tag* represents the HTML tag that defines the object that the event handler will monitor, and attributes are the HTML attributes that the tag supports. Event is the name of the event that triggers the execution of the JavaScript_code, which can be a JavaScript expression or function.

The following example shows how an event handler can be used to call a function:

```
<HTML>

<HEAD><TITLE>Sample Function</TITLE>


<SCRIPT LANGUAGE="JavaScript">


function label1()

{

document.form1.text1.value=("I've been pressed!")

}


</SCRIPT>

</HEAD>

<BODY>

<FORM NAME=form1>

<INPUT TYPE=button NAME="button1" VALUE="Press Me"
onClick="label1()">

<INPUT TYPE=text NAME="text1">

</FORM>

</BODY>

</HTML>
```

The onClick attribute in the button definition tag is the event handler. When this document loads, the Press Me button appears on the page next to an empty text box. Nothing happens until the user clicks the button, which calls the label1 function. The label1 function changes the value of the text box so that it reads "I've been pressed!"

Table 14.12 lists the JavaScript events.

TABLE 14.12

*JavaScript Events*

| EVENT | OBJECTS SUPPORTED | DESCRIPTION |
| --- | --- | --- |
| onAbort | image | The user aborted the loading of an image. For example, the user might have clicked the Stop button or a link. The event handler becomes an attribute of the `<IMG>` tag. |
| onBlur | select, text, textarea | The option list has been deselected. The user clicked another object, pressed the tab key, or pressed Enter. |
| onChange | select, text, textarea | A selected object has been deselected after its value was changed. The user changed the value and then selected another object. |
| onClick | button, checkbox, radio, link, reset, submit | Mouse click on object. |
| onError | image, window | An error occurred while an image or document was loading. This event handler is an attribute of the following tags: `<IMG>`, `<BODY>`, and `<FRAMESET>`. |
| onFocus | select, text, textarea | The object has been selected. The user clicked on the object, pressed the tab key to select it, or pressed Enter and the object was selected. |
| onLoad | window | A browser window has loaded. The event handler becomes an attribute of the opening `<BODY>` or `<FRAMESET>` tag. |
| onMouseOut | area, link | The mouse point moved outside the area defined by the client-side image map or link. This event handler attribute appears in the following tags: `<AREA>` and `<A>`. |
| onMouseOver | link | Mouse pointer has moved over a link on the Web page. The event handler becomes an attribute of the anchor tag that defines the link. |
| onReset | form | The user clicked the reset button. |
| onSelect | text, textarea | The user selected an option or text within the object. |
| onSubmit | form | A user has selected the submit button for a form. |
| onUnload | window | A browser window has been unloaded. The event handler becomes an attribute of the opening `<BODY>` or `<FRAMESET>` tag. |

## USING METHODS

JavaScript methods are functions that are assigned to a JavaScript object. Throughout this chapter, I've demonstrated scripts using the write method, which is a built-in method that displays data in the browser window. To call a method, you use the following statement format:

```
object_name.method_name(args)
```

The procedure for calling a method is almost identical to that for calling a function. The difference is that you specify an object name and method name instead of a function name. In the previous example, *object_name* refers to the complete object name that identifies the object containing the method. The *method_name* refers to a built-in or user-defined method that has been assigned to the object. As with functions, methods can accept and process arguments.

To create a new method, create a function and then assign the function to an object method with a statement, such as the following:

```
object_name.method_name = function_name
```

The *object_name* identifies the object you are assigning the function to, and *method_name* is the name you assign to the method. The method name can be any name that doesn't conflict with the reserved words in Table 14.1 or with other names you've assigned in the script.

Methods are useful because you can use one statement to take action on a single object. Without methods, you would have to enter multiple statements to take action on data and then separately assign it to an object. The following sections describe the write and writeln methods and introduce other built-in methods.

### The Write and Writeln Methods

The write method uses the following form:

```
document.write(message_or_expression)
```

**TIP**

**You can use the + operator within the parentheses to combine messages and expressions. In the following example, the second secret is a variable:**

```
document.write("The secret to success is: " + secret + ".")
```

Two methods for document objects are write and writeln. The difference between these objects is that the writeln method appends a newline character to the end of the message it writes in the document. This newline character is ignored by HTML unless it appears between the preformatted text tags, <PRE> and </PRE>. Consider the following example:

```
<HTML>
<HEAD><TITLE>Writeln example.</TITLE>
</HEAD>
<BODY>
<PRE>
<SCRIPT LANGUAGE="JavaScript">
document.writeln("This is line 1.")
document.writeln("This is line 2.")
</SCRIPT>
</PRE>
</BODY>
</HTML>
```

In this example, the two messages, "This is line 1." and "This is line 2.," appear on separate lines. If the <PRE> tags were omitted, the newline characters would be ignored and the two messages would appear on the same line.

One interesting feature about the write and writeln methods is that their results cannot be printed from the browser. If a browser user prints the document, any data that was displayed using these methods is omitted from the printed document. Some sites use this method to prevent data from being printed. However, the browser user can still copy the text from the browser, paste it somewhere else, and then print it.

### Other Built-in Methods

The write method always writes data to a document, so you'll always see the write method use with the document object. The click method, however, can be used with the following objects: button, checkbox, radio, reset, and submit. The click method simulates a mouse click on the specified object. For example:

```
button.click()
```

JavaScript includes built-in methods for most of the objects that you can use in your scripts. Table 14.13 lists the methods for the Window object. For more information on methods, refer to: developer.netscape.com/library/documentation/communicator/jsguide4/index.htm.

| TABLE 14.13 | METHOD | DESCRIPTION |
| --- | --- | --- |
| Window Methods | alert("*message*") | Displays an alert dialog box that contains a message and an OK button. |
| | confirm("*message*") | Displays a confirm dialog box that contains a message, an OK button, and a Cancel button. |
| | prompt("*message*", "*default value*") | Displays a prompt dialog box that contains a message and an input field. *Default value* specifies the default value for the input field. |
| | open("*URL*", "*windowName*", "*windowFeatures*") | Opens a new browser window. |
| | close() | Closes the current browser window. |
| | setTimeout(*expression, msec*) | Delays the execution of *expression* until the number of milliseconds specified by *msec* has expired. |
| | clearTimeout(*timeoutID*) | Cancels the specified timer. To enable this method for a timer, you must specify a timeoutID when the setTimeout() method is defined as follows: timeoutID=setTimeout(*expression, msec*) |

 **Exercises 14.3 and 14.4: If you're preparing to take the certification exam, or if you want to practice what you learned in this section, turn to the end of this chapter and complete Exercises 14.3 and 14.4. When you are done, continue reading here to prepare for the next exercise.**

## Using the JavaScript Interactive Window

One of the Netscape Navigator features is a special window that you can use to test your JavaScript expressions. To access this window from within Navigator, specify the following URL: `javascript:`. Figure 14.6 shows the JavaScript interactive window that appears. You can also launch the JavaScript window from a Web page link using the HREF attribute as follows: `HREF=JavaScript:`.

**FIGURE 14.6**

*Interactive JavaScript: Window*

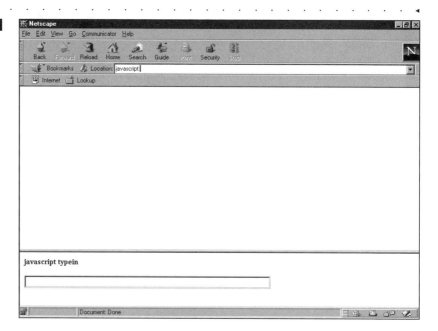

When you use the JavaScript window with expressions that contain variables, the value of the variable on the left side of the equal sign is displayed in the upper window pane. JavaScript displays an error message if you use an undefined variable on the right side of the equal sign. To define a variable for use in another expression, simply enter an expression that assigns the appropriate value to the variable name. Then enter the expression you want to test. JavaScript remembers the values of all of the variables.

Consider the following example:

```
word1="The"
```

```
word2="rain"

word3="falls"

sentence=word1+" "+word2+" "+word3+"."
```

If you enter these expressions in the order listed above, the JavaScript window displays them as shown in Figure 14.7.

**F I G U R E   14.7**

*Using the JavaScript:*
*Window*

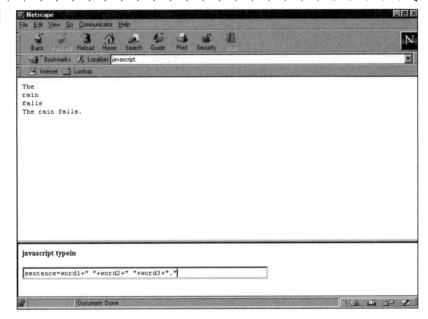

## Linking to JavaScript Functions and Methods

In the previous section, you learned how to open the JavaScript interactive window with the `javascript:` URL. You can also use this URL to execute JavaScript functions and methods when a Web page visitor activates a text or image link. To create a link to a JavaScript function or method, create a link similar to the following:

```
<A HREF="javascript:function(args)>Execute JavaScript
function.</A>
```

You can replace *function* with the name of a function or a method. The *args* variable defines the argument or arguments you want to pass to the function or method.

## Two Kinds of JavaScripts

There are two kinds of JavaScripts: client-side and server-side JavaScripts. The JavaScripts described earlier in this chapter are client-side JavaScripts, which are processed by the browser. As you might guess, server-side JavaScripts are processed by a server.

The most obvious difference between client-side and server-side JavaScripts is the tag you use to start them. Client-side JavaScripts are started with the <SCRIPT> tag, and server-side JavaScripts are started with the <SERVER> tag. Just as client-side JavaScripts can run only on browsers that support JavaScript, server-side JavaScripts only run on servers that support JavaScript. Currently, the following Web servers support server-side JavaScript:

▸ Netscape LiveWire servers

▸ Netscape FastTrack Server for NetWare

▸ Netscape Enterprise Server for NetWare

▸ Netscape FastTrack Server

▸ Netscape Enterprise Server

The differences between client-side and server-side JavaScript are greater than the tags that start them. To create server-side JavaScripts, you need programming experience, and before Web page authors can use them, they must be loaded on the server with the JavaScript Application Manager. Server-side JavaScript offers the following features that are not available with client-side JavaScript:

▸ Support for additional objects including server objects

▸ Support for open database connectivity

▶ Support for the construction of Web site management tools

Client-side JavaScripts can only control the browser interface and cannot access server objects or write data to client files.

The rest of this chapter discusses client-side JavaScripts. For more information on server-side JavaScripts, see the documentation provided with your Web server.

## Modifying JavaScripts

Now that you are familiar with all the parts of a JavaScript, you should be able to create simple JavaScripts on your own. If you aren't ready to write the killer script you need, you can learn more about JavaScript or surf the Web and see if someone else has already written it. Many JavaScripts are published on the Web and are free for the taking. Let's review what is needed to modify a JavaScript for use on your Web page.

To modify a JavaScript, you need to do the following:

1 • If there are any instructions provided with the JavaScript, read them. The procedure you are reading now is a general procedure. JavaScript developers can provide specific instructions that will tell you which variables must be modified, what form elements are required, or which additional files are required.

2 • Copy the script to your HTML document, or copy the entire HTML document that contains the script. In many situations, the best way to copy a script is to copy the complete HTML document in which the script resides. After you verify that the unmodified document works in your environment, you can make changes. If a change breaks the script, you'll know where to begin troubleshooting.

3 • If you did not copy an entire HTML document, do the following:

a. If the script is not a function, copy it to the location, between the `<BODY>` tags, at which you want the script to execute.

b. Review the script for embedded functions that should be moved to the head of the document. If the script is a function, it is a good practice to store it between the <HEAD> tags at the top of the document.

c. Review the script for references to objects that you need in your document.

d. If the script requires objects, such as form elements, create them with HTML tags and set the NAME attributes to match the names used in the script.

**4** • Run the script in your local browser to see if it works as you expect.

If your JavaScript displays errors, refer to the troubleshooting section later in this chapter.

## Security Issues

While it would be unprofessional to tell you how to misuse JavaScripts, it would also be irresponsible to not tell you how others might misuse them. The following are JavaScript features that have the potential to be misused by JavaScript developers:

▶ A JavaScript can track all the URLs that you visit and send them to an Internet host.

▶ A JavaScript can be used to trick a user into entering a password that is not used for authentication. The user's password is compromised when it is sent to an Internet host or when someone captures it with network monitoring equipment.

▶ A JavaScript can be used to trick a user into uploading a file to the Internet.

▶ Some JavaScript programs that are launched by the onUnload method remain active in memory until you quit the browser program.

If you are concerned that a Web site might be misusing JavaScripts, you can disable JavaScript processing as described earlier in this chapter.

## JavaScript Versus Java

In the next chapter, you'll learn how to use Java applets in your Web pages. Although Java and JavaScript sound like close brothers, they are more like step-brothers. These products were developed by different companies and brought together through a partnership. Table 14.14 compares JavaScript and Java.

The difference between object based and object oriented is the relationship between objects. As you've seen in this chapter, the relationship between JavaScript objects is indicated in the object name (for example, frame1.document1.-form1.button1). In JavaScript, that is the extent of the relationship. Objects cannot exchange messages with other objects, and they cannot inherit properties from parent objects. For example, an object does not inherit a background color assigned to its parent object.

In object-oriented Java, however, objects can inherit properties from their parent object. This is called single inheritance. Other programming languages, such as C++, permit multiple inheritance, which enables an object to inherit properties from several parent objects.

In Table 14.14, binding refers to the process of creating an object and making it available to the program. JavaScript uses dynamic binding, which allows objects to be defined while the script is running. Java applets, however, use static binding, so all objects must be defined before the application is compiled.

**TABLE 14.14**

*JavaScript vs. Java*

| JAVASCRIPT | JAVA |
| --- | --- |
| Developed by Netscape Communications Corporation. | Developed by Sun Microsystems. |
| Runs in a JavaScript-enabled browser. | Runs in a Java-enabled browser. |
| JavaScripts can be embedded in HTML files or called from external files. | Java applets are called from HTML files. |

**T A B L E  14.14**

*JavaScript vs. Java*

| JAVASCRIPT | JAVA |
|---|---|
| Client-side JavaScripts are interpreted by the browser. Server-side JavaScripts are interpreted by a server. | Java applets are compiled *bytecode* applications that can be launched by Java-enabled browsers. |
| Nonprogrammers can learn to create client-side JavaScripts. Server-side JavaScripts require programming experience. | To create effective Java applets requires some programming experience. |
| JavaScripts interact with the entire Web page. | Java applets run in a dedicated square area of the Web page, which is unavailable for HTML output. |
| When writing JavaScripts, you do not have to declare variable types (for example, number or string). | When writing Java applets, you must declare variable types. |
| JavaScript is object based. | Java is object oriented. |
| JavaScript uses dynamic binding. | Java applets use static binding. |

# Getting More Information on JavaScript

In this chapter, you've learned to create simple JavaScripts that help you access forms. JavaScripts are frequently used for other purposes too. For example, people have created JavaScript games, calendars, clocks, navigation controls, and more. Take some time to learn more about JavaScript and see what you can do.

**To locate free JavaScripts, visit the following sites:**

**The JavaScript Source:** `javascriptsource.com/`

**WWW.JavaScripts.Com:** `www.javascripts.com/`

**HTML Goodies:** `www.htmlgoodies.com/javagoodies/`

**For more information on JavaScript, browse the following:**

**JavaScript Guide:**
```
developer.netscape.com/library/documentation/
communicator/jsguide4/index.htm
```

**JavaScript FAQ: www.innergy.com/faq/js-faq.shtml**
**Developer.com:**
```
www.developer.com/directories/pages/dir.java.html
```

**JavaScript Sample Code:**
```
developer.netscape.com/library/examples/javascript.html
```

**The following Internet newsgroups provide information about JavaScript:**

```
news://news.livesoftware.com/livesoftware.
javascript.examples
```

```
news://news.livesoftware.com/livesoftware.
javascript.developer
```

## Troubleshooting

The first step in troubleshooting a JavaScript is to look for error messages in the browser window. Table 14.15 lists some common symptoms and the problems that cause them.

**TABLE 14.15**

*Common Problems and
Their Symptoms*

| SYMPTOM | PROBLEM |
|---|---|
| JavaScript error message: *name* is not defined. | The variable or function *name* is undefined. A variable name must be defined on the left side of an expression before it can be used on the right side of an expression. If *name* is used in a function call, the function might be misplaced in the file, or it might be missing. Try using the Find command in your editor program to locate the missing function. If you can't find the function, you'll have to create it, get it from someone else, or remove (or comment out) the function call. |
| A script does not appear to run. | There might be an error in the script. Look for misplaced HTML comment tags that comment out one or both of the `<SCRIPT>` tags. Are both the `<SCRIPT>` tags in place? Your expressions might contain errors. Try executing them in the JavaScript: Interactive Window. |
| A property name does not appear to be working. | The property name does not correctly identify the property. Object and property names are case-sensitive. For example, bgColor is not the same as bgcolor. When an object or property is below the current window in the hierarchy, object and property names must include all objects between the current window and the object or property name. When an object or property belongs to another window in the hierarchy, object and property names must include all objects between the topmost window and the object or property name. |
| The JavaScript interpreter reports an error in a particular line, but the line looks OK. | The error might be in the preceding line. Also, verify that all quotation marks appear in pairs. |
| The document.write method won't print function data in the document window. | The document.write method can only write data in the document window when the Web page is being built. If you need to write data on the Web page after the Web page is built, create a textbox or textarea in which you can display the data. |

**Exercise 14.5: To review your knowledge of the JavaScript topics presented in the latter part of this chapter, turn to the end of this chapter and complete Exercise 14.5.**

## Summary

In this chapter, you learned how to create your first JavaScript. JavaScripts run in the browser and can be placed in a Web page or in a separate file. To run JavaScripts, the browser must be designed to support them. Browser users can choose to disable JavaScript processing.

As with other programming languages, JavaScript has certain punctuation requirements. JavaScript also supports many types of variables, including the variable data entered in HTML forms.

To process data, you can create JavaScript expressions, and you can test these expressions in the JavaScript interactive window. You can use these expressions to build your own JavaScripts, or you can modify other people's JavaScripts.

As with most tools, on the Web, JavaScript has its security issues. People usually figure out a way to misuse everything. If you suspect a mischievous Web site, you can disable JavaScript processing in your browser to eliminate the risk.

Near the end of this chapter, you learned about some of the differences between JavaScript and Java. In the next chapter, you'll get some firsthand experience as you learn to use Java applets.

**PUZZLE 14.1: USING JAVASCRIPTS**

The following word puzzle contains many of the terms discussed in this chapter. See if you can find all the words. As you search for the words, ask yourself why the word is in the list and how it was used in this chapter. If you don't know the answers to these questions, you might want to review the chapter.

```
P  R  E  P  R  O  C  E  S  S  I  N  G  R  B
E  V  I  T  C  A  R  E  T  N  I  W  I  O  O
L  A  R  E  T  I  L  S  T  A  T  U  S  T  O
X  S  E  C  N  E  R  E  F  E  R  P  N  A  L
J  N  P  A  J  I  R  I  H  P  E  E  G  R  E
A  O  A  F  A  P  O  T  Z  M  V  N  Y  E  A
V  I  C  R  R  B  L  R  B  E  E  H  C  P  N
A  S  S  E  Y  L  S  E  M  I  C  O  L  O  N
S  S  T  T  U  T  D  P  L  R  N  A  I  B  T
C  E  E  N  E  D  I  O  A  B  N  T  R  J  N
R  R  N  I  E  F  G  R  H  G  A  U  F  E  E
I  P  N  D  L  I  E  P  U  T  K  I  O  C  R
P  X  N  O  C  I  O  A  O  C  E  F  R  T  A
T  E  W  A  H  O  G  U  O  X  E  M  M  A  P
S  E  L  F  L  E  Q  B  R  O  W  S  E  R  V
```

| | | | |
|---|---|---|---|
| Boolean | interactive | method | properties |
| browser | interface | Netscape | quotation |
| embedded | interpreter | null | security |
| event | JavaScript | object | self |
| expression | language | operator | semicolon |
| flow | literal | parent | status |
| form | logical | preferences | top |
| hierarchy | loop | preprocessing | variable |

## EXERCISE 14.1: JAVASCRIPT BASICS

Review your knowledge of the JavaScript basics presented in this chapter by answering the following questions:

**1** • Compared to the other programming languages discussed in this chapter, how complex is JavaScript?

Answer: . . . . . . . . . . . . . . . . . . . . . . . . . . . . . . . . . . . . . . . . .

**2** • With respect to BASIC, is JavaScript considered to be easier to learn, more difficult, or comparable?

Answer: . . . . . . . . . . . . . . . . . . . . . . . . . . . . . . . . . . . . . . . . .

**3** • What are the benefits of form preprocessing with JavaScript?

Answer: . . . . . . . . . . . . . . . . . . . . . . . . . . . . . . . . . . . . . . . . .

**4** • What should you do if you want to visit a Web site and you are concerned that the Web site is misusing JavaScripts?

Answer: . . . . . . . . . . . . . . . . . . . . . . . . . . . . . . . . . . . . . . . . .

**5** • Which HTML tag do you use to begin or call a client-side JavaScript?

Answer: . . . . . . . . . . . . . . . . . . . . . . . . . . . . . . . . . . . . . . . . .

**6** • Which attribute do you place in the opening script tag to call JavaScript commands in another file?

Answer: . . . . . . . . . . . . . . . . . . . . . . . . . . . . . . . . . . . . . . . . .

**7** • Write the complete opening tag that begins a JavaScript that is embedded in the HTML document.

Answer: . . . . . . . . . . . . . . . . . . . . . . . . . . . . . . . . . . . . . . . . .

8 • What character must appear at the end of each JavaScript statement?

Answer: . . . . . . . . . . . . . . . . . . . . . . . . . . . . . . . . . . . . . . .

9 • What character sequence begins a single-line comment?

Answer: . . . . . . . . . . . . . . . . . . . . . . . . . . . . . . . . . . . . . . .

10 • What character sequence begins a multiple-line comment?

Answer: . . . . . . . . . . . . . . . . . . . . . . . . . . . . . . . . . . . . . . .

11 • Write the characters you can use to begin hiding JavaScript statements from browsers that do not support JavaScript.

Answer: . . . . . . . . . . . . . . . . . . . . . . . . . . . . . . . . . . . . . . .

12 • What happens if you place the characters described in the previous question before the starting script tag?

Answer: . . . . . . . . . . . . . . . . . . . . . . . . . . . . . . . . . . . . . . .

13 • Write the line you can use to end the hiding of JavaScript statements from browsers that don't support JavaScript.

Answer: . . . . . . . . . . . . . . . . . . . . . . . . . . . . . . . . . . . . . . .

14 • Does the line you entered for the previous question belong before or after the closing script tag?

Answer: . . . . . . . . . . . . . . . . . . . . . . . . . . . . . . . . . . . . . . .

## EXERCISE 14.2: USING LATERALS, VARIABLES, AND OBJECTS

Review your knowledge of the JavaScript literals, variables, and objects introduced in this chapter by answering the following questions:

1 • What is *string* data?

   Answer: . . . . . . . . . . . . . . . . . . . . . . . . . . . . . . . . . . . . . .

2 • What are the two possible values of Boolean data?

   Answer: . . . . . . . . . . . . . . . . . . . . . . . . . . . . . . . . . . . . . .

3 • Can variable names begin with a number?

   Answer: . . . . . . . . . . . . . . . . . . . . . . . . . . . . . . . . . . . . . .

4 • Can variable names contain space characters?

   Answer: . . . . . . . . . . . . . . . . . . . . . . . . . . . . . . . . . . . . . .

5 • What are reserved words?

   Answer: . . . . . . . . . . . . . . . . . . . . . . . . . . . . . . . . . . . . . .

6 • What does the object hierarchy define?

   Answer: . . . . . . . . . . . . . . . . . . . . . . . . . . . . . . . . . . . . . .

7 • Is a radio button an object or a property?

   Answer: . . . . . . . . . . . . . . . . . . . . . . . . . . . . . . . . . . . . . .

8 • How can you add objects to a Web page?

   Answer: . . . . . . . . . . . . . . . . . . . . . . . . . . . . . . . . . . . . . .

**9** • Write the property name that refers to the title property in a document named *doc* that appears in a frame named *frame1* in a window named *window1*.

Answer: . . . . . . . . . . . . . . . . . . . . . . . . . . . . . . . . . . . . . . . . .

**10** • Write the property name that accesses the contents of a text box named *comments* in a form named *survey* that appears in the same document.

Answer: . . . . . . . . . . . . . . . . . . . . . . . . . . . . . . . . . . . . . . . . .

**EXERCISE 14.3: PROCESSING DATA WITH JAVASCRIPTS**

Review your knowledge of the data-processing concepts presented in this chapter by answering the following questions:

**1** • What is the difference between an arithmetic expression and an assignment expression?

Answer: . . . . . . . . . . . . . . . . . . . . . . . . . . . . . . . . . . . . .

**2** • What are the possible values for a logical expression?

Answer: . . . . . . . . . . . . . . . . . . . . . . . . . . . . . . . . . . . . .

**3** • List two JavaScript statements that are used for flow control.

a. . . . . . . . . . . . . . . . . . . . . . . . . . . . . . . . . . . . . . . . .

b. . . . . . . . . . . . . . . . . . . . . . . . . . . . . . . . . . . . . . . . .

**4** • What are the two types of functions?

a. . . . . . . . . . . . . . . . . . . . . . . . . . . . . . . . . . . . . . . . .

b. . . . . . . . . . . . . . . . . . . . . . . . . . . . . . . . . . . . . . . . .

**5** • List two benefits of functions.

a. . . . . . . . . . . . . . . . . . . . . . . . . . . . . . . . . . . . . . . . .

b. . . . . . . . . . . . . . . . . . . . . . . . . . . . . . . . . . . . . . . . .

**6** • What is the term used to describe values that are passed from a script to a function?

Answer: . . . . . . . . . . . . . . . . . . . . . . . . . . . . . . . . . . . . .

**7** • Write the opening statement that defines a function name *whoopee* that accepts one value that is stored in a variable named *cushion*.

Answer: . . . . . . . . . . . . . . . . . . . . . . . . . . . . . . . . . . . . .

**8** · Write the JavaScript statement that passes the value named *pin* to the function described in the previous question.

Answer: . . . . . . . . . . . . . . . . . . . . . . . . . . . . . . . . . . . . .

**9** · List the three built-in functions introduced in this chapter.

a. . . . . . . . . . . . . . . . . . . . . . . . . . . . . . . . . . . . . . . .

b. . . . . . . . . . . . . . . . . . . . . . . . . . . . . . . . . . . . . . . .

c. . . . . . . . . . . . . . . . . . . . . . . . . . . . . . . . . . . . . . . .

**10** · Write a JavaScript statement that evaluates an expression stored in a variable named *express* and stores the result in a variable named *result*.

Answer: . . . . . . . . . . . . . . . . . . . . . . . . . . . . . . . . . . . . .

**11** · The onClick attribute is an example of what type of JavaScript control?

Answer: . . . . . . . . . . . . . . . . . . . . . . . . . . . . . . . . . . . . .

**12** · Write an HTML tag that creates a button named *compute* and passes the value of a variable named *expression* to a function named *calculator* when the button is clicked.

Answer: . . . . . . . . . . . . . . . . . . . . . . . . . . . . . . . . . . . . .

**13** · What is the difference between a method and a function?

Answer: . . . . . . . . . . . . . . . . . . . . . . . . . . . . . . . . . . . . .

## EXERCISE 14.4: CREATING A JAVASCRIPT

In this exercise, you will add JavaScript statements to a Web page to turn a form into a simple calculator. To complete this exercise, do the following:

**1** • Use a text-editor or word-processor program to open the following file on this book's CD-ROM:

   *d:/DemoWeb2/Answers/calc.htm*

**2** • In the document head, add a function named *calculator* that accepts an argument named *express*.

**3** • In the calculator function, enter a statement that uses the built-in eval function to evaluate the value in the variable named *express* and assigns this value to the text box named *result*.

**4** • In the tag that defines the Compute button, add the event handler that will respond to a mouse click by calling the calculator function and passing the value of the text box named *expression* to that function.

**5** • Save the edited file to a local drive using the name calc2.htm.

**6** • Open the edited file in your browser, enter an expression (such as 2+2) in the appropriate text box, and click Compute. If you completed the exercise correctly, the JavaScript displays the expression result in the appropriate text box. If you have trouble with this exercise, you can view the answer file on the CD at:

   *d:/DemoWeb2/Answers/calc2.htm*

## EXERCISE 14.5: UNDERSTANDING JAVASCRIPT

Review your knowledge of the JavaScript topics presented in the latter part of this chapter by answering the following questions:

**1** • What is the JavaScript feature you can use to test JavaScript statements without creating a new JavaScript file or Web page?

Answer: . . . . . . . . . . . . . . . . . . . . . . . . . . . . . . . . . . . . . .

**2** • What is the URL that displays the feature described in the previous question?

Answer: . . . . . . . . . . . . . . . . . . . . . . . . . . . . . . . . . . . . . .

**3** • What tag should you use to start a server-side JavaScript?

Answer: . . . . . . . . . . . . . . . . . . . . . . . . . . . . . . . . . . . . . .

**4** • Is JavaScript immune to security attacks?

Answer: . . . . . . . . . . . . . . . . . . . . . . . . . . . . . . . . . . . . . .

**5** • Is JavaScript object based or object oriented?

Answer: . . . . . . . . . . . . . . . . . . . . . . . . . . . . . . . . . . . . . .

**6** • Does JavaScript use static or dynamic binding?

Answer: . . . . . . . . . . . . . . . . . . . . . . . . . . . . . . . . . . . . . .

**7** • Do JavaScript objects inherit properties from other objects?

Answer: . . . . . . . . . . . . . . . . . . . . . . . . . . . . . . . . . . . . . .

**8** • If you suspect that a JavaScript is still running after you change Web pages, how can you stop the JavaScript?

Answer: . . . . . . . . . . . . . . . . . . . . . . . . . . . . . . . . . . . . . . . . .

# CHAPTER 15

# Using Java Applets

In this chapter, you'll learn how to use Java applets to give that extra jolt to your Web pages. As with the chapters on SSI, CGI, Perl, and JavaScript, the goal of this chapter is to help you create dynamic Web pages, which are those Web pages that offer interactivity, animation, sounds, and other features that make your Web page more useful or just plain cool.

## What Is Java?

Java is a programming language that is less complex than C++ and more complex than JavaScript and BASIC. The following list shows how Novell Education rates the complexity of Java with other programming languages:

C++
C
Java
Pascal, Perl
JavaScript, BASIC

As this list shows, shows, Java is considered more complex than Perl and JavaScript, which are described in Chapters 13 and 14. Don't worry about this. Java is more complex for programmers, but we're not going to learn to program Java. We're going to learn how to accent Web pages with Java applets that other people have written.

Java applets are small, precompiled Java applications that run in Java-enabled Web browsers. When a Web page visitor links to your Java-powered Web page, the Web server downloads the Web page first and then downloads the Java applet. As with Web page images, a Java applet is a separate file that the browser calls after it finds an HTML tag in the Web page.

When the browser receives the Java applet, it starts up the applet and displays the applet results in a special Java window within the Web page. As a Web page author, you define the size and location of this Java applet window using HTML tags in your Web document. Unless you are a programmer, you won't ever see the source code for an applet. Instead, you'll configure the applet using HTML tags that the applet supports. Compared to Perl and JavaScripts—this is *easy*!

# Why Use Java?

The main reason to use Java applets on your Web pages is to make them more useful or more fun. With Java applets, you can do the following:

- ▸ Display animations

- ▸ Play audio files

- ▸ Perform calculations and graph results

- ▸ Display controls that allow users to interact with the applet

- ▸ Enable secure communications between the applet and other network applications

Table 15.1 lists some of the advantages of Java applets. Table 15.2 lists some of their disadvantages.

| **T A B L E  15.1** | FEATURE | DESCRIPTION |
|---|---|---|
| *Java Applet Advantages* | Easy to call from Web pages | Easy is better, right? |
| | Built-in security | Java enables higher levels of security than SSI and CGI. Applets can provide secure two-way interaction between hosts and can pass URLs in such a way that they are hidden from Web users. Some of the built-in security features are discussed later in this chapter. |
| | Platform independence | Platform independence enables developers to write one program that runs on many different operating systems. Developers get more customers for their programs, and we get more programs to choose from. |
| | Less complex than C++ and more reliable | Again, this should entice more developers to create programs for us. |

*(continued)*

| TABLE 15.1 | FEATURE | DESCRIPTION |
|---|---|---|
| *Java Applet Advantages (continued)* | Supports both applet and application development | This feature offers more functionality for future applications. Later in this chapter, in the section titled "Java on NetWare," you'll see that Novell has products that allow you to run both Java applets and Java applications on a NetWare server. |
| | Object orientation through extensible classes | This feature offers programmers more opportunities to develop cool applications for us. |

| TABLE 15.2 | FEATURE | DESCRIPTION |
|---|---|---|
| *Java Applet Disadvantages* | Fewer applications available | As Java is relatively new, it will take time to develop a selection of Java applications. |
| | Relatively slow performance | Without a just-in-time (JIT) compiler, Java applets can run up to 20 times slower than equivalent programs that are developed in C or C++. JIT compilers speed up Java processing. |
| | Requires programming skills to develop | If you don't know how to program in Java, you have several choices. You can learn, you can hire a programmer, or you can make do with the applets you find on the Web. |
| | Won't run in Windows 3.x | Java applets run on 32-bit multitasking operating systems that support long filenames. |
| | May require additional memory on NetWare servers | If a NetWare server is not already supporting long filenames for other operating systems, it must be extended to use the longer filenames used by Java programs and applets. You learn more about this later in this chapter. |

# Preparing the Browser

Before you view Java applets with a browser, you must acquire a browser that supports Java. By default, most Java browsers enable Java applet support. However, there may be times when you want to disable Java processing. The following sections introduce browsers that support Java and describe how to enable and disable Java processing.

## CHOOSING A BROWSER

Java is designed to be platform independent and run on multitasking operating systems. Java applets use a five-digit extension, so they must run on operating systems that support long filenames. The following operating systems meet the Java requirements:

- Windows 95

- Windows NT

- Macintosh

- UNIX

- OS/2

To view Java applets in a browser, you must use a Java-enabled browser. The following browsers support Java:

- Netscape Navigator 2.01 or later (32-bit)

- Microsoft Internet Explorer 3.0 or later

- HotJava by Sun Microsystems

## ENABLING AND DISABLING JAVA IN THE BROWSER

Before you can use Java applets, you must have a Java-enabled browser (such as those introduced in the previous section). Later in this chapter, we'll look at some Java security issues. If you want to use Java applets, you must enable the feature in the browser. If you have security concerns, you can disable Java-applet processing.

### Enabling and Disabling Java in Netscape Navigator 4

To enable or disable Java applet processing in Navigator 4, do the following:

1 • Select Edit→Preferences, and then select the Advanced category.

2 • To enable or disable Java applet processing, check or clear the Enable Java checkbox.

3 • Click OK.

**NOTE**

**If you have a Java applet running when you disable Java, simply reloading the page might not stop the applet. Try pressing the Shift key when you click Reload. If this doesn't work, quit and restart the browser to purge the Java applet from memory.**

### Enabling and Disabling Java in Internet Explorer 3.0

To enable or disable Java-applet processing in Internet Explorer 3.0, do the following:

1 • Open Internet Explorer 3.0.

2 • Select View→Options.

3 • Select the Security tab.

4 • Check or clear the Enable Java programs checkbox.

## Preparing the Novell Web Server

Because Java applets use five-digit extensions, the default DOS name space on NetWare server volumes cannot support them. The easy solution to this problem is to add a name space that supports long filenames. The following name spaces support long filenames and are provided with NetWare servers:

▸ LONG.NAM (provided with NetWare 4.11)

▸ OS2.NAM (provided with NetWare 4.1)

Because other operating systems use long filenames, it is best to check your Web server before you install long filename support. It might already be there! If you do need to install the long filename support, you must verify that you have enough server memory to support it. Otherwise, you might lose access to a server volume or the server might shut down. The following sections describe how to verify long filename support, how to calculate the memory you need to support it, and how to enable long filename support.

### VERIFYING LONG NAME SPACE SUPPORT

To find out if the long filename support has been added to your NetWare server, enter the VOLUMES command at the server console prompt. If long filename support has been added to a volume, the Names Spaces column in the report will display either the OS2 or LONG name space.

**The long name space support must be added to each volume that will store the Java applets.**

NOTE

### CALCULATING MEMORY REQUIREMENTS FOR LONG FILENAMES

Adding the long filename support requires additional server memory, which must be added before you add the name space. If you add the name space first and the server runs out of memory, you won't be able to mount the volume.

**WARNING**

**If the server runs out of memory before the SYS volume mounts, you won't be able to start the server.**

To calculate the memory required by the long filename name space, use the following equation:

*Name space memory required = 0.032 × volume size (in MB) / block size (in K)*

Always round up the equation result to the next higher 1MB increment. The total memory required in your NetWare Server will be the total of all the memory required by the NetWare server, all services running on the server, and the long filename name space.

**NOTE**

**The Course 655 exam does not test your ability to calculate the memory requirements for the long name space. This information is provided here so you have the information you need to prepare the server to run Java applets.**

## ENABLING LONG FILENAME SUPPORT

To add the long filename space to a NetWare volume, do the following:

**1** • Locate the long filename space NLM on your server. On NetWare 4.1 systems, the filename is OS2.NAM. On NetWare 4.11 systems, the filename is LONG.NAM. These files are stored in the Sys:System directory.

**2** • At the server console prompt, enter the following commands:

```
LOAD name_space

ADD NAME SPACE name_space TO volume_name
```

Replace the *name_space* variable with either OS2 or LONG. The *volume_name* variable represents the volume to which you want to add long filename support.

After you add the name space to a volume, the name space NLM will automatically load each time the server starts. You do not need to add any commands to AUTOEXEC.NCF.

**NOTE**

The Course 655 exam does not test your ability to install a long filename name space. This information is provided here so you have the information you need to prepare the server to run Java applets.

## Locating Java Applets

When you are ready to use applets in your Web pages, how do you get the applets? Some applets are provided for you on the CD-ROM that comes with this book, but those will probably only whet your appetite for more. Your alternatives are as follows:

▸ Learn to write Java applets

▸ Hire someone to write your applet for you

▸ Buy an applet

▸ Grab a freeware applet

My preference is to get a freeware applet. I'm not ready to write Java applets, and hey, the price is right. Of course, some will argue that you get what you pay for. And let's face it, when you use a freeware applet, you are using the solution to someone else's problem. It might work for you, but it might be worth the money to get a custom applet that caters to your needs. The good news is that whichever solution you choose, you'll find plenty of support on the Web. There are resources for developers, applet developers showing off their wares, and freeware applets for the picking.

Two popular sites for learning about available applets are:
**Java Applet Rating Services:** www.jars.com
**Gamelan:** www-b.gamelan.com/index.shtml

When you locate the applet you want, you'll need to look for a link that enables you to download the applet. Be careful here. Some links give you the Java source code, others give you the applet. The Java source code file usually has a .java extension and won't do you any good if you can't compile it to create the applet. You want to download the applet, which is already compiled and has a .class extension.

Before you grab the applet and run, look for any documentation or support files that accompany the applet. In most cases, these files will be compressed into a single download file with the applet. You simply download the file, run the file to extract the enclosed files, and then work with what you have received.

In some cases, the documentation might be on a separate Web page or in a separate download file. If you don't have time to download all the files you need, or if you are unsure whether you have all the files, bookmark the source so you can get back there if you need to.

 **Exercise 15.1: If you're preparing to take the certification exam, or if you want to practice what you learned in this section, turn to the end of this chapter and complete Exercise 15.1. When you are done, continue reading here to prepare for the next exercise.**

## Calling Java Applets from Web Pages

Once you've located that killer applet for your Web page, how do you use it? To put an applet to work on your Web page, you need to do the following:

► Place the applet and any files that it requires in a directory to which you and your Web page visitors have access.

► Add <APPLET> tags to your Web page to call the applet.

► Test the Web page.

## PLACING THE APPLETS

Your Web pages can access applets on the same Web server or on a remote Web server. You can place an applet in the same directory as the Web page that calls it, or you can place all the applets in a dedicated applet directory. The following sections explore these approaches.

### Placing Applets in the Same Directory as the Web Page

The easiest way to access an applet is to put it in the same directory as the Web page that calls it. The HTML <APPLET> tag is simpler to create and all the related documents are together. You don't have to worry about access rights for the applet because, if users have access to your Web page, they have access to your applet.

### Placing Applets in a Shared Directory

When you plan to use the same applet on a number of Web pages, it makes sense to put one copy in a central location that every Web page can access. Otherwise, you'll have multiple copies of the applet wasting space on your server. And when it's time to update the applet, can you be sure that you've updated all the copies?

When you place an applet in a shared directory, remember to do the following:

- ▸ Choose a directory that is accessible to Web visitors.

- ▸ Specify the directory in the <APPLET> tag with the CODEBASE attribute (which is described later in this chapter).

- ▸ Place all support files for the applet in the same directory as the applet, or use applet-configuration parameters to define the location of the files. (The configuration parameters are described later in this chapter.)

The placement of the applet support files is important. Some applets call graphics files, audio files, or additional applet files. If the applet can't find these files, it won't run as intended and might not run at all. In many cases, the support files must be stored in the same directory as the applet. In other cases, the applet might permit you to configure the location of the support files. The only way to know is to read the documentation provided with your applet, or guess by reviewing other Web pages that use the applet.

If you plan to share applets with multiple Web pages, consider creating an applet directory and then creating a dedicated subdirectory for each applet and its files. This approach makes it easy for you to locate the applet files and keeps applet support files separate from the support files for other applets.

### Using Applets on a Remote Server

Your Web page can call an applet on a remote server, but why would you want to do that? One reason might be that the applet developer will let you use it, but won't give it to you. In general, it is best to store the applet on the same server as your Web page. Otherwise, the success of your Web page is dependent on a server over which you have no control. If the remote server goes down, there goes your Web applet.

When you use an applet on a remote server, remember to specify the URL of the applet's directory in the <APPLET> tag with the CODEBASE attribute (which is described later in this chapter).

## USING THE APPLET TAGS

To call an applet from a Web page, you use an HTML tag called—are you ready for this—<APPLET>. The format for the <APPLET> tag is as follows:

```
<APPLET CODEBASE="http://hostname/path/" CODE="applet.class"
HEIGHT=nn WIDTH=nn>

<PARAM NAME="parameter_name" VALUE="parameter_value">

Alternate_HTML

</APPLET>
```

The opening <APPLET> tag calls the applet and establishes the size of the applet window. Between the opening and closing <APPLET> tags, you might have one or more <PARAM> tags, which configure the applet you are calling. You'll see how these <PARAM> tags are used in the sample code that follows Table 15.3.

After the <PARAM> tags and before the closing </APPLET> tag, you can enter HTML tags and text that appear if the visitor's browser doesn't support Java applets. This alternate HTML code is not displayed if the visitor's browser does support Java applets. Tables 15.4 and 15.5 describe the attributes you can use with the <APPLET> and <PARAM> tags.

| TABLE 15.3 | ATTRIBUTE | DESCRIPTION |
|---|---|---|
| `<APPLET>` *Tag Attributes* | CODEBASE | This optional attribute defines the server directory in which the applet is stored. Enter the complete URL if the applet is stored on a remote server. If the applet is stored on a local server, enter the URL relative to the document root directory. If the CODEBASE attribute is omitted, the applet must be placed in the same directory as the HTML file that calls it. |
| | CODE | This required attribute specifies the name of the applet to be called. The applet name is case-sensitive and always uses the .class file extension. If the CODEBASE attribute is not specified, the applet must be stored in the same directory as the HTML file or in a subdirectory. The CODE attribute does not support a full URL or a relative reference from a directory above the directory in which the calling HTML file resides. |
| | HEIGHT | This required attribute specifies the height in pixels of the window in which the Java applet appears. |
| | WIDTH | This required attribute specifies the width in pixels of the window in which the Java applet appears. |

| TABLE 15.4 | ATTRIBUTE | DESCRIPTION |
|---|---|---|
| `<PARAM>` *Tag Attributes* | NAME | The NAME attribute specifies the name of the Java-applet parameter that the VALUE attribute configures. |
| | VALUE | The VALUE attribute specifies a configuration value for the Java applet. If the value contains any space characters, it must be specified between quotation marks. |

**NOTE**

**You can use the HTML `<COMMENT>` tag, `<!-- comment -->`, to insert comments anywhere between the `<APPLET>` tags. You might want to use a comment tag to note the purpose of a `<PARAM>` tag or the beginning of the alternate HTML text.**

The following HTML document calls a Java applet that displays a marquee with a scrolling message:

```
<HTML>

<HEAD>
```

```
<TITLE>Java Ticker Tape Applet</TITLE>

</HEAD>

<BODY TEXT="#000000" BGCOLOR="#FFFFFF" LINK="#0000EE"
VLINK="#551A8B" ALINK="#FF0000">

<P>

<CENTER><P>Thanks to Chris Cobb for sharing this
applet.</P></CENTER>


<CENTER><P><A HREF="http://www.ccobb.org/javalinks.html">See
Chris Cobb's

Cool Web Page </A></P></CENTER>


<CENTER>

<APPLET CODE="ticker.class" WIDTH="392" HEIGHT="64"
align="absmiddle">

     <PARAM NAME=BorderColor VALUE=128,128,128>

     <PARAM NAME=Pause VALUE=500>

     <PARAM NAME=Speed VALUE="25">

     <PARAM NAME=Text1 VALUE="STRING:Novell's Certified Web
Designer Study Guide">

<P>If you can see this, your browser doesn't support Java,
or Java support is disabled.</P>

</APPLET>

<P>

</CENTER>

</BODY>

</HTML>
```

In this example, the ⟨APPLET⟩ tags call an applet named ticker.class, which is in the same directory as the source HTML file. Look at all the ⟨PARAM⟩ tags. The last ⟨PARAM⟩ tag is named *marquee* and its value defines the message that scrolls in the applet window. You can view this document on the demonstration Web site.

Also note in the example the alternate HTML text before the closing ⟨/APPLET⟩ tag. This text appears in the browser when the browser doesn't support Java, or when the Java support within the browser is disabled. Figure 15.1 shows how this document appears in a Web browser.

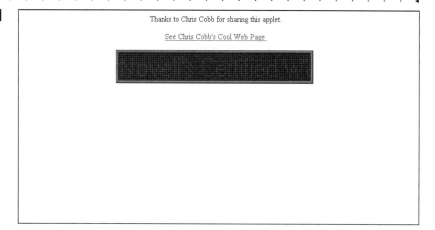

F I G U R E    15.1

*Ticker Applet Web Page*

So, how do you know how to modify the ⟨PARAM⟩ tags? If you don't get any documentation from the programmer who developed the applet, you have to guess. In the case of the Ticker applet, the programmer used descriptive names for the parameters, so most of them are pretty easy to guess. It is much more difficult to work with an applet that has no instructions and no sample Web page to review.

The next sample document is also on the enclosed CD-ROM, and it demonstrates how you can run more than one applet on the same Web page.

```
<HTML>
<HEAD>
    <TITLE>Clock and Date Applets</TITLE>
</HEAD>
<BODY BGCOLOR="#FFFFFF">
```

```
<CENTER><P>

<APPLET CODE="curtime.class" WIDTH="126" HEIGHT="37"
ALIGN="ABSMIDDLE">

</APPLET>

</P></CENTER>


<CENTER><P>Thanks to Chris Cobb for sharing these
applets.</P></CENTER>


<CENTER><P><A HREF="http://www.ccobb.org/javalinks.html">See
Chris Cobb's

Cool Web Page </A></P></CENTER>


<CENTER><P>

<APPLET CODE="curdate.class" WIDTH="174" HEIGHT="37"
ALIGN="ABSMIDDLE">

<PARAM NAME="LEDColor" VALUE="255,0,0">

<PARAM NAME="BorderColor" VALUE="128,0,0">

<PARAM NAME="FullYear" VALUE="1">

<CENTER><P>If you can see this, your browser doesn't support
Java, or Java

support is disabled.</P></CENTER>

</APPLET>

</P></CENTER>


</BODY>

</HTML>
```

The first applet displays a clock using the default applet values. The second applet displays the date using some customized parameter settings. You can view this page on the demonstration Web site. Figure 15.2 shows how this document appears in a Web browser.

F I G U R E   15.2

*Clock and Date Applets Web Page*

Thanks to Chris Cobb for sharing these applets.

See Chris Cobb's Cool Web Page

## TESTING APPLETS

Once you've placed your applet appropriately and entered the applets into your HTML document, it's time to test your Web page. Open your Java-enabled browser and then open the HTML document file.

**NOTE**

**Another way to test Java applets is to use the Java Applet Viewer, appletviewer, that is included in the Java Development Kit (JDK) from Sun Microsystems.**

Because Java applets are processed on the client side of the browser-to-server connection, you can test these documents on a Web server or on your local computer. It is good practice to test your Web pages on the local computer and then transfer them to the Web server when you know they are ready.

**NOTE**

**If you plan to test your documents on a local computer and then transfer them to the Web server, be sure to plan your file references accordingly. If the file structure for the HTML document is the same on both the local computer and on the Web server, the transfer will be painless. If the file structures are different, you'll have to change the source files to get them to work on the Web server.**

If your applet doesn't work correctly, see the Troubleshooting section at the end of this chapter.

**Exercises 15.2 and 15.3: If you're preparing to take the certification exam, or if you want to practice what you learned in this section, turn to the end of this chapter and complete Exercises 15.2 and 15.3. When you are done, continue reading here to prepare for the next exercise.**

## Java Versus JavaScript

In the last chapter, we compared JavaScript to Java. Now that you understand Java applets more, we'll take another look at the differences between Java and JavaScript. Table 15.5 compares Java and JavaScript.

| TABLE 15.5 *JavaScript vs. Java* | JAVA | JAVASCRIPT |
|---|---|---|
| | Developed by Sun Microsystems. | Developed by Netscape Communications Corporation. |
| | Runs in a Java-enabled browser. | Runs in a JavaScript-enabled browser. |
| | Java applets are called from HTML files. | JavaScripts can be embedded in HTML files or called from external files. |
| | Java applets are compiled *bytecode* applications that can be launched by Java-enabled browsers. | JavaScripts are interpreted by the browser. |
| | To create effective Java applets requires some programming experience. | Nonprogrammers can learn to create client-side JavaScripts. Server-side JavaScripts require programming experience. |

| T A B L E   15.5 | JAVA | JAVASCRIPT |
|---|---|---|
| *JavaScript vs. Java* | Java applets run in a dedicated square area of the Web page, which is unavailable for HTML output. | JavaScripts interact with the entire Web page. |
| | When writing Java applets, you must declare variable types. | When writing JavaScripts, you do not have to declare variable types (for example, number or string). |
| | Java is object oriented, which provides more options than object-based JavaScripts. Java objects are organized into classes and benefit from full single inheritance. | JavaScript is object based. |
| | Java applets use static binding. All objects must be defined before the application is compiled. | JavaScript uses dynamic binding, which permits objects to be defined while the script is running. |

▶ · · · · · · · · · · · · · · · · · · · · · · · · · · · · · ◀

## Security Issues

Java is designed to resist many types of security attacks, but no system is perfect. If you are concerned that a Web site might be misusing Java applets, you can disable Java applet processing (as described earlier in this chapter) before you visit that site. This section introduces Java security and describes some known Java security holes.

### JAVA SECURITY

What are the security risks of running Java applets? From a browser user's perspective, there are two primary issues:

▶   Privacy and preservation of local data

▶   Performance of the local computer

### Privacy and Preservation of Local Data

Because Java applets run on the local computer, and because the local computer is connected to other computers, it is technically possible for a remote computer user to copy or destroy data on the local computer. To prevent this from happening, Java applets contain a security manager object, which controls the applet's access to files on the local and remote systems.

The applet security manager object is established when an applet is started and cannot be overridden, replaced, extended, or overloaded. The applet cannot create the security manager, control it, or reference it. The security manager object does the following:

▸ Enables file access to either the local computer or to the remote computer. An applet cannot access files on both computers.

▸ When file access is permitted on the local computer, it is enabled for select directories.

▸ Enables remote computer connections to only the remote computer from which the applet was downloaded. An applet cannot create a connection to a third-host computer.

The Java security features limit what Java applets can do, but the applet is only part of the picture. HotJava browsers support Java security rules, but Netscape Navigator 2.0 prohibits all Java applet access to files on the local computer. Netscape Navigator 4.0, however, does allow Java applets to write data to a local disk, but it prompts the user to approve access first.

### Local Computer Performance

Obviously, any applet that runs on your computer affects the computer's performance. However, applets are miniapplications; they are downloaded over the Internet, so how much can they bog down a computer? The answer is that a carelessly written or maliciously planned applet can bring your computer to its knees. An applet does this by consuming valuable computer resources, such as memory and CPU time.

This type of security issue is called a denial-of-service attack because the applet is preventing you from using your computer effectively. The bad news is that there isn't much that a computer programming language can do to prevent this. The good news is that the solution to a denial-of-service attack is usually as simple as quitting and restarting the browser.

## KNOWN JAVA SECURITY HOLES

Java technology is implemented in Java development tools and in browsers. Every time a new Java tool is developed, there is some potential for a security hole to develop. At the time Course 655 was written, the known security holes were the following:

▶ Select versions of both Netscape Navigator and Internet Explorer have exhibited bugs that allow applets to execute arbitrary machine instructions, execute DOS commands, and access files on a local computer. By the time this book was written, these bugs had been fixed.

▶ Java-enabled browsers can be the targets of denial-of-service attacks as described earlier.

**For more information on Java security, browse the following locations:**
**Sun Java Security FAQ:** `java.sun.com/sfaq`
**Princeton University Secure Internet Programming:**
`www.cs.princeton.edu/sip`

# Java on NetWare

In this chapter, you learned how to call applets from your Web pages and have them run on client computers. Novell's intraNetWare SDK for Java product enables you to run Java programs on a NetWare or intraNetWare server. This Software Development Kit (SDK) supports NetWare 4.1 and later and is available free of charge from the Novell Web site. Table 15.6 lists some of the SDK components.

| TABLE 15.6 | COMPONENT | DESCRIPTION |
|---|---|---|
| *Partial List of intraNetWare SDK for Java Components* | Java virtual machine | The Java virtual machine executes applets and applications on the NetWare server. |
| | Java class libraries | Java classes are like the functions described for the Perl and JavaScript languages in Chapters 13 and 14. The Java class libraries provide interfaces to NDS and to other Novell services, such as licensing, file, and print services. These libraries make it easier for developers to create programs that operate with NetWare and intraNetWare. |
| | Just-In-Time compiler | The Just-In-Time (JIT) compiler enables the server to run uncompiled Java applications. |
| | Java Developer's Kit | Tools and guidelines for creating platform-independent Java applications that run on NetWare and intraNetWare. |

**For the latest information on Novell Java products, refer to the following location:** www.novell.com/java.

## Getting More Information on Java

There is plenty of information on the World Wide Web about Java. To locate it, use a search engine or try some of the links listed below.

For more information on Java-enabled browsers, browse the following:

▸ Netscape Communicator and Navigator: www.netscape.com

▸ Internet Explorer: www.microsoft.com

▸ HotJava: java.sun.com/products/hotjava

For more information on Java, browse the following:

▸ Sun Microsystems: `java.sun.com/docs`

▸ JavaWorld Magazine: `www.javaworld.com`

▸ Java FAQ Archives: `www-net.com/java/faq`

If you want to try Java programming, consider using the following products that are designed to make Java programming easier:

▸ Java Studio (from Sun Microsystems, `java.sun.com`)

▸ JBuilder (from Inprise, `www.inprise.com`)

▸ Visual Café (from Symantec, `www.symantec.com`)

▸ VisualAge for Java (from IBM, `www.ibm.com`)

▸ Super Mojo (from Penumbra Software, `www.penumbrasoftware.com`)

Some of these products use JavaBeans, which are Java software components that you can use as building blocks to create Java applications.

## Troubleshooting

The first step in troubleshooting a Java applet problem is to look for error messages in the browser window. Also, watch the status area at the bottom of the window while the applet is loading. This area displays status messages that can help you determine the source of a problem. Table 15.7 lists some common symptoms and the problems that cause them.

| T A B L E  15.7 *Common Problems and Their Symptoms* | SYMPTOM | PROBLEM |
|---|---|---|
| | I just disabled Java in the browser, but when I reload the Web page, the Java applet is still running. | The Java applet is still running in memory. Quit and restart the browser to clear the applet from memory. |
| | "File not found" message appears in the browser status area. | The applet file might be missing, the path might be incorrect, or the name might be incorrect. The applet name is case-sensitive and must use the .class file extension. |
| | | If the long filename name space support was recently added to the Web server, was the client rebooted after the long name space support was enabled? |
| | The Web page doesn't appear correctly. | A quotation mark or forward slash might be missing. All quotation marks must appear in pairs. Most HTML tags require a forward slash, not a backslash. |
| | I changed some applet parameter settings, but the browser is still using the old settings. | The applet is running in memory and has not been updated. Try the following: |
| | | 1. Make sure you saved the revised HTML file. |
| | | 2. Use the browser Reload command to reload the Web page and applet. In Netscape Navigator, pressing the shift key when you click the Reload button might work. |
| | | 3. If all else fails, quit and restart the browser. |
| | Everything but the Java applet appears in the browser. | The browser is not Java-enabled, or Java is disabled. |

**Exercise 15.4: If you're preparing to take the certification exam, or if you want to practice what you learned in this section, turn to the end of this chapter and complete Exercise 15.4.**

## Summary

In this chapter, you learned how to use Java applets. To create Java applets requires programming skills, but you can find Java applets on the Web. Using other people's applets is as simple as entering `<APPLET>` and `<PARAM>` tags in an HTML file. Using `<APPLET>` tags is much easier when the applet you are using comes with documentation.

To view applets in a browser, you must enable Java-applet processing. As with JavaScript, Java does present some security issues, but you can disable Java processing at the browser if this is a concern.

To support Java applet filenames on a Novell server, you must add the LONG filename space. To run Java applets or programs on a Novell server, you can use the Java Virtual Machine that is included with the intraNetWare SDK for Java product.

## PUZZLE 15.1: USING JAVA APPLETS

The following word puzzle contains many of the terms discussed in this chapter. See if you can find all the words. As you search for the words, ask yourself why the word is in the list and how it was used in this chapter. If you don't know the answers to these questions, you might want to review the chapter.

```
I   D   I   S   A   B   L   E   C   A   P   S   J   C   P
A   G   N   I   D   N   I   B   N   A   M   E   A   O   I
P   Z   H   S   E   R   A   W   T   E   N   C   V   M   X
P   R   E   S   E   R   V   A   T   I   O   N   A   M   E
L   Y   R   O   M   E   M   S   E   L   B   A   N   E   L
E   E   I   D   X   A   Y   V   O   L   U   M   E   N   S
T   Y   T   X   L   S   R   S   E   C   U   R   I   T   Y
G   C   A   A   O   E   S   A   B   E   D   O   C   H   E
P   A   N   R   N   U   S   U   P   C   P   F   L   G   U
M   V   C   M   G   R   R   E   S   W   O   R   B   I   L
E   I   E   D   O   C   E   T   Y   B   C   E   H   E   A
M   R   O   B   J   E   C   T   E   S   T   P   T   H   V
O   P   L   O   A   D   A   B   L   E   L   U   D   O   M
R   A   Y   E   E   D   E   N   I   A   L   X   I   F   L
Y   S   S   A   L   C   D   K   U   N   G   D   W   N   N
```

| | | | |
|---|---|---|---|
| alternate | denial | Microsystems | preservation |
| applet | disable | module | privacy |
| binding | enable | NLM | security |
| browser | height | name | space |
| bytecode | inheritance | NetWare | Sun |
| CODEBASE | Java | object | test |
| CPU | loadable | PARAM | value |
| class | long | performance | volume |
| comment | memory | pixels | width |

## EXERCISE 15.1: JAVA BASICS

Review your knowledge of the Java basics presented in this chapter by answering the following questions:

**1** • With respect to C and C++, is Java considered easier to learn, more difficult, or comparable?

Answer: . . . . . . . . . . . . . . . . . . . . . . . . . . . . . . . . . . . . . . .

**2** • Are Java applets embedded into a Web page?

Answer: . . . . . . . . . . . . . . . . . . . . . . . . . . . . . . . . . . . . . . .

**3** • Where are Java applets displayed?

Answer: . . . . . . . . . . . . . . . . . . . . . . . . . . . . . . . . . . . . . . .

**4** • How does a Just-In-Time (JIT) compiler affect the performance of Java applets?

Answer: . . . . . . . . . . . . . . . . . . . . . . . . . . . . . . . . . . . . . . .

**5** • How can you prevent a Java applet from running in a browser?

Answer: . . . . . . . . . . . . . . . . . . . . . . . . . . . . . . . . . . . . . . .

**6** • What change might need to be made to a Novell server before you can store Java applets on the server?

Answer: . . . . . . . . . . . . . . . . . . . . . . . . . . . . . . . . . . . . . . .

**7** • If a server volume doesn't mount after you extend the volume to support Java applets, what might be the problem?

Answer: . . . . . . . . . . . . . . . . . . . . . . . . . . . . . . . . . . . . . . .

**8** • What program must be loaded on a NetWare 4.11 or intraNetWare server to support Java applets?

Answer: . . . . . . . . . . . . . . . . . . . . . . . . . . . . . . . . . . . . . . .

**9** • What are the first three words in the command that prepares a server volume to store Java applets?

Answer: . . . . . . . . . . . . . . . . . . . . . . . . . . . . . . . . . . . . . . . .

**10** • What is the file extension for Java applet files?

Answer: . . . . . . . . . . . . . . . . . . . . . . . . . . . . . . . . . . . . . . . .

**11** • What is the file extension for Java source code files?

Answer: . . . . . . . . . . . . . . . . . . . . . . . . . . . . . . . . . . . . . . . .

**EXERCISE 15.2: PLACING AND CALLING APPLETS**

Review your knowledge of the procedures for placing and calling Java applets by answering the following questions:

**1** • List three locations where you can store the applets you use on your Web pages.

   a. . . . . . . . . . . . . . . . . . . . . . . . . . . . . . . . . . . . . . . . . . . .

   b. . . . . . . . . . . . . . . . . . . . . . . . . . . . . . . . . . . . . . . . . . . .

   c. . . . . . . . . . . . . . . . . . . . . . . . . . . . . . . . . . . . . . . . . . . .

**2** • Which <APPLET> tag attribute is required when you store applets outside of the directory that contains the Web page that calls them?

   Answer: . . . . . . . . . . . . . . . . . . . . . . . . . . . . . . . . . . . . . . .

**3** • Does access to a Web page automatically give Web page visitors access to applets in other directories?

   Answer: . . . . . . . . . . . . . . . . . . . . . . . . . . . . . . . . . . . . . . .

**4** • Where should applet support files be stored?

   Answer: . . . . . . . . . . . . . . . . . . . . . . . . . . . . . . . . . . . . . . .

**5** • Write an <APPLET> tag that starts an applet named *fun* in an area that is 50 pixels tall and 150 pixels wide.

   Answer: . . . . . . . . . . . . . . . . . . . . . . . . . . . . . . . . . . . . . . .

**6** • Write an <APPLET> tag that calls an applet named *dance* from the shared directory *applets* that is a subdirectory of the document root directory. This applet requires a display area that is 200 pixels tall and 200 pixels wide.

   Answer: . . . . . . . . . . . . . . . . . . . . . . . . . . . . . . . . . . . . . . .

**7** • Write the tag that sets the *speed* parameter for the dance applet to *jitterbug*.

Answer: . . . . . . . . . . . . . . . . . . . . . . . . . . . . . . . . . . . .

**8** • How does the browser process other HTML tags that appear between the starting and ending <APPLET> tags?

Answer: . . . . . . . . . . . . . . . . . . . . . . . . . . . . . . . . . . . .

**9** • When testing your applets, do you need a Web server?

Answer: . . . . . . . . . . . . . . . . . . . . . . . . . . . . . . . . . . . .

EXERCISE 15.3: USING A JAVA APPLET

In this exercise, you will add a Java applet to a Web page. To complete this exercise, do the following:

1 • Use a text-editor or word-processor program to open the following file on this book's CD-ROM:

*d*:/DemoWeb2/Answers/ticker.htm

2 • Between the empty pair of `<CENTER>` tags, enter the following:

▸ An `<APPLET>` tag that starts the ticker.class applet and displays it in an area that is 64 pixels high and 392 pixels wide.

▸ A tag that sets the "BorderColor" parameter to "128,128,128."

▸ A tag that sets the "Pause" parameter to "500."

▸ A tag that sets the "Speed" parameter to "25."

▸ A tag that sets the "Text1" parameter to "STRING:Novell's Certified Web Designer Study Guide."

▸ A text statement that appears only to users of browsers that don't support Java and explains what is happening.

3 • Save the edited file to a local drive using the name ticker2.htm.

4 • Copy the following files to the directory where you saved ticker2.htm:

*d*:/DemoWeb2/Answers/ticker.class

*d*:/DemoWeb2/Answers/tickertext.class

**5** • Open the edited file in your browser. If you completed the exercise correctly, the Java applet displays a scrolling message. If you have trouble with this exercise, you can view the answer file on the CD at:

*d:/DemoWeb2/Answers/ticker2.htm*

**TIP**

**For more information on using the ticker.class applet, see the applet documentation on the CD at *d:/Applets/ticker/ticker.htm***

**EXERCISE 15.4: UNDERSTANDING JAVA CONCEPTS**

Review your knowledge of the Java concepts presented in the later part of this chapter by answering the following questions:

**1** • Can you display Web page elements, such as text or images, over the display area for a Java applet?

Answer: . . . . . . . . . . . . . . . . . . . . . . . . . . . . . . . . . . . . . . . .

**2** • How does a denial-of-service attack deny service to a computer?

Answer: . . . . . . . . . . . . . . . . . . . . . . . . . . . . . . . . . . . . . . . .

**3** • How can you stop a denial-of-service attack from a Java applet?

Answer: . . . . . . . . . . . . . . . . . . . . . . . . . . . . . . . . . . . . . . . .

**4** • What Novell product enables Java applets to run on a NetWare server?

Answer: . . . . . . . . . . . . . . . . . . . . . . . . . . . . . . . . . . . . . . . .

**5** • What component of Novell's server Java product enables applets to run on the server?

Answer: . . . . . . . . . . . . . . . . . . . . . . . . . . . . . . . . . . . . . . . .

**6** • Which component of Novell's server Java product enables the server to run uncompiled Java programs?

Answer: . . . . . . . . . . . . . . . . . . . . . . . . . . . . . . . . . . . . . . . .

**7** • You just disabled Java processing in the browser, but a Java applet is still running. How can you stop the applet?

Answer: . . . . . . . . . . . . . . . . . . . . . . . . . . . . . . . . . . . . . . . .

**8 •** You have just made changes to the settings for a Java applet, but the browser is still displaying the old settings. List three steps you can take to solve this problem.

a. . . . . . . . . . . . . . . . . . . . . . . . . . . . . . . . . . . . . . . . . . . . . . . . . .

b. . . . . . . . . . . . . . . . . . . . . . . . . . . . . . . . . . . . . . . . . . . . . . . . . .

c. . . . . . . . . . . . . . . . . . . . . . . . . . . . . . . . . . . . . . . . . . . . . . . . . .

# Answers to Exercises

This appendix contains answers to all the exercises in this book.

## Puzzle 2.1: Creating Web Pages

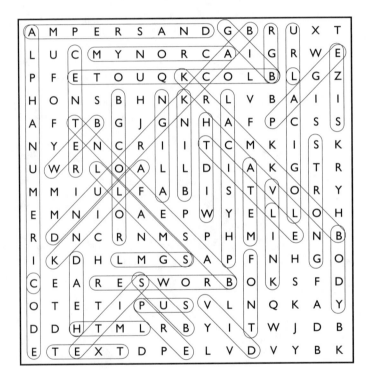

## Exercise 2.5

1 • Standard Generalized Markup Language (SGML).

2 • (a) Head; (b) Body.

3 • Text.

4 • <PRE></PRE>

**5** • (a) at the top of the browser window; (b) in a bookmark list; (c) on search results Web pages.

**6** • (a) subscript: `<SUB></SUB>`; (b) superscript: `<SUP></SUP>`

**7** • ALIGN.

**8** • `<BLOCKQUOTE>`

**9** • ` `

**10** • `&amp;`

▶ · · · · · · · · · · · · · · · · · · · · · · · · · · · · · · · ◀

# Puzzle 3.1: Using Lists, Tables, and Images

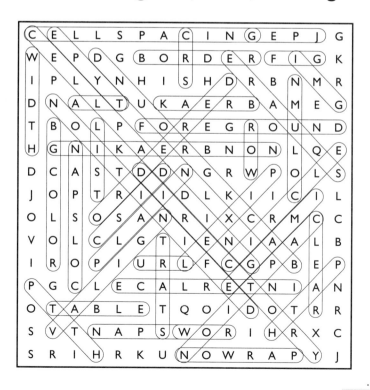

## Exercise 3.4: Understanding Lists, Tables, and Images

**1** • (a) DISC; (b) CIRCLE; (c) SQUARE.

**2** • (a) 1; (b) i; (c) I; (d) a; (e) A.

**3** • A list within a list.

**4** • It appears as an indented list head, with no bullets or numbers.

**5** • Tables are defined one **row** at a time.

**6** • <TH> tags mark heading cells that appear in bold text and <TD> tags mark data cells that appear in the default font.

**7** • (a) ROWSPAN; (b) COLSPAN.

**8** • CELLPADDING

**9** • <TABLE ALIGN=RIGHT BORDER=5>

**10** • (a) Joint Photographic Experts Group (JPEG); (b) Graphic Interchange Format (GIF).

**11** • Thumbnail images.

**12** • Interlaced GIF.

**13** • <BODY BACKGROUND=BACKGROUND.GIF>

**14** • <CENTER><IMG SRC=COOL/WOW.GIF></CENTER>

**15** • <BR CLEAR=RIGHT>

## Puzzle 4.1: Linking Web Pages

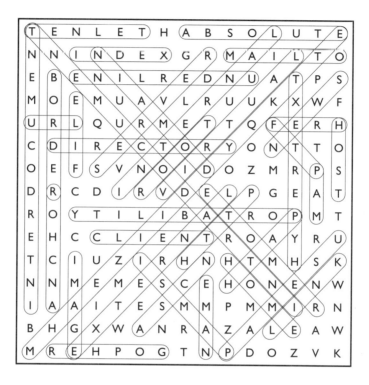

## Exercise 4.5: Understanding Links and Image Maps

**1** • `<A NAME="Doc Brown">`

**2** • `<A HREF="#Doc Brown">Doctor Brown</A>`

**3** • `<A HREF="http://www.novell.com/">Novell</A>`

**4** • `<A HREF="homepage.htm"><IMG SRC="banner.gif"></A>`

**5** • `<A HREF="http://www.acme.com/acmehome.htm">ACME Corporation</A>`

**6** • An **external** link displays a Web page on a different Web server.

**7** • ISMAP.

**8** • MAP.

**9** • USEMAP.

**10** • No. The USEMAP attribute defines the map table where URLs are stored.

**11** • An image map area that has been defined as a link to another file.

**12** • #

**13** • a. Plan the Web site.

b. Create the Web pages.

c. Test the Web pages.

d. Publish the Web site.

e. Maintain the Web site.

## Puzzle 5.1: Using Advanced Web Page Features

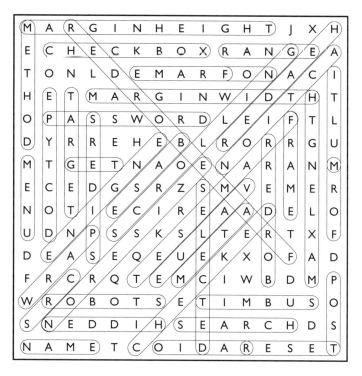

## Exercise 5.3: Understanding Advanced Web Page Features

**1** • No. `<FRAMESET>` tags are ignored if they are placed between body tags.

**2** • `<FRAMESET COLS="25%, *">`

**3** • 250 pixels.

**4** • Look for a row or column that extends from one side of the window to the other. Define the longest row or column first, and then define the others.

**5** • `<NOFRAME>`

**6** • TARGET.

**7** • `<FORM METHOD=POST ACTION=FORM.HTM>`

**8** • (a) checkbox: checked; (b) radio button: checked; (c) menu option: selected.

**9** • The Submit button.

**10** • NAME.

**11** • `<TEXTAREA name=comments cols=60 rows=10> Enter comments here.</TEXTAREA>`

**12** • NAME.

**13** • (a) Author: identifies the Web page author; (b) Classification: provide classification guidelines for search engines; (c) Description: describes the Web site for search engine reports; (d) Generator: identifies the tool used to create the Web page; (e) Keywords: lists words that should be indexed to your Web site.

**14** • In the document head.

**15** • (a) Expires: identifies a cache expiration date for the page; (b) Pragma: tells cache servers not to cache this page.

**16** • CONTENT.

**17** • (a) `<DOCTYPE HTML PUBLIC "-//W3C//DTD HTML 3.2//EN">`; (b) `<DOCTYPE HTML PUBLIC "-//IETF/./DTD HTML 2.0//EN">`

**18** • A, c; B, e; C, b; D, a; E, f; F, d.

## Puzzle 6.1: Creating Web Sites with NetObjects Fusion

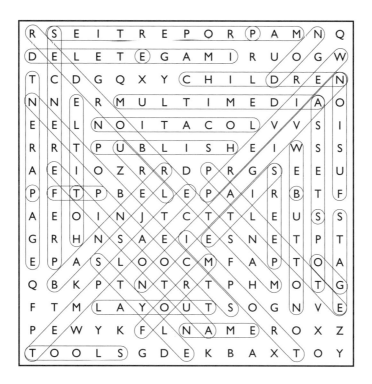

## Exercise 6.4: Using NetObjects Fusion

**1** • (a) Click the New Page button; (b) Select Edit → New Page.

**2** • Position the cursor near the bottom of the page. When the dragged Web page is in the proper position, a red triangle appears upside down on the bottom of the parent page.

**3** • MasterBorders.

**4** • Site styles.

**5** • Use the page changing controls in the lower left corner of the NetObjects Fusion window.

**6** • The Picture tool in the Tools palette.

**7** • The SiteMapper tool in the Tools palette.

**8** • The Preview button.

**9** • Staging.

**10** • File → Import Page.

**11** • In the Tools palette.

**12** • (a) sound files; (b) movie or video files; (c) Java applets; (d) Shockwave files; (e) ActiveX controls.

## Puzzle 7.1: Web Design Basics

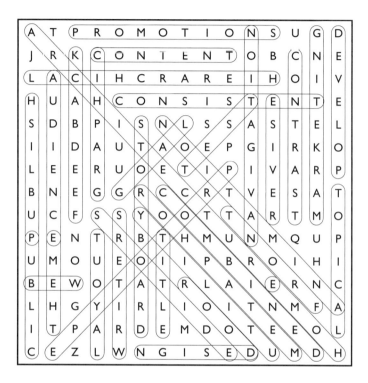

## Exercise 7.1: Understanding Web Design Basics

**1** • (a) publication design (design principles); (b) graphic design; (c) marketing; (d) Web design (Internet experience).

**2** • (a) Define the Web site goals; (b) Create a storyboard; (c) Produce the Web site content; (d) Develop a Web site prototype; (e) Test the prototype; (f) Revise the prototype and publish the finished Web site.

**3** • Feedback.

**4** • Your audience.

**5** • Web site navigation options.

**6** • Home page.

**7** • Linear layout.

**8** • Hierarchical layout.

**9** • Combined layout.

**10** • It displays information you want visitors to see before they see the home page.

**11** • Utility navigation structures.

**12** • Near the home page.

**13** • They are dead ends that provide no links to other pages in your Web site.

**14** • 640 × 480

**15** • Navigation controls.

**16** • To help design team members and management visualize the Web site design.

## Puzzle 8.1: Creating and Adapting Web Graphics

## Exercise 8.1: Understanding Bitmap Images

**1** • (a) bit; (b) pixel.

**2** • 72 dpi.

**3** • Bit depth.

**4** • 256.

**5** • 16.7 million.

**6** • 256.

**7** • 16.7 million.

**8** • A collection of predefined colors that can be used to create and display images.

**9** • No.

**10** • 216.

## Exercise 8.2: Understanding Web Image Problems

**1** • (a) Reduce the image size; (b) Reduce the bit depth of the image (applies to GIFs); (c) Increase the amount of compression (applies to JPEGs).

**2** • Specify the image size with the HEIGHT and WIDTH attributes in the <IMG> tag.

**3** • Interlacing causes the image to display in stages from an initially poorer quality to the true image quality.

**4** • The image might have been created using a resolution larger than the 72 to 100 dpi settings used for Web images.

**5** • Dithering is the display of pixels in multiple colors to create the appearance of another color.

**6** • JPEG.

**7** • A loss of image detail.

**8** • The additional colors introduced in images by anti-aliasing against a background that is a different color from the Web page background.

**9** • Aliased images display **rough** edges and anti-aliased images display **smooth** edges.

**10** • Rectangular.

**11** • Create the irregular-shaped object and fill the image background with the same color used for the background color of the Web page.

**12** • Macintosh and SGI displays.

# Exercise 8.3: Choosing a Web Image Format

**1** • GIF89a.

**2** • GIF and PNG.

**3** • Streaming permits an image, animation, or sound to be displayed or played as it is downloading.

**4** • GIF and JPEG.

**5** • JPEG supports more colors, which provides more image detail.

**6** • Image quality is lost.

**7** • The progressive file format.

**8** • PNG.

**9** • PNG.

**10** • Netscape Navigator. This attribute specifies an alternate file that is displayed before the file specified with the SRC attribute. If the browser can't display the SRC file, it will continue to display the LOWSRC file.

## Exercise 8.4: Using Adobe Photoshop

**7** • (a) 0; (b) 51; (c) 102; (d) 153; (e) 204; (f) 255.

## Exercise 8.5: Creating GIF Images

**1** • Size: 18K.

**7** • HALO2.GIF: 10K; HALO3.GIF: 7K.

## Exercise 8.6: Guidelines for Creating Special Web Page Elements

**1** • Horizontal and vertical object edges.

**2** • Increase or decrease that background area of the image.

**3** • Tiled background.

**4** • A **full-screen** background appears just once on a Web page.

**5** • A full-screen background.

**6** • Make the image wider than the viewing area available to browser users.

## Puzzle 9.1: Adding Multimedia to Web Pages

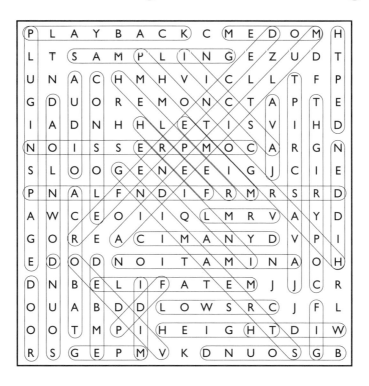

## Exercise 9.1: Understanding Multimedia

**1** • (a) entertainment; (b) education.

**2** • (a) less development effort; (b) faster download times.

**3** • Plug-ins.

**4** • Helper application.

**5** • Portable Document Format (PDF).

**6** • A MIME type.

**7** • The browser user installed a new plug-in that processes that type of media file, and the browser located that plug-in first.

**8** • `<EMBED>`

**9** • `<A>`

**10** • Inline media.

**11** • To specify the size of the image area that displays the sound control panel.

**12** • It hides the media playback control panel.

**13** • It defines a URL for a Web page that enables the user to download the plug-in that plays the media file.

**14** • `<BGSOUND>`

# Exercise 9.2: Understanding Animation Guidelines

**1** • (a) Reduce the number of frames; (b) Reduce the image size; (c) Reduce the number of colors in the animation.

**2** • Whenever you use an animation file that was created by someone else.

**3** • (a) Animate an advertisement, link, or headline to attract viewers to it; (b) Change the appearance of a button or menu when a user activates a Web page control to show a Web page response; (c) To illustrate a dynamic process, or processes, that is difficult to describe with words and static images.

**4** • (a) Animation files are typically smaller than video files; (b) Animation files can cost less to develop.

**5** • Yes. Too many animations are distracting and do not focus the viewer's attention to any particular area.

**6** • Animated GIFs.

**7** • Virtual Reality Modeling Language (VRML).

**8** • Shockwave The Works.

**9** • (a) animated GIFs; (b) Java animations; (c) JavaScript animations.

**10** • It creates vector-graphics images, which can be enlarged without a loss of image quality.

**11** • (a) Java and JavaScripts cannot integrate sound and animations; (b) You have to know how to program to create animations with these tools.

**12** • ASCII text.

## Exercise 9.3: Understanding Guidelines for Sounds

**I** • (a) Reduce the sound bit depth; (b) Reduce the sampling rate; (c) Use monaural sound instead of stereo.

**2** • Place the tag that starts the sound near the end of the HTML page so the page downloads before the sound starts.

**3** • Audio Interchange File Format.

**4** • Musical Instrument Digital Interface (MIDI)

**5** • u-Law.

**6** • Waveform Audio.

**7** • To start RealAudio sounds, you need to link to a metafile that contains the URL of the sound file.

## Exercise 9.4: Understanding Video Guidelines

**I** • The Motion Picture Experts Group (MPEG) file format.

**2** • QuickTime.

**3** • RealVideo.

**4** • The Audio/Visual Interleaved (.avi) format.

**5** • (a) Reduce the image size; (b) Reduce the number of frames.

## Puzzle 10.1: Applying and Publishing Your Design

```
U  G  T  F  J  S  T  N  E  T  N  O  C  Q  I
T  N  A  U  V  Y  N  E  P  F  B  R  U  T  M
I  I  B  N  K  E  E  T  U  O  A  E  I  N  P
L  N  L  C  N  V  R  I  B  N  S  C  N  E  A
I  R  E  T  N  R  A  S  L  T  E  A  D  M  I
T  E  P  I  A  U  P  F  I  S  L  P  E  N  R
Y  K  Y  O  V  S  S  O  C  I  S  X  G  E
H  C  T  N  I  S  N  O  I  S  N  E  M  I  D
F  A  O  A  G  N  A  K  Z  T  E  S  T  L  B
R  B  T  L  A  O  R  R  E  C  N  A  L  A  B
A  D  O  I  T  Y  T  I  L  I  B  A  E  S  U
M  E  R  T  I  G  R  A  P  H  I  C  A  L  Q
E  E  P  Y  O  G  N  I  D  A  E  L  M  T  H
S  F  M  O  N  O  S  P  A  C  E  D  R  O  P
C  A  P  T  I  A  L  A  I  T  I  N  I  V  E
```

## Exercise 10.1: Positioning Text and Graphics

1 • The Macintosh browser.

2 • Test the tag in each of the browsers.

3 • The browser ignores the tag. The tag and its attributes do not appear in the browser window.

4 • Different browsers may assign different names to these controls.

**5** • 640 × 480.

**6** • They are only supported by Internet Explorer.

**7** • Transparent art that is used to create margins on the Web page.

**8** • Set the BORDER attribute to **0**.

**9** • Create a table and leave the corresponding rows or columns empty.

**10** • No, you can only bookmark the frameset. Bookmarks store the location of the frameset file, not the contents a frame might be displaying.

**11** • When the frame is opened in a new window.

**12** • To visually balance a page that has mostly left-justified text.

# Exercise 10.2: Adding Navigation Aids to Web Sites

**1** • A table.

**2** • Replace that button image with a different image that displays the highlighting you want.

**3** • A table of contents or index that displays links for other Web site pages.

**4** • Because the index frame constantly appears in the browser. The Web pages the visitor selects appear in a different target frame.

**5** • (a) overview; (b) orientation; (c) free-form navigation.

**6** • (a) table-based site map; (b) indexed site map; (c) image map-based site map; (d) automatically generated site map.

**7** • (a) quicker downloads; (b) supported in all browsers.

**8** • Use image icons that indicate web page contents. For example, use a movie icon to indicate Web pages that display movies.

**9** • Indexed site map.

**10** • Use special highlighting or animation to make it stand out.

**11** • Some browser users won't be able to use the site maps.

# Exercise 10.3: Using Graphical and HTML Type

**1** • HTML type.

**2** • Graphical type.

**3** • Headings: sans serif font styles; body text: serif font styles; computer text: monospaced font styles.

**4** • **Kerning** is the adjustment of the spacing between the letters in a word.

**5** • **Leading** is the adjustment of the spacing between lines of text.

**6** • Only when the text represents a link.

**7** • (a) aliased and anti-aliased text; (b) kerning; (c) leading; (d) typestyles (fonts).

**8** • `<SMALL>`

**9** • `<FONT>`

**10** • Yes.

▶ · · · · · · · · · · · · · · · · · · · · · · · · · · · · · · · · · ◀

## Exercise 10.4: Testing and Publishing Your Web Site

**1** • ALT.

**2** • Before every major release.

**3** • View your Web page in other types of browsers.

**4** • Disable image display in the browser.

**5** • (a) direct observation during user test sessions; (b) surveys conducted through mail or e-mail; (c) visitor comments through mail or e-mail.

**6** • (1) Set up a Web server or a server account; (2) Copy the Web site files to the Web server; (3) Copy special Web site files to special directories; (4) Establish a feedback channel.

## Puzzle 11.1: Using SSI Commands

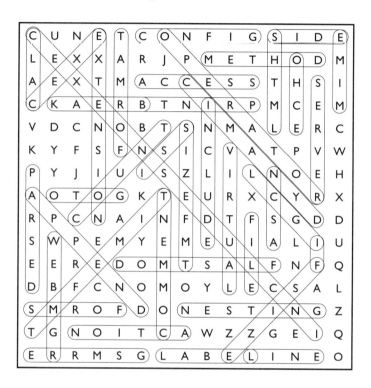

## Exercise 11.1: Enabling SSI Command Processing

**3** • `text/x-server-parsed-html    ssi`

## Exercise 11.2: Understanding the SSI Command Syntax

**1** • No. Nested SSI commands are not permitted.

**2** • #

**3** • No. SSI commands are processed by the server and cannot be processed when a file is not served by a Web server.

**4** • The file argument specifies a file relative to **the directory in which the SSI file is stored**.

**5** • The virtual argument specifies a file relative to **a virtual directory on the Web server where the SSI file is stored**.

**6** • No. The file argument cannot reference a parent directory.

**7** • No. This path implies a reference to the document root directory, not a reference for the SSI file's directory.

**8** • The virtual argument is the only way to reference the file.

**9** • The virtual argument is the only way to reference the file.

**10** • The file argument. The file argument specifies a relative reference that remains valid when the complete file structure is moved on the Web server or to another Web server.

# Exercise 11.5: Understanding SSI Commands

**1** • Dynamic.

**2** • No.

**3** • SSI. It is defined in the MIME.TYPE file on the Web server.

**4** • Another name for an SSI file is a **parsed** HTML file.

**5** • CGI scripts.

**6** • WEBMGR.EXE.

**7** • (a) Enable Includes; (b) Enable IncludesNoExec.

**8** • ACCESS.CFG.

**9** • SSI-command names are not case-sensitive; **variable** names are case sensitive.

**10** • (a) `config`; (b) `echo`; (c) `flastmod`; (d) `fsize`; (e) `include`.

**11** • Whenever the value contains a space character.

**12** • (a) `timefmt`; (b) `sizefmt`

**13** • (a) form variables; (b) calculated variables; (c) environment variables.

**14** • `Var`.

**15** • `REMOTE_ADDR`.

**16** • It includes the contents of a file in a Web page.

**17** • It appends data to the end of a text file on the Web server.

**18** • `<!--#break -->` (don't forget the space after the word *break*)

**19** • Subtraction, addition, multiplication, and division.

**20** • `if`

**21** • `append`

**22** • `&&`

## Puzzle 12.1: Using CGI Programs and Scripts

## Exercise 12.1: Understanding CGI Programs and Scripts

1 • CGI programs.

2 • (a) Use the URL in your browser to request the program in the same way you request a Web page; (b) Use the URL as a link destination within a Web page; (c) Use the ACTION attribute in a <FORM> tag to specify the URL of the CGI program.

**3** • It reads the value of the QUERY_STRING environment variable.

**4** • Novell servers: SYS:\WEB\CONFIG\SRM.CFG; UNIX servers: SRM.CONF.

**5** • (a) C++ or ANSI C; (b) Java; (c) NetBasic; (d) Perl.

**6** • (a) Bourne, C, and Korn shell scripts; (b) C and C++; (c) Java; (d) JavaScript; (e) Perl.

**7** • PERL5.NLM.

**8** • On the Novell Web Server, **RCGI** applications communicate with the Web server through TCP/IP and **LCGI** applications communicate directly with the Web server.

**9** • RemoteScriptAlias.

**10** • LoadableModule.

**11** • (a) host name; (b) port number.

**12** • (a) Install an RCGI daemon; (b) Create a RemoteScriptAlias directive for the remote server program.

**13** • The virtual path name and the script filename.

**14** • The server.

**15** • All rights to all files.

## Puzzle 13.1: Using Perl Scripts

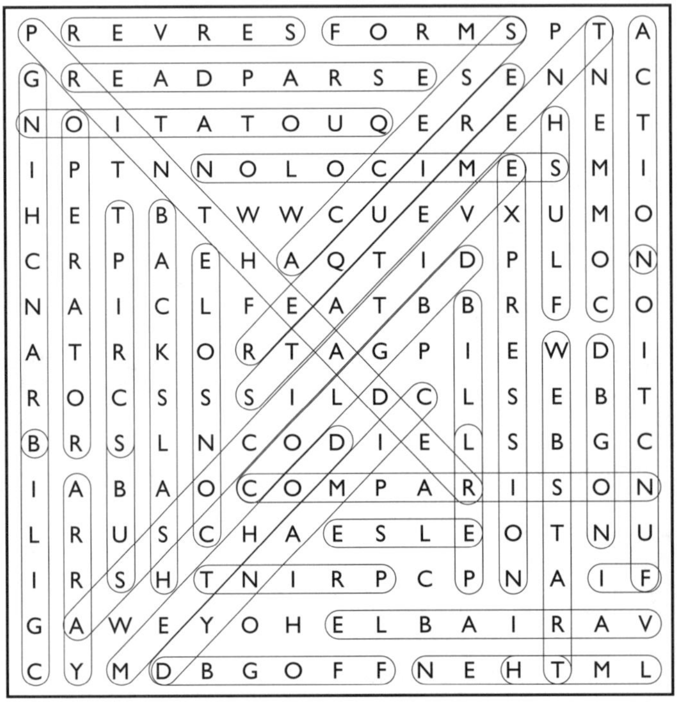

```
P  R  E  V  R  E  S  F  O  R  M  S  P  T  A
G  R  E  A  D  P  A  R  S  E  S  E  N  N  C
N  O  I  T  A  T  O  U  Q  E  R  E  H  E  T
I  P  T  N  N  O  L  O  C  I  M  E  S  M  I
H  E  T  B  T  W  W  C  U  E  V  X  U  M  O
C  R  P  A  E  H  A  Q  T  I  D  P  L  O  N
N  A  I  C  L  F  E  A  T  B  B  R  F  C  O
A  T  R  K  O  R  T  A  G  P  I  E  W  D  I
R  O  C  S  S  S  I  L  D  C  L  S  E  B  T
B  R  S  L  N  C  O  D  I  E  L  S  B  G  C
I  A  B  A  O  C  O  M  P  A  R  I  S  O  N
L  R  U  S  C  H  A  E  S  L  E  O  T  N  U
I  R  S  H  T  N  I  R  P  C  P  N  A  I  F
G  A  W  E  Y  O  H  E  L  B  A  I  R  A  V
C  Y  M  D  B  G  O  F  F  N  E  H  T  M  L
```

## Exercise 13.2: Processing a Form

**FIGURE   13.6**

*Array Variables for
FORM3.HTM*

| Form Element | Variable Name | Value | Associative Array Name |
|---|---|---|---|
| Customer Name | name | | $in {name} |
| Take Out Dining Area | | Take out | |
| Delivery Dining Area | dining | Deliver | $in {dining} |
| Inside Dining Area | | Inside dining | |
| Patio Dining Area | | Patio dining | |

## Exercise 13.3: Understanding Perl Scripts

1 • `require("cgilib.pl");`

2 • `print &PrintHeader;`

3 • `print "`

4 • `";`

5 • (a) Use single quotes to mark the beginning and end of the data to be printed. For example: `print 'data'; ;` (b) Precede each quotation mark to be printed with a backslash character. For example: `\"` .

6 • `#`

7 • The **&ReadParse** function stores form data in two arrays.

8 • (a) `$test` (valid); (b) `#name` (invalid); (c) `$123` (invalid); (d) `$a**` (invalid); (e) `$one_two` (valid).

9 • An array variable.

10 • An associative-array variable.

11 • `if`

12 • Braces: { }

13 • Parentheses: ( )

14 • `else`.

15 • (a) `PERL5 DBGON`; (b) `PERL5 DBGOFF`

16 • `PERL5 SCRIPT`

17 • PERL5 FLUSH

## Puzzle 14.1: Using JavaScripts

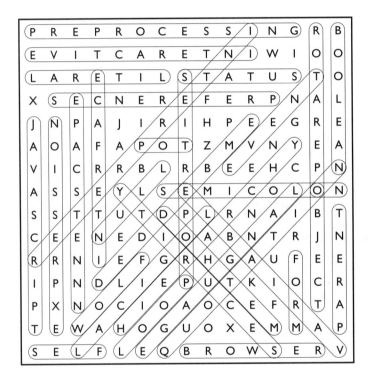

## Exercise 14.1: JavaScript Basics

1 • The least complex.

2 • Comparable.

3 • Form preprocessing provides immediate feedback to users, reduces network traffic, and reduces the load on the Web server.

4 • Disable JavaScript processing in the browser.

5 • `<SCRIPT>`

6 • SRC.

7 • `<SCRIPT LANGUAGE="JavaScript">`

8 • A semicolon: ;

9 • Two forward slashes: //

10 • `/*`

11 • `<!--`

12 • The entire script is ignored in all browsers because it is interpreted as an HTML comment.

13 • `//-->`

14 • Before.

## Exercise 14.2: Using Literals, Variables, and Objects

1 • Data that is interpreted as text, not as numbers.

2 • True and false.

3 • No.

**4** • No.

**5** • Names that cannot be used as JavaScript variables because they already have some other purpose in JavaScript.

**6** • The relationship between the objects in a browser window.

**7** • It is both. The radio button is a property of the form that contains it.

**8** • Add HTML tags that define objects, such as form objects.

**9** • `window1.frame1.doc.title`

**10** • survey.comments.value

# Exercise 14.3: Processing Data with JavaScripts

**1** • An arithmetic expression evaluates to a number, and an assignment expression assigns a value to a variable.

**2** • True and false.

**3** • (a) IF; (b) ELSE.

**4** • (a) built-in; (b) user-defined.

**5** • (a) functions can be shared by many scripts; (b) functions can be called from event handlers.

**6** • Arguments.

**7** • `function whoopee (cushion)`

**8** • `whoopee (pin)`

**9** • (a) `eval`; (b) `parseInt`; (c) `parseFloat`

**10** • `result=eval(express)`

**11** • An event handler.

**12** • `<INPUT TYPE=button VALUE=compute onClick=calculator(expression)>`

**13** • A method is a function that is assigned to an object.

## Exercise 14.5: Understanding JavaScript

**1** • The JavaScript Interactive Window.

**2** • `Javascript:`

**3** • `<SERVER>`

**4** • No.

**5** • Object based.

**6** • Dynamic binding.

**7** • No.

**8** • Quit the browser program.

## Puzzle 15.1: Using Java Applets

## Exercise 15.1: Java Basics

1 • Easier.

2 • No, they are separate files.

3 • In a reserved area within the browser window.

4 • The JIT improves performance.

5 • Configure the browser software to disable Java processing.

**6** • If the server has not been set up to support long filenames, the appropriate name space must be added to each volume that will store applets.

**7** • The server might be out of memory. The addition of long file name space requires additional server memory.

**8** • LONG.NAM.

**9** • ADD NAME SPACE

**10** • class.

**11** • java.

## Exercise 15.2: Placing and Calling Applets

**1** • (a) in the same directory as the Web page; (b) in a shared directory on the same Web server; (c) in a directory on a remote Web server.

**2** • CODEBASE.

**3** • No. To publish Java applets, you must place them in a directory to which visitors have access.

**4** • In the same directory as the Java applet that uses them.

**5** • `<APPLET CODE="fun.class" HEIGHT=50 WIDTH=150>`

**6** • `<APPLET CODEBASE="/applets" CODE="dance.class" HEIGHT=200 WIDTH=200>`

**7** • `<PARAM NAME="speed" VALUE="jitterbug">`

**8** • If Java processing is enabled, the tags are ignored. If Java processing is disabled, the tags are processed with the other HTML tags on the page.

**9** • No. The Web server sends applets to the browser. The browser processes the applets.

## Exercise 15.4: Understanding Java Concepts

**1** • No.

**2** • The attack consumes memory and CPU time so there are no resources available to run other programs.

**3** • Quit the browser program.

**4** • intraNetWare SDK for Java.

**5** • The Java Virtual Machine (JVM).

**6** • The Just-In-Time (JIT) compiler.

**7** • Quit and restart the browser.

**8** • (a) Verify that the changes were saved to the correct file; (b) Reload the Web page; (c) Quit and restart the browser.

# Publishing Web Pages on Web Servers from Novell

The best way to test your progress as a Web page developer is to actually publish on a Web server. For simple Web pages, the results look the same as when you view your Web page on the local computer, but publishing on the Web server is much better. Publishing on the Web server proves to you, and to others, that you are on your way to becoming a Web master.

This appendix describes how to publish Web pages on the following Web servers from Novell:

- Novell Web Server

- Netscape Enterprise Server for NetWare

- Netscape FastTrack Server for NetWare

The following section describes publishing issues that apply to both the Novell Web server and the Netscape Web servers for NetWare. The remaining sections describe issues that are unique to either the Novell Web Server or the Netscape Web servers for NetWare.

**IMPORTANT**

**You might need help from your Web server administrator to complete some or all of the tasks in the following sections. The installation procedure requires file system rights and management rights that might be reserved for the Web server administrator only. If you can't complete the procedures in the following sections, contact your Web server administrator. He or she should be able to explain which directories you should use for Web publishing and assign the appropriate file system rights.**

## Common Web Publishing Issues

As mentioned in Chapter 10, Web publishing is a fancy name for copying files to your Web server. Somewhere on your Web server is that magic directory that is reserved for you. When you place your files in this directory, they are instantly published to your local intranet or to the global Internet. Creating the Web site files is the hard part. Publishing the files is simply a matter of copying them to the right locations and perhaps making a few Web server configuration changes.

If your Web site is the primary Web site for a server or for a virtual server, your Web page files will be stored in the document root directory. If you manage a Web site area, or if you are one of many Web sites sharing a host name, your Web page files might be stored in a subdirectory of the document root directory, or they might be stored in an alias or virtual directory. What is important is that there is a directory somewhere on the server where your files should be placed.

To copy files to one of the Novell Web servers, you can copy files just as you would to a NetWare file server because the Novell Web servers share the NetWare file space. The difference is that Web clients access the file space through the Web server software, and the NetWare clients access the file space through the NetWare software.

To prepare to copy your files through the NetWare software, you need to map a drive to the NetWare server or establish a network connection to the file server through the Network Neighborhood. If you don't know how to do this, ask your network administrator. He or she should be able to configure your computer so it automatically connects to the server whenever you log in.

Once you have a network connection to the file server, you can use your Windows software (Windows Explorer or File Manager, for example) to copy files from your local computer to the file server.

To prepare your Web site for use on any of the Novell Web servers, I recommend that you do the following:

- Save all your standard Web pages with the .html file extension.

- Save all your SSI Web pages with the .shtml file extension (SSI is described in Chapter 11).

If you are using a Windows 3.1 workstation to create your Web site, I recommend that you upgrade it to Windows 95 or Windows NT 4, so you can use the longer filename extensions. While you can use the htm file extension on all Novell Web servers for standard Web page files, you must use the longer .shtml file extension for SSI files on the Netscape Web servers for Novell. If you upgrade your workstation now, you won't have to rename your file extensions every time you copy files to the Web server.

The following sections identify the default document root directories for the Novell Web servers and present the URLs that select the document root directories. These section also include additional guidelines for publishing on the Novell Web servers.

## Publishing on a Novell Web Server

To publish a Web site on a Novell Web Server, you need to do the following:

- Copy files to the appropriate directories.

- Add the index.html index filename to the list of index filenames for the server.

- Configure SSI-command processing for any directories that contain SSI files.

The following sections provide guidelines for copying the files and describe the configuration changes that need to be made.

### COPYING FILES TO THE SERVER

Table B.1 lists where your Web site files should be copied on the Novell Web Server. You can copy these files using a standard NetWare or intraNetWare server connection. If you copied your Web site to the default document root directory for the Novell Web Server, you should be able to open the home page using one of the following URLs:

```
http://server_name/
```

```
http://server_name/index.htm
```

```
http://server_name/index.html
```

**TABLE B.1**

*Copying Web Site Files to a*
*Novell Web Server*

| FILES | COPY FILES TO | COMMENTS |
|---|---|---|
| All Web site files except server-side image maps and CGI scripts (which include Perl scripts) | The document root directory. The default location is: SYS:\WEB\DOCS | The top-level directory in your Web site should contain an index file. The default index filename is index.htm, but I recommend you use index.html. |
| All server-side image map files | The maps directory. The default location is: SYS:\WEB\MAPS | These are the *.map files, and they are introduced in Chapter 4. |
| All Perl programs | The Perl program directory. The default location is: SYS:\INW_WEB \SHARED\DOCS \LCGI\PERL5 | These are the *.pl files, and they are introduced in Chapter 13. |

## ADDING AN ADDITIONAL INDEX FILENAME

Index filenames are introduced in Chapter 4. Index filenames are special names that enable visitors to open a directory home page without specifying the filename. For example, you can enter the URL http://*server_name*/ instead of http://*server_name*/ index.html.

The default index filename for the Novell Web server is index.htm, but you can change this. I recommend that you change it to index.html or add index.html to the configuration. This change prepares your Web site for the future when you might want to upgrade to one of the Netscape Web servers for NetWare.

To change or add an index filename on the Novell Web Server, open the Server Resource Management configuration file (default: SYS:\WEB\CONFIG\SRM.CFG) and edit the following line:

```
DirectoryIndex index.htm
```

You can change the index.htm filename or you can add another name to this line. Be sure to separate the names from each other with space characters. After you edit this file, save it and restart the Novell Web Server to activate your changes. After the change is active, the Novell Web Server searches for index files in the order the names are listed, left to right.

**NOTE**

A complete discussion of Novell Web Server management is beyond the scope of this appendix. For more information, see your Web server administrator, the Novell Web Server documentation, or *Novell's Guide to Web Site Management* from **Novell Press.**

## CONFIGURING SSI PROCESSING

Chapter 11 describes SSI commands and how to use them on the Novell Web Server. If you create Web pages with SSI commands, be sure to enable SSI processing for the appropriate directories when you copy these files to the Web server. For more information, see Chapter 11.

# Publishing on Netscape Web Servers for NetWare

To publish a Web site on either of the Netscape Web Servers for NetWare, you need to do the following:

▸ Copy files to the appropriate directories.

▸ Configure SSI-command processing for any directories that contain SSI files.

The following sections provide guidelines for copying the files and describe the configuration changes that need to be made.

## COPYING FILES TO THE SERVER

Table B.2 lists where your Web site files should be copied on the Netscape Web servers for NetWare. You can copy these files using a standard NetWare or intraNetWare server connection. If you copied your Web site to the default document root directory for the Netscape Web servers for NetWare, you should be able to open the home page using either of the following URLs:

```
http://server_name/
```

```
http://server_name/index.html
```

**TABLE B.2**

*Copying the Demonstration
Web Site to Netscape
Enterprise Server for
NetWare*

| COPY FILES FROM | COPY FILES TO | COMMENTS |
|---|---|---|
| All Web site files except CGIscripts (which include Perl scripts) | The document root directory. The default location is: SYS:\NOVONYX-\SUITESPOT\DOCS | The top-level directory in your Web site should contain an index file. The default index filename is index.html. |
| All Perl programs | The Perl program directory. The default location is: SYS:\NOVONYX\SUITES-POT\DOCS\LCGI\PERL5 | These are the *.pl files, and they are introduced in Chapter 13. |

## CONFIGURING SSI PROCESSING

Chapter 11 describes SSI commands and how to use them on the Web servers. If you create Web pages with SSI commands, be sure to enable SSI processing for the appropriate directories when you copy these files to the Web server. The option for configuring SSI-command processing on the Netscape Web servers is called *Parse HTML*, and it is located on the Content Management configuration page.

For instructions on configuring the Netscape Web servers for NetWare, see the product documentation.

**NOTE**

**The Novell Web Server SSI commands will not operate on the Netscape Web servers for NetWare. As described in Chapter 11, these SSI commands only work on the Novell Web Server.**

# What's on the CD-ROM?

This appendix introduces the software included on this book's CD-ROM and describes how to install the demonstration Web site on Web servers from Novell.

## CD-ROM Contents

DesGuide is the volume name for the CD-ROM that accompanies this book. This CD-ROM includes a demonstration Web site, Netscape Communicator, and software for creating Web pages, Web page images, and Web page animation.

Table C.1 describes the CD-ROM contents and where you can find the appropriate installation instructions. Rather than install all of the software at once, I recommend that you install each component as you encounter it in this book. The information in this book will help you understand the components and get the best use from them. Also, some of this software is trial version software that operates for only 30 days. If you wait to install the software when you are really ready to use it, you can take full advantage of the 30-day trial period.

| TABLE C.1 Contents of Book's CD-ROM | CD-ROM DIRECTORY | CONTENTS | INSTALLATION INSTRUCTIONS |
|---|---|---|---|
| | Applets | Java applets for inserting time, date, and tickertape displays in Web pages | Chapter 15 describes how to use Java applets in Web pages. For instructions on using each of these applets, see the USAGE.HTM file in the same directory as the applet. |
| | Browser | Netscape Communicator 4.04 for Windows 3.1, Windows 95, and Windows NT | Chapter 1 describes how to install the browser software. |
| | DemoWeb2 | Demonstration Web site that contains working examples of the Web pages and Web page features covered in this book | The demonstration Web site can be accessed from the CD-ROM or installed on a Web server. The instructions for installing the Web site on Novell Web servers are provided later in this appendix. |

| | **CD-ROM DIRECTORY** | **CONTENTS** | **INSTALLATION INSTRUCTIONS** |
|---|---|---|---|
| **T A B L E   C.1**<br>*Contents of Book's CD-ROM* | gifMGear | GIF Movie Gear program for creating animated GIF images (30-day trial version) | Animated GIF images and GIF Movie Gear are introduced in Chapter 9. To install GIF Movie Gear, open the GMVGR25.EXE file in this directory and follow the instructions. To access the GIF Movie Gear product documentation, start the program and select Help → Contents. |
| | Mapedit | MapEdit image map creation software (30-day trial version) | Chapter 4 describes image maps. To install MapEdit, open this directory from Windows and open one of the following files: MAPDST.EXE (Windows 3.1) or MAP32DST.EXE (Windows 95 or NT). Follow the onscreen instructions to complete the installation. |
| | MPaper | Morning Paper is a program that tracks and summarizes changes on Web sites you select (30-day trial version) | This program is provided for evaluation purposes from Boutell.Com. To install Morning Paper, open the MORNDST.EXE file in this directory and follow the instructions. To access the Morning Paper product documentation, start the program and click the Help button. |

*(continued)*

| TABLE C.1 | CD-ROM DIRECTORY | CONTENTS | INSTALLATION INSTRUCTIONS |
|---|---|---|---|
| *Contents of Book's CD-ROM (continued)* | NetObjects | NetObjects Fusion Web Site creation software for Windows 95 and Windows NT (30-day trial version) | NetObjects Fusion is introduced in Chapter 6. To install NetObjects Fusion, open the NOF202TRIAL1OF4.EXE program in this directory and follow the onscreen instructions. For additional information, see the README.TXT file in this directory. |
| | PhotoShp | Adobe Photoshop 4.01 for Windows (demo version) | Adobe Photoshop is introduced in Chapter 8. For Adobe Photoshop installation instructions, open the following README file on this book's CD-ROM: PhotoShp\disk1\ Readme.wri |
| | WLater | WebLater URL tracking software, which you can use to return to Web locations you've previously visited (30-day trial version) | This program is provided for evaluation purposes from Boutell.Com. To install WebLater, open this directory from Windows and open one of the following files: WEBLDST.EXE (Windows 3.1) or WL32DST.EXE (Windows 95 or NT). Follow the onscreen instructions to complete the installation. |
| | WUsage5.0 | WUsage Web site analysis software for generating statistical reports from your Web site logs (30-day trial version) | Chapter 5 introduces tools, such as Wusage, as validation tools. For instructions on installing and using WUsage, open the product manual on the CD-ROM at: WUsage5.0\Manual\ Index.html. |

## Installing the Demonstration Web Site on a Web Server

The demonstration Web site on this CD-ROM is a working Web site that demonstrates the concepts presented in this guide. While you can view most of the Web site features directly from the CD-ROM, some features, such as server-side image maps and Perl scripts, require a Web server for processing. The following sections describe how to install the demonstration Web site on the three Web servers offered and supported by Novell:

▸ Novell Web Server

▸ Netscape Enterprise Server for NetWare

▸ Netscape FastTrack Server for NetWare

The procedure for installing the demonstration Web site on the two Netscape Web servers for NetWare is the same. The procedure for installing the Web site on nonNovell Web servers is very similar, but you might have to copy some files to different directories and adjust different configuration settings.

**IMPORTANT**

**You might need help from your Web server administrator to complete some or all of the tasks in the following sections. The installation procedure requires file system rights and management rights that might be reserved for the Web server administrator only. The Web server administrator might also prefer that you install the demonstration Web site in a different directory. If you can't complete the procedures in the following sections, contact your Web server administrator. He or she should be able to install the Web site in any directory using the guidelines presented here.**

### INSTALLING ON A NOVELL WEB SERVER

To install the demonstration Web site on a Novell Web Server, you need to do the following:

▸ Copy files to the appropriate directories.

▶  Configure SSI-command processing for the appropriate directories.

▶  Remove the read-only attributes from some files.

The following sections describe how to copy the files to the Web server, which SSI configuration changes need to be made, and how to modify attributes for the necessary files.

### Copying Files to the Server

Table C.2 lists the files that should be copied from the CD-ROM to the Novell Web Server. You can copy these files using a standard NetWare or intraNetWare server connection.

| TABLE C.2 | COPY FILES FROM | COPY FILES TO | COMMENTS |
|---|---|---|---|
| *Copying the Demonstration Web Site to a Novell Web Server* | *d*:DemoWeb2 | The document root directory. The default location is: SYS:\WEB\DOCS | Copy the directory and all of its contents to the document root directory. |
| | *d*:DemoWeb2\Sites\ Links\travel.map | The maps directory. The default location is: SYS:\WEB\MAPS | Copy just this one file to the MAPS directory. |
| | *d*:DemoWeb2\ Answers\chapters .map | The maps directory. The default location is: SYS:\WEB\MAPS | Copy just this one file to the MAPS directory. |
| | *d*:DemoWeb2\ Programs\CGI\ echo.pl | The Perl program directory. The default location is: SYS:\INW_ WEB\SHARED\DOCS\ LCGI\PERL5 | Copy just this one file to the destination directory. (If you have installed the Novell Web Server Toolkit, this file should already be installed.) |
| | *d*:DemoWeb2\ Programs\Perl\*.pl | The Perl program directory. The default location is: SYS:\INW_ WEB\SHARED\DOCS\ LCGI\PERL5 | Copy all the files with a .pl extension in this directory to the destination directory. These are the example Perl programs. |

| T A B L E   C.2 | COPY FILES FROM | COPY FILES TO | COMMENTS |
|---|---|---|---|
| Copying the Demonstration Web Site to a Novell Web Server | d:DemoWeb2\ Answers\*.pl | The Perl program directory. The default location is: SYS:\INW_ directory. WEB\SHARED\DOCS\ LCGI\PERL5 | Copy all the files with a .pl extension in this directory to the destination. These are the Perl programs created by the exercises. |

Copy the files to the Web server using a Windows 95 or Windows NT 4.0 client. Windows 3.1 clients will not be able to read some of the Java applet and SSI files that use long filenames because they do not conform to the DOS 8.3 filename format (for example, FILENAME.EXT).

If you copied the demonstration Web site to the default directories for the Novell Web Server, you should be able to open the demonstration Web site home page using the following URL:

```
http://server_name/DemoWeb2/
```

### Configuring SSI Processing

After you copy these files, all examples except for the SSI examples should operate with the default configuration of your Novell Web Server. To enable the SSI examples, you must do the following:

- ▶ Add the shtml filename extension to the list of extensions for parsed HTML files.

- ▶ Enable SSI processing for the following directories:

  - ▶ \docs\DemoWeb2\Programs\SSI

  - ▶ \docs\DemoWeb2\Answers

Chapter 11 describes how to complete both of these tasks on a Novell Web Server.

### Removing Read-Only File Attributes

Some of the SSI command examples for Chapter 11 write data to a text file. Because the files are flagged as read-only when saved on the CD-ROM, you must change the file attributes before these examples will work. If you installed the demonstration Web site in the default document root directory, the files that need to be modified are the following:

▸ Sys:\Web\docs\DemoWeb2\Programs\SSI\APPEND.TXT

▸ Sys:\Web\docs\DemoWeb2\Programs\SSI\APPEND2.TXT

▸ Sys:\Web\docs\DemoWeb2\Programs\SSI\COUNT.TXT

▸ Sys:\Web\docs\DemoWeb2\Answers\COUNT.TXT

To remove the read-only attribute from these files with Windows 95 or Windows NT 4.0, right-click the filename in Windows Explorer, select Properties, then clear the checkmark from the read-only box.

To remove the read-only attribute in Windows 3.1, select the filename in File Manager, select File→Properties, clear the checkmark from the Read Only box, and click OK.

## INSTALLING ON NETSCAPE WEB SERVERS FOR NETWARE

To install the demonstration Web site on either of the Netscape Web Servers for NetWare, you need to do the following:

▸ Copy files to the appropriate directories.

▸ Make some configuration changes to the Web server.

▸ Remove the read-only attributes from some files.

The following sections describe how to copy the files to the Web server, which server configuration changes need to be made, and how to modify attributes for the necessary files.

### Copying Files to the Server

Table C.3 lists the files that should be copied from the CD-ROM to the Netscape Web Server for NetWare. You can copy these files using a standard NetWare or intraNetWare server connection.

| TABLE C.3 | COPY FILES FROM | COPY FILES TO | COMMENTS |
|---|---|---|---|
| *Copying the Demonstration Web Site to Netscape Enterprise Server for NetWare* | *d:*DemoWeb2 | The document root directory. The default location is: SYS:\NOVONYX\ SUITESPOT\DOCS | Copy the directory and all of its contents to the document root directory. |
| | *d:*DemoWeb2\ Programs\Perl\ | The Perl program directory. The default location is: SYS:\NOVONYX\SUITESPOT\ DOCS\LCGI\PERL5 | Copy all the files with a .pl extension in this directory to the destination directory. These are the example Perl programs. |
| | *d:*DemoWeb2\ Answers\*.pl | The Perl program directory. The default location is: SYS:\NOVONYX\SUITESPOT\ DOCS\LCGI\PERL5 | Copy all the files with a .pl extension in this directory to the destination directory. These are the Perl programs created by the exercises. |

Copy the files to the Web server using a Windows 95 or Windows NT 4.0 client. Windows 3.1 clients will not be able to read some of the Java applet and SSI files that use long filenames because they do not conform to the DOS 8.3 filename format (for example, FILENAME.EXT).

### Configuring the Server

After you copy the demonstration Web site to the server, most of the examples should operate with the default configuration of your server. To support all example files, you should do the following:

▶ Add the *index.htm* filename to the list of index filenames for the server.

▸ Enable SSI processing the following directories:

   ▸ Sys:\Novonyx\Suitespot\docs\DemoWeb2\Programs\SSI

   ▸ Sys:\Novonyx\Suitespot\docs\DemoWeb2\Answers

The default index filenames for the Netscape servers for NetWare are index.html and home.html. Adding the index.htm filename to the list of index filenames enables you to open the demonstration Web site index file in any directory without specifying the filename. For example, you can enter the URL *server_name*/demoweb2/ instead of *server_name*/demoweb2/index.htm. The option for configuring the index filename on the Netscape Web servers can be found under Document Preferences, and it is located on the Content Management configuration page.

As described in Chapter 11 for the Novell Web Server, the default configuration for the Netscape Web servers for NetWare does not support SSI-command processing. However, you can enable SSI processing for any directory on the Netscape Web server. The option for configuring SSI-command processing on the Netscape Web servers is called *Parse HTML* and is located on the Content Management configuration page.

For instructions on configuring the Netscape Web servers for NetWare, see the product documentation.

**NOTE**    **The SSI command examples for the Novell Web Server SSI commands will not operate on the Netscape Web servers for NetWare. As described in Chapter 11, these SSI commands only work on the Novell Web Server.**

If you copied the demonstration Web site to the default directories for the Netscape Web servers for NetWare, you should be able to open the demonstration Web site home page using the following URL:

```
http://server_name/DemoWeb2/
```

### Removing Read-Only File Attributes

Some of the SSI command examples for Chapter 11 write data to a text file. Because the files are flagged as read-only when saved on the CD-ROM, you must change the file attributes before these examples will work. If you installed the demonstration Web site in the default document root directory, the files that need to be modified are the following:

- Sys:\Novonyx\Suitespot\docs\DemoWeb2\Programs\SSI\Append.txt

- Sys:\Novonyx\Suitespot\docs\DemoWeb2\Programs\SSI\Append2.txt

- Sys:\Novonyx\Suitespot\docs\DemoWeb2\Programs\SSI\Count.txt

- Sys:\Novonyx\Suitespot\docs\DemoWeb2\Answers\Count.txt

To remove the read-only attribute from these files with Windows 95 or Windows NT 4.0, right-click the filename in Windows Explorer, select Properties, then clear the checkmark from the read-only box.

To remove the read-only attribute in Windows 3.1, select the filename in File Manager, select File → Properties, clear the checkmark from the Read Only box, and click OK.

# *I*ndex

## Numbers and Symbols:

2Cool Animations, Web site address for viewing example animated GIFs, 322
8-bit color systems, versus 24-bit color systems, 237
8-bit display adapters, use of dithering to simulate colors not supported, 244
8-bit images, color conversion for, 238
24-bit color systems, versus 8-bit color systems, 237
24-bit image, 235
\* (asterisk), in frameset value list, 128
\*/ (asterisk/forward slash), in JavaScripts, 535
\ (backslash) character, in Perl scripts, 489–490
, (comma) operator, in Perl scripts, 494–495
$ (dollar) symbol
    as Perl scalar variable, 493–495
    using in Web pages, 36
/ (forward slash character)
    using in absolute references, 93
    using in HTML formatting, 19
    using in paths, 68
/\* (forward slash/asterisk), in JavaScripts, 535
// (double forward slash), in JavaScripts, 535
\> (greater than) symbol, 18
    HTML code for, 36
\< (less than) symbol, 18
    HTML code for, 36
% (percent) sign, in Perl associative arrays, 496–497
. (period) operator, in Perl scripts, 494–495
# (pound sign), in Perl scripts, 490
? (question marks)
    HTML code for, 36
    in JavaScripts, 534
    in Perl scripts, 489
    use of with attribute values, 144
; (semicolons)
    in JavaScripts, 534
    in Perl scripts, 489
& (ampersand), HTML code, 36
&gt;, HTML code, 36
&lt;, HTML code, 36
  tag, HTML, 35
&PrintHeader, Perl command, 487
&quote;, HTML code, 36
&ReadParse function
    array data from sample form, 500
    arrays built by, 498–500
    using in Perl scripts, 492–493
&reg;, HTML code, 36
\<!—*comments*\> tag, HTML, 33
    using with \<APPLET\> tag, 601
© (copyright) symbol, HTML code for, 36
~ (tilde character), as reference to user Web page directory, 412
_ (underscore character)
    as part of variable name in JavaScript, 541
    as Perl scalar variable, 493–495
    in variable names, 139

## A

\<A\> \</A\> intradocument link tags, 84–86, 132
\<ABBREV\> \</ABBREV\>, logical style tag, 31
abbreviation, logical style tag, 31
absolute paths, 69
absolute reference
    in URLs, 92–93
    using forward slash (/) in, 93
ACCESS.CFG configuration file, editing, 405–406
Account Setup wizard, Netscape Communicator, 11
acronym, logical style tag, 31
\<ACRONYM\> \</ACRONYM\>, logical style tag, 31
ACTION attribute
    adding to forms, 134
    defining the destination of form data with, 137–138
ActiveX controls, adding to Web pages in NetObjects Fusion, 188–189
Adaptive palette, Photoshop, 260–261
address, logical style tag, 31
\<ADDRESS\> \</ADDRESS\>, logical style tag, 31
Adobe Acrobat Reader, viewing PDF files with, 308
Adobe Distiller, creating PDF files with, 308
Adobe Illustrator EPS (AI, AI3, AI4, AI5, or AI6) format, exporting Photoshop images to, 263
Adobe PageMill, Web site address for, 152
Adobe Photoshop
    Adaptive palette, 260–261
    choosing a color mode, 257–259
    choosing an image file format in, 263–264
    choosing transparent colors for an image in, 274–275
    Color Picker palette, 265–267
    converting a file to a Web image format, 263–264
    creating and adapting Web graphics in, 232–287
    creating aliased text in, 370
    creating and optimizing background images in, 281–284
    creating GIF images, 270–271
    creating graphic images with, 64
    creating graphical text as GIF images in, 368–373
    creating image objects in, 264–265
    creating interlaced GIFs, 274
    creating JPEG images in, 278–279
    creating special text effects, 370–371
    cropping images in, 268–269
    demo versions of program on CD-ROM, 672
    determining the decimal color value in a Web image with, 372
    disabling anti-aliasing in, 265
    displaying alternate images in, 269
    Exact palette, 260–261
    exporting GIF images from RGB color mode, 272–274
    exporting images to different formats, 263–264
    formats for saving image files, 263–264
    indexed color mode, 258–259
    introduction to, 255–256
    loading and choosing Web color swatches in, 265–267
    opening image files in, 257
    reducing image colors while exporting a GIF image, 273–274

*(continued)*

Adobe Photoshop (*continued*)
  reducing image file size, 271–274
  RGB color mode, 258
  RGB color mode conversion and export methods, 272–274
  special palette selections in, 260–261
  specifying image dimensions in, 269
  starting, 256
  Swatches palette, 265–267
  switching or converting images to indexed color mode in, 261–263
  undoing an image crop, 269
  Web site address for, 154
Adobe SiteMill, Web site address for, 153
AgentZ Browser Comparison Page, Web page functionality testing information source, 377
alert("*message*") method, JavaScript Window method, 568
aliased objects and text, 249
aliased text, creating in Photoshop, 370
ALIGN attribute
  document division, 34
  heading style tags, 32
  horizontal rule, 34
  `<IMG>` tag, 66
  table captions, rows, and headings, 59
  `<TABLE>` tag, 58
  `<TC>` `</TC>` tags, 59
alinkColor, document object property, 548
ALT= attribute, `<IMG>` tag, 66
  for specifying display of text instead of images on slower computers, 67
AltaVista, Web site address for registering your Web site, 149
alternate images, displaying in Photoshop, 269
alternate text, displaying in place of images in Web pages, 67
Ameritech.net, Web site address, 13
ampersand (&), HTML tag for, 36
anchor tags, for creating intradocument links, 83–86
Animagic GIF Animator, 323
animated GIFs, 321
  copyright issues and restrictions, 322
  guidelines for creating, 323–324
  locating additional tools for working with, 323
  software products for creating, 323
  Web site addresses for viewing examples of, 322
animation
  adding to Web pages in NetObjects Fusion, 188–189
  displaying with Java applets, 591
  file optimization techniques, 319
  GIF format support for, 250–251
  guidelines for using in Web pages, 320–328
animation file formats, 321
answers to exercises and puzzles, 624–660
anti-aliased text, creating in Photoshop, 370
anti-aliasing
  disabling in Photoshop, 265
  image problems created by, 248–249
appCodeName property, Netscape Navigator object, 547
append SSI command, Novell Web Server

examples, 426
format for, 425–426
AppleScript language, support for CGI programming, 463
`<APPLET>` tags
  adding to Web pages to call applets, 598
  attributes, 601
  format for, 600
  using, 600–605
  using HTML `<COMMENT>` tag with, 601
applets, testing, 605–606
appName property, Netscape Navigator object, 547
appVersion property, Netscape Navigator object, 547
`<AREA>` tag, 132
array variables
  rules for, 496
  in Perl scripts, 495–496
arithmetic operators, in JavaScript, 554
art, aligning Web page content with, 350
Assets directory, Web site, 173
assignment operators, in JavaScript, 554
associative array variables
  rules for names, 497
  in Perl scripts, 496–497
asterisk (*), in frameset value list, 128
asterisk/forward slash (*/), in JavaScripts, 535
attribute values, use of question marks (?) with, 144
audio files, playing with Java applets, 591
Audio Interchange File Format (.aiff, .aif, .aiffc), 329
Audio Player (Netscape), sound file plug-in, 329
AUTH_TYPE environment variable, echo SSI command, 419
Authorware (Macromedia)
  animation format, 321
  plug-in needed to view files, 326
AutoSite templates in NetObjects Fusion, creating new Web sites with, 172

## B

`<B>` `</B>` (bold) tags, 23
BACKGROUND= attribute, `<TABLE>` tag, 58
background images
  adding to Web pages, 63–64, 65
  advantages of full screen, 282
  creating and optimizing in Photoshop, 281–284
  guidelines for creating, 284
  tools for controlling positioning of, 346–347
backslash (\) character, in Perl scripts, 489–490
`<BASE>` tag, specifying a default target for all document links with, 133–134
`<BASEFONT>` tag, HTML 3.2, 26
baseline shift effect, 366
  creating in HTML, 373
  creating in Photoshop, 370
BASIC
  support for CGI programming, 463
  versus Java, 590
Beatnik (Headspace), sound file plug-in, 329, 330

Beginner's All-Purpose Symbolic Instruction Code (BASIC). *See* BASIC
Bell Atlantic Internet Solutions, Web site address for, 13
BellSouth.net Internet Services, Web site address for, 13
bgColor, document object property, 548
BGCOLOR= attribute, `<TABLE>` tag, 58
`<BGSOUND>` tag, playing multimedia files with, 313
`<BIG> </BIG>` tag, HTML 3.2, 26
bit depth, 235–236
    formula for calculating the total number of colors, 236
bitmap graphics, 276–277. *See also* bitmaps
bitmaps
    common bit depths, 235–236
    how they work, 233–239
    image size and resolution, 233–234
    palettes, 238
    primary settings that control how they work, 233–239
bitwise operator, support for in JavaScript, 555
`<BLINK> </BLINK>` tags, Netscape browser, 26
block quote, HTML tag for, 33
`<BLOCKQUOTE> </BLOCKQUOTE>`, HTML tag, 33
BMP (Windows Bitmap) format, saving Photoshop images to, 263
`<BODY> </BODY>` tags, Web pages, 20, 26
`<BOLD> </BOLD>` tags, HTML 2.0, 27
bold text, creating in Web pages, 23
boolean data, in JavaScripts, 539–540
BORDER= attribute
    `<FRAMESET>` tag, 128
    `<IMG>` tag, 66
`<BR> </BR>` tag
    HTML, 34, 54
    as Perl scalar variable, 493–495
break (new line), HTML tag for, 34, 54
`break` SSI command, Novell Web Server, 426–427
break statements, in JavaScript, 558
browser and Web page objects, 542
browser-safe colors, color values table for, 372
browser-safe swatches palette, Photoshop
    downloading a copy of, 267
    loading, 266–267
    selecting colors from, 267
browsers
    enabling and disabling Java in, 594
    enabling and disabling JavaScript in, 531–532, 594
    HTML tags and attributes supported differently in, 345
    image formats supported by, 64–65
    Netscape Communicator, 9–11
    plug-ins and helper applications for Web page visitors, 306–307
    previewing images in before publishing Web pages, 247
    support for multimedia, 306
    supporting multiple in your Web site, 344–346
    supporting no frame, 131–132
    using browser safe colors to fix image color problems, 245, 247
bulleted lists. *See* unordered lists
bullets, guidelines for creating in Photoshop, 280–281
button, guidelines for creating in Photoshop, 281

C

C programming language
    support for CGI programming, 463
    versus Java, 590
C++ programming language
    support for CGI programming, 463
    versus Java, 390
`calc` SSI command, Novell Web Server
    format for, 427–428
    sample commands, 427
`<CAPTION> </CAPTION>` tags, 59
Cascading Style Sheets (CSS), 226
case-sensitivity
    of some URLs, 29
    of Web page tags, 29
CD-ROM in book
    contents, 670–679
    installing demonstration Web site on Netscape Web Servers for
        NetWare, 676–679
    installing demonstration Web site on Novell Web Server, 673–676
    using to view sample files in book, 21
cell width, setting for tables in Web pages, 351
CELLPADDING= attribute, `<TABLE>` tag, 58
CELLSPACING= attribute, `<TABLE>` tag, 58
`<CENTER> </CENTER>`, HTML tag, 33
center line, HTML tag for, 33
Certified Web Designer certificate, preparing for the exam, 4–16
CGI Collection, Web site address for, 469
CGI interpreter
    default directory locations for, 470
    defining a virtual path to in SRM.CFG file, 458
    loading, 474–475
CGI programming, operating systems and programming languages
        that support, 463
CGI programs and scripts
    calling from your Web page, 475–476
    compatible programs, 456
    default directory locations for, 470
    error messages, 477
    how they work, 456–458
    implementing custom solutions to problems with, 455
    importance of placement on server, 470
    loading, 474–475
    obtaining or creating, 468–469
    on the Novell Web Server, 458–462
    placing in directories, 474
    program processing, 458
    reasons for using, 454–456
    sample CGI process results, 462
    sample form processing with, 462
    sample HTML form, 461
    saving form data to, 137–138
    setting up and using, 467–476
    simplified HTML file request, 457
    specifying directories for, 469–474

*(continued)*

CGI programs and scripts *(continued)*
    starting with a URL, 457
    submitting form data to, 457–458
    troubleshooting tips, 477
    types, 463–467
    URLs for program sites, 469
    using <FORM> tag ACTION attribute in, 459
    using, 454–478
    working with, 467–476
CGI program types, 463–467
CGI security, Web site address for information, 477
checkboxes, 143
    creating, 142–143
    option attributes, 142
CHECKED attribute
    checkbox option, 142
    radio button option, 144
checked, property description for objects that appear in forms, 549
child Web page, 170–171
citation, logical style tag, 31
<CITE> </CITE>, logical style tag, 31
CLEAR attribute, new line (break) tag, 34
clearTimeout(*timeoutID*) method, JavaScript Window method, 568
client-side image maps
    adding the image tag, 103
    advantages of, 102
    creating the image, 103
    creating the image map table with a utility, 103–104
    exercise for creating, 117–119
    making in NetObjects Fusion, 184
    tasks needed for using, 102
    verifying browser support for, 102–103
client-side JavaScripts, versus server-side, 571–571
clip art, copyright issues, 319–320
clip sound, copyright issues, 319–320
Clock and Date applets, calling to your Web page, 601–605
close() method, JavaScript Window method, 568
CLUT. *See* color lookup table
code, logical style tag, 31
CODE attribute, <APPLET> tag, 601
<CODE> </CODE>, logical style tag, 31
CODEBASE attribute, <APPLET> tag, 601
color codes
    for five basic colors, 27
    Web site address for RGB Hex Triplet Color Chart, 28
Color Depth drop-down list, Indexed Color dialog box, 262
color lookup table, 237. *See also* palette
color mode, choosing in Photoshop, 257–259
color palette, browser safe, 245
Color Picker palette, Photoshop, 265–267
Colors text box, Indexed Color dialog box, 262
COLS= attribute
    <FRAMESET> tag (Netscape), 128
    <TEXTAREA> tag, 140
columns
    COLSPAN attribute for, 60, 62
    defining number of in a frameset, 127

HTML tags for adding to tables, 57, 59–60
combined (linear and hierarchical) layout, Web site design, 216–217
comma (,) operator, in Perl scripts, 494–495
command interpreter, 460
<!–*comments*> tag, HTML, 33
    using with <APPLET> tag, 601
comments, HTML tag for, 33
Common Gateway Interface (CGI) programs and scripts. *See* CGI programs and scripts
comparison operators
    in JavaScript, 554
    in Perl scripts, 503
CompuServe GIF (GIF) format, saving Photoshop images to, 263
computer graphic types, 276–277
computer system, requirement for supporting Netscape Communicator browser, 8
Concentric Network, Web site address for, 13
config SSI command
    argument values you can use with, 415
    configuring display options with, 414–416
    configuring SSI-error processing with, 416–418
    display option examples, 417
    syntax for, 414
    using onerr and errmsg arguments with, 417
Configure Publish dialog box, 191
    Stage and Publish tabs in, 190
confirm("*message*") method, JavaScript Window method, 568
CONTENT attribute values, <META> tag, 148
CONTENT_LENGTH environment variable, echo SSI command, 419
CONTENT_TYPE environment variable, echo SSI command, 419
continue statements, in JavaScripts, 558
continuous tone images, 246
conversion utilities, converting existing files into Web page files with, 153–154
conversion utility tools, Web site addresses for, 154
2Cool Animations, Web site address for, 322
copyright issues, 319–320
copyright (©) symbol, HTML code for, 36
Corel WordPerfect, Web site address for, 152
count SSI command, Novell Web Server, 428
Crop tool, Photoshop, cropping images with, 268–269
CSE 3310 HTML Validator, Web site address for, 153
CSS. *See* Cascading Style Sheets (CCS)


**D**

daemon application
    directory location on Novell Web Server, 472
    to use CGI script or application on remote server, 472–473
data, processing of in JavaScript, 552–568
DATE_GMT environment variable, echo SSI command, 419
DATE_LOCAL environment variable, echo SSI command, 419
<DD> </DD> HTML tag, 53–54
decorative type effects, 366–367
default index filename, 94
    changing on Novell Web server, 665
default status, window object property, 547

defaultChecked, property description for objects that appear in forms, 549

defaultValue, property description for objects that appear in forms, 549

definition, logical style tag, 31

definition description, HTML tag for, 53–54

definition lists, 53–54

definition topic, HTML tag for, 53–54

`<DEL> </DEL>`, logical style tag, 31

deleted, logical style tag, 31

DemoWeb2, demonstration Web site on CD-ROM, 670
  installing on Netscape Web Servers for NetWare, 676–679
  installing on Novell Web Server, 673–676

Developer.com, Web site address for, 576

`<DFN> </DFN>`, logical style tag, 31

dial-up connection, connecting your computer to the Internet with, 4–5

dial-up Internet Web clients, setting up, 6–15

dial-up network software, requirements for installing Netscape Communicator browser, 8

Director (Macromedia)
  animation format, 321
  plug-in needed to view files, 326

directory tree, sample of how relative references are used, 71

disk space requirements, for installing Netscape Communicator browser, 8

Dither drop-down list, Indexed Color dialog box, 262

dithering, using browser safe colors to minimize, 243–244

`<DIV> </DIV>`, HTML tag, 34

`<DL> </DL>` HTML tags, 53–54

Doctor HTML, Web site address for, 153

document division, HTML tag for, 34

`DOCUMENT_NAME` environment variable, echo SSI command, 419

document object property, alinkColor, 548

`DOCUMENT_URI` environment variable, echo SSI command, 420

document root directory
  storing your Web page files in, 663, 666–667
  URL variable, 91–93
  using the virtual argument to access, 412

document type declaration, including in your Web page, 150–151

dollar ($) symbol
  as Perl scalar variable, 493–495
  using in Web pages, 36

Domain Name System (DNS), 89

double forward slash (//), in JavaScripts, 535

downloading
  Java applets, 598

Dream Catchers CGI Scripts, Web site address for, 469

drop caps effect
  creating in HTML, 373
  creating in Photoshop, 370

drop-down lists, creating, 140–142

`<DT> </DT>` HTML tags, 53–54

Dynamic HTML, 226

**E**

EarthLink Network, Web site address for, 13

echo SSI-command
  calculated variables, 418
  environment variables, 418, 419–421
  form variables, 418
  format argument, 421–422
  syntax, 419
  var argument, 419–421

editing
  ACCESS.CFG configuration file, 405–406

Electric GIFs, Web site address for viewing example animated GIFs, 322

electronic cameras, creating images with, 64

`<EM> </EM>`, logical style tag, 31

`<EMBED>` tag
  calling inline media with, 311
  sample attributes, 313

emphasize, logical style tag, 31

environment variables, echo command, 419–421

EPS (Photoshop Encapsulated Postscript)

error messages
  CGI-related, 477

eval function, JavaScript, 563

events and event handlers, JavaScript, 563–565
  using to call a function, 564

Exact palette, Photoshop, 260–261

exec SSI command, Novell Web Server, 429

Excite, Web site address for registering your Web site, 149

exercises
  adding navigation aids to Web sites, 387–388
  adding special characters, 44–45
  answers to, 624–660
  building Web pages, 196–197
  building tables, 75–76
  choosing a Web image format, 293–294
  converting a Web page into a Perl script, 517–518
  creating a client-side image map, 117–119
  creating a JavaScript, 586
  creating a server-side image map, 114–116
  creating a Web site, 194–195
  creating forms, 161–163
  creating GIF images, 299–300
  creating interdocument links, 112–113
  creating intradocument links, 110–111
  creating lists, 74
  creating Web pages, 39–47
  displaying images, 77–78
  enabling SSI command processing, 440–441
  enhancing and publishing Web pages, 198–200
  formatting text, 41
  guidelines for creating special Web page elements, 301
  Java basics, 615–616
  JavaScript basics, 580–581
  placing and calling Java applets, 617–618
  positioning text, 42–43
  positioning text and graphics in Web sites, 385–386
  processing data with JavaScripts, 584–585

(continued)

exercises *(continued)*
    testing and publishing your Web site, 391
    understanding advanced Web page features, 164–167
    understanding animation guidelines, 338–339
    understanding bitmap images, 289–290
    understanding guidelines for sounds, 340
    understanding Java concepts, 621–622
    understanding JavaScript, 587–588
    understanding links and image maps, 120–121
    understanding lists, tables, and images, 79–80
    understanding multimedia, 336–337
    understanding Perl scripts, 523–525
    understanding SSI command syntax, 442–443
    understanding video guidelines, 341
    understanding Web design basics, 228–230
    understanding Web image problems, 291–292
    updating a Perl script, 519–522
    using a Java applet, 619–620
    using CGI programs and scripts, 480–482
    using frames, 159–160
    using graphical and HTML type, 389–390
    using laterals, variables, and objects, 582–583
    using multimedia, 342
    using NCSA SSI commands, 444–446
    using Novell Web Server SSI commands, 447–448
    using Photoshop, 295–298
    using NetObjects Fusion, 201–202
    using SSI commands, 449–452
    using tags and attributes, 46–47
expiration date and time, for Web pages, 149
explicity path, specifying from a document root directory to an
        image file, 70
explicit references, 71
    in URLs, 88
expressions
    in JavaScript data processing, 553–554
    using operators to process literals and variables in, 554
external links, creating, 92

**F**

fgColor, document object property, 548
`file` argument, sample directory tree and paths to text files, 410
file protocol, for interdocument links, 88
file relative reference, 70
filename, as URL variable, 94–95
files, relative references, 70
Flash (Macromedia)
    animation format, 321
    plug-in needed to view files, 326
`flastmod` SSI command, formats for, 422–423
floating Tools and Properties palettes, customizing Site view
        appearance with, 173–174
`<FONT> </FONT>` tags, HTML 3.2 and 4.0, 25–28
fonts
    HTML tags and attributes for, 25–28
    in Web pages, 345

for statements, in JavaScript, 558
foreground images
    adding to Web pages, 63–64, 65–66
    tools for controlling positioning of, 346–347
form data
    recording, 492–500
    using in JavaScripts, 542–552
form elements
    creating, 138–145
    text input boxes, 138–139
`<FORM> </FORM>` tags, 132, 134
    METHOD attributes, 136–137
form object (single element), 542
    properties, 543
form processing, in Perl
    processing form data, 500–507
    recording form data, 492–500
Form tools, in NetObjects Fusion Tools palette, 185–187, 187
`format` argument, `echo` SSI-command
    examples, 422
    syntax for, 421–422
formatting commands
    for Web page text, 18–19
forms
    adding a submit button to in NetObjects Fusion, 186
    adding ACTION attribute to, 134
    adding other elements to in NetObjects Fusion, 186–187
    common elements, 135
    creating, 134–145
    creating basic, 135–138
    creating a Submit Query button in, 136
    creating elements for, 138–145
    creating in NetObjects Fusion, 185–187
    defining data destination with ACTION attribute, 137–138
    defining the action for in NetObjects Fusion, 186
    GET method, 136–137
    METHOD attribute, 136–137
    POST method, 136–137
    processing with SSI commands, 432–435
    sample, 134
    saving data collected from, 137–138
Forms Plus, Web site address for, 155
forward slash (/) character
    in absolute references, 93
    in HTML formatting, 19
    in paths, 68
forward slash/asterisk (/*), in JavaScripts, 535
`<FRAME>` tag attributes, 129–130
FRAMEBORDER=, `<FRAMESET>` tag attribute, 128
*frame_reference*, property name component in JavaScript, 550
frames
    aligning Web page content with, 352–353
    creating links to using `<FRAME>` TARGET attribute, 132–134
    defining contents of, 129
    disadvantages of using in Web pages, 353
    using, 124–134
    using to display a table of contents for your Web site, 125, 126

frames[*frame*], window object property, 547
frameset, 124
    creating frameset document for, 126–130
    creating nested, 130–131
    defining the number of rows and columns in, 127
    tag attributes table, 128
    tags, 127
    two-frame, 125
frameset documents
    creating, 126–130
    versus Web page documents, 127
<FRAMESET> tags
    attributes, 128–129
    defining a set of frames with, 127
frameset value list, using asterisk in, 128
front door Web page, providing plug-in and helper application
        instructions with, 314–315
fsize SSI command, formats for, 423
FTP, for interdocument links, 88
functionality testing information source, 377
functions, in JavaScript
    benefits of, 558
    built-in, 562–563
    calling from scripts, 561–562
    creating, 559–561
    creating a link to, 570–571

**G**

Gamelan, Web site address for, 597
GET method, METHOD attribute, 136–137
    disadvantages of using, 137
GIF. *See* GIF images
GIF87a, 65
GIF89a (animation) format, 65
    exporting Photoshop images to, 263
GIF Construction Set, 323
GIF images, 64–65
    advantages of using interlaced in Web pages, 241
    animation, 250–251
    converting other image formats to, 275–277
    creating graphical text as, 368–373
    creating in Photoshop, 64, 270–271
    creating interlaced, 274
    detail loss in, 247
    features supported by, 251
    interlaced, 253
    rasterizing, 277
    reducing file size of, 239–240, 271–274
    versus JPEG images, 251
GIF Movie Gear
    creating animated GIFs with, 325–326
    program trial version on CD-ROM, 671
    Web site address for, 154, 323
GMT. *See* Greenwich Mean Time (GMT)
Gopher protocol, for interdocument links, 88
goto SSI command, Novell Web Server, 431

graphic and text links, tying Web site pages together with, 82–108
graphic design, for Web site designers, 208
graphic images. *See* GIF images; images
Graphic Interchange Format (GIF). *See* GIF images
graphic programs and utilities, Web site addresses for, 154
graphical text images, optimizing, 368
graphical type
    enhancing Web pages with, 363
    using, 362–373
graphics programs, creating images with, 64
greater than (>) character, 18
    HTML code for, 36
Greenwich Mean Time (GMT), 419
Guestbook*Star, Web site address for, 155

**H**

<H1> </H1>, logical style tag, 31
<H2> </H2>, logical style tag, 31
<H3> </H3>, logical style tag, 31
<H4> </H4>, logical style tag, 31
<H5> </H5>, logical style tag, 32
<H6> </H6>, logical style tag, 32
halos, preventing appearance of in images, 247–249
HARD option, WRAP attribute, 140
<HEAD> tags, Web pages, 20
heading, logical style tags, 31
HEIGHT attribute, <APPLET> tag, 601
HEIGHT= attribute, <IMG> tag, 66
    adding to Web pages to speed embedded image download
        time, 240
helper applications and plug-ins
    for using and viewing multimedia files in browsers, 306–307
    providing instructions for, 314–315
hidden value, TYPE attribute, 139
hierarchical layout, Web site design, 216
home page, building with NetObject Fusion, 170–171
HomeSite, Web site address for, 152
horizontal rule, HTML tag for, 34
host name, as URL variable, 89–90
hot spots, for image links, 99
HOTBOT, Web site address for registering your Web site, 149
HotDog, Web site address for, 152
HotJava browser by Sun Microsystems
    Java security features supported by, 608
    Java support by, 593
HoTMetaL Pro, Web site address for, 152
<HR> </HR>, HTML tag, 34
HREF attribute, used by link anchor tags, 83–86
HTML
    ampersand (&) symbol code, 36
    <!—*comments*> tag, 33
    copyright symbol code, 36
    defining the version of for Web pages, 150–151
    determining type effects with, 372–373
    examples of Web page coding for text formatting, 24–25
        *(continued)*

HTML (continued)
good reasons for learning, 155–156
greater than (>) symbol code, 36
less than (<) symbol code, 36
tags for publishing Standard Web pages, 13, 18–19
Web site address for viewing online handbooks, 29
Web site address for viewing version 3.2 standards, 18
Web site addresses for information on specific versions, 29
HTML <COMMENT> tags, using with <APPLET> tag, 601
HTML comments, distinguishing from SSI commands, 408–409
HTML documents (Web pages), defining the beginning and end of, 20
HTML editor identification, 148
HTML editors, 151–152
.html filename extension, saving standard Web pages with, 663
HTML files
adding intradocument links to, 83–86
adding special characters to, 36–37
defining the body section of, 20
example of title and text formatting for Web pages, 22
HTML formatting, use of forward slash (/) in, 19
HTML forms. See forms
HTML frames. See frames
HTML Goodies, Web site address for, 575
HTML tags, 20
aligning Web page content with, 349–350
creating combined effects with, 25–28
for nonbreaking spaces, 35
HTML tags and attributes, examples of some supported differently
in browsers, 345
HTML text, selecting browser-safe colors for, 371–372
HTML text links, as Web site navigation aids, 355
HTML Transit, Web site addresses for, 154
HTML type, using, 362–373
HTTP. See HyperText Transfer Protocol (HTTP)
HTTP_ACCEPT environment variable, echo SSI command, 420
HTTP-EQUIV attribute value, <META> tag, 149
HTTP_REFERER environment variable, echo SSI command, 420
HTTP_USER_AGENT environment variable, echo SSI command, 420
hypertext links
tying Web site pages together with, 82–108
versus image links, 86
HyperText Markup Language (HTML). See HTML
HyperText Transfer Protocol (HTTP), between Web browser and
server, 88

**I**

<I> </I> (italic tags), HTML 2.0, 28
if and else branching statements, in Perl scripts, 502–507
format for, 505
if and else statements in JavaScripts, format for, 557
if SSI command, Novell Web Server, 429–431
command operations, 431
command operators, 430
format for, 430
if statements
in JavaScripts, 556–557

in Perl scripts, 502–505
if, then statements, JavaScript, 556–557
image captions, placement tags for, 59, 68
image dimensions, specifying, 64, 269
image file format, choosing in Photoshop, 263–264
image files
opening in Photoshop, 257
Photoshop formats for saving, 263–264
image links
as Web site navigation aids, 355–356
borders tags for, 86
hot spots for, 99
tying Web site pages together with, 82–108
versus hypertext links, 86
image map editor, creating an image map with, 99–100
image-map site map, 361
image maps, 97–98
creating images for, 99
how they work, 98
making in NetObjects Fusion, 184
using server side, 98–101
image maps and links, exercise for testing understanding, 120–121
image objects, creating in Photoshop, 264–265
image pixel measurements, for Web pages, 240
image tags
for alternate text, 67
between anchor tags, 86
using HEIGHT and WIDTH measurements in, 240
images
adding background to Web pages, 65
adding foreground to Web pages, 65–68
adjusting brightness display differences in, 249–250
aligning on Web pages, 67–68
aligning with HTML tags, 349–350
choosing a format to use on Web pages, 250–255
choosing transparent colors for in Photoshop, 274–275
converting from other formats to JPEG, 280
converting PNG to GIF format, 275–277
creating, 64–65
cropping in Photoshop, 268–269
displaying, 62–64
displaying alternate, 269
effects of dithering and noise on, 242–246
fixing halo problems in, 247–249
inline, 63
optimizing (all formats), 268
placing captions for, 68
preventing from overlapping text or another image, 68
previewing in browser before publishing your Web pages, 247
reducing file size of to speed downloading, 239–240
relative path references for, 68
replacing with text for slower computers, 67
setting resolution for faster downloading, 241–242
setting compression levels for JPEG, 252
significant detail loss in, 246–247
specifying dimensions of, 269
specifying height and width of, 68, 269

storing files, 68–70
switching or converting to indexed color mode in Photoshop,
    261–263
thumbnail, 63–64
forward slashes (/) in paths, 68
<IMG> HTML tag, 66
aligning Web page graphics with, 349–350
include SSI command, formats for, 423–424
index file name, 94
changing default or adding new on Novell Web server, 665
index frames, as navigation aids in Web pages, 358
index.htm, default index file name on Novell Web Servers, 94
index.html, default index file name, 94
Indexed Color dialog box, choosing palette for converted image in, 262
indexed color mode, Photoshop
converting or switching images to, 261–263
converting versus switching to, 259
selecting colors you want to keep during conversion, 261
selecting the Web palette file in, 260
switching to, 259–263
undoing mode changes, 263
using, 258–259
Infoseek, Web site address for registering your Web site, 149
initial cap effect
creating in HTML, 373
creating in Photoshop, 370
inline images. See images
<INS> </INS>, logical style tag, 32
inserted, logical style tag, 32
Integrated Services Digital Network (ISDN) Internet connections.
    See ISDN Internet connections
interactive window, JavaScript, 569–570
interdocument links
components of URLs, 87–95
examples of, 95–96
exercise for creating, 112–113
format of with a complete URL, 87
protocols for, 88
interlaced GIFs, 253
creating, 274
internal links, creating within your Web site, 92
Internet access account
setting up using Netscape Communicator, 11–12
setting up for a different browser, 12–14
solving problems with, 14–15
Internet color palette, selecting, 260
Internet connection methods, 4–5
Internet protocol (IP) address, specifying in URLs for accessing
    destination files, 88
Internet Service Providers
custom Web page publishing software from, 13
partial list of, 13
troubleshooting Internet access problems with, 14–15
Web site address for finding, 13
Internet Web site
preparing pages for search engine registration, 146–149
publicizing yours, 145–150

registering with search engines, 150
intradocument links
anchor tags for, 83–86
creating, 83–86
exercise for creating, 110–111
table of contents as, 82–83
tags for, 84–86
intranet Web site, publicizing, 145
intraNetWare
support for CGI programming, 463
IP address. See Internet Protocol (IP) address
ISDN Internet connections, 8
italic <I> </I> tags, HTML, 28

J

Java
animation format, 321
browsers that support, 593
creating animations with, 326–327
defined, 590
enabling and disabling in Microsoft Internet Explorer 3.0, 594
enabling and disabling in Netscape Navigator 4, 594
known security holes, 609
operating systems that support, 593
support for CGI programming, 463
versus JavaScript, 574–575, 590, 606–607
Web site addresses for information about, 611
Java Applet Rating Services, Web site address for, 597
Java Applet Viewer (Sun Microsystems), testing applets with, 605
Java applets
adding to Web pages in NetObjects Fusion, 188–189
advantages of, 591–592
disadvantages of, 592
calculating memory requirements for, 595–596
calling from Web pages, 598–606
downloading, 598
effect on local computer performance, 608–609
enabling, 596–597
installing on Web server, 595
locating, 597–598
long filename name space support, 595
on CD-ROM, 670
placing in a shared directory, 599–600
placing in the same directory as the Web page, 599
playing audio files with, 591
popular Web sites for learning about available, 597
running in Java-enabled Web browsers, 90
security issues, 606–609
security manager object, 608
testing, 605–606
testing on a local computer, 606
troubleshooting problems with, 611–612
using, 590–613
using on a remote server, 600
verifying, 595
Java class libraries, 610

Java Developer's Kit, 610
Java Development Kit (JDK), Java Applet Viewer from, 605
Java-enabled Web browsers
    running Java applets in, 90
    testing Java applets in, 605–606
    Web site address for information on, 610
Java FAQ Archives, Web site address for, 611
Java programming, software products for, 611
Java Studio (Sun Microsystems), Web site address for, 611
Java virtual machine, executing applets and applications on
    NetWare server with, 610
JavaBeans, 611
JavaScript
    accessing object property data, 548
    accessing object property values, 552
    animation format, 321
    arithmetic operators, 554
    assignment operators, 554
    benefits of using, 529–531
    boolean data type in, 539–540
    built-in methods for objects, 567–568
    creating a link to a function or method, 570–571
    creating animations with, 326–327
    creating loops in, 558
    data types, 538–541
    defined, 528–529
    enabling and disabling in the browser, 531–532, 594
    events and event handlers, 563–565
    expressions for data processing, 553–554
    form preprocessing with, 530
    form processing, 530–531
    identification of objects in, 544
    improved user interface controls with, 530
    interactive window, 569–570
    Internet newsgroups that provide information about, 576
    keywords list, 541
    literal data type in, 540
    loop-control statements, 558
    null data type in, 540
    numbers in, 539
    object and property naming conventions, 548–552
    object descriptions, 545–546
    object hierarchy, 543–544, 544
    object properties accessible from, 547–548
    operators in, 554
    processing data in, 552–568
    property descriptions for objects that appear in forms, 549
    property name components, 550
    sample object model, 550
    sample script with punctuation examples, 535
    security issues, 573–574, 607–609
    special Web page features provided by, 531
    support for CGI programming, 463
    use of string data in, 539
    using flow-control statements with, 556–
    using functions in, 558–563
    variables in, 540–541

    variable name rules, 540–541
    versus Java, 574–575, 590, 606–607
    versus other programming languages, 529
    Web site address for information on objects, 547
    Window object methods, 568
    writing your first script, 532–534
JavaScript-enabled browser,
JavaScript FAQ, Web site address for, 576
JavaScript Guide, Web site address for, 576
JavaScript Sample Code, Web site address for, 576
JavaScript Source, Web site address for, 575
JavaScripts
    asterisk/forward slash (*/), 535
    boolean data in, 539–540
    case-sensitivity of statements and variable names, 534
    client-side, 571–572
    common problems and their symptoms, 577
    double forward slash (//) in, 535
    forward slash/asterisk (/*) in, 535
    hiding from JavaScript-disabled browsers, 536–538
    keywords list for, 541
    kinds of, 571–572
    locating free, 575
    modifying, 572–573
    null data type in, 540
    punctuating, 534–535
    question marks (?) in, 534
    security issues, 573–574
    semicolons (;) in, 534
    server-side, 571–572
    string data in, 539
    troubleshooting, 576–577
    use of numbers in, 539
    using, 528–578
    using literal and variable data in, 538–541
    using underscore (_) character in, 541
    variable name rules in, 540–541
    writing, 532–534
JavaWorld Magazine, Web site address, 611
JBuilder (Inprise), Web site address, 611
Joint Photographic Experts Group (JPEG). *See* JPEG (JPE) ; JPEG
    images format
JPEG (JPE) format, 64
    converting other images to, 280
    saving Photoshop images to, 263
JPEG images
    adding special effects to images in, 252
    converting to GIF format, 275–277
    creating and optimizing in Photoshop, 278–279
    disadvantages of using, 253
    effects of dithering and noise on, 244–246
    detail loss in, 247
    features supported by, 252
    opening in browsers, 252
    setting image compression levels, 252
Just-In-Time (JIT) compiler, for running uncompiled Java applications
    on the server, 610

## K

`<KBD> </KBD>`, logical style tag, 32
kerning, 365
    adjusting in HTML, 373
    adjusting in Photoshop, 371
keyboard, logical style tag, 32
keywords, to describe Web site content, 148
Kira's Web Toolbox, CGI Library, 469

## L

`label` SSI command, Novell Web Server, 432
LAN connection, connecting your computer to the Internet with, 4–5
LAN Web client, setting up, 15
large text input areas, creating, 140–142
Lasso tool, enabling and disabling anti-aliasing for, 265
lastModified, document object property, 548
`LAST_MODIFIED` environment variable, `echo` SSI command, 420
Layout area, NetObjects Fusion Web page, 177–178
LCGI (Local CGI)
    executable NLMs, 464
    specifying directories for programs and scripts, 473
    versus RCGI, 467
leading, 365
    changing value in HTML, 373
    changing value in Photoshop, 371
left-justified Web pages, balancing, 354
length
    property description for objects that appear in forms, 549
    window object property, 547
less than (<) character, 18
`<LI>` tag
    ordered lists, 53
    unordered lists, 51–52
line spacing and margins
    adjusting, 44–36
    HTML tags for, 33–35
linear layout, Web site design, 215
link anchor tags, 83–86
linkColor, document object property, 548
linked targets. *See* anchor tags
links, to headings in other documents, 96–97
links and image maps, exercise for testing understanding, 120–121
list end tag, 52
list item tag, HTML code for, 51–52
list start tag, 52
lists
    creating, 50–56
    creating menu option, 140–142
    definition, 53–54
    examples of, 50
    nested, 54–56
    ordered, 52–53
    unordered, 51–52
Live3D sound file plug-in, 321

LiveAudio (Netscape), sound file plug-in, 329, 330
Local Area Network (LAN) connection. *See* LAN connection
Local CGI (LCGI)
    executable NLMs, 464
    versus RCGI, 467
logical operators, in JavaScript, 555
logical style tags, 29–33
    acronym, 31
    address, 31
    example of, 30
long filename name space support
    calculating memory requirements for, 595–596
    enabling, 596–597
    installing on Web server, 595
    verifying, 595
loop-control statements, JavaScript, 558
LView Pro, Web site address for, 154
Lycos, Web site address for registering your Web site, 149

## M

Macintosh operating system
    CGI support by, 463
    Java support by, 593
MacPerl language, support for CGI programming, 463
Macromedia
    multimedia products available from, 326
    sound file plug-ins, 321
Macromedia Backstage, Web site address for, 153
magic targets, 133
magnifying glass tools, Tool palette in NetObject Fusion
    reducing or enlarging the display in the site view window with, 173
MailTo protocol, for interdocument links, 88
map file, creating and placing on the server, 99–100
MapEdit utility
    creating an image map file with, 99–100
    current cost of unlimited use version, 103
    installation instructions for, 100
    trial version on CD-ROM, 671
    Web site address to get latest version, 100, 155
maps directory on Novell Web server, copying all server-side image map files to, 665
MARGINHEIGHT attribute, `<FRAME>` tag, 130
MARGINWIDTH attribute, `<FRAME>` tag, 130
marketing tool, Web site as, 208
Marquee tool, enabling and disabling anti-aliasing for, 265
MasterBorder area, NetObjects Fusion Web page, 177–178
    versus Styles, 178
Matt's Script Archive, Web site address for, 508
MAX attribute, TYPE attribute range, 139
Media Player (Microsoft), sound file plug-in, 329
memory requirements
    calculating for long filename name space support, 595–596
    for installing Netscape Communicator browser, 8
menu option lists, creating, 140–142

`<META>` tags
    defining Web page and Web site information with, 147–149
    HTTP-EQUIV and CONTENT attribute values table, 149
    NAME and CONTENT attribute values table, 148
metacontent structures, 217
METHOD attributes, `<FORM>` tags, 136–137
methods, in JavaScript
    built-in, 567–568
    creating a link to, 570–571
    Write and Writeln, 566–567
    using, 566–468
Microsoft Explorer, Web site address for plug-in information, 322
Microsoft Internet Explorer
    Author's Guide and HTML Reference, Web site address for, 29
    enabling and disabling Java in version 3.0, 594
    Java support by, 593
    PNG image format support by, 254
    table caption tags, 59
Microsoft Media Player, sound file plug-in, 329
Microsoft Windows, requirement for installing Netscape
        Communicator, 8
Microsoft Word, Web site address for, 152
MIDI. *See* Musical Instrument Digital Interface (MIDI)
MIME type configurations, on Web server, 309–310
MIME type definitions, Web server, 308–309
    Web site address for viewing a current list of, 309
MIME types, passing from the Web server to the Web browser, 307
MIN attribute, TYPE attribute range, 139
modem speed requirement, for Netscape Communicator browser, 8
monospaced type style, 363–364
    HTML supported tags for, 373
Morning Paper program, trial version on CD-ROM, 671
Motion Picture Experts Group (.mpeg), video file format, 332
movie files, adding to Web pages in NetObjects Fusion, 188–189
MULTI attribute, `<SELECT>` tag, 140–141
multimedia
    animation guidelines, 320–328
    copyright issues, 319–320
    deciding when to use in Web pages, 317
    designing for minimum download times, 317–319
    file distribution, 306
    file size reduction for faster downloading, 318–319
    general guidelines, 316–320
    how it operates on the Web, 305–310
    need for plug-ins or helper applications with, 305, 306
    plug-ins and helper applications for, 306–307
    reasons for using in Web pages, 304–305
    sound guidelines, 328–331
    video guidelines, 331–333
multimedia files
    additional hardware and software needed for creating, 316
    audio control console, 312
    calling a referenced, 313–314
    calling from Web pages, 311–314
    defining attributes for, 311–312
    file optimization techniques, 319

    obtaining, 310–311
    playing, 310–315
    size of compared to HTML or image files, 316
    skills needed for creating, 316
    using `<EMBED>` tag to start, 311
    versus HTML files, 316
multimedia information dialog box, Netscape Communicator
        installation program, 10
Multipurpose Internet Mail Extension (MIME) types. *See* MIME types
Musical Instrument Digital Interface (MIDI, .midi), 329, 330

## N

name, property description for objects that appear in forms, 549
NAME attribute
    checkbox option, 142
    `<FRAME>` tag, 129
    `<META>` tag, 148
    `<PARAM>` tag, 601
    radio button option, 143
    `<SELECT>` tag, 140–141
    text input boxes, 138–139
    `<TEXTAREA>` tag, 140–142
    used by named anchor tags, 83–86
named anchor tags, 83–86
    format for, 96
naming conventions, object and property, 548–552
National Center for Super Computing Applications (NCSA). *See* NCSA
National Public Radio, Web site address for, 328
navigation aids
    adding to Web sites, 354–362
navigation bars
    aligning text links or image links in, 357
    as Web site navigation aids, 356–358
    highlighting links in, 357–358
navigation support structures, special for Web sites, 217
navigation tools
    adding to Web sites, 354–362
    HTML text links, 355
    individual image links, 355–356
Navigator object, 542
  tag, 35, 36
NCSA Server SSI commands, 413–424
    config, 414–418
    supported by Novell and Netscape Web servers, 413
    URL for additional information, 413
NCSA Web server, as model for Novell Web servers, 99
nested framesets, creating, 130–131
nested lists, 54–56
NetBasic CGI scripts
    default directory locations for, 470
    how they communicate with Novell Web Server, 458–462
    supporting on a Novell Web Server, 458
NetBasic programming language, 464
    support for CGI programming, 463
Netcom, Web site address for, 13

NetObjects Fusion, 103
    adding a site map, 187–188
    adding ActiveX controls to Web pages in, 188–189
    adding graphics to Web pages in, 181–182
    adding multimedia to Web pages, 188–189
    adding text to Web pages in, 180–181
    adding Web site pages in, 175–176
    AutoSite templates, 172
    automatic links created by, 171
    building Web pages in, 176–182
    configuring staging and publishing locations, 189–191
    creating client-side image maps, 184
    creating forms, 185–187
    creating text links in, 183
    creating Web sites with, 170–192
    deleting pages, 176
    displaying floating Tools and Properties palettes in, 173
    importing Web pages from an existing Web site, 185
    making image maps in, 184
    moving pages, 176
    options for creating Web pages, 182–183
    page size settings in, 349
    Picture tab in Properties palette, 182
    previewing a single Web page in, 183
    previewing your Web site in, 182–183
    publishing your Web site, 189–191
    renaming Web site pages in, 175
    selecting a site Style, 178–179
    selecting pages to edit in, 179–180
    staging your Web site, 189–191
    starting a new Web site in, 171–173
    Style view in, 179
    trial version of site creation software on CD-ROM, 672
    Web page architecture, 177–178
    Web site address for, 153
Netscape Account Setup program, setting up an account with, 11–12
Netscape Audio Player, sound file plug-in, 329
Netscape Communicator
    completing the installation, 11
    configuring with Account Setup wizard, 11–12
    custom installation of, 10
    hardware and software requirements for, 8
    installing on standalone or Internet Web client, 9–11
    on CD-ROM, 670
    READ ME dialog box in installation program, 10
    Web site address for, 152
Netscape Enterprise Server for NetWare, 16. *See also* Netscape Web
    Servers for NetWare
    configuring the server for the demonstration Web site, 677–678
    installing demonstration Web site on CD-ROM to, 677–679
Netscape FastTrack Server for NetWare, 16. *See also* Netscape Web
    Servers for NetWare
Netscape Navigator
    enabling and disabling Java in version 4, 594
    enabling and disabling JavaScript in version 3, 531
    enabling and disabling JavaScript in version 4, 532, 594
    how it displays Web pages with no title, 20–21, 21

    Java support by, 593
    object property descriptions, 547
    opening a Web page from the CD-ROM in, 21
    PNG image support by, 253
    table caption tags, 59
    version 4 Web page display area table, 347
    Web site address for online handbook, 29
    Web site address for plug-in information, 322
Netscape Navigator Gold, Web site address for, 152
Netscape sound file plug-in, 321
Netscape Video for Windows plug-in, 332, 333
Netscape Web servers for NetWare
    enabling SSI processing in, 667
    copying Web site files to, 666–667
    index file names for, 94
    installing demonstration Web site on, 676–679
    NCSA Web Server SSI commands supported by, 413
    publishing a Web site on, 666–667
NetWare servers
    enabling long filename support, 596–597
    support for CGI programming, 463
    support for Java applets, 595–597
network interface cards, using to setup LAN Web clients, 15
Network Neighborhood, mapping a drive to the NetWare server
    through, 663
new line (break), HTML tag for, 34, 54
New Page button, NetObjects Fusion home page window, 175–176
New Site dialog box, starting a new Web site with, 172–173
News protocol, for interdocument links, 88
no line break, HTML tag for, 35
NOD filename extension, 173
`<NOFRAME> </NOFRAME>` tags, for supporting no frame
    browsers, 131–132
`<NOBR> </NOBR>`, HTML tag, 34
nonbreaking space, HTML code for, 36
nontiling image, 282
NORESIZE attribute, `<FRAME>` tag, 130
NOSHADE attribute, horizontal rule, 34
Novell Java products, Web site address for information, 610
Novell Web Server
    adding an additional Web site index filename to, 665–666
    CGI components, 459
    CGI on, 458–462
    Configuration dialog box, 403
    copying Web site files to, 664–665
    Directories page in Web Manager, 403
    enabling SSI processing for appropriate Web site directories on,
    666
    index file name, 94
    installation instructions for, 16
    modifying Perl scripts for, 507–509
    NCSA Web Server SSI commands supported by, 413
    opening home page after copying to the default document root
    directory, 664
    preparing for using Java applets, 595–597
    publishing your Web pages on, 664–666

*(continued)*

Novell Web Server *(continued)*
  setting the parsed-HTML extension in the MIME.TYP file, 400
  setting up a LAN Web client on, 4–6
  setting up for testing, 16
  SSI commands supported by, 397, 424–435
  Web Manager utility window, 402
Novell Web Server 3.1 software, 16
Novell Web Server 3.x Examples Toolkit, downloading, 468
Novell Web Server Perl consoles
  Debug, 510–512
  troubleshooting Perl script problems with, 510–513
*Novell's Certified Internet Business Strategist Study Guide*, 213
Novell's Course 654, Web Authoring and Publishing, 18
Novell's Course 660, Designing Effective Web Sites, 207
*Novell's Guide to Web Site Management*, 9
  getting information about the ROBOTS.TXT file from, 376
  using to set up LAN Web clients, 15
  using to troubleshoot Internet access problems, 15
Novell's intraNetWare SDK for Java product
  running Java programs on NetWare or intraNetWare servers
    with, 609–610
NOWRAP attribute, table heading tag, 60
numbered lists. *See* ordered lists

**O**

object and property naming conventions, 548–552
object data
  accessing, 543
  using in JavaScripts, 542–552
object descriptions, JavaScript, 545–546
object model, sample, 550
object property values, accessing in JavaScript, 552
*object_references*, property name component in JavaScript, 550
<OL> </OL> HTML tags, 53
onAbort, JavaScript event, 565
onBlur, JavaScript event, 565
onChange, JavaScript event, 565
onClick, JavaScript event, 565
ONCLICK attribute, button definition tag, 564
onError, JavaScript event, 565
onFocus, JavaScript event, 565
onLoad, JavaScript event, 565
onMouseOut, JavaScript event, 565
onMouseOver, JavaScript event, 565
onReset, JavaScript event, 565
onSelect, JavaScript event, 565
onSubmit, JavaScript event, 565
onUnload, JavaScript event, 565
Open Page dialog box, Account Setup wizard, 12
open("*URL*","*windowName*","*windowFeatures*") method, JavaScript
    Window method, 568
operating system requirements, for installing Netscape
    Communicator browser, 8
<OPTION> tag
  attributes, 142
  adding options to a menu list with, 140–142

ordered lists, 52–53
orders, collecting with Web page forms, 135
OS/2 operating system, Java support by, 593

**P**

<P> </P>, HTML tag, 28, 35
<P>  tag, forcing support for multiple new paragraph tags
    with, 35
Pacific Bell Internet, Web site address for, 13
page design guidelines, for Web pages, 219–224
page size, selecting for Web pages, 347–349
Page View, NetObjects Fusion, 177–178
Paint Shop Pro, Web site address for, 154
Palette drop-down list, Indexed Color dialog box, 262
palettes, 236–238. *See also* color lookup table
  Adaptive, 260–261
  Color Picker, 265–267
  Exact, 260–261
  Swatches, 265–267
paragraph, HTML tag for, 35
<PARAM> tags
  attributes, 601
  using to configure the applet you are calling, 600
parent, window object property, 547
parent directory relative references, 70
parent Web page, 170–171. *See also* home page
parentheses, using in Web pages, 36
parse HTML option, configuring SSI-command processing on
    Netscape Web servers with, 667
parsed-HTML files, 398
  changing the filename extension, 400
  filename extension for, 407
  setting the file extension on Novell Web Server, 400
parseFloat function, JavaScript, 563
parseInt function, JavaScript, 563
parsing, HTML files for SSI commands, 398
password value, TYPE attribute, 139
path, URL variable, 91
PATH_INFO environment variable, echo SSI command, 420
PATH_TRANSLATED environment variable, echo SSI command, 420
paths
  absolute, 69
  in URLs, 91
  relative, 69
  to image files, 68
  using forward slash (/) characters in, 68
PCX format, saving Photoshop images to, 263
PDF files
  creating in Adobe Distiller, 308
  displaying in browsers, 306–307
  popularity of on the Web, 308
  printing, 308
  viewing with Adobe Acrobat Reader, 308
PDFWriter, creating PDF files with, 308
peers, of child Web pages, 171
percent (%) sign, as Perl associative array variable, 496–497

percentage value, using in value list, 127
period (.) operator, in Perl scripts, 494–495
Perl (Practical Extraction and Report Language), 464
    NLMs used to support version 5, 485
    support for CGI programming, 463
    versus Java, 590
Perl associative arrays, percent sign (%) in, 496–497
Perl Debug console commands, 511–512
Perl interpreter
    checking to *see* if it is loaded, 486
    disabling, 485
    starting, 486
Perl program directory
    storing Web site files for Netscape Enterprise Server for
        NetWare in, 667
    storing Web site files for Novell Web Server in, 665
Perl scalar variables, 493–495
Perl Script Debut console, 512, 512–513
    commands, 513
Perl scripts
    array variables, 495–496
    arrays that &ReadParse builds, 498–500
    associative array variables, 496–497
    backslash (\) character in, 489–490
    comma operator in, 494–495
    commands used in example simple program, 487–488
    common script problems, 513–515
    converting a Web page to, 490–491
    creating and modifying, 484–515
    copying to the Perl program directory on the Novell Web server,
        665
    default directory locations for, 470, 485
    error messages and meaning of, 514–515
    for making calculations on form data and displaying result in a
        Web page, 501–502
    form processing, 491–507
    how they communicate with Novell Web Server, 458–462
    if and else branching statements in, 502–507
    modifying for the Novell Web Server, 508–509
    period (.) operator in, 494–495
    platforms available on, 484
    pound sign (#) in, 490
    &PrintHeader command, 487
    punctuating, 488–490
    question mark (?) in, 489
    &ReadParse function, 492–493, 498–500
    scalar variables, 493–495
    semicolon (;) in, 489
    supporting on a Novell Web Server, 458
    troubleshooting using the Novell Web Server Perl consoles,
        510–513
    using on the Novell Web Server, 485–486
    writing one that stores form data and prints it out, 500–502
    writing your first, 486–488
PERL5 NLM, default directory location for, 470
permissions. *See* copyright issues
<PERSON> </PERSON>, logical style tag, 32

photographs, converting to GIF format to use for animation or
    transparency, 250
Photoshop. *See* Adobe Photoshop
Photoshop Encapsulated Postscript (EPS) format
    saving Photoshop images to, 263
physical style tags, 26–28
PICT (PCT or PIC) format, saving Photoshop images to, 263
Picture tab in Properties palette, NetObjects Fusion, 182
pixel count, using in value list, 128
pixels, 234
plug-in dialog box, 315
    options in, 315
plug-ins and helper applications
    for using and viewing multimedia files in browsers, 306–307
    providing instructions for, 314–315
PNG format
    adjusting image brightness display differences with, 249
    browser support for, 253
    converting images to GIF format, 275–277
    features supported by, 253–254
    saving Photoshop images to, 263
    usage guidelines, 254–255
port, URL variable, 90
Portable Document Format (PDF) files. *See* PDF files
Portable Network Graphics (PNG). *See* PNG
portable Web site
    creating, 104–107
    steps for creating, 104–105
POST method,. METHOD attribute, 136–137
PostScript-to-HTML software program, Web site addresses for, 154
pound sign (#), in Perl scripts, 490
Prabhjot Gill's Cool Web Sites, Web site address for, 508
practice environment, setting up, 4–16
Pragma ("no cache") HTTP-EQUIV attribute value, <META> tag, 149
<PRE> </PRE> tags, in Web pages, 20, 35
preformatted text, HTML tag for, 35
Preview button, NetObjects Fusion window, 182–183
Princeton University Secure Internet Programming, Web site
    address, 609
&PrintHeader, Perl command, 487
printing
    PDF files, 308
    variable values, 495, 497
prompt("*message*","*default value*") method, JavaScript Window
    method, 568
Properties palette, NetObject Fusion
    configuration options in, 174
    formatting Web page text using Text tab, 180–181
    image formatting with Picture tab in, 182
    renaming Web site pages in, 174–175
property and object naming conventions, 548–552
property descriptions, for objects that appear in forms, 549
*property_name*, component in JavaScript, 550
protocol, URL variable, 88–89
prototyping your Web site, guidelines for, 375–376
PSD filename extension, 263
public directories. *See* virtual directories

publication design principles, for Web site designers, 207–208

Publish view, 190

publishing your Web site, 191
  common issues, 662–664
  configuring the publishing location, 189–191
  establishing a network connection to the file server for, 663
  on Web servers from Novell, 662–667
  to a FTP server, 190

punctuation, useful for Perl scripts, 488–490

puzzles
  adding multimedia to Web pages, 335
  advanced Web page features, 158
  answers to, 624–660
  applying and publishing your design, 384
  creating and adapting Web graphics, 288
  creating Web pages, 38
  creating Web sites with NetObject Fusion, 193
  linking Web pages, 109
  using CGI programs and scripts, 479
  using Java applets, 614
  using JavaScripts, 579
  using lists, tables, and images, 73
  using Perl scripts, 516
  using Server Side Include (SSI) commands, 439
  Web design basics, 227

**Q**

query string, in URL, 136

QUERY_STRING environment variable, echo SSI command, 420

QUERY_STRING_UNESCAPED environment variable, echo SSI command, 420

QuickTime (Apple Computer)
  sound file plug-in, 329
  video file plug-in and player, 332–333

QuickTime videos
  adding a control panel to, 312
  file format, 331–333

quotation marks (?)
  HTML code for, 36
  in JavaScripts, 534
  in Perl scripts, 489
  use of with attribute values, 144

**R**

radio buttons, 143
  attributes, 143–144
  creating, 143–144

.ram (RealAudio) sound file format, 329, 330

range value, TYPE attribute, 139

rasterizing graphic images, 277

Raw (RAW) format, saving Photoshop images to, 263

Read Me dialog box, Netscape Communicator installation program, 10

README file display, closing in Netscape Communicator installation program, 10

&ReadParse function
  array data from sample form, 500
  arrays built by, 498–500
  using in Perl scripts, 492–493

Real Player (Progressive Networks), sound file plug-in, 329, 330

Real Video (Progressive Networks)
  sound file plug-in, 329
  video file format, 332, 333

RealAudio (.ra, .ram) sound file format, 329, 330

referenced multimedia file, calling, 313–314

referrer, document object property, 548

&reg;, HTML code, 36

registered trademark, HTML code for, 36

registering product users, with Web page forms, 135

relative file references, 70
  sample of how they are used, 71
  using in URLs, 88, 92

relative paths, 69

relative reference, in URLs, 92–93

relative scale, using in value list, 127

REMOTE_ADDR environment variable, echo SSI command, 420

Remote CGI (RCGI)
  executable NLMs, 464–466
  program communications, 465
  sample program, 471–472
  specifying directories for, 471
  versus CGI programs that operate on a remote server, 466
  versus LCGI, 467

remote CGI programs, specifying directories for, 471

REMOTE_HOST environment variable, echo SSI command, 420

REMOTE_INDENT environment variable, echo SSI command, 420

remote server, 90
  using a CGI script or application that runs on, 472–473
  using Java applets on, 600

REMOTE_USER environment variable, echo SSI command, 420

RemoteScriptAlias, 471–473

REQUEST_METHOD environment variable, echo SSI command, 420

Reset button, creating, 145

RGB color mode
  converting from indexed color mode and back, 272
  creating JPEG images in, 278–279
  exporting GIF images from, 272–274
  problems converting to GIF, 259
  reducing color depth with, 272
  using in Photoshop, 258–259

RGB color code text attributes, 27

RGB Hex Triplet Color Chart, Web site address for, 28

Rich Music Format (RMF)

robots, use of by search engines to index Web sites, 147

ROBOTS.TXT file, learning about, 376

root directory, 91–93

rows, defining number of in a frameset, 127

ROWS= attribute
  <FRAMESET> tag, 128
  <TEXTAREA> tag, 140

rules, guidelines for creating in Photoshop, 280–281

**S**

`<S>` `</S>` tags, HTML 2.0, 28
`<SAMP>` `</SAMP>`, logical style tag, 32
sample, logical style tag, 32
sans serif type style, 363–364
    HTML support for, 373
scalar variables, in Perl scripts, 493–495
scanner, creating images with, 64
script directories, setting access rights for, 474
`<SCRIPT LANGUAGE="JavaScript">` tag, 533
SCRIPT_NAME environment variable, echo SSI command, 420
`<SCRIPT>` `</SCRIPT>` tags, 532–534
    starting client-side JavaScripts with, 571–572
scrollable lists, creating, 140–142
SCROLLING= attribute, `<FRAME>` tag, 129
search engines
    preparing your Web pages for, 146–149
    registering your Web site with, 149–150
    use of robots and spiders to index Web sites, 147
security issues
    Java, 607–609
    JavaScript, 573–574
    known Java security holes, 609
    Web site address for information, 609
Select Folder dialog box, Netscape Communicator installation
        program, 10
`<SELECT>` tag
    attributes, 141
    using to create menu option lists, 140–142
SELECTED attribute, `<OPTION>` tag, 140–142
selection tool (arrow) in NetObject Fusion Tools palette, editing
        Web pages with, 173
self, window object property, 548
semicolons (;)
    in JavaScripts, 534
    in Perl scripts, 489
serif type style, 363–364
    HTML support for, 373
SERVER_NAME environment variable, echo SSI command, 420
SERVER_PORT environment variable, echo SSI command, 420
Server Resource Management configuration file (SRM.CFG)
server-side image maps
    creating the image, 99
    creating the map file and placing it on the server, 99–100
    directory to copy all Web site files to on Novell Web server, 665
    entering the link tags, 100–101
    exercise for creating, 114–116
    using, 98–101
    verifying support for, 99
Server Side Include (SSI) commands. *See* SSI (Server Side Include)
        commands
server-side JavaScripts
    saving form data to, 137–138
    versus client-side, 571
server-side link tags, versus other link tags, 101
SERVER_SOFTWARE environment variable, echo SSI command, 420

`<SERVER>` tag, starting server-side JavaScripts with, 571–572
setTimeout(*expression, msec*) method, JavaScript Window method, 568
Setup Association dialog box, Netscape Communicator installation
        program, 10
SGML, 18
shared directory, placing a Java applet in, 599–600
shell scripts (Bourne, C, Korn), support for CGI programming, 463
Shockwave files, adding to Web pages in NetObjects Fusion, 188–189
Shockwave sound file plug-ins, 321
.shmtl filename extension, saving standard Web pages with, 663
Site Mapper tool, NetObjects Fusion Tools palette, 187–188
site maps
    adding to Web sites in NetObjects Fusion, 187–188
    benefits of, 359
    creating as navigation tool for Web pages, 358–361
    indexed, 360
    most common styles for, 359
    table based, 359
    text only, table based, 360
Site view, NetObjects Fusion
    changing the display in, 173–174
    Properties and Tools palettes, 174
SIZE attribute
    horizontal rule, 34
    `<SELECT>` tag, 140–141
    specifying the size of the text box in characters with, 139
small caps effect
    creating in HTML, 373
    creating in Photoshop, 371
`<SMALL>` `</SMALL>` tags, HTML 3.2, 28
SOFT option, WRAP attribute, 140
sound files
    adding to Web pages in NetObjects Fusion, 188–189
    formats for, 329
    guidelines for, 328–331
    optimization techniques, 319
    plug-ins for, 321, 329
source Web page directory, URL variable, 91
Southwestern Bell Internet Services, Web site address for, 13
special characters
    adding to HTML files, 36
    demonstration file for viewing, 36
    Web site address for additional, 37
special operators, support for in JavaScript, 555
special text effects, creating in Photoshop, 370–371
spiders, use of by search engines to index Web sites, 147
Sprint, Web site address for, 13
SPRYNET, Web site address for, 13
SPRYNET Mosaic, PNG image support by, 254
SRC= attribute
    `<FRAME>` tag, 129
    `<IMG>` tag, 66
SSI (Server Side Include) commands
    adding standard boilerplate information with, 396
    adding tags to a new or existing HTML file, 407
    append, 425–426

*(continued)*

SSI (Server Side Include) commands (*continued*)
    `break`, 426–427
    `calc`, 427–428
    case sensitivity of in Netscape Web servers for NetWare, 408
    `config`, 414–418
    `count`, 428
    displaying connection information, 396
    displaying variable information, 396
    distinguishing from HTML comments, 408–409
    `echo`, 418–423
    `exec`, 429
    `flastmod`, 422–423
    `fsize`, 423
    `goto`, 431
    how they work, 398–399
    `if`, 429–431
    `include`, 423–424
    `label`, 432
    Novell Education Course for using, 397
    processing form data and saving the results to files, 396
    processing forms with, 432–435
    saving form data to a Web server text file, 137
    specifying filenames and paths in, 409–412
    supported by the Novell Web Server, 397
    syntax, 407–408
    troubleshooting tips, 435–436
    using, 396–438
    using the `file` argument in, 409
    when to use, 436–437
SSI-command processing, 398, 398–399
    configuring Netscape Web servers for, 667
    enabling, 399–406
    enabling for a specific directory, 401–402
    enabling or disabling with a text editor, 406
    specifying a file extension for parsed-HTML files, 399–401
    using Web Manager utility to enable, 402–404
SSI-error processing, using `config` command to configure, 416–418
SSI files, changing the file extension for, 400–401
SSI Web pages
    preparing for use on any Novell Web server, 663
    system requirements for running, 663
staging Web server, testing Web sites with, 106
staging your Web site, 191
    configuring the location, 189–191
standalone Web clients, setting up, 6–15
Standard Generalized Markup Language (SGML). *See* SGML
Standard Web pages, 13
START attribute, ordered list tags, 53
Start Copying Files dialog box, Netscape Communicator installation
    program, 10
status, window object property, 548
storing, image files, 68–71
storyboarding, before building a Web site, 224–225
`<STRIKE> </STRIKE>` tags, HTML 2.0, 28
string operators, support for in JavaScript, 555
strong, logical style tag, 32
`<STRONG> </STRONG>`, logical style tag, 32

style tags, using logical, 29–33
Style view, NetObjects Fusion, 179
Styles, NetObjects Fusion
    choosing for banners and buttons, 178
    versus MasterBorders, 178
`<SUB> </SUB>` tags, HTML 3.2, 28
subdirectory relative reference, 70
Submit button, creating, 144
Submit It!, Web site address for registering your Web site, 149
Submit Query button, creating in Web page forms, 135–136
subordinate lists. *See* nested lists
subscript tags, HTML 3.2, 28
Sun Java Security FAQ, Web site address, 609
Sun Microsystems Web site address for Java information, 611
`<SUP> </SUP>` tags, HTML 3.2, 28
Super Mojo (Penumbra Software), Web site address for, 611
superscript tags, HTML 3.2, 28
surveys, conducting with Web page forms, 135
Swatches palette, Photoshop, 265–267
switch branching, 507

**T**

table caption tags, 59
table cell data, HTML tags for, 57–61
table columns
    COLSPAN attribute for, 60, 62
    HTML tags for, 57, 59
table data, HTML tags for, 57–61
table heads, HTML tags for, 57–61
table of contents, intradocument link tags for in Web sites, 83–86
table rows
    HTML tags for, 57, 59
    ROWSPAN attribute for, 60, 62
`<TABLE> </TABLE>` tags, 57–62
tables
    aligning Web page content with, 350–352
    building, 56–62
    creating borders in Web pages with, 352
    displaying with no border, 351
    sample table, 56
    guidelines for using to organize Web pages, 351–352
    positioning objects within cells, 351
    setting width of, 352
tag attributes table, framesets, 128
Tagged Image File Format (TIF), saving Photoshop images to, 263
tags, Web page formatting, 18–19
Targa (TGA, VDA, ICB, or VST) format, saving Photoshop images
    to, 263
TARGET attribute, adding to link tags, 132–134
`<TC> </TC>` tags, HTML, 59
TCP/IP port number, specifying in URL, 90
`<TD> </TD>` tags, HTML, 57–61
teletype tags, HTML 2.0, 28
Telnet protocol, for interdocument links, 88
testing applets, 605–606
testing your Web site, 374–379

functionality testing guidelines, 376–377
milestone testing considerations, 374–375
prototyping guidelines, 375–376
user testing guidelines, 377–378
text
    aligning with HTML tags, 349–350
    changing appearance of in Web pages, 23–33
    RGB color codes for, 27
    tools for controlling positioning of, 346, 347
text and graphics links, tying Web site pages together with, 82–108
text file, 18
text formatting, examples of, 24, 24–25
text input boxes
    creating, 138–139
    text object properties that control in JavaScript, 543
text links, creating in NetObjects Fusion, 183
Text tab in NetObjects Fusion Tools palette, adding text to Web
    pages with, 180–181
Text tool, enabling and disabling anti-aliasing for, 265
text value, TYPE attribute, 139
<TH> </TH> tags, HTML, 57–61
ThumbsPlus, Web site address for, 154
Ticker Tape applet, calling to your Web page, 601–606
tilde (~) character, as reference to user Web page directory, 412
tiling image, creating and optimizing, 282–284, 283
title, document object property, 548
<TITLE> tags, in Web pages, 20
™ (registered trademark), HTML code for, 36
Tools palette in NetObject Fusion, tools available in, 173–174
top, window object property, 548
topical navigation links, Web pages, 218
<TR> </TR> tags, 57–62
trademark, HTML code for, 36
transparent colors, 248
    choosing for images in Photoshop, 274–275
troubleshooting
    CGI requests, 477
    common Perl script problems, 513–515
    Internet access problems, 14–15
    Java applets, 611–612
    JavaScripts, 576–577
    Perl scripts using the Novell Web Server Perl consoles, 510–513
<TT> </TT> tags, HTML 2.0, 28
TWAIN-compliant scanners, importing images from, 275–276
TYPE attribute
    ordered list tags, 53
    password value, 139
    Reset button, 145
    text input boxes, 138–139
    values, 139
type effects, decorative, 366–367
type-positioning controls, 364–366
Type Tool dialog box, Adobe Photoshop, 369, *370*
TYPE=checkbox attribute, checkbox option, 142
TYPE=radio attribute, radio button option, 143
typestyles, 363–364
    selecting in Photoshop, 371

**U**

<U> </U> tags, HTML 2.0, 28
<UL> </UL> tag, 51–52
    indenting caption for a list with, 349–350
u-Law (.au) sound file format, 329, 331
Ulead GIF Animator, 323
Underline tags, HTML 2.0, 28
Uniform Resource Locators (URLs)
    case sensitivity of some, 29
    components of, 87–95
    format of, 87
    sample formats with different path specifications, 93–94
    variables, 88–95
UNIX operating system
    Java support by, 593
    support for CGI programming, 463
UNIX systems, case sensitivity of URLs on, 29
underscore character(_)
    as part of variable name in JavaScript, 541
    as Perl scalar variable, 493–495
    in variable names, 139
unordered lists, 51–52
URL, document object property, 548
URL variables
    document root directory, 91–93
    filename, 94–95
    host name, 89–90
    path, 91
    port, 90
    protocol, 88–89
    source Web page directory, 91
    virtual directories, 93–94
URLs
    case sensitivity of some, 29
    components of, 87–95
    examples of links containing, 95–96
    format of, 87
    sample formats with different host name specifications, 90
    sample formats with different path specifications, 93–94
    sample formats with different protocol specifications, 89
user testing guidelines, 377–378
user Web page directory, virtual argument for referencing a file in, 412
userAgent property, Netscape Navigator object, 547
utility navigation structures, Web pages, 217

**V**

validation tools, for Web pages, 153
VALIGN attributes, for table captions, rows, and heads, 59–60
value, property description for objects that appear in forms, 549
VALUE attribute
    checkbox option, 142
    defining default entry for a text box with, 139
    <OPTION> tag, 140–142
    <PARAM> tag, 601

*(continued)*

VALUE attribute (continued)
    radio button option, 143
    Reset button, 145
    Submit button option, 144
value list
    asterisk (*) in, 128
    defining number and size of frames in a frameset with, 127–128
    percentage value in, 127
    pixel count in, 128
<VAR> </VAR>, logical style tag, 32
variable, logical style tag, 32
vector graphics, 277
vertically tiling background image, 283, 283
video files
    adding to Web pages in NetObjects Fusion, 188–189
    formats for, 332–333
    guidelines for, 331–333
    optimization techniques, 319
Video for Windows (.avi)
    file format, 332
    plug-in (Netscape), 332, 333
virtual argument, 410, 411
    syntax for accessing different types of virtual directories, 412
virtual directories
    as URL variables, 93–94
    creating an external link with an absolute reference to a file in, 93
    creating an internal link with an absolute reference to a file in, 93
    using the virtual argument to access, 412
Virtual Reality Modeling Language (VRML)
    animation format, 321
    creating visual three-dimensional worlds with, 327
    versus bitmapped images, 327
Visual Basic, support for CGI programming, 463
Visual Café (Symantec), Web site address for, 611
VisualAge for Java (IBM), Web site address for, 611
visually impaired computer users, supporting on your Web site, 374
vlinkColor, document object property, 548
VOLUMES command, verifying long filename support with, 595

**W**

Waveform Audio (.wav) sound file format, 329, 331
Web browsers. See browsers; Microsoft Internet Explorer; Netscape
        Communicator; Netscape Navigator
Web client
    dial-up Internet with connection and storage space, 4
    LAN with connection to intranet or Internet Web server, 4
    setup flow chart, 7
    standalone with no Web server connection, 4
Web color swatches, loading and choosing in Photoshop, 265–267
Web design
    basics of, 205–226
    challenges of, 208–209
Web designer
    preparing for the certificate exam, 4–16
    responsibilities of, 206–207
Web graphics, creating and adapting in Photoshop, 232–287

Web image design
    how bitmaps work, 233–239
    understanding the issues, 233–250
Web images
    browser safe colors for, 245, 247
    color dots appearing in, 242–246
    common maladies, 239–250
    compensating for color differences in, 249–250
    correcting detail loss in, 246–247
    displaying faster using interlacing, 241
    dithering in, 243–244
    fixing images that appear too large or too small in browsers, 241–242
    noise in, 244–246
    preventing halos around foreground images, 247–249
    reducing delays caused by embedded images, 240
    reducing download time by reducing files sizes, 239–240
    testing, 284–285
Web Manager utility, Novell Web Server
    Directories page, 403
    using on a virtual server, 404
    window, 402
Web page accessory tools, 154–155
Web page development tools, 152
Web page document, versus frameset document, 127
Web page forms. See forms
Web pages
    accessory tools for, 154–155
    adding background images to, 63–64, 65
    adding graphics to in NetObjects Fusion, 181–182
    adding <META> tags to, 146
    adding multimedia to, 304–334
    adding multimedia to in NetObjects Fusion, 188–189
    adding text to in NetObjects Fusion, 180–181
    advantages of using Java applets on, 591–592
    aligning content with art, 350
    aligning content with frames, 352–353
    aligning content with HTML tags, 349–350
    aligning content with tables, 350–352
    aligning text links or image links in a navigation bar, 357
    anatomy of, 19–23
    balancing left-justified, 354
    basics, 18–19
    building in NetObjects Fusion, 176–182
    calling CGI programs from, 475–476
    calling Java applets from, 598–606
    calling multimedia files from, 311–314
    changing text appearance in, 23–33
    choosing an image format for, 250–255
    content guidelines, 223–224
    content references to avoid when designing, 346
    creating, 17–37
    creating site maps for, 358–361
    creating text and image-based navigation bars in, 356–358
    defining frames that display, 129
    defining the HTML version for, 150–151
    deleting in NetObjects Fusion, 176

design guidelines for, 219–224

development tools for, 153

disadvantages of using Java applets on, 592

displaying alternate text in place of images in, 67

exercises for creating, 39–47

formatting commands, 18–19

graphics programs and utilities for developing, 154

guidelines for creating graphical type for, 367–360

HTML editors for, 151–152

importing into NetObjects Fusion Web site, 185

including document type declaration in, 150–151

linking, 81–108

minimum set of tags needed for, 19

moving in NetObjects Fusion, 176

page layout guidelines, 220–223

placing Java applets in the same directory as, 599

PNG image format support in, 254–255

positioning text and graphics on, 346–354

preparing for search engine registration, 146–149

puzzle, 38

renaming in NetObject Fusion, 174–175

selecting a page size, 347–349

selecting pages to edit in NetObjects Fusion, 179–180

storing in the document root directory, 663

setting up workstation for creating and viewing, 4–16

using advanced features, 124–157

using graphical and HTML type in, 362–373

using HTML text links in, 355

using index frames in, 358

using individual image links in, 355–356

using Java applets on, 591

using SSI command on, 407–412

Web palette file, selecting, 260

Web Promotion Spider, Web site address for, 155

Web server

    MIME type definitions, 308–309

    restricting CGI directory access on, 476–477

    sample directory, 71

    setting up for testing, 16

    well-known port number for, 90

Web site addresses

    Adobe PageMill, 152

    Adobe Photoshop, 154

    Adobe SiteMill, 153

    Alta Vista, 149

    Ameritech.net, 13

    animated GIFs, 322

    Assets directory, 173

    Bell Atlantic Internet Solutions, 14

    BellSouth.net Internet Services, 13

    CGI security information, 477

    conversion utility tools, 154

    2Cool Animations, 322

    Corel WordPerfect, 152

    CSE 3310 HTML Validator, 153

    Dream Catchers CGI Scripts, 469

    for finding Internet Service Providers, 13

    for information on JavaScript objects, 547

    Gamelan, 597

    GIF Movie Gear, 154, 323

    graphic programs and utilities, 154

    HOTBOT, 149

    HotDog, 152

    HTML Transit, 154

    HTML, 18, 29

    Java Applet Rating Services, 597

    Java FAQ Archives, 611

    Java Studio, 611

    Java, 611

    Java-enabled Web browser information, 610

    JavaScript FAQ, 516

    JavaScript Guide, 576

    JavaScript Sample Code, 576

    JavaScript Source, 575

    JavaWorld Magazine, 611

    JBuilder, 611

    LView Pro, 154

    Lycos, 149

    MapEdit utility, 100, 155

    Matt's Script Archive, 508

    Microsoft Explorer plug-in information, 322

    Microsoft Word, 152

    MIME type definitions, 309

    National Public Radio, 328

    NetObjects Fusion, 153

    Netscape Communicator, 152

    Netscape Navigator Gold, 152

    Netscape Navigator online handbook, 29

    Netscape Navigator plug-in information, 322

    Pacific Bell Internet, 13

    Paint Shop Pro, 154

    PostScript-to-HTML software program, 154

    Prabhjot Gill's Cool Web Sites, 508

    Princeton University Secure Internet Programming, 609

    RGB Hex Triplet Color Chart, 28

    security issues information, 609

    Southwestern Bell Internet Services, 13

    Sprint, 13

    SPRYNET, 13

    Submit It! for registering your Web site, 149

    Web Promotion Spider, 155

Web sites

    adding navigation aids to, 354–362

    architecture, 213–219

    Assets directory, 173

    building with NetObject Fusion, 170–176

    changing the storage location of the files, 172

    copying files to Netscape Web Servers for Netware, 666–667

    copying files to a Novell Web server, 664–665

    copying files to a Web server, 380

    copying special files to special directories, 380–381

    creating a portable, 104–107

    creating site maps for, 358–361

*(continued)*

Web sites (continued)
creating Web pages for, 18–47
creating with NetObjects Fusion, 169–192
defining goals of, 211–212
deleting pages with NetObjects Fusion, 176
design basics, 205–226
design guidelines, 213–224
directory to copy all files except server-side image maps and CGI scripts to, 665
establishing a feedback channel, 381
for learning about available Java applets, 597
guidelines for adding navigation controls to, 361–362
how to design, 210–211
moving pages with NetObjects Fusion, 176
preparing SSI Web pages for use on Novell Web servers, 663
preparing standard for use on Novell Web servers, 663
publicizing, 145–150, 381
publishing, 379–381
registering yours with search engines, 149–150
setting up the Web server or server account for publishing, 379–381
showing off at interview, 4
skills needed by design team, 206–209
starting new with New Site dialog box, 172–173
storyboarding before building, 224–225
supporting multiple browsers in, 344–346
supporting visually impaired visitors to, 374
testing, 374–379
using AutoSite templates to create, 171–172
using index frames for navigation control in, 358
using scanned images in, 253
Web site architecture, 213–219
architectural guidelines, 217–219
combined layout, 216–217
front door or entry Web page in, 217
hierarchical layout, 216
linear layout, 215
metacontent structures, 217
special navigation support structures, 217
storyboarding before building, 224–225
topical navigation links, 218–219
utility navigation structures in, 217
Web site development tools, 153
Web site management tools
conversion utilities, 153–154
development tools, 153
graphics programs and utilities, 154
HTML editors, 151–152
using, 151–155

validation tools, 153
Web page accessory tools, 154–155
WebCrawler, Web site address for registering your Web site, 149
WebLater URL tracking software, trial version on CD-ROM, 672
Weblint, Web site address for, 153
while statements, in JavaScripts, 558
WIDTH attribute
adding to Web pages to speed embedded image download time, 240
<APPLET> tag, 601
horizontal rule, 34
<IMG> tag, 66
<TABLE> tag, 58
WinCIM CompuServe, PNG image format support by, 254
window object, 542
window object property descriptions, 547–548
window_reference, property name component in JavaScript, 550
windows, creating links to using <FRAME> TARGET attribute, 132–135
Windows 3.x,
Windows 95, Java support by, 593
Windows Bitmap (BMP or RLE) format, saving Photoshop images to, 263
Windows dial-up networking software, installing on a Windows NT workstation, 9
Windows NT, Java support by, 593
Windows operating system, CGI programming support, 463
WinGIF, Web site address for, 154
wireless modems, connecting to the Internet with, 8
workstation
need to upgrade to run SSI Web pages, 663
setting up, 4–16
World Wide Web Consortium, Web site address for viewing HTML 3.2 standards, 18
WRAP attribute, <TEXTAREA> tag, 140
write and writeln methods, for document objects in JavaScript, 566–567
WUsage5.0 Web site analysis software, trial version on CD-ROM, 672
WWW GIF Animator, 323
WWW.JavaScripts.Com, Web site address for, 575

## Y

Yahoo!
Web site address for registering your Web site, 149
Web site address for viewing examples of animated GIFs, 322
Younis Graphics Web Page Monitor Tester, functionality testing information source, 377

# my2cents.idgbooks.com

## Register This Book — And Win!

Visit **http://my2cents.idgbooks.com** to register this book and we'll automatically enter you in our fantastic monthly prize giveaway. It's also your opportunity to give us feedback: let us know what you thought of this book and how you would like to see other topics covered.

## Discover IDG Books Online!

The IDG Books Online Web site is your online resource for tackling technology — at home and at the office. Frequently updated, the IDG Books Online Web site features exclusive software, insider information, online books, and live events!

### 10 Productive & Career-Enhancing Things You Can Do at www.idgbooks.com

- Nab source code for your own programming projects.
- Download software.
- Read Web exclusives: special articles and book excerpts by IDG Books Worldwide authors.
- Take advantage of resources to help you advance your career as a Novell or Microsoft professional.
- Buy IDG Books Worldwide titles or find a convenient bookstore that carries them.
- Register your book and win a prize.
- Chat live online with authors.
- Sign up for regular e-mail updates about our latest books.
- Suggest a book you'd like to read or write.
- Give us your 2¢ about our books and about our Web site.

You say you're not on the Web yet? It's easy to get started with IDG Books' *Discover the Internet,* available at local retailers everywhere.

# IDG BOOKS WORLDWIDE, INC.
# END-USER LICENSE AGREEMENT

**READ THIS.** You should carefully read these terms and conditions before opening the software packet(s) included with this book ("Book"). This is a license agreement ("Agreement") between you and IDG Books Worldwide, Inc. ("IDGB"). By opening the accompanying software packet(s), you acknowledge that you have read and accept the following terms and conditions. If you do not agree and do not want to be bound by such terms and conditions, promptly return the Book and the unopened software packet(s) to the place you obtained them for a full refund.

1. **License Grant.** IDGB grants to you (either an individual or entity) a nonexclusive license to use one copy of the enclosed software program(s) (collectively, the "Software") solely for your own personal or business purposes on a single computer (whether a standard computer or a workstation component of a multiuser network). The Software is in use on a computer when it is loaded into temporary memory (RAM) or installed into permanent memory (hard disk, CD-ROM, or other storage device). IDGB reserves all rights not expressly granted herein.

2. **Ownership.** IDGB is the owner of all right, title, and interest, including copyright, in and to the compilation of the Software recorded on the disk(s) or CD-ROM ("Software Media"). Copyright to the individual programs recorded on the Software Media is owned by the author or other authorized copyright owner of each program. Ownership of the Software and all proprietary rights relating thereto remain with IDGB and its licensers.

3. **Restrictions on Use and Transfer.**
   **(a)** You may only (i) make one copy of the Software for backup or archival purposes, or (ii) transfer the Software to a single hard disk, provided that you keep the original for backup or archival purposes. You may not (i) rent or lease the Software, (ii) copy or reproduce the Software through a LAN or other network system or through any computer subscriber system or bulletin board system, or (iii) modify, adapt, or create derivative works based on the Software.

**(b)** You may not reverse engineer, decompile, or disassemble the Software. You may transfer the Software and user documentation on a permanent basis, provided that the transferee agrees to accept the terms and conditions of this Agreement and you retain no copies. If the Software is an update or has been updated, any transfer must include the most recent update and all prior versions.

4. **<u>Restrictions on Use of Individual Programs.</u>** You must follow the individual requirements and restrictions detailed for each individual program in Appendix C of this Book. These limitations are also contained in the individual license agreements recorded on the Software Media. These limitations may include a requirement that after using the program for a specified period of time, the user must pay a registration fee or discontinue use. By opening the Software packet(s), you will be agreeing to abide by the licenses and restrictions for these individual programs that are detailed in Appendix C and on the Software Media. None of the material on this Software Media or listed in this Book may ever be redistributed, in original or modified form, for commercial purposes.

5. **<u>Limited Warranty.</u>**
   **(a)** IDGB warrants that the Software and Software Media are free from defects in materials and workmanship under normal use for a period of sixty (60) days from the date of purchase of this Book. If IDGB receives notification within the warranty period of defects in materials or workmanship, IDGB will replace the defective Software Media.

   **(b) IDGB AND THE AUTHOR OF THE BOOK DISCLAIM ALL OTHER WARRANTIES, EXPRESS OR IMPLIED, INCLUDING WITHOUT LIMITATION IMPLIED WARRANTIES OF MERCHANTABILITY AND FITNESS FOR A PARTICULAR PURPOSE, WITH RESPECT TO THE SOFTWARE, THE PROGRAMS, THE SOURCE CODE CONTAINED THEREIN, AND/OR THE TECHNIQUES DESCRIBED IN THIS BOOK. IDGB DOES NOT WARRANT**

**THAT THE FUNCTIONS CONTAINED IN THE SOFTWARE
WILL MEET YOUR REQUIREMENTS OR THAT THE
OPERATION OF THE SOFTWARE WILL BE ERROR FREE.**

(c) This limited warranty gives you specific legal rights, and you may have other rights that vary from jurisdiction to jurisdiction.

6. <u>Remedies.</u>

(a) IDGB's entire liability and your exclusive remedy for defects in materials and workmanship shall be limited to replacement of the Software Media, which may be returned to IDGB with a copy of your receipt at the following address: Software Media Fulfillment Department, Attn.: *Novell's Certified Web Designer Study Guide,* IDG Books Worldwide, Inc., 7260 Shadeland Station, Ste. 100, Indianapolis, IN 46256, or call 1-800-762-2974. Please allow three to four weeks for delivery. This Limited Warranty is void if failure of the Software Media has resulted from accident, abuse, or misapplication. Any replacement Software Media will be warranted for the remainder of the original warranty period or thirty (30) days, whichever is longer.

(b) In no event shall IDGB or the author be liable for any damages whatsoever (including without limitation damages for loss of business profits, business interruption, loss of business information, or any other pecuniary loss) arising from the use of or inability to use the Book or the Software, even if IDGB has been advised of the possibility of such damages.

(c) Because some jurisdictions do not allow the exclusion or limitation of liability for consequential or incidental damages, the above limitation or exclusion may not apply to you.

7. <u>U.S. Government Restricted Rights.</u> Use, duplication, or disclosure of the Software by the U.S. Government is subject to restrictions stated in paragraph (c)(1)(ii) of the Rights in Technical Data and Computer Software clause of DFARS 252.227-7013, and in subparagraphs (a) through (d) of the Commercial Computer—

Restricted Rights clause at FAR 52.227-19, and in similar clauses in the NASA FAR supplement, when applicable.

8. **General.** This Agreement constitutes the entire understanding of the parties and revokes and supersedes all prior agreements, oral or written, between them and may not be modified or amended except in a writing signed by both parties hereto that specifically refers to this Agreement. This Agreement shall take precedence over any other documents that may be in conflict herewith. If any one or more provisions contained in this Agreement are held by any court or tribunal to be invalid, illegal, or otherwise unenforceable, each and every other provision shall remain in full force and effect.

# CD-ROM Installation Instructions

Here are basic instructions for installing the various products on the accompanying CD-ROM in this book. For more detailed instructions, please refer to Appendix C.

**Demonstration Web Site**  The demonstration Web site can be accessed from the CD-ROM or installed on a Web server. Detailed instructions for installing the Web site on Novell Web servers are provided in Appendix C.

**GIF Movie Gear (animated GIFs)**  To install GIF Movie Gear, run the GMVGR25.EXE file in the gifMGear folder and follow the instructions. To access the GIF Movie Gear product documentation, start the program and select Help → Contents.

**MapEdit (image maps)**  To install MapEdit, open the Mapedit folder and run one of the following files: MAPDST.EXE (Windows 3.1) or MAP32DST.EXE (Windows 95 or NT). Follow the onscreen instructions to complete the installation.

**Morning Paper (Web site tracking)**  To install Morning Paper, run the MORNDST.EXE file in the MPaper folder and follow the instructions. To access the Morning Paper product documentation, start the program and click the Help button.

**NetObjects Fusion (Web site creation)**  To install NetObjects Fusion, open the NOF202TRIAL1OF4.EXE program in the NetObjects directory and follow the onscreen instructions. For additional information, see the README.TXT file in this directory.

**Netscape Communicator**  The instructions for installing Netscape Communicator are provided in Chapter 1.

**Adobe Photoshop 4.01 for Windows**  For Adobe Photoshop installation instructions, open the following Readme file: PhotoShp\disk1\Readme.wri.

**WebLater (URL tracking)**  To install WebLater, open the WLater folder and run one of the following files: WEBLDST.EXE (Windows 3.1) or WL32DST.EXE (Windows 95 or NT). Follow the onscreen instructions to complete the installation.

**WUsage (Web site analysis)**  For instructions on installing and using WUsage, open the product manual on the CD-ROM: WUsage5.0\Manual\Index.html.